Theoretical
Perspectives
in Sociology

Theoretical Perspectives in Sociology

EDITED BY

SCOTT G. McNALL

UNIVERSITY OF KANSAS

ST. MARTIN'S PRESS
NEW YORK

ACKNOWLEDGMENTS

Thomas Baumgartner, Tom Burns, and Philippe DeVillé, "Actors, Games, and Systems:
The Dialectics of Social Action and System Structuring" from R. Felix Geyer and Johan
van der Zouwen (eds.), *Sociocybernetics: An Actor-Oriented Social Systems Approach.*
Martinus Nijhoff Social Sciences Division, Leiden, Boston, London, 1978, Vol. I, pp.
27–54. Reprinted by permission. Revised version of a longer paper.

Acknowledgments and copyrights continue at the back of the book on page 562, which
constitutes an extension of the copyright page.

To John and Peggy

Preface

Theoretical Perspectives in Sociology began as a special issue of *The American Sociologist*. I had wanted to put together an issue on alternative theoretical perspectives, and in 1977 I undertook a search for articles. My idea was to encourage people who were experts in, or advocates of, some of the "new" sociologies—semiotics, critical theory, phenomenology, and so forth—to explain, as simply as possible, what their particular approach was and how it illuminated a portion of social reality. The essays were to be essentially primers rather than fully elaborated statements. Their purpose was to provide some guidelines that would help nonspecialists, or newcomers to a particular perspective, make sense of the sometimes confusing professional literature.

The special issue of *The American Sociologist*, comprising eight essays, was published in the spring of 1978. However, a considerable number of excellent articles had to be omitted, most of them simply because the authors did not have time, before the deadline, to revise in response to comments from the journal's reviewers. Many of those articles, now revised, are included in the present volume along with the original eight, and a few additional articles have been solicited to fill gaps in crucial areas. More than two-thirds of the articles in this volume are published here for the first time.

This is not a collection of essays in social theory that purports to demonstrate once and for all how we got where we are, what we can do about it, and what's in store for us. These articles are intended, instead, to explain what is essential about particular theoretical frameworks, how they can be used, and why they should be given attention. Some of the pieces clearly reveal the cutting edge of social theory, while others are enlightening statements about theories, or perspectives, in need of clarification or reformulation. Such essays can provide the creative reader with new ways to perceive reality. Some of the approaches discussed will appeal more than others, but they are all worthy of serious consideration. All of the authors have written with both the student and the professor in mind, and each has provided an annotated bibliography to accompany his or her text. In itself, the compilation of more than three hundred annotated references for the study of contemporary sociological theory is, I believe, a unique resource.

This enterprise is, of course, a collective one. In acknowledging my debts I regret that the reviewers of *The American Sociologist* must remain anonymous, for they are owed special gratitude. In my introduction to the special issue, I praised Allen Grimshaw, the editor, for his help. Being a modest man, he edited my praise. That does not alter the fact that neither that issue nor this volume would have been possible without him. Thank you, Allen. Thanks go also to my wife, Sally Allen McNall, who assisted with the final editing of the manuscript.

Scott G. McNall

Contents

PART VI. THE INDIVIDUAL AND HUMAN CONSCIOUSNESS   323

PART VII. BIOLOGY AND HUMAN BEHAVIOR   397

PART VIII. SOCIETY AND THE ENVIRONMENT   463

PART IX. ANNOTATED BIBLIOGRAPHY   515

Theoretical
Perspectives
in Sociology

INTRODUCTION: ALTERNATIVE THEORETICAL PERSPECTIVES IN MODERN SOCIOLOGY

Although anyone approaching modern social theory is struck by the richness of offerings, this can also be a source of frustration for anyone who is systematically inclined. One problem with attempting to make sense of social theory is that one has to begin by asking, "What *isn't* social theory?" Are essays on manners and morals social theory? Are the works of certain authors—Marx or Weber—social theory? Is a discussion of the concept of territoriality and its application to an understanding of male/female power relations social theory? Or should one simply say that social theory is a set of interrelated propositions in which lower-order propositions are derived from higher-order propositions? The answer is probably that anything which seems to illuminate some portion of social reality in a new way can be treated as social theory. This is, needless to say, a general answer. For particular schools of thought, only propositions framed in a certain way are deserving of the name *theory*. Yet that sort of dictatorial nonsense prevents us from understanding why there is so much social theory. One or two explanations, which will necessarily and unfortunately involve categorization, may help.

When I began the enterprise of collecting a set of articles on contemporary social theories, I was struck by two things. First, reviewers, apparently could not agree about any given paper. One would state that an article contained "the best thing I've seen in this area," while another claimed it contained the worst. Also, the references for articles in an area differed widely from article to article. The reason? Sociologists, especially those who call themselves social theorists, often do not draw on a common body of information, nor do they have common standards for deciding what is or is not useful. They have very different perceptions of what theory is, and what it should do.

My own feeling is that there are six different kinds of general theory or perceptions of what the function of social theory is. These are: (1) theory as *science*; (2) theory as *method*; (3) theory as a *technique of illumination*; (4) theory as *ideology*; (5) theory as a *critique*; and, finally, (6) theory as *praxis*. Let us examine them independently, ignoring, for the moment, the inevitable overlaps.

When one speaks of theory as *science*, one means that the sociologist, usually of a positivist bent, believes that formal laws underly human behavior, and that these laws can be discovered, codified, and put into propositional form. A theory, then, becomes a system in which explanation consists of deducing lower-order propositions from higher-order ones. These propositional systems may range (using Merton's terms [1957]) from low, to middle, to high. There are a number of these formal systems in sociology, ranging from Parsonian "action" theory through "exchange" theory and others of the "middle range," to axiomatic "theories" of deviance, suicide, and criminology. General systems theorists, exact theorists, network analysts, and their brethren continue to refine their work in the hope of discovering laws about human behavior. These theories do not dominate the discipline, for reasons that also apply to some of the other approaches. First, formal theory doesn't seem to be about the world in which we live. This was one of Phillips' points (1971:xi) in *Knowledge from What*, when he took the rather pessimistic position that "sociology in no way represents some codified, cumulative body of knowledge," and that "individuals acquainted with certain sociological theories are unlikely to know any more about the real world than people who are unfamiliar with these theories." I would suggest that this dim view might apply only to certain types of theory. Another related criticism that is applied to formal or deductive theory is perhaps best represented by C. Wright Mills's condemnation (1959) of both grand theory and abstracted empiricism. Grand theory is not historically grounded, and abstracted empiricism, which sometimes forms the basis for such things as axiomatic theory, never goes beyond the data set with which it begins. The problem, though, is the same: we don't understand contemporary social reality or our place in it.

Theory also exists as *method*. A we–they dichotomy characterizes much of sociological thinking. "We" can understand what "they" are up to by putting ourselves in their place. Blumer (1956:686), speaking for symbolic interactionists, nicely summarized the relationship between theory and method, when theory *is* the method. "We can, and I think, must, look upon human life as chiefly a vast interpretative process in which people, singly and collectively, guide themselves by defining the objects, events, and situations which they encounter. . . . Any scheme designed to analyze human group life in its general character has to fit this process of interpretation." Though the level of sophistication varies greatly, many ethnomethodologists and phenomenologists see their theories as methods, or statements, about the way in which research is to be conducted and human behavior is to be understood.

The we–they perspective enters in another way, as Goudsblom (1977:181) has demonstrated. In 1783 Condorcet wanted to study human society as a naturalist would study bees, and Durkheim in *The Rules of the Sociological Method*, and again in *Suicide*, proposed to study behavior from a detached, analytic perspective. To Durkheim's credit he failed, for much of the richness of his two works comes from the fact that he attributed meaning to his actors by virtue of the fact that he, too, was one. Fortunately, some social theories, unlike those of the behaviorists or positivists, stress the necessity of considering actors' inner mental states.

Theory as a *technique of illumination* refers to the ways in which sociologists use "little" theories, or concepts, to illuminate portions of reality. If we accept the notion that language is an abstraction of reality, then any means of examining the world in some specialized fashion is a theory. Often what is interesting at one moment of history isn't at another. In a sense the concept of the melting-pot, a popular theory during the early 1900s, did explain the behavior of some ethnics, although the theory of concept, if you will, of ethnic awareness better describes what happened in the 1960s and 1970s. Sociology and social history have provided a number of such concepts or theories, such as the authoritarian personality, folkways, the Protestant ethic, capitalism, taboos, and *embourgeoisement*, that allow us some grasp of a historical moment. In her introduction to Benjamin's work, *Illuminations*, Hannah Arendt (1969:51) explains the value of insightful comment and the use of unique concepts. "And this thinking, fed by the present, works with the 'thought fragments' it can wrest from the past and gather about itself. Like a pearl diver who descends to the bottom of the sea, not to excavate the bottom and bring it to light but to pry loose the rich and the strange, the pearls and the coral in the depths, and to carry them to the surface . . ." Social theory in this context, then, seeks not to excavate the whole of reality, but merely a few valuable portions.

A fourth way of conceptualizing theory is to see it as Mannheim (1936) did, as a belief system, or an *ideology*. Sometimes these world views are rooted in particular classes, and will obviously change from one historical period to another, as when Marx alluded to the fact that the dominant ideas of an age are the ideas of the ruling class. Such theories, about how one *ought* to view the world, are sometimes called metatheories. (Followers of Kuhn [1962] could argue that the shared paradigms of a scientific community represent metatheories.) Gouldner (1974), in discussing Marxism and social theory, noted that the often overlooked metaphorical character of Marxism has been of primary importance in the struggles of revolutionaries such as Lenin and Castro. Gouldner (1974:17) wrote: "Theory thus becomes a sub- or counter-culture, a basis for community solidarity among those theorists, whose predominant effect is to encourage and support a profoundly aware and pervasive anticapitalist attitude and perspective." Under this category is humanistic sociology, black sociology, and sociology informed by a feminist perspective. These may not be explanatory systems, but they can be powerful models of interpretation.

Closely related to theory as illumination and ideology is theory as *critique*, which refers to a theory that serves simultaneously as ideology, critique, and illumination. Here theory addresses itself to the facts of the human condition or the ways in which the social world has become unbearable (Berger, 1972:51) for many. The task of good social theory has always been to explain human suffering. The aim of critical social theory is to demystify the world, to show contemporary men and women what constrains them and what their routes to freedom are. Though he might resist the label "critical theorist," this is the role that Peter Berger (1963) identified for sociology in *Invitation to Sociology*, when he talked about the emancipatory possibilities that were available through sociological understanding. A number of sociological concepts have an emancipatory or demystifying character, as do notions such as social class, bourgeoisie, sexism, or racism.

Finally, there is theory as *praxis*, or the wedding of thought and action. This vision of theory as the obligation to take action is normally associated with a Marxist tradition, though there is no reason why symbolic interactionism, or an ethnomethodological vision, would not cause one to take action. The point is that theory, generated from an analysis of a specific historical situation, may be an argument for intervention. Such theory demystifies, clarifies, shows people the source of their misery, and the means of overcoming it. This is Marx's point in *The Poverty of Philosophy* (MEGA,I,6).

> Just as the economists are the scientific representatives of the bourgeoisie, so the socialists and communists are the theorists of the proletariat. . . . But as history proceeds and as the struggle of the

proletariat takes shape more clearly, [these theorists] need no longer look for science in their own mind; they only have to give account of what is happening before their eyes, and make themselves its voice. As long as they seek science and only create systems, as long as they are the beginning of the struggle, they see in misery nothing but misery, without recognizing its revolutionary and subversive aspect, which will overthrow the old society. But from this point on, science, produced by the historical movement and consciously associated with this movement, has ceased to be doctrinaire and has become revolutionary.

Formal theory, concepts, ideological statements, and pure vision are grouped together under the heading of social theory, for only this initially broad categorization permits one to capture the spirit of what has been done and is being done in sociology under that name. With due respect to Robert Merton, the functions of contemporary social theory are to provide:

1. The elements of a *science*, or theory as a propositional system.
2. A *methodology* for analyzing society.
3. An *illumination* of the dark corners of the world.
4. An *ideology* to guide one's work and to create a subculture.
5. A *critique* of human social reality.
6. A *praxis* that dictates intervention.

One could argue that a good social theory should encompass all aspects of this list, though it is unusual to find such efforts. What is generally asked of a social theory is that it give us some practical handle on the world, particularly on our individual lives. Theory is a form of imagination, in the sense that Mills (1959) used the concept. For Mills there were three basic questions with which sociologists should concern themselves. The first relates to the structure of industrial society: what are its essential components, how are they related, and how does our society differ from others? The second relates to history: where does our society stand in human history, and where and how is our society changing? The third relates to personality: what types of men and women prevail in society, and what types will come to prevail? The answers to such questions help individuals better understand their lives. Social theory from this perspective simply—although it is no simple matter—means "making sense of things." For a given individual, any of the six functions of social theory could meet this criterion, and perhaps only one of them would serve this purpose. This is a powerful argument for not restricting the vision of what social theory should be. Gouldner's criterion (1970) for a good theory is a gut-level feeling that the explanation makes sense. This is why much of Goffman's work (1959), though difficult to put into propositional form, receives such wide acceptance. Erikson's book (1977) on how people reacted to a community disaster would also fall into this category.

Yet one is still left with the question of why it is that sociology has so many versions of theory, and why few theories serve all of the six functions. The problem of social theory is partly epistemological and partly historical. First, consider some of the roots of this situation.

During the Enlightenment, social theorists believed, among other things, that humankind would progress because of a combination of human (which also meant humane) reason and empirical methods. This distinction eventually led to a split between the objective and subjective views of human existence. Social theorists often took into account only one realm of human existence, at considerable cost to their theories, and to their understanding of man. In Durkheim's work, for instance, there is a general dissociation of subject and object. Moreover, modern sociology has carried to this dissociation to its logical extreme in the areas of theory and method. Survey research represents an extreme of the mind-body division, as does the elevation of methodological techniques to the status of theories, as sometimes occurs in discussion of path analysis.

Other social theorists seem to have abandoned the social world as objective reality. Aristotle and Plato both said that one becomes an individual through society. In contrast, some contemporary thinkers argue that one becomes an individual in spite of society. This celebration of self is represented in the United States by subjective social theories, of which ethnomethodology is one type. These are based on the philosophies of hermeneutics and phenomenology, though some may argue that Garfinkel (1967) is attempting to forge the links between the objective and subjective realms. It should be noted that this preoccupation with the self is primarily an American idiosyncracy; among continental social theorists, hermeneutics deals with events beyond the individual.

There are a number of other ways to characterize the kinds of sociologies that grew out of this vision of the nature of humans. Alan Dawe (1970), for instance, argued that there are now two sociologies—a sociology of social action and a sociology of social system. These sociologies are grounded in a historical concern with order and control. One theory, that of humanists, sees human beings as spontaneous actors, able to create their own worlds when freed from unnatural constraints. The other stresses control. The neat division into humanists and anti-humanists has its problems, as Morris (1977:175) noted. It might be more useful, she suggests, to see the two sociologies not necessarily as opposing political philosphies but merely as having different foci. "The one sees society from the outside in, the other from the inside out."

Epistemological difficulties are exacerbated by the historically specific bases of social theories. Mannheim holds that ideologies vary from one historical moment to another; my observation shows that theories have a distinct political appeal. Often social theorists are caught up in their own history, and their theories become statements of personal belief. A statement of personal belief even occasionally assumes the status of a social theory. This problem relates to the age-old one of relevance, and, consequently, trivialization.

If one goes no further back than the nineteenth century, one finds sociologists attempting to make their social theories relevant to the times. One of the main objections raised today (Schwendingers, 1974)· against such people as Spencer is that he and others often wrote for a growing bourgeoisie with whom they were all too happy to identify. But relevance need not limit theory to the interests of one section of the population. In the 1960s, when new sociological theories were flourishing, a relevant theory was one directed at the inequalities in the structure. There is, of course, nothing wrong with a social theory that deals with this question, but the historical specificity of some work sometimes renders it trivial. Goudsblom (1977:196) summarized the dilemma of the modern sociologist as follows:

> As the dilemma of trivialization shows, sociologists are faced with a set of goals that seem at times incompatible. They are expected to produce knowledge which is precise in its factual references, systematic in its manner of classification and explanation, of far-reaching scope, and relevant to a variety of purposes.

The problem of relevance will not disappear, for it is rooted to one of the fundamental purposes of social theory, which is to make sense of things. The theories which arose in the 1960s and continue to be developed to deal with "political" problems, as well as some of the older theories which were resurrected at that time (such as those of the rediscovered continental theorists, particularly those members of the Frankfurt school who had settled in New York), do not always explain the times or our anxieties. Some of the trends which emerged during this period were preoccupied with problems of political legitimacy, a general debunking of values and tradition, and a concomitant celebration of the self. Hermeneutics, phenomenology, and ethnomethodology certainly reflect these trends.

It is possible to list some of the trends of the late 1960s and early 1970s which persist to the moment. Hinkle (1978:67–69), for example, identified seven trends in modern social theory. (There is some legitimate disagreement about what constitutes a real trend [Turner, 1978:81–82].) A greater variety of topics are being dealt with at the present time, but in spite of the diversity, many of the theorists are still concerned with the assumptions of positivism and empiricism. There is also renewed attack on the notion that a value-neutral sociology is workable. In order to escape the problems of positivism, many schools are reexamining their ontological assumptions. We also find an increasing acceptance of topics that were once considered philosophical, and, consequently, a greater awareness of the work of such men as Hegel, Husserl, and Heidegger. There is increasing contact and awareness between American and continental sociologists. Finally, there is a growing exchange of ideas with other disciplines such as science and the arts (also see Warhsay, 1975). This diversity in the field, though one can cavil about directions and strengths, is a direct outgrowth of the epistemological and historical problems identified earlier.

Heroic efforts are always made to bridge the objective–subjective gap in social theory. Marx's system clearly involved an understanding of the individual situated in a historical setting, and his concept of *praxis* specifically addressed this question. I believe that this was Weber's intention, also, in his writing on *verstehen*. In his now famous introduction to *Economy and Society* (1968:3), Weber defined sociology as "a science which seeks to understand social action interpretively, and thereby to explain it causally in its course and its effects." The discovery of causal laws is the ultimate goal of sociology, but understanding of human motives is central. Like the phenomenologist, then, Weber regarded as important the study of the ways in which individuals, constrained by others, manage to act; like Marx, he believed in the importance of the historical context. To jump ahead in our argument, one can anticipate that a social theory which is to have transhistorical validity, and which is to be satisfactory to social beings, must deal with the reality of the social actor.

Along these lines, Appelbaum (1978:76) described the power of Marxist dialectics.

> What distinguishes Marxism from positivist social science is its ability to move simultaneously on two levels: it formulates the laws of the "natural history" of capitalist economic organization, and at the same time demonstrates the ideological (i.e., historically situated) character of those laws so that they might be repealed by self-conscious workers organized collectively in their own interests.

It would not be inappropriate to note that sociology has drifted considerably from what Marx, Weber, and other major social theorists saw as the mission of sociology.

Are there any truly new social theories? The issues are the same.

Consider Hinkle's comments (1978) on trends in sociological theory. Much that is labeled new is really an attempt to clarify an older theory or is a comment about what ought to be emphasized. There is also a growing tendency in sociology to talk about how one ought to perceive reality rather than about the nature of reality itself. A consequence of this is an inability to *do* theory—to create a system to explain the social order and to test that system. Perhaps we have enough social theory. Whatever their faults, Parsons, Durkheim, Marx, Weber, Simmel, Toennies, Tocqueville, and Veblen did provide us with total images of reality. I do not want my remarks on the diversity of social theory to encourage a theoretical free-for-all, nor are they to be taken as a statement in support of theoretical relativity. We must do our best to examine the truth value of any given assertion. There must be some way of adjudicating between competing definitions of what is real. To stretch things to the political arena, we need to know when we are—and when we are not—being lied to.

Of course, it is not easy to create a theory and to examine it under the harsh light of social reality. Marx, Weber, Durkheim, and others devoted their lives to clarifying, applying, changing, and reformulating their visions of social order. Their systems have transhistorical validity because they tried to consider the relations and contradictions between the political, economic, cultural, educational, and familial structures, as well as humans' biological nature in a historical setting. Modern theories are often about specific, and increasingly limited, portions of reality which cannot be integrated with one another. There is little, if any, indication that theorists are aware of the historical moment and its effects on perception, or of what the epistemological issues are. Dealing with limited portions of the social order may be appropriate and necessary, but that cannot excuse failure to deal with larger questions. Small questions may be a step to approaching greater issues, but we cannot get big answers to small questions.

The other extreme poses its problems, too. Global cosmologies are as bad as atomized empiricism (Mills, 1959). Sociologists need to seek the reality that lies in between. Nisbet (1976) suggested that there are a number of schemes common to the social sciences (community, masses, power, and so forth), and that these themes extend across the ages. They comprise a central part of major social theory, and they must be dealt with anew in each historical period. Similarly, Marx claimed that in order to understand the historical moment, one must examine political and social institutions and generate laws for the explanation of what one finds, understanding that they will be time-bound if they are to have any utility. (This is why it is not legitimate to apply Marx's theories of economics to any social system other than a capitalist one.) In this sense new theories are not really built on the theories of the past in the way that people normally think of advancing knowledge.

> ... Of all the Idols of the Mind of Profession regnant today the worst is that which Bacon might have placed among his Idols of the Theatre: the belief, first that there is something properly called theory in sociology, and second, that the aim of all sociological research should be that of adding to or advancing theory (Nisbet, 1976:20).

The grand theories of Comte, Spencer, and Ward are in the past. What remain are the insights gleaned from the use of those theories. For Nisbet theory is the illumination of the sense of discovery that accompanies any genuinely fresh study of a piece of the world we live in. That is why Simmel's *Secret Society*, Riesman's *The Lonely Crowd*, Goffman's *Asylums*, Anderson's *Passages from Antiquity to Feudalism*, and Wallerstein's *The Modern World System* fall under the heading of theory. They provide us with fresh insights. According to Nisbet, this is the best that sociology can aspire to. The function of social theory is to provide new portraits: surreal, post-modern, it does not matter what; as long as they are new. Once sociologists have seen them, the ways in which they perceive reality are forever changed. Nisbet (1976:7) wrote: "What artist of the period gave us role-types in his novel or painting more evocative than what we draw from Marx about the bourgeois and the worker, from Weber about the bureaucrat, or from Michels on the party politician?"

One can agree with Nisbet, and at the same time, entertain the notion that social theory should be other things as well. I mentioned earlier that social theory should make sense to individuals by allowing them to retrospectively explain their lives and I made an assumption that sociologists should have something to say about modern human dilemmas. These two assumptions are not generally grounded in the realities of contemporary social theory. To take but a few examples, behavioral sociology and general systems theory illuminate only small portions of reality. They could address large issues, but they do not. Critical theory, which sensitizes us to the concepts, images, and language used in constructing theory, fails to provide a grounding and often results in a deep pessimism about the possibility of change (Clecak, 1973). Ethnomethodology offers useful insights into the means by which rules are constructed, but is often ahistorical and fails to deal with problems of power. The varieties of Marxist sociology call attention to the inherent contradictions within capitalist states and to some of the ways in which the system guarantees its own survival, but its images of human beings are nowhere as valuable as its dialectics, which could provide a means of understanding how total systems operate. In short, most modern social theories are limited. Most books dealing with modern social theory note a need for a synthesis; some even attempt it.

One way to approach a new synthesis would be to address ourselves again to the supposedly irreconcilable mind/body split that was introduced to sociology by the Kantians, and confused by the neo-Kantians. Benton (1977:138), in what I believe is one of the clearest discussions of the problems of positivism, argues that ". . . the principal, Neo-Kantian, humanist tradition of thought fails to establish its thesis of a fundamental divide between the natural sciences and the 'human,' 'cultural' or 'historical' studies." According to Benton, the thesis fails on two essential counts. First, it unwittingly accepts the positivist interpretations of what science should be and how it operates. (One of the enduring contributions of the phenomenologists is their critique of positivism and their lament over its absence in the scientific process.) Second, it tried to show that the social sciences required a different methodology when all that was required was a method and form "adequate to the specificity of their object." The implication of Benton's analysis is that there might well be an alternative to anti-humanistic positivism and anti-positivistic humanism in the social sciences.

Benton's answer is a materialist theory of knowledge, the roots of which I will not trace here. Suffice it to say that he takes the idea of a materialist philosophy from Durkheim, adds *verstehen*, concepts relative to a theory of ideology, and non-positivist concepts of causality appropriate to the social sciences. What Benton takes to the bosom of a materialist theory of knowledge is well thought out. The theory of materialist knowledge is as follows (Benton, 1977:171):

1. It recognizes the reality of the object of knowledge, the independence of the "knowing subject," the process of production of knowledge, and the knowledge itself.

2. Its adequacy to the object of knowledge is the ultimate standard by which the cognitive status of thought is to be assessed.

3. It recognizes the existence of ideas as realities in their own right.

4. It theorizes these realities not as *sui generis*, but as the result of underlying causal mechanisms.

My objection to Benton's well-thought out schema is that, while not denying the need for a *praxis*, it does not give it its due. My own perference, then, is for a combination of critical theory and Marxist structuralism: critical theory, because it sensitizes us to the process of theory construction, how we perceive reality, and the fact that theories are political; Marxist structuralism, because it sensitizes us to the historical realm and the contradictions inherent in modern life and provides a viable image of what can be.

This is the project that Fay (1975:92–110) outlined when he spoke to the development of a critical social science. For him a critical social science is characterized by three main features. First, it accepts the interpretive categories of social science, which means that it is essentially anti-positivist. (This is similar to Benton's definition of a materialist knowledge, which accepts the reality of the social actor. Second, a critical social science accepts the fact that people perform many actions they have no control over. This is an attempt to address the Marxist critique of the ethnomethodological or phenomenological assumption that people are manipulators of social reality.) Finally, a critical social theory is interconnected with social practice, "such that what is to count as truth is partially determined by the specific ways in which scientific theory is supposed to relate to practical action" (Fay, 1975:94). This means that social theory has a *responsibility*. It must explain the sufferings and needs of actors in a fashion that they can understand and so they will know what has caused things to be the way they are. Finally, it must allow them to understand what might be done to change things.

What passes for social theory should be evaluated in terms of these criteria, though one must remember that any given theory illuminates different portions of reality. This does not mean that theories are relative, but that now is not the time for dogma within the discipline. I personally recommend and argue for a combination of Marxism and critical theory, but whatever allows us to plumb the depths and return is valuable. In that spirit I believe the collection of works that follows is without peer.

REFERENCES

APPLEBAUM, RICHARD
1978 "Marxist method: Structural constraints and social *praxis.*" The American Sociologist 13 (February):73–81.
ARENDT, HANNAH (ed.)
1969 "Walter Benjamin: 1892–1940." Introduction in Walter Benjamin, Illuminations. New York: Schocken Books.
BENTON, TED
1977 Philosophical Foundations of the Three Sociologies. London: Routledge and Kegan Paul.
BERGER, JOHN
1972 Selected Essays and Articles. Harmondsworth: Penguin.
BERGER, PETER
1972 Invitation to Sociology. New York: Doubleday.

BLUMER, HERBERT
  1956 "Sociological analysis and the variable." American Sociological Review
         19 (December):683–690.
CLECAK, PETER
  1973 Radical Paradoxes. New York: Harper & Row.
DAWE, ALAN
  1970 "The two sociologies." British Journal of Sociology 21 (June):207–218.
ERIKSON, KAI
  1977 Everything in Its Path. New York: Simon & Schuster.
FAY, BRIAN
  1975 Social Theory and Political Practice. London: George Allen and Unwin.
GARFINKEL, HAROLD
  1967 Studies in Ethnomethodology. Englewood Cliffs, N.J.: Prentice-Hall.
GOFFMAN, ERVING
  1959 The Presentation of Self in Everyday Life. New York: Doubleday.
GOUDSBLOM, JOHN
  1977 Sociology in the Balance. Oxford: Basil Blackwell.
GOULDNER, ALVIN W.
  1970 The Coming Crisis in Western Sociology. New York: Basic Books.
  1974 "Marxism and social theory." Theory and Society 1:17–35.
HINKLE, GISELA J.
  1978 "Seeing trends in recent sociological theory." Wisconsin Sociologist
         15 (Spring/Summer):63–74.
KUHN, THOMAS
  1962 The Structure of Scientific Revolutions. Chicago: University of Chicago
         Press.
MANNHEIM, KARL
  1936 Ideology and Utopia: An Introduction to the Sociology of Knowledge.
         New York: Harcourt, Brace and World.
MARX, KARL
  1847 The Poverty of Philosophy. Moscow: Foreign Languages Publishing
         House. (Translated from the 1847 French edition, n.d.)
MERTON, ROBERT K.
  1957 Social Theory and Social Structure. Glencoe, Ill.: The Free Press.
MILLS, C. WRIGHT
  1959 The Sociological Imagination. New York: Oxford University Press.
MORRIS, MONICA B.
  1977 An Excursion into Creative Sociology. New York: Columbia University
         Press.
NISBET, ROBERT
  1967 Sociology as an Art Form. New York: Oxford University Press.
PHILLIPS, DEREK L.
  1971 Knowledge from What? Chicago: Rand-McNally.
SCHWENDINGER, HERMAN, and JULIA SCHWENDINGER
  1974 The Sociologists of the Chair. New York: Basic Books.

TURNER, JONATHAN H.
   1978 "Some problematic trends in sociological theorizing." Wisconsin
        Sociologist 15 (Spring/Summer):80–88.
WARSHAY, LEON H.
   1975 The Current State of Sociological Theory. New York: McKay.
WEBER, MARX
   1968 Economy and Society. Translated by Guenther Roth and Claus Wittich.
        New York: Bedminster Press.

PART I
WORLD VIEWS

The title "World Views" may annoy some, coming as it does at a time when theoretical frameworks are attempting to deal with a number of historical, philosophical, economic, and political problems in a transhistorical fashion. Yet the two articles in this section deal with capitalism, which is certainly a worldwide phenomenon; Marxism and world-system theory are two ways of dealing with it.

Because of its diversity, Marxist theory is often difficult to define, and it is not clear to some just where or how Marxism might be applied. Burawoy illustrates some of the issues dividing Marxists and how these controversies stem from Marx's own work. In the first part of his paper, he looks at the family, law, and the world capitalist system from two perspectives on social structure. In the second part, the dynamics of capitalism, the struggles between classes, races, and genders are seen as sources of change. Marx's view of history and Marxist theories of the modern state are also dealt with.

Wallerstein's discussion of world-system theory has been elaborated in his book on *The Modern World-System*. In this article he demonstrates the need to understand human behavior, particularly economic behavior, with a vision that trenscends the nation-state. A world-system perspective assumes, to use Wallerstein's words, that social action takes place in an entity within which there is an ongoing division of labor, and it seeks to discover empirically whether or not such an entity is unified either culturally or politically. This perspective is especially valuable for understanding the means by which the capitalist world system developed during the sixteenth century, as well as how it operates today in terms of creating a worldwide division of labor.

15

1. Contemporary Currents in Marxist Theory

MICHAEL BURAWOY

Four convictions inform this essay. First, there is no Marxist alternative. There are only a plethora of Marxist alternatives—the accumulation of over a century of debate, struggle and evolution. Second, Marxism has overtaken Marx. But it still remains true to his methods, his categories and his concerns, and that is what makes it Marxist. Third, Marxism provides total portraits of the world, leaving no arena of social life unexplored. Fourth, Marxism systematically links the practical and the theoretical, the concrete and the abstract. Each particular theoretical perspective within Marxism is reshaped through the exploration of the problems it identifies. In this short paper I can only begin to sketch the basis for these assertions. For reasons of space I shall confine myself to contemporary issues within Marxism, and even then I shall cover only a small number of the current controversies. The paper is divided into four sections. Each section begins with a theoretical introduction, which is followed by one or two illustrations of the concrete research generated by different perspectives. In the first section, I deal with two notions of social structure which produce different Marxisms, and I illustrate these by reference to two very different phenomena—the family and the world system. In the second section, after outlining the implications of the different notions of totality for the understanding of history I examine class, race and sex as possible agents of change. In the third section, I discuss the idea of "reproduction" and examine it with reference to

Source: Reprinted from *The American Sociologist* 13 (February 1978):50–64.

different theories of the capitalist state. In the final section, I discuss Marx's projection of history into the future and contemporary Marxist notions of passages out of the present.

TOTALITY: STRUCTURED OR EXPRESSIVE?

Whatever else they may be, Marxists are not empiricists.[1] This, of course, does not mean that they do not confront the empirical world. Rather, it means they do not measure for the sake of measuring. They do not mistake appearance for essence, ideology for reality. On the contrary, Marxists make a radical distinction between the two. They try to penetrate everyday experience to its underlying structure. By searching for a totality, they try to show that what appears as common sense—as natural, inevitable, and necessary—in fact rests on the existence of certain conditions which are not immutable but socially produced. The concrete empirical world is not "received" as given or viewed as separate from the apparatus used to understand it. Just as astronomers are not deceived by the apparent movements of celestial objects but seek to transform and explain appearances; just as Freud developed a theory which both transformed and explained the phantasmagoria of dream life; so Marxists following Marx attempt to unveil the hidden secrets behind lived experience, behind common sense, that is, behind the world of ideology. More specifically, they try to advance a *theory* of social structure; they try to show how networks of social relations into which we enter as individuals are produced by an *underlying structure*. This underlying structure then becomes the object of analysis: its dynamics, its contradictions, and its effects on the experience of particular individuals.

Within Marxism there are two distinct notions of how a social structure should be theoretically constructed. On the one hand, there is the idea of a Hegelian totality in which a single "essence" or dominant principle comes to pervade the entire society. Each part of the social structure becomes an expression of the whole, of the defining "spirit." For Lukács (1971)"commodification" or "reification," for Marcuse (1964) "one dimensionality," for Braverman (1974) Taylorism (the separation of mental and manual labor and workers' loss of control over their labor)—these are the dominant principles which both order and are expressed through social relations, not merely within the economic realm, but in leisure, in the family, in politics, in the cultural realm—in short, throughout capitalist society. On the other hand, there is the idea of a structured totality, in which a single part (the economic) determines the *relations* among all parts.[2] The economy, by virtue of its functional requirements (or, as Marxists say, conditions of reproduction), defines the contributions of different parts of society and thus the relations among those parts. Thus, it is a condition of existence of the capitalist economy that the legal system protect private property, that the family reproduce the labor force, that ideology legitimate capitalist relations, that the state enforce law and order, and so forth. The relations among the parts are established on the basis of their distinctive contributions to the working of the whole. Furthermore, the "function" of each part defines its form or structure, and in so doing, endows it with an autonomy and a logic of its own. Three illustrations of the different types of totality follow.

The Law

The "function" of the legal system is to define a set of formal rules which regulates and preserves capitalist relations. But in order to do this its operation must appear legitimate. The law must define and enforce "fair" rules. That is, it must treat all people as though they were equal and not distinguish between capitalists and workers; it must treat all property as though it were the same and not distinguish between property involved in the production of profit, such as machines, and property that is simply consumed unproductively, such as shirts. Moreover, changes in the law must appear to emerge from its own logic and not in response to particular interest groups. In short, the law possesses a coherence and autonomy of its own so it can effectively perform its function. It obeys principles and creates categories of people different from those in other parts of the totality.

By contrast, in an expressive totality the legal system is regarded as an expression of the single logic or essence that defines capitalism. Thus, if commodification and the universalization of exchange are regarded as the defining essence of capitalism, then the law will appear as an expression of that essence—it will operate on universalistic and impersonal criteria. There is little sense here of the legal system performing particular needs in the maintenance of capitalism. The legal system is not endowed with an autonomy of its own. Rather, its existence embodies the essence of capitalism.[3] Functional interdependence is replaced by a principle of domination. I shall illustrate these differences with two further examples—the family and the world system.

The Family

From the point of view of the capitalist economy the family performs a number of definite and necessary functions. It maintains and renews the laboring population, that is, it reproduces labor power. It sends that labor power off to factories and offices. It prepares youth for the alienating experience of work. It socializes children for their future procreative and reproductive roles. It is a labor reservoir prepared for increased demands for industrial labor, as when women enter the wage labor force. It engages in consumption work, such as shopping. In the structured totality, the family not only changes with the changing requirements of the capitalist economy, but it also possesses a structure of its own and therefore a certain relative autonomy which allows it to engage in the activities mentioned above (see, for example, Mitchell, 1971; Dalla Costa and James, 1972; Weinbaum and Bridges, 1976). Alternatively, the expressive totality may depict the family as a victim of commodification, in which the cash nexus enters the family; of reification, in which members of the family treat one another as objects; of Taylorization, in which domestic work becomes fragmented and de-skilled; of whatever is defined as the essence of capitalism. That is, the essence of capitalism, its defining spirit, thrusts itself out from the core to penetrate the entire fabric of social life. Even the family, as one of the last arenas of potential resistance, succumbs, is stripped, and loses what little autonomy it had (for examples, see the Frankfurt Institute of Social Research, 1972; Braverman, 1974; Ewen, 1977).

The World System

If capitalism has managed to prevade and incorporate the farthest corners of social life within many Western societies, has it also incorporated the farthest corners of the world? Is the "world system" itself an expressive totality, in which each nation is subordinated to and devastated by the expansion of capitalism (Wallerstein, 1974)? Or is the world system a structured totality, in which different nations exhibit a political independence and an economy constituted out of a combination of capitalist and noncapitalist modes of production (Genovese, 1971; Mandel, 1975)? The answer depends in part upon what is being explained (the origin of capitalism, the dynamics of contemporary imperialism, national liberation movements, etc.) and in part upon the notion of capitalism. (Of course, the two are not unrelated.) Does capitalism refer to the particular relations men and women enter into as they transform nature, that is, a mode of production? Or does capitalism refer to the particular relations men and women enter into as they exchange the products of their labor, that is, a mode of exchange?[4]

The latter position leads to a discussion of the progressive subordination of peripheral regions of the world to the core regions (Baran, 1957; Frank, 1969; Wallerstein, 1974), and to the examination of the forms of unequal exchange between powerful capitalist nations and the third world (Emmanuel, 1972). What is missing from such analyses is a specific elaboration of the response and possible resistance to the spread of capitalism, or at least to the uneven development capitalism brings in its wake. The underdeveloped world becomes a dependent appendage of the advanced world with little power to resist subordination. Nairn's (1977) analysis of nationalism is one of the few attempts to come to terms with modes of resistance. Nationalism—always a thorn in Marxist flesh—can be understood, argues Nairn, as the attempt of a rising or weak bourgeoisie to stimultaneously harness resources for the development of capitalism and resist subordination to a powerful international bourgeoisie. To this end, the emergent capitalist class of the periphery and semiperiphery mobilizes the only resource at its disposal, namely, the people. It does this through the ideologies of nationalism and populism. Nairn convincingly demonstrates the link between the combined and uneven nature of capitalist development, and the appearance of Scottish nationalism and the nationalism of Western Europe in the nineteenth century. Without much effort his ideas can be extended to contemporary Asia, Africa and Latin America. Yet the particular form and content of those nationalisms have still to be examined.

This can be more appropriately accomplished through a vision of the "world system" as composed of a combination of capitalist and noncapitalist modes of production (see, for example, Lenin, 1960). The particular arrangement of modes of production (capitalist, petty commodity, primitive communist, etc.) within peripheral or semiperipheral territories provides a specific material basis for different forms of resistance, particular types of nationalist movements, and so forth. What becomes significant in this structured totality is not the erosion of all precapitalist modes of production by capitalist modes of production, but the political and ideological forms which facilitate the coexistence of precapitalist and capitalist modes of production (Wolpe, 1972; Laclau, 1971) and the transfers of labor and surplus from one mode of production to another through, for example, a system of migrant labor. The second perspective, therefore, emphasizes the *interdependence* of precapitalist and capitalist modes of production whereas the first perspective stresses the *destruction* of precapitalist modes of production.

HISTORY: WITH OR WITHOUT A SUBJECT?

Like social structure, history also has to be constructed. It is not received as a succession of events but rather is constituted out of its premises. And the first premise is that men and women must be able to live in order to make history, that is, they must transform nature into the means of their existence. Therefore, history is conceived as the succession of ways of producing the means of existence, that is, as the succession of modes of production—primitive communist, ancient, feudal, capitalist, etc. Each mode of production is defined by a set of relations into which men and women enter and the corresponding form of consciousness. Accordingly, history has two aspects: (1) the dynamics of a given mode of production—how it changes while remaining the same; and (2) transitions from one mode of production to another. I shall consider the latter in the final section, while this and the following section will be largely devoted to the dynamics of capitalism.

Marxists constitute the history of the capitalist totality out of its essence or underlying structures. Thus, the expressive totality sees the history of capitalism as the unilinear unfolding of an essence, a single principle (commodification, Taylorism, etc.), as it invades and incorporates ever greater expanses of social life. As portrayed in the works of Marcuse (1964), Lukács (1971), Aronowitz (1973) and Braverman (1974), capitalist domination possesses an ineluctable logic which eliminates resistance, absorbs alternatives and assimilates critique. Because it leaves largely unexamined the *problematic conditions* of domination, this perspective inevitably leads towards utopianism, determinism and pessimism. Therefore, commentators such as Marcuse tend to embrace almost any potentially emancipatory challenge to domination the occasion offers—students, new working class, women, etc.

The structured totality produces a very different notion of social change. Here history is marked by an indeterminacy. It is not unilinear or unidimensional but uneven; it is the combination of the disparate histories of its separate parts, namely the political, the ideological, the economic, and so on. Since these parts move with their own relatively autonomous dynamics, revolutionary situations or conjunctures can appear with a degree of unpredictability. Thus, the expressive totality directs our attention to *arenas of resistance*, that is, to particular places; the structured totality focuses on *times of crisis*, that is, particular conjunctures.[5]

Thus far we have conceived of the history of capitalism as the unfolding of some irrevocable logic or combination of logics. But logics, structures, and principles do not *make* history. Who does? And furthermore, does it matter who does? Does history take place behind our backs, beyond our control, or are there agents who consciously shape the movement of history? This is the terrain of classical Marxist debate expressed through the dichotomies of freedom and necessity, revolution and science, voluntarism and determinism. Is the historical process an unwinding of irrevocable laws inscribed in the structure of the mode of production, such as the falling rate of profit, whose pace may be temporarily halted or even reversed, but whose ultimate direction and destiny is preordained? Or are there no such laws and is history contingent on unconstrained class struggle? Of course, these polarizations are crude, presenting false dichotomies which Marx warned against—men and women make history, but under conditions not of their own choosing. Marx ackowledged these constraints, but he still regarded class as the agent and class struggle as the motor of history. What then has become of Marx and Engels' opening to the *Communist Manifesto:* "The history of all hitherto existing society is the history of class struggles"? Let us see.

Class: Historical Actor or Sociological Category?

Within the Marxist tradition two notions of class have emerged: class in itself—a sociological *category* designating particular places in relation to the means of production; and class for itself—a social *force* which makes history, perhaps even marches through history. The problem is to connect the two concepts both in theory and in practice. Marx tended to presume some inevitability about the association of particular places in the social structure with particular historical actors. And there have been some brilliant "demonstrations" of the logical and historical necessity for a class in itself to turn into a class for itself. Both Lukács (1971) and Thompson (1963)—one in an abstract theory and the other in a concrete account—identify the proletariat as the subject of history, the subject whose presence comes to dominate all areas of society. The totality comes to be identified with the emergence of the proletariat, in whom science and revolution, necessity and freedom, object and subject, are unified. But history has confounded brilliance and created, if anything, a widening gap between the two notions of class. After all, what happened to the English working class after 1830, where Thompson's account stops? What happened to its revolutionary consciousness? What has happened to revolutionary proletariats of Western Europe during the last fifty years? Faced with a proletariat which is not revolutionary, or with agents of social change who do not constitute a class, that is, who are not defined by a unique relationship to the means of production, Marxists find themselves embracing one notion of class or the other— hanging from one pole while stretching for the other as it recedes into the distance. Those who vacillated have dropped into the gorge between the two.

Accordingly, some Marxists are beginning to develop different class maps of the capitalist social structure. Erik Wright (1976), for example, treats the United States as a combination of capitalist and petty commodity modes of production, which gives rise to three classes: capitalists, workers, and petty bourgeoisie. By introducing the notion of contradictory class location to represent "intermediary" positions between these classes (small employers, managers, supervisors, etc.), he has begun to forge new tools for illuminating the capitalist social formation.[6] These new Marxist class categories seem to promise a new theory of social structure, that is, of the production, linkages and dynamics of places in that structure which emerge from the tendencies of the capitalist mode of production and its reproduction requirements. For example, how do changes in the labor process (proletarianization and expropriation of skills) and in the economic structure (rise of service industries) create and destroy positions in the social structure (Braverman, 1974)? However, it should not be forgotten that such formulations lead right back to history without a subject. They ignore the fact that the production of places in the social structure becomes the object of struggle. Struggles among classes and other groups must be incorporated into a theory of social structure.

Alternatively, some Marxists cling to class as a historical force (Poulantzas, 1973; Przeworski, 1977; Balibar, 1977). Class in itself drops out, leaving only class for itself. Unfortunately, losing sight of the location of actors in relation to the means of production may lead to lumping together workers and capitalists into a single "class," or constituting women and blacks as a class denuded of its explicit link to the economic. To avoid such a predicament it may be necessary to bring back a weak notion of class in itself. Thus, one possibility is to restrict class as a historical force to politically organized agents of production. But these still may not be the significant historical actors. A second possibility is to regard historical actors as coalitions or alliances of classes defined in terms of agents of production. This would lead to a discussion of the organization and reorganization of relations among classes. The utility of these approaches would have to be explored empirically.

Sex and Race: The Achilles' Heel?

Not surprisingly, some Marxist thinkers (particularly in the United States) have been content to abandon class altogether, although this may have cast them outside the ambit of Marxism. Others, in trying to understand the quiescence of the working class, or at least the absence of revolutionary consciousness, have turned to gender and race as alternative sources of polarization and struggle, and as historical forces in their own right. Marx expected relations between classes to assimilate relations between nations, sexes and races, but for contemporary Marxists this is no longer a viable position. The creation and reproduction of these relations represent a theoretical challenge they have met with varying success. They have posed a number of questions. In what way, if any, can relationships of gender and race be linked to class and modes of production? Or do the social distinctions of gender and race transcend any periodization of history by class and mode of production? Are relations between men and women prior, historically or logically, to the relationship between dominant and subordinate classes?

Of course, this is no abstract issue. With the disappearance of classes under a putative communism, can we also be assured of the disappearance of other forms of oppression based on gender and race? What is the link between class and gender or class and race, not at an empirical level but at a theoretical level? In response to this problem, one avenue of investigation has been to ascertain whether there is male dominance in all precapitalist classless societies: whether there have been societies in which men did not dominate women (see Reiter, 1975 and Rosaldo and Lamphere, 1974, for two different sides of the debate over the universality of male dominance). The debate appears inconclusive due to ambiguity in the concept of dominance. Moreover, although such studies may shed light on the relationship between gender and oppression under primitive communism, it is quite another matter to generalize their results to any future form of communism.

Similar arguments can be made with respect to race, although they have been less well elaborated because of the seemingly accidental appearance of racial divisions. Jordan (1968) has traced racism to psycho-social attributes of the precapitalist era and before the emergence of slavery in the United States. But these issues do not broach the question critical to a Marxist understanding of race, namely, is it more helpful to look at the continuity of racial oppression through history and across modes of production, or is it more appropriate to examine racial oppression in terms of the particular mode of production in which it is found, such as slavery (Genovese, 1976) or capitalism? The question is not whether capitalism is the original source of racism, but whether the form racism assumes under capitalism is sufficiently different from its form under slavery to warrant an entirely separate treatment.

How have Marxists linked racial divisions, oppression and discrimination to the capitalist mode of production? Theorists of the dual economy, such as Harrison (1972), have tentatively suggested that racism may be reproduced through a segmented labor market linked to different fractions of capital (monopoly, competitive and service sectors). There is a tendency, it is argued, for blacks to fill places in the competitive and service sectors, while whites are awarded preference in the monopoly sectors. That the matching of race and labor market is not perfect only serves to obscure the class basis of race relations. Alternatively, race could be viewed in terms of modes of reproduction of labor power. The ghetto represents a particular system of reproducing labor power, just as the Mexican village constitutes a different mode of reproducing labor power. In both instances, ethnic or racial labeling obscures the different ways through which the labor force is maintained and renewed. Yet another possibility is to look at patterns of race relations as the product of the interrelationship among different modes of production. Thus, Wolpe (1972) argues that the apparatus of South African apartheid is a mechanism of reproducing a precapitalist mode of production alongside a capitalist mode of production. Marxism has not, and, I would argue, cannot develop a general theory of race relations. Instead, particular or local theories are generated to explain how different forms of race relations express and conceal the specific conjuncture and context in which they are produced and reproduced.

Therefore, the discovery that racism and male dominance are universal attributes, or at least exhibit a continuity across modes of production, would not of itself deal a death blow to Marxist analysis. But it would mean that two types of analyses would have to be developed: one concerned with understanding the reasons for the generality of the phenomenon irrespective of the historical context, and a second concerned with the particular forms it assumes in relation to any given mode or modes of production.[7]

REPRODUCTION AND DOMINATION

Whatever its dynamics, capitalism both changes and remains the same. How did Marx and how do Marxists talk about the continuity over time of those social relations which define the capitalist mode of production? Unlike much contemporary sociology, Marx did not "solve" the problem of order by focusing on a commitment to capitalism generated by the internalization of certain values and norms.[8] Values and norms are the product of social relations.[9] Capitalists accumulate and workers work because they are enmeshed in a set of social relations indispensible and independent of their will. But once established, social relations do not spontaneously maintain themselves; they do not persist of their accord, but rather have to be continually perpetuated, that is, reproduced. This notion of reproduction of social relations can be illustrated with a simple example. Within the capitalist mode of production there are two fundamentally different places. *Workers*, dispossessed of the means of gaining an independent livelihood, have to sell their capacity to work—their labor power—to *capitalists*, who own and control the means of production. In selling their labor power for a wage, workers renounce their power to appropriate the products of their labor. Instead, the capitalist expropriates the products of labor as commodities and transforms them into (gross) profit and future wages. In other words, as a result of producing a "thing," workers produce (earn) a wage which allows them and their families to survive, but only until the next working day; and they produce a profit which not only keeps the capitalist rich but also keeps him in business, and therefore guarantees the prospect of future wages. The production of things, therefore, produces on the one side the worker and on the other side the capitalist, that is, it *reproduces* the relationship between capital and labor.

This, in fact, is Marx's conception of the reproduction of capitalist relations. Marxists have proposed a number of reasons why it is no longer adequate to look upon the relations between capital and labor as automatically reproducing themselves through the production of commodities. I shall deal here with only two. First, there are relations among capitalists which tend to make the production, circulation and consumption of commodities more and more difficult. Second, there is a tendency for the reproduction of relations between capital and labor to generate different forms of class struggle, which in turn threaten to undermine those relations. These two sets of tendencies towards the dissolution of relations of production give rise to two types of theories of the state: interventionist theories, which attempt to explain how, why, and when the state is able to counteract tendencies toward economic crises; and theories which aim to show how class struggles are organized, contained, or suppressed by the state.[10]

Interventionist Theories of the State

What are the "crisis" tendencies of the capitalist economy which threaten to undermine the reproduction of relations of production? The most conventional are the various elaborations of Marx's "tendency for the rate of profit to fall" as a law inscribed in the structure of the capitalist mode of production. However, no matter how sophisticated the mathematics in these elaborations (for example, Yaffe, 1973), it is always possible to discover some empirically untenable assumptions underlying the inferences. The question rests on the relative strength of the tendency for the rate of profit to fall and the counter-tendencies (such as increasing the rate of exploitation, capital saving innovations, cheapening raw materials, etc.), in which the state plays an important role. There does not seem to be any obvious way of demonstrating that the tendencies are stronger than the counter-tendencies, so many look upon the movement of the rate of profit as the product of contingent historical forces (Mandel, 1975).

By contrast, Baran and Sweezy (1966) maintain that the falling rate of profit may apply to the era of competitive capitalism, but under monopoly capitalism it is replaced by the tendency for the absolute level of surplus to rise above the capacity of capitalism to absorb it. The problem is not too little surplus but too much surplus. Of course, the two "laws" are by no means incompatible, for the amount of surplus can increase relative to consumption while falling relative to the quantity (measured in socially necessary labor time) of labor and capital employed. Baran and Sweezy argue that the tendency towards over-production brings into play state mechanisms for surplus absorption, such as the expansion of military capacity. Hence, they point to underlying economic imperatives leading towards the warfare state.

Other crisis theories focus on the problematic nature of exchange and circulation, in particular the problem of ensuring that what is required for consumption (productive or unproductive) is also produced in the right proportions (Mandel, 1975). How is this accomplished through the market? When the market fails, as it does under monopoly capitalism, what agencies intervene to assure proportionality? O'Connor (1973) suggests that the state must intervene to provide forms of "social capital" (roads, transportation, communications, research and develop-ment, subsidized housing, etc.) to guarantee those prerequisites of accumulation which individual capitalists cannot afford.

O'Connor argues that the state is also responsible for "legitimating" capitalism through the distribution of concessions to the working classes (welfare, social security, etc.). But the costs of social capital and social expenses (concessions) tend to outstrip revenues, precipitating a "fiscal crisis of the state." Although economic in origin, the crisis manifests itself in the political arena. Yet is is not clear how the crisis can be recognized and whether there is an inherent tendency towards its exacerbation.

Habermas (1975) extends O'Connor's ideas to other realms, claiming that there are tendencies towards economic, rationality, legitimation and motivational crises, but he does not explain why, when, how and under what conditions these crises appear. Nevertheless, the idea that contra-dictions can be displaced or externalized from one sphere to another is a definite advance on earlier formulations of the Frankfurt School, which were based on the assumption of the durability of the capitalist economy, focused on the cultural realm, and chose to ignore the dynamics of the economy.

All these theories assume a similar form. A crisis is identified, a functional gap discovered, a contradiction revealed, and the state is invoked as the agency of restoration. This is an unsatisfactory functionalism. First, each theory of the contradictions of the capitalist economy gives rise to a different theory of the state, which means that Marxists have to direct attention to developing more comprehensive theories of the economy: nothing short of rewriting the three volumes of *Capital*! Second, the conditions under which the state endeavors, or even possesses the capacity, to counteract crisis tendencies are left unformulated. Such questions revolve around the issue of class struggle, which has yet to be systematically incorporated into these frameworks.

Class Struggle Theories of the Capitalist State

The second set of theories, inasmuch as they examine the relationship between class struggles and the state, complement the interventionist theories. These theories have emerged out of different interpretations of Marx and Engels' celebrated formulation in the *Communist Manifesto:* "the executive of the modern state is but a committee for managing the common affairs of the whole bourgeoisie" (Tucker, 1972:337). The conventional understanding of this passage is that the state acts as a coercive instrument for the dominant class (Miliband, 1969). The state is defined in terms of its various branches or "apparatuses"—the military, the police, the judiciary, the government, civil service, and so on. This *instrumentalist* perspective is linked, albeit weakly, to the notion of the expressive totality, in which all arenas of society are subordinated to the power of capital, thereby losing their individual autonomy.

In contrast, theories linked to the structured totality examine the *functions* of the state, that is, they focus on the "common affairs of the whole bourgeoisie" rather than on the *institutions* through which those functions are carried out. Poulantzas (1973), for example, translates the common affairs of the whole bourgeoisie into the unity and cohesion of the entire social formation. To preserve this unity and cohesion, he argues, it is necessary for the state to assume a *relative autonomy* with respect to individual capitalists or fractions of capital (finance, competitive, monopoly, commercial, etc.). For, in siding with this or that capitalist or group of capitalists, the state may jeopardize the *common* interest of all capitalists, that is the interests of the *capitalist class*, the interest in the reproduction of capitalist relations of production, and in organizing class struggles in ways which do not threaten the capitalist order. This is not to say that the state never sides with a particular fraction of capital. It is often forced to do so to protect the common interest of the capitalist class, for example, in subsidies to agriculture. On the other hand, when the state becomes an instrument of one or another fraction, and this obviously does happen, then the ability of the state to preserve its legitimacy is impaired.

The state must also assume an autonomy vis-à-vis the entire capitalist class. For the state must be in a position to grant material concessions to subordinate classes at the expense of the immediate economic interests of the dominant classes, for example, in the New Deal; to erect a hegemonic ideology which presents the interests of the dominant classes as the interests of all; to constitute the citizen/individual as the essential social category which the state establishes and recognizes in its structure so as to disorganize the dominated classes; and so on. Even individual branches of the state must operate with their own autonomy if they are to secure the consent of the people to the capitalist system, as in the Watergate hearings and the operation of the Watergate Special Prosecution Office. Poulantzas (1974, 1976) extends these formulations to examine the concrete forms the capitalist state can assume under, for example, fascism, dictatorships and parliamentary democracy. In each instance, he tries to identify a characteristic relative autonomy of the state as determined by different arrangements among the dominant classes and the balance of power between dominant and subordinate classes. Then the conditions can be examined under which a relative autonomy breaks down and yields to a state that becomes the instrument of a particular fraction of the dominant economic class. Chile, before, during and after Allende, provides an interesting case study of ways in which different apparatuses of the state can be "seized" by different classes and of the implications this absence of relative autonomy has for the survival of a particular type of regime.

The weakness of the structuralist view of the state, as it is presently formulated, is its functionalism. How is it that the state does what it is supposed to do? How does it secure and protect its relative autonomy? How does it dispense concessions? What are the mechanisms through which it preserves the hegemony of the dominant classes? Moreover, it is here that the instrumentalist perspective appears to be strong because it provides an explanation for the policies executed by the various branches of the state. Unfortunately, many of its assumptions are too crude. For example, Miliband (1969) incorrectly infers the existence of a cohesive, class conscious, enlightened bourgeoisie based on a relative homogeneity of attitudes, education, social origins, and so on. Irrespective of their common backgrounds, capitalists, both as groups or fractions, and as individuals, compete and conflict with one another, and thereby continually jeopardize their common interests. Furthermore, the state frequently acts in opposition to the declared and defended interests of the capitalist class or its fractions. The struggles over the Factory Acts, or the day to day commentary in the *Wall Street Journal* are obvious illustrations of the state acting with an autonomy of its own. In an attempt to rescue an instrumentalist perspective, some have followed the theorists of the corporate liberal state, such as Kolko (1963), Weinstein (1968), and Williams (1961) who postulate and try to demonstrate the existence of a hegemonic and enlightened fraction of the capitalist class which directs the state for the preservation of the interests of the whole capitalist class, even where this involves economic sacrifices. A second problem confronting the functionalist formulation is the mapping between function and concrete institution. Are all institutions which promote the functions of the state also part of the state? The family, for example, clearly contributes to the cohesion of the entire social forma-tion, but does that necessarily place it within the orbit of a state apparatus?

Significantly, the two theories—structuralist and instrumentalist—offer very different perspectives on the "transition to socialism" and the current debate over "Euro-communism." In writing about a *state in capitalist society* Miliband implies that the state he describes can be wielded by any economically dominant class (bourgeoisie or proletariat) to protect its specific interests. If the proletariat or its representatives can only seize the state, by electoral or any other means, then socialism can be inaugurated. Poulantzas (1973) and Balibar (1977), by contrast, refer to a *capitalist state* as distinguished from a feudal state or a socialist state. Because of its very structure, because of the social relations of which it is composed and which are independent of the will of those who (wo)man its apparatuses, the capitalist state will continue to protect and reproduce capitalist relations of production even if a socialist or communist party gains power. Thus, conquering or gaining access to the state through electoral means cannot lead to socialism since the working class party, when it takes over the government, becomes a prisoner of the very system it attempts to overthrow. Rather, in the "transition to communism," the capitalist state has to be dismantled and replaced by a socialist state which has the capacity to dissolve itself.

THE FUTURE AS HISTORY

For sociology, history ends with capitalism.[11] For Marxism, history ends with communism. Or, more accurately prehistory ends with commu-nism and "true" history begins, that is, men and women begin consciously to shape their own lives. Peculiar to all Marxisms is a vision of the future which is fundamentally at odds with the present. But how is that future to be realized? Marx uncovered a logic or telos to history, to the succession of different modes of production, which made socialism and communism the inevitable successors of capitalism. His logic rested on the development of the forces of production, that is, the increasing capacity of human beings to transform nature. This notion of progress is what linked past, present and future. Marx also sketched the general process by which one mode of production both *made necessary* and *laid the basis* for the next mode of production. As the forces of production — the manner of transforming or appropriating nature — advance, sô they enter into conflict with the relations of production — the way surplus is appropriated by a dominant class, or, as Marx wrote, the particular way of pumping surplus out of the direct producers. When the relations of production are no longer compatible with the development of the forces of production they become so many fetters and are burst asunder. A period of social revolution is inaugurated and class struggle becomes the driving force in the transition to a "higher" mode of production. The new relations of production become forms of development of the productive forces until again an incompatibility arises, and another revolutionary period brings forth the next mode of production.

How does Marx apply this theory to the capitalist mode of production? Individual capitalists privately appropriate unpaid labor, or what Marx calls surplus value, in the form of profits, realized through the sale of commodities in the market. Competition among capitalists drives them, on pain of extinction, to the continual transformation of technology and of the labor process, that is, of the productive forces. The transformation of labor increasingly assumes a "social" or collective form with the interdependence of labor increasing at the same time as its homogeneity. The process of accumulation leads on the one side to the concentration and centralization of capital, and thus to the elimination of small employers; and on the other side to the production of surplus laborers as the capital intensity of technology increases. A polarization grows between those who own the means of production and who privately appropriate surplus, and those who own only their labor power and who collectively appropriate nature. At the same time, the productive forces develop a power beyond the capacity of society to consume their products, causing crises of overproduction and hindering further expansion of those productive forces. Crises of overproduction combine with a decline in the rate of profit (linked to increasing proportion of capital relative to labor) to lay the objective basis for the inevitable dissolution of capitalism. In addition, the expansion of the productive forces creates the foundation for socialism because it presents the possibility of a regime of plenitude in which individual and collective talents can be developed to the full through engagement in varied types of work. However, the realization of these potentials (that is, the overthrow of capitalism and the construction of socialism) rests not only on the development of objective contradictions, but also on the level of struggle which is shaped in ideological and political arenas. This was Marx's theory.

The entire corpus of twentieth century Marxism—from Kautsky to Colletti, from Lenin to Althusser, from Gramsci to Habermas, from Luxembourg and Trotsky to Mao, from Lukács and Korsch to Marcuse—can be understood as reformulating and reinterpreting this theory of the transition to socialism. Informed by the ability of capitalism to confound Marx's prognoses, Marxists have increasingly looked upon his optimism with a certain ambivalence. And just as Marx sought to justify his vision of the future in a teleology, a hidden (or not so hidden) purpose of history, so Marxists have returned to history as a means of reexamining passages out of the present. How, then, do Marxists conceive of transitions from one epoch to another? They have questioned the idea of one mode of production being born in another. Anderson (1974) suggests that the feudal mode of production arose out of the catastrophic collision and fusion of two dissolving modes of production, namely the primitive Germanic and the ancient Roman. In the transition from feudalism to capitalism, according to Balibar (1970), the meeting of capital and wage labor, that is, the genesis of capitalism, has to be conceived of as occurring *outside* the decline of the feudal mode of production. In dislocating the genesis of one mode of production from the dissolution of its predecessor the idea of progress is lost. There is no theoretical reason why feudalism could not have been followed by the ancient mode of production, or even by socialism. Such a position is taken to its logical conclusion by Hindess and Hirst (1975). In their analysis of precapitalist modes of production they argue that while history may offer a sense of alternatives and thus of what is possible, at the same time there is no logical or teleological way of ordering those possibilities. History is not a fortune teller. What is left is a radical indeterminacy in the transition from one mode of production to another. Outcomes, including socialism, depend on struggle.

Gramsci's (1971) formula—"pessimism of the intelligence and optimism of the will" (taken from Romain Rolland)—resonates not only with historical studies but also with contemporary analyses of capitalism. I have already referred to the gap between class as a sociological category and class as a historical force, and to the capacity of the state to cushion and counteract crisis tendencies through the organization of politics and ideology. Other critics have invaded Marx's scheme at an even deeper level, arguing that the forces of production develop in ways that reinforce and reproduce rather than threaten capitalist relations. Gorz (1976), for example, shows how the labor process, and even technology, can serve to prevent the formation of class consciousness through the fragmentation, atomization and hierarchization of relations in the factory and office. These factors not only divide the working class into individuals and competing groups, but also obstruct the penetration of immediate experience to the totality of relations which shape people's lives. Gorz (1976), Marglin (1976), and Braverman (1974) are ambiguous in their assessment of capitalist technology—whether or not it has an emancipatory potential and could be used under socialism. Marcuse (1964), on the other hand, maintains that the very technology is tainted. Capitalist productive forces, far from being neutral or innocent, embody a form of domination incompatible with notions of a true socialism. Socialism requires socialist machines and even a socialist science. Capitalist technology is irretrievably contaminated. Responding to Marcuse in a now celebrated debate, Habermas (1970) tries to restore neutrality and continuity to the development of the productive forces. In themselves they are neither innocent nor guilty. Thus Habermas can redirect his attention to the political as the arena of emancipation. His vision of the future rests on a return to genuine consensus politics—what he calls the repoliticization of the public realm.

All these sorties into world history, the dynamics of capitalism and alternative technologies have been prompted by very definite historical experiences of the twentieth century. From among these, attempted transitions from capitalism to socialism hang heavily in the minds of Marxists—in the Marxist collective consciousness. An important lesson of the last hundred years is that it is one thing to speak of alternative futures or even of repressed potentialities in the present; it is quite another matter to move towards such visions even when a revolutionary crisis presents itself. Strong socialist and communist movements in Germany and in Italy led not in the direction of socialism, but in the direction of fascism. Contemporary events also illustrate the precariousness of left wing movements fighting a capitalism constituted on a world scale. The examples of Chile and Portugal suggest the ease with which counter-revolution, restoration or dictatorship can be established.[12] It remains to be seen what will happen in Spain, France, Italy and Greece. Labor governments, such as the one in England, find themselves fighting for the survival of capitalism.

Even if counter-revolution in any of its guises and the social democracy of welfare capitalism are averted, the path to socialism is still filled with daunting and seemingly insuperable obstacles. Some form of capitalist restoration is always possible, even likely. Widespread disillusionment with the unfolding of events in the Soviet Union has made Marxists even more cautious in their speculations and prognoses. In such a historical context, critical theory affords an understandable retreat, particularly in the United States where the future appears so hopeless. By stressing the widening gap between what is and what could be, critical theory aims to undermine the seeming naturalness and inevitability of everyday life and reveals common sense as ideology. But in bridging the divide between "reality" and potentiality, between the present and the future, critical theory has little to offer.

In nations such as France and Italy, with traditions of revolution and class struggle, Marxist debate takes place on a different terrain than in the United States, and directly confronts the issues of the transition to socialism. Accordingly, new directions in Marxist studies revolve around the reexamination and reinterpretation of the history of the Soviet Union. It is no longer enough to "critique," condemn, or lament the fate of the October Revolution; or to lay the blame at the feet of individuals or accidents of history. However disturbing it is, Marxists have been forced to examine precisely how, when and why it went wrong (see, for example, Bettleheim, 1976). But these reconstructions have to be a real history—a Marxist history—not a crude vindication of the status quo or an apology for the Soviet ruling class. Such endeavors, combined with the recent withdrawal of many European communist parties from beneath Soviet hegemony, can only augur well for the extension and deepening of Marxist discourse on the prospects and nature of socialism. Presumably, that has something to do with its realization.

NOTES

1. Lest there be any confusion, let me say at once this does not mean that Marxists are not positivists. Some are positivists, some are not. Inasmuch as they proceed deductively from certain premises and arrive at certain conclusions which they then attempt to relate to the concrete world, they are positivists. Such theories find their validity in *accounting* for what exists and what does not exist, what has been and what has not been, what will be and what will not be. Inasmuch as critical or any other theory justifies itself by reference to a preordained *goal* or *purpose*, it is not positivist. In contrast to both these approaches, empiricism draws conclusions about the concrete world on the basis of *induction*. It treats the world of appearance as the only world.

2. The notion of a structured totality is most fully elaborated by the French Marxists associated with Althusser. The concept is developed, although not called by this name, in Althusser (1969) and Althusser and Balibar (1970). These

writers have also coined the term "expressive totality" for their portrait of the "historicist school" of Marxism, in which they include Gramsci, Lukács and Korsch. They tend to caricature these writers in their attempt to elucidate their own "complexly determined" or "overdetermined" notions of totality.

3. Some works present an uneasy coexistence of both totalities. Thus, Baran and Sweezy (1966) emphasize the functional interdependence of the economy and the state in the first part of their book, while in the last chapters they shift into an analysis which portrays capitalist society as permeated by commodification and irrationality. They switch from monopoly capitalism conceived of as a mode of *production* to monopoly capitalism conceived of as a mode of *domination*. Similar tensions between expressive and structured totality can be found in Max Weber (Rheinstein, 1954). The modern legal system is seen both in terms of its autonomy and contribution to the needs of an industrial economy, and as an expression of the legal-rational spirit which defines the essence of the industrial society. The same ambiguity is found in the work of Talcott Parsons, who tries to stress both dominant values and functional subsystems.

4. A similar issue has gained prominence in the debate over feudalism and the transition from feudalism to capitalism. Is the distinction between feudalism and capitalism to be seen in terms of production for use rather than production for exchange *or* in terms of the extraction of surplus through rent rather than through wage labor? See the classic contributions in Hilton (1976).

5. I follow Przeworski (1977:39) in viewing crises as ". . . moments of uncertainty, the periods of decision when forms of organization of society become the object of struggles and when relations of organized physical force come to the fore."

6. It should be noted that his notion of contradictory class location does in fact smuggle back, however surreptitiously, class as a historical force, and the problem of "class in itself/class for itself." For Wright, the significance of the contradictory class location rests on the ambiguity of the incumbent's relationship to two "fundamental" classes, that is, ambiguity as to which class the incumbents will support in class struggle. This indeterminacy is resolved by the intervention of political and ideological factors. Therefore, Wright's class map is by no means a purely "sociological" map, but contains all sorts of assumptions about historical actors.

7. Thus Rubin (1975), recognizing the specific subordinate roles that women occupy under capitalism, seeks to explain why it is women rather than men who fill those places. To answer this question it is necessary to go beyond capitalism and to seek the source of allocation of women to subordinate positions in their exchange through marriage rules. This, she argues, transcends all modes of production, while the concrete forms of male dominance are linked to a particular mode of production.

8. This is a juncture where Marxism has frequently parted with Marx. Thus, a major contribution of the Frankfurt School has been the Marxist appropriation of Freudian psychology. It is interesting to note the convergence of the psychoanalytic descriptions of contemporary society as found in Marcuse (1955) and in Parsons (1954). Of course, they differ in their evaluations of the potentiality for transcending the repressive aspects of capitalist society.

9. This is not to say that values and norms, or, as Marxists would say, ideology, do not have a structure and autonomy of their own. They do. Moreover, ideology is not uniquely determined by social relations. Indeed, ideological struggle reflects the ambiguous relationship of ideology and social relations. Nor does this mean that ideology is unimportant. On the contrary, as Marx wrote and Gramsci continually emphasized, it is ideology that shapes class struggle.

10. Tendencies toward economic crises and class struggles have been counteracted not only by the state but also by changes in relations among capitalists and in the labor process, both brought about by the emergence of the large corporation. See, for example, Baran and Sweezy (1966) and Braverman (1974). I have commented at length on these changes elsewhere (Burawoy [1978] and [1979]).

11. To refer to the "post-industrial society," "post-capitalist society," "advanced industrial society," etc., as "socialism" is to denude that concept of its Marxist meaning.

12. The possible resurgence of fascism as a reactionary response to the strengthening of European socialist and communist parties has prompted Marxists to reexamine the origins and nature of National Socialism. See, for example, Mason (1968); Rabinach (1974); Poulantzas (1974); Abraham (1977); Goldfrank (1977).

REFERENCES

ABRAHAM, DAVID
1977 "State and classes in Weimar Germany." Politics and Society 7:3.
ALTHUSSER, LOUIS
1969 For Marx. London: Allen Lane, The Penguin Press.
ALTHUSSER, LOUIS AND ETIENNE BALIBAR (eds.)
1970 Reading Capital. New York: Pantheon.
ANDERSON, PERRY
1974 Passages from Antiquity to Feudalism. London: New Left Books.
ARONOWITZ, STANLEY
1973 False Promises: The Shaping of American Working Class Consciousness. New York: McGraw-Hill.
BALIBAR, ETIENNE
1970 "The basic concepts of historical materialism." Pp. 201–308 in L. Althusser and E. Balibar (eds.), Reading Capital, New York: Pantheon.
1977 On the Dictatorship of the Proletariat. London: New Left Books.
BARAN, PAUL
1957 The Political Economy of Growth. New York: Monthly Review Press.
BARAN, PAUL, and PAUL SWEEZY
1966 Monopoly Capital. New York: Monthly Review Press.
BETTLEHEIM, CHARLES
1976 Class Struggles in the USSR: 1917–1923. New York: Monthly Review Press.

BRAVERMAN, HARRY
1974 Labor and Monopoly Capital. New York: Monthly Review Press.
BURAWOY, MICHAEL
1978 "Towards a Marxist theory of the labor process: Braverman and beyond."
Politics and Society 8.
1979 Making Out on the Shop Floor: Changes in the Labor Process under
Monopoly Capitalism. Chicago: University of Chicago Press.
DALLA COSTA, MARIAROSA, and SELMA JAMES
1972 The Power of Women and the Subversion of the Community. Bristol
(England): Falling Wall Press.
EMMANUEL, AGHIRI
1972 Unequal Exchange. New York: Monthly Review Press.
EWEN, STUART
1977 Captains of Consciousness: Advertising and the Social Roots of The
Consumer Culture. New York: McGraw-Hill.
FRANK, GUNDER
1969 Capitalism and Underdevelopment in Latin America. New York:
Monthly Review Press.
Frankfurt Institute for Social Research
1972 Aspects of Sociology: Boston: Beacon Press.
GENOVESE, EUGENE
1971 The World the Slaveholders Made. New York: Vintage Books.
1976 Roll, Jordan, Roll: The World the Slaves Made. New York: Pantheon.
GOLDFRANK, WALTER
1977 "Fascism and the world economy." Paper presented at the Annual
Meetings of the Society for the Study of Social Problems, Chicago.
GORZ, ANDRE (ed.)
1976 The Division of Labor. Atlantic Highlands, N.J.: Humanities Press.
GRAMSCI, ANTONIO
1971 Selections from Prison Notebooks. New York: International Publishers.
HABERMAS, JÜRGEN
1970 Towards a Rational Society. Boston: Beacon Press.
1975 Legitimation Crisis. Boston: Beacon Press.
HARRISON, BENNETT
1972 "Public employment and the theory of the dual economy." Pp. 41–76 in
H.L. Sheppard, B. Harrison and W. J. Spring (eds.), The Political
Economy of Public Service Employment. Lexington, Mass.: Heath-
Lexington.
HILTON, RODNEY (ed.)
1976 The Transition from Feudalism to Capitalism. London: New Left
Books.
HINDESS, BARRY, and PAUL HIRST
1975 Pre-Capitalist Modes of Production. London: Routledge & Kegan Paul.
JORDAN, WINTHROP
1968 White Over Black: American Attitudes towards the Negro 1550–1812.
Chapel Hill: University of North Carolina Press.

KOLKO, GABRIEL
1963   The Triumph of Conservatism. New York: Free Press.

LACLAU, ERNESTO
1971   "Feudalism and capitalism in Latin America." New Left Review 67:19-38.

LENIN, V. I.
1960   The Development of Capitalism in Russia. Collected Works, Vol. 3. Moscow: Progress Publishers.

LUKÁCS, GEORG
1971   History and Class Consciousness. Cambridge: M.I.T. Press.

MANDEL, ERNEST
1975   Late Capitalism. London: New Left Books.

MARCUSE, HERBERT
1955   Eros and Civilization. Boston: Beacon Books.
1964   One Dimensional Man. Boston: Beacon Press.

MARGLIN, STEVEN
1976   "What do bosses do?" Pp. 13-54 in A. Gorz (ed.), The Division of Labor. Atlantic Highlands, N.J.: Humanities Press.

MASON, TIM
1968   "The primacy of politics—politics and economics in National Socialist Germany." Pp. 165-195 in S. J. Woolf (ed.), The Nature of Fascism. London: Weidenfeld and Nicolson.

MILIBAND, RALPH
1969   The State in Capitalist Society. New York: Basic Books.

MITCHELL, JULIET
1971   Women's Estate. Harmondsworth: Penguin Books.

NAIRN, TOM
1977   The Break-Up of Britain. London: New Left Books.

O'CONNOR, JAMES
1973   The Fiscal Crisis of the State. New York: St. Martin's Press.

PARSONS, TALCOTT
1954   Essays in Sociological Theory. New York: Free Press.

POULANTZAS, NICOS
1973   Political Power and Social Classes. London: New Left Books.
1974   Fascism and Dictatorship. London: New Left Books.
1976   The Crisis of the Dictatorships. London: New Left Books.

PRZEWORSKI, ADAM
1976   "The process of class formation: From Karl Kautsky's Class Struggle to recent controversies." Politics and Society 7.
1977   "Towards a theory of capitalist democracy." Unpublished manuscript, University of Chicago.

RABINBACH, ANDREW
1974   "Toward a Marxist theory of fascism and National Socialism: A report on developments in West Germany." New German Critique 1(3):127-153.

REITER, RAYNA (ed.)
1975 Toward an Anthropology of Women. New York: Monthly Review Press.
RHEINSTEIN, MAX (ed.)
1954 Max Weber: A Law in Economy and Society. Cambridge, Mass.: Harvard University Press.
ROSALDO, MICHELLE, and LOUISE LAMPHERE (eds.)
1974 Woman, Culture and Society. Stanford, Calif.: Stanford University Press.
RUBIN, GAYLE
1975 "The traffic in women: Notes on the 'political economy' of sex." Pp. 157-210 in R. Reiter (ed.), Toward an Anthropology of Women. New York: Monthly Review Press.
THOMPSON, EDWARD
1963 The Making of the English Working Class. London: Victor Gollancz.
TUCKER, ROBERT (ed.)
1972 The Marx-Engels Reader. New York: Norton.
WALLERSTEIN, IMMANUEL
1974 The Modern World-System: Capitalist Agriculture and the Origins of the European World-Economy in the Sixteenth Century. New York: Academic Press.
WEINBAUM, BATYA, and AMY BRIDGES
1976 "Monopoly capital and the structure of consumption." Monthly Review, 28(3):88-103.
WEINSTEIN, JAMES
1968 The Corporate Ideal in the Liberal State: 1900-1918. Boston: Beacon Press.
WILLIAMS, WILLIAM APPLEMAN
1961 The Contours of American History. Cleveland and New York: World Publishing.
WOLPE, HAROLD
1972 "Capitalism and cheap labor power in South Africa: From segregation to apartheid." Economy and Society 1:425-456.
WRIGHT, ERIK OLIN
1976 "Class boundaries in advanced capitalist societies." New Left Review 98:3-41.
YAFFE, DAVID
1973 "The Marxian theory of crisis, capital and the state." Economy and Society 2:186-232.

2. A World-System Perspective on the Social Sciences

IMMANUEL WALLERSTEIN

It is in the nineteenth century and the early twentieth that the organizational structures of the sciences of man which we use today became fixed. In 1800 the categories (or 'disciplines') which today are standard—history, economics, sociology, anthropology, political science—did not for the most part exist as concepts, and certainly were not the basis of sharply differentiated groups of teachers and researchers. The somewhat tortuous process by which certain combinations of concerns and concepts took particular forms resulted in major 'methodological' debates, which we sometimes still hear about under the rubric, 'philosophy of history'. Among the debates, one of the most influential was that between so-called nomothetic and idiographic knowledge, between the possibility and impossibility of generalizations about human behaviour, between the universalizers and the particularizers.

The universalizers spoke of themselves as 'scientists'. They tended to argue that human behaviour was a natural phenomenon like any other, and could therefore be studied on the same basis as any other natural phenomenon, using the same rules of logic ('the scientific method') and capable eventually of yielding precise results comparable to those achieved in the natural sciences. The particularists, in contrast, often termed themselves 'humanists'. They tended to argue that human life,

SOURCE: Reprinted from *British Journal of Sociology* 27 (September 1976): 343–352.

being thinking life, could not be viewed in the same way as other natural phenomenon, for one of two reasons. Either it was because, said some, humans have souls and are therefore resistant to arbitrary uniformities, or it was because, said others, the human researcher inevitably distorted the human subject of analysis in the very process of observing him and therefore the generalizations would never be valid.

Like all such grand debates, there is just so much that can be said on the subject, and it has largely been said. This does not mean that the debate is over or forgotten but simply that the divisions have been institutionalized and thereby contained. *Grosso modo*, the universalizers were assigned the departments of economics, sociology, and political science, and the particularizers the departments of history and anthropology. Obviously, given the high capriciousness of the organizational dividing lines, there were dissidents in each 'disciplinary' structure (such as political 'theorists' in political science, and linguists in anthropology). But no matter! Spheres of influence had been demarcated, and the status quo enshrined.

This crude picture has to be qualified by taking into account regional variation. My description works best for the Anglo-American core of the world-system. The Germans chafed at British definitions of social knowledge and gave birth to an uncertain cross-breed, *Staatswissenschaft*. Some French chafed at the failure of other Frenchmen to chafe, which led to the birth of the *Annales* school. And the Western European working classes chafed at the system in general, and nourished outside the academy a critical perspective, Marxism, which challenged the universality of the 'universals'.

Underlying the dominant institutionalization of the great methodological split, universalizer versus particularizer, there turned out to be, as there usually is, a hidden but very important consensus, the concept of the individual society as the basic unit of analysis. Everyone seemed to agree that the world was composed of multiple 'societies'. They disagreed about whether it was the case that all societies pursued *similar* paths down the road of history (albeit at differing rates) or that each society went its own historic way. They disagreed whether society in question took the form of a 'state' or a 'nation' or a 'people', but in any case it was some politico-cultural unit.

The period after World War II saw in this field, as in so many others, the culmination of these intellectual tendencies in the elaboration of a perspective we may call 'developmentalism', which for most of its devotees went hand in hand with 'behaviorism'. This perspective assumed that all states were engaged in 'developing' (which for many meant 'becoming nations'), that their progress along this path could be measured quantitatively and synchronically, and that on the basis of knowledge derived from such measurements, governments could in fact hasten the process, which was a highly commendable thing to do. Since these states were proceeding down parallel paths, *all* states were intrinsically capable of achieving the desired results. The only serious intellectual question was why many resisted doing so.

This viewpoint swept the scholarly world—not only of the hegemonic power, the United States, and its allies, old Europe, but also of its chief antagonist, the U.S.S.R. The theories of what governmental actions would promote development, and what social forces impeded it varied widely, but the plausibility of 'development' as a matrix of analysis reigned supreme until the mid-1960s, when it foundered on one economic reality and two political developments.

The economic reality was that, despite all the theories, and all the presumed effort (aid, technical assistance, human investment), the so-called 'gap' between the 'developed' and the 'developing' countries was growing bigger, not smaller.

The two political developments were in fact ultimately a reflection of this economic reality. One was the emergence of national liberation movements throughout the world which engaged in armed struggle with more or less success—Vietnam, Algeria, Cuba. Their struggle had a resonance within the United States and Western Europe—among students, professors, and the 'Third World within'—which in fact shook the up-to-then facile dominance of the developmentalists in the academy.

But this same political upheaval affected the Communist countries as well, where a long series of interrelated crises—the XXth Party Congress of the C.P.S.U., the 'upheavals' in Eastern Europe, the split between the Chinese and the Russians, the cultural revolution, the rise of 'Eurocommunism'—similarly has undermined the internal credibility of the Stalinist version of developmentalism, the crude sequence through which each state was destined to 'pass'.

When a theory no longer seems to serve an adequate *social* function, scholars usually begin to question its intellectual credentials. As 'developmentalism' seemed less and less to explain the social reality through which we are living, various authors criticized one or another of its premises, groping towards an alternative framework of explanation, which I shall call a 'world-system perspective'.

The key difference between a developmentalist and a world-system perspective is in the point of departure, the unit of analysis. A developmentalist perspective assumes that the unit within which social action principally occurs is a politico-cultural unit—the state, or nation, or people—and seeks to explain differences between these units, including why their economies are different. A world-system perspective assumes, by contrast, that social action takes place in an entity within which there is an ongoing division of labour, and seeks to discover *empirically* whether such an entity is or is not unified politically or culturally, asking *theoretically* what are the consequences of the existence or nonexistence of such unity.

By throwing overboard the *presupposition* that there is a 'society' we are forced to look at the alternative possibilities of organizing the material world. We in fact rapidly discover that there are a limited number of possibilities, which we may call varying 'modes of production', meaning by that something very close to what the phrase seems on the surface to convey: the way in which decisions are made about dividing up productive tasks, about quantities of goods to be produced and labour-time to be invested, about quantities of goods to be consumed or accumulated, about the distribution of the goods produced.

One mode, historically the earliest, we may call the reciprocal-lineage mode. It is based on limited and elementary specialization of tasks in which the products are reciprocally exchanged among producers. In this mode the chief productive resource is human labour and therefore the chief guarantee of sub-group survival the control of reproduction (via the control of women and their offspring). Production over a certain level is politically unsettling by enabling younger persons to escape the control of elders and therefore inequalities though real are limited.

Empirically, it is the case (and I think it could be established that theoretically it must be the case) that such systems are small in physical scope, and that the economic boundaries are largely identical with political and cultural boundaries. Mini-systems seem a reasonable name. I believe it is the case that such mini-systems are not only small in physical scope but short-lived historically (meaning a life of say six generations or so). This short life can be accounted for in various ways: the dangers for such a technologically primitive group of physical extinction (through warfare or natural calamity); the possibility of conquest; fission of the group as the result of slow growth in accumulated stock; reorganization of the division of labour resulting from physical flight and consequent ecological adjustment.

If this is an accurate description, the world has known countless such groups over historical time and has virtually no historical records of how they functioned. Some ethnologists claim to have recorded such groups, but for the most part I am sceptical that the units studied were truly autonomous systems, since one of the preconditions of most such study has in fact been imperial control of the area studied by a larger political entity which in turn existed within a far wider division of labour.

Our empirical knowledge is largely limited to larger divisions of labour which I shall term world-systems, using the word 'world' to signify larger space and longer time than mini-systems, and operationally to mean an arena, or division of labour, within which more than one 'cultural' grouping exists, but which may or *may not* be politically unified.

There have in fact, up to now, been two basic forms of world-systems. Since in one form the prototype is the unified political system, we shall call this type the 'world-empire', by contrast with the other type which is precisely defined by the continuing absence of such political unity, the 'world-economy'.

The 'world-empire' has many variations in terms of the political superstructure and the cultural consequences. A large part of Weber's *Economy and Society* is a morphology of these variations. But the mode of production is common to these variant forms. It is a mode of production which creates enough of an agricultural surplus (based therefore on a more advanced technology than the reciprocal-lineage mode) sufficient to maintain both the artisans who produce non-agricultural goods and, in the widest sense, an 'administrative' stratum. Whereas the agricultural and artisanal producers in some sense 'exchange' goods, either reciprocally or in local markets, goods are transferred from producers to 'administrators' by a forced appropriation, 'tribute', which is centralized by someone or some institution—how remote this institution is from the producer is one of the major variables of the differing forms—and thereupon 'redistributed' to the 'administrative bureaucracy'.

The principal difference in this mode of production from the reciprocal-lineage mode was the fact that a class which did not produce 'goods' was supported (and indeed supported well). But there was a major similarity common to both pre-modern forms. In neither mode of production was maximal production desirable or desired. The reason is clear. Since the channel upward of the surplus appropriation in the redistributive-tributary form was the same 'bureaucracy' to whom the top of the structure 'redistributed' this surplus, too large a surplus created a strong temptation for 'pre-emption' of this surplus on the way upward. This of course constantly happened. But it meant that the ruling groups were always caught in the contradiction of wanting more, but not 'too much'.

The consequences were manifold. Technological advance was not desirable *per se*. It no doubt occurred, but it was probably less the desire

to expand production than the need, when it occurred, to *stem a decline*
in real production that served as its spur. Secondly, the contradictory
needs of the ruling groups (more, but not too much) were communicated
to the direct producers in terms of socially-fixed as opposed to socially-
open quotas of appropriation. That is not to say that these quotas never
changed. They changed constantly, but discontinuously, and the myth
of the constant rate was a central ideological motif of the social structure.

In this mode of production, inequalities were enormous in comparison to the reciprocal-lineage mode, but there were some inbuilt limits.
The ruling groups might have the power of life and death by the sword
over the direct producers, but they were normally concerned to prevent
starvation, since the 'fixed' income of the ruling groups was dependent
on a 'fixed' level of appropriation from a 'fixed' estimated total production. Starvation might occur despite the efforts of the local ruling groups
but seldom amidst their indifference.

Empirically it is the case (and again I think it could be established that
theoretically it must be the case) that such systems were larger in
physical size than the reciprocal-lineage forms (and occasionally very
large, as for example the Roman Empire at its height). Within the
economic division of labour, multiple 'cultures' flourished—parallel
groups of agricultural producers, 'world'-wide trading groups, endoga-
mous trans-local 'administrative' groups. But the keynote of this mode
of production was the political unity of the economy, whether this
'unity' involved extreme administrative decentralization (the 'feudal'
form) or relatively high centralization (an 'empire' proper).

Such 'world-empires' have existed ever since the Neolithic Revolution, and right up to very recent times. The number was large, but not
'countless'. The life of such systems varied according to their size, their
isolation, their ecological base, and so forth. But the *pattern* of such
systems was a cyclical one—expansion of size and hence total surplus-
appropriation to the point where the bureaucratic costs of appropriating
the surplus outweighed the surplus that could, in socio-political terms,
be effectively appropriated, at which point decline and retraction set in.

The cycle of expansion and contraction involved the perpetual
incorporation and releasing of 'units' which, when outside the 'world-
empire', formed reciprocal-lineage mini-systems, but which when incorporated within it, formed merely one more *situs* out of which tribute was
drawn and whose socio-economic autonomy was thereby eliminated.
Thus these two modes of production co-existed on the earth for thou-
sands of years.

'Civilization' is a term which is often used to mean the patterns of 'high culture' developed by the ruling and 'administrative' strata in such 'world-empires'. And since there was a certain 'revival' of the forms of a particular culture each time a new world-empire was created in the same geographic zone, we can also use the concept 'civilization' to connote those cultural forms that are common to *successive* world-empires in the same zone. (China is the model-case of a long series of such successive world-empires.)

Since the needs of world-empires were facilitated by 'rationality' in administration, the development of 'records' was normal and we have considerable 'documentation' from which to reconstruct the workings of such systems, which we may thus 'observe' across historical time (or rather reconstruct in terms of our contemporary needs).

The 'world-economy' is a fundamentally different kind of social system from a 'world-empire' and *a fortiori* from a mini-system—both in formal structure and as a mode of production. As a formal structure, a world-economy is defined as a single division of labour within which are located multiple cultures—hence it is a *world*-system like the world-empire—but which has no overarching political structure. Without a political structure to redistribute the appropriated surplus, the surplus can only be redistributed via the 'market', however frequently states located within the world-economy intervene to distort the market. Hence the mode of production is capitalist.

A capitalist mode is one in which production is for exchange; that is, it is determined by its profitability on a market, a market in which each buyer wishes to buy cheap (and therefore that which is, in the long run, most efficiently produced and marketed) but in which each seller wishes to sell dear (and therefore is concerned that the efficiencies of others are not permitted to reduce his sales.) Thus the individual as buyer rewards efficiency and as seller uses his political power to thwart it.

The basic contradiction that informs capitalism as a social system results from the simultaneous desirability of freedom for the buyer and its undesirability for the seller—freedom of labour, freedom of the flow of the factors of production, freedom of the market. The combination of freedom and unfreedom that results is the defining characteristic of a capitalist world-economy. This ambivalence about freedom pervades its politics, its culture, its social relations.

Whereas the quantities of production in a redistributive-tributary mode were more or less socially 'fixed', precisely the opposite is true of a capitalist mode. There is no social limit to profit, only the limit of the market: of competitive sellers and inadequate numbers of buyers. An individual producer produces not a fixed amount but as much as he can, and anything that can aid him to produce more, and more efficiently— science and technology—is welcome. But once produced, it must be sold, or no profit is realized. And once profit is realized, the less that is consumed immediately, the more future profit will be possible.

But as everyone proceeds this way—the 'anarchy of production'— there will soon come a point where additional production offers not profit but loss. Hence there are cycles here too—not the political cycles of the world-empires but the economic cycles of the world-economies.

There are to be sure profound inequalities of distribution too, and probably *greater* inequalities than in world-empires (although liberal social science has always argued the opposite). The reason has to do with the greater wealth to be maldistributed (as a result of technological advance) and the technique by which the maldistribution is enforced.

In a redistributive system, the primary weapon of the powerful is the sword. Thus death to the political resistant, but minimal life for the acquiescent producer is the basic law of political life. But in a capitalist mode, with *economic* cycles, the life of the producer can be more unprofitable as consumer of surplus than profitable as producer of surplus. Thus the politico-military machinery can frequently best serve to maximize profit by permitting starvation, both literally and figuratively.

Historically, world-economies were very fragile institutions whose life-spans were probably less than a century and hence had little opportunity to become an ongoing, capital-expanding system. They lacked the political structures to prevent withdrawal of regions from the system and hence the world-economies that emerged from time to time often disintegrated. Or, if they did not, it was because a member state expanded to fill the boundaries of the division of labour, the world-economy thus being transformed into a world-empire, and the beginnings of a capitalist mode rapidly reverting to a redistributive-tributary mode of production.

What is remarkable then about the modern world is the emergence of a capitalist world-economy *that survived*. Indeed it did more than survive: it has flourished, expanded to cover the entire earth (and thereby eliminated all remaining mini-systems and world-empires), and brought about a technological and ecological 'explosion' in the use of natural resources.

There are three separate intellectual questions that may be asked about this modern world-system. The first is the explanation of its genesis: how is it that the sixteenth-century European world-economy survived, unlike previous such systems. The second question is how such a system, once consolidated, operates. The third is what are the basic secular trends of a capitalist system, and therefore what will account for its eventual decline as a social system.

Each of these three questions is a long and complex one and cannot be answered briefly with any degree of satisfaction. Since, however, I have attempted longer answers to these questions elsewhere, I will merely outline my position of these three issues here in the most summary of fashions.

The genesis is to be located in the process of 'decline' of a particular redistributive world-system, that of feudal Europe, which seems to have 'exhausted its potential' in its great socio-economic spurt of 1100–1250. In the 'crisis' of contraction of the following two centuries, the real income of the ruling strata seemed to take a real fall. One reason was the rising real wages of the producers, the result of demographic disasters. A second was the destruction that occurred because of widespread peasant revolts (consequence of the previous exaggerated level of exploitation) and the internecine warfare of the ruling strata (consequence of their long-term proportional expansion, reaching the conjuncture of economic decline). The prospect was collapse.

Had there been a world-empire on the edges capable of conquering the core of the system (the old 'dorsal spine' of Europe), or had feudal Europe itself been more centralized, there might have been a more traditional political reorganization of 'empire'. But there wasn't. Instead there was a sort of creative leap of imagination on the part of the ruling strata. It involved trying an alternative mode of surplus-appropriation, that of the market, to see whether it might serve to restore the declining real income of the ruling groups. This involved geographical expansion, spatial economic specialization, the rise of the 'absolutist' state—in short, the creation of a capitalist world-economy.

The genesis of capitalism was not in the triumph of a new group, the urban burghers, over the landed feudal nobility. Rather it should be seen as the reconversion of seignior into capitalist producer, an essential *continuity* of the ruling families. Furthermore, it worked magnificently, as any look backward from say 1800 to 1450 can show. The 'crisis of seigniorial revenues' was no more. The crisis was now located in the revenues of the producers. The 'poor' had been created as a major social category.

The operation of the system, once established, revolved around two basic dichotomies. One was the dichotomy of class, bourgeois versus proletarian, in which control by ruling groups operated primarily not through lineage rights (as in the mini-systems) nor through weapons of force (as in the world-empires), but through access to decisions about the nature and quantity of the production of goods (via property rights, accumulated capital, control over technology, etc.)

The other basic dichotomy was the spatial hierarchy of economic specialization, core versus periphery, in which there was an appropriation of surplus from the producers of low-wage (but high supervision), low-profit, low-capital intensive goods by the producers of high-wage (but low supervision), high-profit, high-capital intensive, so-called 'unequal exchange'.

The genius, if you will, of the capitalist system, is the interweaving of these two channels of exploitation which overlap but are not identical and create the cultural and political complexities (and obscurities) of the system. Among other things, it has made it possible to respond to the politico-economic pressures of cyclical economic crises by rearranging spatial hierarchies without significantly impairing class hierarchies.

The mechanism by which the capitalist system ultimately resolves its recurrent cylical down-turns is expansion: outward spatially, and internally in terms of the 'freeing' of the market—remember the basic ambivalence about the free market, good for the buyer and bad for the seller—via the steady proletarianization of semi-proletarian labour and the steady commercialization of semi-market-oriented land.

Both of these processes have logical limits. In the case of geographical expansion, these limits were largely reached by the beginning of the twentieth century. In the case of internal expansion, there is still much room. The world is probably halfway, more or less, in the process of freeing the factors of production. But here too the world eventually approaches an asymptote, at which point the possibility of resolving economic crises will largely disappear, and thereby we will enter into a true crisis of the system as such.

Linked to these structural limits are the curves of political repression. A system of unequal distribution (all known systems hitherto) is only possible by repression, which is a function of the relation of two curves, the ability and willingness of the upper strata to repress, the ability and willingness of the lower strata to rebel.

But over historical time, within the capitalist world-economy, the first curve is continually going down in strength and the second curve is continually rising. The reason is simple. The 'cost' of repression is the partial redistribution of the surplus to the repressors, who are in fact the intermediate strata. The process is called 'co-optation'. But each co-optation is less 'worthwhile' than the previous one, since it involves further deductions from a *declining percentage* of the surplus controlled by the top strata, in order to buy off once again the intermediate strata. (One does not 'buy off' lower strata. The whole point is to exploit them, whence comes the money with which one 'buys off' others, that is, shares the spoils.)

Let us be clear what we are saying. Even if the *world-wide* appropriation of the producers has remained about as high in recent decades as in earlier periods of the capitalist world-economy, the distribution of this surplus has begun to shift from the top to the intermediate strata. This is politically crucial. The so-called 'rise of the middle classes' is often seen as politically stabilizing, because it is alleged this is depriving the lower strata of their leadership. I see it quite differently. It is politically destabilizing because it is depriving the top strata of a prize high enough to be worth struggling for. This is the 'failure of nerve' that is setting in.

Conversely, the lower strata are in fact becoming ever better organized, not *despite* but *because of* the 'rise of the middle classes'. This rise has in fact made it ever clearer that the interests of the producers are *not* tied to the needs and demands of the intermediate strata (as expressed historically in reform movements and ethno-national demands for *spatial* reorganization of the distribution of profits).

However the continuing technological advances of the capitalist economy are creating possibilities of *political* organization of direct producers unknown in previous eras. Furthermore, in rebellion, success leads to success in the sense of revealing its potentials.

To resume this simple and simplified picture, the transition from a capitalist world-economy to a socialist world-government in which we are living and which will take a long time to complete, is theoretically the consequence of two secular trends: the potential exhaustion of the limits of structural expansion which is required to maintain the economic viability of the capitalist system; the closing of the gap between the two political curves of the will to fight of the ruling groups and the direct producers *on a world level.*

What is crippling about a developmentalist perspective is the fact that these large-scale historical processes are not even discussable, if one uses the politico-cultural entity (the 'state') as the unit of analysis. It is only by recognizing that it is world-systems we must study that we can begin to locate the data of modern history, both those that are 'universal' and those that are 'particular', within the process of the social structures the world has seen over historical time.

It is only then, too, that we can begin to be 'scientific' about a central natural phenomenon, the human group, and 'humane' in opting for the possible choices that will in fact enable us, all of us, to reach our potentials and create our worlds within our limits.

PART II
COUNTERPERSPECTIVES

Counterperspectives are not so much a complete theoretical system as they are statements to the effect that sociologists have neglected important aspects of reality. This is why Lemert's piece on semiotics has been placed in this section. It is an unusual perspective that deserves attention for the rich insights it yields.

Traditionally, alternative perspectives have been taken to be critical theory, or dialectics, or phenomenology. Yet, all of these traditions are part of a Western, rational mode of thought. Bell encourages us, through her explication of Buddhist thought, to examine how another mode of thought can open new avenues to us. She examines the sociological enterprise from within the perspective of Eastern disciplines.

There is now a wealth of literature dealing with women's issues. Segal and Berheide examine the current state of feminist sociology and note its underlying assumptions. They show that this view has provided new ways of examining some old issues, such as occupational mobility and family behavior, while encouraging new research, and how it has been useful as a critique of a male-dominated enterprise.

It has been argued that a traditional sociological perspective is a conservative force, sheltering the students who learn it from the realities of the world. Hoult argues that, on the contrary, a humanistic perspective is necessary in understanding the undesirable social conditions which exist, and what to do about them.

The final piece, on semiotics, covers a growing and complex area.

Lemert, drawing on the work of Lévi-Strauss, Althusser, Derrida, Foucault, and others, makes semiotics more accessible than usual by seeing it as a basis for picturing sociological work as a reading of society. Just as one reads a book, one ought, when applying semiotics, to read a society or a social setting in order to achieve a clearer understanding of it.

1. Buddhist Sociology: Some Thoughts on the Convergence of Sociology and the Eastern Paths of Liberation

INGE POWELL BELL

For years the overwhelming influence in sociology has been positivism and neo-positivism. In recent years this orientation has come under fire from neo-Marxist radicals and from a school that might be called humanist–existentialist, which is perhaps best represented by the work of Peter Berger. In this essay I would like to suggest yet another alternative tradition from which sociology might draw to its great benefit: the esoteric cores of Hinduism and Buddhism, which have lately come to Western shores in the form of the yoga, Zen Buddhist and Tibetan Buddhist movements, the teachings which Alan Watts has called the Eastern paths of liberation.[1]

In this essay I would like to depart from the more usual practice of looking at these thought systems from a sociological perspective. Instead, I would like to look at the intellectual enterprise and social organization of sociology from within the perspective of the Eastern disciplines. Here is a body of ideas which deal with the human condition and the attainment of wisdom about human life from a standpoint completely different from the science-based enterprise of the West. Just as one who travels to another country learns much about his own, so I hope that a brief trip to this "other country" may yield some useful insights to sociologists.

The Eastern paths may instruct us from several perspectives: their view of man and his relationship to society questions some of the basic theoretical assumptions of our field, while their concept of liberation introduces us to a dimension of human experience which has remained largely hidden from us. Even more important are the potential contributors of the Eastern paths to our basic methodological assumptions. In his commentary on "reflexive sociology," Gouldner (1970) points again to the need to find a way to go beyond the distortions created by self-interest, yet we have nothing in our arsenal more powerful than the incantation of one's possible biases in the introductions to our writings. I believe that the disciplines of the Eastern paths speak precisely to this question of overcoming self-interested bias. Finally, and most important, I believe that the insights of Eastern thought provide us with a criticism of our practice as sociologists, professionals, and academicians. In the following pages I would like to speak to the three areas of theory, methodology, and practice as they are illuminated by Eastern philosophy.

SOCIALIZATION

The process of socialization is a central concern of Western sociology and of the Eastern ways of liberation, but these two approaches to the fundamental human experience see socialization from diametrically opposing viewpoints. Sociology occasionally regards adult socialization as demeaning or damaging—when, for example, people are socialized into prison or the army. Usually, though, the concept refers to the process by which a child is made a member of society, and it is here that the process is seen in a wholly favorable light. Socialization is what makes a child human. Without this process the child would remain an animal. Furthermore, "Socialization helps explain how society is possible at all" (Elkin & Handel, 1960:6). Sociologists have tended to view socialization as a process by which an essentially passive and receptive child, whose main desire is for acceptance by others, is easily imprinted with society's messages. The very term "socialization" implies a process which simply makes the individual fit to live with other human beings. The term "conditioning," for example, immediately suggests quite a different process.

Psychologists have traditionally been far more aware than sociologists of the destructive aspects of socialization. For example, in *Metamorphosis*, Schachtel (1959:188, 319-20) decries the fact that adults have been so trained by society that they come to experience reality in the very cliches which they will use to tell their friends about it. The myth of a happy childhood reflects the truth that "there was a time before animalistic innocence was lost, before pleasure-seeking nature and pleasure-forbidding culture clashed in the battle called education, a battle in which the child always is the loser. . . . If they [childhood experiences] were remembered, man would demand that society affirm and accept the total personality with all its potentialities. . . ."

Perhaps our inability to see the socialization process as destructive, or at least as conflict-providing, arises out of a general lack of interest in the subjective quality of experience. Very little can be found in sociology, for example, under the rubric of happiness.[2] Sociology seldom addresses itself to the fact which most of us living in this society suspect: that most people are not very happy. Socialization often transforms happy, spontaneous children into tense, emotionally mutilated adults.

In his excellent article "The Oversocialized Conception of Man," Wrong (1967:136) points out that, unlike psychoanalytic theory, which has always seen a tension between society's demands and the pull of instincts, sociology has underemphasized the forces in man which struggle against the acceptance of social discipline. Wrong sees only "drives" or "the body" as sources of nonconformity; he feels they come from totally different sources within the personality. The enlightened man is one who is inwardly free to deviate from societal norms. Yet nothing within compels him to do so. He may choose conformity or nonconformity with equal ease and according to his larger interests.

For the Eastern paths enlightenment[3] is a process of desocialization: the unlearning of everything society has taught us (Watts, 1961:19–21). This is because the Eastern ways see socialization as the weaving of that web of illusion, or *Maya*, which binds the individual to the inventions and distortions, the motives and purposes, of society, which are the causes of his attachment, striving, and suffering. The process of undoing socialization extends even to the most essential conceptualizations, as, for example, dividing the world into good and evil or subject and object; to push even beyond this, learning to see the world without human concepts such as comparison and typology—i.e., seeing the world anew, even as a child would see it. What is recognized here is that not only do society's codes turn into "hang-ups" for the individual, but the very freshness of experience is dulled and grayed by the conceptual web which societies weave.

The question naturally arises: Is all socialization deleterious? Can or should it be avoided altogether? Obviously, socialization into some culture is an inevitable part of the human condition. Parts of the process are wholly valuable: when we learn a language, we can communicate;

when we learn technology, we can manipulate the environment; when we learn the social rules, we can maneuver in society. The dangerous component of socialization is illusion which arises out of an unwilling-ness to accept reality. For example, we have many illusions of life after death, and, in our own society, we have the illusion that we can become immortal or emotionally secure through fame and celebrity. Then there are the myths of legitimation by which we are taught to fear or worship or lust after power. And above all is the master illusion of a self separate from its environment, an object separate from its ground, a free will by virtue of which society can hold us responsible for breaking its rules.

The distinction between useful and harmful or illusion-forming socialization parallels Krishnamurti's distinction between technological and psychological thought. The former is obviously useful to man, while the latter is tied to and generated by concern for the fate of the "self." It is from this type of thought that the Eastern paths seek to free us (Linssen, 1958:119).

The process of desocialization envisaged by the Eastern paths implies no resocialization. If the Westerner has merely exchanged Western culture for Japanese or Indian culture, the process has gone wrong. In *Invitation to Sociology* Berger (1963) refers to the Eastern concept of *Satori* as being just like any conversion to a new belief system, but this is a fundamental misunderstanding. *Satori* is a consciousness beyond culture and beliefs. One piece of evidence on this score is the practice common in most Eastern disciplines of providing the student with a lengthy period of isolation from all human contact. Resocialization, on the other hand, always involves immersion in a new social setting. The attainment of *Satori*, while often accompanied by immersion into a new group, hinges strongly on an individual's experience of himself, by himself. It involves an implicit assumption that the human being can regain contact with an "original" or "authentic" self which lies behind the overlay of culture.

That the core of the teachings is separate from accompanying Oriental cultural practices is brought out clearly by Trungpa (1966:249, 252) as he describes the process of adapting Tibetan Buddhism to the Western setting. He says of his Tibetan teachers: "They taught about a basic sanity that has nothing to do with time and place. They taught about the neurotic aspects of the mind and the confusion in political, social, and other structures of life, which are universal." After an auto accident Trungpa shed the last trappings of Tibetan culture: "This led to my taking off the robe. The purpose of this was to gain for me personally the strength to continue teaching by unmasking, and also to do away with the exotic externals which were too fascinating to students in the West. . . ."

The student is not learning a new thought system in the usual sense, but is assimilating a thought system which denies the validity of all thought systems. Negation, rather than assertion, is the hallmark of this enterprise. "The spiritual life represents a process of disengagement from the tyrannical thought symbols which dominate our life and actions. This disengagement is not, however, the giving up of one enslaving thought habit and its substitution by another. . . ." (Powell 1967:134). As Krishnamurti (1978) has said: "Thought must put an end to itself." The possibility of desocialization without resocialization is nowhere recognized in sociology, but it is precisely this which constitutes enlightenment or liberation in the Eastern sense.

The liberated person, by attaining a higher consciousness, has regained the qualities of childhood. "To such, his every deed expresses originality, creativity, his living personality. There is in it no conventionality, no conformity, no inhibitory motivation. He moves just as he pleases. His behavior is like the wind which bloweth as it listeth. He has no self encased in his fragmentary, limited, restrained, egocentric existence. He is gone out of this prison. . . ." (Fromm, 1960:16)

THE SELF

One of the most heavily stressed ideas of the Eastern paths is the necessity of dropping the ego, or the concept of no-self. This easily leads to confusion because the term "ego" is not used here to designate the intergrative, controlling, and reality-testing aspects of self which social scientists usually mean by that term. Rather "ego" or "self" refers to the conflict between an "ideal self"—who I ought to be—and a "real self"—who I think I really am—both of which are obviously acquired from society. As we pit these two illusory images against each other, we generate tension, emotional imbalance, and a constant concern with the self.

Sociologists recognize that socialization normally results in the creation of an ideal self. Although they see that anxiety may be caused if the ideal and real selves are too divergent, this is considered an abnormal or unusual outcome, and the ideal self is viewed as necessary in enabling the individual to develop self-disciplined, goal-directed action (Broom and Selznick, 1955:92). For the Eastern ways, on the other hand, the ideal self is merely another refusal to accept reality fully, while the whole syndrome of self is an invention of society which creates constant and fruitless concern.

Sometimes sociologists do explicitly recognize the fact that anxiety is a prevalent condition. Broom and Selznick (1955:89) believe that the long period of dependency during which socialization takes place makes man the "anxious animal." What is implied here is that such anxiety is an inevitable part of being human. Watts (1961:71) notes more precisely what society does to make the individual anxious: "Social conditioning as we know it depends entirely on persuading people not to accept themselves. . . ." But there is a way out. The liberated person is as human as anyone else, but "his liberation lies in the fact that he is not in conflict with himself for being so. . . ."

Put in terms of role theory, sociology holds that certain roles are central to the integration of one's personality; the individual stakes his self-respect on the successful carrying out of such roles. The role thus creates a burden of anxiety, while at the same time limiting the person's outlook to the perspective on the world he gets from his particular role. This is seen as normal and inevitable. But the liberated individual is precisely one who "no longer confuses his identity with his social role. . . . He plays his role instead of taking it seriously." Watts points out that at the moment when we cease to take the role seriously, "it is possible to go on behaving as rationally as ever—but with a remarkable sense of lightness" (Watts 1961:49).

Of course, sociologists see that a particular role may be false. The con man who "cools out the mark" (Goffman, in Rose, 1962) does not believe a word he is saying, but he is motivated by a serious need to be successful in another role, namely, that of a con man. What sociology seems to miss is that an enlightened person may have at his disposal a collection of roles, none of which he takes seriously and none of which he uses to confer identity on himself.

The Eastern ways regard as fictitious and misleading the notion that there is a person whose actions we can control, an entity which exists over time. There is only a series of occurrences or experiences. This difficult notion may perhaps be glimpsed in the experience of anyone over forty who looks back on himself at thirty or twenty or fifteen and says to himself, "That was really somebody else; how I felt about life then bears almost no resemblance to how I feel now." It is only social structure which imposes on the individual the definition of a continuously existing person who is the same at twenty, forty, and eighty. After discussing the way an individual rewrites his own life history with every new perspective he attains, Berger (1963:106) sees that "the self is no longer a solid, given entity that moves from one situation to another. It is rather a process, continuously created and re-created in each social situation that one enters, held together by the slender thread of memory. . . ." Although the clarity of Berger's insight is rare, most sociologists do see that the self is a social construction, but they assume it is a necessary construction, one without which the individual could not function. Symbolic interactionists such as G. H. Mead (1934) and Herbert Blumer (1934) emphasize that the self is a process rather than a fixed entity. Still they see the self as a real identity and structure that underlies the growth process—that is, the concept of self for the symbolic interactionists presupposes a structure from which growth can be evaluated.

The Eastern paths tell us that in our normal socialized state we are victims of ignorance or forgetfulness (*Avidya*) of our true nature (often described as our true God-like nature). During our formative years, we adopt certain personality traits as ways of dealing with our environment. For example, a child with a bullying parent learns to play depressed to get that parent's sympathy or buy his or her neutrality. Eventually, the depressive role becomes habitual. The individual now feels trapped inside the role. It looms before him as if it were an alien power, and it buffets him about. He has forgotten that he invented this response—that once he "was God," i.e., he was and is the shaper of his own soul.

Berger (1963:140–45, 147 and 148) comes very close to the Eastern view when he uses the model of society as drama. He writes that "deception and self-deception are at the very heart of social reality. . . ." Then he introduces the strictly Western notion of existential despair to explain why everyone cooperates in the deception. It is because society hides from us "the naked terrors of our condition." These terrors seem to consist of a mixture of the fear of death and the fear of discovering ourselves alone in a vast, impersonal universe. "In the end we must return to that nightmare moment when we feel ourselves stripped of all names and all identities." What Berger does not seem to see is that this fear of death and of the cosmos, a psychological fear, is also a social invention which has been particularly strong in Western civilization. Many societies do not share our horror of death, and the Eastern paths of liberation regard as the most precious *Satori* that moment when we "feel ourselves stripped of all names and all identities."

The Western view generally ignores the enlightenment dimension, just as it often ignores the quality of experience. In terms of role theory, this means that nowhere in our analysis do we have the tools which might enable us to tell the difference between the role-playing of Watts's or Suzuki's enlightened man and the performance of one who is so attached to the illusion of his role that he suffers a heart attack or an ulcer. We touch upon this hidden dimension frequently in indirect ways: when, in the sociology of knowledge, we study the way thought is shaped by society, we are looking at the creation of *Maya*, of illusion.

When we study the causes and treatment of mental illness, we are involved in trying to move people toward enlightenment; when we study Maslow's (1962) work on self-actualizing people we are looking at some of the characteristics of higher consciousness. Yet the underlying dimension is seldom explicitly recognized. It is, of course, a dimension that cannot be summarized in a few words. Indeed, since the enlightened state is a state beyond language, it is impossible to pinpoint through language alone. Becoming enlightened is not primarily an intellectual process, and, although the intellect may help, it may also hinder. Keeping one's emotional balance in life or becoming adept in the use of "skillful means" of living resembles the process of learning to ride a bicycle or play a musical instrument. You cannot learn this by reading books about it. You can learn only by practice. In order to recognize what enlightenment is, we must ourselves be enlightened. We can judge enlightenment only to the point where we have ourselves arrived.

With Eastern views of socialization and self, we have moved beyond the intellect. But might not sociology be the discipline which is willing to ask the question: In understanding human life, just how far can pure intellect take us? And if it can take us only so far, what else is there? Eastern philosophy suggests that there is something more valuable than the conceptualizing, knowledge-accumulating intellect. This is sometimes called "basic intelligence": our ability to perceive and deal with reality without reference to accumulated idea systems. Basic intelligence is what gets us out of a burning building. The question for us is whether sociology can incorporate into its framework the development of such an intelligence.

METHODOLOGY

The Eastern paths also speak to us on the most basic questions of our methodology. Having accepted the positivist approach, Western social science has also accepted the idea that the scientist qua scientist has little to do with the scientist as a person. The separation supposedly goes in two directions: who I am is not supposed to influence my study of human behavior, and my study is not expected to reflect back on who I am. We lack a tradition, a system, which would enable us to develop a meaningful perspective on this problem.

Unfortunately, sociologists have made the mistake of putting mechanical methodologies in the center of their objectivity training rather than developing a far more fruitful line of thought initiated by Mannheim's sociology of knowledge,[4] C. Wright Mills's insistence that the sociologist must understand his own position in history and how this shapes his perception, or the more recent ideas of Gouldner's reflexive sociology (1970:511–512): a sociology of sociology.

Gouldner points out that most sociological theorizing is an effort to cope with the feeling of being threatened by one's world, and that objectivity is possible only when the theorist rises above these personal feelings. But how can he do this? Neither Mannheim nor Mills nor Gouldner tells us. They imply that we must develop an intellectual understanding of our self-interest and the processes by which this shapes our ideas. But is intellectual understanding enough to neutralize the powerful emotions of self-preservation? I think not. Mannheim (1936) is the perfect case in point. In *Ideology and Utopia* he develops a brilliant analysis of how social position forms ideology and then falls into the same trap himself by arguing that the "floating intelligentsia" is somehow not rooted in society in the same way as social classes and is thus, alone, able to see objectively. He has rescued the transcendent role of the scholar from the suspicion he cast upon it and enshrined his own group as the only one capable of this saving grace. All his intellect did not avail against the pull of his personal commitments.

Because self-interest is rooted in emotion, it cannot be overcome by intellect alone. The Eastern parths offer an ancient and highly developed discipline which can liberate us from the pull of self-interest and develop an attitude which accepts the often threatening world and its inevitable flow of change. Self-interest will loose its hold over our minds only as we disengage ourselves from self.

Because "men's highest values, no less than their basest impulses, may make liars of them" (Gouldner, 1970:499), we must liberate ourselves from our noblest as well as from our basest desires. Eastern mysticism sets out to do this, to free us from *all* opinions, values, and preconceptions. What I am asserting is that clear insight into society begins with detachment from one's own emotions. The self cannot be, as in the positivist model, sealed off from the material it studies; it can only be made fully open to every aspect of that material. Only then can we attain the kind of awareness which Gouldner (1970:494) refers to as "an openness to bad news."[5]

TOWARD AN ENLIGHTENED SOCIOLOGY

Just as enlightenment does not come through intellect alone, so its fruits cannot be purely theoretical. To be real, enlightenment must revolutionize the practice of sociology. One conclusion which is implied by enlightened self-appraisal is that teaching must be restored as a central value of our profession. The furtherance of enlightenment requires personal contact between teacher and student, and it is in this relationship that we can offer the greatest contribution to society.

As a teacher, I have for years been frustrated by how little study of sociology tells students about living a satisfying life. As critics of the social structure, we can stimulate students to generate ideas about changing society in order to make life better for larger numbers of people. And, indeed, this is an invaluable contribution; perhaps it is the major contribution to be expected from a science which sees how irrevocably the individual's life is tied to the whole fabric of society. But what do we say to students who have to live their lives right now and in the future in a world they never made and perhaps cannot affect very much? Shouldn't the field which claims to study people in their totality—as citizens, producers, consumers, parents, lovers, friends— have something to say about how to raise the quality of life for the individual? Students who have not yet been schooled in what the field consists of continue to have expectations of gaining insight and wisdom for their own lives. For the most part they continue to be disappointed.[6]

The Eastern ways of liberation speak precisely to the question of how to live a satisfying life in given circumstances. For contrary to popular Western opinion, these schools of thought do believe in changing what can be changed, and they also concentrate on how to live with what cannot be changed.[7] This involves developing a gut-level understanding and acceptance of what the universe is about and what our place in it is. Because we are self-centered, we believe that there is a right and wrong to everything, right being whatever makes us comfortable, safe, and happy, and wrong being whatever threatens our safety, pleasure, or desire for control. The Eastern ways tell us that we cannot control the universe to suit our egotistical fantasy. Change is constant and is the way of the universe. To accept this is also to accept our losses and our eventual demise with equanimity. Fortunately, sociology does in some ways contribute to the development of this type of enlightenment.

The development of objectivity in the student can be a discipline at least somewhat similar to the disciplines of the Eastern paths. It involves a systematic attempt to expand self-centered awareness beyond the parochial situation in which everything in society is judged according to whether it fulfills or frustrates our desires. The wealthy student must learn to see the society through the eyes of the poor (Mills, 1959); the young must understand how the world looks to the old. This is not a purely intellectual process, but it involves learning how the other feels by becoming, if only momentarily, the other.[8]

Another important contribution of social science to objectivity is cultural relativism, the insight that no social codes or systems are intrinsically right or wrong. Rather, they are all divergent manifestations of humans' culture-building capacity.[9] This is certainly an excellent foundation for the difficult process of learning to see through the absolutes of one's own culture.

We must design the learning experience to educate the heart as well as the head. I would suggest, as just one example, that we require of every sociology major a year living in some part of society never before experienced by that student. I would discourage any reading before this field placement. Let the student experience without prejudgment. Afterward, there will be no need to urge them to read what others have said about their field environment. On a lower level sociodrama can simulate the experience of taking other social roles; so can meetings with young workers, welfare mothers, millionaires, and others.

Toward a Practicing Sociology

For the Eastern paths, "Physician heal thyself" is a primary dictum. This is learning what must be judged by the practice to which it leads. In sociology, though, our practice fails to reflect our expertise in human relations and group behavior. Although sociologists have studied academic institutions and the workings of many academic disciplines, we appear to have drawn few lessons which we can apply to ourselves. Human relationships in sociology are not markedly better than those in other disciplines.

We are full of ideas for reforming society but make little connection between these ideas and our day-to-day actions. We deplore the effects of careerism in big business, at the same time that we groan under the strain of careerism ourselves.[10] We theorize about "community" while our junior colleagues live in fear of losing their jobs. We argue for greater equality in America while despising our own students as unworthy of our attention. We believe that we want to improve society, but our immediate personal motive is career advancement. We acquiesce in a viciously competitive system of publish-or-perish which floods our field with an indigestible and actually obstructive body of material, most of which, produced under competitive duress, only demeans those who write it while wasting the time of those who read it. We seem unconcerned with the possibility that the emphasis on academic research is designed by the power structure to neutralize us as an influence on the young or within the wider community. Our research is funded by the Ford Foundation, Rockefeller, and the Department of Defense, as if the sociology of knowledge did not clearly tell us what sources of funding do to the bias of the recipients. We learn sociology, but we do not learn *from* sociology.

These contradictions reflect on our professional practice and on ourselves. Consciousness of institutional oppression begins with an awareness of one's own situation. Where this awareness is radically enhanced, opposition to oppressive institutions must follow. Far from being a recipe for privatization or inaction, the Eastern paths provide insights and suggestions for effective social change, beginning precisely in that arena which we are best able to influence—ourselves and our immediate environment.

Sociologists are good at questioning the values of mainstream America, but we generally remain blind to the myths of our own academic subculture. To the extent that we demythologize American culture for the student, we lift the veil, but we quickly follow this act of desocialization with an act of resocialization. In place of the myths and values of the dominant culture, we put the myths and values of the Academy. We create a new illusion, *academaya*. We cannot see through the role of the professional, with all its striving, competition, and deadly seriousness. We do not see that a career is a highly developed form of concern with the ego, nor do we show how easy it is to control a person who is intent on career success. To the extent that we take ourselves seriously as sociologists and academicians, we continue to propagate the illusion, the goal attachment, and the suffering. Like our popular and high culture, which features almost exclusively the activities of obsessively goal-oriented heroes, American sociology accepts and practices goal-orientation as the only possible mode of human conduct.

Put in terms of power and authority, the ways of enlightenment seek to liberate the individual from the authority of society and those who rule it, from scripture, and even from religious tradition. We enlighten our students to the edge of liberation only to ensnare them again in the authority structure of the academy and the related professions. Insofar as these structures are ultimately tied by a thousand threads to the power structure of the larger society, we make them and even their very vision of reality subservient to those who rule.

NOTES

I would like to thank Ted Hoffman for his help in the area of Eastern thought; Ellin Ringler, for her editing of the manuscript; and to give special thanks to Glenn Goodwin for his help in sociological theory and his constant encouragement.

1. This article purposely does not begin with the traditional review of the literature. The standard review is a rigid and largely empty formula which keeps us from communicating with each other directly with fresh and new ideas. It discourages breadth, rewards overspecialization, and constantly ties our thought to the past. I would prefer to strive for that state of lucid awareness which Krishnamurti (1969) refers to as "Freedom from the Known."

Since I urge sociologists to look into Eastern thought, I would also like to recommend some books which I have found valuable in beginning my explorations into this subject. First, I suggest any of the works of Alan Watts. Although some purists consider him a hedonist, he speaks to us as a Westerner and is fairly easy to understand. Second, any of the works of Krishnamurti. In both these cases I say "any work" by these authors, because all their books are segments of the same running commentary. Also: D. T. Suzuki, *An Introduction to Zen Buddhism*; Fromm and Suzuki, *Zen Buddhism and Psychoanalysis*; Chogyam Trungpa, *Meditation in Action, Cutting Through Spiritual Materialism*, and *The Myth of Freedom and the Way of Meditation*; Tarthang Tulku, *Gesture of Balance*; Eugen Herrigel, *Zen in the Art of Archery*; and Robert Powell, *Zen and Reality*.

Since this is not a discipline which can be mastered by purely intellectual means, those serious about pursuing it should also become conversant with the practice of meditation, as it is explained in these books or taught by one of the many applied schools of Eastern thought in this country.

2. Although, of course, the issue of happiness is implicit in much sociological writing, the only book-length work explicitly related to the subject is Bradburn and Caplowitz, *Reports on Happiness*.

3. Some readers of this article have indicated that the terms "enlightenment" or "liberation" (I use them here interchangeably) are not fully defined. This is difficult because the term "enlightenment" is much like the term "sociology": if you could fully define it, you would be a fully trained sociologist; if you could fully understand enlightenment, you would be fully enlightened. I try throughout this article to indicate what enlightenment is by tying it into the theory and practice of sociology. For those who like short definitions, however, I offer the following: enlightenment or liberation is freedom from desire, total acceptance of reality, including the reality of self; it is freedom from all egotistical concern, what Krishnamurti calls "psychological thinking" as opposed to "technical thinking" (i.e., I think technically about the substance of my field, but have no thoughts as to how I rank in relation to others). Ultimately, it is a seeing beyond the concepts and categories of one's culture. The following quotations may also be helpful: "a certain silence of the mind, an inner transparence, a mental relaxation" (Linssen, 1958); "Understanding the nature of bondage results in liberation." ("Understanding" here means something broader than the action of intellect alone.) "*Satori* may be defined as intuitive looking into, in contradistinction to intellectual and logical understanding. Whatever the definition, *satori* means the unfolding of a new world hitherto unperceived in the confusion of dualistic mind . . ." (Suzuki, 1964).

4. One reader of this essay criticized it for not subjecting the Eastern teachings

to the analysis of the sociology of knowledge, but this would be seeing the teachings through our own social science thought system. This is precisely what I avoid in speaking from within the assumptions of Eastern thought. From these assumptions the sociology of knowledge does not hold because Eastern thought differs from other philosophies in that it is a negation of all philosophy. In that sense it takes the implications of the sociology of knowledge that all thought has irrational roots more seriously than we do.

5. In terms of Krishnamurti's distinction between technical and psychological thought, sociology is a mixed case. Our information processing becomes entangled with the personal needs which we project onto our material.

6. Once I was asked by a class of young prison inmates what sociology had to tell them about how to save their lives. After much thought I finally came up with the following contribution: since upward mobility involves, above all, learning to take on another class-culture, those desiring mobility should make informal, friendship contacts with middle-class people. This was probably a truthful suggestion, but the setting only brings out the usual irony: people are stuck in existing social situations. How can they survive them?

7. The Western stereotype of the yogi sitting in his Himalayan cave only applies to some Western practitioners. From others we have a very different example. Gandhi and his present Indian followers are probably the most dramatic instances of social action. But we have innumerable other examples of yoga and Buddhist teachers who have founded schools, mental hospitals, and similar institutions, and of those many who have generally spent their lives teaching. Nor have their teachings always ignored social ills. Krishnamurti's speeches and writings are filled with critical comments on the functioning of modern society.

8. This is, of course, not the kind of learning envisaged by those who regard sociology as parallel to natural science. I am reminded of a class in race relations I taught in the 1960's. The students had read Baldwin and other very angry black intellectuals without much comment. Then I invited a black radical to class who was so angry he almost failed to communicate altogether on a verbal level. Afterward all sorts of students came up to me and said, "You know, they're really mad!" and "For the first time I think I grasp what Baldwin was all about." When sociology functions at this level, it is fully in tune with the way of experiental knowledge, which is the way of the Eastern paths (Fromm, 1960:118). It should be emphasized that I am not arguing for a totally subjectivist position, but only that the kind of knowledge necessary for the study of people must be both intellectual and emotional.

9. For those who fear that cultural relativism will leave us without any standard of judgment, and hence paralyzed, the Eastern paths offer an answer. The truly enlightened can see through the myriad cultural forms to a more ultimate underlying reality.

10. In his excellent book on careerism in corporations, Michael Maccoby follows his description of corporate careerism with this observation: "Comparing my own experience in universities, I would say that although academics consider themselves more 'humane' than businessmen, the engineers and

managers we interviewed are no more competitive and a lot more cooperative with one another than most professors. If corporate managers engaged in the nitpicking and down-putting common in universities, little would be created and produced. If managers treated their subordinates with the neglect and contempt common in the attitude of professors to graduate students, no one would work for them" (Maccoby 1976:209).

REFERENCES

BERGER, PETER L.
  1963 Invitation to Sociology: A Humanistic Perspective. Garden City: Doubleday-Anchor Books.
BLUMER, HERBERT
  1934 "Society as symbolic interaction." In Arnold Rose (ed.), Human Behavior and Social Processes. 1962, Boston: Houghton Mifflin.
BRADBURN, NORMAN M., and DAVID CAPLOVITZ
  1965 Reports on Happiness. Chicago: Aldine.
BROOM, LEONARD, and PHILLIP SELZNICK
  1955 Sociology, 4th ed. New York: Harper & Row.
ELKIN, FREDERICK, and GERALD HANDEL
  1960 The Child and Society: The Process of Socialization. New York: Random House.
FROMM, ERICH, D. T. SUZUKI, and RICHARD DE MARTINO
  1960 Zen Buddhism and Psychoanalysis. New York: Harper & Row.
GOULDNER, ALVIN W.
  1970 The Coming Crisis of Western Sociology. New York: Basic Books.
HERRIGEL, EUGEN
  1971 Zen in the Art of Archery. New York: Vintage, Random House.
KRISHNAMURTI, J.
  1969 Freedom from the Known. New York: Harper & Row.
  1978 Lecture at Ojai, Calif., April 11.
LINSSEN, ROBERT
  1958 Living Zen. New York: Grove Press.
MACCOBY, MICHAEL
  1976 The Gamesman. New York: Simon & Schuster.
MANNHEIM, KARL
  1936 Ideology and Utopia: An Introduction to the Sociology of Knowledge. New York: Harcourt Brace.
MASLOW, ABRAHAM
  1962 Toward a Psychology of Being. Princeton: Van Nostrand.
MEAD, GEORGE HERBERT
  1934 Mind, Self and Society. Chicago: University of Chicago Press.
MILLS, C. WRIGHT
  1959 The Sociological Imagination. Oxford: Oxford University Press.

POWELL, ROBERT
1961 Zen and Reality. Middlesex, England: Penguin Books.
1967 Crisis in Consciousness. Greenwood, S.C.: Attic Press.
SCHACHTEL, ERNEST
1959 Metamorphosis. New York: Basic Books.
SUZUKI, D. T.
1964 An Introduction to Zen Buddhism. New York: Random House.
TARTHANG TULKU
1977 Gesture of Balance. Emeryville, Calif.: Dharma Publishing.
THAKAR, VIMALA
1970 Towards Total Transformation. Fairfax, Calif.: Tamal Land Press.
TRUNGPA, CHOGYAM
1966 Born in Tibet. Baltimore: Penguin Books.
1969 Meditation in Action. Berkeley: Shambhala Publications.
1976 The Myth of Freedom and the Way of Meditation. Berkeley: Shambhala
      Publications.
1973 Cutting Through Spiritual Materialism. Berkeley: Shambhala Publica-
      tions.
WATTS, ALAN W.
1961 Psychotherapy East and West. New York: Ballantine.
WRONG, DENNIS
1967 "The Oversocialized Conception of Man." In Peter I. Rose, The Study of
      Society: An Integrated Anthology. New York: Random House.

2. Towards a Women's Perspective in Sociology: Directions and Prospects

MARCIA TEXLER SEGAL
CATHERINE WHITE BERHEIDE

A women's perspective in sociology has been trying to emerge since the publication of Viola Klein's *The Feminine Character* (1971, originally published in 1946) and Helen M. Hacker's "Women as a Minority Group" (1951). These works received little serious attention when first published, but two decades later, when many more women have become openly disillusioned with their options in society, the works are being reconsidered. Women in sociology (see, for an early example, Rossi, 1964) were expressing concern with the inability of the social sciences to provide an analysis of the position of women upon which a program for change could be built. A women's perspective in sociology developed as an attempt to provide such an analysis.

The women's perspective in sociology focuses on the lifestyles, interests, and activities of women in our gender-differentiated society. Women-oriented sociology examines the behavior and attitudes of the previously invisible half of humanity. Consequently, research is now being done on subjects such as housework, sexual inequality, and women's health care—subjects that were formerly defined as unworthy of study because of their almost exclusive association with women. Empirical data from these studies provide the basis for inductively building a women's theoretical perspective with clearly stated assumptions and propositions. The construction of a comprehensive feminist social theory has begun.

A comprehensive feminist social theory would involve a description

69

and explanation of women's oppression and assess implications for social change. The women's perspective currently consists of a critique of women's place in contemporary society and some tentative explanations of it. Feminist theory is interested in how the social structure affects women's lives and in how women perceive their position in the social structure. The women's perspective attempts not only to describe the sex roles in a society but to reveal their social, economic, and political functions. The ideology of sexism, its structural bases, and its effects on the position of women are examined. Feminist theory has begun to elucidate the interactional and structural aspects of the oppression of women.

Thus, the women's perspective in sociology involves both a macrosociological and a microsociological approach to understanding the conditions of women's lives. It is concerned with the study of sex differences, gender roles, women as a minority group, and women as a class or caste (Hochschild, 1973). Research in the areas of sex differences and gender roles emphasizes the relationship of individuals to the social structure. In microlevel analyses gender role socialization is used to explain the position of women. Proposals for social change are directed towards altering socialization patterns. Research in the areas of women as a minority group and women as a class emphasizes the organization of society. In macrolevel analyses social structure is used to explain the position of women. Proposals for social change are directed towards altering the structure of society. At the present time feminist sociologists need to develop theories which connect the conclusions of the social psychological and social structural research. Unfortunately too many feminist sociologists take an exclusively gender role/socialization or sexual inequality/social structure approach.

Women have not been the exclusive focus or the exclusive producers of sociological work from a feminist perspective. Doris Entwisle's current work (1977) on prenatal and neonatal-stage families is unprecedented in its focus on the father during this crucial time. David Tresemer (1975) and Warren Farrell (1974) are among the men who are re-evaluating men's roles from the perspective of women's roles.

Empirical research using a feminist framework has sometimes revealed the inadequacies of other sociological theories for explaining some part of reality and at times has suggested new explanations of social reality. And yet, the women's perspective is not incompatible with other perspectives. Clearly, it has much in common with conflict perspectives as it focuses on women as a disadvantaged class/caste/interest group category.[1] Sociologists investigating sexual inequality follow the conflict perspective when they assume that differences in power explain differences between the sexes, and that social change will result from the attempts of women to redress the imbalance. Improving the position of women requires an accurate description of women's present position and of the power structure which maintains that position. Thus, the feminist perspective also involves a political critique of society (e.g., Oakley, 1974b).

Social psychological perspectives such as symbolic interaction and labeling can help us to understand the microdynamics of women's place, and are, therefore, compatible with a women's perspective. Research on sex roles is informed by established sociological theory concerning roles and socialization, although there is considerable controversy surrounding the use of the term "sex roles." Gould and Kern-Daniels (1977) argue that "gender roles" rather than "sex roles" is the more appropriate term, because gender refers to the socially defined masculine and feminine attitudes and behavior, while sex refers to the biologically defined differences between males and females. Currently, "gender" and "sex" are applied inconsistently and sometimes inter-changeably in the women's perspective literature. Lopata and Thorne (1978) go one step further and argue that "role" is also inappropriately applied to the sociology of gender and sex. They see gender as a pervasive identity which defines the characteristics and roles women and men are assigned by society.

Feminists have criticized many of the conclusions of functionalist theorists (e.g., Parsons, 1959) for assuming that the status quo is neces-sary. Functionalists argue that the traditional sexual division of labor is functional for society; feminists have countered by noting that while the traditional sexual division of labor may have been functional in the past, it is no longer necessary and cannot be justified in a post-industrial society. Still, the women's perspective is compatible with general functionalist notions that social systems have certain basic needs which are filled by social institutions, and that social systems are characterized by a degree of normative and functional integration (see Safilios-Rothschild, 1976, on articulating changes in family and occupational spheres).

How the emerging biosocial perspective fits with a women's perspec-tive is open to question. Biosocial views have often been little more than scientific sexism (e.g., Tiger, 1970) or well-meaning but misguided fictions (e.g., Morgan, 1972). Yet there is a biological component to social life, which feminists such as Tanner and Zihlman (1976) and Rossi (1977) are just beginning to seek. For example, in her discussion of parenthood, Rossi combines an evolutionary perspective with recent biological findings regarding the interactions of the endocrine system with the central nervous system and the social and psychological environment. She suggests that evolution has better equipped women than men for parenthood. Women learn the needed skills and establish the requisite bonds more easily because they build upon a biological base that men lack. She argues for restructuring social institutions in ways which will work with, not against, biology.

The women's perspective is not a single, unified, homogeneous perspective. Feminist researchers belong to many schools of thought—Marxist, symbolic interactionist, functionalist—and many disciplines—sociology, history, political science. Much feminist scholarship is cross-disciplinary in character, but psychological and economic variables must be integrated still more with more strictly sociological ones. In addition, the questions asked by woman-oriented researchers require historical and cross-cultural perspectives. Sociologists are doing some of this work themselves and are cooperating with colleagues in other disciplines as well. Sociological variables and frames of reference are being used by feminist scholars in other disciplines (e.g., economists Ross and Sawhill, 1975). Other attempts are being made to bring the perspectives of more than one discipline to bear on particular issues (e.g., Segal and Segal, 1976, present both anthropological and sociological perspectives on two-occupation families). A women's perspective is a broad one which can lead to the incorporation of new variables into an essentially sociological framework.

What then is new about sociology from a feminist perspective? One thing that those who take this perspective regard as axiomatic is that there is no official line, and there are no official spokespersons. What follows represents the views of the authors, who focus first on the underlying assumptions of the women's perspective as they see them and then on the women's perspective as a basis for a thorough critique of past, and finally, on the ongoing work which stems from other perspectives. New areas of study are brought into focus by the perspective for the discipline, some brief examples of theoretical discussions of women's oppression are presented.

UNDERLYING ASSUMPTIONS

The women's perspective assumes that the relative positions of women and men are social, not biological, facts. We presuppose this in part because we are social scientists who begin with the assumption that most aspects of society and culture are social, not biological, in origin. Some feminists would deny biology any role in explaining the positions or the behavior of women. But the majority of authors would not go that far. Rather, we would maintain that the role of biology is a relatively minor and undifferentiated influence which can be expressed in terms of behavioral tendencies or limits. The normative and structural factors which differentiate the lives of women and men are specific and readily observable. The women's perspective seeks to identify these factors and explain their effects.

The women's perspective further assumes that the subordination of women is unjust. Since the inferior position of women is socially enforced, it can and should be improved. While social systems may have certain basic requirements which must be met if they are to continue to exist, any given arrangement has functional alternatives. Thus, no existing arrangement is inherently unalterable, and both the alternatives to the current sexual division of labor and the means of implementing them are legitimate objects of investigation. As this implies, feminist sociology has both political and theoretical aims. Rather than support the existing social arrangements, the women's perspective seeks to improve the quality of women's lives.

The women's perspective maintains that gender is an important variable in explaining behavior. Indeed, women and men have unique life experiences, they inhabit separate social worlds, and they perceive social reality differently. Bernard (1972) speaks of his and her marriages, recognizing that to the extent that they have different responsibilities and goals, the relationships among family members appear differently to husbands and wives. The language used by and to women and men differs (Warshay, 1972), and different norms govern their behavior in the same social settings (Walum, 1974). Even behavior itself differs (Broverman et al., 1972).

The opportunity structure of any particular organization or community is different for females and males. This results in differing realities within which to set goals and predict one's success or failure (see the "fear of success" debate beginning with Horner, 1972, and continuing with Levine and Crumrine, 1975, and Tresemer, 1976). The ways in which women and men are tied to social networks, and the networks to which they are tied, differ. Men are linked to the society primarily through occupational roles, while women tend to forge the links between family and community by being the principal consumers of goods and services and the performers of much unpaid labor at home and in organizations. These and other differences between females and males are at least as pervasive as those between females of different economic strata or different ethnic backgrounds. These differences produce world views which only partially overlap, though each may be based on accurate assessments of the social environment (cf. Smith, 1977).

Because the expectations, rewards, and options available to women and men are so different, some writers (Goetz, 1978; Lee and Gropper, 1974) speak of sex-role cultures. They point out that because society operates largely according to the norms of the male culture, females, like members of other minority groups, may become bicultural so that they can interact successfully in a wider range of settings. More typically, females and males are seen as analytically separate social categories or classes, the former subordinate to the latter.

Some of the assumptions of the women's perspective parallel those made by other sociological perspectives; however, they are made with regard to groups—women and men—who are initially differentiated by ascribed criteria rather than categories—like economic strata—which are differentiated on purely social grounds. Ultimately, the women's perspective should lead to a revision of other social theories so that women's lives are incorporated into the analysis of society. Once such revisions occur, a separate women's perspective will be unnecessary, because gender and the sexual division of labor will be adequately accounted for by the established sociological perspectives.

THE IMPACT OF THE FEMINIST CRITIQUE

Feminist critiques of other theoretical perspectives and of empirical research make at least implicit alternative theoretical assumptions about society and social life. First, the women's perspective criticizes sociology for studying men almost exclusively (see Oakley, 1974a). Established sociological models which are based on the male world distort women's social reality. Too often sociological theory and research have assumed that what is true for men is true for women. In contrast, the women's perspective assumes that there are important differences between the experiences of men and women which need to be investigated. Thus, feminist sociologists call for new theories, models, concepts, and methods with which to analyze the heretofore neglected half of humanity. Second, the women's perspective argues that by ignoring women, sociology has left whole areas of social life unexplored. In particular, sociology has overlooked the informal private side of social life, which is dominated by women, and instead, has emphasized the formal public side of life, which is dominated by men (Millman and Kanter, 1975). The women's perspective assumes that informal and interpersonal networks are critical parts of society that have an influence on formal and official arrangements. This influence needs more study.

The feminist critique of sociology has begun to have an impact on research in several ways. First, it has led sociologists to look at the position and behavior of women in areas of social life where we have previously studied only the behavior of men. Second, traditional women's areas such as the family have been re-examined. Third, the women's perspective has encouraged researchers to investigate areas of special interest to women. Finally, research is looking into the ways in which women are made into and maintained as a class.

Under the impetus of the women's perspective, critical re-evaluations of previous scholarship have appeared (e.g., Lofland, 1975, on community and Simon, 1975, on crime). Much effort has been devoted to a challenge of the sexist assumptions about the place of women in the study of stratification and social mobility (see Acker, 1973, and Duberman, 1976, for discussions of the sexist bias in stratification and mobility research). These assumptions about women have been treated as empirical questions and tested. For example, Ritter and Hargens (1975) question the assumption that family social status is determined solely by the husband's occupation. The attempt has been made to develop new models to account for the data on women as well as men. Studies which compare male and female occupational and marriage mobility patterns have thus far produced inconsistent results, partly because they have been based on secondary analysis of data gathered for other purposes and have used different techniques (cf. De Jong et al., 1971; Tyree and Treas, 1974; and others).

The second area of research stimulated by the women's perspective involves a new look at some areas traditionally associated with women. For example, the sociology of the family is undergoing major revisions, as studies of family power and household division of labor are re-examined by feminist researchers who do not assume that housework is shared because most husbands/fathers do sometimes wash dishes or babysit, or that decision making is egalitarian because he buys the cars while she buys the groceries (Berheide et al., 1976; Gillespie, 1971).

Studies of pink-collar work (Howe, 1977) belong to the third category of new research areas—that is, studies of settings and issues of female-dominated occupations and of patterns of behavior generally thought to be more characteristic of women at work than of men. Issues relating to women's health (Bart, 1968), child care (Roby, 1973), aging (Lopata, 1973), and resuming one's education (Katz et al., 1974) belong in this category. Studies of women's organizations, whether feminist, nonfeminist, antifeminist, straight, or gay, also fall into this cagegory (Cassell, 1977).

Finally, some research is geared toward describing in detail the social mechanisms by which females become members of a subordinate class in our society. There are many theoretical, particularly Marxist, discussions of the causes and consequences of women's oppression. Those formulations that explain gender differences in terms of social structure follow Rubin's paraphrase (1975:158) of Marx: "A woman is a woman. She only becomes a domestic, a wife, a chattel, a playboy bunny, a prostitute, or a human dictaphone in certain relations." There are, of course, differences of opinion regarding what the determining relations are and whether, by becoming domestics, dictaphone operators, or bunnies, women thereby become an exploited class of themselves, or merely the lesser half of whatever exploited class their fathers, brothers, husbands, and sons belong to. Marxist feminists argue that the oppression of women is an outgrowth of capitalism and its oppression of the working class. Other feminists maintain that women can be subordinated even in a classless society. Still other feminists believe that the division of society into sexes is even more fundamental than its division into classes.

Another common thread in most treatments of gender differences as products of social structure is the distinction between public and private spheres of activity, interest, and influence. The distinction grows sharper as one moves from foraging societies through horticultural ones to agricultural and industrial ones. In preclass societies, men and women may have different tasks and responsibilities. As Reiter (1975:272) said: "Kinship-as-politics belongs to men, kinship-as-household-organization belongs to women." Kinship, however, is society's most pervasive organizing principle, and community and family functions are not conceptually or physically separate.

In this view the distinction is sharpened in class societies, because instead of each kin unit providing for itself, some are exploited for the benefit of others. The labor of males is more readily exploited than that of females because men are more mobile and do not have the burden of reproduction and maintenance of children. Males gain skills and power even as they are exploited. They act to maintain their positions. Females (and children) become secondary sources of exploitable labor, less productive and of lower value because of the limitations of family responsibilities (and immaturity, in the case of children). The church and the law reinforce and sanctify the structures which emerge.

Some writers are more concerned than others with the traditional Marxist distinction between kinds of value (Benston, 1969; Sacks, 1975). The private sphere produces only personal use value; the public sphere, exchange value. So long as males and females contribute to the production of different kinds of value, their contributions can be esteemed and rewarded differentially. Men can be considered social adults and given rights that socially dependent women lack (Sacks, 1975). In addition, as women are rendered dependent on men, they are forced into marriage, which justifies their treatment as marginal labor, as well as their sporadic employment at lower wages (Benston, 1969; Hartmann, 1976).

Those who use cross-cultural materials, especially those who look at non-Western and nonindustrial societies, are pursuing the question of the specific conditions under which females have more or less power vis-à-vis males (see, for example, Collins, 1975). Lipman-Blumen (1976) focuses on how and why male dominance, once established, is maintained. Her homosocial theory might be called exchange theory from a women's perspective. She notes that to the extent that males control all socially valued resources, it is only for the procreation of children that women are needed. There are few factors to motivate men, or even other women, to interact with women. The process is circular: women lack skills and material resources because they are excluded from all male groupings; they are excluded because they are unable to provide anything that a male could not provide as well or better.

Empirical studies of the factors affecting women's position in society are needed in addition to such theoretical treatises. Stewart and Winter (1977) report a quantitative analysis of cross-cultural data which suggests that women have higher status in societies with high educational levels and socialist governments. Other materials in this area include those which seek to explain sex-role socialization primarily in terms of sociological variables (see, for example, Walum, 1977, part 1), those which view violence toward women as social control mechanisms (Holmstrom and Burgess, 1975, on rape; Pagelow, 1977, on wife beating), and those which seek to account for the unequal positions of males and females in the marketplace, whether industrial (Oppenheimer, 1970), academic (Rossi and Calderwood, 1973), or military (Goldman, 1973).

CONCLUSION

Feminist sociologists have generally been interested in changing both the discipline and the society, by improving the position of women in both. A strong policy orientation is apparent in many of the writings associated with the women's perspective, beginning with Rossi (1964). The proposals have been as diverse as the abolition of the nuclear family (Oakley, 1974b), an alteration of the hierarchical nature of organizations (Kanter, 1976), and voluntary parental leaves with pay for care of infants (Safilios-Rothschild, 1974).

We do not claim that the current increase in the volume of research in which women are the subjects, or gender is a variable, is solely the result of the introduction of a women's perspective in sociology, or that all such studies qualify as women's perspective research. As Warshay noted (Berheide and Segal, 1977), many current social problems involve women. Legislatures and social welfare agencies are confronted with such phenomena as the increasing participation of women with husbands and children in the labor force, the increasing proportion of female-headed households, and the growing awareness of the prevalence of physical abuse of women and children. The demand for reliable relevant data is large. Some researchers are led to focus on women mainly because there is money available to do so. Such research is welcome if it adds to the pool of data available for feminist sociologists to interpret, or if it helps policy-makers improve the position of women in society. To the extent that it perpetuates stereotypes, those who take the women's perspective are obligated to be openly and constructively critical of it.

The women's perspective has performed a valuable task in making women visible in sociological research. Explanations about the position of women in society have implications for men. Thus, in trying to fill in the other half of the picture, feminist sociologists are working toward a general theory of human behavior. One question such a theory will have to address is the part biology plays in shaping social structure.

NOTES

We gratefully acknowledge the input from the members of two panels held on this topic: Jeanne Ballantine, Wendy Carlton, Jackie Macaulay, Martha Thompson, and Diana Wortman Warshay. We have also benefited greatly from unusually lively audiences at both the panel presentation at the May 1977 North Central Sociological Association meetings and the one at the August 1977 Sociologists for Women in Society meetings.

1. Which label is appropriate depends upon one's definition of these terms. To avoid debate on an issue peripheral to our topic, we use them interchangeably to mean an identifiable segment of the society which is treated categorically; has multiple common interests which are, in importance, equal to or greater than the interests stemming from cross-cutting memberships in other segments; and has at least a potential for developing consciousness of those interests.

REFERENCES

ACKER, JOAN
   1973 "Women and social stratification: a case of intellectual sexism." Pp. 174–184 in Joan Huber (ed.), Changing Women in a Changing Society. Chicago: University of Chicago Press.

BART, PAULINE
  1968 "Social structure and vocabularies of discomfort: what happened to female hysteria?" Journal of Health and Social Behavior 9:188–193.
BENSTON, MARGARET
  1969 "The political economy of women's liberation." Monthly Review 21 (4):13–27.
BERHEIDE, CATHERINE WHITE, SARAH FENSTERMAKER BERK, and RICHARD A. BERK
  1976 "Household work in the suburbs: the job and its participants." Pacific Sociological Review 19:491–518.
BERHEIDE, CATHERINE WHITE, and MARCIA TEXLER SEGAL (organizers)
  1977 "The emerging women's perspective in sociology: directions and prospects." Panel discussion at the September meeting of Sociologists for Women in Society, Chicago.
BERNARD, JESSIE
  1972 The Future of Marriage. New York: World.
BROVERMAN, I. K., D. M. BROVERMAN, F. E. CLARKSON, P. S. ROSENKRANTZ, and S. R. VOGEL
  1972 "Sex rôle stereotypes and clinical judgments." Pp. 320–324 in J. Bardwick (ed.), Readings on the Psychology of Women. New York: Harper & Row.
CASSELL, JOAN
  1977 A Group Called Women. New York: David McKay.
COLLINS, RANDALL
  1975 Conflict Sociology: Toward an Explanatory Science. New York: Academic Press.
DEJONG, PETER Y., MILTON J. BRAWER, and STANLEY S. ROBIN
  1971 "Patterns of female intergenerational mobility." American Sociological Review 36:1033–1042.
DUBERMAN, LUCILE
  1976 Social Inequality: Class and Caste in America. Philadelphia: J. B. Lippincott.
ENTWISLE, DORIS
  1977 Paper prepared for Thematic Panel: "The impact of contemporary trends in the family on socialization." Presented at the September meeting of the American Sociological Association, Chicago.
FARRELL, WARREN T.
  1974 The Liberated Man. New York: Random House.
GILLESPIE, DAIR
  1971 "Who has the power? the marital struggle." Journal of Marriage and Family 33:445–458.
GOETZ, JUDITH PREISSLE
  1978 "Theoretical approaches to the study of sex-role culture in schools." Anthropology and Education 9:3–21.
GOLDMAN, NANCY
  1973 "The changing role of women in the armed forces." Pp. 130–149 in Joan Huber (ed.), Changing Women in a Changing Society. Chicago: University of Chicago Press.

GOULD, MEREDITH, and ROCHELLE KERN-DANIELS
  1977 "Toward a sociological theory of gender and sex." The American
       Sociologist, 12:182–189.
HACKER, HELEN M.
  1951 "Women as a minority group." Social Forces 30:60–69.
HARTMANN, HEIDI
  1976 "Capitalism, patriarchy, and job segregation." Signs 1:137–169.
HOCHSCHILD, ARLIE R.
  1973 "A review of sex role research." American Journal of Sociology
       78:1011–1023.
HOLMSTROM, LYNDA L., and ANN W. BURGESS
  1975 Rape reconsidered: the victim's view. Remarks prepared for roundtable
       discussion at the August meeting of the American Sociological Associa-
       tion, San Francisco.
HORNER, MATINA A.
  1972 "Toward an understanding of achievement-related conflicts in women."
       Journal of Social Issues 28:157–176.
HOWE, LOUISE KAPP
  1977 Pink Collar Workers. New York: Avon.
KANTER, ROSABETH M.
  1976 "The impact of hierarchical structures on the work behavior of women
       and men." Social Problems 23:415–431.
KATZ, NAOMI, MURIEL MYERS, RAE LYKER, and BONNIE PETERSON
  1974 "The subject as object: a study of the returning woman student." Paper
       presented at the November meeting of the American Anthropological
       Association, Mexico City.
KLEIN, VIOLA
  1971 The Feminine Character. Chicago: University of Illinois Press.
LEE, PATRICK C., and NANCY B. GROPPER
  1974 "Sex-role culture and educational practice." Harvard Educational Re-
       view 44:369–410.
LEVINE, ADELINE, and JANICE CRUMRINE
  1975 "Women and fear of success: a problem in replication." American
       Journal of Sociology 80:964–974.
LIPMAN-BLUMEN, JEAN
  1976 "Toward a homosocial theory of sex roles: an explanation of the sex
       segregation of social institutions." Signs 1:15–30.
LOFLAND, LYN
  1975 "The 'thereness' of women: a selective review of urban sociology." Pp.
       144–170 in Marcia Millman and Rosabeth Moss Kanter (eds.), Another
       Voice. Garden City, N.Y.: Anchor.
LOPATA, HELENA
  1973 Widowhood in an American City. Cambridge, Mass.: Schenkman.
LOPATA, HELENA A., and BARRIE THORNE
  1978 "On the term 'sex roles.'" Signs 3:718–721.

MILLMAN, MARCIA, and ROSABETH MOSS KANTER
  1975 "Editorial introduction." Pp. vii-xvii in Marcia Millman and Rosabeth
      Moss Kanter (eds.), Another Voice. Garden City: Anchor.
MORGAN, ELAINE
  1972 Descent of Woman. New York: Stein and Day.
OAKLEY, ANN
  1974a The Sociology of Housework. New York: Pantheon.
  1974b Woman's Work: The Housewife, Past and Present. New York: Pantheon.
OPPENHEIMER, VALERIE K.
  1970 The Female Labor Force in the United States. Population Monograph
      Series, No. 5. Berkeley: University of California.
PAGELOW, MILDRED DALEY
  1977 "Women and violence: battered women." Topical session at the Septem-
      ber meeting of Sociologists for Women in Society, Chicago.
PARSONS, TALCOTT
  1959 "The social structure of the family." Pp. 241-274 in R. N. Anshen (ed.),
      The Family: Its Function and Destiny. New York: Harper & Row.
REITER, RAYNA R.
  1975 "Men and women in the South of France: public and private domains."
      Pp. 252-282 in Rayna R. Reiter (ed.), Toward an Anthropology of
      Women. New York: Monthly Review Press.
RITTER, KATHLEEN V., and LOWELL L. HARGENS
  1975 "Occupational positions and class identifications of married working
      women: a test of the assymmetry hypothesis." American Journal of
      Sociology 80:934-948.
ROBY, PAMELA
  1973 Child Care: Who Cares? New York: Basic Books.
ROSS, HEATHER L., and ISABEL V. SAWHILL
  1975 Time of Transition: The Growth of Families Headed by Women.
      Washington D.C.: Urban Institute.
ROSSI, ALICE
  1964 "Equality between the sexes: an immodest proposal." Daedalus
      93:607-652.
ROSSI, ALICE
  1977 "A biosocial perspective on parenting." Daedalus 106:1-31.
ROSSI, ALICE S., and ANN CALDERWOOD (eds.)
  1973 Academic Women on the Move. New York: Russell Sage Foundation.
RUBIN, GAYLE
  1975 "The traffic in women: notes on the political economy of sex." Pp.
      157-210 in Rayna R. Reiter (ed.), Toward an Anthropology of Women.
      New York: Monthly Review Press.
SACKS, KAREN
  1975 "Engels revisited: women, the organization of production, and private
      property." Pp. 211-234 in Rayna R. Reiter (ed.), Toward an Anthropol-
      ogy of Women. New York: Monthly Review Press.

82   MARCIA TEXLER SEGAL AND CATHERINE WHITE BERHEIDE

SAFILIOS-ROTHSCHILD, CONSTANTINA
1974 Women and Social Policy. Englewood Cliffs, N.J.: Prentice-Hall.
1976 "Dual linkages between the occupational and family system: a macrosociological analysis." Signs 1:51–60.
SEGAL, MARCIA TEXLER, and EDWIN S. SEGAL
1976 "Sharing: two worker families." Paper presented at the April Pioneers
for Century III Conference, Cincinnati.
SIMON, RITA JAMES
1975 The Contemporary Woman and Crime. National Institute of Mental
Health, DHEW Publication No. (ADM) 75–161. Washington, D.C.:
Government Printing Office.
SMITH, DOROTHY E.
1977 "Some implications of a sociology for women." Pp. 15–29 in Nona
Glazer and Helen Youngelson Waehrer (eds.), Women in a Man-Made
World: A Socioeconomic Handbook, 2nd ed. Chicago: Rand McNally.
STEWART, ABIGAIL J., and DAVID G. WINTER
1977 "The nature and causes of female suppression." Signs 2:531–553.
TANNER, NANCY, and ADRIENNE ZIHLMAN
1976 "Women in evolution. Part I: innovation and selection in human
origins." Signs 1:585–608.
TIGER, LIONEL
1970 Men in Groups. New York: Vintage.
TRESEMER, DAVID
1975 "Assumptions made about gender roles." Pp. 308–339 in Marcia Mill-
man and Rosabeth Moss Kanter (eds.), Another Voice. Garden City, N.J.:
Anchor.
TRESEMER, DAVID
1976 "Do women fear success?" Signs 1:863–74.
TYREE, ANDREA, and JUDITH TREAS
1974 "The occupational and marital mobility of women." American Sociological Review 39:293–302.
WALUM, LAUREL RICHARDSON
1974 "The changing door ceremony: notes on the operation of sex roles."
Urban Life and Culture: 506–515.
1977 The Dynamics of Sex and Gender: A Sociological Perspective. Chicago:
Rand McNally.
WARSHAY, DIANA WORTMAN
1972 "Sex differences in language style." Pp. 3–9 in C. Safilios-Rothschild
(ed.), Toward a Sociology of Women. Lexington, Mass.: Xerox.

3. The Humanist Perspective

THOMAS FORD HOULT

Imagine that it is customary for each year's crop of freshly graduated sociologists, coming from various universities across the land, to gather together for a collective *rite de passage*. This year, I have been asked to give the commencement speech. I aim to address the issue of the nature and promise of humanistic sociology. This is, of course, not a new view—it was advocated by the founder of sociology himself. But humanistic sociology comes and goes, popular one year and scorned the next. It has recently experienced a rebirth of energy and interest, as exemplified in the new organization the Association for Humanist Sociology and the inauguration of the journal *Humanity and Society*. Still, many questions remain unanswered and uncertainties abound. With all these factors in mind, I speak.

THE LAST OF THE HUMANOIDS

It is difficult, is it not, to entertain seriously the idea that you are part of an era which a cosmic historian may some day title "The Last of the Humanoids"? Yet this possibility is so near to becoming reality that only those who see it as a frightening probability can be termed meaningfully educated. To paraphrase historian Warren Wagar (1971:3), the human species in the latter days of the twentieth century is best likened to a baby in a basket placed on the doorstep of doom.

Consider this brief summary of disturbing conditions now

prevailing—and please forgive me if, in my attempt to make sure we have a common understanding, I mention matters that are well known to some of you:

• The superpowers confront one another armed so that each can readily kill at least fifteen times the total population of the others. When nations are so primed, history suggests, they reach a state of tension that makes war almost inevitable even under conditions where there can be no "winner," as in the present nuclear standoff. Yet the SALT talks and agreements, meant to limit the deployment of strategic weapons, have degenerated into a cover for an intensified arms race. Those who control the weapons of mass destruction include generals like the one who, when asked about the fact that nuclear war will make it impossible for any survivors to live, replied ritualistically, "At least our national honor will live on." We are led by senators like the one who, when told nuclear war would depopulate the entire Northern Hemisphere, responded to this effect: "Well, in that case, when we start all over, at least there'll be a chance for the new Adam and Eve to be Americans." Meanwhile, Herbert York notes (1975), we are gripped by two absurdities: (1) although the military power of the Soviet Union and the United States has constantly increased since the end of World War II, the national security of both nations has steadily diminished; and (2) in the United States (and perhaps also in the Soviet Union), weapons systems have become so complex and widespread that efforts to make them fail-safe have prompted a transferral—from high-level statesmen, to low-level technicians, and finally to machines—of the power to decide when doomsday has arrived. But, says York, neither nation can really rely on the other's fail-safe measures to prevent an unauthorized use of nuclear missiles. Nor can either solve the contradiction inherent in the need for a "hair trigger," required for quick response, and a "stiff trigger," required to prevent accidental activation of the systems. We thus arrive at the ultimate absurdity—uncontrollable conditions have led us to place our fate in the "hands" of an unreliable nonhuman process. Hence, Frank Barnaby (1977:11) observes, in his role as director of the independent Stockholm International Peace Research Institute:

> The probability of a nuclear world war is steadily increasing. If just the consequences of recent advances in military technology are considered, this conclusion is virtually inescapable.

• Fully two-thirds of the world's population is both hungry and angry—hungry because the population explosion has in many areas produced far more people than local technology can support and angry because most exploited people now know they have long been the hapless victims of the greed and racism of developed nations. "That's not our problem now," some complacent persons observe; others, beguiled by short-term changes in the population growth rates of relatively wealthy nations, remark that we have come to the end of the population explosion. Yet *each day* they so remark, 250,000 *additional* people take a place at the world's dinner table. Also, is it not a frightening thought that though it took countless generations for world population to reach the one billion mark in 1850, just one hundred years were needed to add the second billion? And it has taken only a quarter of a century to *double* the 1950 figure. Thus, each increase further widens the base for additional massive increases. As for those who say the plight of the world's poor is "not our problem," are there any knowledgeable persons who believe that the hungry hordes in depressed areas—such as India, China, Mexico, and Africa will indefinitely refrain from pressing—at times in a state of panic and rout, and despite their own governments' opposition—into more prosperous adjoining areas? And is there any doubt about what will be the response of those who are invaded, or that other nations will eventually become involved in the conflagrations?

• We live in a closed ecosystem, one which cannot be expanded in the slightest, yet those who constitute the one-third of the world's population accustomed to living "fat" seem determined to continue their lifestyle even though it is doomed to self-destruction. It cannot continue because, as William R. Catton notes (1974), it depends on fast-disappearing "ghosts." That is, many Westerners have been able to live especially well during the last couple of centuries not only because they have exploited the weak but because they have been profligate in using, in a few generations, energy that is a product of life forms that took countless centuries to accumulate. The result is, in the words of Harry Caudill (1970:165), "We are inflicting a doleful list of disasters on the only life-supporting planet known to astronomy." The disasters include, among other things, noxious emissions from exhaust pipes that have "buried our cities at the bottom of vast and oppressive sewers"; streams, rivers, and lakes poisoned by toxic wastes; sewage disposal methods which force downstream communities to use, in effect, chlorinated urine for drinking water; gigantic oil tankers that are ecological disasters looking for a place to happen; lumber firms that clear-cut, turning green forests into deserts with long-term and massive climatic implications; agribusinesses, in search of the quick dollar, saturating the land with chemical pesticides and fertilizers that exact high ecological costs over the long run; conversion to a nuclear economy that biologist Paul Ehrlich (1975) predicts will mean the end of civilization. And, perhaps most significant of all, we are tied to an economic system—capitalism—that demands precisely the kind of constant growth and unending exploitation that nature can least tolerate.

• We have governments determined to maintain the nation-state system that prevents any concerted attack on the many problems that cross national borders; young people who have become conservatives, not to preserve fine old customs but to insure the continuation of a maldistribution system they hope will give them an outsized share of strictly limited resources; religious and therapy movements that encourage converts to feel free of any responsibility for the less fortunate; tax systems that are hypocritically termed "progressive," yet charge the poor at far higher real rates than those applied to the rich; a health system that subsidizes medical worker education, which is then used as a basis for exploiting the public that paid for the education; a business system called "free enterprise" which, in its large-scale manifestations, is actually a publicly subsidized, monopolistic procedure that makes it relatively easy for those who have to get more, while those who have not must struggle simply to stay even.

CUSTOMARY TRAINING

In the face of such momentuous events and trends, what has been the nature of your education? Has it prompted you to face reality? Has it inspired you to play a reasonable part in altering the course of history? Have you, with any intensity, been taught "We don't have much time. Maybe social scientists ought to behave as if they have only one career to fling away on a world heading for disaster" (Dumont, 1969:20)? Or, as seems more likely, have you been sheltered from the facts, encouraged instead to consider yourself above the battle, uniquely suited and trained simply to measure events rather than to participate in them? Were you taught that you should be more concerned with the definitions of problems than with alleviation of them? Have you been urged to concentrate on the positive aspects of society—and, of course, there *are* many good things to say about it—leaving the negatives to "doomsayers"? Am I not right in guessing that many of you, when studying American society, were assigned a famous book which does not even suggest that the most fundamental fact of American life is that, however democratic it may be politically, it is built on ruthless exploitation—of humans and the environment—as exemplified by the gross income differential between whites and most nonwhites? And were not most of you, when studying our institutions, guided to literature that analyzed political and economic affairs, religion, and education pretty much in the abstract, focusing on their formal functions rather than on their realities?

By realities, I refer to the fact that governments today, despite their alleged primary role as even-handed protectors of all, typically collaborate with the powerful few to exploit the weak many—as in the collusion between regulatory boards and the industries they supposedly regulate (Mintz and Cohen, 1971). I refer to the fact that contrary to the formal function of religion as a method for believers to "get right with God," it actually tends to serve as a means of rationalizing and sanctifying the ways of society's ruling groups, as illustrated by the business connections of the controlling boards of many large religious groups (e.g., see Hoult, 1968). And education, instead of teaching people to think, aims primarily to fit them into the profit needs of the corporate society, as shown by Bowles and Gintis (1976) in their discussion of the part that education plays in perpetuating the class structure.

With regard to methods of study, I suspect that most of you were encouraged to think of objectivity and involvement as irreconcilables. "We must choose," Robert Nisbet wrote (1970), "between the ideals of objectivity and intellectual anarchy." At one extreme you were perhaps told that the methodological rigor of your studies is more important than the subject matter; at the other extreme, you may have attended a large West Coast university where some methodology classes have been treated as encounter groups which taught that the sole effective method is introspective testimonials. In either case, you were given few if any hints about the real state of the world or your responsibility regarding it. You seldom had an opportunity to take courses dealing specifically and searchingly with the phenomena that threaten the continued existence of human society—war, exploitation, the abrogation of civil liberties, racism, poverty, nationalism, and pollution.

QUESTIONS AND ANSWERS

I have perhaps maligned some of you. No doubt a number of you have had the kind of training I obviously favor, or you have, on your own, arrived at a point where you are as concerned with what is wrong with the world as you are with what is right. You have studied and fully appreciated the hard-hitting, often radical, analyses of Lynd, Lee, Marx, Maslow, Mills, Szasz, Gouldner, Stein, Vidich, Galbraith, Bottomore, Commoner, Lens, Domhoff, Kolko, Deutsch, Szymanski, Zeitlin, Friedrichs, Birnbaum, and others. Thus, you are so well read that I can teach you little of note.

To the rest of you, I ask only that you seriously consider this point: for reasons I will indicate, it is logical and in your own long-term interest, as well as in that of society, for you to move in the direction of a sociological point of view that radically confronts conditions such as those I have described. This kind of sociology can be termed *humanist*. It is called this because the research and teaching of its practitioners have one ultimate purpose—to help develop a society where the best potential of *all* humans is most likely to be realized, in short, to develop a *humane* society. Thus, humanist sociologists are not, as are so many scholars, interested primarily in analysis; we are more concerned with progressive reform (although, in my opinion, the latter is often dependent on the former). Our interest in reforms that will build a humane society is not based on a sentimental attachment to social betterment. It springs, rather, from our conviction that since a humane society would increase everyone's chance to lead a more fulfilling life, we could not help but benefit personally, and we know from cross-cultural and historical evidence that social science worth having cannot exist in a social order where there is insufficient faith in the potential worth of every individual.

The desire for a humane society and a safe environment is such a patently worthy goal that many of you probably have an inclination to join the humanist ranks. But you hesitate because you are bothered by a number of humanism's seeming contradictions and its sometimes tenuous relationship to rigorous scientific method. Let me try to set your mind at rest on these and other issues, using a question and answer format.

QUESTION: How can one reconcile value commitment with the norms of science?

ANSWER: Medical scientists do it routinely. Are we less capable? The value commitment of medical researchers involves, for example, the idea that cancer is an evil. They set out to find a substance that will eradicate the disease. In their search they adhere strictly to the norms of scientific method, carefully separating fact and value, using controlled experiments involving data that are systematically collected and as representative as possible, and analyzing and cautiously interpreting results. We could and, in my view, should, proceed in a comparable manner, understanding, of course, that in the social sciences it is not always possible to be as objective as one might wish. Where humans are concerned, for example, differentiating between fact and value is by no means a simple matter. Still, if we proceed as the medical researcher does, insofar as that is possible, our values will be manifest *and*, where appropriate, we will be guided by scientific standards. If we are committed to the elimination of poverty, our quest for a means to reach our goal must—if we are to have any realistic hope for success—adhere to all the relevant strictures of scientific method. (The fact that poverty may be more complicated than cancer does not, I submit, alter the basic point that value commitment and scientific norms are not necessarily at odds.)

QUESTION: Even if one can reconcile science and values, is it not preferable for a social scientist to remain above ideological battles? Is there not a compelling risk that those who take sides will simply descend to using selected data that would more accurately be called propaganda?

ANSWER: There is such a risk, and I know no certain way to avoid it other than careful training that stresses how vitally important it is for researchers to remain ideologically neutral when they gather and analyze data. Without this type of value neutrality, one person has observed, our inquiries (no matter how elegant and insightful) "produce garbage." At the same time it is naive to think that, with the possible exception of narrowly defined and carefully conducted research activity, one can really stay clear of wide-ranging ideological contests. If measured in terms of consequences—and what is more significant than consequences?—ideological neutrality aids those currently in power and is thus not neutrality at all. Max Weber, often cited as the premier advocate of value-free sociology, observed (1949:53), "All action and naturally, according to circumstances, inaction, imply in their consequences the espousal of certain values—and herewith—what is today so willingly overlooked—the rejection of certain others."

QUESTION: What about the claim of some humanists that we should not use scientific methods to study humans because such methods manipulate and make objects of people?

ANSWER: This *is* the feeling of some humanists, but by no means all. A. M. Lee (1970), John Glass (1971:193), and I (1979:Ch. 4)—to cite just three individuals who have published a number of humanistic works—have all gone on record as favoring the use of major aspects of scientific method. Nevertheless, I hope it is clear that we respect the integrity of those who disagree with us; we agree fully that it is vital to be concerned about "science for whom?" Further, it seems obvious that there is much to be gained by soft methods, such as participant observation and depth interviewing. Also, I know that much scientific rigor is actually a cover for fiddling with inconsequentials. Thus, I hail C. Wright Mills's question (1958:125): "What Western scholar can claim to be part of the big discourse of reason and yet retreat to formal trivialities and exact nonsense, in a world in which reason and freedom are being held in contempt, being smashed, being allowed to fade out of the human condition?" At the same time, I deplore abuse of the perfectly legitimate term "qualitative research" when it is used as a disguise for unwillingness to gather data systematically and/or analyze it rigorously; and I am not favorably impressed by those who scorn all research as having no immediate practical application—they would no doubt have sneered at Mendel's interest in breeding sweet peas; and I shudder to think of what the consequences would be if we followed the advice of a few radical ethnomethodologists who assert that since every event is unique, we are not justified in summarizing data in terms of averages and trends; and I am appalled when I consider what could be the results if we confined ourselves, as some advocate, to "research" consisting solely of intuition, philosophic speculation, or contemplation of "the poetry of existence." These methods of obtaining knowledge, based as they are on a distrust of reason, undermine the discipline of which they are a part (Bendix, 1970:841). In addition, the methods provide no standards for estimating the accuracy of a variety of claims and conclusions. Furthermore, I am not convinced that studying people as one would other phenomena necessarily makes the people objects or unduly manipulates them. As Elliot Aronson has shown at length (1976), even experimental methods—provided they safeguard subjects and involve full debriefing—can be quite benign while adding significantly to our store of knowledge about human behavior.

QUESTION: Would not the sociological-deterministic view that personality is largely a product of sociocultural environment be undermined by the belief of some humanists that we have free will?

ANSWER: Yes, if such a belief were to become general in the discipline. But how can it? Belief in free will is, in essence, a conviction that important aspects of human behavior are uncaused. How can any educated person believe such a thing? In contrast, determinism is simply the philosophy that all phenomena, including human behavior, are best explained in terms of the conditions antecedent to them. This does not mean we are puppets who are inexorably victims of fate—the environment that affects us, much of which we ourselves help to create, often contains elements negating the effects of seeming "iron laws"—but our behavior is *caused*. I declare, it puzzles me how anyone can reasonably believe anything else.

QUESTION: What is the justification for the claim that since social science worth having cannot exist in a totalitarian environment, it is a professional duty of social scientists to do what they can to help create and preserve the needed political milieu?

ANSWER: There are two parts to this question. First, regarding the claim that respectable social science is dependent on what may be termed a civil libertarian environment, can be substantiated merely by pointing to the near laughable (when not tragic) state of sociology in Nazi Germany, Stalinist Russia, and present-day China. In the Soviet Union it was typical for research articles to defer to the opinions of "our brother Stalin"; in China, the editorial guidelines for an influential journal read thus: "Our publication welcomes all manuscripts which . . . exalt the great, glorious, and infallible Chinese Communist party" (Leys, 1977:15–16). As for the last part of the question, relating to the claim that it is a professional activity for social scientists to help preserve civil liberties, I use the analogy of a physical scientist supervising the construction of a laboratory. It is not science per se for physicists to build their own work spaces, but since they must have them, it is a professional act to develop the needed facilities. Similarly, a social scientist's contributions to building and maintaining a relatively open society are not science as such, but they are professional acts, since they help to build the "laboratory" wherein alone genuine social science can survive. As Robert S. Lynd observed (1939:249):

> Social science cannot perform its function if the culture constrains it at certain points in ways foreign to the spirit of science; and at all points where such constraints limit the free use of intelligence to pose problems, to analyze all relevant aspects of them, or to draw conclusions, it is necessary for social science to work directly to remove causes of these obstacles.

QUESTION: What is your reaction to the claim of some humanists that we have had too many despairing debunkers, too much emphasis on the repressive aspects of society, and, therefore, too little on the human potential for greatness?

ANSWER: Let each of us emphasize that which we individually conclude is most important. Perhaps out of the mix of doomsaying and whistling in the dark will come a well-rounded picture.

QUESTION: Widely varied types call themselves or their efforts humanist. Who and what is genuinely such?

ANSWER: It would be unseemly for me to try to make an authoritative declaration on this point. Therefore, the most I can do to answer the question is to indicate how *I* decide who is and who is not a humanist. To me, the core, the essence, of the humanist philosophy is commitment to the belief that all individuals have potential and should have the fullest opportunity to develop it, short of hurting others. If this is a person's central motivating creed—allowing generously for variations in expression—then I call her or him a "humanist." I use the same standard for judging political organizations, religions, and educational techniques. Those which seem to promise the most effective aid to the greatest number of individuals in developing their potential are, it seems to me, justifiably called humanist and therefore worthy of support. This point, incidentally, is a living demonstration that although humanists are relativists in most things, they have a comforting philosophical rock on which to stand, a standard for measuring the degree of decency of almost anything—not an inconsequential fact in these anomic times.

QUESTION: "The moral worth of humanism as you describe it seems beyond question," a friendly critic has written, "but how does such a philosophic stance translate into a distinctive set of sociological practices?"

ANSWER: Humanist sociologists make a particular effort to show how the sociological point of view and its concepts and research findings are potentially powerful weapons for unmasking exploitation and tyranny and guiding efforts at social reform. Thus, humanist sociologists, like all their fellows, stress systematic study of social interaction and structure, but the humanists give special emphasis to pointing out how certain types of structure and interaction are inhumane and how they might be made less so. Humanist sociology, as compared with a more conventional type, tends to be less abstract and less identified with the established order, and it tends to be more iconoclastic in its analysis of political and economic institutions and trends. Conventional sociology often gives the distressing impression that its practitioners are complacently unaware of the political-economic-ecological precipice on the edge of which the world teeters. In contrast, humanist sociologists, motivated by a keen sense that we have so little time, actively try to "scare hell out of people," as was recommended by Samuel H. Day, Jr., in his final editorial for *The Bulletin of the Atomic Scientists* (December, 1977).

QUESTION: You say that humanist sociologists are interested in progressive social reform. But how are humanist sociologists unique in this regard? Isn't every sensible person interested in such reform?

ANSWER: I think the critical thing here is a matter of degree, of depth of commitment. Surely every reasonable person favors forward-looking social reform. But to genuine humanists such reform takes first priority, because only to the degree that we have it can the ultimate goal of a society that maximizes individual opportunity for self-development be reached. For others—nonhumanists, if you will—social reform is viewed as "nice if you can get it," but hardly the center of interest and effort.

QUESTION: A number of sociological perspectives appear to be similar to the humanists' view—the radical, the reflexive, the critical, and the Marxist. What, if any, are the differences among these perspectives?

ANSWER: I agree that these viewpoints are in some respects similar and overlapping. All, for example, are at least neo-Marxist. But, depending on particular circumstances and practitioners, there are subtle differences and unique emphases. To me, however, the differences are insignificant. I happen to prefer the term "humanist" because of its long history and honorable associations, but a humanist sociology that is not radical is not meaningfully humanist. And a genuinely humanist sociology—besides being radical—is also, to a considerable degree, reflexive, critical, and Marxist. I suspect one could rightly make a parallel statement about the other perspectives.

QUESTION: Some view ethnomethodology, phenomenology, and symbolic interactionism as humanistic. Do you agree with this evaluation?

ANSWER: Mostly no. In their research methods there is a strong strain of humanism in the sense that there is usually concern for the individual as such, but proponents of the perspectives, with their microstudies and their attention to the attitudes of individuals, do not in general stress the political concerns so characteristic of activist humanist sociology.

QUESTION: Is "assaulting the barricades" a necessary part of humanistic sociology?

ANSWER: Yes, but often only in a metaphoric sense. The designation "humanist" is meaningless if those who claim it do not, at a minimum, speak out forcefully and clearly against injustice, individual and collective, against oppression and needless exploitation. But there are various ways of speaking out, and people have widely differing talents, temperaments, and timidity inclinations. So what we do depends on a multitude of variables. Some of us may find it most congenial to confine our efforts to inspired teaching; others may choose direct political action; still others, quiet and methodical analysis.

THE PROMISE

Now I come to the final matter: what is humanistic sociology's promise? Here I must self-consciously restrain myself lest my enthusiasm appear to be overpraise. Therefore, I will say just this: humanistic sociology is an honest, reasonable, constructive, and exciting perspective. It is honest in the sense that its proponents openly proclaim relevant political values; reasonable because it is not trapped in the illogic of the "value-free" position; constructive because it ruthlessly, radically analyzes even the most sensitive aspects of society; and exciting because students are keenly aroused by it and because its practitioners are frequently in hot water, since, given the activism and openness of the perspective, the toes of the mighty get trampled.

But even when beleaguered, the humanist social scientist has the deep satisfaction of knowing he or she has a favorable relationship with history's most inspiring apostles of outspokenness—those whom society "put down" but whose accomplishments we still celebrate. It would be falsely boastful to claim too close a relationship; most of us can do no more than be on the side of the angels rather than take wing ourselves. But it is heartening to know one has at least a tenuous connection with the social science mavericks who fought for human dignity—Karl Marx, Thorsten Veblen, Charles A. Beard, Robert S. Lynd, C. Wright Mills. Such people were not perfect. But what human is? Despite their shortcomings, we remember their work in detail, rather than the efforts of their detractors. The five have thus achieved a degree of immortality. And as immortals, they exemplify the transcendental promise of humanistic social science, a promise that humankind, given proper conditions, can rise far above its crippled state to achieve beauty and greatness for all. This is a promise that even the least of us can help to realize. In Markham's words:

> . . . the task that is given to each one, no other can do;
> so the errand is waiting; it has waited through the ages for you.
> And now you appear; and the hushed ones are turning their gaze,
> To see what you do with your chance in the chamber of days.

REFERENCES

ARONSON, ELLIOT
   1976 The Social Animal. 2nd ed. San Francisco: W. H. Freeman.
BARNABY, FRANK
   1977 "The mounting prospects of nuclear war." Bulletin of the Atomic Scientists 33(June):11–20.
BENDIX, REINHARD
   1970 "Sociology and the distrust of reason." American Sociological Review 35(October):831–843.
BOWLES, SAMUEL, and HERBERT GINTIS
   1976 Schooling in Capitalist America: Educational Reform and the Contradictions of Economic Life. New York: Basic Books.
CATTON, WILLIAM R., JR.
   1974 "Depending on ghosts." Humboldt Journal of Social Relations 2(Fall/Winter):45–49.

CAUDILL, HARRY W.
  1970 "Are capitalism and the conservation of a decent environment possible?"
        Pp. 165-183 in Harold W. Helfrich, Jr. (ed.), Agenda for Survival: the
        Environmental Crisis—2. New Haven: Yale University Press.
DUMONT, MATTHEW P.
  1969 "Social science and the survival of cities." Psychiatry and Social Science
        Review 4(October):16-20.
EHRLICH, PAUL
  1975 "Cheap nuclear power could lead to civilization's end." Los Angeles
        Times (27 May).
GLASS, JOHN F.
  1971 "Toward a sociology of being: the humanist potential." Sociological
        Analysis 32(Winter):191-198.
HOULT, THOMAS FORD
  1968 "Exorcism, middle class church style." The Christian Century 85(6
        March):294-295.
  1979 Sociology for a New Day. 2nd ed. New York: Random House.
LEE, ALFRED McCLUNG
  1970 "On context and relevance." Pp. 3-16 in Glenn Jacobs (ed.), The
        Participant Observer. New York: George Braziller.
LEYS, SIMON
  1977 "China's war on the mind." Saturday Review 4(25 June):14-19.
LYND, ROBERT S.
  1939 Knowledge for What: The Place of Social Science in American Culture.
        Princeton: Princeton University Press.
MILLS, C. WRIGHT
  1958 The Causes of World War III. New York: Simon and Schuster.
MINTZ, MORTON, and JERRY S. COHEN
  1971 America, Inc.; Who Owns and Operates the United States. New York:
        Dell.
NISBET, R. A.
  1970 "Subjective si! objective no!" New York Times Book Review (5 April):1,
        2, 36.
WAGAR, W. WARREN
  1971 Building the City of Man: Outlines of a World Civilization. San
        Francisco: W. H. Freeman.
WEBER, MAX
  1949 The Methodology of the Social Sciences. Translated and edited by
        Edward A. Shils and Henry A. Finch. Chicago: The Free Press of
        Glencoe.
YORK, HERBERT F.
  1975 "Are nuclear command and control systems fail-safe?" Center Report
        8(April):6-7.

4. Structuralist Semiotics and the Decentering of Sociology

CHARLES LEMERT

One must write of *structure* and *structuralism* with care. The terms are tricky because sociologists and others have used them in diverse ways. They are, of course, important to structural–functionalism. In other contexts sociologists as different as exchange theorists and Marxists speak of structural analysis when referring to phenomena as dissimilar as systematic variance in status and social rank (Blau, 1970:203) and structured relations of production. In more technically precise usages, there are two reasonably well-developed structuralist schools in sociology: Harrison White's formal mathematical structuralism (White, 1963, 1970; cf. Mullins, 1973: Ch. 10) and Peter Blau's exchange structuralism (Blau, 1960, 1964; cf. Homans, 1958, Ekeh, 1974). Finally, there are several sociological critiques of or experiments with the structuralism of Lévi-Strauss (Bourdieu and Passeron, 1968; Boudon, 1971; Rossi, 1974; Turner, 1974; Stinchcombe, 1975).

These structural theories are not the primary concern of this paper. The topic here is structuralist semiotics, the label I will use to describe the recent European intellectual movement identified with the work of such diverse writers as Louis Althusser, Roland Barthes, Jonathan Culler, Jacques Derrida, Umberto Eco, Julia Kristeva, Michel Foucault, Jacques Lacan, Philippe Sollers, and others. This is not a unified school. Many reject the label *structuralist*; others do not describe themselves as semioticians. Whatever unity there is to structuralist semiotics exists in its loose consensus on several general assumptions pertinent to all the human and social sciences. Among these assumptions are the following: (1) that discourse is the principal topic and resource of the human sciences; (2) that the latent metaphysics of strongly subjectivist social theories (existentialism, phenomenology, historicism) are obstacles to be overcome by the human sciences; (3) that the rules governing the production (writing) and reception (reading) of literary texts are of special importance for the critical analysis of what we sociologists would call social structures. This list does not, by any means, exhaust the assumptions of interest to these writers; but it does accurately represent central intellectual tendencies.

Issues related to these assumptions are not unfamiliar to sociologists. Recent sociological literature has paid considerable attention to such related problems as the effect of natural language on coding and measurement techniques; the place of the social subject in the construction and maintenance of social order; and the inadequacy of traditional, formal, and uncritical strategies for the analysis of social structures. Therefore, my reason for recommending an examination of structuralist semiotics is not that these European authors have discovered something entirely new.[1] Their potential contribution is in the way they have handled problems similar to those discussed by sociologists. In other words there is not at the moment a structuralist sociology (in my sense of the term), but rather, the theoretical resources for such a sociology exist. I want to outline here some of the ways in which these resources could be used.

Before presenting that outline, however, it is necessary to qualify further the label *structuralist semiotics*. This involves several brief remarks on its various uses by Lévi-Strauss.

Sociologists and others who have studied the writings of Lévi-Strauss tend to focus on two features of his work: the technique of binary–oppositional analysis and the concept structure itself. Perhaps the most widely read of Lévi-Strauss's texts is *The Structural Study of Myth* (Lévi-Strauss, 1967, Ch. 11). Here he uses a model borrowed from phonetics to decompose Greek oedipal and Zuni creation myths into distinctive units which are subsequently rearranged into logically opposing pairs. The meaning of myths is attributed to the structured oppositive relations thus invented (see Lévi-Strauss, 1966: Ch. 1). This process, says Lévi-Strauss, suggests a technique capable of yielding a formal structural theory. "When we have succeeded in organizing a whole series of variants into a kind of permutation group, we are in a position to formulate the law of that group" (Lévi-Strauss, 1967:255). This ideal of formalization is most clearly found in Lévi-Strauss's early kinship studies (1969 [1949]) and has been attractive if not convincing to sociologists interested in formal logical or mathematical studies, e.g., White, 1963; Homans and Schneider, 1955; Stinchcombe, 1975.

Closely related is the tendency to interpret the structure in structuralism as a universal feature of human thought and culture. This view often makes structuralism a cross-cousin to all systematic, holistic theoretical methods, including systems theory, Greek metaphysics, and Chomsky's grammar. Lane (1970:11–39), Piaget (1970), and Boudon (1971) are examples of this interpretation. To be sure, such an emphasis is encouraged by Lévi-Strauss's often cited declaration that he is looking for the universal "constraining structures of mind" (1969a:10). What is at stake here is the difference between structural and structuralist strategies (Glucksmann, 1974). To date, the sociological theories have been structural and only accidentally structuralist.

This is not the place to evaluate what Lévi-Strauss really intended. Such an assessment would require a consideration of such difficult problems as the place of linguistics in his thought (Mounin, 1970); the semiological aspects of his method (Culler, 1975:40–54), especially in the later, post-kinship studies of myth; and the extent to which his work might be seen as an attack on any metaphysical formal science (Derrida, 1970).

I note these problems of interpretation in order to sharpen the distinction between structuralist semiotics and the structural sociological theories previously cited. To this end one can say with tolerable accuracy that Lévi-Strauss is at most a meeting ground for two different intellectual activities. Those sociologists intrigued by the formalist technique and the holistic structural principle in Lévi-Strauss have minimized the importance of his semiological analysis of myths. For example, Stinchcombe (1975, note 1) wrote: "I have borrowed a few things from his analysis of mythology . . . , but have been able to use very little of it because I do not understand it." On the other hand, European structuralist semiotics is among other things a post-structuralist critique of Lévi-Strauss, which rebels precisely against the formalist themes. Where there is appreciation, it is guarded (e.g., Derrida, 1970) and mixed with serious criticisms (Derrida, 1976; part 2). This group shares with Lévi-Strauss only a common interest in linguistic and discursive structures in the tradition of Saussure's structural linguistics (Saussure, 1959; Culler, 1976; Lemert, in press[b]). Were it not for the fact that the structuralist tag is so fixed in the minds of most readers (see, e.g., Foucault, 1972:11), it would have been more accurate to drop the term.[2] In the same spirit of accommodation, I will sometimes use the term *structuralist* as a convenient though imprecise label for *structuralist semiotics*.

LANGUAGE, DISCOURSE, AND SOCIAL RESEARCH

If there is one topic common to most recent (post-1960) sociological innovations, it is language (Lemert, in press[a]). The most obvious example is ethnomethodology, which bases its study of social rule making on the analysis of conversational settings (e.g., Cicourel, 1974; Garfinkel and Sacks, 1970; cf. Labov, 1978:90; Lemert, in press[a]). In a different theoretical context, Habermas and other critical theorists have sought to reconstruct Marxist materialist social theoriest with reference to the idea of communicative competence (Habermas, 1970; McCarthy, 1973; Mueller, 1973; Gouldner, 1976; and Han's article elsewhere in this book). In still another realm one can say that theory constructionism is a metatheory of the rules governing the translation of verbal theory into formal logico–mathematical statements (e.g., Blalock, 1968; cf. Lemert, 1979: Chs. 2, 3; Lemert, in press[b]). In addition, one thinks of the interest in language found in such diverse activities as Goffman's (1974) frame analysis, Duncan's (1968) dramaturgical theory, Berger and Luckmann's (1967) phenomenology of symbolic interaction, various uses of communication theory in causal modeling theory, and the tentative but growing sociological interest in sociolinguistics (Bernstein, 1975; cf. Labov, 1978).

Structuralist semiotics more than shares this interest in language, though from a different point of view. Whereas in sociology, many of the language theories are either implicit or accidental, European semiotics has employed from the beginning an explicit theory of language and its place in society. This remark is more than the truism that structuralism derives from Saussurian linguistics (Saussure, 1959; cf. Barthes, 1970; Eco, 1976; Culler, 1975, 1976). The self–consciousness of its theory of language means at least two things of special importance to sociology: structuralism includes an explanation of the emergence of language as a topic, and it suggests in concrete examples the ways in which discourse can be both resource and topic in social research.

The term *linguicity* (Said, 1971:61) conveys the structuralist claim that language has "invaded the universal problematic" (Derrida, 1970:249). Michel Foucault (1973:306) wrote: "The whole curiosity of our thought now resides in the question: What is language, how can we find a way around it to make it appear in itself, in all its plentitude?" When Foucault speaks of "our thought," he has in mind all contemporary thought. The universality of the question "What is language?" is not coincidence but necessity.

The most explicit available discussions of the connection between linguicity and the modern human sciences are Foucault's (1973) and Derrida's (1970; cf. 1976) presentations of psychoanalysis and ethnology as the two uniquely modern human sciences. In both presentations the study of the human abandons nineteenth-century homocentrism—that is, the hermeneutical and historicist ideals of investigating people with reference to inner subjective and cultural meanings. The structuralist argument is that hermeneutics and historicism are, in effect, crypto-metaphysics because they assume that human action is deducible from prior principles. The irony in the structuralist critique is the claim that these nineteenth-century strategies actually hide humans by overextending their importance (Foucault, 1972; cf. Lemert, 1979).

According to Foucault and Derrida, the alternative proposed by psychoanalysis and ethnology—that is, by Freud and structural anthropology (including but not confined to Lévi–Strauss)—is to consider the human not as a primary object in itself but as a product of human discourse. From the point of view of language, "things attain to existence only insofar as they are able to form the elements of a signifying system (Foucault, 1973:382)." One reasonably clear example is Lacan's insistence (1977) that it is improper to read Freud's psychoanalytical works as a hermeneutical interpretation of dreams representing deeper unconscious meanings. Instead, according to Lacan (1977:159; cf. Ch. 3), Freud's *Interpretation of Dreams* is the program for a linguistics and semiotics of dream talk. If "the unconscious is the discourse of the Other" (Lacan, 1977:172), then psychoanalysis must be governed by the rules of discourse which explain dream images with reference to the patient's ex-centric use of conscious talk. Symptoms are not signs of inner, hidden meanings, but are products of the standard rules of discourse applied to biographically specific desires. The unconscious becomes, thereby, a scientific object to be studied via nonmysterious rules.

Discourse becomes the proper topic of the human sciences because it is the one distinctively human product which operates at the boundaries between the cultural and the natural, that most crucial of nineteenth-century distinctions. Discourse relies always on noncultural material and natural (bodily) supports (or, *signifiers*: phonetic signals, graphic marks) to produce cultural ideas (*signifieds*). Thus, from the structuralist view of language, the human sciences cannot idealize people as the strictly human, cultural, meaning-producing center of social life. Accordingly, the universality of discourse reminds us that we are actually a decentered product of both material and ideal, both natural and cultural factors. (Here one detects the influence of Marx on structuralist thought.)

Discourse is the proper topic of the human sciences, because discourse puts the human in its proper, decentered place in the order of things. At the same time discourse is analyzable only in terms of its own rules of formation. In the Saussurian (1959) tradition speaking is not motivated; it is a grammar-governed selection of its own paradigmatic terms, rules, and sounds. Thus, when language becomes the primary topic, it then must be its own primary resource. "Language bears within itself its own critique" (Derrida, 1970:254; cf. Kristeva, 1968:83; Eco, 1976:71; Saussure, 1959).

Although this discussion necessarily omits the details important to the appreciation of a complex argument, I hope to clarify how structuralism's interest in discourse derives from an acknowledged desire to use language as the basis for a reconstruction of social theory. Here is one of its potential contributions to sociology.

The example of structuralism suggests that the language-interested sociologies just mentioned are facing the same problems (see Lemert, in press[a]). One of the few things that most sociologists will agree upon is that their discipline has never stopped searching for a method. Structuralism's critique of the nineteenth-century human sciences implies that sociology's long frustration might be historically limited and thus within reach of a solution. In this connection it is interesting to note that the three major new language-interested sociologies—ethnomethodology, critical theory, and theory constructionism—are all critiques of methods associated with their own traditions. Ethnomethodology, in addition to its critique of formalism, is also a critique of traditional hermeneutical sociologies, which rely on the prior givenness of meaningful order (e.g., Zimmermann and Wieder, 1970). Likewise, Habermas's critical theory is also a rejection of materialist reductionism (e.g., Habermas, 1973: Ch. 6), and theory constructionism is a critique of naïve empiricism (e.g., Blalock, 1968).

What traditional sociological naturalism (e.g., symbolic interactionism), historical materialism, and naive empiricism (e.g., operationalism) have in common is that each assumes that the human is reducible to some prior principle: subjective meaning, economic factors, and measurement instruments, respectively. It is perhaps not by accident that each of the recent sociological innovations uses language (conversation, the ideal speech act, and the formal proposition) to develop their critiques.

The purpose of this observation is not to celebrate these new sociologies but merely to call attention to the possibility that their interest in language, like that of structuralism, may be anything but accidental. Their use of language as a resource for solving methodological problems suggests that sociology could benefit from structuralist semioticians' prior experience with similar methodological problems. I turn, therefore, to two of structuralism's most distinctive and substantive themes: the problem of subjectivity and the nature of structures.

SUBJECTIVITY AND SOCIAL STRUCTURES

Subjectivity has been a more visible intellectual topic in Europe (especially in France) than in the United States (see Bourdieu and Passeron, 1968). Structuralism, in the late 1950's and the 1960's, was, in large part, a critical reaction to the postwar influence of subjectivist philosophies such as existentialism and phenomenology. The issue was not narrowly conceived. The very idea of practical, political action was under examination. In the background was the question of left-wing intellectuals' attitudes toward the idea of a new historicism associated with various humanistic Marxisms (Sartre, Gramsci, Lukács, among others; see Althusser and Balibar, 1970: Ch. 5). In part the structuralist position was that even a Marxist historicism founded on a strong subjectivity is a crypto-metaphysics (the limitation of the free play of scientific theory and political action by the hegemony of first principal [Derrida, 1970]). Thus, Lévi–Strauss strongly rejected Sartre's historicism: "I believe the utlimate goal of the human sciences to be not to constitute but to dissolve man" (Lévi–Strauss, 1966:246; cf., Foucault, 1973:373–387).

The structuralist critique of homocentrism (Lemert, 1979) has taken many forms. The most immediately interesting, however, is the argument that when subjectivism is its central principle, human science is caught in a hopeless reductionism which virtually eliminates the possibility of structural analysis (Derrida, 1970; Foucault, 1972: 3–17). Stated this way, the problem is more familiar to American sociologists. How can sociology study social structures and, at the same time, account for the subjective intentions of social actors? Interpretivist critiques (e.g., Garfinkel and Sacks, 1970) of formalism, and formal sociology, and macrosociology's critique (e.g., Etzioni, 1970:72) of social psychologism have revolved around this dilemma. One structural sociologist puts it this way: "The problem is to derive the social processes that govern the complex structures of communities and societies from the simpler processes that pervade the daily intercourse among individuals and their interpersonal relations" (Blau, 1964:2).

Sociology has not yet found a convincing solution. In general there are three standard strategies: (1) structural deductivism, (2) methodological individualism, and (3) subject reductionism. Blau represents the first, which takes a structural feature of inter-subjective relations (such as exchange) as a generalizable attribute "from which more complex structures are derived (1964:2)." The weakness of this approach is that the range of subjective intentions considered is drastically and artificially reduced, in Blau's case (1964:4–5), to reward-seeking intentions. Here the interest in structural theory virtually eliminates subjectivity as is seen when Blau explicitly ignores subjective motives in his formal theory of organizational structures (Blau, 1970:203).

Methodological individualism is also closely related to structural deductivism, both logically and in its attempt to account for the subject as the source of social action.[3] Homans (1967:61–64) is one example, but Parsons is the more interesting because he analyzes social structures explicitly. Parsons maintains that "all concrete behavior is the behavior of individuals" (1961:33, n. 4). Yet this concrete behavior can be explained only by means of the "analytically isolated individual" who is an analytic "member" of social systems (1961:33; 1970:29; 1951:3–6). The result is that subjective motives are not the source of action, but the product of social structures. Parsons's strong theory of socialization produces a weak theory of concrete actions (as opposed to action as such).

Sociological interpretivism (interactionism, phenomenology, ethnomethodology, and the like) makes subjective (and inter-subjective) motives the originating source of all social order, with the consequence of providing a weak metaphoric theory of social structures, such as Blumer's joint lines of action.

These three sociological approaches set up the problem in a way that forces them to be either strongly structural or strongly subjectivist. Subjective action is, in effect, either nothing or everything.

Structuralist semiotics provides an alternative which, ironically, is based on its critique of subjectivity itself. In rough terms, the structuralist model is that the subject uses social structures, but is neither their simple product nor their original source. In Lévi–Strauss's terms (1966: Ch. 1) the subject is a *bricoleur* (handyman) whose action is a borrowing of the used "junk" of social structures. I will explain this model by referring to Saussure.

The structuralist subject is the speaking subject, and the model to which I allude is a theory of language and sign production. Saussure's famous distinction between *la langue* and *la parole* views the speaking subject as one who selects from structured paradigms. The subject's speech (*la parole*) is the articulation of linguistic materials (terms, phonetic codes, rules) provided by language (*la langue*) (Saussure, 1959:13). *La langue* is, for Saussure, an entirely social fact (Saussure, 1959:14, 113). Language survives entirely by its usage in *la parole*; but, conversely, speech does not create language. *La langue* is, therefore, a complexly structured set of social conventions.

Translated into sociological language, this means that social structures (cf. *la langue*) provide the contents of subjective action (cf. *la parole*). Paradigms for action are pre-established as community structures. In this model the subject is socialized only insofar as these paradigms are learned by community members. This, however, is a weak theory of socialization. The actor, as selector, is free to reject or modify structured paradigms according to the needs of specific contexts. Just as the speaker may combine linguistic elements in unusual patterns (neologisms, malapropisms, intentional errors, accents, dialects, style, etc.), so one would visualize the actor as free to gloss social structures (see Garfinkel and Sacks, 1970; Cicourel, 1974). Norms (cf. syntactical rules) are provided, but they have no capacity to guide action (cf. speaking) unless they are selected by the actor (cf. speaker). Culture exerts no cybernetic control, in Parsons's sense. Nor are social structures (cf. *la langue*) created by the subject (Saussure, 1959:14). In other words, the subject is decentered, is never the source of either action or structures. In more precise terms subjective motives explain nothing (Saussure, 1959:69). Action is selection, not invention.

The implications of this model, presented elsewhere (Lemert, in press[b]), cannot be detailed here.[4] What I can show, on the basis of this sketch, is that the structuralist theory of the speaking subject is an alternative which reveals that sociology's inability to develop a positive theory of the subject-in-social-structures may be due to a latent but ubiquitous homocentrism. Nineteenth-century homocentrism, to which sociology is obviously indebted, made the subject virtually the sole source of action (see Lemert, 1979). Obviously, structuralism leads to a frontal attack on interpretivism's subject reductionism, but it also allows us to see that both structural deductivism and methodological individualism may suffer from a similarly strong theory of the subject. Even though Blau and Parsons offer essentially structural theories, they share with interpretivism the idea that the source of society is micro-, inter-subjective action. For Blau, complex structures are derived from elemental interpersonal exchanges; for Parsons, the real action of individuals provides the energy for the social system, an analytic construct. Thus, sociology's dilemma is that the subject, if it cannot be the source, must be either ignored or oversocialized. In both cases the subject is a problem, and in both cases the subject is seen as the original source of the social system. On the other hand, structuralism's decentered self is the mere user, selecter, borrower, or *bricoleur* of structures and their paradigms for action. It is a subject which gives up absolute freedom for free play (Derrida, 1970).

STRUCTURES, INDETERMINACY, AND READING

The immediately apparent problem with this model of the post-metaphysical, decentered subject is how to account for agency. This is the freedom/determinism problem discussed by Applebaum elsewhere in this book. If structure is viewed as the supplier of elements borrowed by the individual, then is not structural analysis merely the analysis of static, pregiven forms? This is a familiar sociological problem, which usually takes the following form: one shifts sociological analysis from the subject, who is the concrete actor, to structures, in order to provide macroanalyses of social complexes. But since structures are not observables, as are concrete actors, how does one avoid making the measure of structures the measure of mere forms—analytic abstractions existing only in sociology's technical vocabulary but not in the real world? For example: "By social structure I refer to population distributions among social positions along various lines" (Blau, 1974:616).

Several early structuralisms failed to avoid this problem, but such recent developments as the *Tel Quel* group have taken it very seriously (see Caws, 1973; Culler, 1975: Ch. 10; Sollers, 1972). Julia Kristeva (1968, 1974, 1977), for example, describes a revolutionary subject which is not the source of meanings but, roughly, the juncture at which the chaotic and creative forces of both psyche and social relations meet. The subject is pictured as a productive agent who is simultaneously the product of social relations. The image here is comparable to and derivable from Marx's laborer, except for the fact that, with Kristeva, the decentered subject is the writer (*scripteur*), the producer of texts (*phenotextes*), which, in turn, are conditioned by a textual field (*genotextes*).

Kristeva's complex argument cannot be fully presented here, so I will turn to a less radical and sociologically more accessible model, Umberto Eco's theory of culture as conventional codes (1976).

Of particular interest to sociologists is Eco's claim that every act of human communication involves a text. Throughout recent structuralism, the idea of the text has been a crucial concept. The text emerged as a primary topic as a result of structuralist semiotic's criticism of early formalistic and linguistic semiologies in which analysis was focused on the linguistic sign (see Derrida, 1970; Sollers, 1968; Kristeva, 1974). The text differs from the sign because it is a more explicitly social product. A text is the product of elements from a multiplicity of codes (literary, political, biographical, historical). As a result, the text as a unit of analysis tends to avoid the formalism of the linguistic sign by virtue of being a necessarily contexted object. Flaubert's novel *Le médecin de campagne* is a complex social product, and to an extent that the sentence with which it ends (*"Priez pour lui!"*) is not.

The structuralist text is a generic concept for which the literary and artistic text is a primary model, but the structuralist text is also intended as a way of conceptualizing the relationship between *any* expression of social labor and the structured social relations within which that labor produces. Thus, Philippe Sollers (1968:405), speaking of and for the *Tel Quel* group, once said; "We propose to consolidate a 'science of writing (*écriture*)' which would treat different practices (philosophical, scientific, aesthetic, and social) as texts." [5]

Naturally, the sociological use of such a concept must face up to an obvious problem. Is the text-as-a-product-of-social-structures (codes) to be a literal object of sociological investigation—that is, are we to follow Sollers in saying that social action is textual in nature? Personally, I believe that such an argument can be made, but not here (Lemert, in press [b]). There is, however, a more modest version, that can be made here, namely, that social action can best be understood when conceived from the point of view of textual theory. This is Eco's position in his general theory of codes: "Humanity and society exist only where communicative and significative relationships are established" (1976:22). Eco does not claim that society is *nothing but* intertextual communication; he wishes more simply to argue that a science of society is complete only when it uses a science of signs (semiotics) to develop a theory for the reading of social action as textual productivity. Thus, the essential activities of society (tool making, kinship, economic exchange) are all, in effect, text-producing activities insofar as they are sociologically interpretable only when viewed as structured, code-specific activities (Eco, 1976:21–28). A material object—such as a new Cadillac—can make sociological sense only to the extent that one is able to situate it in a codal system—that is, in the economic and cultural structures that provide it with meaning as a produced and purchased commodity, as a fetish, as an index of economic productivity, and as a measure of personal income. In this respect, social actions toward objects like Cadillacs are readable in the same way as are purely cultural products like a poem by Baudelaire. Poems and Cadillacs are read as textual products of structural conventions (poetic figures in one case, socioeconomic relations in the other). It is in this sense that Eco justifies his statement "that culture can only be studied completely under a semiotic profile" (1976:28). No phenomenon can be sociologically interesting unless it signifies. The task of social science is to explain these signifying processes whether they be ideas or tons of wheat.[6]

This scheme avoids formalism by means of a theory of codes (that is, structures) which, in Saussurian fashion, views them as social conventions and as, thus, historically relative. Here the model straddles the freedom/determinism dilemma in a fruitful way. Instead of attributing freedom to certain stages in history outside of structurally determined epochs (as does Appelbaum elsewhere in this book), freedom is taken into the semiological process by virtue of a methodological decision. As in Saussure's tactical distinction (1959) between diachronic and synchronic linguistics, structuralism assumes that scientific explanation applies to synchronic slices of structural relations in a certain form at a certain moment in history. The structures arise historically (diachronically), but are studied synchronically. Their historical origin is not considered a primary source of their explanation, although historical analysis is necessary in order to identify a given structural arrangement. This is, however, essentially only a descriptive prelude to explanation. Explanation is the analysis of relations between structures and between structures and actions at a given historical moment (Eco, 1976:125–129). This analysis of synchronic structures is not absolutistic, because the structures, isolated by an analytic procedure, are historically contexted, and thus, ultimately indeterminate.

> Semiotics must proceed to isolate structures *as if* a definitive general structure existed; but to be able to do this, one must assume that this global structure is simply a regulative hypothesis, and that *every time a structure is described something occurs within the universe of signification which no longer makes it completely reliable.*
>
> But this condition of imbalance and apparent lack of stability puts semiotics on a par with other disciplines such as physics, governed—as this latter is—by such a methodological criteria (*sic*) as the indeterminacy or complementarity principles. Only if it acquires this *awareness of its own limits,* and avoids aspiring to an absolute form of knowledge, will one be able to consider semiotics as a *scientific* discipline (Eco, 1976:129; emphasis in original).

The same can be said of and for sociology.

NOTES

1. They have discovered something new, but in this article I wish to emphasize structuralism's points of contact with sociology.

2. Other designations in use are: poetics (Culler, 1975), grammatology (Derrida, 1976), and archaeology (Foucault, 1972).

3. The distinction between structural deductivism and methodological individualism is analytic and not meant to deny the actual closeness of the two in some cases. Homans, for example, belongs to both groups.

4. It should be noted that later structuralist semiotics has severely criticized Saussure for having incompletely abandoned phonocentric subjectivism.

5. In the background of this interest in the text is the strong intellectual affiliation of left-wing structuralists with the literary and artistic avant-garde in France (Kristeva, 1974; Caws, 1973).

6. Among the most fruitful applications of this model is to measurement theory (Lemert, in press[b]).

REFERENCES

ALTHUSSER, LOUIS
1970 For Marx. New York: Vintage Books.
ALTHUSSER, LOUIS, and ÉTIENNE BALIBAR
1970 Reading Capital. New York: Pantheon Books.
BARTHES, ROLAND
1970 Elements of Semiology. Boston: Beacon Press.
BERGER, PETER, and THOMAS LUCKMANN
1967 Social Construction of Reality. New York: Doubleday.
BERNSTEIN, BASIL
1975 Class, Codes, and Control. New York: Schocken Books.
BLALOCK, HUBERT M.
1968 "The measurement problem: A gap between the languages of theory and research." Pp. 5–27 in Hubert M. and Ann B. Blalock (eds.), Methodology in Social Research. New York: McGraw-Hill.
BLAU, PETER
1960 "Structural effects." American Sociological Review 25:178–193.
1964 Exchange and Power in Social Life. New York: John Wiley.
1970 "A formal theory of differentiation in organizations." American Sociological Review 35:201–218.
1974 "Parameters of social structure." American Sociological Review 39:615–636.
BOUDON, RAYMOND
1971 Uses of Structuralism. London: Heinemann.
BOURDIEU, PIERRE, and JEAN-CLAUDE PASSERON
1968 "Sociology and philosophy in France since 1945: Death and resurrection of a philosophy with subject." Social Research 34:162–212.
CAWS, MARY ANN
1973 "Tel Quel: Text and revolution." Diacritics 3:2–8.
CICOUREL, AARON
1974 Cognitive Sociology. New York: Free Press.
CULLER, JONATHAN
1975 Structuralist Poetics. Ithaca, N.Y.: Cornell University Press.
1976 Saussure. Glasgow: Fontana/Collins.
DERRIDA, JACQUES
1970 "Structure, sign and play in the discourse of the human sciences." Pp.

247-265 in R. Macksey and E. Donato (eds.), The Structuralist Controversy. Baltimore: Johns Hopkins University Press.

1976 Of Grammatology. Baltimore: Johns Hopkins University Press.

DUNCAN, HUGH D.

1968 Symbols in Society. London: Oxford University Press.

ECO, UMBERTO

1976 A Theory of Semiotics. Bloomington: Indiana University Press.

EKEH, PETER P.

1974 Social Exchange Theory: The Two Traditions. Cambridge, Mass.: Harvard University Press.

ETZIONI, AMITAI

1970 "Toward a macrosociology." Pp. 69-97 in John C. McKinney and Edward Tiryakian (eds.), Theoretical Sociology. New York: Appleton-Century-Crofts.

FOUCAULT, MICHEL

1972 Archaeology of Knowledge. New York: Random House.

1973 The Order of Things. New York: Vintage Books.

GARFINKEL, HAROLD, and HARVEY SACKS

1970 "On formal structures of practical actions." Pp. 337-366 in Theoretical Sociology. New York: Appleton-Century-Crofts.

GLUCKSMANN, MIRIAM

1974 Structural Analysis in Contemporary Social Thought: A Comparison of the Theories of Claude Lévi-Strauss and Louis Althusser. London: Routledge & Kegan Paul.

GOFFMAN, ERVING

1974 Frame Analysis. New York: Harper Colophon Books.

GOULDNER, ALVIN

1976 The Dialogue of Ideology and Technology. New York: Seabury.

HABERMAS, JÜRGEN

1970 "Toward a theory of communicative competence." Pp. 115-145 in H. P. Drietzel (ed.), Recent Sociology No. 2. New York: Macmillan.

1973 Theory and Practice. Boston: Beacon Press.

HOMANS, GEORGE C.

1958 "Social behavior as exchange." American Journal of Sociology 63:597-606.

1961 Social Behavior: Its Elementary Forms. New York: Harcourt, Brace & World.

1967 The Nature of Social Science. New York: Harcourt, Brace & World.

HOMANS, GEORGE C. and DAVID M. SCHNEIDER

1955 Marriage, Authority, and Final Causes: A Study of Unilateral Cross-Cousin Marriage. New York: The Free Press.

KRISTEVA, JULIA

1968 La sémiologie: science critique et/ou critique de la science." Pp. 80-94 in Tel Quel, Théorie d'ensemble. Paris: Éditions du Seuil.

1974 La révolution du language poétique: l'avant-garde à la fin du XIXe siècle. Paris: Éditions du Seuil.

1977 Polylogue. Paris: Éditions du Seuil.

LABOV, WILLIAM
  1978 "Crossing the gulf between sociology and linguistics." The American
        Sociologist 13:93–103.
LACAN, JACQUES
  1977 Écrits: A Selection. New York: W. W. Norton.
LANE, MICHAEL (ed.)
  1970 Structuralism: A Reader. London: Cape.
LEMERT, CHARLES
  1979 Sociology and the Twilight of Man: Homocentrism and Discourse in
        Sociological Theory. Carbondale: Southern Illinois University Press.
  In   "Ethnomethodology and structuralism: Linguicity and the decentering
  Press[a] of core-values." Theory and Society. [1978]
  In   "Language, structure, and measurement: Structuralist semiotics and
  Press[b] sociology." American Journal of Sociology. [1979]
LÉVI-STRAUSS, CLAUDE
  1966 The Savage Mind. Chicago: The University of Chicago Press.
  1967 "The structural study of myth." Pp. 202–228 in C. Lévi-Strauss,
        Structural Anthropology. New York: Anchor Books.
  1969a The Raw and the Cooked. New York: Harper Torchbooks.
  1969b[1949] The Elementary Structures of Kinship. Boston: Beacon Press.
McCARTHY, T. A.
  1973 "A theory of communicative competence." Philosophy of the social
        sciences 3:135–156.
MOUNIN, GEORGES
  1974 "Lévi-Strauss' uses of linguistics." In I. Rossi (ed.), The Unconscious in
        Culture. New York: Dutton.
MUELLER, CLAUSS
  1973 The Politics of Communication. London: Oxford University Press.
MULLINS, NICHOLAS C.
  1973 Theories and Theory Groups in Contemporary American Sociology.
        New York: Harper & Row.
PARSONS, TALCOTT
  1951 The Social System. New York: The Free Press.
  1961 Theories of Society. Glencoe: Ill.: The Free Press.
  1970 "Some problems of general theory in sociology." Pp. 27–68 in John C.
        McKinney and Edward Tiryakian (eds.), Theoretical Sociology. New
        York: Appleton–Century–Crofts.
PIAGET, JEAN
  1970 Structuralism. New York: Basic Books.
ROSSI, INO (ed.)
  1974 The Unconscious in Culture. New York: Dutton.
SAID, EDWARD
  1971 "Abacedarium culturae: Structuralism, absence, writing." Tri-Quarterly
        20:33–71.
SAUSSURE, FERDINAND DE
  1959 Course in General Linguistics. New York: Philosophical Library.

SOLLERS, PHILIPPE
  1968 "L'Écriture fonction de transformation sociale." Pp. 399-405 in Tel
       Quel, Théorie d'ensemble. Paris: Éditions du Seuil.
  1972 "Ébranler le systeme." Magazine Littéraire 65:10-17.
STINCHCOMBE, ARTHUR
  1975 "A structural analysis of sociology." The American Sociologist 10:57-64.
TURNER, STEPHEN
  1974 "Structuralist and participant's view sociologies." The American Sociol-
       ogist 9:143-146.
WHITE, HARRISON C.
  1963 An Anatomy of Kinship: Mathematical Models for Structures of Cumu-
       lated Roles. Englewood Cliffs, N.J.: Prentice-Hall.
  1970 Chains of Opportunity. Cambridge, Mass.: Harvard University Press.
ZIMMERMAN, DON H., and D. LAWRENCE WIEDER
  1970 "Ethnomethodology and the problem of order: Comment on Denzin."
       Pp. 285-298 in J. Douglas (ed.), Understanding Everyday Life. Chicago:
       Aldine.

PART III
FORMAL THEORY

In the introduction social theory as a science was discussed. This is the attempt to develop propositional systems that are empirically grounded. For those who have succeeded in doing more than providing summations of their empirical observations, the pay-off has been high. To study human behavior in this fashion means using a fairly high level of abstraction, so that what is developed can be applied cross-culturally, as well as across time.

Ball sees general systems theory (GST) as a method of inquiry, though the goal of inquiry in this area is clearly the development of formal theory. GST overcomes the problems of such theoretical frameworks as functionalism, sees relationships in a processual fashion rather than an Aristotelian one. It makes assumptions about the ways in which human behavior should be analyzed and develops an appropriate methodology.

Following along these lines, Baumgartner, Burns, and DeVillé outline what they call a systems theoretic approach. Their goal is to describe and analyze how, and under what conditions, processes and social systems develop, stabilize, decay, or otherwise change. They draw on modern systems theory, of the kind described by Ball, to accomplish their task. Social systems are seen as processual, dialetical systems, which require a specific mode of analysis. In a way this kind of work reflects difficulties involved in the construction of social theory, because of the vast array of variables that need to be taken into account. Their virtue is that they serve to remind us what we have omitted, or might include, in developing models.

The article by Black reflects a different level of analysis, for he seeks to develop a theoretical framework for the study of all social behavior. As he says, "Pure sociology is the study of social variation without regard to other aspects of social reality." Social reality, then, has a space of its own, with vertical, horizontal, symbolic, corporate, and normative dimensions. Taking examples from law, medicine, ideas, and art, he demonstrates his strategy. Pure sociology overcomes a number of the assumptions and problems that beset the social sciences today.

The enterprise of Hingers and Willer is similar to that of the other sociologists in this section in that they wish to demonstrate that sociology can develop laws of human behavior, and that sociologists have the ability to do so now. Social exchange theory, which is of growing importance in the discipline, challenges the assumptions of older theories such as functionalism. Until now, however, the writing in this area has been difficult and laden with jargon. This article clearly articulates the prevailing postulates and shows how these assumptions can be applied to such activities as economic behavior and organizational behavior.

Like Hingers and Willer, Michaels and Green wish to make accessible a form of doing sociology—behavioral sociology. Their task is also not unlike that of Burawoy in showing the sources of the apparent confusions in Marxist theory and what essentials one might reasonably grasp. These authors trace the unique features of behavioral sociology and show why they have caused some confusion. They outline its history and then show how the concepts in this area have been applied to the analysis of such things as complex organizations. Finally, they deal with criticisms of behavioral sociology.

1. Sociology and General Systems Theory

RICHARD A. BALL

Sociology has been intensely concerned with the issue of "systems," and a great deal has been written on the subject. There are literally dozens of different systems perspectives, each developed by particular exponents of a given point of view. Some theories stress the patterns of social organization, others the dominant cultural configurations, still others emphasize factors such as religion, economic circumstances or geography. Into this tangle has come general systems theory (GST), a framework which has developed across a variety of sciences but which hopes to deal with a major problem common to them all: the scientific treatment of organized complexity. Just as there are many different "systems theories," there are some wide variations within GST itself. No one proponent can hope to speak definitively. My intention in this brief space is to outline something of the ongoing enterprise of GST. If what follows is at all successful in stimulating interest within our discipline, then I may be forgiven for a treatment which will undoubtedly overlook some of the most important features of GST while perhaps overemphasizing others.

General systems theory is "essentially a cluster of strategies of inquiry" (Berrien, 1968:13) which attempts to overcome the limitations of traditional positivism without sacrificing conceptual clarity, parsimony, precision and pragmatic attention to the natural world (Laszlo, 1972). It is not a new theory, but a paradigm shift, and it can be applied to the

SOURCE: Reprinted from *The American Sociologist* 13 (February 1978):65–72.

sciences generally. Although GST is directly applicable to problems of systems technology (Von Bertalanffy, 1968), it must not be confused with the conventional practice of "Systems Analysis," which has retained the reductionistic narrowness so characteristic of extreme positivism (Boguslaw, 1965). Those attracted to GST find it a particularly powerful framework for applied research and theory construction. It can contribute to traditional functionalism and conflict theory, as well as to such schools of thought as symbolic interactionism, and may eventually help sociology to deal more effectively with the problems of these different traditions. I will outline some potential contributions of GST, taking examples from two important areas of research—social deviance and social change. I will argue that GST can begin to resolve some of the major dilemmas which have impeded research and theory construction in sociology. Among these are the tendency toward reification, the constant threat of reductionism, the presistence of metaphysical dualism, the dominance of narrowly linear thought patterns, and the limitations inherent in the concept of homeostasis.

BEYOND REIFICATION

Western epistemology has been plagued by what Whitehead (1929) has called the "bifurcation of nature"—that arbitrary division of the realms of mind and matter which produces either idealists or materialists. Both of these schools of thought are based on an essentially Aristotelian logic. This is a logic preoccupied with taxonomy, which proceeds by isolating analytical categories and ordering these abstract categories by a method of subsumption and aggregation similar to the way bricks are cut out and then laid upon one another to form an artificial wall. System builders who work within this tradition try to divide reality into internally consistent, boundary-maintaining categories, and then to construct relatively timeless, closed systems out of these parts. Idealists may engage in rhetorical construction, often ending in scholasticism. Materialists may attain to the taxonomic achievements of, for example, a Linnaeus. But in both cases, further progress is blocked. The source of the impasse is the latent tendency toward reification of categories.

As van den Berghe (1963:98) has stressed, the most serious shortcomings of functionalism, even of the more "cautious" functionalism which he identifies with Parsons (1951), Merton (1957) and Davis (1959), result from "looking at social structure as the 'backbone' of society, and considering structural analysis in social science as analogous to anatomy or morphology in biology." One result of this classificatory mode is a tendency toward the fallacy of misplaced concreteness, toward the reification of what "is" (Buckley, 1967). GST does not reject conventional functionalism, however, but recognizes it as a contribution limited by unnecessarily rigid categories. GST is *holistic*; it begins with the concept of *organization*—not of parts which happen to be related, but of relationships which may be studied by examining relevant subfields.

In recent decades, following the work of logicians such as Peirce (1934), Dewey (1938) and Whitehead (1929), and scientists such as Weiner (1948) and Von Bertalanffy (1968), it has been generally conceded that the older classificatory logic must give way to some form of *processual* logic. Older frameworks have begun with theoretical entities, and then tried to relate them by a categorical logic; GST begins with a processual conception of reality as consisting fundamentally of relationships among relationships, as illustrated in the concept of "gravity" as used in modern physics. The term "gravity" does not describe an entity at all. There is no such "thing" as gravity. It is not even a force. Gravity is *a set of relationships*. To think of these relationships as entities is to fall into reification. GST recognizes "social facts," but in the same sense that gravity is a fact. This means, for example, that those sociological perspectives which treat social life as a continuous "negotiation of reality" are generally more congenial to GST than is the older notion of a specific set of norms systematically derived from a more abstract set of values. The GST approach demands that sociologists develop the logic of relationships and conceptualize social reality in relational terms.

Conflict theory seems to be most powerful when it treats social reality in relational terms. This is where Marx is often misunderstood. As Ollman (1971:15-25) has shown, Marx's conception of reality follows the tradition of the "philosophy of internal relations":

> The relation is the irreducible minimum for all units in Marx's conception of social reality. This is really the nub of our difficulty in understanding Marxism, whose subject matter is not simply society conceived of 'relationally'. Capital, labor, value, commodity, etc., are all grasped as relations . . .
>
> Thus capital in a situation where it functioned as interest would be called 'interest,' and vice versa. However, a change in function only results in a new name . . . if the original factor is actually conceived to be what is is now functioning as . . .
>
> Generally speaking, we understand why Marx has used a particular name to the extent that we are able to grasp the function referred to . . .

What emerges from the interpretation is that the problem Marx faces in his exposition is *not* how to link separate parts but how to individuate instrumental units in a social whole which finds expression everywhere. (emphasis in original)

It is important to note that the term "function" is applicable only in the mathematical sense—not in the more usual sense of "consequence" or "purpose." A variety of illustrations may be drawn from statistics, which deals not with the "parts" (e.g., individuals), but with relationships in the aggregate. A correlation coefficient is a relationship; an intercorrelation is a relationship between relationships. Factor analysis treats reality in relational terms. The problem of "massaging" sociological data is a problem of "how to individuate instrumental units in a social whole which finds expression everywhere" (Ollman, 1971:25).

Marx was quite familiar with the philosophy of internal relations, especially as it had been developed in Hegelian dialectics; in fact, the idea goes back to the ancient Greek philosophers. Its most recent expressions include the formulations of philosophers such as Dewey (1938) and Whitehead (1929), and the work of the biologists, physicists, engineers and others who have constructed GST as a way of dealing with practical scientific problems.

What is the approach to a reality consisting of shifting relationships? Those who continue to adhere strictly to Aristotelian logic tend to fall into one of two different traps of categorical logic. This can be illustrated by the running battle over the definition of "deviance." Deviance is not some sort of entity inherent in the act itself as the realists contend. But does this necessarily lead to the nominalistic position in which deviance is merely a label? In GST, the term is defined by examining various relationships and relational properties—not by imputing certain structural properties to the "deviant" or to those who are "labeling" him. Neither functionalism nor conflict theory has grasped this logic; the former tends to the errors of realism and the latter to the errors of nominalism.

In research on Mexican medicine hucksters (Simoni and Ball, 1975), close attention to actual empirical *processes* has made it apparent that although society *treats* the medicine huckster as a "deviant" and a "marginal man," hucksterism is better described as an "interstitial" role mediating between subsystems which are in a state of latent conflict. The medicine huckster is a colorful character who works the village market circuits of the Mexican hinterland, selling medicinally worthless products by a remarkably effective sales pitch which captivates his audiences. His operations are illegal, yet he is allowed to work unmolested. While the concept of marginality implies a social system with certain deviants to be found along the outer edges, the concept of the interstitial role emphasizes that what is called *the* system is comprised, in this empirical instance, of a variety of differentiated social fields in shifting relationships to one another. What happens in the space between dominant fields (e.g., the development of medicine hucksterism) is a function of the relationship between the fields (in this case, the historically shifting relationship between the health care establishment on the one hand and the mass of the poor on the other). Marx (1906:784–848) has treated peddlers, vagabonds and "nomad workers" in such terms. A GST approach suggests that medicine hucksterism reduces pressure on the health care establishment due to rising expectations among the Mexican poor. Functionalism might emphasize that the medicine huckster is therefore "functional" to Mexican society. Conflict theory might describe him as another "opiate for the masses," a social technique employed by the powerful against the exploited peasantry. GST can combine these two perspectives, acknowledging the partial truth contained in each. The result is neither an implicit acceptance of the status quo nor an explicit call for social revolution; rather it is an exploration of various ways in which the obvious effectiveness of the medicine huckster might be directed into more socially useful channels. This approach has proved practical enough to suggest means by which effective huckster techniques might be employed to enhance the communication of badly needed health information to the Mexican poor, and to open up communication between the poor and the traditionally aloof establishment (Simoni and Ball, 1975).

BEYOND REDUCTIONISM

According to GST, the various sytems sociologists are concerned with (e.g., biological, psychological, or sociocultural) form a hierarchy of multiple levels, each level emerging from the previous. GST supports Spencer's notion that evolution proceeds from systems of "incoherent homogeneity" to systems of "coherent heterogeneity." Systems at advanced hierarchical levels achieve increased flexibility (wider "freedom") through the process of "complexification": increasingly sophisticated and integrative feedback loops lead to greater and greater internal differentiation. This means that although systems higher in the hierarchy are based upon those beneath them, they cannot be reduced to lower levels, because the principles of organization have become different. A sociocultural system, for example, is bound together by more complex relationships than is the material system upon which it rests. If we conceptualize society in hierarchical terms, with the symbol systems of religion, art and even law evolving from the economic level, GST tells us that (a) these "superstructures" are *based* upon the economic sub-system, but (b) they cannot be *reduced* to that level without a loss of understanding. Do the different aspects of capitalism, for example, follow *logically* from one another? Marx has disclosed some of the major internal contradictions which make capitalism "illogical" in any formal sense. GST allows us to make use of such conflict theories as Marxism without succumbing to their limitations, which are often reductionistic. GST might therefore accept certain formulations based upon a Marxist approach, but it would reject a strict economic determinism even as it would reject a psychologistic reductionism. The challenge is to explore the ways in which systemic processes at one level build upon different but related processes at another. We must spell out the "relationships" and the "differences" in rigorous terms which can be replicated in various empirical contexts. This is easier to propose, of course, than it is to accomplish.

BEYOND DUALISM

In an attempt to overcome our persistent metaphysical dualism, Laszlo (1972:119) has provided a logically powerful explanation of the manner in which so-called "physical events" and "mental events" can be systematically related by GST. He describes a method of searching for their common features. As a practical framework which succeeds in escaping metaphysical dualism, GST may offer us one basis for a more systematic social psychology.

The methodological implications of any rejection of dualism are immense. GST insists that consciousness, having emerged as one aspect of the evolutionary process, has an affinity for the world precisely because it is a part of it; society is understandable precisely because it has been constructed by and is being constantly modified by the very beings which seek to understand it. This is not some mysterious phenomeno-logical sensitivity. General systems theorists assume a stance of *radical empiricism* in the Jamesian sense. They "live in the experience," but also attempt to describe and measure it. The phenomenological impres-sionist, by taking only the first course, is rarely able to apply his personalized data to change the reality he encounters. The pure positiv-ist, on the other hand, holds reality at a distance, contenting himself with reading his instruments. GST aims at the systematic translation of experience into communicable models. The individual and society are treated equally, not as separate entities but as mutually constitutive fields, related through various "feedback" processes. This is not a revolutionary idea; the potential contribution of GST lies in its comprehensive attention to a wide variety of systems and its attempt to draw analogies which may clarify the processes operating in one system by reference to another.

The connection between GST and the tradition of symbolic interactionism is now obvious. Shibutani (1968:330–331) has applied the GST perspective in a way which illuminates the more "cybernetic" Meadian concept of the act as an organized whole, pointing out that social action "is seen not as response to stimulation, as relief from tension, nor as the accomplishment of symbolized intent; it is something that is *constructed in a succession of self-correcting adjustments to* changing life conditions" (emphasis in original). As he also emphasizes, the relative openness of the process means that the same final action may result from different initial conditions in different ways, according to the GST principle of *equifinality*. Shibutani (1968:333) goes on to stress that "the key to all such self-correcting adjustments is *feedback*; all purposeful behavior requires negative feedback" (emphasis in original). The 'Me' is the self-image built up in feedback from others; the 'I' is the evoked response. These "inner experiences" do not take place in some introspective vacuum, for society is a complex net of feedback loops uniting individual members into a whole.

GST may also offer symbolic interactionism an opportunity to transcend its oft-criticized preoccupation with the purely interpersonal to the neglect of macrosociological factors through the concept of the image. Shibutani (1968:333) clarifies the Meadian appreciation of cognitive functions through his treatment of imagery or cognitive mapping of information: "Any impulse that is not immediately consummated is transformed into an *image*, which serves as the basis for reflection" (emphasis in original). The economist and GST advocate Boulding (1961:14), has employed the concept of "imaging" at the societal level, in a way which ties together sociocultural and interpersonal dynamics. He draws heavily upon information theory, which has contributed a great deal to GST. In place of the positivist conception of social facts as immovable entities, he employs the concept of information flow, emphasizing that many so-called social facts are "only messages filtered through a changeable value systems" (Boulding, 1961:14). Culture itself is treated largely in terms of such images. The parallel with Shibutani is clear. "Culture" is conceived of as the "image" of the society, the collective information by which the society attempts to organize itself.

BEYOND LINEARITY

GST does not follow a linear logic; it therefore denies *both* idealistic formalism and materialistic determinism. Those who lean toward idealistic formalism often see "normal" social action as consisting entirely of purposive, ends-means behavior. One influential example may be seen in Parsons (1937), where the "unit act" is conceptualized as if it were merely a "means" to realize a priori cultural ends called "values". The Meadian approach, especially as clarified by GST, highlights the inadequacies of the strictly unilinear ends-means view of idealistic formalism, emphasizing, among other things, the reciprocal relationship between individual and society.

The linearity of materialistic determinism is evident in the reflex arc (S-R) models of the Skinnerians, which treat social action as a set of conditioned responses. Recent work with the GST concept of "biofeedback" has called into question the strictly unilinear behaviorist position, demonstrating that "states of consciousness" can actually control what were once regarded as involuntary organic processes. This is not to say that people do not engage in instrumental actions, nor is it to say that we are not also creatures of habit. The problem is to find the terms which will clarify the relationship between these complementary processes.

The linearity of conventional sociological analysis is clearly illustrated in Merton's (1957) classic definition of social order in terms of institutionalized means-ends. Linear logic makes it almost inevitable that social disorganization, or anomie, will be treated as means-ends discontinuity. Social problems are then defined in terms of departure from this purely abstract construction. But much of the complexity of social change is reduced to the problem of anomie.

GST tries to use empirical research to develop formulations which reflect the processes of change as clearly as those of stability. GST has shown that most empirically normal systems follow a naturalistic logic of *multilinear discontinuity* rather than a formalistic logic of linear continuity (Boulding, 1956). The equifinality principle referred to above states that the goal may remain relatively constant while the means shift in response to internal and external feedback on developmental progress. For example, there is a genetic code for the development of an organism, but in actual operation this plan shifts *within certain limits* so as to accomplish essentially the same end in the face of varying environmental conditions. Another empirically common pattern is one in which the means remain relatively stable while the goals shift. Through the concept of displacement, this process has already achieved considerable importance in organizational theory. It can be described even more generally, however, in terms of the GST process of *equistasis*. Merton has done a great deal to clarify the problems which arise when institutionalized means are not adequate to permit realization of internalized cultural goals, but research which is restricted by Mertonian premises is likely to treat both equifinality and equistasis as disorganization. Research which begins from a more comprehensive GST framework may be more alert to the variety of organizational and relational possibilities and to the empirical factors surrounding each of them.

BEYOND HOMEOSTASIS

The GST approach may be further clarified by turning again to conventional functionalism, which has contributed a great deal to GST by its insistence on the importance of the "system" concept. I will consider the most common criticism of functionalist theory: the limitations of an equilibrium concept which cannot account for such obvious empirical facts as the existence of internal conflict, deepening malintegration, maladaptive reactions to external change, and revolution (van den Berghe, 1963:697). From Malinowski's (1945) position, functionalism has developed a perspective much like Weiner's (1948) cybernetics. Weiner's use of the feedback concept has made an immense contribution to the resolution of many problems resulting from the traditional unilinear, causal analysis. He saw cybernetic processes as self-stabilizing, controlled by error-reducing *negative* feedback (Laszlo, 1972:38). The thermostat is the most frequently cited example of a control mechanism which keeps a flexible system in "dynamic equilibrium" between designed tolerance limits: an increase or decrease in temperature provides the negative feedback. In functionalist theory it is value consensus which provides the negative feedback which maintains a changing society in dynamic equilibrium. This dynamic equilibrium is called *homeostasis*.

According to GST, it is not that functionalism has been in error, but that it has not gone far enough. If the collapse of the controlling negative feedback were the only source of social change, all change would result in increasing chaos. However, the actual empirical processes of evolution involve not only negative feedback loops which operate to restore the "natural order," but also *positive* feedback loops which amplify "deviant" tendencies. Much of the strength of conflict theory lies in its appreciation of these processes. The problem is that conflict theory has neglected sources of legitimate integration and has generally failed to see the *reciprocity* of conflicting relationships (see the discussion of victimology below). A system characterized by both positive and negative feedback is in a state of *homeorhesis*. Positive feedback changes the system, while negative feedback provides the integration necessary to maintain it. Analogies drawn from biological systems may clarify the nature of positive feedback.

In the empirical relationships between subsystems and suprasystems, certain types of biological environments favor certain types of mutants, which in turn produce changes in their environments. The phenomenon of "secondary deviation" (Lemert, 1951:77), which has become the basis of labeling theory, is such a process of positive feedback: the same environment which has fostered a variety of behavioral variations reacts to certain of them with counterproductive severity, thereby fostering a pattern of further compensating variations, while reducing the effectiveness of its own negative feedback as a constraining factor. Subsystem-to-subsystem relationships often reflect a mutually positive feedback process of escalation, as when an increase in the protective capacity of one species fosters increased predatory capacities in another, producing a spiral of further protective capacities in the first. (A sociocultural analogy may be found in the mathematics of arms races, in which the moves of each international subsystem—i.e., nation-state—provoke counter moves by others [Richardson, 1960].) Element-to-element relationships within a particular subsystem (e.g., within a species) often develop processes by which mates of certain types are favored, fostering offspring with particular characteristics. All of these are "deviation-amplification" processes which propel change by way of *positive* feedback loops (Maruyama, 1963).

Of course, neither stability nor change is to be posited as desirable in itself. GST helps us to distinguish between the *power* of a particular process and its *result* in a way which illuminates both conventional functionalism and traditional conflict theory. A particular process is not necessarily functional merely because it is powerful. Actually, power may be directly correlated with dysfunctionality so that the more dysfunctional a process becomes, the more powerful it becomes; an example is the growth of cancerous tissue in an organism.

The field of "victimology," which has developed since WW II, is another example of increased attention to the reciprocity of feedback relationships. Victimology suggests that crimes should not be viewed simply as actions springing from sources in the offender, but as "transactions" which can be explained in part by the behavior of the victim. In its early years, victimology often amounted to an attempt to depict the victim as the cause of his own victimization, sometimes to the extent of excusing the offender (Schafer, 1968). The reasoning remained essentially linear, except that what had been seen as cause came to be seen as effect, and vice versa. More recently, victimology has profited by a GST approach which breaks down the cause-effect distinction by emphasizing the process of interaction: a reciprocal flow of positive feedback between victim and offender, which often makes it difficult to decide just who should be charged with instigating the offense. The idea of transactions originated in the process theory of Dewey and Bentley (Buckley, 1967). Through modifications of game theory (which has made major contributions to GST), it has become applicable to the therapy context as well as to the study of crime. Berne (1964) describes various "games people play" as patterns of sustained relationships built on *mutually* dysfunctional exploitation. These represent "negative-sum" games in which all players lose. There is little to be gained by defining these relationships as functional on the basis of their empirical endurance. At the same time, there is little to be gained by treating one side as the exploiter and the other as the exploited, for the exploited will often seek another similar relationship immediately after attaining freedom from the first. The nature of the feedback loops and the particular "information" being transmitted are problems which need to be approached through research.

CONCLUSION

GST combines a suitable epistemological position with a workable methodological strategy. It has drawn heavily on the prior contributions of other theoretical perspectives, while attempting to avoid their respective limitations. There are pitfalls to be avoided. A move toward a purely positivistic systems analysis would place undue limitations on GST, and that is one reason why the broader possibilities have been stressed in this review. The problem of system jargon, perennial to our discipline, must not be allowed to lead to more reinventions of the wheel, or to a drift into obscurantism. Above all, GST must prove itself in practice. What is needed more than anything else at this moment is the help of methodologically inclined sociologists who are more interested in learning from empirical problems than they are in producing elegant abstractions to be admired for their own sakes.

REFERENCES

BERNE, ERIC
1964 Games People Play. New York: Grove Press.
BERRIEN, KENNETH
1968 General and Social Systems. New Brunswick, N.J.: Rutgers University Press.

BOGUSLAW, ROBERT
1965 The New Utopians: A Study of System Design and Social Change. Englewood Cliffs, N.J.: Prentice-Hall.
BOULDING, KENNETH
1956 "Towards a general theory of growth." General System Yearbook 1:65–75.
1961 The Image. Ann Arbor: University of Michigan Press.
BUCKLEY, WALTER
1967 Sociology and Modern Systems Theory. Englewood Cliffs, N.J.: Prentice-Hall.
DAVIS, KINGSLEY
1959 "The myth of functional analysis as a special method in sociology and anthropology." American Sociological Review 24:757–772.
DEWEY, JOHN
1938 Logic: The Theory of Inquiry. New York: Holt, Rinehart and Winston.
LASZLO, ERVIN
1972 Introduction to Systems Philosophy. New York: Harper & Row.
LEMERT, EDWIN
1951 Social Pathology. New York: McGraw-Hill.
MALINOWSKI, BRONISLAW
1945 The Dynamics of Culture Change. New Haven: Yale University Press.
MARUYAMA, MAGORAH
1963 "The second cybernetics: Deviation-amplifying mutual causal processes." American Scientist 51(2):164–199.
MARX, KARL
1906 Capital. A Critical Analysis of Capitalist Production. Samuel Moore and Edward Aveling (trans.). New York: Random House.
MERTON, ROBERT K.
1957 Social Theory and Social Structure, Revised Edition. Glencoe, Ill.: Free Press.
OLLMAN, BERTELL
1971 Alienation: Marx's Conception of Man in Capitalist Society. London: Cambridge University Press.
PARSONS, TALCOTT
1937 The Structure of Social Action. New York: McGraw-Hill.
1951 The Social System. Glencoe, Ill.: Free Press.
PEIRCE, CHARLES S.
1934 Collected Papers of Charles Sanders Peirce. Charles Hartshorne and Paul Weiss (eds.). Cambridge, Mass.: Belknap Press.
RICHARDSON, L. F.
1960 Arms and Insecurity. London: Stevens.
SCHAFER, STEPHEN
1968 The Victim and His Criminal. New York: Random House.
SHIBUTANI, TAMOTSU
1968 "A cybernetic approach to motivation." Pp. 330–336 in Walter Buckley (ed.), Modern Systems Research for the Behavioral Scientist. Chicago: Aldine.

SIMONI, JOSEPH J., and RICHARD BALL
   1975   "Can we learn from medicine hucksters?" Journal of Communication 25
      (3):124–181.
VAN DEN BERGHE, PIERRE L.
   1963   "Dialectic and functionalism: Toward a theoretical synthesis." American
      Sociological Review 28 (5):695–705.
VON BERTALANFFY, LUDWIG
   1968   General System Theory. New York: Braziller.
WEINER, NORBERT
   1948   Cybernetics: Or Control and Communication in the Animal and Ma-
      chine. Cambridge, Mass.: M.I.T. Press.
WHITEHEAD, ALFRED N.
   1929   Process and Reality. New York: Macmillan.

2. Actors, Games, and Systems: The Dialectics of Social Action and System Structuring

TOM BAUMGARTNER, TOM R. BURNS, and PHILIPPE DeVILLÉ

This paper outlines a systems theoretic approach with which to describe and analyze how and under what conditions processes and structures of social systems develop, stabilize, and decay or undergo transformation. Our theoretical perspective draws on and attempts to develop modern systems theory (Ashby, 1957; Buckley, 1967, 1968; Deutsch, 1963; Katz and Kahn, 1966) and game theory (Luce and Raiffa, 1957; Rapoport, 1960; von Neumann and Morgenstern, 1953) as well as Marxist theory and research.

This first part outlines the general assumptions of the *actor-oriented systems analysis.*[1] This approach addresses itself to: (1) systems, including social institutions as sources of constraint and the regulation of social action and interaction, and, in particular, as determinants of the varying opportunities of different actors or classes of actors, and (2) actors and their activities as driving forces for the maintenance and change of system structures and processes, thereby shaping the conditions for social activity. In this sense one may speak of the dialectical relationship between social action and systems. The second part suggests a few applications of such an approach; the third part, key conceptual

SOURCE: A longer version of this paper appears in R. Felix Geyer and Johan van der Zouwen, eds., *Sociocybernetics. An actor-oriented social systems approach.* Martinus Nijhoff Social Sciences Division, Leiden, Boston, London, 1978, vol. 1, pp. 27–54.

elements are presented; and in the fourth part methodological features and research guidelines of the approach are summarized.

ACTORS AND SYSTEMS

Two fundamentally different conceptions of human action underlie most modeling of social behavior and social systems. In one social actors are viewed as the essential force that structures and restructures social systems and the conditions of human activity. The individual, the historic personality, as exemplified by Schumpeter's entrepreneur, enjoys an extensive freedom to act within and upon social systems, and in this sense is independent of them. In the other view, social actors are faceless, rational automata following the iron rules of optimal choice theory in a world of constraints over which they lack any control. This perspective excludes conflicting interests and values, divided loyalties, heterogeneous and incompatible goals, and true uncertainty, which is not the same as probabilistic uncertainty.

To a large extent social systems theories have been based on the second view,[2] reflecting its affinity to systems engineering and, possibly, the influence of the deterministic natural science paradigm. This type of approach tends to deny free decision and action space to human actors, since this leads to indeterminism. System maintenance and reproduction, rather than being treated as problematical, are considered "natural" and taken for granted in system modeling and analysis.[3] Purposeful action to assure system reproduction is seen as unnecessary; struggles to transform social systems are given minimal attention. In addition to addressing itself to system properties and dynamics, social system modeling and analysis can, as we mean to show, entail concepts and a methodology which will specify the decision making and strategic capabilities of actors as purposeful, self-reflective beings. Their relation to system dynamics and stability will also be shown.

In traditional game theory and its various offshoots in the social sciences, games are conceptualized and analyzed as *closed systems.* This neglects an important feature of real-life games, or interaction situations, namely, that actors often can and do attempt to transform unsatisfactory game structures (Buckley et al., 1974).

Actor-oriented systems analysis, while trying to incorporate the valuable analytical approach provided by game theory, treats games as open, multilevel systems of social action. They change and develop. Game structuring and restructuring processes are identified as metalevel operations that can maintain or change components of a game or system of social action. Our investigations of such *game transformation processes* have had two major concerns:

1. To specify and analyze the various constraints on conflict situations or games, and conflict patterns and developments.

2. To ground game analysis in a theory of social action, which, above all, stresses the transformational potentialities and tendencies of such action, in particular the capacity to structure and transform games.

In the first instance attention is given to the ways in which specific aspects of the game context structure and restructure games. In particular, this includes the actors' definition of the social situation, their goals and preferences, available options, and interaction outcomes. In the second instance one investigates the extent to which actors with different social relationships and cultural understandings not only respond and interact differently in the context, for example, of "zero-sum," "prisoners' dilemma," or other objective game conditions,[4] but also the extent to which they act differently on the context, structuring and transforming games. ("Actor" refers not only to individuals, but also to social groups, organizations, communities, and nations.).

ACTOR-ORIENTED SYSTEMS ANALYSIS

This approach takes as its point of departure—and attempts to elucidate—the fundamental duality of the human situation: freedom and determinism. Human individuals and groups are subject to material, social structural, and cultural constraints on their actions, yet they are at the same time creative, active forces who, in part, make their own history. Social science research in general, and social systems analysis in particular, should, in our view, try to avoid the danger of reifying institutions, as well as the danger of assuming human powerlessness in the face of natural and environmental forces, which in any case are partly shaped by human activity. This leads to unjustifiably underestimating the capability of humans to diminish or overcome constraints through creative restructuring (Zeitlin, 1973:257). At the same time, one should not attribute an unrealistic power to human actors to shape and transform their conditions.

The focus on the interrelatedness of freedom and determinism of human action suggests the similarities and differences between Marxist analysis and our approach. Within the Marxist tradition two different approaches to the problem of the reproduction and transformation of the capitalist system were developed. The first, as exemplified by the structuralist formulation of Louis Althusser, is to a large extent a deterministic, causal-explanatory approach. The fundamental structures of the capitalist system are the basis on which system maintenance and system transformation are explained. The structural dominance of one class over the other reproduces itself through a spectrum of economic, ideological-cultural, political and social institutional mechanisms. The structural antagonisms between the classes—continuously generated by the contradictions between the relations and forces of production—are postulated to lead deterministically to a fundamental discontinuity in history, the revolution which destroys the self-reproducing nature of the system. In such a framework purposeful, self-reflective human action is almost totally absent.

In contrast to structuralist Marxism, one finds also within the Marxist tradition a much more idealistic-voluntaristic approach, as is seen, for example, in the works of George Lukács. Here the focus is on proletarian man, who, through adequate consciousness of his own exploitation, assumes the revolutionary nature of his historical role—the abolishment of capitalism—and acts on this basis. The emphasis is on the inherent rationality of the proletarian as "universal man" who is able to transcend the structural contradictions of the capitalist system.

These two poles have yet to be systematically and effectively integrated within Marxist theory. One strategy with which to tackle this problem may be, as suggested here, to relate a systems approach to a more developed *theory of social action.*

Our approach entails the development of methods, concepts, and models suitable for investigating and describing how and under what conditions processes and structures in social systems are formed, reproduced, and transformed. Particular attention is given to incompatibilities and conflicts in the systems and to human intentionality and social action as they are related to system stability and change. System stability, in particular, implies purposeful action to maintain the system, which, in the absence of such activity, would tend to change (DeVillé and Burns, 1977). Such an approach goes beyond the usual assumptions and features of modern systems and cybernetical modeling, which give minimal attention to incompatibility, conflict and structure changing, or transformational tendencies in systems.

Research based on actor-oriented systems analysis has focused particularly on the following:

1. System maintaining (reproduction) and system changing (transforming) processes, that is, structuring processes and their relationship to what are referred to as process-level conditions and activities, e.g. conflict and exchange activities.

2. The capability of social actors to partially structure and restructure social systems and societal development. The dual nature of social action; that is, as a system maintaining and system changing force, is particularly stressed.

3. The simultaneous conflict and harmony of interests among actors in a social system.

STRUCTURING OF SOCIAL SYSTEMS

A social system consists of interdependent spheres of social action, e.g., political and economic spheres or subsystems.[5] System components are linked to one another in the usual causal relationships and feedback loops, as well as through structuring processes and linkages. Structuring generally is an operator on processes, functions, and relationships rather than on variables (Baumgartner et al., 1977a, 1976a). In this sense structuring represents a higher form of determination or causality.

Structuring factors shape and regulate process-level conditions, processes, and activities, that is, the opportunities and constraints, incentives, and meanings within which production, exchange, influence, and conflict, as understood in traditional interaction analysis, take place.[6] Our approach entails specifying the higher order structuring processes and variables and their relation to lower relationships and processes in a social system. We try to formulate a *multi-level model* of social system stability and change, which accounts for particular system structures and processes in different contexts or in different time periods.

Some key structuring factors examined in our research are the following:

1. Deliberate human action and planning, the exercise of metapower and relational control by social actors.

2. Cultural and ideational factors.

3. Structuring processes as unintended or secondary consequences of social action.

4. Technology and material conditions.

5. Uncontrolled or exogenous natural and social conditions, such as climatic and international factors, respectively.

We present examples of our investigation and analysis, to suggest the concrete applicability of the approach, as well as to point up properties of social relations and processes which are structured. Structuring through the manipulation or management of systems of social action is particularly stressed.

STRUCTURING OF CONFLICT AND COOPERATION

Here we have tried to describe and analyze social conflict, which is the possible involvement of multiple actors (with varying perspectives and interests) at different levels and in different spheres of social action, the formation of new collective actors, and the fragmentation or collapse of others (Baumgartner et al., 1975b, 1977b, 1978c). In general the form, course, and outcome of conflict processes depend on contextual factors such as the following (Baumgartner et al., 1978c; Coleman, 1957; Deutsch, 1973; Kriesberg, 1973; Simmel, 1964):

1. The type of social relations the actors have or develop, in particular, the extent to which they have solidary relations, the number and strength of cooperative linkages.

2. The normative and value context of a conflict—specifically, the extent to which the actors share a common vision or image of the appropriate institutional framework or rules within which conflicts are to be settled.

3. The social matrix, for instance, cross-cutting identifications, common allegiances and memberships, and above all, the likelihood of effective third-party intervention and structuring of the conflict process.

Established social relationships are a major factor in structuring conditions and activities on the process level. Consider a conflict, for instance, between management and labor in the context of a production setting, where no outcome acceptable to both sides appears feasible within the existing set of options, rules of the game, or other institutional conditions. Typically, in such a case, actors try to generate new options, change game rules, or restructure institutional features. At least two families of transformation pattern may be distinguished. On the one hand, if the relationships between the actors are antagonistic, each will try to increase his or her chances of gaining ground or avoiding losses at the expense of others in the situation. Mutually satisfying conflict settlements will be unlikely in such cases. This contributes to reproduction of the antagonistic social relations. On the other hand, if the actors have solidary social relations, they will probably cooperate in transforming conflict situations so as to obtain mutually satisfactory outcomes and, thereby, reinforce and reproduce their solidary relationships. If actors share a common set of values and norms guiding the structuring and restructuring of institutional arrangements, they can probably agree to an institutional change to settle a conflict which does not appear resolvable within the existing institutional set-up. Third parties may intervene to transform game conditions and rules either to develop or resolve conflict. The conflict-settlement role is frequently institutionalized, as in many industrial and industrializing societies, where the state intervenes and regulates capital/labor interactions and disputes and also other potentially conflicting relationships through the use of legislation, mediation, and arbitration, as well as other strategies,[7] (e.g., see our analysis of the Lip factory conflict [Besançon, France]) which shows the effect of a specific social structural context (government, the judicial system, powerful industrial interests, and national labor unions) on the course and outcome of an escalating management/labor conflict (Baumgartner et al., 1978c).

STRUCTURING OF POWER SYSTEMS

Actor-oriented systems analysis has been applied to the study of the structuring and restructuring of systems of stratification (e.g., Alker et al., 1978; Baumgartner et al., 1978a,b; Burns, 1976). This approach to the study of social power entails investigation and analysis of structuring processes which have led historically to the emergence and development of social control hierarchies and more systemic forms of power. The research focuses on (1) positive feedback loops that link initial power differences to differential accumulation of power resources among actors or categories of actors, and (2) the contexts of such feedback loops, as, for example, in situations where opportunities for subordinate actors and groups to withdraw or emigrate are minimal, or where possibilities for subordinate actors to communicate, organize, and act collectively to constrain accumulation processes are absent or problematical.

Social differentiation among actors in a social system in terms of resource control and action capability typically contributes to differential accumulation of resources through processes of social interaction (exchange, conflict, and influence processes).[8] Small initial differences in positional advantage and resource control may be amplified into major institutionalized class structures. These developments, combined with intersocietal exchange, competition, and conflict, tend to reinforce internal and external social stratification. Such processes have been examined in our research in relation to the emergence and development of the state and empire (Baumgartner et al., 1976b). The overall process entails the differential accumulation and uneven development of action capabilities and resource control among actors; it may take the following characteristic forms, among others:

1. Initial differences in action possibilities or in resource control among actors lead to unequal payoffs through conflict, exchange, and influence processes (or social interaction generally), and the unequal payoffs make for future differentials in action capabilities and resource control. This is particularly the case where there is little or no institutional or normative regulation to prevent or limit such amplification.

2. These differences in action capabilities and resource control translate into differential probabilities for further accumulation. For instance, advantaged actors can generate or exploit new action or exchange opportunities, prevent or control negative consequences or developments, structure themselves and their environments to their advantage, and produce, maintain, and change social networks and social institutions to their own benefit. They can transgress or overcome institutionalized and normative constraints on power accumulation.

By using their power to define the rules of the game and to shape the matrix of action possibilities and payoffs, they can attract supporters and weaken opponents. Supporters and dependents, in turn, can be used on yet a larger scale in exercising and structuring power and relational control. Ultimately, an elite or power group A in such a position may be able to construct and control a hierarchical system of loyal or compliant supporters or participants. At the same time A and his agents may, through divide-and-rule strategies, erode or weaken competing or opposing segments of society and the structures and processes which they control. In this way conditions and processes which might countervail and restrict A's power and power development are socially impeded or regulated.

3. As a result of processes such as those described in 1. and 2., A gains advantages in systemic power relative to competing or potentially competing groups. A highly differentiated social structure and network system under A's hegemony emerges and develops.

Such a positive feedback loop between initial power differences and differential accumulation of resources and societal power occurs in different social structural, material, and cultural contexts (Baumgartner et al., 1976b). Below, we try to specify a few of these settings or contexts:

a. Where increasing surplus resources are available, for example, by virtue of the expansion of production (through new technology, increases in the labor force or in other factors of production), territorial conquest, trade expansion, or new bases for legitimizing taxation.

b. Where ownership and inheritance rules and rights (as opposed to norms of redistribution and corrective institutional devices to limit or prevent accumulation processes) sustain and legitimize differential accumulation of resources. A power group or elite A often uses an initial power advantage to strengthen ownership and inheritance concepts and practices.

c. Where weaker actors lack group consciousness and organization or control over important resources, and thus are not in a position to oppose the accumulation processes or the restructuring of social conditions by the power group or elite A. Processes and conditions which fragment or weaken opposition groups permit a process of power accumulation to continue or even to accelerate. Of course, powerful actors may initiate or maintain such conditions of fragmentation through divide and rule strategies (see footnote 7).

d. Where demographic movements across societal boundaries amplify the power of A. The import of persons or groups who are or become dependent on A can contribute to A's power to organize collective action within the society. A's power position also is improved and stabilized by the emigration or exile of opposition persons and groups who countervail or restrict A's power and its development,[9] provided the resulting loss of population does not undermine significantly the economic base of the society. Such emigration opens up opportunities for the selective recruitment and promotion of loyal persons and groups into political and economic roles vacated by emigrants (Hardin, 1976).

e. Where social hierarchization is facilitated by constraints on the emigration (or withdrawal) possibilities of subordinate individuals and groups, whose productive capabilities and resources are not replaceable. For instance, historically, the emergence and development of classical state and empire formations have been associated with a dense growing population practicing agriculture in a fertile region which is circumscribed geographically or socially (Caneiro, 1970; Baumgartner et al., 1976b).

Military, economic, or other constraints enable their labor and the products of their labor to be mobilized and appropriated by those in superior positions. Such constraint may also arise from physical environments. For example an ecological setting of fertile lands suitable for farming surrounded by infertile, arid, or mountainous areas, constrained farming populations, at least in early history, from leaving the area. The constraints also may be structural in nature: members of a community are prevented from moving to neighboring areas or alternative territorial systems by the presence of other ethnic, religious, national, or cultural groups capable of blocking passage, or there are powerful incentives to stay close to allies or potential allies for protection in case of attack. Sometimes an area, relative to its surrounding areas, is highly developed or abundant with resources and economically ties persons or groups to it. Religious beliefs may tie them to an area.

The establishment of national frontiers has been a major instrument of structuralization (Finer, 1975; Baumgartner et al., 1976b, 1975d; Schumacher, 1973). Societal boundary control to prevent or inhibit migratory movements is maintained by the administrative and police powers of a more or less well-developed state. This may also entail limitations on internal movement.[10]

If subordinate actors are able to exit—to use the metaphor of Hirschman (1970)—then an elite is limited to manipulating payoff structures and making normative appeals in order to establish and maintain hierarchical structures and to accomplish its ends. But power based on the manipulation of payoffs does not usually provide opportunities to establish *absolute* domination.

If in a particular social context, A has sole access to valuable resources, e.g., trade, slaves, land, or money, then A can establish social relationships in which subordinate actors are to some extent dependent on those resources. If there are alternative sources of the resources ultimately available—frontier land or other social systems or collectivities to migrate to or to participate in—then it is impossible for A to absolutize the relationships, since the use of the resources is still limited to the manipulation of payoffs.[11] For subordinate actors in this case, submission to A's power is marginally better than attempting to obtain the necessary goods from another source. An element of choice is still involved: if A pushes B (or the Bs) too far, the latter simply leaves. Hence, hierarchical structure will tend to be limited in the degree of stability it achieves. This suggests that differential control over resources in and of itself is not a sufficient condition to create lasting power structures. In the absence of real scarcity, it is difficult, if not impossible, to structure systems of extreme social domination or hierarchy in any permanent way be means of using resources-for-inducement.[12]

To the extent that A's resource accumulation and power development depends on the production of resources by B, which A then appropriates—for example through unequal exchange—then opportunities for Bs to emigrate limit accumulation and stratification *to a level which B finds acceptable or tolerates.* One may argue that, *in general, the more readily subordinate actors have access to basic resources outside of an A/B superordinate–subordinate system of relationships, the less A will be able to dominate B, exploit his labor or the products of his labor, and develop hierarchical control structures.*

In sum, geographic and technologic conditions, as well as those of a social structural and ideological character, contribute to shaping the formation and development of social structure. In our framework this is seen to take place by their facilitating or constraining action opportunities and influencing payoffs, particularly in a manner so as to differentiate groups in society. Again, emphasis should be placed on how elites and power groups themselves try to manipulate social action and interaction conditions in order to structure social relationships, processes, and their behavioral consequences in a manner favorable to themselves. The evolution of higher-level social control strategies, techniques, and institutions has occurred through the discovery by individuals and groups of various methods of control, as well as the development of the ability to adopt methods discovered by others. Of particular interest in this regard has been the development of more sophisticated strategies for planning, metamanagement, and integration of multiple social structures and networks.

CONCEPTUAL AND METHODOLOGICAL FEATURES

Several general theoretical and methodological premises provide a point of departure for the actor-oriented systems approach. These are considered basic to any attempt at model building and analysis in the social sciences. Although the discussion which follows is abstract, the concepts and principles suggest specific guidelines for the construction of models of social structures and processes.

SYSTEMS OF SOCIAL ACTION

Social action systems consist of patterned social action and interaction, which are shaped and influenced by material, social structural, and cultural constraints at the same time that they produce, reproduce, and transform. Such systems are characterized by the following components:

1. A set of actors.

2. Activity, problem or issue area(s) with respect to which the actors have certain interests and goals (not necessarily compatible).

3. Rules, norms, guiding concepts, and assumptions ("the rules of the game") defining the situation, and the type of game the actors are to play.

4. Interests and goals of the actors in relation to one another in the context of the activity area, their evaluative bases, and perceptual models in the situation.

5. The distribution of action and interaction possibilities, including resource control, among different actors or categories of actors.

6. The likely outcomes or costs and benefits, including spinoff and spillover effects, of actions and interactions for different actors or categories of actors.

INTERRELATEDNESS OF THINGS

A social system consists of interdependent spheres of social action and subsystems which are partially autonomous with respect to one another. Such systems possess properties and modes of action distinct from those of the constituent elements. Social processes, actions, and interactions have multiple and varied ramifications, because actors and resources are constituent elements of two or more spheres of social action (e.g., economic, political, social, and cultural subsystems). Thus, social processes of production and distribution generate multiple effects, spinoffs and spillovers. This is the basis of the multistranded linkages among spheres and subsystems and of the unintended consequences of purposeful human action.[13]

POWER, METAPOWER, AND DEVELOPMENT

Property rights, and control rights more generally, and the different positions and roles of actors or classes of actors in social systems give them qualitatively and quantitatively different relationships to the socially valued products (including their spinoffs and spillovers) of social activity. These valuables include not only material goods and resources, but also labor power, knowledge and capabilities, and social characteristics such as status, authority, and charisma.

Control over valuables provides controlling actors with power and metapower. Power is the ability of actors to bring about or influence social actions and outcomes favorable to their interests within an institutionalized social action context. Metapower or structuring power is the ability to influence and structure an institutionalized framework of social action. The exercise of metapower entails the manipulation or change of rules of the game, distribution of resources and action possibilities, interaction outcomes, and cultural orientations—in general, the conditions of social action in a particular system.

Structuring of Systems

A social system is not necessarily well-integrated and self-regulating. Rather, societal processes and forces within and between spheres may often operate in opposition to one another. Attainment of stability in one subsystem may produce instability in other subsystems. Achievement of a goal or objective in one part can mean failure to achieve goals or objectives in other parts. Thus, the system, when viewed as a complex, dynamic totality, is rarely, if ever, in equilibrium. System stability must be explained in the face of ever-present tendencies for structures to reform, change, or evolve. The stress is therefore on the transformation potentialities and tendencies of social systems in a dynamic world of flux.

Structuring factors, whether arising from a social system's environment, system-environment dynamics, or internal dynamics of the system affect directly or indirectly multiple factors, components, or subsystems of the social system; multiple components or subsystems differentially; and often in *incompatible or contradictory ways*. Multiple effects are produced, and some of these work at cross-purposes or in opposition to one another, as, for instance, when tending both to maintain and to change system properties at the same time. In such ways changes in material, social structural, cultural or social features of a social system produce divergent developments.

Dialectical processes in social systems also entail contradictory or conflicting social processes as well as dialogue-like competing social forces.[14] Contradictory processes entail two or more processes or structuring factors which come into relation to one another and work inconsistently or at cross-purposes. It is possible for the same process to do this by generating multiple effects, some of which work in opposition to one another. The role of human cognition and reflection in social processes also suggests that contradictions be interpreted literally to include as well oppositions in symbolically communicated principles of social organization.

SOCIAL REPRODUCTION AND TRANSFORMATION

Social systems are the products of human action. They are artificial, and subject to continual pressures to transform. Maintenance of system stability, therefore, requires continual reproductive and structuring activities in response to system contradictions, patterns of conflict, and changes in system environments.[15] We speak of social reproduction when stability or continuity of characteristic social structures and processes occur. This entails not only their maintenance during a given time period but also the production or acquisition of necessary and possible sufficient resources for their perpetuation in subsequent time periods. Thus, social reproduction depends on replacing the instruments or other means of activity (production) as well as on the maintenance and replacement of actors (reproduction of labor power). It also involves structuring the context of social activity, e.g., in the case of economic production, the structuring of the political, and sociocultural spheres.

Social reproduction depends on three factors (Burns, 1976):

1. Possession on the part of actors engaged in structuring activity of a model of society to guide activities involved in reproducing a particular social structure, process, or other feature.

2. Interest and commitment on their part to mobilize and use resources in the reproduction process.

3. Sufficient resources, capabilities, and power and metapower to carry out effective reproduction.

The metapower capability of actors to initiate and control processes of producing and reproducing institutional arrangements has, of course, to be itself reproduced, and, in a changing environment, typically requires adapting models, interests, and resource capabilities. Even so, power and metapower redistributions, continuous environmental interference, and a contradictory integration of subsystems may make reproduction impossible. Often there are unintended consequences of the policies and actions of dominant groups. Such contradictions may emerge because the model used by the actors does not enable evaluation of conditions and processes which erode the system; that is, new possibilities of social action emerge which are *incompatible* with the existing institutional set-up.

Incentives may tempt actors into the pursuit of interests or activities incompatible with the maintenance and reproduction of the system. Frequently, actors become engaged in other institutional areas and social relationships which make competing claims on their loyalties and interests. This then erodes their commitment to or interest in social reproduction of a particular institutional set-up. Finally, the actors may lack the action capability or powers to carry out effective structuring activities in the face of restructuring forces or action on the part of others. In particular, when shifts in power favor those with a different model or blueprint of the system, and those actors perceive a net gain in bringing about a change, restructuring will occur against the will of those committed to the previous institutional set-up.[16]

Institutionalized social relationships and social relational ideology, the basis for which actors expect certain patterns of behavior from one another and are disposed to interact in patterned ways, shape concrete interaction settings among actors by structuring action opportunities, payoffs, and social orientations of the actors to one another. At the same time the social relationships and ideology may be incompatible with the very interactions they produce in the concrete action settings.

The established or institutionalized social relationships and relational ideology only partially determine the conditions of action and interaction. Other social factors, as well as material conditions (geographical, climatical, technological, and other aspects of the physical environment) outside the domain or control inherent in the social relationships and relational ideology, structure and influence action and interaction patterns.[17]

The relationships between human actors and the social and cultural worlds, and their products, is a dialectical one. Human institutions, which may appear "objective and overwhelming" are a humanly constructed objectivity (Godelier, 1973). Rules and institutional arrangements are more or less open to frequent reinterpretation, reappraisal, and reconstruction for practical purposes, while at the same time they shape action possibilities and consequences, often in unintended ways. Thus, they become an impersonal power—much like the natural environment—although they have been created and are maintained through human activities.

CONFLICT AND SOCIAL TRANSFORMATION

As already suggested, social systems cannot be assumed to be well integrated and automatically self-regulating. Divergent developments will occur, and conflicting social forces will operate in any social system. Different social actors and classes are likely to be associated in differing degrees and in qualitatively different ways to the discordant developments. Those adversely affected by the operation or development of the institutional set-up may be able to socially articulate their disadvantage and deprivation, e.g., in terms of norms and values about fairness or equity or on other ideological grounds. They may also organize and mobilize to carry out collective action to change the institutional set-up. These activities usually bring them into conflict with those having an interest or commitment to system reproduction. Such conflict can interfere with reproduction processes, setting the stage for social transformation.

CONTEXTUAL ANALYSIS AND MULTILEVEL MODELING

The language and methodological approach developed and used in our work describes and analyzes system stability and change.[18] Two general principles underlie the approach:

1. In social life the existence of space and time invariances or lawful connections cannot be taken for granted (Herbst, 1971; Baumgartner et al., 1977a). Human systems are typically self-transforming systems as opposed to being mechanical systems.

2. Changes in social system processes and structures can best be conceptualized, modeled, and analyzed from a multilevel perspective.

Since a social process often takes the specific form it does because of its context, it will undergo transformations as a result of changes in context. Of particular interest are rules and patterns of social action and interaction which are dependent on specific settings. Such a contextual approach to the study of social phenomena calls for the development of models and tools which can show the specific ways in which contexts structure or operate on the phenomena. For this purpose we use multilevel concepts and models.

A multilevel system or process is composed of subsystems, one or more of which stand in subordinate relationship to a dominant variable, process, or subsystem. The latter regulates, operates upon, or changes the relationships or processes at the lower level, for example, by changing the parameters or coefficients of such relationships or the relationships themselves. The system-changing and system-maintaining tendencies are seen as outputs either of metalevel processes or of lower subsystems structuring the processes, relationships, and parameters. The metalevel processes may actually depend on or be influenced either by system inputs or outputs or developments inherent to the system, that is, by lower-level events or processes.

We have suggested a fairly general and systematic framework for organizing and understanding social processes and events. Our particular action-oriented systems analysis is offered as a useful beginning; it appears to organize a large mass of often unrelated data and is compatible with the more dynamic and structural theories of social science. Some readers may prefer a larger and more refined set of system components, and we hope that they may be inspired to develop them and carry further the present and obviously limited effort.

NOTES

We are grateful to Walter Buckley, Eivind Jahren, and Scott G. McNall for their comments and suggestions on an earlier draft.

1. A number of published papers developing and applying various concepts of actor-oriented systems analysis are listed in the references under Alker, Baumgartner, Buckley, Burns, DeVillé and Meeker.

2. Important exceptions to the general pattern are found in the works of Buckley (1967) and Geyer (1974, 1977).

3. This type of approach tends to separate system processes and structures. Although consideration may be given to how environment (and structure) determine processes, the processes and their outputs, in turn, are rarely seen to affect or transform the structures through dynamic feedback and feed-forward linkages. This is the case, for example, with economic growth models, whose mathematical structure remains unaffected by model output. Similarly, macro-economic models have to be frequently re-estimated, particularly during periods of actual structural transformations, so that newer data "bends" coefficients, at least somewhat, in the right direction (Baumgartner et al., 1977a, 1976a).

4. Objective game situations are defined by the rules of the game, e.g., rules concerning communication and the making of binding agreements, by the action and interaction possibilities, and their outcomes.

5. The abstract concept of a system is defined as a set of elements or components together with the set of relationships and processes connecting the elements. The network of linkages between elements is the organization of the system.

6. Structure-level processes may themselves be structured by metalevel processes. In general, factors, relationships among variables, and processes in a social system depend on the context in which they occur (See Parts 3 and 4).

7. Third-party intervention aimed at maintaining or developing competitive or conflict processes is observable in divide-and-rule strategies such as are used by governments in anticartel regulation of markets. This entails determining the "rules of the game"; structuring the aggregate action and interaction possibilities of those involved in the situation, by, for instance, limiting their opportunities to associate or communicate; structuring the gains and losses associated with particular interactions in order to promote conflict or competition, as in the creation of payoff structures such as "zero-sum" or "prisoners' dilemma"; or it can entail promoting distrust among the actors or an individualistic self-interest ideology (Burns and Buckley, 1974; Buckley et al., 1974).

This study of the social structuring of conflict relationships has focused on an investigation of the use of divide-and-rule strategies of differing degrees of sophistication in several social contexts. Although many historical and contemporary processes can be examined in such terms, slave, factory, and imperialist systems have provided particularly fruitful areas for this type of investigation (Baumgartner et al., 1975b; 1977f). We have also tried to explore how accidentally or historically derived social fragmentation may contribute to the maintenance of a system of domination.

8. For example, a common pattern in the historical emergence of the state is the availability and acquisition by the central leadership of surplus resources which can be used for purposes of societal structuring. Typically, the center is enabled to attract and support a body of followers and dependents, using resources gained through warfare, trade and other economic activity, political alliance as well as various legitimation devices. The followers and dependents are the "king's men," supporting him and executing his will. Through them he gains the possibility of extending his capability to obtain additional resources (through taxation, tribute, territorial conquest, etc.) and to carry out structuring activities.

9. For example, the export of warriors in the early Norman states (twelfth and thirteenth centuries) may have contributed to stable internal structure. Also, emigration to the United States probably reduced internal turbulence in nineteenth-century Europe and facilitated the trend to stable representative democracies.

10. Groups within the society may oppose the socially imposed constraints on the freedom of movement of particular groups or persons, since such conditions affect the distribution of power in society. Such opposition strengthens the stratification in some domains and possibly weakens it in others.

Resources are required to carry out such boundary control, and hence, represent costs not borne by societies which have naturally occurring environmental constraints or social constraints arising exogenously (hostile or alien neighbors). These differences often have long-term economic and political implications.

11. The unavailability of alternative sources is equivalent to monopoly over the distribution of resources. This constrains the action possibilities of those lacking such resource control; in other words, they lack the alternative of going outside the system to realize their goals or needs. Dominant actors also try to make subordinates believe that there is no viable alternative source of the necessary resources.

12. There are degrees of replaceability. In a more complete discussion, one would have to take up general demographic factors.

13. Subsystems and spheres of social action in a social system are partially autonomous with respect to one another, that is, they are differentiated from one another at the same time that linkages and interactions, particularly structuring linkages, are found among them. In this way they provide context for one another. Therefore, changes in one or more subsystems produce changes in context of other context-dependent subsystems. Changes in the context of a system may be incompatible with the maintenance of that system.

14. Incompatible processes may have the character of dominant and recessive tendencies, which are simultaneously embodied in a particular social system or its different subsystems. Dialectically transformative restructurings, somewhat like Hegelian syntheses, may then be thought of as relatively sudden switches in positions of dominance of such co-occurring tendencies or organizing principles.

15. The development of social systems and their institutions depends to a substantial degree on two basic dialectical relationships: the relationship between human societies and nature, or the physical or biological environments on which societies depend; and the dialectical relationships between actors in and between societies. Humans' necessary contacts with their natural environment create the conditions for this environment to shape their action and interaction possibilities and experience. In turn human consciousness and activity shape the natural environment, often in unintended ways.

16. Such power shifts may be initiated in a variety of ways. All have in common the failure of existing institutional arrangements and dominant groups to fully control innovations, resource distributions, and development of action capabilities which are incompatible with the existing social structure and systems of social action. These developments often occur as a result of events or changes external to the system, but they also emerge through the logic of internal system development, that is, where the seeds of destruction are contained within the existing system, for instance, as in the case of system growth leading to resource exhaustion and shifts in control over remaining resources (Burns, 1976).

17. Ideologies and models of social action reflect, to some extent, physical and social environments and may serve as guidelines for the structuring and transformation of such environments. But social action itself may, in turn, alter the physical and social environments in such a way as to contradict the model that gave rise to action in the first place.

18. Much of contemporary social science methodology is predicated on the assumption of closed, structure-maintaining systems for which laws and principles are invariant. Data analysis is often limited to a time span of observation that permits the transformational potentialities of social systems to remain undetectable (that is, relationships among variables appear to be stable). If the time span allows detection, the models in which data are used tend to overlook instability. In many instances, the very choice of time and research setting will determine whether, and to what degree, there is apparent system closure and structural stability.

REFERENCES

ALKER, H., JR., T. BAUMGARTNER, and T. R. BURNS
   1978   "Center/periphery relationships in the world system." Alternatives: A Journal of World Policy, in preparation.
   1976   "Introduction and overview." In T. R. Burns and W. Buckley (ed.), Power and Control: Social Structures and Their Transformation. London and Beverly Hills: Sage.

146   BAUMGARTNER, BURNS, AND DEVILLÉ

ASHBY, W. R.
1957 An Introduction to Cybernetics. New York: Wiley.
BAUMGARTNER, T.
1976 The Political Economy of International Economic Exchange and Devel-
      opment: A Systems Approach to the Structuring of the International
      Economic System. Ph.D. dissertation. University of New Hampshire,
      Durham.
BAUMGARTNER T., W. BUCKLEY, and T. R. BURNS
1975 "Relational control: the human structuring of cooperation and con-
      flict." Journal of Conflict Resolution, 19:417–440.
BAUMGARTNER, T., W. BUCKLEY, and T. R. BURNS
1976 "Unequal exchange and uneven development." Studies in Comparative
      International Development, 11:51–72.
1975 "Meta-power and relational control in social life." Social Science Infor-
      mation, 14:49–78.
BAUMGARTNER, T., W. BUCKLEY, T. R. BURNS, and P. SCHUSTER
1976 "Meta-power and the structuring of social hierarchies." In T. R. Burns
      and W. Buckley (eds.), Power and Control. London and Beverly Hills:
      Sage.
BAUMGARTNER, T., and T. R. BURNS
1977 Wildcat Strikes: The Cases of Sweden and Switzerland. Scandinavian
      Institutes of Administrative Research, Research Report. Lund, Sweden.
1975 "The structuring of international economic relations." International
      Studies Quarterly, 19:126–159.
BAUMGARTNER, T., T. R. BURNS, and P. DEVILLÉ
1978a "Work, politics and structuring under capitalism." In T. R. Burns, L.
      E. Karlsson, and V. Rus (eds.), The Liberation of Work and Political
      Power. London: Sage, in preparation.
1978b "Conflict resolution and conflict development: a theory of game restruc-
      turing with an application to the LIP conflict." In L. Kriesberg (ed),
      Research in Social Movements, Conflict and Change. Greenwich, JAI.
1977a "The oil crisis and the emerging world order: the structuring of institu-
      tions and rule-making in the international system." Alternatives: A
      Journal of World Policy, 3:75–108.
1977b "Autogestion and planning: dilemmas and possibilities." Paper pre-
      sented at the Second International Conference on Participation, Work-
      ers' Control and Self-Management. Paris.
1977c "Divide et Impera." Unpublished manuscript.
1975 "Middle East scenarios and international restructuring: conflict and
      challenge." Bulletin of Peace Proposals, 6:364–378.
BAUMGARTNER, T., T. R. BURNS, P. DEVILLÉ, and D. MEEKER
1975a "A systems model of conflict and change in planning systems." General
      Systems Yearbook, 20:167–183.
BAUMGARTNER, T., T. R. BURNS, and D. MEEKER
1977 "The description and analysis of system stability and transformation:
      multi-level concepts and methodology." Quality and Quantity 11.

BAUMGARTNER, T., T. R. BURNS, D. MEEKER, and B. WILD
  1976 "Open systems and multi-level processes: implications for social research." International Journal of General Systems, 3:25–42.
BAUMGARTNER, T., T. R. BURNS, and D. SEKULIE
  1978 "Self-management, markets and political institutions in conflict." In T. R. Burns, L. E. Karlsson, and V. Rus (eds.), The Liberation of Work and Political Power. London: Sage, in preparation.
BUCKLEY, W.
  1967 Sociology and Modern Systems Theory. Englewood Cliffs, N.J.: Prentice-Hall.
  1968 Modern Systems Research for the Behavioral Scientists. Chicago: Aldine.
BUCKLEY, W., T. R. BURNS, and D. MEEKER
  1974 "Structural resolutions of collective action problems." Behavioral Science, 19:277–297.
BURNS, T. R.
  1977 "Unequal exchange and uneven development in social life: Continuities in a structural theory of social exchange. Acta Sociologica, 20:217–245.
  1976 Dialectics of Social Systems: Their Reproduction and Transformation. Working Papers Nr. 50. Oslo: University of Oslo, Institute of Sociology.
BURNS, T. R., and W. BUCKLEY
  1974 "The prisoners' dilemma game as a system of social domination." Journal of Peace Research, 11:221–228.
BURNS, T. R., and D. MEEKER
  1977 "Conflict and structure in multi-level, multiple objective decision-making systems." In C. A. Hooker (ed.), Foundations and Applications of Decision Theory. Dordreen-Holland: Reidel.
CANEIRO, R. L.
  1970 "A theory of the origin of the state." Science, 169:733–738.
COLEMAN, J. S.
  1957 Community Conflict. Glencoe, Ill.: Free Press.
DEVILLÉ, P., and T. R. BURNS
  1977 "Institutional responses to crisis in capitalist development: A dialectical systems approach." Social Praxis, 4:5–46.
DEUTSCH, K. W.
  1963 The Nerves of Government. New York: Free Press.
DEUTSCH, M.
  1973 The Resolution of Conflict: Constructive and Destructive Processes. New Haven and London: Yale University Press.
FINER, S.
  1975 "State building, state boundaries, and border control." Social Science Information, 13:79–126.
GEYER, R. F.
  1977 "Individual alienation and information processing: a systems theory conceptualization." In pp. 189–223 of R. F. Geyer and D. Schweitzer (eds.), Theories of Alienation—Critical Perspectives in Philosophy and the Social Sciences. Hague: Martinus Nijhof.

1974 "Alienation and General Systems Theory." Sociologica Neerlandica 10:18–40.

GODELIER, M.
1973 Rationality and Irrationality in Economics. New York: Monthly Review.

HARDIN, H.
1976 "Stability of statist regimes: industrialization and institutionalization." In pp. 147–168 of T. R. Burns and W. Buckley (eds.), Power and Control. London: Sage.

HERBST, P.
1971 Behavioral Worlds. London: Tavistock.

HIRSCHMAN, A. O.
1970 Exit, Voice and Loyalty. Cambridge, Mass.: Harvard University Press.

KATZ, D., and R. KAHN
1966 The Social Psychology of Organizations. New York, Wiley.

KRIESBERG, L.
1973 Sociology of Social Conflicts. Englewood Cliffs, N.J.: Prentice-Hall.

LUCE, R. D., and H. RAIFFA
1957 Games and Decisions. New York: Wiley.

MURPHY, R.
1971 The Dialectics of Social Life. New York: Basic Books.

RAPOPORT, A.
1960 Fights, Games and Debates. Ann Arbor: University of Michigan Press.

SCHUHMACHER, E. F.
1973 Small is Beautiful. New York: Harper & Row.

SIMMEL, G.
1964 The Sociology of Georg Simmel (ed.), K. H. Wolff. New York: Free Press.

ZEITLIN, I.
1973 Rethinking Sociology: A Critique of Contemporary Theory. Englewood Cliffs, N.J.: Prentice-Hall.

VON NEUMANN, J., and O. MORGENSTERN
1953 Theory of Games and Economic Behavior, 3rd ed., Princeton, N.J.: Princeton University Press.

3. A Strategy of Pure Sociology

DONALD BLACK

Science is the study of variation. Variation is also known as behavior, as in the behavior of matter in physics, molecules and compounds in chemistry, plants and animals in biology, or persons in psychology. In its pure form, each branch of science is a study of a particular kind of variation in its own terms. Pure physics ignores chemical and biological variation as such, for instance, and so does pure psychology. Accordingly, sociology is the study of the behavior of social life, and pure sociology is the study of this behavior without regard to biological, psychological, or other variation (compare, e.g., Ward, 1903).

The purpose of this paper is to outline a strategy of pure sociology. The strategy first appeared in a study of law (Black, 1976), but it applies to other phenomena as well. It takes for granted that social life of every kind is, in principle, measurable as a quantitative variable. It also takes for granted the importance of formulations that predict and explain as much variation as possible, as simply as possible. It does not, however, include a number of assumptions and implications about people as such, and about society as such, now found in social science. It has no concept of human nature, for example. It neither assumes nor implies that people are rational, goal-directed, pleasure-seeking, or pain-avoiding. It has nothing to say about how people experience themselves, their freedom of choice, or the causes of their actions. And it does not assume

SOURCE: This paper was presented at the 73rd Annual Meeting of the American Sociological Association, San Francisco, California, September, 1978.

149

150   DONALD BLACK

or imply that social life is a system with needs and functions (compare, e.g., Radcliffe-Brown, 1935), that it rests upon a consensus or tends toward equilibrium (compare, e.g., Parsons, 1951), or that conflict, coercion, or change inheres in it (compare, e.g., Dahrendorf, 1959:157–165; 1968). It does not assume or imply that society as a whole, or any segment of society, ultimately benefits from any kind of social life. It is a way to predict and explain the behavior of social life, and that is all.

SOCIAL SPACE

In science of all kinds, a major strategy is to predict behavior with the setting in which it occurs. When deduced from a general statement, and successful, this may be understood as explanation (see, e.g., Braithwaite, 1953; Hempel, 1965; Homans, 1967: Chapter 1). Thus, it is possible to predict and explain behavior with every aspect of its environment, that is, with its location and direction in space, whether physical, biological, or psychological space, past or present. All else constant, the distance from the earth predicts and explains its velocity of a falling object, for example; temperature and pressure predict and explain the volume of a gas; conditions for reproduction predict and explain the population of a species; and the training of a child predicts and explains his or her personality as an adult. This strategy has been followed in the study of social life as well, but for the most part it has been implicit if not unconscious, without a program of its own, without its own imagery, concepts, and questions.

Social life is a reality in its own right, a space with dimensions of its own, with locations, directions, and distances defined by human interaction itself. Social space includes vertical. horizontal, symbolic, corporate, and normative dimensions, each describing social life in its own terms. Each is itself variable across social settings, from an encounter between two persons to a gang or organization, from a household to a neighborhood, community, or society. And each predicts and explains the behavior of social life.

Vertical Space

The vertical dimension of social space is present wherever people have an uneven distribution of wealth, or stratification. When they do, their social life may be described by its vertical location, whether it is higher or lower in the distribution of wealth. Is there more crime higher or lower in the distribution of wealth, for instance, or more religion, friendship, or sport? In addition, a social phenomenon may have a vertical direction, moving downward from a higher to a lower location, or upward from lower to higher. A particular crime may be upward or downward, for example, and the same applies to a gift, vote, request, or protest. And apart from the vertical direction of a phenomenon, the difference in wealth itself, or vertical distance, is also variable. Whether it is higher or lower in a distribution of wealth, or downward or upward in its direction, a crime may span a greater or lesser distance in vertical space. The vertical dimension of social space includes other aspects as well, such as the shape of a distribution of wealth, its degree of segmentation, range, origin, stability, and age.

Horizontal Space

The horizontal dimension is defined by the distribution of people in relation to each other, or social morphology. It includes any division of labor across people, or differentiation. It also includes the pattern by which people participate in social life itself, as by working, raising children, or simply by conversing with their neighbors. Every activity describes a circle of participation, with people closer or farther from the center, and, accordingly, every social phenomenon has a radial location. It may also have a direction in radial space, moving in a centripetal or a centrifugal direction, inward or outward from the center, as when a marginal person complains about someone who is more integrated, or vice versa. The difference in integration, or radial distance, varies as well. Another aspect of horizontal space is intimacy, or relational distance, measured by the degree to which people participate in each others' lives, the scope of their interaction, its frequency, duration, and their proximity in a wider network. The structure of intimacy varies in many ways, and its history varies as well.

Symbolic Space

The symbolic dimension of social space is known by expressions of all kinds, aesthetic, intellectual, and moral, whether arts, ideas, ideologies, religions, languages, or ceremonies. This is culture, and it is a space of its own. If the total quantity of culture is unevenly distributed, for instance, so that one person or group has more than another, a social phenomenon may be described by its location in this distribution, and by the direction and distance in this space that might be involved. The location of a phenomenon may also be more or less conventional, measured by the relative frequency of its culture. Again a direction and distance in cultural space might be involved, from more to less conventionality or from less to more, as in an election where a member of the cultural mainstream votes for a minority member, or vice versa. Still another distance in cultural space is known by the content of culture, apart from its quantity or frequency. For example, a Hindu is more distant from a Protestant or a Catholic than is either of these from the other. Just as there is religious distance of this kind, there is also aesthetic, intellectual, and linguistic distance, even culinary and musical distance, with every expression of culture closer or farther from the next.

Corporate Space

The corporate dimension of social space is known by the capacity for collective action, or organization. The quantity of organization varies across social settings, with some centralized to a point of autocracy, others democratic; some a plurality of groups, others individuals only, each on his or her own. Beyond this, whatever its location in corporate space, a phenomenon may have a direction from more to less organization or from less to more. A group might help an individual, for instance, or vice versa. And the more or less organized the group, the more or less organizational distance this involves. Corporate space presents itself in many forms, with groups nesting within other groups, for example, memberships overlapping, or alliances linking one group to another. All of this defines a reality in its own right.

Normative Space

Yet another dimension of social life is normative space, the world of social control, including whatever defines or responds to deviant behavior. The quantity of social control varies across social life, with many expectations, complaints, and punishments in some settings, few in others. There are different varieties of social control, such as law, psychotherapy, bureaucracy, and etiquette. These correspond to particular styles of social control, including penal, compensatory, therapeutic, and conciliatory styles. And authority—the capacity for social control—may be more or less unevenly distributed in a hierarchy, so that a social phenomenon may be described by its hierarchical location. It may have a direction in this space as well, from more to less authority or from less to more, with the hierarchical distance variable in each case.

Another location in normative space looks backward in time, describing the degree to which people have been subject to social control, or their respectability. Some persons and groups have long records of deviant behavior, defined as more or less serious; others have reputations beyond question, without blemishes of any kind. Hence, a social phenomenon may be located in normative space of this kind, a space of respectability, created by social control itself. A normative direction and distance may also be involved. Thus, in several ways, social control defines its own dimension of social space.

A Note on Status

The location of a person or group in social space, seen in relation to others, is a status. Each person has a status in vertical space measured by his or her wealth, for instance, a radial status measured by his or her participation in social life, a normative status measured by the social control to which he or she has been subject, and so on. In relation to others, each has more or less status of every kind. One individual might have more vertical but less radial or normative status, for example, more cultural or organizational status, or some other combination. And all of these together may be compared, so that one person may have, overall, more or less social status than another (see, e.g., Baumgartner, 1978). It might also be noted that, strictly speaking, a biological characteristic such as age, sex, or race is not a social status, since it is not in itself a location in social space. This is not to deny that in some settings one or more of these biological characteristics may correspond to one or more social locations, and so may be indicators of social status for all practical purposes.

THE BEHAVIOR OF SOCIAL LIFE

Pure sociology predicts and explains the behavior of social life with its location and direction in social space. In fact, a tradition of social theory corresponds to each dimension of social space, and the importance of each has been established for many years in sociology and related sciences. The strategy of pure sociology outlined here incorporates all of these traditions, discarding their peculiarities, keeping what is valuable in each, and showing how they contribute to a single body of theory.

At least since Tocqueville (1840) and Marx (1846, with Engels), for example, one tradition has understood social variation with its location and direction in vertical space. Since Spencer (1876), Durkheim (1893), and Simmel (1908), the horizontal dimension of social space has been given prominence, whether the division of labor, patterns of social participation, or the structure of intimacy. Among others, Hegel (1821) and Sorokin (1937) established a tradition around the symbolic dimension, Michels (1911) and Weber (1922) around the corporate dimension, and Ross (1901) and Sumner (1906) around the normative dimension. Much recent theory has followed these traditions, interpreting social variation with one or more aspects of a single dimension of social space, such as networks of interaction (Bott, 1957; Mitchell, 1969), the distribution of authority (Dahrendorf, 1959), or the structure of group life (Swanson, 1971; Smith, 1974). Whatever the tradition it follows, the best theory of this kind is symmetrical in design and broad in application; yet it is limited to its own dimension, or only an aspect of a dimension, ignoring other variables of proven value. By contrast, another kind of theory includes variables from any and all of these traditions, taking the world as it presents itself, working up from the facts (see, e.g., Glaser and Strauss, 1967; Stinchcombe, 1968). Eclecticism such as this is a strategy of its own. Indeed, sociology and related sciences polarize between these extremes of one-dimensional theory and eclectic theory, the first often elegant and general but weak in its ability to predict and explain variation, the second often powerful, but arbitrary in design and narrow. The strategy of pure sociology presented here attempts to transcend these extremes, to have the best of each at once. Consider a few examples.

The Behavior of Law

Pure sociology asks how law varies with its location and direction in social space. (This section draws upon Black, 1976.) Law is known by every instance of governmental social control (Black, 1972:1096), whether an arrest, a lawsuit, a judgment in behalf of a plaintiff, a punishment, or compensation. It includes legislation, litigation, and adjudication of every kind. Law is a quantitative variable, measurable everywhere, from a single dispute to the evolution of social life over the centuries, from an encounter between two people to a neighborhood, community, society, or the world as a whole. It is possible to describe all of these settings in the language of social space, and to predict and explain the quantity of law accordingly.

It is possible to specify how law varies with its location in vertical space, for instance, whether it increases or decreases with the wealth of the parties, and whether it is greater in an upward than in a downward direction, from less to more wealth or from more to less. In fact, the quantity of law increases as its location in vertical space is higher. This means that, all else constant, a dispute between wealthy people is more likely to result in litigation than a dispute between poor people (see, e.g., Mayhew and Reiss, 1969). It also means that if a wealthy person injures someone equally wealthy, this is more serious than if a poor person injures someone equally poor: a conviction is more likely, for example, and so is a severe punishment (e.g., Johnson, 1941; Myrdal, 1944:550–555). If the injury is accidental, the wealthier victim is likely to be awarded more compensation. In every way, law defines the well-being of a wealthier person as more important. Moreover, down-ward law is greater than upward law. This means that if one party is wealthier than the other, he or she has an advantage at every stage of the legal process. If a poor person offends a wealthy person, then, this is defined as more serious than an offense in the opposite direction (e.g., Johnson, 1941; Garfinkel, 1949). And the greater the difference in wealth, the more downward law increases and the more upward law decreases, so that, all else constant, law varies directly with the wealth of the victim and inversely with the wealth of the offender. It might also be observed that law varies directly with stratification itself. Hence, apart from differences across cases, a society or community with more inequality of wealth has more law as well (see Engels, 1884: Chapter 9; Fried, 1967).

The same variables predict and explain the style of law: downward law is more penal than upward law, for instance, and the conciliatory style decreases as stratification increases. Beyond all of this, law varies with its location and direction along every other dimension of social space—horizontal, symbolic, corporate, and normative. It varies directly with status of every kind. It is greater from more to less status than from less to more status, increasing with social distance in the first case and decreasing in the latter. It also varies with other properties of social life: its relationship to cultural and relational distance is curvilinear, for example, with the least law at the extremes (e.g., Black, 1970:740–741; 1971:1097–1098). It varies directly with organization (e.g., Wittfogel, 1957: Chapters 3–7; Bergesen, 1977). It varies in other patterns with the quantity of culture, the division of labor, and other social control. What is more, these patterns apply not only to law but to social control of other kinds, such as etiquette, ethics, bureaucracy, and the treatment of mental illness.

It might also be noted that since social control defines deviant behavior, theory of this kind predicts and explains deviant behavior itself. Crime is conduct that is subject to criminal law, for example, and so the location and direction of crime in social space is defined by the location and direction of criminal law (see Kitsuse and Cicourel, 1963; Black, 1970). The theory of criminal law therefore addresses the same facts as does the theory of crime. For instance, the deprivation theory of deviant behavior predicts that a poor person is more likely than a wealthier person to commit a crime (e.g., Bonger, 1916: Part 2, Book 2, Chapters 1-2; Merton, 1938), and the facts support this prediction (see, e.g., Sutherland and Cressey, 1960:189-193). But the theory of law predicts these facts as well, since law varies inversely with the wealth of the offender. The same applies to the facts predicted by other theories of deviant behavior, such as marginality theory (e.g., Hirschi, 1969), subcultural theory (e.g., Miller, 1958), and labeling theory (e.g., Lemert, 1967). The theory of law predicts the same facts as every successful theory of deviant behavior, but explains them in a different way.

The Behavior of Medicine

Just as social control defines and responds to deviant behavior, medicine defines and responds to illness, injury, and related problems (compare Parsons, 1958; Freidson, 1970: Chapters 10, 12). It defines who needs care and treatment, and, by giving help, how much is needed in each case. Medicine is found in every society to some degree, and it is possible in every setting, in a family, friendship, or among strangers. It may be an aspect of folklore, practiced by anyone, or the responsibility of someone defined as an expert, such as a shaman, physician, or other professional.

Medicine is a quantitative variable. In each setting its magnitude is seen in whether a particular condition is defined as a problem at all, and, if so, by how much care and treatment is prescribed and given in each case. This includes attention of every kind, whether diagnostic, therapeutic, or convalescent. In a modern society, for instance, a person may receive more or less professional attention, from a specialist or only a general practitioner, as an emergency or not, with or without drugs, surgery, or other techniques, in or out of a hospital, with or without intensive care, or for a longer or a shorter period of time. The greater the attention in each case—whether by admission to a hospital or other medical setting, application of the latest techniques, by physicians, nurses, or anyone else—the greater is the quantity of medicine. In these and other ways, medicine varies with its location and direction in social space. It varies across and within societies and communities. It varies up and down the distribution of wealth, across networks and circles of interaction, from one subculture to another, and from the organized to the unorganized. No expense is spared for some; others are ignored.

Medicine varies directly with the status of the patient. It varies, for example, with his or her wealth, integration, education, authority, and respectability (see, e.g., Duff and Hollingshead, 1968: Chapters 7-9, 11;

Richardson, 1969; Bice et al., 1972; McKinlay, 1975; Roth, 1975). In addition, medicine varies inversely with the cultural and relational distance between the patient and whoever might provide help (see Freidson, 1970: Chapter 13). It might be noted as well that, all else constant, professional medicine varies inversely with folk medicine. This applies to the evolution of medicine over the centuries, and also from one case to another. The more care and treatment a person receives at home, for instance, the less likely he or she is to visit a physician. People who live alone, the unmarried and the widowed, are therefore more likely to see a physician. And, in a society where women care for men more than men care for women, women are more likely to seek the help of a professional (see, e.g., Andersen and Anderson, 1967: Chapter 2).

Those who receive more help are also more likely to ask for it in the first place. Accordingly, just as people of higher status are more likely to receive medicine of every kind, so they are more likely to define themselves as sick or injured to begin with; their associates are more likely to urge them to see a professional; and they are more likely to follow this advice (see, e.g., McKinlay, 1975). People of higher status seek and receive more preventive medicine, such as physical examinations and immunizations (e.g., Moody and Gray, 1972; Coburn and Pope, 1974), and more cosmetic medicine, such as plastic surgery and dentistry done only for the sake of appearance (e.g., Koos, 1954: Chapter 8). Higher-status people also have higher standards of public health regarding sanitation and other strategies for the control of communicable disease (see Simmons, 1958: Chapter 4). People in organizations have more health care, those in higher-status organizations still more—as do those in higher-status communities and societies. The same formulations predict and explain all of this at once.

It might seem that medicine varies not only with its location and direction in social space, but also with who needs it, who is sick or injured, and how seriously. But who needs help is an evaluation, not a question of fact (compare, e.g., Mechanic, 1968:141–142). Just as science can tell us only who is subject to social control, not who deserves to be, so it can tell us only who is defined and treated as sick or injured, not who ought to be. Who needs medicine is a question for medicine itself, not science.

The Behavior of Ideas

An idea is a statement about the nature of reality. It is a statement of fact, of what is the case, and not of value or emotion. It may appear in any setting, whether religious, scientific, political, economic, or sociable. It may be recognized as true or false, important or not. In this sense, every idea has a life of its own, with more or less success.

An idea is a quantitative variable, its magnitude a question of its contribution to knowledge, measured by how people define and respond to it. The reception of an idea may be informal, as in a round of applause or the nodding of a head, or more formal, as in the acceptance of a manuscript for publication, its citation in an article or book, or an honorific award bestowed upon its author. People may relate to an idea as true but unimportant, as often occurs at a party or other sociable gathering (compare Simmel, 1908:112–113), or even significant but false, as sometimes occurs in a review of a book or other publication in the scientific literature. In any given setting, then, the quantity of ideas depends upon the truth and importance of each idea presented, measured by the recognition that each receives. Ideas also vary in other ways, by whether they are theoretical or practical, for example, or by whether they are supernatural, metaphysical, or empirical (see Comte, 1830:1–8).

Pure sociology predicts and explains the behavior of ideas with their location and direction in social space. It is possible, for instance, to predict and explain the success of an idea with the location of its source and audience in social space. Thus, an idea moving from more to less status is more likely to succeed than one moving in the opposite direction, from less to more status. This applies to status differences of every kind, vertical, horizontal, cultural, organizational, or normative. And the greater the difference between the source and the audience, the greater this variation is. All else constant, the success of an idea varies directly with the status of its source and inversely with the status of its audience. The higher the status of a scientist, for example, the more likely are his or her ideas to be recognized. If two scientists co-author a paper, or make the same discovery at the same time, the one with more status prior to the event is more likely to be recognized—at the other's expense—for this achievement (Merton, 1968). And the higher the status of a scientist, the more likely is publication, citation, and every other kind of recognition of his or her work (see, e.g., Crane, 1967; Allison and Stewart, 1974; compare Cole and Cole, 1973). Scientists may therefore have difficulty winning recognition in their early years, even while they do the work for which they may later be celebrated (see, e.g., Manniche and Falk, 1957). In any given case, though, the chances of a younger scientist will improve if a more eminent colleague steps forth as a sponsor. Sponsorship is itself a kind of recognition, however, predictable from other variables, such as the degree of relational distance between the younger scientist and his or her senior colleague and the degree to which the younger scientist is conventional in lifestyle and respectable in the bureaucracy of science.

Patterns such as these appear not only in science but everywhere that people make statements about the nature of reality. Among the members of a jury, for instance, those of higher status have more to say about the verdict (Strodtbeck et al., 1957). In a factory, even in one meant to be run by the workers, white-collar employees are treated as more knowledge-able (e.g., Obradović, 1972). In politics the more organized faction is more likely to win acceptance of its ideology (e.g., Gamson, 1975: Chapter 7). In conversation an adult's remark is taken as more impor-tant than a child's, a man's as more important than a woman's, a white's as more important than a black's (see, e.g., West and Zimmerman, 1977). Everywhere, people of higher status of all kinds are defined as more intelligent, and whatever they say is recognized as more useful and interesting. Hence, across history, ideas rise and fall with the status of their sponsors (see Mannheim, 1927), and in every epoch the ruling ideas are the ideas of the ruling class (Marx and Engels, 1846:39).

The success of an idea also varies inversely with the relational distance between its source and audience. The more intimate people are, the more value they find in each other's ideas. In science, for instance, the recognition of ideas is concentrated within networks of interaction, or "invisible colleges" (see Price, 1963: Chapter 3; Crane, 1972; Kadushin, 1976). In medicine, a new drug is more likely to be adopted by a physician if it is suggested by a friend or colleague (Coleman et al., 1966: Chapters 6–9). Among the public at large, information of all kinds follows a "two-step flow," first to an informal leader and then to his or her intimates, such as kinfolk, friends, and neighbors (Katz and Lazars-feld, 1955). And the longer people know each other, the more they share a view of the world, and the more they agree about everything (see, e.g., Berger and Kellner, 1964). Relational distance even explains why students find seminars more valuable than larger classes and why teachers give better grades to their smaller classes. Ideas of all kinds evolve and spread in small groups (see Mead, 1964: Chapter 8). People renounce their old beliefs as their old relationships come apart, and, especially when unattached and adrift, convert to new beliefs as they find new relationships (see Lofland and Stark, 1965). An idea may thus be successful in one setting but not another, true and interesting to some but not others.

It might be added that the quality of an idea, including its truth, is not a matter of fact. Regardless of the degree of consensus among scientists, for example, it is not possible to measure the importance of a scientific idea, but only how it is evaluated by the participants themselves. To do otherwise is to participate in the evaluation itself. Thus, from an observer's standpoint, how well a scientific theory orders the facts is not an empirical question, and so it cannot explain the success of the theory (compare, e.g., Kuhn, 1970). Scientifically speaking, the truth of an idea can never explain its success. Similarly, the career of a scientist cannot be explained with the quality of his or her work (compare Cole and Cole, 1973). Like the seriousness of deviant behavior or the need for medicine, a contribution to knowledge is a question of value, not a fact in itself. The same applies to the beauty of art.

The Behavior of Art

Art is a creation defined as beautiful. It might include music, dance, literature, painting, sculpture, photography, architecture, furniture or other interior decoration, clothing or other body adornment, or the preparation and presentation of food. Whatever people do, they may do more or less artistically. But this is a matter of taste, not fact (compare, e.g., Shils, 1960; Jaeger and Selznick, 1964; Adorno, 1968).

It is possible to measure the degree to which people define and respond to any creation as artistic, that is, whether they appreciate it as beautiful, and to what extent (see Gray, 1966). In this sense, art is a quantitative variable. If, for instance, an object is defined as beautiful at all, the degree of appreciation might range from a word of praise to acquisition, private display, or even display in a museum. If acquired, its price might be great or small, and this is a measure of appreciation as well. In the case of a performance, attendance might be more or less costly for the audience, and the performers themselves might receive more or less compensation. Although the essence of art is not a matter of fact, then it is possible to measure the success of any creation in quantitative terms. And this varies with its location and direction in social space.

For example, the success of art varies directly with the status of its patrons. This means that in a modern society the work appreciated by the wealthier and more educated people is more likely to be recognized as genuine art, and the best of its genre. It is more likely to be exhibited in museums, staged in concert halls, studied in universities, praised in the mass media. It is defined as fine art rather than popular art, high culture rather than mass culture or low culture (e.g., Gans, 1974), even superior or refined culture rather than mediocre or brutal culture (Shils, 1960; see also Shils, 1957). The literature, music, and films appreciated by high-status people are defined as more serious, their food as *haute cuisine*, their clothing as *haute couture*. In everything, their taste is defined as better. This applies, however, only when all else is constant.

Among themselves, for instance, the people of each social location generally have their own taste. In modern America, taste varies between the wealthy and the poor, one ethnic group and another, adults and younger persons, men and women, in short, between social locations of all kinds. It may therefore seem that a question of aesthetics is different from, say, a question of science, where there is so much more consensus about what is important. It may seem that the quality of scientific work is more obvious. But this is only because people from so many different locations in social space actually participate in the evaluation of art, whereas this is not the case in science. What is a good book or movie is a question addressed by practically everyone, not merely by a small network of similar people such as those who evaluate the work in a branch of science. In fact, whatever the topic, the degree of consensus varies inversely with the range of social locations involved. It also varies inversely with the cultural and relational distance among and between the participants. This is why the people of a simple tribe agree so much about everything, and about beauty as much as truth. The same applies to many enclaves of a modern society, such a families, colleagues, or cliques of teenagers. Disagreements do not arise because art or anything else is inherently difficult to evaluate, but because of the social location of evaluation itself.

Pure sociology also predicts and explains the nature of art. It is possible to predict and explain the kinds of art found across societies (see, e.g., Kroeber, 1944: Chapters 5-9, 11; Gray, 1972) and across the settings of a single society (see, e.g., Ridgeway, 1976). Some people have more music than others, or more visual or literary art, and the particular expressions of each kind of art vary as well. In the case of music, for example, lyrics, rhythm, harmony, and instrumentation vary in their complexity directly with the stratification of a society (Lomax, 1968). The same applies to dance, with more parts of the body becoming active as the distribution of wealth is less equal (Lomax et al., 1968). Within a society too, dance is more elaborate where the dancers are less equal among theselves. Finally, it is possible to predict and explain similarities and differences in art across history. When simple societies become more complex, for example, so does their music and dance. But in some respects modern art has come to resemble the art of the earliest societies, with some modern painting and sculpture resembling tribal art, even prehistoric cave drawings (see Giedion, 1956; McLuhan and Parker, 1968:197, 209). Perhaps this is because social life has begun to evolve into a stage with characteristics similar to those of the simplest societies (see Black, 1976: Chapter 7; see also McLuhan, 1964; Douglas, 1970: Chapter 4). In any event, art is orderly, and all of it is subject to pure sociology.

CONCLUSION

Pure sociology is the study of social life in its own terms. It predicts and explains the behavior of social life with its location and direction in the space of interaction itself, including vertical, horizontal, symbolic, corporate, and normative space. It predicts many known facts about human conduct, but explains them without regard to the individual as such. It is possible to predict and explain deviant behavior as the distribution of social control, for example, the use of health services as the distribution of medicine, intellectual and aesthetic achievement as the distribution of ideas and art. It is possible to predict and explain status of every kind, including its attainment and loss, as the distribution of locations in social space. What has always been seen as the behavior of persons may thus be seen as the behavior of social life (compare, e.g., Winch, 1958; Homans, 1964). And every kind of social life is a quantitative variable, with more or less in one location or direction than in another. Every kind is a matter of degree, like heat or sound or light.

This strategy of pure sociology is a synthesis of earlier traditions, an effort to be as simple and general as each, as powerful as all together. Pure sociology also has its own conception of social reality and its own logic. But is is forever ready to change, to include dimensions of social space now unseen, new locations and directions, undiscovered principles, unknown implications. It has possibilities without end.

NOTE

For commenting upon an earlier draft, I thank M. P. Baumgartner, Herbert L. Costner, George Farkas, Alan Horwitz, Arthur G. Lindsay, Scott G. McNall, W. Russell Neuman, and F. P. Romo.

REFERENCES

ADORNO, THEODOR W.
  1968 Introduction to the Sociology of Music. 2nd ed. New York: Seabury Press, 1976.
ALLISON, PAUL D., and JOHN A. STEWART
  1974 "Productivity differences among scientists: evidence for accumulative advantage." American Sociological Review 39 (August):596-606.

ANDERSEN, RONALD, and ODIN W. ANDERSON
  1967 A Decade of Health Services: Social Survey Trends in Use and Expenditure. Chicago: University of Chicago Press.
BAUMGARTNER, M. P.
  1978 "Law and social status in colonial New Haven, 1639-1665." Pp. 153-174 in Rita J. Simon (ed.), Research in Law and Sociology: An Annual Compilation of Research. Volume 1. Greenwich, Conn.: JAI Press.
BERGER, PETER L., and HANSFRIED KELLNER
  1964 "Marriage and the construction of reality: an exercise in the microsociology of knowledge." Diogenes 46 (Spring):1-25.
BERGESEN, ALBERT JAMES
  1977 "Political witch hunts: the sacred and the subversive in cross-national perspective." American Sociological Review 42 (April):220-233.
BICE, THOMAS W., ROBERT L. EICHHORN, and PETER D. FOX
  1972 "Socioeconomic status and use of physician services: a reconsideration." Medical Care 10 (May-June):261-271.
BLACK, DONALD
  1970 "Production of crime rates." American Sociological Review, 35 (August):733-748.
  1971 "The social organization of arrest." Stanford Law Review 23 (June):1087-1111.
  1972 "The boundaries of legal sociology." Yale Law Journal 81 (May):1086-1100.
  1976 The Behavior of Law. New York: Academic Press.
BONGER, WILLIAM ADRIAN
  1916 Criminality and Economic Conditions. Boston: Little, Brown.
BOTT, ELIZABETH
  1957 Family and Social Network: Roles, Norms, and External Relationships in Ordinary Urban Families. London: Tavistock Publications.
BRAITHWAITE, RICHARD BEVAN
  1953 Scientific Explanation: A Study of the Function of Theory, Probability and Law in Science. New York: Harper & Row, 1960.
COBURN, DAVID, and CLYDE R. POPE
  1974 "Socioeconomic status and preventive health behavior." Journal of Health and Social Behavior 15 (June):67-78.
COLE, JONATHAN R., and STEPHEN COLE
  1973 Social Stratification in Science. Chicago: University of Chicago Press.
COLEMAN, JAMES S., ELIHU KATZ, and HERBERT MENZEL
  1966 Medical Innovation: A Diffusion Study. Indianapolis: Bobbs-Merrill.
COMTE, AUGUSTE
  1830 Introduction to Positive Philosophy. Indianapolis: Bobbs-Merrill, 1970.
CRANE, DIANA
  1967 "The gatekeepers of science: some factors affecting the selection of articles for scientific journals." The American Sociologist 2 (November):195-201.

1972 Invisible Colleges: Diffusion of Knowledge in Scientific Communities. Chicago: University of Chicago Press.

DAHRENDORF, RALF

1959 Class and Class Conflict in Industrial Society, 2nd ed. Stanford, Calif.: Stanford University Press.

1968 "In praise of Thrasymachus." Pp. 129–150 in Essays in the Theory of Society. Stanford, Calif.: Stanford University Press.

DOUGLAS, MARY

1970 Natural Symbols: Explorations in Cosmology. New York: Pantheon.

DUFF, RAYMOND S., and AUGUST B. HOLLINGSHEAD

1968 Sickness and Society. New York: Harper & Row.

DURKHEIM, EMILE

1893 The Division of Labor in Society. New York: Free Press, 1964.

ENGELS, FRIEDRICH

1884 The Origin of the Family, Private Property and the State: In the Light of the Researches of Lewis H. Morgan. New York: International Publishers, 1942.

FREIDSON, ELIOT

1970 Profession of Medicine: A Study of the Sociology of Applied Knowledge. New York: Harper & Row.

FRIED, MORTON H.

1967 The Evolution of Political Society: An Essay in Political Anthropology. New York: Random House.

GAMSON, WILLIAM A.

1975 The Strategy of Social Protest. Homewood, Ill.: Dorsey Press.

GANS, HERBERT J.

1974 Popular Culture and High Culture: An Analysis and Evaluation of Taste. New York: Basic Books.

GARFINKEL, HAROLD

1949 "Research note on inter- and intra-racial homicides." Social Forces 27 (May):369–381.

GIEDION, SIGFRIED

1956 "Space conception in prehistoric art." Explorations: Studies in Culture and Communication 6 (July):38–55.

GLASER, BARNEY G., and ANSELM L. STRAUSS

1967 The Discovery of Grounded Theory: Strategies for Qualitative Research. Chicago: Aldine.

GRAY, CHARLES EDWARD

1966 "A measurement of creativity in Western civilization." American Anthropologist 68 (December):1384–1417.

1972 "Paradoxes in Western creativity." American Anthropologist 74 (June):676–688.

HEGEL, GEORG WILHELM FRIEDRICH

1821 Hegel's Philosophy of Right. London: Oxford University Press, 1952.

HEMPEL, CARL G.

1965 "Aspects of scientific explanation." Pp. 331–496 in Aspects of Scientific

Explanation and Other Essays in the Philosophy of Science. New York: Free Press.

HIRSCHI, TRAVIS
  1969 Causes of Delinquency. Berkeley: University of California Press.

HOMANS, GEORGE CASPAR
  1964 "Bringing men back in." American Sociological Review 29 (December):809-818.
  1967 The Nature of Social Science. New York: Harcourt, Brace and World.

JAEGER, GERTRUDE, and PHILIP SELZNICK
  1964 "A normative theory of culture." American Sociological Review 29 (October):653-669.

JOHNSON, G. B.
  1941 "The Negro and crime." The Annals of the American Academy of Political and Social Science 271 (September):93-104.

KADUSHIN, CHARLES
  1976 "Networks and circles in the production of culture." American Behavioral Scientist 19 (July-August):769-784.

KATZ, ELIHU, and PAUL F. LAZARSFELD
  1955 Personal Influence: The Part Played by People in the Flow of Mass Communications. Glencoe, Ill.: Free Press.

KITSUSE, JOHN I., and AARON V. CICOUREL
  1963 "A note on the uses of official statistics." Social Problems, 11 (Fall):131-139.

KOOS, EARL LOMON
  1954 The Health of Regionville: What the People Thought and Did About It. New York: Hafner, 1967.

KROEBER, A. L.
  1944 Configurations of Culture Growth. Berkeley: University of California Press.

KUHN, THOMAS S.
  1970 The Structure of Scientific Revolutions. enlarged ed. Chicago: University of Chicago Press.

Lemert, EDWIN M.
  1967 "The concept of secondary deviation." Pp. 40-64 in Human Deviance, Social Problems, and Social Control. Englewood Cliffs, N.J.: Prentice-Hall.

LOFLAND, JOHN, and RODNEY STARK
  1965 "Becoming a world-saver: a theory of conversion to a deviant perspective." American Sociological Review 30 (December):862-875.

LOMAX, ALAN
  1968 "Song as a measure of culture." Pp. 117-169 in A. Lomax (ed.), Folk Song Style and Culture. Washington, D.C.: American Association for the Advancement of Science, Publication Number 88.

LOMAX, ALAN, IRMGARD BARTENIEFF, and FORRESTINE PAULAY
  1968 "Dance style and culture." Pp. 222-247 in A. Lomax (ed.), Folk Song Style and Culture. Washington, D.C.: American Association for the Advancement of Science, Publication Number 88.

MANNHEIM, KARL
1927   "Conservative thought." Pp. 74–164 in Paul Kecskemeti (ed.), Essays on Sociology and Social Psychology. New York: Oxford University Press, 1953.

MANNICHE, E., and G. FALK
1957   "Age and the Nobel Prize." Behavioral Science 2 (October):301–307.

MARX, KARL, and FRIEDRICH ENGELS
1846   The German Ideology. New York: International Publishers, 1947.

MAYHEW, LEON, and ALBERT J. REISS, Jr.
1969   "The social organization of legal contacts." American Sociological Review 34 (June):309–318.

McKINLAY, JOHN B.
1975   "The help-seeking behavior of the poor." Pp. 224–273 in John Kosa and Irving Kenneth Zola (eds.), Poverty and Health: A Sociological Analysis, rev. ed. Cambridge, Mass.: Harvard University Press.

McLUHAN, MARSHALL
1964   Understanding Media: The Extensions of Man. New York: McGraw-Hill.

McLUHAN, MARSHALL, and HARLEY PARKER
1968   Through the Vanishing Point: Space in Poetry and Painting. New York: Harper & Row.

MEAD, MARGARET
1964   Continuities in Cultural Evolution. New Haven: Yale University Press.

MECHANIC, DAVID
1968   Medical Sociology: A Selective View. New York: Free Press.

MERTON, ROBERT K.
1938   "Social structure and anomie." American Sociological Review 3 (October):672–682.
1968   "The Matthew effect in science." Science 159 (January 5):55–63.

MICHELS, ROBERT
1911   Political Parties: A Sociological Study of the Oligarchical Tendencies of Modern Democracy. New York: Collier Books, 1962.

MILLER, WALTER B.
1958   "Lower class culture as a generating milieu of gang delinquency." Journal of Social Issues 14 (Number 3):5–13.

MITCHELL, J. CLYDE
1969   "The concept and use of social networks." Pp. 1–50 in J. C. Mitchell (ed.), Social Networks in Urban Situations: Analyses of Personal Relationships in Central African Towns. Manchester, England: Manchester University Press.

MOODY, PHILIP M., and ROBERT M. GRAY
1972   "Social class, social integration, and the use of preventive health services." Pp. 250–261 in E. Gartly Jaco (ed.), Patients, Physicians and Illness: A Sourcebook in Behavioral Science and Health, 2nd ed. New York: Free Press.

MYRDAL, GUNNAR
  1944 An American Dilemma: The Negro Problem and Modern Democracy.
        New York: Harper and Brothers.
OBRADOVIĆ, JOSIP
  1972 "Distribution of participation in the process of decision making on
        problems related to the economic activity of the company." Pp. 137–164
        in Eugen Pusić (ed.), Participation and Self-Management, vol. 2. Zagreb,
        Yugoslavia: Institute for Social Research, University of Zagreb.
PARSONS, TALCOTT
  1951 The Social System. New York: Free Press.
  1958 "Definitions of health and illness in the light of American values and
        social structure." Pp. 165–187 in E. Gartly Jaco (ed.), Patients, Physi-
        cians and Illness: Sourcebook in Behavioral Science and Medicine.
        Glencoe, Ill.: Free Press.
PRICE, DEREK J. DE SOLLA
  1963 Little Science, Big Science. New York: Columbia University Press.
RADCLIFFE-BROWN, A. R.
  1935 "On the concept of function in social science." Pp. 178–187, in Structure
        and Function in Primitive Society: Essays and Addresses. New York: Free
        Press, 1965.
RICHARDSON, WILLIAM C.
  1969 "Poverty, illness, and the use of health services in the United States."
        Hospitals 43 (July):34–40.
RIDGEWAY, CECILIA L.
  1976 "Affective interaction as a determinant of musical involvement." Socio-
        logical Quarterly 17 (Summer):414–428.
ROTH, JULIUS A.
  1975 "The treatment of the sick." Pp. 274–302 in John Kosa and Irving
        Kenneth Zola (eds.), Poverty and Health: A Sociological Analysis. 2nd ed.
        Cambridge, Mass.: Harvard University Press.
ROSS, EDWARD ALSWORTH
  1901 Social Control: A Survey of the Foundations of Order. New York:
        Macmillan.
SHILS, EDWARD
  1957 "Daydreams and nightmares: reflections on the criticism of mass cul-
        ture." Sewanee Review 65 (October–December):586–608.
  1960 "Mass society and its culture." Daedalus 89 (Spring):288–314.
SIMMEL, GEORG
  1908 The Sociology of Georg Simmel, edited by Kurt H. Wolff. New York:
        Free Press, 1960.
SIMMONS, OZZIE G.
  1958 Social Status and Public Health. New York: Social Science Research
        Council, Pamphlet 13.
SMITH, M.G.
  1974 Corporations and Society. London: Gerald Duckworth.

SOROKIN, PITIRIM A.
1937 Social and Cultural Dynamics. New York: American Book Company.
SPENCER, HERBERT
1876 The Principles of Sociology, vol. 1. London: Williams and Norgate.
STINCHCOMBE, ARTHUR L.
1968 Constructing Social Theories. New York: Harcourt, Brace and World.
STRODTBECK, FRED L., RITA M. JAMES, and CHARLES HAWKINS
1957 "Social status in jury deliberations." American Sociological Review 22
(December):713–719.
SUMNER, WILLIAM GRAHAM
1906 Folkways: A Study of the Sociological Importance of Usages, Manners,
Customs, Mores, and Morals. New York: New American Library, 1960.
SUTHERLAND, EDWIN H., and DONALD R. CRESSEY
1960 Principles of Criminology, 6th ed. Philadelphia: J. B. Lippincott.
SWANSON, GUY E.
1971 "An organizational analysis of collectivities." American Sociological
Review 36 (August):607–624.
TOCQUEVILLE, ALEXIS DE
1840 Democracy in America, vol. 2. Garden City, N.Y.: Anchor Books, 1969.
WARD, LESTER F.
1903 Pure Sociology: A Treatise on the Origin and Spontaneous Development
of Society. New York: Macmillan.
WEBER, MAX
1922 The Theory of Social and Economic Organization, edited by Talcott
Parsons. New York: Free Press, 1964.
WEST, CANDACE, and DON H. ZIMMERMAN
1977 "Women's place in everyday talk: reflections on parent–child interac-
tion." Social Problems 24 (June):521–529.
WINCH, PETER
1958 The Idea of a Social Science and Its Relation to Philosophy. London:
Routledge and Kegan Paul.
WITTFOGEL, KARL A.
1957 Oriental Despotism: A Comparative Study of Total Power. New Haven:
Yale University Press.

4. Prevailing Postulates of Social Exchange Theory

R. H. HINGERS and DAVID WILLER

Social exchange theory has become an important theoretic orientation in sociology, which, unlike functionalism, has at its nexus a concept of social relationship. This can be seen as a return from the functionalist perspective to the classical tradition of Marx and Weber, for the concept of social relationship was also central to their work. Unlike the theories of Marx or of Weber, however, which included formulations for a variety of forms of social relationship, social exchange theory has concentrated upon the relationship of exchange, and in so doing, has for the most part excluded from its scope other relational types. Furthermore, as will be maintained in this paper, social exchange theory has concentrated upon only a very narrow range of exchange relations and conditions of their occurrence.

There are sound scientific reasons for developing conceptions of a narrow scope, particularly when the aim is to gain an understanding of that which falls within the narrower focus before moving to broader-ranging problems. Yet, as we hope to point out, the narrow scope of exchange theory is not a consequence of a planned scientific procedure, but is instead a consequence of certain stereotypic conceptions concerning the nature and form of exchange and other social relationships. Following Merton, we call these stereotypic conceptions "prevailing postulates." Three prevailing postulates of social exchange theory are discussed here: (1) universal exchange, or the relationship of exchange that effectively subsumes all social relationships; (2) universal balanced reciprocity, or the motion that all social exchanges are balanced by

169

norms of reciprocity; and (3) universal commensurability, the idea that all exchanges are of items which are measurable by a common standard by those engaged in the relationship.

Social exchange theory is not a monolithic paradigm (for reviews see Mulkay, 1971; Simpson, 1972; Ekeh, 1974), but certain common views are shared by its most central theorists: Homans, Blau, and Emerson. Portions of these shared views are discussed throughout this article. Social exchange theory has been fruitful in generating experimental research (see, for example: Emerson, 1964; Crosbie, 1972; Michener and Cohen, 1973; Burgess and Nielsen, 1974; Michener, et al., 1975). It has been less successful in its applications to historical and contemporary societies because its scope has been drawn too narrowly to explain those cases which are at the core of its concern. If social exchange theory is to become a theory of sufficient scope to be applied precisely to nonexperimental systems, certain additions and revisions must be made. This paper is intended as a first step in that direction.

WHAT IS SOCIAL EXCHANGE?

Before proceeding further, a brief review of the nature of social exchange as formulated by Homans, Blau, and Emerson is needed. For Homans the fundamental description and explanation of social exchange is contained in his set of propositions (1961:31). These are:

1. If in the past the occurrence of a particular stimulus-situation has been the occasion on which a man's activity has been rewarded, then the more similar the present stimulus-situation is to the past one, the more likely he is to emit the activity, or some similar activity, now (1961:53).

2. The more often within a given period of time a man's activity rewards the activity of another, the more often the other will emit the activity (1961:54).

3. The more valuable to a man a unit of the activity another gives him, the more often he will emit activity rewarded by the activity of the other (1961:55).

4. The more often a man has in the recent past received a rewarding activity from another, the less valuable any further unit of that activity becomes to him (1961:55).

5. The more to a man's disadvantage the rule of distributive justice fails of realization, the more likely he is to display the emotional behavior we call anger (1961:75).

The first three propositions are drawn from operant psychology. The cycle emanating from these propositions is one in which two actors generate a social relationship characterized by increased exchanges of a mutually rewarding nature. Romance might exemplify such a process, as might any activity which manifests relative stability over time, in which mutual rewards lead to increased exchanges. Proposition four deals with the rule of marginal utility or an organism's satiation, and is concerned with the reduction in rate or termination of an exchange. The final proposition, which deals with distributive justice, holds that the individual actor compares the rewards and costs engendered with those of the exchange partner. After the comparison is made, the actor may display emotional behavior such as anger or guilt (1961:74–76).

While Blau does not give a formal set of theoretic propositions akin to those of Homans, he explicitly defines the nature of social exchange as he sees it. His central definition maintains that "social exchange . . . refers to voluntary actions of individuals that are motivated by the returns they are expected to bring and typically do, in fact, bring from others" (Blau, 1964:91). Although not as formal as Homans's central notion of social exchange, Blau's definition has a similar basis in that both use a cost-benefit formula. Both claim that motivation by rewards or expectation of rewards is at the nexus of social exchange. Consistent with Homans, it is Emerson's position that rewards are characteristic of the "mutual dependence which binds actors together in social systems" (1962:40). All three theorists, then, contend that social exchange is behavior in which each actor transmits something perceived as rewarding by the recipient in order to motivate the other to act.

THE POSTULATE OF UNIVERSAL EXCHANGE

The postulate of universal exchange is that social exchange subsumes, in effect, all socially significant and durable relationships. This includes all historically important relations whereby societies differentiate and advance.

The issue to be addressed here, then, pertains to the scope of social exchange theory as a general theory of social relationships. Do the exchange formulations of Homans, Emerson, and Blau claim to subsume effectively all social relationships, and is this claim sound? Homans has maintained that:

> either two persons reward one another in more than one way, like each other on more than one count, and increase their interaction, or they will hurt one another in more than one way, dislike one another, and decrease interaction (1967:46).

Emerson states that "the concept of an exchange relation, and the principles which surround it, provide a basis for studying the formation and change of social structures as enduring relations among specified actors, with the exchange relation as the structural unit" (1972:60). Blau states: "In brief, social exchange may reflect any behavior oriented to socially mediated goals" (1964:5). Blau delimits subsumable social behavior as social exchange with two exclusions; those of physical coercion and pure gifts (see Blau, 1964:91).

Leaving aside pure gifts, which will be considered again under reciprocity, let us consider to what extent coercion can be considered a physical relation, and to what extent it must be considered social. Consider the instance of a mugger and his victim. Here the two extremes are clear. At the one extreme is the mugger who shoots his victim and lifts the wallet from the body. Clearly, this is an instance of physical coercion, which, like Weber's colliding cyclists, "may be compared to a natural event" (Weber, 1947:113). At the other extreme is the mugger who, by threat, has successfully extracted the victim's wallet, which has been handed to him by his victim. Clearly, this is, however transitory, a social relationship and is worthy of study by the sociologist.

Now consider long-standing coercive social relationships, those relationships in which the threat of harm, whether physical or psychic, is used as a means initiating and maintaining a flow of positive sanctions. No one would deny that slave states existed and persisted for generations. In contradistinction to the quotation from Homans, slaves were undoubtedly hurt and undoubtedly would have preferred to decrease their interactions with their masters. That they generally did not do so is an historic fact which cannot and should not be ignored by sociological analysis. Taxation by Oriental despots, feudal lords, theocracies, and modern political states is a form of coercive social relationship that is fully operative as social exchange. Coercive relations are not merely transitory, then, as social exchange theory maintains.

While coercion, or the potential for punishment, can be quite durable, the effectiveness of coercion is also obscured in social exchange theory. For example, according to Blau (1964:224) "Punishment is not a very effective method of influencing behavior."

On the other hand Goode (1972:511) has pointed out that "the importance of force and force threat in human behavior is richly demonstrated by the rarity of its use." Indeed, force and force threat have traditionally been an effective and prevalent means of imposing or establishing social order. The effectiveness (and relative inexpensiveness) of negative sanctions is further evidenced as Goode noted (1972), since in stable systems the threat or potentiality of the sanction alone is sufficient. We pay taxes routinely, not because of a history of negative reinforcements by our government upon us, but in order to avoid possible future punishments. Lacking for the most part the means for negative sanctioning, the citizens of modern states are limited almost exclusively to exchange as a basis for their social relationships—not because, as has been claimed, that exchange is the only effective social relationship, but because other options have been precluded.[1]

Furthermore, the importance of coercion as an ongoing condition for exchange systems has not been recognized by social exchange theory. Consider two typical exchange systems; those which are "legal contractual" systems and "communal" exchange systems based upon "norms." In modern societies the economic sector uses legal contracts as the most pervasive method of conducting exchanges. What, then, is the sociological nature of a contract? A contract is characterized by the inclusion of a third party to an agreement between the exchanging parties, the third party being the state. A violation of the terms of the contract render the violating actor open to coercion by the state. If one violates a contract, the state can, through its legal system, demand that restitution be made, and if it is not, it can coerce the violator with fines and/or imprisonment. These potential consequences are of importance even when they do not occur—for in the absence of contracts, many exchanges which do occur would not occur. How then are the occurrences of modern exchange relations to be theoretically treated independent of the potential coercive role of the state in contracts?

Turning to exchange systems based upon norms, a similar set of conditions is found. In small communities there can be a basis other than contracts for the assurance that the obligations of a mutual agreement regarding exchange will be fulfilled This basis is the normative system of the community. Those who do not carry out their obligations normally find their status reduced in the community. Those who have routinely ignored their exchange obligations may find themselves at the point of convergence of a very large number of negative sanctions, and in far greater distress than that experienced by those who go to great lengths to fulfill their obligations. If the violation is great enough, the individual may be excluded from the community and its network of exchange. Thus, at least in small systems, the normative community as a whole can perform the role provided by the state in large contractual systems. How then are the exchanges which occur in normative systems theoretically to be treated independently of the potential coercive role of the normative system?

An analogy at this point may have some heuristic value. Homans, Blau, and Emerson attribute a significant portion of their work to operant psychology. For example, Emerson illustrates his theory of power-dependence with the case of Skinner and the pigeon (1969:389). Emerson notes that Skinner rewards the pigeon for orderly behavior and, in turn, the pigeon rewards Skinner by behaving in an orderly way. This situation supposedly exemplifies how mutual rewards lead to the maintenance of an exchange relationship. Yet, this illustration ignores conditions fundamental to the relationship. How did Skinner, the Skinner box, and the pigeon in the box get there in the first place? Clearly, there is an exchange relation of a sort between the bird and Skinner, but it is not maintained solely by exchange but, rather, by coercion in the form of the box. A counterpart to this example is found in the labor camp described by Solzhenitsyn in *One Day in the Life of Ivan Denisovich* (1971). Constant exchanges are integral to the social behavior in the camp as the daily routine unfolds. Ongoing exchanges occur in networks in which individuals are included or excluded apparently as a social exchange theory would posit. Nevertheless, the potential coercion of the labor camp is evident in the demeanor of the silent guards with their mute automatic weapons. This coercive factor is easier to ignore with Skinner's pigeon. In both cases the critical question is, what reproduces the system? And in both cases the potential and actualized coercion would appear to be the crucial conditions.

It should now be clear that no theory of social exchange can adequately explain its data without consideration of the coercive relations upon which exchange is predicated. Including only the actual flows of sanctions that occur in any system is not theoretically adequate. The undergirding potential flows of the system must also be included as part of the network. Take the case of a circumscribed group such as that in the labor camp. If only the sanctions that did flow were considered, how would one differentiate between forced labor and that freely given as a gift? Potential relations are as important for the analysis of conflict as they are for analysis of exchange and coercive relations, but conflict is virtually ignored by social exchange theory. Potential conflict, which can have important long-term effects on an exchange system, e.g., the military-industrial complex and the arms race, is theoretically considered insignificant. We feel this treatment has led to grave confusion in present exchange frameworks, Macrolevel dynamics, e.g., international relations and the role of the state, appear beyond the scope of exchange theories as they presently stand. The same problems are manifested on the microlevel, e.g., marriage and the role of normative systems. Clearly, universal exchange is a myth, and until the limited scope of exchange theories is recognized and remedied, no further progress will be made in understanding social exchange.

The Postulate of Universal Balanced Reciprocity

A working definition of reciprocity is necessary before we examine it further. As Gouldner (1960) indicated, the concept of reciprocity had been assigned vast importance in social life, but it had not been defined. In an "effort to clarify the diverse meanings of reciprocity," Gouldner turned to "Malinowski's seminal contribution" (1960:169). Briefly, Gouldner stated Malinowski's position this way: "Reciprocity, therefore, is a mutually gratifying pattern of exchanging goods and services" (1960:170). Since this definition takes the basic format of social exchange itself, let us attempt to add a finer distinction. Reciprocity occurs during social exchange relations when the transmission of a reward is accompanied by the expection that the recipient will, in turn, transmit a reward to the actor initiating the exchange, and when that expectation actually governs the actions of the recipient. Balance is the property of conditional expectations in an exchange relationship where the mutual flows of positive sanctions tend toward equality.

The postulate of universal balanced reciprocity holds that all social exchanges are balanced reciprocally. According to Blau, "Reciprocity is an equilibrating force, the assumption being that every social action is balanced by some appropriate counteraction" (1964:336). Although Blau does use a dialectic in which reciprocity results in imbalances outside of reciprocation, he nevertheless maintains that "social structures are governed by equilibrating forces" (1964:338). Hence, Blau assumes that while nonreciprocal and imbalanced relations can occur as isolated incidents, social exchange can persist only through reciprocity. For example,

> individuals who receive needed benefits from others are obligated, lest the supply of benefits cease, to reciprocate in some form, whether through expressions of gratitude, approval, material rewards, services, or compliance. If persons are obligated to accede to another's wishes because he renders essential services to them for which they cannot otherwise compensate him, their compliance reciprocates for the unilateral services they obtain, and in this sense restores balance, but it also creates an imbalance of power (Blau, 1964:336).

Emerson states that "viable exchange relations are reciprocal by

definition" (1969:389). Like Blau, who uses Emerson's balancing operations for his own purposes, Emerson also discusses balance and imbalance. Emerson claims "in short, exchange relations tend to change
toward balance" (1972:66). Indeed, Emerson presents an exchange theory
in which balancing operations play a major role, e.g., the division of
labor, stratification, social circles, and coalitions are generated by the
tendency toward balance (1972:79–86). Emerson's unique balancing
operations take us farther afield than space and present concerns allow,
and recognizing that Emerson's position on the viability of social
exchanges assumes that reciprocity is an act which balances and thus
maintains the relationship is all we need here.

Homans and Emerson both base their work on operant principles.
With Homans, reward and reinforcement are virtually inseparable.
Reward and reinforcement are indexed and used by Homans (1961), but
reciprocity is not.[2] It is in the proposition on distributive justice that we
find Homans's use of a rule analogous to balanced reciprocity:

> A man in an exchange relation with another will expect that the
> rewards of each man be proportional to his costs—the greater the
> rewards, the greater the costs—and that the net rewards, or profits, of
> each man be proportional to his investments—the greater the
> investments, the greater the profit. This means that unless the
> investments of the two men are greatly different, each man will
> further expect the following condition to hold good: the more
> valuable to the other (and costly to himself) an activity he gives the
> other, the more valuable to him (and costly to the other) an activity
> the other gives him. Finally, when each man is being rewarded by
> some third party, he will expect the third party to maintain this
> relationship between the two of them in the distribution of rewards
> (1961:75).

Homans, Blau, and Emerson all stipulate that a viable social exchange relation is characterized by reciprocity.

But is balanced reciprocity an empirically necessary component of
social exchange? Since much of the literature on social exchange
considers primitive systems to be prototypical (cf. Emerson, 1976), a brief
examination of Sahlins's work (1972) may be of some assistance at this
point. His use of the term "reciprocity" is considerably broader than
those discussed earlier. Sahlins points out that Malinowski originally
described a continuum of reciprocal relations among the Trobriand
Islanders. Based on this and a considerable amount of data compiled
from ethnographies, Sahlins has developed a typology of "reciprocity"
for primitive exchange. First, he defines generalized reciprocity, of which

"a good pragmatic indication . . . is a sustained one-way flow. Failure to reciprocate does not cause the giver of stuff to stop giving: the goods move one way, in favor of the have-nots for a very long period" (1972:194). He defines balanced reciprocity as where an equivalent return is calculated "so the pragmatic test of balanced reciprocity becomes an inability to tolerate one-way flows; the relations between people are disrupted by a failure to reciprocate within limited time and equivalence leeways" (1972:194). Finally, he defines negative reciprocity as "the attempt to get something for nothing with impugnity. . . . indicative ethnographic terms include 'haggling' or 'barter,' 'gambling,' 'chicanery,' 'theft,' and other varieties of seizure" (1972:195). Clearly, the type of reciprocity employed in the social exchange theories of Blau, Emerson, and (by imputation) of Homans is balanced reciprocity. Neither of the other type is intended. Yet, generalized reciprocity and not balanced reciprocity is seen by Sahlins (1972:223) as the type most prevalent in kinship groups, tribes, and chiefdoms.

Apparently for many primitive exchange systems, balanced reciprocity is not a necessary empirical condition for the existence of persisting social exchange relations. In generalized reciprocity a failure to reciprocate is often inconsequential in comparison with the overriding social relationship upon which the exchanges are based. In these cases the exchanges are predicated on the relationship, rather than the relationship being predicated on the exchanges (Sahlins, 1972:191–275). Similarly, in modern families parents do not expect their children to pay them back for their support. Even in capitalist systems parents do not keep account books to be balanced at a future date by their children. Further, the importance of a normative system or of a state is underscored in the case of balanced reciprocity by Sahlins's concern for the "special conditions" necessary for its continuity.

While elements of some of the foregoing relationships might be interpretable from the point of view of distributive justice and similar formulations, generalized reciprocity, considered as a sustained one-way flow, is clearly beyond the scope of these notions. In fact, in generalized reciprocity the flow is sustained in a direction directly opposite to that expected from the point of view of the distributive justice formulation. For example, in primitive systems, the hunter has the sole investment in the activity; the recipient, none. Yet, for the relationship, all that is received is profit for the recipient and loss for the hunter. Nor are these relations necessarily balanced by gratitude as expressed in the form of symbolic rewards from the recipient to the hunter, for it is often the case that such symbolics (including obsequiousness) are proscribed in primitive systems. It is simply bad manners to thank those who provide sustenance. Generalized reciprocal exchanges are, we feel, properly treated by Sahlins and other anthropologists as exchange relationships and as such, they should be central to the concern of social exchange theory and not read out as merely free gifts, as Blau seems to imply.

Specifically balanced reciprocity, as suggested by Sahlins, requires special conditions for its continuity. Primitive systems are not systems composed only of exchange relations. As discussed in the foregoing section, exchange relations are governed by overarching normative systems—these being coercive in nature. Consider the possible fate in such a system of a successful hunter who did not share his catch with others as expected. Would this action be ignored, or would there be consequences from others? Thus, for primitive systems, as well as familial interaction and contractual relations, exchange and coercive relations must be considered together as analytically essential features of the empirical system. When such systems are operating smoothly, coercion will remain potential. The successful hunter who magnanimously shares his catch with the group may give a false impression to the uninitiated that these are free gifts. Yet it is the normative system, i.e., the mutual contingencies which the group has generated, that prescribes and proscribes which social actors shall share with one another and under what conditions.

On the other end of Sahlins's continuum is negative reciprocity. Haggling and barter may be interpreted as processes of balance. Such an interpretation is not, however, generally sound for chicanery, theft, and seizure.

Balanced reciprocity seems to be a comparatively limited and sometimes fragile process in the working of exchange relationships. A serious question may be raised about reciprocity *per se* as a motive in perpetuating social exchange. If reciprocity were always a sufficient human motive, the potential coercive normative and contractual systems within which social exchange flourishes would be superfluous. Yet, the ubiquity of such coercive systems shows the inadequacy of reciprocity in sustaining exchange relationships. Perhaps the conditions under which balanced exchange is most likely to attain a durable character are not systems governed by reciprocity but modern legal-contractual systems.

It is clear, then, that all social exchange relations are not balanced. It is further evident that they do not necessarily tend toward balance in either the short or the long run, nor are all social exchange relations based wholly or in part on reciprocity as a motivating force in the relationship. In fact there is reason to suppose that the vast majority of social exchange relations take forms distinct from that which would have been expected from the point of view of the postulate of universal balanced reciprocity. Clearly, if errors of interpretation are to be avoided, and if analyses and interpretations are to have nontrivial scope, a broader conception of exchange is needed.

THE POSTULATE OF UNIVERSAL COMMENSURABILITY

Commensurate social exchange means that the items in exchange are measured according to a common standard by those engaged in the exchange. Hence, commensurability raises the question as to whether or not certain items can be exchanged for one another. Perhaps the most familiar context available for illustrating the idea of commensurable exchange is the modern economic market. Marx saw the development of capitalism as a transition in which formerly incommensurable items (land, labor, and capital) became commensurable items as money became the universal standard for negotiating exchanges. This transition is illustrated in Marx's discussion of the Trinty Formula of capitalism:

> First, the alleged sources of the annually available wealth belong to widely dissimilar spheres and are not at all analogous with one another. They have about the same relation to each other as lawyer's fees, red beets and music.
> Capital, land, labour! However, capital is not a thing, but rather a definite social production relation, belonging to a definite historical formation of society, which is manifested in a thing and lends this thing a specific social character.
> Capital is rather the means of production transformed into capital, which in themselves are no more capital than gold or silver in itself is money (1967:814–815).

That which is seen as commensurable will vary among societies. In certain primitive exchange systems, a bachelor would see as commensurable an exchange of female cousins with another member of the tribe for a comparable number of females for marriage. Similarly, an exchange of a particular type and number of domestic animals has been seen as commensurable with a desirable marriage. Yet such exchanges would be predicated on the common ideological standards of prestige, honor, or propriety in that system. In contradistinction, while these primitive systems may consider land, labor, and capital incommensurable, modern capitalist systems would normatively and legally not consider humans as items for exchange.

Not all items available in any system are commensurate. Even in the capitalism which Marx and Engels see as having "resolved personal worth into exchange value, and in the place of the numberless, indefeasible chartered freedoms, has set up that single, unconscionable freedom—Free Trade" (1948:11), definite proscriptions pertaining to exchange are still found. It would thus seem that a notable effect of ideologies upon any system of social relations is their role in defining what is commensurable and what is not. Ideologies, then, are in one respect qualitative prescriptive and/or proscriptive guidelines for exchange relations within a system. The ideology of a given system delineates its commensurability, thereby proscribing certain exchanges, and even permitting certain incommensurate items to be exchanged.

In cases of incommensurate exchange, social actors perform certain acts because their statuses and roles define a given act as proper or obligatory, not because of expected reward or simple habit. In incommensurable social exchange, the question the social actor may ask is not, "Is this profitable?", but "Is this right?" Actors whose behavior is actually guided by such notions as right and wrong will not consider the cost/profit involved in their actions. When the exchange involves incommensurate items which by definition cannot be measured by a common standard the actors cannot make calculations of loss and gain.

Modern families, for example, are generally characterized by the belief that actions performed for one another should be done out of love and not out of selfish or profit-oriented motives. The husband who treats his wife like a maid is comically ridiculed in Western industrial nations. The wife who treats her husband solely as a source of income has been traditionally vilified as a shrew. Sexual behavior can provide a good indicator of the state of a marriage in terms of whether the partners are preoccupied with who does more investing and who gains more benefits. Such considerations suggest marital difficulties. Sexual behavior in which pleasure is the major consideration precludes comparisons based on egoistic profit/loss concerns, for it is this identification with general happiness or well-being that gives the status and roles of marriage partners their specific character.

Feudal society represents a case of an entire social system for which the fundamental basis of exchange was incommensurate exchange. Conquerors parceled out land or fiefs to their distinguished warriors as rewards for duty fulfilled. But fulfillment of duty and lands had no common standard. After the collapse of the Roman Empire, neither the state nor the family provided security or protection from various sources of conflict and coercion. Hence, the more powerful accepted homage and service from the less powerful, creating strong obligations for mutual assistance and protection. Oaths of vassalage became the overriding bonds of mutual dependence throughout the feudal structure. Such oaths were, at the apex of feudalism, considered as seriously as contemporary marriage vows and to disregard the bond, according to Bloch, "was the most terrible of sins" (1961:232).

Regarding premodern systems, Polanyi has emphasized that "in spite of the chorus of academic incantations so persistent in the nineteenth century, gain and profit made on exchange never before [capitalism] played an important part in human economy" (1968:3). One might add that, not only is gain and profit a recent addition to the exchange process, but also much of what researchers using contemporary theories and terminology call exchange is defined in premodern groups not as exchange, but as obligations or bonds of a highly personal nature. For example, employers in New Guinea found that the indigenous tribes did not conceptualize the performance of contractual work as an impersonal, limited transaction based upon calculations of gain, but rather, as part of an encompassing social relationship for the common welfare of both parties that went beyond the contractual arrangement (Schwimmer, 1973:72).

In many cases, though, we may find that there is no conceptualization of exchange by those engaged in the relationship, nor is it seen as a process motivated by costs and profits. How are these social relationships to be properly understood? Schwimmer has pointed out the significance of complementarity in determination of transactions within specified complementary status and role relations (1973):

> This notion of complementarity is inseparable from all our discourse about giving and receiving. For instance, in the present work I shall write a good deal about the exchange relationships between mother's brother and sister's son, husband and wife, son-in-law and father-in-law, friend and friend, creditor and debtor, victor and vanquished. Not only have the patterns of relationship linking these dyads been laid down by Orokaiva custom, but the complementary nature of these relationships is already implicit in the words I have used to describe them (Schwimmer, 1973:4).

Closely related to the concept of complementarity is the concept of exchange sphere. According to Schwimmer, the anthropological study of how viable social relationships are established generated a distinction between exchanges of items belonging to the same sphere and exchanges of items belonging to different spheres; "Firth, Steiner, Bohannan, Salisbury and others have distinguished between transactions of this type and more complex ones called translations (Steiner) or conversions

(Bohannan)" (1973:5). As Schwimmer notes, these translations or conversions are characteristic of incommensurate exchanges designated between complementary status and role relations:

> A person who gives a service receives influence, but the person who "gives" the influence cannot "receive" influence in return; he receives only service. Being inferior in status, any service he gives will gain him, not influence, but perhaps material goods, or perhaps a service of a different kind. Conversions are a normal phenomenon in social exchange (1973:5).

Thus, it can be seen that commensurable and incommensurable exchanges are distinctly separate phenomena. When exchange items are commensurable, calculations of profit and loss can be made, and, as a consequence, can govern the occurence of such exchanges, the frequency of their reoccurence, and the rates of exchange for the items. When exchange items are incommensurable, questions of profit and loss cannot arise. Thus, incommensurable exchanges are governed not by profit and loss but by conceptions of right and wrong as they are defined by the ideologies of those engaged in the exchange. As social analysts we can say that these latter activities are in fact exchanges (1) because the services and goods exchanged are desired by those receiving them, and (2) because through complementary statuses and roles, the flows of these goods and services are mutually contingent. Because those engaged in the relationships do not see the parts as measurable by the same standard, though they will see beyond the obligations for morally right action to the underlying complementarity of the system, that is, they will not necessarily see themselves as engaged in social relations of exchange.

In relatively small systems the transfer of resources is organized along the principle of complementarity. Large systems can be made up of large numbers of such small systems with complementary relations between groups, as in feudalism. In other words the right or obligation affixed to the individual's position in the group, along with the incommensurability of the items, eliminates the motive of calculable exchange. As any given group or subgroup expands, though, the personal bonds embedded in the status and role relations can become tenuous. The usual concomitant to such expansion is the development of more complementary relationships. Feudalism exemplified such a process with its enormous weblike system of interlocking personal commitments, as many a person was both man and master to others in the hierarchy. As a group increases in size, the individual becomes cognizant of a limited area in the system of relationships. The utility of a standard measure of exchange items, by which one could circumvent traditional complementarity and create new, albeit impersonal and purely economic relations, becomes evident. Money, for example, becomes a universal standard for exchange in regions and social strata formerly inaccessible to outsiders. Capitalism, as an ideological system, represents an entirely new means of social organization. Capital provides the means for establishing a vast market in which the personal bonds engendered in former systems diminished to familial and communal units. What transactions one could participate in no longer wholly adhered to personal bonds, but also took on the impersonal unit of commensurability called money. Thus, the separation of social and economic exchange is a basic distinction between incommensurate and commensurate exchange. The difference between the two is found in the ideological method of conversion. Either the status and role relations are personalized bonds within which incommensurate items flow or an impersonal item is used as a commensurate standard for the flow of exchange items.

SUMMARY

Perhaps it is not overly harsh to assert that social exchange theory contains a stereotypical conception of social relationships. Taken as a whole, that conception asserts that all important and durable social relationships are balanced reciprocally. The actors engaged in the relationship make certain calculations of gain and loss, and consequently, the items exchanged are always commensurable. Because of the claims for the empirical universality of this type of relationship, it cannot be seen as a consciously constructed ideal type which is intended to be compared to reality for purposes of interpretation—thus, the term stereotypical seems justified.

Social exchange theory in the form in which it has been critically examined here is operant exchange theory. We have not dwelled on its operant basis in the foregoing remarks, for a critical examination of operant psychology and sociology would require space far beyond the limits of this article. Nevertheless, we would be remiss not to point out that the postulates of exchange theory are related to its operant beginnings as interpreted by Homans. Operant social actors, if they can be so called, are typically seen as avoiding punishments, calculating losses and gains, and maintaining certain types of balances. Whether these interpretations of operant psychology are in fact sound is itself open to discussion.

Quite apart from the question of the soundness of operant interpretations of human behavior and of their applications to social relationships, there appears to be need for a fundamental extension and reformulation of social exchange theory. Coercion and conflict are simply not adequately dealt with, and they cannot be ignored because they are themselves governing mechanisms for ongoing systems of exchange. Clearly, relations of exchange may or may not be based wholly or in part upon motives of reciprocity, and may or may not be balanced in either the short or the long run.

Finally, some social relationships, which are properly called exchange relations, are simply not recognized as such by those engaged in them and, consequently, cannot be based upon ideas of profit and loss, cannot be balanced, and cannot be reciprocal, at least as those terms are presently interpreted in exchange theory. If serious social analysis is to follow from social exchange theory, then a fundamental reformulation is necessary.

NOTES

1. Not all means of negative sanctioning are state-regulated, yet the legal codes of most states do consider crimes against the person and crimes against property as violations of one's inviolable rights as a citizen. Less intense means of negative sanctioning are numerous, ranging from the off-cited sociological study of "arm-binging" in a work group as discussed in the Hawthorne studies, to everyday insults (i.e., symbolic negative sanctions). Our argument should not be construed as one in which coercion is regarded as a rarity; indeed, quite the contrary is intended.

2. Homans does briefly touch on reciprocity in his earlier work. For example, in his discussion titled, "An example: The Control of Reciprocity" (1951:284) Homans states: "We shall, in this book, continue to use the conventional language of reward and punishment" (1951:285). It would appear that this position has been maintained throughout his later work as well. Furthermore, Homans skirts a number of sociological problems regarding reciprocity and commensurability by stating:

> Let us choose a norm that is one of the world's commonest: if a man does a favor for you, you must do a roughly equivalent favor for him in return. Unlike economists, we do not need to go into the question of what constitutes equivalence or price—how many yams are worth a fish in one society, how many votes are worth a job in another. Equivalence varies from favor to favor and from group to group. Let us take the different equivalences as given for a particular group (1951:285).

REFERENCES

BLAU, PETER M.
1964 Exchange and Power in Social Life. New York: Wiley & Sons.
BLOCH, MARC
1961 Feudal Society. London: Routledge & Kegan Paul.

BURGESS, ROBERT L., and JOYCE McCARL NIELSEN
  1974 "An experimental analysis of some structural determinants of equitable and inequitable exchange relations." American Sociological Review 39:3, 427–443.
CROSBIE, PAUL V.
  1972 "Social exchange and power compliance: A test of Homans' propositions." Sociometry 35:1, 203–222.
EKEH, PETER P.
  1974 Social Exchange Theory. London: Heinemann Educational Books.
EMERSON, RICHARD M.
  1962 "Power-dependence relations." American Sociological Review 27:31–41.
  1964 "Power-dependence relations: Two experiments." Sociometry, 27: 282–298.
  1969 "Operant psychology and exchange theory." In Robert L. Burgess and Don Bushell, Jr. (eds.), Behavioral Sociology: The Experimental Analysis of Social Process. New York: Columbia University Press.
  1972 "Exchange theory, Part II: Exchange relations and network structures." In Joseph Berger, Morris Zelditch, Jr., and Bo Anderson (eds.), Sociological Theories in Progress, Vol. II. Boston: Houghton Mifflin.
  1976 "Social exchange theory." In Alex Inkeles (ed.), Annual Review of Sociology, Vol. II. Palo Alto, Calif.: Annual Reviews Inc.
GOODE, WILLIAM
  1972 "Presidential address: The place of force in human society." American Sociological Review 37:5, 507–519.
GOULDNER, ALVIN, W.
  1960 "The norm of reciprocity: A preliminary statement." American Sociological Review 25:161–178.
HOMANS, GEORGE C.
  1951 The Human Group. London: Routledge & Kegan Paul.
  1961 Social Behavior: Its Elementary Forms. New York: Harcourt, Brace and World.
  1967 "Fundamental social processes." In Neil Smelser (ed.), Sociology: An Introduction. New York: Wiley.
  1974 Social Behavior: Its Elementary Forms. New York: Wiley.
MARX, KARL, and FRIEDRICH ENGELS
  1948 Manifesto of the Communist Party. Ed. F. Engels. New York: International Publishers.
MARX, KARL
  1967 Capital, Vol. III. Ed. F. Engels. New York: International Publishers.
MICHENER, ANDREW, H., and EUGENE D. COHEN
  1973 "Effects of punishment magnitude in the bilateral threat situation: Evidence for the deterrence hypothesis." Journal of Personality and Social Psychology 26:427–438.
MICHENER, ANDREW H., JERRY J. VASKE, STEPHEN L. SCHLEIFER, JOSEPH G. PLAZEWSKI, and LARRY J. CHAPMAN
  1975 "Factors affecting concession rate and threat usage in bilateral conflict." Sociometry 38:G2–80.

MULKAY, M. J.
  1971 Functionalism, Exchange and Theoretic Strategy. New York: Schocken Books.
POLANYI, KARL
  1968 Primitive, Archaic and Modern Economies: Essays of Karl Polanyi. Ed. George Dalton, Boston: Beacon Press.
SAHLINS, MARSHALL
  1972 Stone Age Economics. Chicago: Aldine.
SCHWIMMER, ERIK
  1973 Exchange in the Social Structure of the Orokaiva: Traditional and Emergent Ideologies in the Northern District of Papua. New York: St. Martin's Press.
SIMPSON, RICHARD L.
  1972 Theories of Social Exchange. Morristown, N.Y.: General Learning Corporation.
SOLZHENITSYN, ALEXANDER
  1971 One Day in the Life of Ivan Denisovich. New York: Ballantine Books.
WEBER, MAX
  1947 The Theory of Social and Economic Organization. Glencoe, Ill.: Free Press.

5. Behavioral Sociology: Emergent Forms and Issues

JAMES W. MICHAELS and DAN S. GREEN

We wish to provide an introduction to behavioral sociology by briefly describing its origins, major forms, and the features that have made it attractive to some, but unattractive to others. Although we cannot describe all that falls under the broad heading of behavioral sociology in this brief paper, our intent is to provide a representative view of a major perspective that, according to Ritzer (1975:vi), remains unfamiliar to most sociologists.

Ritzer (1975:145) defines behavioral sociology as the "theoretical effort to apply the principles of psychological behaviorism to sociological questions." Thus, a behavioral sociologist is one who uses the concepts and principles of operant conditioning for the purpose of examining, explaining, and sometimes altering human social behavior. Behavior analysis may be applied to the socially relevant behavior of individuals, the interaction of individuals in groups, or the behavior of groups, organizations, or even societies as units. Behavioral sociologists are interested in how the social behavior of individuals or collectives is influenced by social and nonsocial environments.

ORIGINS AND DEVELOPMENT

The basic concepts and principles used by behavioral sociologists are those of operant conditioning, empirically derived by B. F. Skinner and his students (e.g., Skinner, 1953). Operants are behaviors that "operate"

SOURCE: Reprinted from *The American Sociologist* 13 (February 1978):23-29.

on the environment, producing some consequence which may alter subsequent behavior. In short, operants are behaviors that are maintained or altered by their consequences. The functional relationships between operants and their consequences (relationships which are usually expressed as contingency statements) provide the foundation for operant analyses and behavior modification. Behaviorists generally explain behavior by specifying the conditions that reliably produce it. This means identifying the consequences (i.e., reinforcers and punishers) of behavior, their sources, and the contingencies or conditions on which they are based. Identification, in turn, frequently requires the experimental manipulation of consequences and contingencies to effectively control the behavior under examination. Thus, distinctions between explanation, prediction, and control become somewhat blurred. Although the principles and procedures of operant conditioning cannot be presented here (see Reynolds, 1975 for a brief introduction), it is important to note that behavioral sociologists have gotten much mileage from only a few basic principles.

Ritzer (1975:142) considers Skinner the major exemplar of social behaviorism (not to be confused with Mead's social behaviorism). But George Homans (1961), directly influenced by Skinner, stimulated the adoption of these principles by developing and elaborating five general behavioral propositions which form the foundation for his social exchange approach. Perhaps the major significance of this early attempt was that it provided the groundwork for the transition from controlling the nonsocial behavior of pigeons to analyzing the social exchange behavior of humans. This transition was based partly on the simple observation that people in interaction establish contingencies for rewarding and punishing one another. However, Homans clearly indicated that the explanatory power of these principles was not confined to face-to-face interaction, but extended to macro-sociological phenomena as well. In fact, according to Homans (1964:818), the only *general explanatory* propositions are "not about the equilibrium of societies but about the behavior of men."

Although Homans's writings may not have led *directly* to behavioral sociology as it appears today, he was adopted as sociological exemplar by a group of sociologists primarily at Washington University. This group (which also included Robert Burgess, Don Bushell, David Schmitt, and James Wiggins) had independently become interested in applied behavior analysis under the influence of Keith Miller and later of Robert Hamblin. They were instrumental in developing behavioral sociology as it appears today. One substantial contribution was Burgess and Bushell's (1969) book (which included contributions from Homans,

Kunkel, and Skinner, as well as from the Washington University group), which coined the label, defined the forms and scope of the perspective, and still serves as a major textbook for courses in behavioral sociology (see Hamblin and Kunkel, 1977, for more recent readings on behavioral theory and research in sociology).

Major Forms

Research and writings described in this section are divided into three categories: (1) applied behavior analysis in complex organizations; (2) experimental analyses of social exchange and social process; and (3) behavior macrosociology and theoretical extensions. These categories correspond to work done primarily by psychologists, social psychologists, and sociologists, respectively.

Applied Behavior Analysis in Complex Organizations

Although complex organizations constitute a major analytical domain within sociology, few sociologists have become involved in, or even paid attention to, applied behavior analysis in such settings. Applied behavior analysis began by examining and altering the idiosyncratic behaviors of individual mental patients; its application has gradually shifted to normals, to complex social behavior, and toward total systems (e.g., see Goodall, 1972, for a brief overview).

Behavior analysts have worked with "captive subjects" in mental hospitals, as well as in educational and correctional settings. In all such settings the token economy is the most popular systemic program. For example, Hamblin and his colleagues (Hamblin, *et al.*, 1971) used a token economy system to alter the behavior of inner-city school children who had been labeled culturally deprived, disturbed, and unteachable. Students were awarded tokens for meeting previously defined behavioral objectives. Tokens earned could be exchanged for a variety of goods or opportunities. Bizarre and disruptive behaviors were treated by terminating reinforcement for the behaviors (extinction procedures) and simultaneously reinforcing other, more accepted social behaviors. Although occasionally a "time out" procedure (brief removal of the opportunity to earn tokens) was used, the use of aversive stimuli or punishment was avoided. Among the behaviors strengthened were reading, writing, correct language use, good work habits, peer tutoring, constructive interaction with teachers and peers, and even better performance on IQ tests.

Since Nord (1969) outlined the transition from educational to management applications, similar reinforcement procedures (though not token economies) have been used to strengthen attendance, punctuality, and quality and quantity of performance by both workers and supervisors. For example, Emery Air Freight was able to substantially improve sales, responses to customer queries, and appropriate container usage by instituting a worker administered performance feedback system, and by reinforcing performance improvement with praise and recognition (Business Week, 1971).

A recent text (Nietzel, *et al.*, 1977) suggests that behavior analysis can also be applied at the community level to a wide range of problems including drug abuse, alcoholism, community mental health, aging, unemployment, and the environment. Applications aimed at reducing environmental problems (littering, recycling, energy conservation, and pollution, for example) show particular promise for immediate adoption on an even larger scale (e.g., see the review by Tuso and Geller, 1976).

It is easy for the sociologist to dismiss applied behavior analysis on the basis that, although behavioral, it is not sociology. After all, the principles and procedures used were developed and are applied primarily by psychologists. Furthermore, the fact that the analyses occur in organizational and community settings does not make them inherently sociological. On the other hand, both the settings and the problems addressed have also been analytically addressed by sociologists. Thus, there are several reasons why the application of behavior analysis should at least be regarded as sociologically relevant. First, these applications go beyond descriptive and correlational analyses to deal with variables that directly affect behavior; therefore, they may provide a more complete understanding of organizations and communities. Second, because these settings constitute major analytical domains within sociology, sociologists should have something to contribute. Third, the more sociologists do become involved, the more the applications will involve social structural variables, and thus become more sociological. Finally, as funding becomes more contingent on demonstrable utility, applied sociology may become more attractive.

Experimental Analyses of Social Exchange and Social Process

Recent behavior social exchange formulations combine operant principles and procedures with the early social exchange frameworks of

Thibaut and Kelley (1959) and Homans (1961). In one of the first attempts in this area, Emerson (1972) used balanced and unbalanced power-dependence relations between actors to address such traditional sociological concerns as values, cohesion, norm formation, role and status, stratification, and division of labor, as applied to both small and large groups.

The more recent social exchange formulation by Molm and Wiggins (1977) is even more explicitly operant, using a strictly operant model rather than a rational choice model. They have investigated the conditions under which social exchange is established, maintained, disrupted, and re-established. Other laboratory-experimental analyses of social exchange which address the same concerns include those by Burgess and Nielsen (1974), Marwell and Schmitt (1975), and Michaels and Wiggins (1976).

The major independent variables in most of these studies involve structural power-dependence relations between actors which produce variations in profit, inequity, and social exchange. Procedural paradigms involve a series of trials during which subjects choose to obtain rewards independently, through exchange, or cooperatively.

The work of Marwell and Schmitt (1975) best exemplifies the cumulative nature of this research; they have done more than 30 interrelated experiments on factors affecting cooperation. Two persons in separate rooms could earn money by operating plungers on consoles. Both could earn money cooperatively only if *both* pushed their switches to "Work with other person" and operated their plungers for mutual benefit. Otherwise, each could earn money (usually somewhat less) by pushing the switch to "Work alone" and operating the plunger solely for individual benefit. Factors found to interfere with cooperation included payoff inequity, risk, and the opportunity to "rip-off" one another. Factors found to facilitate cooperation included unconditional cooperation by other, the opportunity for verbal communication (visual presence had no effect), and, of course, higher payoffs for cooperation.

Other laboratory-experimental analyses of social process have examined macrosociological concerns using larger groups. For example, Wiggins (1966) examined some of the functions of the stratification issue raised by Davis and Moore by controlling how status differentiated groups allocated group rewards (differentially or equally) as a function of the external consequences of the allocations. Leik, Emerson, and Burgess (1968) examined social stratification by controlling the internal stratification of groups as a function of structurally determined exchange outcomes of various coalitions. Finally, Burgess' (1968) experiments on problem solving communication networks resolved long-standing inconsistencies regarding the relative efficiency of various networks. In these experiments, the Circle (a decentralized network) and the Wheel (a centralized network) were found to be equally effective when reinforced for speed and accuracy of solutions, and when the groups operated until steady state performance was reached. During early trials without reinforcement, however, the Wheel was superior.

But are such studies sociological? Not if sociology is restricted to the analysis of existing social systems in their natural settings. However, if sociology involves the analysis of general social processes such as stratification and functional differentiation, such studies are definitely sociological. It is important to note, however, that such studies should be regarded as demonstrations of how the behavior of social systems can be controlled by exogenous consequences and contingencies; not as explanations for how any particular social system got to be the way it is.

Behavioral Macrosociology and Theoretical Extensions

According to Friedrichs (1974:4–5), if behavioral sociology is to make the headway he predicts for it, it will demand a subtler mediator than Skinner or Homans. In terms of empirical research, he nominates for this role James S. Coleman, whose work involves both a policy research orientation and mathematical models appropriate to the macroscopic settings and problems faced by sociologists. However, although Coleman's (e.g., 1973) work does involve elements found in social exchange formulations (e.g., rational choice and profit maximization assumptions), he explicitly disavowed any connection with Skinnerian psychology during his address at a plenary session of the ASA convention (Montreal, 1974). Robert Hamblin may be a more willing nominee. His previous work may be considered from the behavioral perspective, and his recent mathematical-empirical research falls into the same tradition. Unlike Coleman, Hamblin uses inductively derived (curve fitting) mathematical equations and an explicit reinforcement interpretation in his analysis of cultural innovation and diffusion (Hamblin, et al., 1973). His first step in explaining "use diffusion," for example, is to find the equations (usually exponential or logistic) which best describe the diffusion of activities (e.g., number of automobile registrations, academic degrees conferred, marriages and divorces, and various leisure activities) over time. Although these equations yield the expected high level of explained variance (median r^2 is .98), many will no doubt consider the equations descriptive rather than explanatory. However, these equations are then integrated into an axiomatic mathematical theory with a reinforcement interpretation. For example, the power function equation of Axiom 2 states that the level of behavioral steady state is a positive monotonic function of the level of reinforcement (Hamblin, et al., 1973:198).

In terms of theoretical explications, Friedrichs (1974:6) nominates John Finley Scott (1971) as the exemplar (perhaps because the title of his book, *Internalization of Norms*, gave little hint of its contents—a social learning approach to socialization). Indeed, social learning formulations such as Scott's may be more attractive to sociologists than strictly operant formulations because they provide more familiar elaborations, and they more closely approximate what sociologists regard as relevant theory. In this regard Kunkel's (1970, 1975) social learning formulation addresses such traditional sociological concerns as social structure and anomie, cultural deprivation, social change and economic growth, and social problems.

Theoretical elaboration of behavioral principles has been applied to other areas of traditional sociological concern. Burgess and Akers's (1966a) behavioral reformulation of Sutherland's differential association theory of criminal behavior states, in essence, that criminal behavior is likely to be adopted whenever the opportunities, and magnitudes and frequencies of reinforcement, are greater for criminal than for noncriminal behavior. This reformulation was later expanded (Akers, 1973) as a general social learning theory of deviant behavior that complements other deviance theories such as anomie, conflict, control, and labeling. In another example, Michaels (1974) described the similarities between human ecology and behavioral psychology and considered the desirability and feasibility of linking the two behavioral approaches. Similarities discussed included the recognition of the interaction between behavior and environment, the view that change is externally determined, and quantitative analyses involving aggregated behaviors. Rather striking parallels between the general concepts and principles of the two approaches were also described.

Clearly, behavioral macrosociology has shown substantial variation and elaboration in form and substance, as well as convergence with more established sociological approaches. There are two reasons for this: (1) operant principles lack the cultural substance necessary to explain particular social phenomena; and (2) social systems include characteristics and processes different from those found in individual learning (Kunkel, 1975:186). Thus, emergence, elaboration, and convergence are likely to remain the dominant patterns in behavioral sociology.

ISSUES

Perhaps no other perspective appears so completely different, even antithetical to traditional sociological training and practice, as the behavioral perspective. The unique features of this perspective are major attractions for some, but have evoked major criticism from others.

In a recent survey of behavioral sociologists (Green, 1975), respondents were asked to give reasons they were attracted to this perspective. Typical answers were: (1) it is a rigorous scientific approach, methodologically strong, theoretically parsimonious and sound; (2) it makes sense and is a useful alternative for the study of human social behavior; and (3) it is objective, replicable, experimental, and cumulative, and thus offers techniques that can be used to make significant changes in social behavior. The need for a social technology has been expressed by Tarter (1973:153): "A science without a technology is doomed to the monotony of repetitive observation and idle speculation."

However, other sociologists utterly reject the possibility that behavioral principles have anything to offer sociology. Several features of behaviorism have been issues of concern in psychology as well as sociology. Although space constraints preclude lengthy consideration of these issues, we would be remiss if we failed to consider them, however briefly.

Tautology

There is considerable confusion regarding the logical status of reinforcement principles. There is disagreement not only over whether or not they are tautological, but also over whether the use of tautologies should be admired or condemned. Regarding the first question, reinforcement definitions and principles can be stated in both tautological and non-tautological forms (e.g., Burgess and Akers, 1966b). Regarding the second question, tautologies have been admired for their utility in other disciplines such as physics and economics. If reinforcement principles are tautological, they are relational tautologies, rather than logical tautologies (Chadwick-Jones, 1976:214–218). Finally, a conclusion either way would seem to make little difference at the operational level.

Reduction

Because the term "reduction" has been used in many ways, its meaning for sociologists is not entirely clear. The classical (some say only) case of *complete reduction* was the reduction of thermodynamics to statistical mechanics; yet both still constitute separate disciplines. Because the requirements for complete reduction are very demanding of both sides, sociology and psychology seem unlikely candidates.

On the other hand, Homans, when he attempts to explain or interpret sociological principles by induction, correlating them to more abstract, corresponding psychological principles, is engaging in *logical reduction* (Chadwick-Jones, 1976:367). Although some sociological principles can be "explained" or accounted for in this way, it should be obvious that the consequent reduction will be devoid of the original sociocultural concepts or referents.

Finally, some critics apparently fear that behavioral sociologists intend to atomize or nominalize emergent phenomena. Yet, as suggested by Kunkel (1975:47), behavioral sociology naturally leads to social structural, rather than individualistic, explanations.

The Omission of Internal States

Behaviorists generally, but not universally, omit internal states as relevant data. The resulting interpretation of behavior appears to move the locus of control from inside the actor to outside stimuli that are directly observable. Thus, autonomous and purposive man is no longer the initiator of his own action, but a responder to external stimuli. Regardless of the utility of such a model of man, it is apparently a discomforting one for many. Although behaviorists manage without involving internal states, any sociologist bent on explaining behavior by the cognitive processes that precede it can, on this basis alone, rightfully reject behavioral sociology.

The Issue of Behavior Control

Although the principles and procedures of the behavior perspective can be used solely for the analysis of social process, this perspective, more than any other, implies behavior modification and control. London (1969:208), states "The ethical challenge is that of how to preserve or enhance individual liberty under circumstances where its suppression will frequently be justified not only by the common welfare but for the individual's happiness." Kunkel (1975:116) has expressed a somewhat different view. He believes that when there is widespread agreement that a particular problem exists, it makes little sense, moral or otherwise, to leave it as it is.

CONCLUSION

The dominant pattern in the development of behavioral sociology has clearly been one of emergence. Behavioral sociology has shown great variability, elaboration, and even convergence with more established sociological perspectives. It is applicable to both micro- and macrosociological research problems. Thus, we agree with Warland's (1971:576) statement that behavioral sociology may be "best viewed as a critical step toward a future synthesis of theoretical and methodological views in the social sciences which hopefully will produce a more meaningful sociological perspective than our present one."

REFERENCES

AKERS, RONALD L.
  1973 Deviant Behavior: A Social Learning Approach. Belmont, Calif.: Wadsworth.
BURGESS, ROBERT L.
  1968 "Communication networks: An experimental re-evaluation." Journal of Experimental Social Psychology 4:324–337.
BURGESS, ROBERT L. and RONALD L. AKERS
  1966a "A differential reinforcement theory of criminal behavior." Social Problems 14 (Fall):128–147.
  1966b "Are operant principles tautological?" The Psychological Record 16:305–312.
BURGESS, ROBERT L. and DON BUSHELL (eds.)
  1969 Behavioral Sociology: The Experimental Analysis of Social Process. New York: Columbia University.
BURGESS, ROBERT L. and JOYCE M. NIELSEN
  1974 "An experimental analysis of some structural determinants of equitable and inequitable exchange relations." American Sociological Review 39 (June):427–443.
Business Week
  1971 "New tool: Reinforcement for good work." December 18:68–69.
CHADWICK-JONES, J. K.
  1976 Social Exchange Theory. New York: Academic Press.
COLEMAN, JAMES S.
  1973 The Mathematics of Collective Action. Chicago: Aldine.
EMERSON, RICHARD M.
  1972 "Exchange theory." Pp. 38–87 in Joseph Berger, Morris Zelditch, Jr., and Bo Anderson (eds.), Sociological Theories in Progress, Vol. 2. Boston: Houghton Mifflin.

FRIEDRICHS, ROBERT W.
1974 "The potential impact of B. F. Skinner upon American sociology." The American Sociologist 9 (February):3-8.
GOODALL, KENNETH
1972 "Shapers at work." Psychology Today 6 (November):53-138.
GREEN, DAN S.
1975 "Behavioral sociology: A new perspective." Paper presented at the 1975 meeting of the Midwestern Sociological Association, Chicago.
HAMBLIN, ROBERT, DAVID BUCKHOLDT, DANIEL FERRITOR, MARTIN KOZLOFF and LOIS BLACKWELL
1971 The Humanization Process: A Social, Behavioral Analysis of Children's Problems. New York: Wiley.
HAMBLIN, ROBERT L., R. BROOKE JACOBSEN and JERRY L. L. MILLER
1973 A Mathematical Theory of Social Change. New York: Wiley.
HAMBLIN, ROBERT L. and JOHN H. KUNKEL (eds.)
1977 Behavioral Theory in Sociology. New Brunswick, N.J.: Transaction Books.
HOMANS, GEORGE C.
1961 Social Behavior: Its Elementary Forms. New York: Harcourt, Brace and World.
1964 "Bringing men back in." American Sociological Review 29 (December):808-818.
KUNKEL, JOHN H.
1970 Society and Economic Growth: A Behavioral Perspective of Social Change. New York: Oxford University Press.
1975 Behavior, Social Problems, and Change. Englewood Cliffs, N.J.: Prentice-Hall.
LEIK, ROBERT K., RICHARD M. EMERSON and ROBERT L. BURGESS
1968 The Emergence of Stratification in Exchange Networks. Seattle: Institute for Social Research, University of Washington.
LONDON, PERRY
1969 Behavior Control. New York: Harper & Row.
MARWELL, GERALD and DAVID R. SCHMITT
1975 Cooperation: An Experimental Analysis. New York: Academic Press.
MICHAELS, JAMES W.
1974 "On the relation between human ecology and behavioral social psychology." Social Forces 52 (March):313-321.
MICHAELS, JAMES W. and JAMES A. WIGGINS
1976 "Effects of mutual dependency and dependency asymmetry on social exchange." Sociometry 39 (December):368-376.
MOLM, Linda D. and JAMES A. WIGGINS
1977 "A behavioral analysis of the dynamics of social exchange in the dyad." Paper presented at the Annual Meeting of the American Sociological Association, Chicago.

NIETZEL, MICHAEL T., RICHARD A. WINETT, MARIAN L. McDONALD and WILLIAM
    S. DAVIDSON
  1977 Behavioral Approaches to Community Psychology. New York: Per-
    gamon Press.
NORD, WALTER R.
  1969 "Beyond the teaching machine: The neglected area of operant condition-
    ing in the theory and practice of management." Organizational Behavior
    and Human Performance 4 (November):375–401.
REYNOLDS, G. S.
  1975 A Primer of Operant Conditioning. Glenview, Illinois: Scott, Foresman.
RITZER, GEORGE
  1975 Sociology: A Multiple Paradigm Science. Boston: Allyn and Bacon.
SCOTT, JOHN FINLEY
  1971 Internalization of Norms: A Sociological Theory of Moral Commit-
    ment. Englewood Cliffs, N.J.: Prentice-Hall.
SKINNER, B. F.
  1953 Science and Human Behavior. New York: Macmillan.
TARTER, DONALD E.
  1973 "Heeding Skinner's call: Toward the development of a social technol-
    ogy." The American Sociologist 8 (November):153–158.
THIBAUT, JOHN W. and HAROLD H. KELLEY
  1959 The Social Psychology of Groups. New York: John Wiley & Sons.
TUSO, MARGARET A. and E. SCOTT GELLER
  1976 "Behavior analysis applied to environmental/ecological problems: A
    review." Journal of Applied Behavior Analysis 9 (Winter):526.
WARLAND, REX
  1971 "Review of Behavioral Sociology: The Experimental Analysis of Social
    Process by Robert L. Burgess and Don Bushell, Jr." Rural Sociology 36
    (December):575–576.
WIGGINS, JAMES A.
  1966 "Status differentiation, external consequences, and alternative reward
    distributions." Sociometry 29 (June):89–103.

PART IV
DIALECTICS

Theory is also method. It is a demand that the world be approached in a particular way. Generally, dialectics, following the Marxist tradition, attacks positivistic social science. Applebaum explicates certain portions of Marxist methodology and philosophy in order to demonstrate the utility of a historical, dialectical method for understanding contemporary society. He considers Marxism as philosophy and method and suggests that the concept of *praxis* can bridge the gap between them. In the introduction Marx's concept of *praxis* was seen as one way of handling the mind/body split that had been introduced into the discipline. Applebaum argues that Marx's work, as exemplified in *Capital*, provides a methodology capable of responding to the need for laws and the humanistic concerns of the neo-positivists.

Walls extends these concerns by pointing out that a dialectical social science goes beyond the concerns of the political left. By outlining and then synthesizing two approaches to dialectics, Walls defines the dialectic in terms of the subject–object dialectic in history, as derived from Marx and expressed by Berger and Luckmann in terms of the processes of externalization, objectivization, and internalization.

To say that dialectics is anti-positivistic is not a rejection of scientific possibilities. It means, rather, that one tries to understand how the social world is constructed. Wardell and Benson show how this view stresses the social production of social arrangements, how contradiction is a central feature of social formation, and how societal totalities are related. Because this method is sensitive to change, and sees the world as socially constructed, it has profound implications for action.

1. Marxist Method: Structural Constraints and Social *Praxis*

RICHARD P. APPELBAUM

The antimony between freedom and determinism can be viewed as strictly parallel to that between idealist philosophy and science as conventionally conceived. Science, according to notions prevalent among social scientists, seeks universal determinate laws embedded in the very structure of the universe itself. Such laws operate "behind our backs"—that is, they govern the universe whether or not we are aware of them. Freedom, according to such a formulation, is very limited: it is the ability to recognize the operation of those laws, impartially study their operation, and then govern our behavior accordingly. The laws of ballistics can never be abrogated, but, if we understand them, we can send a missile halfway around the world with unerring accuracy. In one sense Marx unquestionably saw himself as a scientist—a person concerned with understanding the "laws of motion" of capitalist economic production. But at the same time Marx could not accept a determinist version of science which ultimately—pushed to its logical limits—left no room for free, conscious activity. Such thinking would appear to be directly antithetical to the revolutionary project. Revolution is no simple mechanical activity of spelling out in accurate detail the complex of forces operating at a given moment, constructing a course of action that respects those forces, and then pressing a button which starts the process towards its final outcome. For Marx, revolutionary struggle entailed not only a clear understanding of the social forces operating to

SOURCE: Reprinted from *The American Sociologist* 13 (February 1978):73–81.

produce social change, but it also involved continual choices, commitment, and an openness to the moment. It involved, in a word, freedom as
well as necessity. Freedom is the traditional concern of idealist philosophy, which emphasizes intellectual emancipation through reflection and
contemplation. It is not surprising that Marx spent his early years
studying philosophy, that his first works were heavily "philosophical"
in nature, and that he continually returned to "philosophic" themes
throughout his life. Before understanding Marx as a scientist, it is
necessary to understand the significance of philosophy for Marxist
thought.

MARXISM AS CRITICAL THEORY

For Hegel, the purpose of dialectical thought was to take dogmatic
notions about reality and render them transparent. Freedom, for Hegel,
was inward: it resulted from a certain kind of contemplation which
Hegel termed Reason. In the chapter on "sense-certainty" in the *Phenomenology*, Hegel (1967:149–160) argued that the immediate sensual
perceptions, which seem "to be the truest, the most authentic knowledge," the "bare fact of certainty," are really the "abstractest and poorest
kind of truth." This is because both subject and object are continually
changing, and—appearances to the contrary—exist only in relation to
one another. The only real sense-certainty, as Hume demonstrated, is a
congeries of unconnected point-instants: it is through mental processes
that we secure the reality of an object in time and space.

Hence, the immediate appears real to the senses, but it is not. The
radical implications of this position account for Hegel's appeal to Marx
and to the circle of left-Hegelians who surrounded him, as well as to
critical theorists today. In the chapter on "Commodities" in volume I of
Capital, Marx sought to demonstrate how something as seemingly real
and tangible as a commodity is actually something quite different from
what it appears:

> A commodity appears, at first sight, a very trivial thing, and easily
> understood. Its analysis shows that it is, in reality, a very queer
> thing, abounding in metaphysical subtleties and theological nice-
> ties.
>
> A commodity is . . . a mysterious thing, simply because in it the
> social character of men's labour appears to them as an objective
> character stamped upon the product of that labour; because the
> relation of the producers to the sum total of their own labour is
> presented to them as a social relation, existing not between them-

selves, but between the products of their labour. . . . There is a definite social relation between men that assumes, in their eyes, the fantastic form of a relation between things.

This Fetishism of commodities has its origin . . . in the peculiar social character of the labour that produces them (Marx, 1967:71-72).

What Marx meant by this last sentence is that the apparent social relationship between two inanimate objects (the fact that two commodities exchange for one another) is due in reality to the fact that both embody specific amounts of human labor time, and hence reflect a particular social organization of production. The three volumes of *Capital* begin with the chapter on commodities; the commodity is the immediate, "sense-certain" experience which we all take for granted. Using the commodity as a foil, Marx then sought to unravel the many threads that constitute the relations of capitalism; in so doing he demonstrated that simple commodity exchange presupposes a complex set of social, political, and economic conditions which had been quite invisible in the beginning.

Capital thus moves simultaneously on two levels. On one level, it is a scientific analysis. In Marx's terms, of capitalist economic production—a showing forth of underlying relationships and the special types of laws that govern them. On a second level, *Capital* is a critique of taken-for-granted thought—primarily of the categories of classical political economics, but also of popular notions of economic organization. *Capital* is appropriately subtitled "A Critique of Political Economy." It thus serves an important didactic purpose: it breaks through the veils of reification whereby people bestow naturalistic qualities on a world they themselves actually produce, as in the "mist-enveloped regions of the religious world [where] the productions of the human brain appear as independent beings endowed with life, and entering into relations both with one another and the human race" (Marx, 1967:217).

Critique, then, involves dissolving the seeming facticity of the conceptual categories that underlie our perceptions of the world—rendering "facts" transparent. To achieve such transparency, a "fact" must be situated within a concrete sociohistorical totality. Only by locating the commodity-form within capitalist economic production can its real nature be understood, and its seeming facticity thereby dissolved. The strength of critical theory is its unremitting emphasis on self-conscious human activity as the key to political emancipation. Reification—false consciousness—is the central concern; no automatic progression of society through inevitable stages of transition to a communist utopia is assumed, since an understanding of society is viewed as a necessary condition for its revolutionary transformation. But a weakness of critical theory has been its excessive preoccupation with philosophical issues, to the neglect of the empirical study of the structural conditions Marx believed to contain the possibilities for social change. Marx believed such study would entail a "scientific" approach to political economy.

MARXISM AS SCIENCE

Marx's desire to develop a unified science of man and nature was expressed as early as 1844, when he wrote that "natural science will in time incorporate into itself the science of man, just as the science of man will incorporate into itself natural science: there will be *one* science" (Marx, 1964:143). This "orthodox scientistic position identifies all possible knowledge with scientific knowledge" (Habermas, 1971:4). While Marx undertook no systematic study of the natural sciences (that task fell to Engels), it is clear that he had a positivist's view of their procedures, and that, furthermore, he felt them to be an appropriate model for his own emerging science. In the afterword to the second German edition of *Capital*, published in 1873, Marx approvingly quoted a Russian reviewer, who, discussing Marx's method, observed that

> ... Marx only troubles himself about one thing: *to show by rigid scientific investigation, the necessity of determinate orders of social conditions, and to establish as impartially as possible, the facts that serve him for fundamental starting points.* For this it is quite enough if he proves, at the same time, both the necessity of the present order of things, and the necessity of another order into which the first must inevitably pass over; and this is all the same, whether men believe it or do not believe it, *whether they are conscious or unconscious of it.* Marx treats the social movement as a process of natural history, *governed by laws not only independent of human will, but rather, on the contrary, determining that will, consciousness, and intelligence* ... in his opinion, every historical period has laws of its own. ... As soon as society has outlived a given period of development, and is passing over from one given stage to another, it begins to be subject also to other laws (Marx, 1967:18, emphasis added: see also pp. 8–9).

"What else," Marx asked, "is he [the reviewer] picturing but the dialectical method?" (p. 19)

As suggested in the quotation from the Russian reviewer, Marx moderated his scientistic position only to the extent that he at times argued that economic laws are historically specific, that is, different laws apply to different historical periods. Thus, in criticizing Malthus in Volume I of *Capital*, Marx observed that "every special historic mode of production has its own special laws of population, historically valid within its limits alone" (Marx, 1967:632). According to some who view Marx as a scientist, Marx's laws are more akin to those of biology than those of physics and chemistry, inasmuch as the latter "apply across the board in all places and at all times" whereas the former are seen as analogous to "historically specific laws" in that they apply to each species separately (Szymanski, 1973:31).

In actual practice, whatever his self-understanding, Marx's *usage* of the dialectic differs significantly from the scientistic mode suggested in these quotations. Marx's methodological understanding was limited by his lack of concentrated attention to methodological issues, as well as his limited knowledge of the practice of natural science. Marx failed to come to grips with the differing requirements for the study of social and physical phenomena (see Habermas, 1971: esp. pp. 25–42); indeed, the debate within European scholarship over the two "sciences" occurred after his death. Nonetheless, he did seek to bridge his two concerns— science and philosophy—throughout his writing; and his attempt is best understood by utilizing the notion of *praxis*, which I shall now consider.

Praxis: *The Dialectic of Subject and Object*

Marx, particularly in his earlier writings but in *Capital* as well, regarded man as a world-producing creature: that which distinguishes man from other animals is his ability to erect a project in imagination and subsequently realize it in practice. In achieving such a project man is constrained by the external conditions he encounters, including the limits of his knowledge; furthermore, those conditions (as well as his knowledge) are altered in the very process of realizing the project. Thus, Marx conceived of the labor *process* as an ongoing reciprocal relationship between objectification and reappropriation, with both theoretical and practical moments internally related. Human labor is thus conceived, ideally, as *praxis*. As Colletti (1971:84–85) observes, both causality and teleology are ideally operative according to Marx's conceptualization: *causality* because within ascertainable limits actions have determinate consequences, and *teleology* because action is consciously goal-oriented and therefore intentional effects may precede and govern efficient causes. Marx's entire work of criticism can be regarded as an attempt to demonstrate how the teleological aspects of human activity have been lost through the reification of the social world (and the consequent congealing of its laws). At the level of critique, it was Marx's intention to restore man's understanding of his potential role in the world, and thereby initiate the revolutionary project.

What distinguishes Marxism from positivist social science is its ability to move simultaneously on two levels: it formulates the laws of the "natural history" of capitalist economic organization, and at the same time demonstrates the ideological (i.e., historically situated) character of those laws so that they might be repealed by self-conscious workers organized collectively in their own interests. Criticism is not enough, nor is a theoretical understanding of how the laws of political economy operate and what they portend for the future of the capitalist economy. Nor is blind struggle; history does not move automatically towards socialism or any other predetermined end. Early in his writing Marx recognized that both critical awareness *and* scientific understanding were necessary to guide radical social change—as well as organized revolutionary activity. Science, criticism, organized class struggle—all are required, as Marx noted in 1843 when he wrote:

> It is clear that the arm of criticism cannot replace the criticism of arms. Material force can only be overthrown by material force; but a theory itself becomes a material force when it has seized the masses (From *Critique of Hegel's 'Philosophy of Right,'* in 1972a:18).

Marx used "science" in a very restricted sense: his science was not the predictive science of physics or chemistry. The future cannot be predicted; rather, in Sartre's words, it is "a project to be accomplished" (Sartre, 1971:115). Our knowledge of the future occurs only through activity oriented towards realizing that future; the future itself becomes concrete to us to the extent that we participate in shaping it (Lukács, 1971:11). Sartre captures succinctly the meaning of *praxis*, when he observes that "what is essential is not that man is made, but that he makes that which made him" (Sartre, 1971:115).

Marx himself distinguished natural and social history when he echoed Vico in observing that *"Human history differs from natural history in this, that we have made the former, but not the latter"* (Marx, 1967:372; emphasis added). Later in the same passage, Marx noted that the "abstract materialism of natural science . . . excludes history and its process"; this he regarded as a "weak point," which becomes evident whenever natural scientists "venture beyond the bounds of their own specialty" (373). Human history, for Marx, thus has a double nature: it is at once a project of human activity and a constraint on that activity, a social construct and an apparently natural condition of such construction.

Men make their own history, but they do not make it just as they please; they do not make it under circumstances chosen by themselves, but under circumstances directly found, given, and transmitted from the past. The tradition of all the dead generations weighs like a nightmare on the brain of the living (1972b:437).

Praxis is the union of theory and practice, the mutual transformation of subject and object, the precondition for reappropriating the social dimension of naturalized human history—these are the meanings of the term imparted by the Marxist tradition of critical theory. The utility of a "*praxis* orientation" for empirical social research will be demonstrated in the concluding section of this paper, by referring to Marx's treatment of what he regarded as a fundamental "law" of capitalist economic production: the tendency of the overall rate of profit to decline over time, thereby producing unavoidable economic crises. Before proceeding, however, it will be necessary to briefly introduce some of the basic terms of Marxist economic analysis.

The "Law" of the Falling Rate of Profit[1]

Marx analyzed the value of commodity production in terms of three elements: (1) *constant capital* (C), the value of the means of production used up during the production process (primarily the depreciated value of machines, buildings, and raw materials); (2) *variable capital* (V), the value of the labor-power applied to the production process (primarily the wage bill); and (3) *surplus value* (S), the value of unpaid labor appropriated by the capitalist during the production process (workers' labor time beyond that which is "socially necessary" to sustain the standard of living of the working class). Surplus value is the key to capitalist economic production, for it is the source of all profits, including (and most importantly) those which are reinvested in enhanced productive capacity (capital accumulation). During the period of competitive capitalism (with which Marx was primarily concerned), individual capitalists were under continual economic pressure to increase the efficiency of production—to produce commodities at lower unit costs. While this could be achieved by economizing on either of the two principal component costs of production—constant or variable capital—Marx believed that in the long run the key to lowering production costs was mechanization, which meant increasing C relative to V (1967:265; 1972b:186). Thus, driven by the economic imperative to undersell competitors in order to remain afloat, individual capitalists would be forced to substitute increasingly efficient machines for human labor. Throughout the economy, therefore, there is a long-run tendency for what Marx termed the "organic composition of capital" to rise, as denoted by the symbol Q, where $Q = C/(C + V)$.[2] This tendency, in turn, made it possible for the remaining workers to produce ever-larger quantities of goods with ever-decreasing labor-time; as a consequence there is a parallel tendency for the rate of surplus value (S′)—defined as the ratio of unpaid to paid labor time (S/V)—to rise as well.

How do these tendencies affect the overall rate of profit in capitalist economic production? Marx defines the rate of profit (P) as the ratio of surplus value to total capital advanced, or

(1) $p = S/(C + V)$

from which it follows algebraically that the rate of profit can be decomposed into two terms comprised of the rate of surplus value and the organic compsoition of capital:

(2) $P = S′(1 - Q)$ where $S′ = S/V$ and $Q = C/(C + V)$

Marx argued that a rising organic composition was the hallmark of capitalist production (1967:449; Marx and Engels, 1972:338). It follows that as Q approaches 1, $(1 - Q)$ approaches 0, with a consequent depressing effect on the overall rate of profit. On the other hand, inasmuch as the reason for mechanization in the first place is to increase S, the downward pressure on profitability resulting from rising Q will be partially offset: to the extent that S′ rises as Q simultaneously rises, the value of P is indeterminate. Marx was well aware of these considerations, but argued on logical grounds that as the organic composition reaches a high level, additional increases in productivity (hence S′) are inadequate as a strategy to maintain profitability (1967:247; see also 1973:338–340 for a crude mathematical 'proof').[3] Since capitalism is production for profit, once the overall rate of profit (or at least that obtaining in key economic sectors) drops below some minimally acceptable level, production ceases: factories close down, and an economic crisis ensues. The profit-maximizing strategy of individual capitalists has resulted in a profitability crisis for the class of capitalists as a whole. This is, for Marx, a structural imperative of capitalist economic production.[4] Yet despite the compelling nature of such an imperative, its actual working-out depends on concrete sociohistorical circumstances; the declining rate of profit is a *tendency* that manifests itself within and through class struggle, and not a *law* which operates automatically outside of human practice.

UTILITY OF THE PRAXIS ORIENTATION

I believe the distinction between "tendency" and "law" is the central feature of interest in Marx's theory and method. I have argued that Marx sought to avoid both the determinism of a completely materialist science, and the voluntarism of idealist philosophy. He achieved this by conceptualizing the material conditions of action as embedded within interrelated social, economic, and political structures, while regarding human action itself as capable of modifying the underlying structures (and hence the conditions of future action). In the example of the declining rate of profit during the period of competitive capitalism, the principal structures of analytic interest are economic. Marx did not treat these structures as obeying universal laws that lead to precisely predictable outcomes: he was not developing a social physics. Rather, he advanced the position that while the economic structures of competitive capitalism impose certain requirements on economic actors, those requirements lead to contradictory outcomes which undermine the structures themselves, creating opportunities for conscious political action. Marx's treatment of economic "laws" or "tendencies" can be characterized as follows:

(A) Laws constitute theoretical statements concerning the structures of principal interest in understanding capitalist economic production. When expressed formally, as in equation (2), they draw attention to predictable outcomes (such as a declining rate of profit) given certain conditions (such as a rising organic composition which outstrips the rising rate of surplus value).

(B) These conditions are theoretically conceived as socially accomplished rather than naturalistically given (although they may be perceived as the latter by economic actors). Thus, both a rising organic composition and a rising rate of surplus value result from the behavior of capitalists (who strive to economize labor) and labor (which organizes to oppose and reverse such efforts). However, such behavior is by no means freely chosen; rather, it is more-or-less restricted and hence more-or-less determined in the short run. The restrictions stem from the "givens" of a particular mode of production (for example, capitalists must remain competitive to survive, given the existence of a market economy; this in turn entails strong pressures to introduce technologies which economize the cost of production, producing a rising organic composition; and so on)—they are thus experienced as social facts. The "more-or-less" quality of the restrictions reflects the fact that during times of crisis, the range of freedom is greatly extended. For example, during crisis periods large and powerful capitalists are able to acquire the more marginal enterprises, thereby reducing competitive pressures through monopolization (Wright, 1975; Yaffe, 1973; Cogoy, 1973). Following a crisis, according to Marx, the range of action is again circumscribed—although the requirements of the new phase (e.g., monopoly capitalism) may involve different restrictions than those of previous one (e.g., competitive capitalism). During periods of particularly acute crisis, a great many restrictions on action may be relaxed. Such times are revolutionary times, and a properly organized and politically conscious working class has the potential of totally abrogating the laws of capitalist economics (Marx believed) through the establishment of a planned, socialist economy.

(C) Within a mode of production, laws are conceived as depicting structured instabilities or contradictions. Capitalism—conceived ideally-typically by Marx as a closed economic system—entails contradictory elements which work to undermine the system despite the intentions (and, indeed, even awareness) of its ruling sectors. Thus, for example, the logic of production as I have described it implies an eventual decline in profitability for capitalists as a whole: rational, survival-oriented behavior on the part of individual capitalists spells long-term disaster for the capitalists as a class. (A similar argument can be made with regard to the Keynesian problem of insufficient aggregate demand, according to which the necessary economizing of labor-costs reduces the purchasing power of the working class, thereby producing tendencies towards overproduction and underconsumption; see, for example, Sweezy, 1968, 1974; Hodgson, 1974.) According to Marx, such contradictions are an inevitable feature of production in all class-based societies, that is, in all societies where surplus value is produced by one class and appropriated by another. Since one result of such contradictions is a persistent tendency towards recurrent economic crisis, the resolution of contradiction cannot be predicted; final outcomes depend on the action taken by the principal classes involved in production.

(D) Thus, while Marx may express economic relationships in the form of seemingly lawful equations such as (2), the terms of these equations— S, V, and C—must be taken as denoting social relations rather than purely formal economic ones. In particular, C, V, and S are indicators of the degree of class consciousness and class struggle, and this is an important feature of their role in Marx's economic equations. Surplus value (S), for example, is the arena of the struggle between workers and capitalists (or their managerial representatives) over the length of the working day and the intensity of the labor process; the outcome of that struggle is ultimately the product of such historically unique circumstances as the degree of economic crisis or stability, the level of working-class consciousness and political mobilization, the possibilities for substituting inexpensive foreign labor through capital export, and the extent to which capital enjoys monopoly control over production. Variable capital (V) is the arena of struggle over wages and subsistence; its outcome similarly reflects the relative power of labor and capital at a particular conjuncture—the extent to which capital can "deliver the goods" cheaply while incorporating key elements of the labor movement, and the degree to which labor can press its claims for a higher standard of living in a unified fashion. Finally, constant capital (C) denotes the extensiveness of capitalist economic relations—the ability of capitalists to economize capital through appropriate technologies or foreign investment, the intensity of competition among capitalists, and the degree of class-conscious organization among the owners of large capital (for an elaboration of these examples, see Appelbaum, forthcoming).

The struggles over workers' share in output, the disposition of the surplus, and capitalists' control over the productive process; these are merely different aspects of the class struggle. That struggle is not purely economic, although it depends to a large extent on economic conditions, and affects those conditions most directly. The class struggle, as seen by Marx, also moves at the political and cultural levels. The possibilities of delegitimation of the state and dereification of both popular and scientific culture flow from economic struggles, and shape those struggles. That is why "theory itself" becomes a material force when it has "seized the masses" (Marx, 1972a:18).

CONCLUSION

There is nothing automatic about the processes of social change. This is true of the broadest historical view (i.e., the "state of societal development" often attributed to Marx), as well as of more historically bounded economic "laws" (e.g., that of the falling rate of profit under capitalism). Changes in concrete societies occur within well-defined structural limits; those limits are given for capitalist forms, within Marxist political economy, by the hypothesized relationships among the parameters C, V, and S. But those limits can be changed, the relationships among the parameters can be altered, and the parameters themselves can change in value independently of their necessary connection within formal equations. This is because C, V, and S, while serving as economic parameters, were ultimately conceptualized by Marx as signifying social relations, of which the quantitative economic measures (hours of labor time, price) are merely surface indicators. Social relations can be altered, within bounds. Those bounds were, for Marx, first and foremost the structural conditions of economic production. The structural conditions generate problems (contradictions), while setting limits to the solution of those problems. The likelihood and efficacy of any economic solution depend,

in large part, on the legitimacy accorded to the growing state intervention (with its mounting economic costs) and on political consciousness
and class militancy in general. Crises of legitimation, dereification, class
organization and struggle may grow out of adverse economic conditions
(or equally adverse "solutions" to such conditions), but they are not
reducible to economic factors. The future cannot be predicted from
within a Marxist framework. It can only be shaped and guided by
adequate theoretical understanding, but it is ultimately dependent on
the behavior and conscious understanding of organized social classes.

NOTES

1. Marx's theory of the falling rate of profit is only one aspect of his overall
theory of the crises of capitalist production. The other principal aspects have to
do with realization crises (see especially Sweezy, 1968)—those resulting from the
overproduction of capital and commodities relative to demand. Recent reformulations of Marxist economic theory have identified further sources of crisis
appropriate to the phase of monopoly capitalism; these include the theory of the
profit squeeze (Glyn and Sutcliffe, 1971) and theories focusing on the role of the
state in absorbing surplus and stimulating accumulation (e.g., O'Connor, 1973;
Mattick, 1969; Baran and Sweezy, 1966; Offe, 1973; Altvater, 1973).

2. Marx generally spoke of the proportion or ratio of C:V: the organic
composition of capital is expressed by some writers as C/V (e.g., Mattick, 1969;
Mandel, 1968). I shall follow Sweezy's (1968) usage, which defines the organic
composition as the ratio of constant capital to total capital advanced.

3. See Wright (1975:37, footnote 7) and Yaffe (1973:202) for a mathematical
demonstration that "as the organic composition of capital rises, the rate of profit
becomes progressively less sensitive to changes in the rate of exploitation [i.e.,
surplus value]" (Wright, 1975:16). Marx also detailed a number of empirical
influences which may for a time counteract the tendency of the organic composition to rise (see 1967:232–240), but these are judged insufficient in the long run to
mitigate the overall process.

4. The crisis itself is an integral part of the dynamic of capitalist production.
While it temporarily restores profitability through lowering the organic composition (see Yaffe, 1973:205–206 for an elaboration), it does so by altering the
framework of production itself, through contributing to the centralization of
capital: economic crises thus abet the transition from competitive to monopoly
capitalism (Marx, 1967:250–251; see Wright, 1975 for an excellent discussion of
these processes).

REFERENCES

ALTVATER, ELMAR
1973 "Notes on some problems of state interventionism," Parts I and II.
Working Papers on the Kapitalistate, 1-2.

APPELBAUM, RICHARD P.
Forth- "Marx's theory of the falling rate of profit: Towards a dialectical analysis
coming of structural social change." American Sociological Review.
BARAN, PAUL, and PAUL SWEEZY
 1966 Monopoly Capital. New York: Monthly Review Press.
COGOY, MARIO
 1973 "The fall of the rate of profit and the theory of accumulation: A reply to
       Paul Sweezy." Bulletin of the Conference of Socialist Economists (Win-
       ter):52–67.
COLLETTI, LUCIO
 1971 "The Marxism of the Second International." Telos 8 (Summer):84–91.
GLYN, ANDREW, and BOB SUTCLIFFE
 1971 "The critical condition of British capital." New Left Review 66 (March-
       April):3–33.
HABERMAS, JÜRGEN
 1971 Knowledge and Human Interests. Boston: Beacon Press.
HEGEL, G. W.
 1967 The Phenomenology of Mind. New York: Harper & Row.
HODGSON, GEOFF
 1974 "The theory of the falling rate of profit." New Left Review 84 (March-
       April):55–82.
LUKÁCS, GEORG
 1971 "Moses Hess and the problems of the Idealist dialectic." Telos 10
       (Winter):3–34.
MANDEL, ERNEST
 1968 Marxist Economic Theory (2 volumes). New York: Monthly Review
       Press.
MARX, KARL
 1964 The Economic and Philosophic Manuscripts of 1844. New York: Inter-
       national Publishers.
 1967 Capital, Volume 1. The Process of Capitalist Production. New York:
       International Publishers.
 1972a "Critique of Hegel's Philosophy of Right. "Pp. 11–23 in Robert C.
       Tucker (ed.), The Marx-Engels Reader. New York: W. W. Norton.
 1972b "The Eighteenth Brumaire of Louis Bonaparte." Pp. 436–525 In Robert
       C. Tucker (ed.), The Marx-Engels Reader. New York: W. W. Norton.
 1973 Grundrisse. New York: Vintage.
MARX, KARL, and FREDERIK ENGELS
 1972 The Communist Manifesto. Pp. 331–362 in Robert C. Tucker (ed.), The
       Marx-Engels Reader. New York: W. W. Norton.
MATTICK, PAUL
 1969 Marx and Keynes: The Limits of the Mixed Economy. Boston: Porter
       Sargent.
O'CONNOR, JAMES
 1973 The Fiscal Crisis of the State. New York: St. Martin's Press.

Offe, Claus
1973 "The abolition of market control and the problem of legitimacy," Parts I and II. Working Papers in the Kapitalistate 1-2.

Sartre, Jean-Paul
1971 "Replies to structuralism: an interview." Telos 9 (Fall):110–116.

Sweezy, Paul
1974 "Some problems in the theory of capitalist accumulation." Monthly Review 26 (May):38–55.
1968 The Theory of Capitalist Development. New York: Monthly Review Press.

Szymanski, Albert
1973 "Marxism and science." The Insurgent Sociologist 3 (Spring):25–38.

Wright, Eric Olin
1975 "Alternative perspectives in the Marxist theory of accumulation and crisis." The Insurgent Sociologist 6 (Fall):5–39.

Yaffe, David S.
1973 "The Marxian theory of crisis, capital and the state." Economy and Society 2 (May):186–232.

2. Dialectical Social Science

DAVID S. WALLS

Friedrichs (1970:51–56; 1972b) has hailed the prospect of a dialectical sociology as an alternative to mainstream social theory, and has suggested the possibility of a dialectical paradigm to mediate the split between system and conflict theorists as well as between Marxists and non-Marxists. Although Friedrichs calls for a reformulation of the epistemological basis of sociology, his exemplar (1972a) leaves this necessary foundation undeveloped. Despite the emergence of a radical sociology and anthropology and a parallel post-behavioral movement in political science, no school of dialectical social science has yet found a wide recognition as such. This lack of recognition may be due less to the challenge of a "renaissant behavioralism," as Friedrichs (1974) recently argued, than to a continued lack of understanding about what theories are found within dialectical social science. The association of "dialectical" with "materialism," and thus, with orthodox Marxism, may make many academicians wary, as Friedrichs (1970:326) suggests. A more important source of confusion is the fact that not all theories within dialectical social science are radical, and not all radical or Marxian theories are dialectical. A dialectical social science is not simply an ideological project of the political left. By outlining two approaches to dialectical social science, which share certain assumptions about the nature of human society but have ontological assumptions with vastly different ideological implications, I will show that the concept of dialectical social science encompasses far more than the tradition of critical Marxism and deserves a methodological elaboration in its own right.

Confusion over the status of dialectical social science is evident, for example, in the popular recent work on sociology by Ritzer (1975). He sees it as a multiple paradigm science, but does not acknowledge a dialectical paradigm. Ritzer's analysis is particularly valuable in distinguishing theories from broader paradigms, and in recognizing that the fundamental split in sociology is not between structural-functionalism and conflict theory. Setting aside the problematic application of the paradigm concept in this context, at least two major problems emerge from Ritzer's discussion. First, he chooses to emphasize the arbitrary and irrational elements underlying the formulation of paradigms, taken from the first edition of Kuhn (1962), but he rejects Kuhn's (1972:174–210) revision, which places added emphasis on the scientific foundations of paradigms. This leads Ritzer away from basing his distinctions of contending paradigms on the alternative epistemological foundations of social science, and he is consequently distracted by the current partisan debates within sociology. The limitations of this approach are evident when one looks beyond the discipline of sociology to the social sciences as a whole. Second, Ritzer's notion of "paradigm bridgers," including such great figures in the field as Marx, Weber, and Parsons, is inadequate, as it offers only an eclectic rather than a theoretical basis for paradigm reconciliation. Ritzer fails to see dialectical social science in its own right, and he establishes only a residual category for such schools as critical theory.

DEFINITION OF DIALECTIC

Since much confusion exists over the use of the term "dialectic," I will attempt to clarify the way in which it is to be understood in speaking of dialectical social science. Dialectic has a distinguished conceptual history dating back as far as the pre-Socratic philosophers (Abbagnano, et al., 1971). The wealth of significations of dialectic has been indicated by Gurvitch (Bosserman, 1968), Schneider (1971), and Sorokin (1964). Included are immanent change, contradiction, paradox, negation, complementarity, ambiguity, polarization, and reciprocity. Van den Berghe (1963) and Turner (1974; 1975) use dialectic to refer to what is better described as conflict theory, while Gross's (1961) neodialectical approach aims at synthesizing a pluralism of views. To many dialectic is identified with the notorious triad "thesis-antithesis-synthesis," which is, in turn, associated with Marxism, despite the fact that this formula was popularized by Fichte, never used by Hegel, and seldom employed by Marx (Mueller, 1958; Lichtheim, 1970:7).

For our purposes here, the term "dialectic" will be used to refer to the mutual formative process between humans and society. North American sociologists may be most familiar with this usage in the work of Peter Berger and his associates, who have given a succinct summary of the three dialectical moments of externalization, objectivation, and internalization: "Society is a human product. Society is an objective reality. Man is a social product" (Berger and Luckmann, 1966:61). This dialectical theory combines what Berger calls a quasi-Weberian emphasis on subjectivity and a quasi-Durkheimian emphasis on objectivity, both "the subjective foundation and the objective facticity of the societal phenomenon" (Berger, 1967:187).

As Berger and Luckmann (1966:196–201) acknowledge, the social dialectic, which is the essence of man's self-production, was identified by Karl Marx in his early writings. Marx critiqued Hegel's idealism, as in the famous statement in *Capital* that Hegel's dialectic was "standing on its head" and must be "turned right side up again" to "discover the rational kernel within the mystical shell" (Marx, 1967:20). Yet Marx also distinguished his position from earlier versions of mechanistic materialism in his first and third "theses on Feuerbach" (Marx and Engels, 1959:204; see also Avineri, 1970:68–9). Marx's method is dialectical: "As society itself produces man as man, so is society produced by him" (Marx, 1964:137). This understanding of Marx's theory has begun to gain a wider acceptance by sociologists, as exemplified by recent articles by Appelbaum (1978a, 1978b).

The dialectical heritage disappears in the popular stereotype of Marxian social theory as a variety of economic determinism. Although Marx never used the term, the positivistic orthodoxy of "dialectical materialism" was developed by his successors (see Wetter, 1958). Considerable responsibility for the positivistic interpretation rests with the official versions of Marxism propagated by the Second (Socialist), Third (Communist), and Fourth (Trotskyist) Internationals. These variations on orthodox Marxism emphasize a deterministic approach modeled after the natural sciences. One explanation of this deviation is that several of Marx's important works written between 1844 and 1860 were not published until the late 1920s and 1930s and were thus not available when the various versions of orthodox Marxism crystallized. Other accounts point to a latent positivism in Marx's theory (Wellmer, 1971:67–119) or to Engels's infatuation with the natural sciences (Hodges, 1965; Coulter, 1971). The development of the dialectical heritage of Marx is found in the tradition of Western Marxism, a lineage that begins with Lukács's critique in 1923 of Engels's positivist interpretation of the dialectic: "He does not even mention the most vital interaction, namely the dialectical relation between subject and object in the historical process" (Lukács, 1971:3).

ALTERNATIVE METHODOLOGICAL BASES FOR SOCIAL SCIENCE

This definition of dialectic as the mutually formative relationship between humans and society allows us to situate dialectical social science in relation to earlier efforts, overlooked or ignored by Ritzer, to ground a classification system for sociological theories in alternative epistemological bases for social science. Wagner (1963) proposed a grouping of theories into three broad categories. Positive sociological theories approach sociology as a natural science (including neo-positivism, human ecology, structural functionalism, social behavioralism, and bio-psychological theory of culture). Interpretative sociology approaches sociology as a *social* science as opposed to a natural science (including theory of cultural understanding, interpretative sociology of action and interaction, interpretative social psychology, and social phenomenology). Nonscientific or evaluative social theories (including social-philosophical, humanitarian reform, and ideological social theories) is a category that includes some theories which are covered by the rubric of our dialectical social science.

Wilson (1970) distinguishes between the normative paradigm, based on the natural science model (including social behavior, structural-functionalism, and conflict theories), and the interpretive paradigm, based on a recognition of meanings by the social actor (including symbolic interaction and ethnomethodology theories). The distinctions made by Wagner and Wilson parallel the split between what Radnitsky (1973) terms the "Anglo-Saxon" and "Continental" schools of meta-science. Habermas (1972) distinguishes among the empirical-analytic sciences in the natural science tradition of Anglo-American positivism, the historical-hermeneutic sciences in the tradition of Continental idealism, and the critical sciences of the Hegelian-Marxian tradition. Following Habermas, Fay (1975) terms the alternative approaches as positivist, interpretive, and critical social science. Table 1 presents a comparison of several of these systems of classification of social theory, organized to contrast what I would call positivistic and interpretive social science and dialectical social science.

In the systems compared in Table 1, there appears to be a consensus about the character of interpretive social science (Ritzer's social definitions paradigm). On the other hand, whether positivistic theories are best viewed as comprising one positivistic paradigm will undoubtedly remain a subject for further debate. In distinguishing between the social

Table 1
A Comparison of Systems of Classification of Social Science

	Positivistic Social Science	*Interpretive Social Science*	*Dialectical Social Science*
Wagner (1963)	Positive sociological theories	Interpretative sociologies	Nonscientific or evaluative social theories
Wilson (1970)	Normative paradigm	Interpretive paradigm	
Habermas (1972)	Empirical-analytic sciences	Historical-hermeneutic sciences	Critical sciences
Fay (1975)	Positivist social science	Interpretive social science	Critical social science
Ritzer (1975)	Social facts paradigm Social behavior paradigm	Social definitions paradigm	
	Biologism		Critical theory

facts and social behavior paradigms, for example, Ritzer appears to be assigning different names to the Continental collectivistic positivist and the Anglo-American individualistic positivist traditions (see Parsons, 1961:85–97), a distinction that has been elaborated in the case of exchange theory by Ekeh (1974). To clarify the meaning of dialectical social science, I will differentiate two varieties, the conservative humanism of the Berger group and the dialectical tradition of Western Marxism. I contrast these with various theories sometimes termed dialectical, which may be better understood as existing within positivistic social science.

THE CONSERVATIVE HUMANISM OF THE BERGER GROUP

The major theoretical statement of the theory group or cluster (see Mullins, 1973) centered on Berger is the treatise on the social construction of reality as a problem in the sociology of knowledge (Berger and Luckmann, 1966). In this work the authors synthesize several streams of sociological thought. Externalization as an anthropological necessity derives from Hegel and Marx. Objectivation as reality *sui generis* is taken from Durkheim. Internalization is analyzed in terms of Mead's social psychology. Weber's concern for the subjective meaning of social action is interpretated via Schutz (see Schutz and Luckmann, 1973); habitualized human actions become institutionalized through reciprocal typifications. Social institutions require a "canopy of legitimations" ranging from "simple traditional affirmations" to "symbolic universes" of great complexity (Berger and Luckmann, 1966:62, 94–97). For the Berger group a biological imperative for institutionalization and objectivation is outlined in Gehlin's notion of the lack of a specialized instinctual structure in humans; this world-openness requires the stability of institutionalized social structures (Berger and Kellner, 1965). A symbolic universe has the nomic function of ordering the world, thus providing a defense against "anomic terror" and chaos (Berger, 1967:22–4).

Berger's concern for anomie draws on Durkheim's notion of *homo duplex*, the split of humans into a socialized self and a passionate, egoistic, nonsocialized self (Berger, 1967:83–84; see also Durkheim, 1964). For Berger (1971:3), "Sociology leads to the understanding that order is *the* primary imperative of social life." Little wonder then that objectivation quickly becomes reification, the situation in which people lose sight of the social world as a human production, and that social roles and institutions are taken for granted. "Reification in this way comes close to being a functional imperative" (Berger and Pullberg, 1965:208; see also Berger, 1966). While his humanistic perspective is debunking, ironic, and relativizing toward the status quo, Berger (1963:39) is most skeptical of "all kinds of revolutionary utopianism." Distinguishing himself from American "conservatism" (a variety of classical liberalism), Berger (1972) characterizes his political stance, with some irony, as that of one of the last Habsburgian monarchists.

Berger's account of externalization in the service of Gehlen's imperative for order has been challenged by critics who point out its distinction from the Hegel-Marx version of externalization as human practical activity (Lafferty, 1977), or the psychoanalytical assumption of natural human tendencies and potentials (Carveth, 1977). Berger's version of objectivation is disputed by critics who charge that his account of communication and language in the processes of mutual typification and legitimation lacks a sense of the distortions that result from conflicting interests and disparities in power (Lichtman, 1970; Dreitzel, 1970). Berger develops an order vocabulary around the concept of anomie, in contrast to the Marxists, who develop a conflict vocabulary around the concept of alienation (see Horton, 1964, 1966). Berger attacks ideological mystifications in the domain of consciousness, but denies a Marxian concept of alienation that seeks its origins in historical modes and relates to production (Brewster, 1966; Walton et al., 1970).

The theory group around Berger has achieved the most striking success in applying this conservative humanistic dialetical approach to the analysis of a variety of problems of everyday life: marriage as a mutual redefinition of the world through conversation (Berger and Kellner, 1964); the separation of public and private spheres in industrial society and its impact on identity formation (Luckmann and Berger, 1964); psychoanalysis as a technique for identity repair and maintenance (Berger, 1965). Largely on the basis of this work, the Berger group has often been classified, when it is considered at all, within such schools of interpretive social science as social phenomenology, symbolic interactionism, and ethnomethodology (Mullens, 1973; Ritzer, 1975). Being out of step with both the apologetics for capitalism of American conservatives and the technocratic elitism of American liberals, the Berger theory group may not develop beyond a small cluster into the wider movement of professional specialization. But if the idiosyncratic stance of Berger is not widely imitated, the work of his associated theory group certainly provides a stimulating introduction to dialectical social science. The Berger group has synthesized several important strands of contemporary sociological theory. Although it holds sharply different ontological assumptions and ideological commitments from the Marxists, the Berger cluster may help bridge the group between North American interpretive social science and the dialectical tradition of Western Marxism.

THE DIALECTICAL TRADITION OF WESTERN MARXISM

The term "Western Marxism" was first used by Korsch (1970:120) in 1930 to contrast with Russian or Soviet Marxism; it was popularized by Merleau-Ponty's (1973:30–58) essay of that title on Lukács. Such alternative designations as "humanistic," "Hegelian," or "critical" Marxism can be construed more narrowly, and thus give a less satisfactory characterization of the broad tradition than does "Western Marxism." Two anthologies give a representative sampling: Grahl and Piccone (1973) and Howard and Klare (1972), although the latter includes chapters on Della Volpe and Althusser, structuralist Marxists whose work falls more within positivistic than dialectical social science. Only two monographs consider the tradition of Western Marxism, one hostile account (McInnes, 1972) and one mixed assessment by Anderson (1976), which also treats structuralists Della Volpe, Althusser, and Colletti.

An important contribution made by social theorists working within the tradition of Western Marxism has been the explication of the dialectical foundation of Marxism in Marx's ideas of alienation and praxis, an interpretation not popular with orthodox Marxists (see Hoffman, 1976). While social democrats (Bell, 1960; Feuer, 1963) and structuralist Marxists (Althusser, 1969:51–86) have found common ground in asserting a split between the "young Marx" and the "mature Marx," the contemporary dialectical theorists have pointed out the essential continuity of Marx's concerns (Marcuse, 1941; Petrovic, 1967:31–51; Avineri, 1968; Meszaros, 1970:217–53; Ollman, 1971:290; Bernstein, 1971:11–83). Although the differences between orthodox and Western Marxism are often put in terms of varying interpretations of the relationship between Marx and Hegel, the question is complicated. The early Marxists most attracted to the natural science model—such as Engels, Plekhanov, and, later, Lenin—also saw themselves as Hegelian Marxists. But as Jacoby (1971:135) points out, "The Hegel that was important to these Marxists was not the same Hegel important to Lukács, et al.; to the former it was the Hegel of the universal movement of contradictions, of quantity to quality, of the processes of quasi-automatic transformation; to the latter it was the Hegel of the historical movement of consciousness, of the subject-object dialectic" (see also Fetscher, 1971:40–147).

At a time when the early figures in the tradition of Western Marxism—Lukács, Korsch, and Gramsci—were forced to work as isolated individuals, the Frankfurt School emerged in the early 1930s as the first major theory cluster within the tradition. The Frankfurt School has been closely identified with the idea of critical theory. As Lichtheim (1971:174) summarizes, critical theory "measures social actuality against historical possibility." According to Schroyer, a leading interpreter of the Frankfurt School to North American sociology, what distinguishes critical from positivistic and interpretive sciences is critical science's "concern with the assessment of the socially unnecessary modes of authority, exploitation, alienation, repression. The interest of a critical science is the emancipation of all self-conscious agents from the seemingly 'natural' forces of nature and history" (Schroyer, 1970:225; 1973). Critical science exposes the ideological uses of technocratic consciousness: "the scientistic image of science has become the dominant legitimating system of advanced industrial society. . . . the fundamental false consciousness of our epoch" (Schroyer, 1970:212–3; see also Habermas, 1970:81–122).

Efforts to combine the existential and phenomenological traditions with Marxism (on post-war France, see Poster, 1975) show promise of illuminating the analysis of such features of everyday life as culture, the family, sexuality, and work. For Merleau-Ponty (1964a:134) Husserl's emphasis on intersubjectivity opened the prospect of a social theory that is neither positivistic nor idealistic, but truly dialectical: "Man no longer appears as a product of his environment or an absolute legislator but emerges as a product-producer, the locus where necessity can turn into concrete liberty." Merleau-Ponty (1964b:20) brings to phenomenology a sense of the life-world as an historical world: "We are in the field of history as we are in the field of language or existence" (see also O'Neill, 1970, 1972). His triad of existence, language, and history suggests Habermas's triad of work, language, and domination as the three media of human existence, although—with the exception of Marcuse—the Frankfurt theorists have been skeptical of phenomenology (see Rovatti, 1973). Sartre's "open Marxism" (1963:57–67) analyzes the mediations between individuals and social classes, seeking concrete categories to replace abstract universals. The Italian theorist Paci (1972) has been an influential interpreter of the importance for Marxism of the later work of Husserl (1970), which describes the occluded precategorial foundations of the life-world. In North America Piccone (1973) and the journal *Telos* have developed phenomenological Marxism as the most fruitful ground for revitalizing the Western Marxist tradition (see also Dallmayr, 1973; Reid and Yanarella, 1974; Smart, 1976; Reid, 1977).

Another important stream of thought, not identified with a particular theory cluster or group in sociology, derives from Gramsci's analysis of hegemony in Western societies. Williams (1960:587) summarizes Gramsci's notion of hegemony as "an order in which a certain way of life and thought is dominant, in which one concept of reality is diffused throughout society in all its institutional and private manifestations." Hegemony emphasizes the obtaining of consent rather than the use of force in establishing and maintaining relations of dominance in society. Wolpe (1969:117) calls attention to the similarity of hegemony as "the set of guiding ideas which permeate consciousness and legitimate the social arrangements" to Berger's concept of a symbolic universe. The ramifications of Gramsci's concept of hegemony are beginning to be studied closely (see Martinelli, 1968; Femia, 1975), and the implications of the concept for sociology developed (Sallach, 1974; Livingstone, 1976). Gramsci's work has been an important influence on Genovese (1972:391–422), whose study of "the world the slaves made" (1974) is an exemplar of dialectical analysis in social history.

The perspectives of Western Marxism have informed and influenced a number of writers working within the traditions of North American social science, including Birnbaum (1969, 1971) on the sociology of advanced industrial society, Gouldner (1976) on ideology and technology, and Schwartz's (1976) dialectical analysis of a social movement.

Other writers have developed perspectives on dialectical theory through a confrontation of the Hegelian-Marxian tradition with the work of Gurvitch (Bruyn, 1974) or with Schutz's social phenomenology (Rasmussen, 1973).

DIALECTIC IN POSITIVISTIC SOCIAL SCIENCE

This rapid survey of Berger's conservative humanism and the tradition of Western Marxism should be adequate to establish the distinction between dialectical social science and other varieties of orthodox Marxism and conflict theory. Szymanski's (1972, 1973) assertion that Marxism is a version of functionalism and a deterministic materialism with a methodology modeled after the "hard" sciences is clearly a claim to a position within positivistic social science. A similar formulation was made in 1921 by Bukharin (1969) in his presentation of historical materialism as a system of sociology; the argument drew a rebuttal from Lukács and from Gramsci (1971:419–72). Outside the boundaries of Marxism, the label of dialectic to describe duality, polarity, conflict, and contradiction in Blau's exchange theory (Weinstein and Weinstein, 1972; Blau, 1972) is not sufficient to remove this school of thought from the positivistic social science. A case in point is the hostile reaction of positivistic exchange theorists (Abbott et al., 1973) to the effort by Singelmann (1972) to develop a dialectical synthesis of exchange and symbolic interaction theories.

One might expect the insights of the developing structural Marxism to make an important contribution to dialectical social science. Thus far, however, adherents of structural Marxism have remained opposed to integrating an analysis of human subjectivity into their theories. They persist in dichotomizing Marxism into expressive and structural approaches (Burawoy, 1978) and maintaining that "a synthesis of 'objective' and 'subjective' components is impossible within the Marxist tradition" (Burawoy, 1977:16). Therborn (1970, 1971) charges the Frankfurt school with reducing science and politics to philosophy, and with severing theory and practice. In general, orthodox and structural Marxists join in dismissing the dialectical tradition of Western Marxism as critical idealism.

CONCLUSION

I have attempted a brief sketch of two varieties of dialectical social science that share certain premises about the nature of human society while holding distinct ontological assumptions with sharply differing political and ideological consequences. Both the Berger group and the dialectical tradition of Western Marxism view the social world as the intersection of active human subjects confronting objective, historical structures. The conservative humanism of the Berger group posits an imperative for order based on a human need to avoid anomie. The dialectical tradition of Western Marxism seeks emancipation from historically unnecessary forms of alienation produced by a class-structured society. The strands of theory developed by the Frankfurt school, the existential and phenomenological Marxists, and the Gramscians have by no means been successfully synthesized to date, nor have they been fully integrated with the traditions of sociological theory. The Berger group has made an important contribution by synthesizing a dialectical perspective within sociological traditions. Contrary to the assertions of the structural Marxists, the prospect of a synthesis within the dialectical tradition of Western Marxism holds great promise (see Sallach, 1973a, 1973b) for illuminating studies ranging from social history to the analysis of everyday life.

Several recent studies on the methodology of the social sciences, from a variety of standpoints, appear to be converging on a methodological framework for dialectical social science. The revival of a methodological controversy in German sociology (Adorno et al., 1976) and the discussion of the relationship between Marxism and social science in France (Sartre, 1963; Goldmann, 1969) are examples from continental Europe. Fay (1975:92–110) has elaborated the methodological implications for the tradition of critical theory. Bernstein (1976) considers the contributions of empiricism, language analysis, phenomenology, and critical theory to a dialectical social and political theory. Giddens (1976) offers new rules of sociological method beginning from an interpretive position, while Keat and Urry (1975), beginning from a structuralist Marxist perspective, leave room for a synthesis of subjective and objective theories in positing a realist conception of the philosophy of social science. The differences that remain to be reconciled are many, but the outlook is hopeful. The choice is not "for sociology" or "for Marx," as some would have it, but for an understanding of the obdurate reality of the socially constructed world that can assist human subjects in the transformation of that world.

REFERENCES

ABBAGNANO, NICOLA, et al.
1971 La Evolucion de la Dialéctica. Barcelona: Ediciones Martínez Roca.

ABBOTT, CARRELL W., CHARLES R. BROWN, and PAUL V. CROSBIE
  1973 "Exchange as symbolic interaction: for what?" American Sociological
    Review 38 (August):504–506.
ADORNO, THEODOR W., et al.
  1976 The Positivist Dispute in German Sociology. New York: Harper & Row.
ALTHUSSER, LOUIS
  1970 For Marx. New York: Vintage.
ANDERSON, PERRY
  1976 Considerations on Western Marxism. London: New Left Books.
APPELBAUM, RICHARD P.
  1978a "Marxist method: structural constraints and social praxis." The Ameri-
    can Sociologist 13 (February):73–81.
  1978b "Marx's theory of the falling rate of profit: towards a dialectical
    analysis of structural social change." American Sociological Review 43
    (February):67–80.
AVINERI, SHLOMO
  1968 The Social and Political Thought of Karl Marx. Cambridge: Cambridge
    University Press.
BELL, DANIEL
  1960 The End of Ideology. New York: Free Press.
BERGER, PETER L.
  1963 Invitation to Sociology: A Humanistic Perspective. Garden City, N.Y.:
    Doubleday.
  1965 "Toward a sociological understanding of psychoanalysis." Social Re-
    search 32 (Spring):26–41.
  1966 "Response to Brewster." New Left Review No. 35 (January–Febru-
    ary):75–77.
  1967 The Sacred Canopy: Elements of a Sociological Theory of Religion.
    Garden City, N.Y.: Doubleday.
  1971 "Sociology and freedom." The American Sociologist 6 (February):1–5.
  1972 "Two paradoxes." National Review 24 (May 12):507–511.
BERGER, PETER L., and HANSFRIED KELLNER
  1964 "Marriage and the construction of reality." Diogenes No. 46 (Sum-
    mer):1–24.
  1965 "Arnold Gehlen and the theory of institutions." Social Research 32
    (Spring):110–5.
BERGER, PETER L., and THOMAS LUCKMANN
  1966 The Social Construction of Reality: A Treatise in the Sociology of
    Knowledge. Garden City, N.Y.: Doubleday.
BERGER, PETER L., and STANLEY PULLBERG
  1965 "Reification and the sociological critique of consciousness." History and
    Theory 4 (2):196–211.
BERNSTEIN, RICHARD J.
  1971 Praxis and Action. Philadelphia: University of Pennsylvania Press.
  1976 The Restructuring of Social and Political Theory. Philadelphia: Univer-
    sity of Pennsylvania Press.

226 DAVID S. WALLS

BIRNBAUM, NORMAN
1969 The Crisis of Industrial Society. New York: Oxford University Press.
1971 Toward a Critical Sociology. New York: Oxford University Press.
BLAU, PETER M.
1972 "Dialectical sociology: comments." Sociological Inquiry 42 (2):182–188.
BOSSERMAN, PHILLIP
1968 Dialectical Sociology: An Analysis of the Sociology of George Gurvitch. Boston: Sargent.
Brewster, Ben
1966 "Comment on Berger and Pullberg." New Left Review No. 35 (January-February):72–75.
BRUYN, SEVERYN T.
1974 "The dialectical society." Cultural Hermeneutics 2 (April):167–209.
BUKHARIN, NIKOLAI
1969 Historical Materialism: A System of Sociology. Ann Arbor, Mich.: University of Michigan Press.
BURAWOY, MICHAEL
1977 "Marxism and Sociology." Contemporary Sociology 6 (January):9–17.
1978 "Contemporary currents in Marxist theory." The American Sociologist 13 (February):50–64.
CARVETH, DONALD L.
1977 "The disembodied dialectic: a psychoanalytic critique of sociological relativism." Theory and Society 4 (Spring):73–102.
COULTER, JEFF
1971 "Marxism and the Engels paradox." Pp. 129–56 in Ralph Miliband and John Saville (eds.), The Socialist Register 1971. London: Merlin.
DALLMAYR, FRED R.
1973 "Phenomenology and marxism: a salute to Enzo Paci." Pp. 305–56 in George Psathas (ed.), Phenomenology and Sociology: Issues and Applications. New York: Wiley.
DREITZEL, HANS PETER
1970 "Introduction: patterns of communicative behavior." Pp. vii–xxii in Hans Peter Dreitzel (ed.), Recent Sociology No. 2. New York: Macmillan.
DURKHEIM, EMILE
1964 "The dualism of human nature and its sociological conditions." Pp. 325–40 in Kurt H. Wolff (ed.), Essays on Sociology and Philosophy. New York: Harper Torchbooks.
EKEH, PETER P.
1974 Social Exchange Theory: The Two Traditions. Cambridge: Harvard University Press.
FAY, BRIAN
1975 Social Theory and Political Practice. London: George Allen and Unwin.
FEMIA, JOSEPH
1975 "Hegemony and consciousness in the thought of Antonio Gramsci." Political Studies 23 (March):29–48.
FETSCHER, IRVING
1971 Marx and Marxism. New York: Herder and Herder.

FEUER, LEWIS
  1963 "What is alienation? the career of a concept." Pp. 127-47 in Maurice
    Stein and Arthur Vidich (eds.), Sociology on Trial. Englewood Cliffs,
    N.J.: Prentice-Hall.
FRIEDRICKS, ROBERT W.
  1970 A Sociology of Sociology. New York: Free Press.
  1972a "Dialectical sociology: an exemplar for the 1970s." Social Forces 50
    (June):447-55.
  1972b "Dialectical sociology: toward a resolution of the current 'crisis' in
    Western sociology." The British Journal of Sociology 23 (Septem-
    ber):263-74.
  1974 "The potential impact of B.F. Skinner upon American sociology." The
    American Sociologist 9 (February):3-8.
GENOVESE, EUGENE D.
  1972 In Red and Black: Marxian Explorations in Southern and Afro-
    American History. New York: Vintage.
  1976 Roll, Jordan, Roll: The World the Slaves Made. New York: Vintage.
GIDDENS, ANTHONY
  1976 New Rules of Sociological Method: A Positive Critique of Interpretative
    Sociologies. New York: Basic Books.
GOLDMANN, LUCIEN
  1969 The Human Sciences and Philosophy. London: Jonathan Cape.
GOULDNER, ALVIN W.
  1976 The Dialectic of Ideology and Technology: The Origins, Grammar and
    Future of Ideology. New York: Seabury Press.
GRAHL, BART, and PAUL PICCONE (eds.)
  1973 Towards a New Marxism. St. Louis: Telos Press.
GRAMSCI, ANTONIO
  1971 Selections from the Prison Notebooks. New York: International
    Publishers.
GROSS, LLEWELLYN
  1961 "Preface to a metatheoretical framework for sociology." The American
    Journal of Sociology 67 (September):125-43.
HABERMAS, JÜRGEN
  1970 Toward a Rational Society: Student Protest, Science and Society. Boston:
    Beacon Press.
  1972 Knowledge and Human Interests. Boston: Beacon Press.
HODGES, DONALD CLARK
  1965 "Engels' contribution to Marxism." Pp. 297-310 in Ralph Miliband and
    John Saville (eds.), The Socialist Register 1965. London: Merlin.
HOFFMAN, JOHN
  1975 Marxism and the Theory of Praxis: A Critique of Some New Versions of
    Old Fallacies. New York: International Publishers.
HORTON, JOHN
  1964 "The dehumanization of anomie and alienation: a problem in the
    ideology of sociology." British Journal of Sociology 14 (4):283-300.

1966 "Order and conflict theories of social problems as competing ideologies." The American Journal of Sociology 71 (May):701–713.

HOWARD, DICK, and KARL E. KLARE (eds.)
1972 The Unknown Dimension: European Marxism Since Lenin. New York: Basic Books.

HUSSERL, EDMUND
1970 The Crisis of European Sciences and Transcendental Phenomenology. Evanston: Northwestern University Press.

JACOBY, RUSSELL
1971 "Toward a critique of automatic marxism." Telos No. 10 (Winter):119–146.

KEAT, RUSSELL, and JOHN URRY
1975 Social Theory as Science. London: Routledge and Kegan Paul.

KORSCH, KARL
1970 Marxism and Philosophy. New York: Monthly Review Press.

KUHN, THOMAS S.
1970 The Structure of Scientific Revolutions, Second edition, enlarged. Chicago: University of Chicago Press.

LAFFERTY, WILLIAM M.
1977 "Externalization and dialectics: taking the brackets off Berger and Luckmann's sociology of knowledge." Cultural Hermeneutics 4 (April):139–161.

LICHTHEIM, GEORGE
1970 Marxism: An Historical and Critical Study, 2nd ed. New York: Praeger.
1971 From Marx to Hegel. New York: Herder and Herder.

LICHTMAN, RICHARD
1970 "Symbolic interactionism and social reality: some Marxist queries." Berkeley Journal of Sociology 15:75–94.

LIVINGSTONE, DAVID W.
1976 "On hegemony in corporate capitalist states." Sociological Inquiry 46 (3–4):235–250.

LUCKMANN, THOMAS, and PETER BERGER
1964 "Social mobility and personal identity." European Journal of Sociology 5 (2):331–344.

LUKÁCS, GEORG
1971 History and Class Consciousness: Studies in Marxist Dialectics. London: Merlin.

McINNES, NEIL
1972 The Western Marxists. New York: Library Press.

MARCUSE, HERBERT
1941 Reason and Revolution: Hegel and the Rise of Social Theory. New York: Oxford University Press.

MARTINELLI, ALBERTO
1968 "In defense of the dialectic: Antonio Gramsci's theory of revolution." Berkeley Journal of Sociology 13:1–27.

MARX, KARL
1964 The Economic and Philosophic Manuscripts of 1844. Edited by Dirk J.
      Struik. New York: International Publishers.
1967 Capital. Volume I. New York: International Publishers.
MARX, KARL, and FRIEDRICH ENGELS
1959 Basic Writings on Politics and Philosophy. Edited by Louis S. Feuer.
      Garden City, N.Y.: Doubleday.
MERLEAU-PONTY, MAURICE
1964a Sense and Non-Sense. Evanston, Ill.: Northwestern University Press.
1964b Signs. Evanston: Northwestern University Press.
1973 Adventures of the Dialectic. Evanston, Ill.: Northwestern University Press.
MESZAROS, ISTVAN
1970 Marx's Theory of Alienation. London: Merlin.
MUELLER, GUSTAV E.
1958 "The Hegel legend of 'thesis-antithesis-synthesis.'" Journal of the
      History of Ideas 19 (June):411-414.
MULLENS, NICHOLAS C.
1973 Theories and Theory Groups in Contemporary American Sociology.
      New York: Harper & Row.
OLLMAN, BERTELL
1971 Alienation: Marx's Conception of Man in Capitalist Society. Cambridge:
      Cambridge University Press.
O'NEILL, JOHN
1970 Perception, Expression and History: The Social Phenomenology of
      Maurice Merleau-Ponty. Evanston, Ill.: Northwestern University Press.
1972 Sociology as a Skin Trade: Essays Toward a Reflexive Sociology. New
      York: Harper & Row.
PACI, ENZO
1972 The Function of the Sciences and the Meaning of Man. Evanston, Ill.:
      Northwestern University Press.
PARSONS, TALCOTT
1961 "Editorial foreward: the general interpretation of action." Pp. 85–97 in
      Talcott Parsons et al. (eds.), Theories of Society: Foundations of Modern
      Sociological Theory. New York: Free Press.
PETROVIC, GAJO
1967 Marx in the Mid-Twentieth Century. Garden City, N.Y.: Doubleday
      Anchor.
PICCONE, PAUL
1971 "Phenomenological marxism." Telos No. 9 (Fall):3–31.
POSTER, MARK
1975 Existential Marxism in Postwar France: From Sartre to Althusser.
      Princeton, N.J.: Princeton University Press.
RADNITSKY, GERARD
1973 Contemporary Schools of Metascience. Third enlarged. Chicago: Henry
      Regnery.

RASMUSSEN, DAVID M.
1973   "Between autonomy and sociality." Cultural Hermeneutics 1 (November):3–45.

REID, HERBERT G.
1977   "Critical phenomenology and the dialectical foundations of social change." Dialectical Anthropology 2 (May):107–130.

REID, HERBERT G., and ERNEST J. YANARELLA
1974   "Toward a post-modern theory of American political science and culture: perspectives from critical marxism and phenomenology." Cultural Hermeneutics 2 (November):91–166.

RITZER, GEORGE
1975   Sociology: A Multiple Paradigm Science. Boston: Allyn and Bacon.

ROVATTI, PIER ALDO
1973   "Critical theory and phenemonology." Telos No. 15 (Spring):25–40.

SALLACH, DAVID
1973a   "Class consciousness and the everyday world in the work of Marx and Schutz." The Insurgent Sociologist 3 (Summer):27–37.
1973b   "Critical theory and critical sociology: the second synthesis." Sociological Inquiry 43 (2):131–40.
1974   "Class domination and ideological hegemony." The Sociological Quarterly 15 (Winter):38–50.

SARTRE, JEAN-PAUL
1963   Search for a Method. New York: Vintage.

SCHNEIDER, LOUIS
1971   "Dialectic in sociology." American Sociological Review 36 (August):667–678.

SCHROYER, TRENT
1970   "Toward a critical theory for advanced industrial society." Pp. 210–34 in Hans Peter Dreitzel (ed.), Recent Sociology No. 2. New York: Macmillan.
1973   The Critique of Domination: The Origins and Development of Critical Theory. Boston: Beacon Press.

SCHUTZ, ALFRED, and THOMAS LUCKMANN
1973   The Structures of the Life-World. Evanston, Ill.: Northwestern University Press.

SINGELMANN, PETER
1972   "Exchange as symbolic interaction: convergences between two theoretical perspectives." American Sociological Review 37 (August):414–424.

SMART, BARRY
1976   Sociology, Phenomenology, and Marxian Analysis. London: Routledge and Kegan Paul.

SOROKIN, PITIRIM A.
1964   "Comments on Schneider's observations and criticisms." Pp. 401–431 in George W. Zollschan and Walter Hirsch (eds.), Explorations in Social Change. Boston: Houghton Mifflin.

SCHWARTZ, MICHAEL
1976   Radical Protest and Social Structure: The Southern Farmers' Alliance and Cotton Tenancy, 1880–1890. New York: Academic Press.

SZYMANSKI, ALBERT
1972 "Dialectical functionalism: a further answer to Lidz." Sociological Inquiry 42 (2):145-153.
1973 "Marxism and science." The Insurgent Sociologist 3 (Spring):25-38.
THERBORN, GÖRAN
1970 "The Frankfurt school." New Left Review No. 63 (September-October):65-96.
1971 "Jürgen Habermas: a new eclecticism." New Left Review No. 67 (May-June):69-83.
TURNER, JONATHAN H.
1974 The Structure of Sociological Theory. Homewood, Ill.: Dorsey.
1975 "A strategy for reformulating the dialectical and functional theories of conflict." Social Forces 52 (March):433-444.
VAN DEN BERGHE, PIERRE L.
1963 "Dialectic and functionalism: toward a theoretical synthesis." American Sociological Review 28 (October):695-705.
WAGNER, HELMUT R.
1963 "Types of sociological theory: toward a system of classification." American Sociological Review 28 (October):735-742.
WALTON, PAUL, ANDREW GAMBLE, and JEFF COULTER
1970 "Philosophical anthropology in Marxism." Social Research 37 (Summer):259-274.
WEINSTEIN, MICHAEL A., and DEENA WEINSTEIN
1972 "Blau's dialectical sociology." Sociological Inquiry 42 (2):173-182.
WELLMER, ALBRECHT
1971 Critical Theory of Society. New York: Herder and Herder.
WETTER, GUSTAV A.
1958 Dialectical Materialism. New York: Praeger.
WILLIAMS, GWYN A.
1960 "The concept of 'egemonia' in the thought of Antonio Gramsci: some notes on interpretation." Journal of the History of Ideas 21 (October-December):586-599.
WILSON, THOMAS P.
1970 "Concepts of interaction and forms of sociological explanation." American Sociological Review 35 (August):697-710.
WOLPE, HAROLD
1969 "The problem of the development of revolutionary consciousness." Telos No. 4 (Fall):113-144.

3. A Dialectical View: Foundation for an Alternative Sociological Method

MARK L. WARDELL and
J. KENNETH BENSON

The dialectical view of social life provides the foundation for a new sociological method.[1] The dialectical view consists of a series of related statements about social life which have implications for how an empirical discipline such as sociology should be constructed. These implications are methodological in the broad sense of stating how the empirical discipline should address the social world, defining the basic elements of its stance toward the social world. (While such a stance has implications for methods in the narrow sense of techniques for collecting and analyzing data, these are not the concern of the present article.)

The dialectical view derives from the Hegelian–Marxian tradition; more specifically, from a strand of critical-dialectical Marxism.[2] While for some purposes, one might emphasize differences among these figures (e.g., see Howard, 1978), our purpose is to express a point of view shared within the tradition. The dialectical view, we contend, is the stance which runs through Marx's work as a whole and which guides his specific empirical investigations of early industrial capitalism. The dialectical view, then, can be extracted from the specific analyses of capitalism and applied to other social formations, including modern state capitalism and state socialism.

SOURCE: An earlier version of this paper was presented at the Annual Convention of the Midwest Sociological Society, Omaha, Nebraska, April, 1978. We acknowledge helpful comments on earlier drafts by Scott McNall, T. R. Young, and several anonymous reviewers.

The dialectical view provides the basis for a distinctive approach to sociological work, i.e., an alternative methodological stance which we will term "the dialectical method." We contend that methodological stances are theory-laden in the sense that they rest upon often unstated assumptions about social life. These underlying and often hidden assumptions guide and restrict inquiry by narrowing the range of substantive propositions that can be entertained and the research procedures that can be used. We propose to make our orienting assumptions explicit and to define, at least in broad terms, their methodological implications. The dialectical view and its major methodological implications can be outlined in the following statements.

1. Human societies are socially produced through the joint actions of people mediated by their social contexts; therefore, sociological work must deal with the production of society, and explanations must be consistent with its socially produced character.

2. The social production of society is a contradictory and problematic process characterized by potentiality rather than by determination; therefore, sociological work must be sensitive to contradictions in the social formation and to the potential for new social constructions.

3. The contradictory and problematic character of social production is occasioned by the multiple relations constituting a total social formation; therefore, sociological work must be concerned with the total social formation in which production takes place. These three commitments of the dialectical view—production, contradiction, and totality— will serve as the divisions of our argument.[3]

PRODUCTION

Social life is characterized by production, an ongoing process through which people construct the conditions of their existence. This includes the construction of material artifacts, such as tools, machinery, commodities, and buildings, as well as ideological systems and forms of social organization. Through the cooperative efforts of human beings to produce a material means of sustaining everyday life, various social organizations are needed to coordinate everyday life activity. Because of the productive dimension in social life, the means of existence, material and social, are potentially subject to modification or alteration by further social production.

Fundamental to the dialectical view is the conception that human beings actively produce their social and material world. In doing so, they objectify themselves in the form of social relations and material objects. This productive dimension of social life exists because human beings are able to imagine future social arrangements and then engage in purposeful activity to create those arrangements. Unlike other animals, human beings can separate themselves from their surroundings by taking their own activity as an object of consciousness (Marx, 1964:113). The instability of societies stems from this conscious reflexive process since human beings may set out to intentionally reconstruct their world. This production process undermines established arrangements, edging them toward fundamental change. And at critical junctures people may act jointly to construct alternatives. These interruptions are somewhat unpredictable, but they are crucial to the historical development of societies (Marković, 1974). Yet, because of the form of the present social structure, human beings may be only partly conscious of themselves, others, and the alternative possibilities when producing their social world.

It is important to distinguish this notion of human activity from two other notions that often prevail in sociological literature. First, even though human beings have the potential to produce the social and material means of their existence, they cannot do it in isolation or as individuals. Production is necessarily a social process whereby individuals join—and not necessarily in a voluntary fashion—their activities and form coordinated social relationships (Marx and Engels, 1947:18). Second, while production is more than a summation of individual efforts, it is a social event rather than a predetermined or necessitated activity. Unlike sociologistic viewpoints, whether in Marxism or sociology, the dialectical method suggests that human activity is not determined by factors which are external and coercive. Further, the outcomes of activity are not fixed in advance.[4] Neither Althusser's (1969) notion of overdetermination nor Durkheim's (1964) notion of social facts is compatible with the dialectical method.

This does not imply, however, that the production of social life is random or relative. The social structure of any society sets limitations upon what can be produced and by whom. Production takes place within an existing social structure, which is a complex of differentiated social contexts tied together in a more or less coordinated manner.

These distinct contexts or sectors of society provide a basis for common experiences and thus common interests, assumptions, and definitions of reality not fully shared with other sectors.[5] Members incorporate these assumptions and definitions into their everyday routines, with varying degrees of awareness (Lefebvre, 1971), as they define their present existence and future possibilities. All the while, their consciousness is limited by their present social context and so are their imaginative projectiońs. Therefore, the imaginative construction of an object, material or social, is limited as well.

In addition, the central structure coordinates the actual division of labor. Sectors of society differ not only in terms of their consciousness, but also in terms of their actual productive activities. This established form of organization may provide some contexts with a dominant role in the control of society and others with a subordinate role. The basic social structure, then, may specify an array of advantages and disadvantages accruing to certain participants, which provides them with a particular range of opportunities for shaping the production of the material and organizational content in society.

Indeed, many settings are the potential basis for constructing alternative perspectives and actions. For example, university students preparing for technocratic careers, and inner-city residents subjected to urban redevelopment, may produce forms of life that contest the hegemony of the present social order (Lefebvre, 1969). While this innovative production is often disjointed, events may combine in ways that permit movements of more general significance to develop such as the May 1968 movement in France (Lefebvre, 1969; Touraine, 1971). In such situations a general contestation of the established order is possible because the people withdraw from the routines and rituals that sustain the established order of everyday life. Any social structure will limit and restrain the production of future alternatives, but the same structure contains openings through which human beings may construct innovative alternatives to the present limitations.

The dialectical method implies that the organization of any society is socially produced. The order which is observed is not produced and sustained by need-fulfilling tendencies. Hence, systems theory, which emphasizes the "givenness" of society, fails to grasp the process through which a social formation is produced. It deals instead with the orderly relations within a produced formation. Systems theory may usefully describe some societies at particular times, but it does not adequately account for the emergence and persistence of a society, nor does it deal adequately with a society's contradictions and potential transformation (Lefebvre, 1971; Djilas, 1957). The emphasis on production in the dialectical method directs attention to the created, constructed character of human societies and undermines the sense of inevitability and the natural order associated with systems theory and similar views. Yet, at the same time, the dialectical method directs attention to structuring of the production process by the historically deposited social arrangements. The future is neither fully open nor thoroughly programmed. Its course is problematic, and depends ultimately upon human actions to define its direction (Marković, 1974).

CONTRADICTION

The process of social life, historicity, is dynamic and open-ended because of the contradictory tendencies found within the central organizing structure of a society. The dialectical method implies that any social order, while socially produced, contains the origins of its own replacement, as well as the basis for its own existence (Marković, 1974). On the one hand, the structure encourages the reproduction of the present social arrangement, while on the other it negates that order and encourages the creation of alternatives.

Within a capitalist society, the basic means of organizing everyday activity is exchange relations (Marx, 1967). Within these relations, the various participants strive to maintain themselves by contracting with each other. Exchange is not generic to the history of human life; its centrality in industrial capitalism is unique (Polanyi, 1944). The exchange relations under capitalism are organized in such a way that various sectors have differing advantages. Owners of industry strive to maintain surplus value by incorporating greater amounts of regimentation for their workers, using advanced technologies that replace workers, and controlling material production as efficiently and effectively as possible in order to predict monetary profits (Habermas, 1970; Braverman, 1974).

This structural arrangement contains several contradictory tendencies. First, the striving for surplus value is opposed to the useful application of science and technology. Rather than providing greater freedom from meaningless labor, exchange relations foster the displacement of laborers from central to marginal, and more meaningless, areas of the labor market (Braverman, 1975). Second, performance and achievement standards tend to be negated by the increasing concern for efficiency of production. As surplus value becomes more difficult to attain, labor becomes more segmented, resulting in a disjunction between components and levels of organization. This makes it more difficult to directly assess the quality of performance, and consequently, the evaluation of labor activity is focused more on conformity to the rules of the organization than performance per se (Offe, 1976). In addition, management personnel tend to be drawn from outside rather than from within the rank-and-file, blocking upward mobility from within the organization regardless of performance (Offe, 1976). Finally, and from a more general perspective, the concern for surplus value encourages the use of controlled consumption, which is conjoined with the rational-technical form of material production. The major outcome is the maintenance of the "quotidian" by control of the everyday life activity of the human beings involved (Lefebvre, 1971). This control tends to oppose any active and conscious involvement in the construction of everyday life by most human beings. Yet, were they consciously and collectively to pursue the production of an organization which objectified their interests, their activity would tend to negate the controlling order. Furthermore, the social formation produces tendencies toward the formation of consciousness and the development of alternatives to the present order.

These contradictory tendencies have their origin in the basic exchange structure of industrial-capitalism. The particular form of this arrangement, where surplus value is extracted primarily from labor power, on the one hand, encourages a more efficient use of labor, but, on the other hand, makes it more difficult to extract profit. Concomitantly, this arrangement fosters an increasing use of marginal labor, but the type of productive activity this involves limits the potential of most workers to objectify themselves in their material and social existence. Marx (1964) concluded that the basic contradictory relation of all societies exists between the species essence, i.e., the tendency of human beings to objectify or produce themselves, and the actual social arrangements which they constructed in the past, but which now limit their further use of their creative potential.[6]

Because contradictory relations are comprised of opposing tendencies rather than opposing concrete forces, the maintenance of the industrial-capitalist arrangement is problematic. This is a point that has plagued many Western Marxists, who must confront the relative stability of capitalism and the failure of a proletarian revolution in industrial-capitalist nations. The historical materialist orientation often found in the more orthodox Marxisms is not capable of handling this persistence mainly because it implies that contradictions are natural forces which lead inevitably to certain outcomes. The dialectical method, however, suggests that contradictions do not run a natural or inevitable course, and therefore, a social arrangement, even though it fosters contradictory tendencies, may continue to exist.

The maintenance, or reproduction, of the exchange relations is part and parcel to the contradictory tendencies. The stratified nature of exchange relations within industrial-capitalism provides more advantage to certain sectors. They may consciously act to preserve and defend the present social structure and their position within it. These actions may vary from modifying the core structure (Lefebvre, 1971) to blocking certain decisions while enforcing others or legitimating certain events while delegitimating others (Clegg, 1977). In addition, the basic nature of exchange relations which tie the society together influence the nature of other institutions in such ways that the base structure is maintained. For example, educational institutions come to support and maintain the existing division of labor and consciousness of corporate capitalism (Bowles and Gintis, 1976; Bourdieu and Passeron, 1977). The effectiveness of these reproductive tendencies may be so great that human beings involved come to accept the social arrangement as natural, i.e., reification adds to the reproduction process.

Even though reification is one of the less noticeable means of reproduction, it is no less important than the deliberate acts of the dominant sectors in contributing to the maintenance of society (Gramsci, 1971; Lukács, 1971). It is crucial because it stands opposed to the production of alternative social arrangements by influencing the activity of those whose interests are best represented in alternative forms of organization. Reified notions about the nature of social reality are constructs created in response to the present form of existence. When the form of the social structure greatly restricts the possible alternatives, the structure of society may appear to be independent of human activity, and the routines of everyday life may be taken as natural (Lukács, 1971). In other words, the range of alternatives may appear quite limited, and the actual possibilities may indeed be limited. In response to these circumstances, human beings may regard the existing social arrangement as a necessary or even universal requirement. They might construct notions which claim the present is due to uncontrollable biological or ecological forces or to inherent laws of the economy. Regardless of the content, reified notions emphasize the permanence of the present, focus practical activity on its maintenance, and limit alternative conceptions of social reality.

Despite the reproductive tendencies within an established order, there is always a potential for change, even for a thorough reconstruction of the social arrangement (Marković, 1974). The potential for constructing alternatives is not open but is limited to the historical context; it resides in the ability of people to become aware of the limitations of their social arrangements and the possibility for alternatives. They must assess which alternatives are feasible within the present context and coordinate their activity to produce them. Imaginative construction of alternatives in thought, along with strategic coordinated action, will not necessarily produce the desired alternative. If the contingencies between those working toward alternatives and the dominant sector can be blocked effectively, then the productive activity may produce an alternative social arrangement.

While efforts to produce alternative social arrangements may conflict with efforts to reproduce the extant arrangement, the dialectical method should not be construed as a variation of conflict theory, especially that typified by Coser (1967) and Dahrendorf (1959). The conventional conflict theory position suggests that conflict arises because of an unequal share in power or wealth accompanied by the imposition of the dominant group's values upon the subordinate group. In contrast, the dialectical method suggests that conflicts between superordinate and subordinate sectors of society stem from the basic contradiction residing in the limitations of the social structure. More important, from a conventional conflict perspective, the conflict itself is seldom viewed as a struggle concerning a fundamental reorganization of the established structure; hence, the resolution of conflict from this view is an adaptation of the structure to competing interests. The resolution is typically viewed as a realignment and, therefore, a contribution to the reproduction of the existing social structure. The dialectical method, however, implies that potential always exists for radical changes in the social structure. The particular form of social structure which exists at any given point is the key factor in assessing the degree to which an alternative arrangement is possible.

There is no guarantee what form the alternative social arrangement will take. From a dialectical perspective, specific social arrangements vary in the extent to which people can rationally produce alternatives. Alienation characterizes one logical extreme; *praxis*, the other. Alienation is a condition of social existence in which people generally are unable to be creative, i.e., the social organization is so limiting that they cannot create their own interests into objective forms. The established order is reproduced, and the opportunities for creative production are quite limited. At the opposite extreme *praxis* refers to a condition of social existence in which people are able to construct their imaginations into objective forms. Here the established order gives way to a more rational means of social organization as human beings consciously try to produce a social arrangement that facilitates their creative activities (Lefebvre, 1971). Wherever a society stands in its history, the potential always exists for people to construct a society characterized more by alienation or more by *praxis*. Because the process of production and reproduction is problematic, the specific outcome of any alternative movement is unpredictable.

This makes predicting the future, a typical goal of most social scientists, a precarious endeavor. Attention should be given to the constructed nature of social relationships, and the means by which they are sustained, instead of expecting the present relationships to be characteristic of future arrangements. This involves describing the main limitations of the control structure within a given historical setting, the concomitant forms of consciousness, and the ideological apparatus which supports them, e.g., schools. The analysis must also include a consideration of the potential consciousness of people (Goldmann, 1969) and of the social movements through which they may actualize their consciousness (Touraine, 1977). Above all, the contingencies of the present, as well as the uncertainty of the future, must be taken into account. This can be done only by describing the present nature of social relationships and the potential alternatives; it cannot be done by searching for a seemingly universal set of propositions.[7] Sociologists must restrict their empirical efforts to describing the historical whole.

TOTALITY

Although there is an explicit concern for empirical description, the dialectical method takes the totality of the present as the main unit of analysis (Marković, 1974). Totality is the whole set of social relationships and practices that characterize a particular historical setting. It includes not only the observed order but also the emerging ones, plus the entire set of contradictions through which production is taking place (Goldmann, 1969; Lefebvre, 1968).

Because of historicity, the systematic study of social life is necessarily limited to the existing totality. Although Nisbet (1966; 1976) has pointed out the existence of themes running through the development of social thought, and although others have argued for the development of universal, ahistorical statements (e.g., Gibbs, 1972), the dialectical method suggests that human activity is organized historically. Various aspects of social life have been widely observed, e.g., division of labor, bureaucracy, alienation, conflict, and families, but even if these are universal phenomena, there is no reason to expect the means by which they exist within a particular society to resemble the means by which they may exist in some other society two hundred years hence. As Marx (1963; 1973) argued, the division of labor within capitalism exists in a different form than its appearance in precapitalist societies or in a community society. Similarly, bureaucracies in socialist nations differ from bureaucracies in capitalist nations in some fundamental ways which make the formulation of a universal theory of bureaucracy a perilous task. Division of labor and bureaucracy are social products which are remade in different historical totalities, and each totality has a nature unique to its development and maintenance (Touraine, 1977).

Methodologically, totality requires the placing of social events into a larger context by understanding the complex ties between events. People produce social arrangements in contexts of established relationships characterized by particular forms of consciousness. The products, then, reflect the context of their production and must be understood relationally, i.e., by going beyond the boundaries of a limited field of study to learn how the events are contingent upon the larger, more inclusive arrangement. When these events are abstracted from the totality, their constructed, historical nature is ignored. In general, any sociological endeavor, from the study of complex organizations (Benson, 1977) and urban sociology (Pickvance, 1975) to that of sex roles and small groups, would be substantially modified if the key analytical principle were totality instead of generalizations based on the abstraction of social phenomena within their historical context.

Totality, however, is not reducible to the notion that everything is functionally related to everything else, nor that the whole is the summation of individual parts. Totality is characterized by significant disjunctions wherein sectors, in effect, are working toward opposite goals. Some sectors may be planning and building alternative social organizations while others are reproducing the foundations of the present. Also, some social events may be tenuous, requiring extensive negotiation, while others may be highly routinized and ritualized. Hence, the totality of any present society is not an integrated system fluctuating in and out of balance, nor is it the simple compilation of myriad face-to-face encounters. Yet, no social event can be properly understood unless its connection to the larger context is taken into account. To view society as a social system is to grasp an abstraction rather than a historical whole, and to view it as an aggregate of interactions is to grasp an abstracted segment by denying the relational quality of the whole.

This does not mean that sociologists must study all relationships or all social events at any one particular time. Clearly, these are impossible tasks. But adopting totality as a main analytical principle requires that any sociological investigation contain a deliberate effort to place observed events within the central organizing structure of society. In order to assess the significance of any social event, the event must be related to the larger structural arrangement and to the way in which this arrangement limits it. If this larger context is sheared off for analytical convenience, the present may be reified because the observed human activity may be considered subject to uncontrollable forces.

In general, then, totality represents the qualitative whole of a society. The quality is specified by the basic organizing structure, which, within capitalism, is exchange relations, and the concomitant contradictions and forms of consciousness. Empirical investigations, guided by the ontological categories of the dialectical method, use pieces of social life to press for a more general understanding or characterization of the present totality. The dialectical method is the basis for asking certain questions about the nature of the present totality. Empirical observations are the first step in answering the questions. The next step is theoretical generalizations about the whole of society. Clearly, this involves some form of abstraction via the making of theoretical generalizations, but the generalizations are intended to characterize the means by which the present arrangement limits the rational development of human activity, rather than to specify a set of ahistorical principles based on universal tendencies.

SOME IMPLICATIONS

The dialectical view provides a methodological foundation for developing an alternative sociology. It is the foundation for a science of social behavior rather than a science of material objects. This has implications for theory construction, data analysis, and verification. First, theory construction cannot proceed wholly in the logico-deductive form. Theory must grasp the total complex of relations in which variables are imbedded, as well as the concrete social practices from which variables are abstracted. Furthermore, theory must treat observed regularities in social arrangements as temporary constructions. While formal theory may be useful for summarizing regularities in an arrangement at a particular time, an adequate theory will encompass these statements in a more complicated totality. For example, formal theories of occupational mobility may be useful for describing order within a particular small segment of an encompassing system (for example, see Bowles and Gintis, 1976). Yet a dialectical analysis would require the grounding of such relationships in the intersubjectively understood practices of people (Turner, 1977) and the locating of the relationships in a complex, changing totality. Such encompassing statements, we think, must be qualitative and interpretive.

Second, both qualitative and quantitative data may be appropriately used in dialectical analysis. Quantitative data are useful in describing repetitive patterns resulting in part from reification and the foreclosing of creative action. Qualitative data are necessary for analyzing the processes through which new social forms emerge. Both *erklären* and *verstehen* are important (Marković, 1974).

Third, dialectical theory receives confirmation of its usefulness in pointing to the central limitation of an existing social arrangement and suggesting alternatives which transcend the limitation.[8] Usefulness in this sense can only be determined as people act to reconstruct their social world. Predicting observations in a produced social order is important, but is inadequate alone as the basis for evaluating dialectical theory. Thus, one must supersede empirical theory (Bernstein, 1976) and construct a critical theory of society.[9]

CONCLUSION

The dialectical view provides a basis for an alternative sociological method. A sociology based on this method would be concerned with the processes of production and reproduction through which social formations are constructed and maintained. This would take us beyond approaches which merely map and describe the orderly relations within an established social order and would instead attend to the total set of relations making up the social formation. This would take us also beyond sociological work that only analyzes segments of social life abstracted from their relational contexts. In dealing with the totality, a dialectical sociology would be concerned with the contradictions which are inherent in a social formation and which provide openings for its reconstruction. A dialectical sociology would be concerned with the potentialities for change and with the potential alternatives to established social arrangements. Rather than contributing to the reification and reproduction of a social formation, a dialectical sociology would contribute to its reconstruction.

NOTES

1. Discussions of the dialectical method are not new to sociology. Some sociologists have suggested it would be a suitable partner to existing sociologies (van den Berghe, 1963; Schneider, 1971), but only a few have seen it as a major alternative (Tucker, 1969; Friedrichs, 1972). Still, there is a meager showing of support for its adoption. Benson (1977) and Heydebrand (1977) argue for its incorporation into the study of complex organizations, while Sherman (1976) develops a more general orientation. Several recent statements provide brief summaries of the intellectual tradition or sociological significance of the dialectic (Sewart, 1978; Burawoy, 1978; Appelbaum, 1978).

2. This discussion is grounded within the Hegelian-Marxian tradition of the dialectic. Among the representatives of this tradition are Lukács (1971), Lefebvre (1971), Goldmann (1969), Horkheimer (1972), Marković (1974), and Petrović (1967). This particular Marxian perspective emphasizes the totality of Marx's

work as indicative of a dialectical method rather than stressing either the "young" or "mature" Marx as having all the answers.

3. The dialectical method is more than a basic philosophy of science and world view. It also involves a commitment to changing social organizations which do not limit the development and rational use of human potentiality. Toward this end, a major concern is the development of critiques of the present social arrangements (e.g., Lefebvre, 1971; Braverman, 1974) and the so-called rational-technical tools which further the maintenance of the existing limitations (e.g., Horkheimer, 1972; Habermas, 1970; 1973).

4. Most assuredly, this does not suggest that the physical environment does not restrain production, be it material or social. Marx (1967) was well aware that labor can only work on material furnished by nature, but it is the nature of the social relations which specify how the material will be used. As Touraine (1977:25) argues, "Man molds his environment and his social organization. . ."

5. Again, the use of terms may raise some questions. Traditionally, a Marxian discussion would refer to "classes" rather than to "sectors", but the focus of this discussion is upon developing a generalizable method which can be used for analysis within any society. Social classes, as they are usually conceived, represent sectors in historically specific societies. More generally, this discussion is intended to formulate the mode of reasoning behind Marx's analysis of capitalism.

6. The notion of creative potential (or species-being), like many other Marxian concepts, is often used in a vague, ambiguous manner. For this reason many sociologists have found little utility in Marxian thought, especially the thought expressed by the "young" Marx. The "young Marx" is considered philosophical rather than scientific, thus making his early work unacceptable to the scientific study of societies. "Species-essence" was used by Marx when developing a philosophical anthropology, but it is crucial to understanding his later works (Petrović, 1967; Avineri, 1971; Ollman, 1971). As Marx used it, the dialectical method is an ontology, epistemology, and ideology (Marković, 1974), and consequently, the philosophical bent of his earlier work provided the general framework for his later analyses. His investigations of capitalism maintained the assumption that human beings are creative producers; e.g., Marx (1967) claims human beings are qualitatively different from bees because their productive activity is purposive; whereas bees produce because of instinctual patterns. Marx's criticism of capitalism, then, is an application of the general conceptions found in his philosophical anthropology, which are filled up with historical-empirical content. He provides historical answers to the more general, abstract questions of his early works. The particular form of social relations (exchange) found in capitalism prevents most persons from objectifying their own interests in their daily productive activity. Exchange relations in capitalism, according to Marx, restrain the development of human activity as *praxis*. But this may raise a question about the origin of the creative potentiality. To answer this, one might start with Marx's *Economic and Philosophic Manuscripts of 1844*.

7. Around 1970 a flood of discussions attempted to provide rules and proce-

dures for discovering theories with universal qualities (Zetterberg, 1965; Stinch-combe, 1968; Blalock, 1969; Dubin, 1969; Gibbs, 1972; and Hage, 1972). These efforts were designed to improve the scientific status of sociology, but from a dialectical perspective, they appear to be searching for a natural order that does not exist.

8. This raises one of the more crucial issues in theory construction, i.e., verification. Where most traditional sociologies are predicated upon prediction and control of future events to establish verification, the dialectical method requires an alternative means. Since theories are valid only insofar as the social conditions from which they were derived continue to exist, theoretical generalizations are valid only insofar as they help to produce an alternative social arrangement. The importance of this issue deserves a more lengthy discussion, which is not possible at this time.

9. While most sociologists have contemplated the ethical implications of their work, they continue to maintain an objective or neutral stance toward its practical implications. If sociological theories are constructions within specific historical totalities, and if, like other objects of production, they are incorporated into the ongoing processes of social life, then it is imperative that the practical implications be a major consideration (Ollman, 1971; Venable, 1945).

REFERENCES

ADORNO, THEODOR W.
1976 "Sociology and empirical research." Pp. 68–86 in Theodor W. Adorno, et al., The Positivist Dispute in German Sociology. Translated by Gleyn Adey and David Frisby. New York: Harper Torchbooks.
ALTHUSSER, LOUIS
1969 For Marx. Translated by Ben Brewster. New York: Vintage.
APPELBAUM, RICHARD P.
1978 "Marxist method: Structural constraints and social praxis." The American Sociologist 13 (February):73–81.
AVINERI, SHLOMO
1968 The Social & Political Thought of Karl Marx. Cambridge: Cambridge University Press.
BENSON, J. KENNETH
1977 "Organizations: a dialectical view." Administrative Science Quarterly 22 (March):1–21.
BERNSTEIN, RICHARD J.
1976 The Restructuring of Social and Political Theory. New York: Harcourt Brace Jovanovich.
BLALOCK, HUBERT M.
1969 Theory Construction. Englewood Cliffs, N.J.: Prentice-Hall.
BOURDIEU, PIERRE, AND JEAN-CLAUDE PASSERON
1977 Reproduction in Education, Society, and Culture. Translated by Richard Nice. London and Beverly Hills: Sage Publications.

BOWLES, SAMUEL, AND HERBERT GINTIS
1976   Schooling in Capitalist America. New York: Basic Books.
BRAVERMAN, HARRY
1974   Labor and Monopoly Capital. New York: Monthly Review.
BURAWOY, MICHAEL
1978   "Contemporary currents in Marxist theory." The American Sociologist
       13 (February):50–64.
CLEGG, STEWART
1977   "Power, organization theory, Marx and critique." Pp. 21–40 in Stewart
       Clegg and David Dunkerley (eds.), Critical Issues in Organizations.
       London: Routledge and Kegan Paul.
COSER, LEWIS A.
1967   Continuities in the Study of Social Conflict. New York: Free Press.
DAHRENDORF, RALF
1959   Class and Class Conflict in Industrial Society. Stanford, Calif.: Stanford
       University Press.
DJILAS, MILOVAN
1957   The New Class. New York: Praeger.
DUBIN, ROBERT
1969   Theory Building. New York: Free Press.
DURKHEIM, EMILE
(1895)   The Rules of Sociological Method. Translated by Sarach A. Solovay and
1964   John H. Mueller. New York: Free Press.
FRIEDRICHS, ROBERT W.
1972   "Dialectical sociology: toward a resolution of the current "crisis" in
       Western sociology." The British Journal of Sociology (Septem-
       ber):263–274.
GIBBS, JACK
1972   Sociological Theory Construction. Hinsdale, Ill.: Dryden Press.
GOLDMANN, LUCIEN
1969   The Human Sciences and Philosophy. Translated by Hayden V. White.
       London: Jonathan Cape.
GRAMSCI, ANTONIO
1971   Selections From the Prison Notebooks. Translated by Quintin Hoare
       and Geoffrey Nowell Smith. New York: International Publishers.
HABERMAS, JÜRGEN
1970   Toward a Rational Society. Translated by Jeremy J. Shapiro. Boston:
       Beacon Press.
1973   Theory and Practice. Translated by John Viertel. Boston: Beacon Press.
HAGE, JERALD
1972   Techniques and Problems of Theory Construction in Sociology. New
       York: Wiley.
HEYDEBRAND, WOLF
1977   "Organizational contradictions in public bureaucracies: toward a Marx-
       ian theory of organizations." The Sociological Quarterly 18 (Winter):
       83–107.

HORKHEIMER, MAX
1972 Critical Theory. New York: Herder and Herder.
HOWARD, DICK
1977 The Marxian Legacy. New York: Urizen Books.
LEFEBVRE, HENRI
  1968 Dialectical Materialism. Translated by John Sturrock. London: Jonathan Cape.
  1969 The Explosion: Marxism and the French Upheaval. Translated by Alfred Ehrenfeld. New York: Modern Reader.
  1971 Everyday Life in the Modern World. Translated by Sacha Rabinovitch. New York: Harper & Row.
LUKÁCS, GEORG
  (1923) History and Class Consciousness: Studies in Marxist Dialectics.
  1971 Translated by Rodney Livingstone. Cambridge, Mass.: MIT Press.
MARKOVIĆ, MIHAILO
  1972 "The problem of reification and the verstehen-erklären controversy." ACTA Sociologica 15: 1:27–38.
  1974 From Affluence to Praxis: Philosophy and Social Criticism. Ann Arbor, Mich.: University of Michigan Press.
MARX, KARL
  (1847) The Poverty of Philosophy. New York: International Publishers.
  1963
  (1844) The Economic and Philosophic Manuscripts of 1844. Dirk J. Struik (ed.).
  1964 Translated by Martin Milligan. New York: International Publishers.
  (1867) Capital, vol. I. Translated by Samuel Moore and Edward Aveling. New
  1967 York: International Publishers.
  (1939) Grundrisse: Foundations of the Critique of Political Economy. Trans-
  1973 lated by Martin Nicolaus. New York: Vintage.
MARX, KARL, and FRIEDRICH ENGELS
  (1932) The German Ideology, parts I and II. Edited by R. Pascal. New York:
  1947 International Publishers.
NISBET, ROBERT
  1966 The Sociological Tradition. New York: Basic Books.
OFFE, CLAUS
  1976 Industry and Inequality. The Achievement Principle in Work and Social Status. Translated by James Wickham. London: Edward Arnold.
OLLMAN, BERTELL
  1971 Alienation: Marx's Conception of Man in Capitalist Society. Cambridge: Cambridge University Press.
PETROVIĆ, GAJO
  1967 Marx in the Mid-Twentieth Century. New York: Anchor.
PICKVANCE, C. G.
  1975 "Review essay: Toward a reconstruction of urban sociology." American Journal of Sociology 80:1003–1008.
POLANYI, KARL
  1944 The Great Transformation. Boston: Beacon Press.

SCHNEIDER, LOUIS
  1971 "Dialectic in Sociology." American Sociological Review 36 (August):667–678.
SEWART, JOHN J.
  1978 "Critical Theory and the critique of conservative method." The American Sociologist 13 (February):15–22.
SHERMAN, HOWARD
  1976 "Dialectics as a method." The Insurgent Sociologist 6 (Summer): 57–64.
STINCHCOMBE, ARTHUR L.
  1968 Constructing Social Theories. New York: Harcourt, Brace and World.
TOURAINE, ALAIN
  1971 The May Movement, Revolt and Reform, New York: Random House.
  1977 The Self-Production of Society. Translated by Derek Coltman. Chicago: University of Chicago Press.
TUCKER, CHARLES
  1969 "Marx and sociology: Some theoretical implications." Pacific Sociological Review 12 (Fall):87–93.
TURNER, STEPHEN P.
  1977 "Blau's theory of differentiation: is it explanatory?" The Sociological Quarterly 18 (Winter):17–32.
VAN DEN BERGHE, PIERRE
  1963 "'Dialectic and functionalism: toward a theoretical synthesis." American Sociological Review 20 (April):173–180.
VENABLE, VERNON
  1945 Human Nature: The Marxian View. New York: Meridian Books.
ZETTERBERG, HANS L.
  1965 On Theory and Verification in Sociology. Totowa, N. J.: Bedminster Press.

PART V
CRITICAL THEORY

The intent of a critique of society is, usually, human emancipation. Although such a critique, like dialectics, has an anti-positivistic strain, the focus of critical theory is on human enlightenment and political emancipation.

Brown, tracing the conditions for the success of a critical sociology, argues that positivistic empiricism must be eliminated, and a dialectical mode of analysis adopted. That position is, of course, remarkably like that sketched in the papers in the previous section; however, Brown adds that there must be a methodology which sensitizes one to the plight of the observed and commits one to doing something about it. He sees critical theory as maintaining the perspective of historically limited human reason and constantly searching for the means by which human relations transform themselves. Its method is a sympathetic awareness, and its topics are alienation, reification, domination, and the relationship between knowledge and domination. Its object of inquiry is late capitalist society.

The general problem for most critical theory is how human beings come to be dominated and what can be done about it. Halley, in looking at the problem of domination, focuses on art and shows how it must be viewed as part of the totality of society. Drawing on the works of Benjamin, Adorno, Goldmann, and others, he develops a critical sociology of culture.

The title of Han's piece might give the impression that it should go with those on dialectics, yet the discursive method that he elaborates is aimed at overcoming the problems that all critical theorists identify. He explores the problems and limits of Marxism, functionalism, and positivism. Discursive method, which is offered as an alternative, is derived from critical theory and structural semiotics. Ideology is seen as a distorted language game with which the discursive method can deal. Han addresses himself to the all-important questions that torture Habermas, i.e., how we ground critical theory, and how we develop realistic, non-elitist solutions to the problems of human communication. In Han's words, "Discursive method advocates the politics of enlightenment, anticipating the unity of theory and practice in a way distinctive from both Stalinist Marxism and bourgeois technocracy."

The writings of the Frankfurt school are central to an understanding of critical theory. Sewart briefly examines the main themes of this school, their attacks on positivism, and their solutions. The concept of societal totality, as it is defined by members of the school, is considered. Because of the centrality of Habermas to this enterprise, his work is dealt with. The role of critical theory in social change, the problems inherent in the perspective, and the likely future directions of this school are described.

1. Sociology as Critical Theory

MICHAEL E. BROWN

"The acceptance of an essential unchangeableness between subject, theory, and object . . . distinguishes the Cartesian conception from every kind of dialectical logic" (Horkheimer, 1976:222).

Critical theory refers to a body of social and philosophic writings identified with the Frankfurt *Institut für Socialforschung* (Frankfurt, 1972), also known as the Frankfurt school. The overall problem of this literature is the relationship between enlightenment and political freedom. Its methodology is critical and interpretive. The most prominent contemporary representative of the school is Jürgen Habermas, who has written on subjects ranging from technical sociology (including survey research) to philosophy, history, political economy, and the social psychology of language.

While critical theory is broader than sociology, its significance for sociology lies in its rigorous and patient use of dialectical reason in critiquing modern, late capitalist society. Its inquiry takes place against and draws much of its force from a political-intellectual opposition, generally identified as positivist (cf. Adorno, 1976b; Lukowsky, 1977; Schroyer, 1970; Jay, 1973).

It is mostly via the Frankfurt sociologists that we have access to the rich but neglected works of nineteenth-century phenomenology, dialectics, and hermeneutics; it is by virtue of those efforts that history has remained as a possible foundation for a genuinely human social science (cf. for discussions of the concept and problem of history, Lukacs, 1971; Goldmann, 1964; Lefebvre, 1968; Connerton, 1976, has collected a number of articles within the tradition of critical theory that illuminate the problems of historical social science). The current prominence of critical theory and the recent translation of much of the work of Horkheimer, Adorno, Marcuse, and Habermas, have clarified the profound and radical difference between prevailing tendencies in American sociology and the aims, conceptions, and methodologies of dialectical materialism. This difference and the corresponding fact that basic and apparently common concepts such as "society," "history," "the individual," and "action," have meanings that do not translate from one school to the other, have made it difficult to locate critical theory within American sociology, and even more difficult to make it intelligible to the practitioners of a discipline thoroughly grounded in positive philosophy and confident that the history of science is precisely the rejection of the philosophic, social, and political traditions that are the foundations of dialectical materialism (cf., for example, Catton, 1964).

Critical theory becomes intelligible primarily through and within its practice—the concrete urgencies and social formations in regard to which it can be considered as theory and intervention. To recognize this in regard to any theory is to begin to comprehend theory as a historic force in the sense of being part of the practical determination and implementation of values and interests. This is the first proposition that critical theory offers both by way of defense and as a substantive and methodological assertion. It is by virtue of this proposition that critical theory forgives its opponents, without forgetting their opposition and its temptation, and displays itself as an instance of dialectical reason.

The appreciation of critical theory is made all the more difficult by a culturally overriding empiricism that subjects all public knowledge to identical sets of criteria and canons of methodology. Consequently, a dialectical method that uses both interpretation and intervention—dialogue—appears to be one-sided, subjective, and arbitrary.[1] This is because it rejects the possibility of the radical distance that positivism requires between the object that displays data and the observer who collates and summarizes it. It thereby fails to maintain a positively reliable basis for claims of objectivity in research, that is, to maintain a constant consciousness independent of its objects and therefore capable of observational innocence. Even its dual objects, history and society, appear to be either a nineteenth-century globalism of uncertain or metaphysical universality or an abstraction beyond any possible objective determination (Catton, 1964).

This difficulty—opposition of positivism and critical theory—is not simply resolvable within a shared discourse. Rather, it is one of the critical theorist's objects of study. The analysis of that difficulty, that opposition, has led to two important conclusions: (1) the complexity of human experience that warrants a social science in the first place has been reduced by positive reason to a particular and uninteresting version of itself, involving factors of instrumental action and decision; (2) the hegemony of science and technology as a societal practice and an administrative ideology, as capitalism's contemporary form of reason in action and its mystification of power and violence, has made it all but impossible to comprehend human experience and its possibilities without taking exception to capitalist society as a whole (Habermas, 1971; Adorno and Horkheimer, 1972).

In order that these conclusions not be taken simply as self-serving, they must be drawn from a plausible analysis of contemporary society that demonstrates the crisis of interests and institutions that makes technocracy and its restrictions on enlightenment, and hence freedom, both necessary and unreasonable (Lukowsky, 1977).

THE RATIONAL AND THE PRIMITIVE

Horkheimer, Adorno, and Habermas have reformulated the problem of knowledge and rationality in a way that corrects the invidiousness of the distinctions between science and common sense, institutional acts and collective behavior, and organizational behavior and everyday life (Horkheimer and Adorno, 1972; Habermas, 1971; cf. Brown and Goldin, 1973). Rationality is a property of all these forms, and each can claim objectivity in its knowledge. One must recognize that there is no abstracted rationality but only concrete and therefore limited, rationalities of human interests. To establish this, the critical theorists re-engage the classical questions of the relations of knowing and the will, theory and practice, fact and value, and the good and the true. This means a return to Kant and to Hegel, and to subsequent formulations of the relationship of knowledge to freedom (Habermas, 1971).

Because the critique of rationality has so fundamentally expressed the problematic relationship between enlightenment and freedom, and because the idea of a social system has come to depend so thoroughly upon a generalized model of scientific rationality, Parsonian sociology has been the principal opposition to critical theory in the United States (cf. Gouldner, 1970; Therborn, 1976: ch. 1). Parsons's book *The Structure of Social Action* (1937) provided philosophic and historic justification for the already available categorical distinctions between the formal and informal, the institutional and non-institutional, social action and collective behavior, the primary and the secondary, social control and social solidarity, and rational action and everyday life. Each of these expresses the poles of American sociology's most general analytic dimension, rationalization, and the fundamental distinction between the rational (the formal and the instrumental) and the primitive (the informal, expressive, interested, collective, and the deviant). Parsons' work (1937, 1951, 1958) provides the theoretic language to which most American sociologists—critical and positive—have recourse in one way or another. It states more thoroughly than any other literature the position whose very implementation in theoretic work denies the possibility of critique.

For Parsons the institutional analysis of society as a system of goal-directed action depends upon two presuppositions: (1) the problem of power has been solved so that social life is controlled by universal values realized in generalizable norms rather than by coercion; (2) human action evolves and develops only insofar as it is instrumentally geared to the pursuit of ends chosen from among means more or less adapted to the ends and the conditions of their possible attainment. Replicative forms or self-elaborating forms are identified as sources of maladaptation, even as they are taken to provide a certain stability and identity for the evolving system of action. The coordination and ultimate elimination of difference are the internal problems of the social system. Its external problems are the establishment of direction in the face of environmental obstruction and varying access to potential system resources. From the standpoint of the system and from the standpoint of theory, any particular system can be analyzed in terms of *authority*, which replaces coercion as an explanatory concept; *values*, which replace motives; *norms* and *forms of organization*, which replace tradition, conflict, and manipulation; and *societal resources*, which replace the acquisition, distribution, use, and accumulation of wealth. These concepts represent both a theoretic gain over their alternatives and, in Parsons's later work their referents constitute a real historical accomplishment of capitalist industrial society.

If human action can develop only as instrumental action controlled by goals and the choice of means under conditions of urgency, the development of a system of action depends upon its cultivation of technique and its gradual and normatively controlled elimination of the nontechnical. The increasing rationalization of society is, then, both its necessary movement and an inevitable succession of approximations known as science. In fact the real future of society, the ideal to which it must tend if it is to survive as an instrumentally oriented and coordinated system of action, is science. Parsons summarizes the historic dimension of modern society:

> Action is rational in so far as it pursues ends possible within the conditions of the situation, and by the means which, among those

available to the actor, are intrinsically best adopted to the end for reasons understandable and verifiable by positive empirical science (1937, p. 58).

As a system of increasing flexibility and internal unity, society is also deathless, and history is the record of its continuation and development.

Yet, the identification of this deathless entity whose foil (and origin) is the primitive, and whose ultimate end is science, is made possible by the concepts of *boundary* and *state* (cf. Brown, 1978). "Boundary" specifies the social system's spatial circumstance in reference to other systems and in regard to the unsystemically organized environment. "State" specifies its overriding problem in relation to former and succeeding problems by identifying the system as a concrete solution and a deliberation. Time, for Parsons, is the relationship between a given state of the system and an ideal state.

Society appears poised between the possibility of being science and the possibility of being primitive. The former is its hope and development; the latter is its essential danger, which is why Parsons identifies the basic dimension of societal practice as conformity-deviance, and why his theory entails at its highest level of abstraction a theory of collective behavior. Smelser (1963) has developed this logic and has shown how Parsonian sociology, indeed, how all institutional analysis, must treat as historically regressive the very forces that Marx and Engels identified as progressive (Marx and Engels, 1948). The struggle of classes is, for the Parsonians, one of the primitivisms of society, and the crowd and the social movement are displays of the insurgent primitive against society. History for them is not the play of contradictory interests in a production aimed at the private accumulation of wealth, but is the gradual consolidation of rational action and its authorities. Thus, domination is radically eliminated as a political and theoretical problem, and with this is eliminated the possibility of critique, though certainly not criticism, and the possibility of knowing the everyday life *praxis* beneath the idealizations and appearances of institutional control (Habermas, 1971a, 1975; see, for a related formulation, Lefebvre, 1971).

THE LOSS OF SOCIOLOGY'S OBJECT AS THE LOSS OF SOCIOLOGY

Aside from the identification of rationality in action with the practices of a technically limited science, to the detriment of the daily life and critical practices that are nevertheless the foundation of the sociological enterprise, Parsonian theory dismisses the problem of subjectivity precisely at the moment that it raises it in newly critical terms; the theory of action shows unmistakably that social action, indeed action in general, cannot be accounted for in any respect by reference to individual consciousness or mechanically combined ensembles of individual actors.

A critique of idealism might well have followed from this recognition of the difference between consciousness and subjectivity and the irreducibility of the latter to the former, and Parsons might have found more and other in Weber, Husserl, Marx, and Durkheim than he did. It was by no means certain, from the text of *The Structure of Social Action*, that *The Social System* (1951), with its casual violations of Parsons's own earlier warnings against the reification of the theory of action, would have followed. The result of this lapse was that Parsons found social unity where he ought to have been suspicious of a perception so easily attained. Instead of establishing the concrete interest base of societally totalizing practices (those of capital, administration, and labor), he showed capitalist society as the realization of a universal interest and therefore as the only legitimate subject (representative agency) of the history of humanity's relation with nature. His conclusions reify nature as the wild source of goods and dangers, the calculation of which is society's work; they reify subjectivity as either calculation or the primitive. Subjectivity is drawn, at best, on the model of the survivor in the wilderness; so far as practice is concerned, antagonisms of interest express only the primitive whose survival is, in principle, impossible.

This way of raising the problem of historical subjectivity by formulating a conception of system beyond social and material relations, and therefore, by showing that subjectivity is a false problem, has engaged quite a few critics. While they have raised the issue of power, and occasionally the issues of ideology and interest, few have been able to avoid the temptations of exploring "system" at the most abstract and strategically significant level of their theorizing. One finds constant recourse to the Parsonian conception of history with its abstractions of time and space. American sociology, including its indigenous critical moments, is institutional analysis at its core. Consequently, it is limited by implicit reference to system and models of adaptation in its comprehension of a human experience, the main part of which lies on the side of what both sociology and administration must take as system's internal and mortal danger, namely the insurgent primitive, that which is before and beyond calculation.

The materially human (labor) and the historically social (struggle), twin concepts at the origin of sociology, suddenly missing from texts by the end of the 1920s, fade in significance. History is ultimately realized in technocracy, and society ultimately ceases to be historic: what remains of materiality and history is society's name, its wealth and its record. Subjectivity becomes a matter of form and sociology an idealism. Adorno comments in this regard: "No society which contradicts its very notion—that of mankind—can have full consciousness of itself" (1976:268).

Sociology, then, loses its coherence as a theory of human action and as a form of societal self-consciousness. It loses its position in the very history of ideas invoked by historians of its enterprise. Comte, Mill, Spencer, Maine, Sumner, Durkheim, Weber, Thomas, and Park become little more than advocates of method, as if method were inherently indifferent to its subject matter and had a history distinct from the more transient objects of its concern. What appears to be the hostility of critical theory to science is, rather, a hostility to a particular science and to the overgeneralization in philosophies of science and knowledge of what is actually a particular "knowledge-constituting interest" (Habermas, 1971). The science that it confronts:

> wishes with the aid of a single harmonious system to remove the tension between the universal and the particular from a world whose unity is founded in inconsistency (Adorno, 1976a:247).

But, according to the Frankfurt sociologists, the "tension between the universal and the particular" can no longer be expressed in classically Marxian terms. Dialectical reason must go beyond that.

THE CRITIQUE OF MARX:
THE DIALECTIC OF DIALECTICS

Having shown that positive sociology uses an idealization of science to demonstrate the irrationality of critique and the irrelevance of interest to an account of knowledge and human affairs, the critical theorists reaffirm the fundamental idea of the socially human. Positivism expresses a concrete, historically limited, interest; society must be understood historically and therefore in terms of social-material contradictions; and dialectical materialism has a more general and historically suitable foundation than that provided by the classical radical analysis of nineteenth-century liberal capitalism and its ideologies. Since the issue of human emancipation is so thoroughly and apparently conclusively developed in the writings of Karl Marx, however; the reaffirmation of the social human requires a critique of Marxian political economy from the standpoint of its concept of freedom.

Habermas's basic assertion against Marx (and against Parsons's version of Weber's critique of Marx) is that human association cannot be understood as founded in either production or culture, but must be considered in relation to both. The dominance of one over the other is an historic fact and not a law of nature. Marx, Habermas argues, overemphasized work to the exclusion of the symbolic communication that grounds collectivity and establishes the subjective basis of all action. As a result, Marx found himself forced into a positivism in his theories of crisis, and finally identified the possibility of human liberation with the development of instrumental technique (cf. Wellmer, 1971; Howard, 1977:127–135). The class struggle expressed concrete limitations on the elaboration and use of technique by a capitalism that differentiated people within the sphere of production according to their control over production and the market. The proletariat held an interest in control, which was identical to the interest of its class enemy. Labor was differentiated from capital by the limits that each could place on the other's control over a socially produced surplus. Thus, neither group— labor nor capital—possessed human interests as Habermas uses the term, but particular interests in some thing. The proletariat and the class enemy are identifiable within the totality of capitalism only in a one-sided and historically limited view of human affairs. The self-emancipation of the proletariat is the emancipation of a statistical majority; it is not a universally human emancipation, an emancipation in principle of the human in principle.

Marx was not, however, incorrect. His critique was, Habermas acknowledges, the specific critique of capitalist production aimed at the end of capitalist exploitation. It was occasioned by the real obstacles to human solidarity that capitalist relations of production had constructed in the nineteenth century. The regular and increasingly severe crises of the uncontrolled private accumulation of wealth led to the interventionist state, and this became the overriding force in capitalist societies of the twentieth century. It is in this context that science and technology become legitimating ideologies for administrative practice, and the public sphere comes to exclude the collective expression of human values, needs, and solidarity in favor of the representation of false unities, official reason, and the denigration of social life. It is in this period of late capitalism that the element of communication becomes as important as production had been in the nineteenth century, but now it takes the form of distorted communication and a false consciousness. Though capitalism remains the seat of the problem, the class struggle ceases to be the historic axis of society, and the proletariat ceases to be the agency for human liberation (Habermas, 1971; 1975).

Nevertheless, production and communication remain separated as societal facts and the practical logic of production still dominates the formation of human consciousness to the detriment of a genuinely collective will (Habermas, 1970; 1975). It is because of the contemporary contradiction of work and communication that Habermas can identify three knowledge-constituting interests and specify the historic limitations on the truth of positive science and the truth of Marxism, and it is because of this contradiction that he can locate the crises that constitute late capitalist society and singularly provide the opportunity and necessity for a critical sociology. I will discuss each of these in turn.

KNOWLEDGE AND HUMAN INTEREST

The critique of positivism is, for critical theory, the critique of idealism and the interests that sustain it. Ultimately, it is a critique of domination (Leiss, 1974). As such, it offers its own science and affirms a distinctive and real human interest (Habermas, 1971).

The fundamental distinction between work—instrumental action—and symbolic communication—acts that construct a social reality as a self-conscious reality—entails a distinction between technical rules that enable an individual to control events and social norms that are ongoing accomplishments, that provide for collectivity as a practice. The interest in control limits the truth of positivism; the interest in practice (collectivity) specifies and limits the truth of hermeneutical understanding (interpretation). Collectivity provides the sense of things that makes positive science possible. Positive science, which is the science that posits things within a constant, reliable, and objectifying consciousness, then, investigates certain collective referents as objects of possible control.

At this point it is clear that Habermas, who has explicitly developed this analysis, means something other than particular motivation or desire by the term "interest." Interest is not something people either have or do not have, nor is it an interest in some thing that is ontologically independent of interest. The human interests represent an analysis of what it is to be human. The set of such interests constitutes a minimal conception without which we could make little sense of the history of what passes for knowledge of human experience and action. People must act instrumentally and communicate not in order to survive, but because they would otherwise not be human (Habermas, 1971; cf. O'Neill, 1972; cf. Howard, 1977:139).

Habermas's formulation is not a functionalism at this stage of analysis. The truth of positivism as a philosophy that would supersede all others is a one-sided truth, which is, as Adorno says, contradictory to the very notion of the human that allows one to think of philosophy and sociology at all. If it were to be made general as theory and practice, if life were to be ordered totally in regard to the possibility of control over things, society would be a system of resolution without consensus, and people would be objects with measurable and static traits that define usefulness rather than subjects. "Social control" would mean bringing these objects into line, and it is what various social psychologies of socialization mean when they speak of taming the primitive, replacing the wild nature of the presocietal human object with specific and functional location.

Positive sociology can be a human science only if it is reformulated in the light of a full analysis of the human, in particular, in the light of a recognition of work and communication as essential and contradictory aspects of human life. Interpretative sociology would also be a false consciousness if it simply described the forms of life within collectivity that are publicly expressed and officially explicit. In fact, it would become a positivism if it were to treat collective life as a static and closed set of replicating practices, routines, norm-governed types of action, or institutions. Interpretation can only complement technical knowledge if it reflects upon the possibility of change as the essence of its subject matter.

Thus, another human interest is stated by Habermas that justifies the analysis of knowledge and human interest and establishes as a matter of history and critique the distinction between the interest in control and the interest in collective practice. Interest informs critical theory as a human science and makes it a foundation for all science within the context of capitalism (Habermas, 1971). This interest is what Habermas calls the emancipatory interest in reconciling knowledge and freedom by overcoming domination. The possibility of a false consciousness cannot be rectified either by a positivism that only refers to things or by a hermeneutics that only knows familiar and publicly acknowledged forms of action. Collectivity appears to be no more than a possible source of bias; it also is impossible to distinguish unity in reality from unity in theory or from the ideological representation of unity. Only the emancipatory interest accounts for the distinctions between substantive discourse and ideology, real subjectivity and false consciousness, objects of knowledge and things, and theory and practice so that they can all be aspects of the same reality.

At this point Habermas has shown how Weber's separation of formal and substantive rationality can be overcome, how theory can recognize the validity of discourse about values and the rationality of that discourse in regard to a human interest. Habermas has also shown a possible basis outside of production for the history of society. The dialectic of domination is a critique of late capitalism, which places sociology on a new footing in terms of the substance of its propositions and its methods of inquiry. Research cannot claim to be detached and neutral. Rather, it must always be seen as an intervention. Instead of transforming human activity and its products into a world of independent things, as positivism had unknowingly done, or reducing history to the expression of rules and cultural forms, as interpretation had done in answer to positivism, critical sociology intervenes against both of those interventions. It deprives each of its claim to be generalizable as a philosophy and establishes for each its historical limitations. The history of the emancipatory interest is shown in the critique of domination, and the science of that knowledge-constituting interest is dialogic (intersubjective) rather than monologic (a relation of a subject to a thing). It is "the process of becoming aware of the truth and untruth of the self-image that the observed object is attempting to realize" (Adorno, 1976a:253). Since only an intentional awareness of an object reflects upon itself, critique is the process of the observer becoming self-aware as an aspect of what is observed. This is the sense one must make of the idea of a reflexive sociology (Gouldner, 1970) that is also engaged (Mills, 1961).

Habermas argues that science and technology are not simply ideological, but rather, that they are material forces within the totality of late capitalism. The instrumental steering mechanisms of society have become dominant in late capitalism, bypassing the capacity of the proletariat to achieve a universalizing liberation. Because of the one-sidedness of this development, and because it has taken place against the expression of human need and against collectivity, late capitalism experiences crises of legitimation and rationalization (Habermas, 1975; Schroyer, 1973; O'Connor, 1973). Rationalization collapses in the face of the irrepressible problem of values, and legitimation fails in the face of a lack of authentic consensus. Consequently, all deliberation over questions of value is usurped by technocratic administration and subjected to the particular logic of science and technology. Domination lies in this suppression of intersubjectivity by means of the management of communication (Mueller, 1973; cf. Aronowitz, 1973). Critical sociology investigates the technology of that domination, including the media within which it takes place and the myths and images of unity that are displayed within those media. It also investigates the contradictions that constantly erupt within the instruments of domination by clarifying ambivalence and difference without showing them to be solvable by instrumental action. Critical sociology is, then, the theory of late capitalism's crises in all their details and in all their possibilities for enlightenment and freedom. It is also the theory of capitalism's evolution in such a way that its crises are given historic dimension in the fullest possible sense.

LATE CAPITALISM AND ITS CRISES

Crisis appears as a turning point (Brown and Goldin, 1973). It expresses contradiction (Habermas, 1975), which is a totalizing difference, a difference without which the whole cannot be imagined, but with which the whole cannot be sustained. This is the basis for Marx's radical distinction of labor and capital as an expression of the capitalist division of production into purpose and activity. In capitalism activity must be subordinated to purpose, labor to capital. The freedom of capital is limited by its own anarchism and by the class struggle. Private accumulation of wealth requires control over socialized labor and socialized resources. That labor and resources are social does not, however, appear to be the case within the logic of capitalism. Moreover, accumulation takes·place within a market that appears to the individual capitalist as a series of emergencies that can only be dealt with through competitive action within the perspective of the immediate situation (Marx, 1967, Volume II, Parts 1 and 2). Labor must, in this account, be totally subordinated and placed wholly within the market as "free labor." Yet labor's freedom is no more than its separation from all possibility of intersubjectivity. When Marx was writing, this meant the separation of the worker from region, family, craft, and feudal loyalties. The removal of these obstacles to exchange meant that the worker was free in the same sense that commodities were free: the movement of both was to be determined exclusively by market factors. Need and collectivity were to be given no forms of expression within the logic of capitalist accumulation, and in relation to that logic, they were considered subversive. The inhumanity of capitalism lies, then, not simply in economic exploitation, but also in the suppression of human reality in favor of the reality of things governed by laws of exchange. This exploitation and suppression appears only in the later development of capitalism, when adminis-tration and its ideology have superceded the class struggle. In late capitalism the nineteenth-century anarchism of the market has for Habermas been replaced by the interventionist state; crises of accumulation have been transformed into contradictions between steering and collectivity. Domination is no longer the control of productive labor by capital but the control of all social life by the institutions of the capitalist state.

One must deal with the consolidation of capital and the formation of the system exclusively within the steering mechanisms of society. Habermas describes the contradiction as one between "social integration" or symbolically structured life worlds and "system integration" or instrumental systems of action involving steering mechanisms (Habermas, 1975:20–24). The concrete dilemmas of this contradiction have to do with the unpredictability of nature, with the difficulty of achieving consensus within an enforced individualism, and the problem of implementation—coordinating communication and control. Critique (critical theory and critical action) poses a threat for system integration precisely because it expresses the possibility of a genuine social integration, which could determine the values that govern decisions. Under capitalism, systemic coordination is mechanical. It involves manipulation and coercion directed at the supression of social integration. This prevents public scrutiny of value determinations, in part by establishing a discourse that can be both public and exclusive of the problem of value. For science and technology as the rational form of this discourse, questions of value appear unresolvable and as expressions of particular motivations of particular groups. Discussions of such issues and the attempt to establish a rational basis for such discussions are seen within this framework as polemical.

Thus, according to Habermas, a genuine and continuing value consensus cannot be established within late capitalism. The values and needs in relation to which the legitimacy of the state can be produced and recognized are excluded from public communication except in the distorted form enforced by agencies of control. Domination is immediately and directly the control of persons as members, as instances of setting, role, office, and group. The increasing coordination of domination and the emphasis within that coordination on communication make social manipulation intrinsically psychological. The rationality of membership, this official "daily life," involves an attitude of waiting and an upward gaze. The member looks to the official and the expert, and looks beyond the situation to the continual refinement and expansion of technique, the principle of that situation's order. This consciousness is at home with futuristic thought. Its folklore is futurology; its attitude toward the world is fantastic and spectacular; its coherence is the coherence of the image. Public discourse among such members within late capitalism is increasingly sterile and therefore increasingly vulnerable to manipulation. This very result, aimed for as a good, becomes, however, further justification for the denigration of daily life that characterizes so much of the literature of positivism: ordinary life appears to be arbitrary and unreliable in contrast with administration.

This discourse, which is scientific and managed, is conceived, at best, as reactionary in the sense of simply condensing official consciousness and official practice. It becomes public opinion, predictable on the basis of the messages it receives. Like the masses of early nineteenth-century conservative theory, this public provides evidence that supports the technocratic hostility to and contempt for democracy, even as its existence provides justification for the existence of the bourgeoise state. The survey comes to be seen as that public's truest expression, as well as its most comic aspect (Wellmer, 1971; Adorno, 1976b:30), and survey research becomes the comprehensive instrument not only of bourgeoise social science but bourgeoise democracy itself.

Habermas's description (1975:16–17) of the evolution of late capitalism as the transformation of societal crises brings together political economy and critical sociology. He argues that it is necessary to formulate a "principle of organization" that accounts for the primacy of any particular institution (the economy, for example) in society rather than one that begins from the standpoint of a particular institutional dominance. Late capitalism is a transformation of the economic domination that characterized an earlier liberal capitalism. Liberal capitalism, in turn, developed from a primitive form whose institutional core was kinship and whose organization resulted from combinations of age and sex. Legitimacy in the early form depended upon myth and religion. For Habermas this evolution from primitive to late capitalism takes place through the clarification and overcoming of crises rather than as an accumulation of new formations alongside of older ones that are thereby gradually modified.

Primitive forms were not geared to surplus production and were therefore susceptible to external factors and to changes in population caused by such factors. In contrast, class societies were organized around the production of surplus. Traditional class societies had internally-determined identity crises due to the politicality and inherent instability of rule. Under late, more liberal, capitalism, the economy controlled society. Its anchor was bourgeoise law, and its essential problem was the control of social life in order that labor be freed for the market and capital freed from the class struggle. As class relations were depoliticized and the market consolidated as a money-dominated price-making market, the origin of class power became mystified, appearing as authority and market-constituted wealth. Exchange became the primary steering mechanism. Rather than expressing different interests, class conflict seemed to constitute unjustifiable interference with the natural operations of the market, and the occasionally necessary planning that was required by nature's vicissitudes and the possibility of monopolization. In this society,

> Economic growth takes place through periodically recurring crises because the class structure, transplanted into the economic steering system, has transformed the contradiction of class interests into a contradiction of system imperatives (Habermas, 1975:26).

Thus, late capitalism goes beyond the separation of economics and politics and the distinctions of class to determine consensus through the agencies that articulate public needs in terms of prevailing ideologies and exclude unarticulated needs from having influence on societal action (cf. also Howard, 1977:120–127; Meuller, 1973; Wolfe, 1973). This exclusion inevitably mythicizes both the public and the domain of the scientific-official:

> Then we cannot be astonished by the ultimate desperate attempt to secure socially binding precommitments on practical questions institutionally by a return to the closed world of mythic images and powers (Habermas, 1976:337).

Positivism's theory, and the administrative practice that it ratifies, has thereby reintroduced the very dogma that it set out to criticize. Rather than a secularization of the life world, as Weber had thought would occur, late capitalism shifted the referents of myth from religion to science and administration. This latter enchantment is at the expense of the collective totality for which the original enchantment of the world had collective force and was part of the interiorization of society.

Habermas's coordination of the sciences within his conception of an emancipatory interest and his analysis of the evolution of late capitalism has made the literature of American sociology and "administrative science" available to critical theory. This is particularly true for symbolic interactionism, which has testified to the mythic dimension of modern life, and qualitative organizational analysis, which continually reopens questions of the relationships of norms to coercion, boundaries to membership, and order to solidarity. But Habermas's main purpose and accomplishment is to show that the split between substantive and formal rationality is a contradiction of late capitalism rather than an unspecifiable complementary relationship or a hierarchy of forms of reason. Habermas has clarified the problem of crisis for a critical sociology and has raised the issue of domination in connection with the possibility of its being overcome as a theoretic and practical matter.

DISTORTED COMMUNICATION, IDEAL
SPEECH, EMANCIPATION

Communication has become decisive in late capitalism's attempt to establish and manage consensus in order to justify itself, but since this consensus cannot be real, and since justification assumes the possibility of a discourse on values within a critical and genuinely cohesive public of interacting subjects, this attempt must amount to no more than an attempt to institute a false consciousness. This takes place at two levels: (1) control over the media within which a public language is sanctified and given its topics and logic, including the obligation to exclude discourse on questions of value as either already decided or beyond sense; (2) the structure of ordinary language, that builds in as matters of syntax, meaning and use, the particularization of experience, the reification of social relations and social accomplishments, the denigration of the subjective, and the alienation of need and desire as states that can only be legitimately attributed to an observer detached from need and desire. The certification of the official and the expert occurs in the myths provided by mass media and in the decisiveness of "ordinary" language's objectivism; and it occurs in relation to the illusions of group, organization, authority, and the other intrinsically hierarchical unities that are used to ground experience by denying a relationship between subjectivity (intersubjectivity) and real events.

Ordinary language contains within it, as Lefebvre has pointed out (1971) and Goffman has demonstrated (1963), precisely the uncertainty that must immobilize any actor as speaker: one can never be clear as to whether one acts on one's desires or under compulsion (cf. Habermas, 1970a). This inability to tell whether or not an act is controlled is the experiential counterpart to the domination contained within language itself, and it is an inability that directly expresses for the individual the crisis of late capitalism (Habermas, 1970). In formulating this problem, critical theory denies in principle the reduction of subjectivity (intentionality in action) to individual consciousness (psychology). This denial remains programmatic within the body of Habermas's work. In my opinion its development depends on the establishment of a working relationship between critical theory and contemporary French readings of Freud, structuralist and post-structuralist critique, Sartre's analysis of dialectical reason, and the work of the original ethnomethodologists (cf. Deleuze and Guattari, 1977; Derrida, 1976; Lacan, 1968; Sartre, 1976; Garfinkel, 1967).

Communication is, then, the point of departure for critical sociology (Connerton, 1976). For Habermas (1970) it raises the problem of the transformation of distorted communication by means of establishing the conditions of a genuine intersubjectivity. For other critical sociologists it raises the problem of the distortion of intersubjectivity and the possibility of a critical public as matters of concrete social organization (cf. in particular, Mueller, 1973; Offe, 1972), the social training of children (Aronowitz, 1973; Hearn, 1976; Poster, 1978), and the interrelationships among effective social formations—in particular, official agencies and the agencies of capital—occasionally under the rubric of a theory of the state (Balbus, 1973; Ewen, 1976; Habermas, 1970a; Marcuse, 1964; Offe, 1972; Wolfe, 1973).

Communication is not studied as human behavior, that is, what individuals *do* in the presence or under the influence of one another, as if it is an example of creature movements lacking internal principles of development and change, but rather, communicative *action* is seen as controlled simultaneously by its objects, its objectifications of itself, and the constant and troubled interplay between the instance (the utterance) and the whole (meaningful talk), the individual and the collectivity, the prospective and the retrospective, and the speaker (who ostensibly originates talk) and the socially constituted author of a particular discourse (Habermas, 1970; cf. Derrida, 1976).

Thus, a phenomenology of objectivity would show the relations of an object to the contradictory and complex mediations that make it concrete as an object of intention and that make its objectivity a history. Goffman has done this sort of research in *Stigma* (1963). Garfinkel's work consistently sustains this dialectic (Garfinkel, 1967; Brown, 1979), as does Lefebvre's work on the commodity as a form of life and on the city (cf. Lefebvre, 1971; Leiss, 1976; Brown, 1978; and cf. Marx, 1967, Vol. I, Chapter 1; Barthes, 1972).[2]

Habermas's work (1970, 1971a), and it is programmatic at this point, deals with the self-objectification of communication as discourse or ideology, the relationship between speaker and collectively constructed meaning that is itself mediated within the contradictions of late capitalism, and the relationship between ordinary language and the ideal speech situation that is implicit in the very possibility of ordinary language. He hopes to establish a "universal pragmatics" as the basic analytic tool for the emancipation of consciousness. This involves (1) showing how ordinary language presupposes an ideal speech situation that constitutes the possibility of communication; (2) showing how it is distorted so as to suppress this presupposition and thereby to constitute both a particularization of consciousness (as belonging to individuals) and a manageable public; (3) describing the ideal speech situation itself

268 MICHAEL E. BROWN

and situating it within the history of political freedom; and (4) specifying the ideal speech situation as a competence to intersubjective communication that can be concretely and methodically attained.

He has found it useful to appropriate a vast literature to this effort, including elements of symbolic interactionist social psychology, phenomenology, ethnomethodology, linguistic philosophy, structuralism, sociolinguistics, and linguistic theory. The danger for Habermas and for critical theory is that the solution will be premature. By that I mean that he may have failed to purge those theories, metatheories, and methodologies of the traces of positivism that could lead to the idealism of a strictly logical inquiry on the order of Parsons's use of standard categories of psychology, sociology, and cultural studies, or to the reductionism of behavioristic analyses of communication as an isolated activity (cf. Foucault, 1970, 1972:148; Brown and Goldin, 1973). The results so far seem promising, and it is at least clear that the critique of communication is, while in the hands of the critical theorists, neither psychology nor culturology.

Having specified ideal speech as a set of conditions (presumably historically concrete) of intersubjectivity, Habermas attempts to illustrate his conception of a critical science that both discloses the distortion in communication as systematic and affords a politicizing methodology, a *praxis*, for overcoming it. Such a science cannot consist of a set of techniques that can be applied to any object by a subject (healer, philosopher, teacher, researcher) that is itself entirely free of distorted communication since such a subject cannot be established by a non-idealist theory. It must be dialogic rather than monologic: the enlightener becomes enlightened in the process of rehabilitating the intersubjective.

Habermas's example (1970, 1971), and it is only provisional, is psychoanalysis. Here, his interpretation must be put in some relation to recent French readings of Freud, from Lacan (1968) to Deleuze and Guattari (1977), if only because it is in that literature that one finds a radical approach to the problem of subjectivity that remains psychoanalytic. For Habermas the analyst begins as an external, dominating, mediator of the patient's talk, confronting the patient with his or her double meanings, inexplicit presumptions, and false detachments and rationalizations. Soon the analytic situation becomes part of the problem in the course of overcoming distortion and false consciousness. The patient's dependence upon the analyst eventually becomes a reproduction, at a higher level, of a distorted communication in which the objectification and critique is the work of the analyst and patient together. At this moment metacommunication becomes possible so that the psychoanalytic process becomes a historic condition rather than a method of cure.

In the possible generalization and sociological correction of this example, Habermas believes that a critical public can be constituted within the strictures and opportunities of late capitalism, initially correcting the imbalance between instrumentality and collectivity and ultimately establishing the interpenetration of the two in an egalitarian society for which questions of value are recognizably capable of rational discourse and in which consensus is socially grounded rather than hierarchically manipulated. It is at this point that the history of humanity's self-conscious relation with nature can begin.

But distortion is not simply a phenomenon of language. Intersubjectivity is suppressed by agencies and apparatuses whose connection with class has not been adequately disclosed by the social sciences or by political economy. In addition the maintenance of this suppression is accomplished through the manifestation of a variety of false unities (family, authority, the city, the nation, economy, society, public opinion, the disciplines, organization, social control, role-structures, etc.) that must be studied as ideological products and as coerced obligations. The analysis of communication must, then, be coordinated with a more embracing critical materialism.

There is, it appears, an element of utopianism in Habermas, as in all the critical theorists from Horkheimer and Adorno to Marcuse. One might defend it by claiming that it is not a utopianism that denies history and politics altogether (Marx and Engels, 1948), but the limited and practical utopia that represents the possible resolution of an historically articulated crisis.

CONCLUSION

The conditions of success for a critical sociology are, primarily (1) the rigorous elimination of positivist empiricism, the study of human activities and products as things, in favor of an objectivity that never loses sight of its subjective base; (2) the methodic incorporation of the totality of late capitalist relations at given levels of abstraction in any inquiry; (3) the maintenance of the possibility of engagement throughout any analytic operation, both on the part of the observer and on the part of the observed; (4) the appropriation of the critical features of contemporary intellectual and political work without simultaneously incorporating the anticritical elements; and (5) the presentation of classical issues and its own inquiry within a dialectic that is intrinsically political. This last assumes that current movements to restrict the teaching of Marxism (as in the Ollman case at the University of Maryland) are temporary and manageable.

In emphasizing the available work of Habermas and its relevance to sociology, and in leaving unstated current and classical debates among critical theorists, I have given a limited view of the sociological program of critical theory (cf. Howard, 1974, 1977; Lichtheim, 1971; McCarthy, 1973; Ricoeur, 1973; Schapiro, 1977; Connerton, 1976). Marcuse is in some respects more radical (1969); Horkheimer (1976) and Adorno (1976) are more rigorous in their dialectical reasoning. Habermas is a more than adequate representative figure for an essay introducing critical theory as a possible foundation for sociology (Howard, 1977:118). He has tried to deal with contemporary sociology, and American sociology in particular, as he finds it. He is trained in the field and is familiar with its models, hypotheses, research strategies, technologies, and literature. Finally, his works provide access to a wide range of critical research and theory, as well as to the intellectual tradition of Hegel and Marx which has been so neglected in the sociological curriculum, the profession, and the journals of American sociology.

Some criticisms can be made of Habermas's work. It seems to me that his critique of Marx appears to neglect many points that Marx clarifies in the later volumes of *Capital* and elsewhere. The split between work and communication is a forced interpretation of Marx that responds less to the original texts than to the development of Marxism in the twentieth century. The challenge to the labor theory of value is entirely problematic, since it provides nothing to replace it as a foundation for historical materialism and the evolution of late capitalism that is so important to the structure of Habermas's argument. The obscurity of Habermas's political position and his ambivalent evaluations of political action are understandable from that point of view. Like the false socialists of a century ago, Habermas seems to want liberation without struggle and would give too much credit to intellectuals for the attainment of enlightenment (cf. Howard, 1977:146–152 for Habermas's attempt to deal with the political question). He has too easily written off the proletariat as a progressive force and too easily accepted the description of late capitalism as a state-controlled society beyond the interactions of classes and the development of material production.

These criticisms are of a piece. The critique of Marx is insufficiently developed in Habermas's works and in the works of his associates (cf. Wellmer, 1971). The relationship between this critique and the critique of the theory of value is unclear. Consequently, it is not possible to evaluate his descriptions of late capitalism and the present state of class interactions. Without greater sensitivity to these issues, Habermas's politics (1973:40) appears to be arbitrary and ultimately to constitute a defense of the institution of higher learning which legitimizes his own work. His specifically political writings show less sensitivity to political struggle than one might wish, in particular in his analysis of the student movement of the 1960s, which nevertheless is vastly superior to what appeared during that time in the United States. They also show a willingness, once again, to bring the reactionary concept of "collective behavior" into the theoretical view (Habermas, 1970a).

Habermas is encyclopedic. He seems to have great faith in the possibility of synthesis, but his capacity to embrace so much of the contemporary literature in social science and philosophy and to give it an interesting and suggestive slant within a critical materialism risks an overreliance on categories whose development and significance were originally established uncritically. This seems to me to have been the case in his writings on language and psychoanalysis as well as in his work on the evolution of late capitalism. He ends, in the latter, by looking more like a Parsonian than a consistent critical materialist. He is left with stages of development, functions, and strains interpreted as contradictions. In order to justify these formulations, he ultimately takes recourse in a philosophical anthropology that does not answer the Marxian and neo-Marxian criticisms of that position in bourgeoise social science. He reopens the question of evolution precisely as he excludes the only available alternative to idealism (the labor theory of value) so far as a metatheory of history is concerned.

Still, the fact that Habermas has raised so many questions within the general framework of dialectical materialism and has contributed so much to the revitalization of neo-Marxist thought provides new prospects for intellectual and political work, including the work of becoming acquainted with contemporary European developments in sociology, philosophy, psychoanalysis, and the analysis of discourse. What is no doubt difficult to face, but what must be faced, is the overwhelming fact that critical theory affords a basis for and requires a total re-evaluation of what most American sociologists have taken for granted as the intellectual equipment and fundamental conceptualizations of their field. Critical sociology is real sociology when reality is history.

NOTES

1. "A rigorous dialectical thinker should not in fact speak of method, for the simple reason . . . that the method should be a function of the object, not the inverse" (Adorno, 1976b:131).

2. The classical analysis is Marx's phenomenology of the commodity-form. It begins inside ordinary language as talk of the relationship between countable and useful goods and wealth, and ends with the disintegration of that talk's innocence in the text itself. The object, commodity, is finally shown to be a contradiction (of use value and exchange value) that expresses a particular mode of production with its particular division of production and its articulation as a class relation. The contradiction is shown, within Marx's text, as the history of a consciousness (a reading) of the commodity as an autonomous thing, given to the senses and subject to the laws that govern the interaction of things. The reader is driven to the recognition of the contradiction not simply by argument and proof, but by the exhaustion of the very categories in terms of which it is expressly denied. The method is that of Hegel's *Phenomenology of Spirit*, and it constitutes reading as a concrete history of a concrete consciousness rather than appeals to the reader. At the end the *reader* has had the idea, and the contradictory character of the commodity is unforgettable (This, it seems to me, is Goffman's procedure in *Stigma*, 1963).

REFERENCES

ADORNO, THEODOR
  1976 "Cultural criticism and society." Pp. 258-276 in P. Connerton (ed.), Critical Sociology. Middlesex: Penguin.
  1976a "Sociology and empirical research." Pp. 237-257 in P. Connerton (ed.), Critical Sociology. Middlesex: Penguin.
  1976b "Introduction." Pp. 1-67 in T. Adorno, H. Albert, R. Dahrendorf, J. Habermas, H. Pilot, and K. Popper. The Positivist Dispute in German Sociology. New York: Harper & Row.
  1976c "Appendix III." Pp. 131-136 in L. Goldmann, Cultural Creation. St. Louis: Telos Press.
ARONOWITZ, STANLEY
  1973 False Promises. New York: McGraw-Hill.
BALBUS, ISAAC
  1973 The Dialectics of Legal Repression. New York: Russell Sage Foundation.
BARTHES, ROLAND
  1972 Mythologies. New York: Hill and Wang.
BROWN, MICHAEL
  1978 "The new city and the myth of the primary." Journal of Comparative Research, forthcoming.
  1978 "Society against the state: the fullness of the primitive." Forthcoming.
BROWN, MICHAEL and AMY GOLDIN
  1973 Collective Behavior. Santa Monica, Calif.: Goodyear.
CATTON, WILLIAM
  1964 "The development of sociological theory." Pp. 912-950 in R. Faris (ed.), Handbook of Modern Sociology. Chicago: Rand McNally.

CONNERTON, PAUL (ed.)
1976 Critical Sociology. Middlesex: Penguin.
DELEUZE, GILLES, and FELIX GUATTARI
1977 Anti-Oedipus. New York: Viking Press.
DERRIDA, JACQUES
1976 Of Grammatology. Baltimore: Johns Hopkins University Press.
EWEN, STUART
1976 Captains of Consciousness. New York: McGraw-Hill.
FOUCAULT, MICHEL
1970 The Order of Things. New York: Pantheon.
1972 The Archaeology of Knowledge. New York: Harper & Row.
Frankfurt Institute for Social Research
1972 Aspects of Sociology. Boston: Beacon Press.
GABEL, JOSEPH
1975 False Consciousness. London: Blackwells.
GARFINKEL, HAROLD
1967 Studies in Ethnomethodology. Englewood Cliffs, N.J.: Prentice-Hall.
GOFFMAN, ERVING
1963 Stigma. Englewood Cliffs, N.J.: Prentice-Hall.
GOLDMANN, LUCIEN
1964 The Human Sciences and Philosophy. London: Jonathan Cape.
GOULDNER, ALVIN
1970 The Coming Crisis of Western Sociology. New York: Avon.
HABERMAS, JÜRGEN
1970a "Toward a theory of communicative competence." Pp. 115-148 in
      H. Dreitzel (ed.), Recent Sociology #2. Patterns of Communicative
      Behavior. New York: Macmillan.
1970b Towards a Rational Society. Boston: Beacon Press.
1971a Knowledge and Human Interest. Boston: Beacon Press.
1971b Toward a Communication Theory of Society. Unpublished Gauss
      lectures. Princeton, N.J.: Princeton University Press.
1973 Theory and Practice. Boston: Beacon Press.
1975 Legitimation Crisis. Boston: Beacon Press.
1976 "Theory and practice in a scientific civilization." Pp. 330-347 in
      P. Connerton (ed.), Critical Sociology. Middlesex: Penguin.
HEARN, FRANCIS
1976 "Toward a critical theory of play." Telos 30:145-160.
HORKHEIMER, MAX
1976 "Traditional and critical theory." Pp. 206-224 in P. Connerton (ed.),
      Critical Sociology. Middlesex: Penguin.
HORKHEIMER, MAX, and THEODOR ADORNO
1972 Dialectic of Enlightenment. New York: Seabury Press.
HOWARD, DICK
1974 "A politics in search of the political." Theory and Society I:271-301.
1977 The Marxian Legacy. New York: Urizen Books.

274 MICHAEL E. BROWN

JAY, MARTIN
1973   The Dialectical Imagination. Boston: Little, Brown.
LACAN, JACQUES
1968   The Language of Self. New York: Delta.
LEFEBVRE, HENRI
1968   Dialectical Materialism. London: Jonathan Cape.
1971   Everyday Life in the Modern World. New York: Harper & Row.
LEISS, WILLIAM
1974   The Domination of Nature. Boston: Beacon Press.
1976   The Limits to Satisfaction. Toronto: University of Toronto Press.
LICHTHEIM, GEORGE
1971   From Marx to Hegel. New York: Herder and Herder.
LUKÁCS, GEORG
1971   History and Class Consciousness. Cambridge: Mass.: MIT Press.
LUKOWSKY, JEFFREY
1977   Emancipatory Communication. Unpublished Ph.D. dissertation, City University of New York.
MARCUSE, HERBERT
1964   One-Dimensional Man. Boston: Beacon Press.
1969   An Essay on Liberation. Boston: Beacon Press.
MARX, KARL, and FRIEDRICH ENGELS
1948   The Communist Manifesto. New York: International Publishers.
1967   Capital. New York: International Publishers.
McCARTHY, THOMAS
1973   "A theory of communicative competence." Philosophy of the Social Sciences, 3:135–156.
MILLS, C. WRIGHT
1961   The Sociological Imagination. New York: Evergreen.
MUELLER, CLAUS
1973   The Politics of Communication. New York: Oxford University Press.
O'CONNOR, JAMES
1973   The Fiscal Crisis of the State. New York: St. Martin's Press.
OFFE, CLAUS
1972   Strukturprobleme des Kapitalistischen Staates. Frankfurt: Suhrkamp.
O'NEILL, JOHN
1972   Sociology as a Skin Trade. New York: Harper.
PARSONS, TALCOTT
1937   The Structure of Social Action. New York: Free Press.
1951   The Social System. New York: Free Press.
1958   "An approach to psychological theory in terms of the theory of action." Pp. 612–712 in S. Koch (ed.), Psychology: a Study of a Science, Volume 3. New York: McGraw-Hill.
POSTER, MARK
1978   Critical Theory of the Family. New York: Seabury.
RICOEUR, PAUL
1973   "Ethics and culture: Habermas and Gadamer in dialogue." Philosophy Today, 17:151–160.

SARTRE, JEAN-PAUL
  1976 Critique of Dialectical Reason. London: New Left Books.
SCHAPIRO, JEREMY
  1977 The Unknown Dimension: European Marxism Since Lenin. New York: Basic Books.
SCHROYER, TRENT
  1970 "The critical paradigm." Pp. 210–234 in H. Dreitzel (ed.), Recent Sociology #2. Patterns of Communicative Behavior. New York: Macmillan.
SCHROYER, TRENT
  1973 The Critique of Domination. Boston: Beacon.
SMELSER, NEIL
  1963 Theory of Collective Behavior. New York: Free Press.
THERBORN, GORAN
  1976 Science, Class and Society. London: New Left Books.
WELLMER, ALBRECHT
  1971 Critical Theory of Society. New York: Seabury.
WOLFE, ALAN
  1973 The Seamy Side of Democracy. New York: McKay.

2. Beyond the Sociology of Art: Recent Interdisciplinary Developments in the Critical Analysis of Culture

JEFFREY A. HALLEY

In the United States the sociology of art and culture typically puts the artist and the work of art in the context of the social structure. Consequently, most research has been concerned with art as occupation, institution, or milieu, with special attention devoted to the socialization of the artist (Albrecht et al., 1970; Wilson, 1964). A major stream of thought in the Marxist analysis of culture, influenced by Plekhanov (1953) and the Second International, has looked at art and culture as part of the ideological superstructure reflecting the material base of society.

Both of these approaches reduce art to a reflection of the social structure. The social significance of cultural production—the art work itself and the process of its production—becomes an issue only to the extent that it is an epiphenomenon. The empirical studies that characterize the sociology of art, therefore, lose the significance of culture within the societal totality. Even in atypical cases, as for example, Bell (1976), contemporary culture is seen as merely dysfunctional to the given order of society. One loses track of what is distinctly modern in culture, and what cultural production really is. In particular one of the crucial issues in modern culture lost to the sociology of art is the relation between creativity and the historically changing character of subjectivity.[1]

One position develops a radically different approach. In Marxian and neo-Marxian tradition, one finds works directly addressing the issues of artistic production and creativity and the relation of art, consciousness,

276

BEYOND THE SOCIOLOGY OF ART 277

history, and the economy. Among the major contributions to this critical sociology of culture are the early works of Lukacs, the Frankfurt school, and the Marxist structuralists. To display some major themes of this tradition, I will draw upon the works of the following people: Walter Benjamin, Theodor Adorno, Jean Baudrillard, Adolpho Sanchez Vazquez, Pierre Macherey, Lucien Goldmann, Julia Kristeva, Gilles Deleuze, and Felix Guattari.

These theorists share the view that art is an activity that can go beyond its origins and also be critical of those origins. This view of art is possible in a context of totality, that is, when culture and society are not mechanically hypostatized into two discrete realms, but are part of a total, dynamic, historical system. Thus, in critical analysis, art and culture are not analyzed in a reductive, empirical manner within a sociology of pregiven institutions that confine a sociology of consciousness to a sociology of knowledge (Williams, 1977), but rather, they are seen as a material production and process embedded in the totality of capitalist social relations.

One of the seminal texts is Lukacs's *History and Class Consciousness* (1971), in which he wrestles with the problem of domination in the form of alienation and reification. From Marx's analysis of the commodity (1967), Lukacs sees that in a capitalist system, human relationships are reduced to the function of the exchange of commodities, and commodities take on a life of their own, over and against their producers; they become reified. (As Brecht wrote in the song of the merchant called "The Measures Taken": "What is this thing called rice? . . . I don't know what rice is. I only know its price" [Brecht, 1967:650].) Lukacs is influenced here not only by Marx but also by Weber, especially his theory of the development of bourgeois rationalization. Thus, to Lukacs, reification implies the increased calculability of instrumental reason, which Weber felt led to the disenchantment of the world. But where the growth of this formal rationality was for Weber both neutral and fated, Lukacs characterizes it as a form of domination that is part of the process of capitalism's very development.

In the face of this increasing domination in capitalism, the question posed by these critical theorists of art is the possibility of recovering human freedom. A number of these analysts suggest that art has a special role in this process, for art both transcends it social origins and acts back upon them. Thus for Marcuse, art is political in that its form subverts perception and thereby indicts the established reality (1978). And, as Habermas wrote:

Only bourgeois art, which has become autonomous in the face of demands for employment extrinsic to art, has taken up positions on behalf of the victims of bourgeois rationalizaton. Bourgeois art has become the refuge for a satisfaction, even if only virtual, of those needs that have become, as it were, illegal in the material life-process of bourgeois society.

I refer here to the desire for a mimetic relation with nature; the need for living together in solidarity outside the group egoism of the immediate family; the longing for the happiness of a communicative experience exempt from imperatives of purposive rationality and giving scope to imagination as well as spontaneity. Bourgeois art . . . did not take on tasks in the economic and political systems. Instead, it collected residual needs that could find no satisfaction within the "system of needs." Thus, . . . art and aesthetics (from Schiller to Marcuse) are explosive ingredients built into the bourgeois ideology (Habermas, 1975:78).

The common conception of these writers, expressed in a variety of ways, can be summed up as follows: art and culture are part of the totality of society. Modern culture takes a critical stance toward the development of alienation, reification, and the rationalization of late capitalism, while at the same time it is not entirely free of these elements. The dialectic of art is one of a commodity that resists being a commodity. Both are seen not as reflections of society but as creative human interventions that are part of the dialectic of society. And in the creative act the status of the individual and the social collective in late capitalism is questioned.

CULTURAL PRACTICE AS RESISTANCE TO RATIONALIZATION

In avant-garde art and literature, the problem of rationalization and resistance is the thesis of the work and the discussion of work. Critics examine the possibility that cultural production can provide a basis for a liberating practice, and their own practice rejects the positivist method of separating the observer from the observed, since they believe, with Adorno, that the function of the critic is "to awaken congealed life in frozen objects" (1967:233).

Walter Benjamin grapples with this problem throughout his writings. In fact the unifying theme of his work is a search in modern art for techniques which would break objects from their reified spell as commodities, or delegitimate instrumental rationality. This rationality, though, is conceived of as a false whole of domination. For Benjamin and others these liberating practices champion the fragment, the collage, the particular, in order to attack this generalized and dominating rationality.

Benjamin points to Baudelaire's use of gambling, chance, strolling in the city, and the literary device of "correspondences" as possessing the element of shock that detaches the artist from the context of experience. Like Simmel, Benjamin argues that the shock of contact with art and the nineteenth-century metropolitan masses gave rise to a new subjectivity; the stroller in the city takes it all in, creatively recombining the fragments "like a kaleidoscope equipped with a consciousness" (1968:176). Similarly, Baudelaire's "correspondences" attack the congealed language of the bourgeoisie by the shock of new juxtapositions of images. In Benjamin's essay on surrealism, the loss of self in the ecstasy of language, as well as the use of hashish and love, break through the conventions of the bourgeois individual and develop a new public of collective desire. Extending Baudelaire's poetic techniques, the use by surrealism of chance and imaginary combinations of words releases us from the automatism of language and points to new emancipatory possibilities.

Benjamin further develops this notion of the part as a liberating agent of the reified whole. He was one of the first to see that German fascism developed new forms of total domination through the mobilizing power of the new electronic media. He called this false, mystified whole in art "the aura." The aura is the dead weight of tradition that mystically halos a work of art, lending it a quasi-religious authority. The museum becomes a cultist shrine, and bourgeois art develops a fetishistic character. Fascist art wanted to intensify the aura by mystifying politics and making them appear to have esthetic value, dramatically exemplified in the Nazi movie, "Triumph of the Will."

For Benjamin intensification of the aura is the basis of the cult of the Fuehrer, and it leads to war. The Italian fascist Marinetti states as one of the principles of his futuristic esthetic: "War is beautiful because it initiates the dream of metalization of the human body" (1968:243). Benjamin proposes, on the contrary, to demystify the aura by politicizing art. His model is the theater of his friend Bertolt Brecht, which lays bare the device; reveals, rather than mystifying it (Benjamin, 1973). In "The Work of Art in the Age of Mechanical Reproduction," Benjamin develops the position that the new techniques of photomontage and reproducibility of art have dealienating possibilities. Like Dada's juxtaposition of objects, the process of reproduction in art breaks the aura by separating the art object from its traditional framework (Benjamin, 1968:219–254).

Benjamin is aware, however, of contradictions in the artistic practice of the avant-garde. He notes that even as new poetic techniques attack the reified world, they are nonetheless developed in a literary market that functions to put other poets in the shade (Benjamin, 1968). In other words, even as avant-garde art functions to resist commodification, it becomes simultaneously a new marketable commodity. One can make the same comment about Dada's entry into the museum; an art conceived as the rejection of art becomes absorbed by the market.

Theodor Adorno disagrees with Benjamin's characterization of the breakdown of the aura. Adorno sees it as a regression and intensification rather than an advance of the fetishism of commodities. Adorno thus shares the same concern for the dealienation of art as Benjamin does, but is more sensitive to the increasingly administered nature of capitalist instrumental rationalization. For him the culture industry:

> . . . demonstrates the regression of enlightenment to ideology which finds its typical expression in cinema and radio. Here enlightenment consists above all in the calculation of effectiveness and of the techniques of production and distribution; in accordance with its content, ideology expends itself in the idolization of given existence and of the power which controls technology (Horkheimer and Adorno, 1972:xvi).

Commercial music shares this fetishistic character, through which our sense of hearing regresses in the service of commodities (Eisler and Adorno, 1947:21). In terms of cultural production as a liberating practice, Adorno argues that Schoenberg's music makes great demands on the listener and does not yield to easy assimilation. Resisting the increasingly hegemonic culture industry, Schoenberg's music is progressive in its break with reified forms. To take another example, commenting on Baudelaire's artistic technique of "correspondences," Adorno notes all modern art's liberating attempts are a means of breaking with traditional form:

> By occluding the division between different realms of sense perception, they simultaneously try to efface the rigid classification of different kinds of objects, as it is brought about under the practical requirements of industrial civilization. They rebel against reification (Adorno et al., 1950:746).

Here, as with his comment that "the whole is untrue," Adorno is attacking the administered world of instrumental rationality as totalitarian. Along with Benjamin, he thus sees, in art as in philosophy, that the fragment, the collage, the particular, can be a force for dereification. For Adorno, then, in a world increasingly dominated by instrumental reason, art preserves a moment of resistance to alienation, and offers a vision of the possibility of a different and unalienated future existence.

Benjamin and Adorno conclude that the artistic attack on formal rationality can be absorbed as a marketable commodity. Polony (1974) and Sanguinetti (1973) have argued this last point to the extreme, saying that art only expresses the formal negation of commodification. The work of art is only the possibility of critique; it leaves what is criticized untouched. Thus a liberating practice seems to accomplish nothing and therefore lacks any real historical content. In this way the work of art readily becomes a marketable commodity, best exemplified by Dada, now found only in the museum.

Yet this is a false conceptualization. Polony and Sanguinetti lose sight of the fact that the process of commodification and capital is a dilemma facing every liberating activity. Even though liberating acts reproduce the logic of capital, they do so on a different level. A movement that temporarily dislocates language from objects puts the whole problem of socialization for the market in a historically new form—a form that challenges and resists the very society of which it is a part.

For example, Willener (1970) argues that a particular conjuncture between politics and culture was crucial to the French student revolution of May 1968. Dada, surrealism, free jazz, Marxism, and anarchism surfaced in "cultural politicization," and together, they amounted to a total contestation of the established social order.

Jean Baudrillard also grapples with the problem of what he calls "terrorist rationality" and resistance to it. Baudrillard sees that the trajectory of modern art, from Baudelaire through surrealism to the present, has tried to dereify—to make problematic what the status quo treats as given—by fragmenting the rationality of the whole. One of the decisive methods of dereification has been to separate words from concepts, signifier from signified. This has entailed, as well, an attack on the repressive unity of the nineteenth-century bourgeois ego.

The end of the tonal system in music and the dissolution of perspective in painting are, in Baudrillard's terms, the loss of referentials to reality, but this very separation of signifier from signified becomes part of the development of commodification, for language becomes fractured, autonomous, and beyond stable reference: "The code no longer refers back to any subjective or objective reality, but to its own logic . . . all reality is a place of . . . manipulation" (Baudrillard, 1975:127–8).

In late capitalism, then, what should be the final reference of a product, its use value, disappears. Consumption loses its original interest in human need and becomes manipulated by the demands of the system of production. Instrumental rationalization plans all socialization through manipulation, the most notable example being advertis-ing. This manipulation of symbols is also systematized into a code, which, by collapsing the signified into the signifier, attempts to com-mand acceptance by leaving no room for criticism or judgment, as seen in such statements as, "You are in the Pepsi Generation" or "We are in the Free World" (Baudrillard, 1975:10).

In this manner Baudrillard conceives of modern society as a totality beyond the divisions imposed by the logic of capitalism. Thus, the key to capitalism's continuance is the manipulation of consumption through the code; the locus of domination shifts from the political economy of production to the political economy of the sign. This notion of the political economy of the sign cuts across the distinctions of base and superstructure. Indeed, Baudrillard argues that divisions of base/super-structure, exploitation/alienation, and individual/society are reifica-tions required by the general system of exchange (1976). The code, then, operates as a "terrorist rationality," because it marks off whole groups, producing "the radical distinction of the masculine and the sexual objectification of the feminine," the factory, asylum and ghetto, and the "racial" domination of social groups (Baudrillard, 1975:135). But again, the victims are operating within a code, and therefore no emancipation is possible. Baudrillard argues that the revolt must be against the "capitalist social reality principle" itself, rather than merely against exploitation (1975:134).

In terms of a liberating practice, the problem with this solution is that it implies that the cultural code is beyond material human production and social relations and beyond any human action. What must be established is a critical interest that recurrently resists instrumental rationality, this Baudrillard has not done. One has also to look to other writers, for example, Henri Lefebvre (1971), who has tried to rehistori-cize the total domination that has seemed to flow from capitalist development. He argues that domination in late capitalism can never be total; it always generates oppositional needs and interests. The assertion of desire in the midst of domination is a feature of everyday life that preserves the possibility of critique. I will return to this notion of desire in the last section of this paper.

ART AND THE CRITIQUE OF REFLECTION

It is interesting to note that Adorno's sociology of music finds that the form of the work reveals the social: for him "the task would be to decipher art as the medium in which the unconscious historiography of

society is recorded" (Frankfurt Institute for Social Research, 1972:101).
In analyzing tensions and contradictions, he does more than merely
situate the work of art. Analysis of the social within the artistic practice
and product is missing from most sociology of art, which sees art merely
as a reflection of the given. This idealist thought has penetrated certain
forms of Marxism, which, rather than seeing culture as a constitutive
social practice, separate culture from material life. Yet, both Adorno and
Benjamin see art, in its resistance to the rationalizing tendencies of
capitalism, as an active, demystifying *praxis*, one that reflects and
transcends.

The work of Adolpho Sanchez Vazquez (1973) addresses this theme.
He states that the specific nature of art lies in its transcendence, that art is
a manifestation of creative *praxis* which goes beyond the given, and that,
as such, its expression of real needs is a force for dereification. Sanchez
Vazquez attacks the notion that art is only ideology. (Marx himself goes
beyond this position in his discussion of the appreciation of Greek art in
different historical conditions, and on the uneven development of art
and society.) A work of art endures and outgrows its class origins.
Sanchez Vazquez opposes Lukacs's later sociologistic reasoning that "art
is decadent when it expresses or portrays a decadent society" (Sanchez
Vazquez, 1973:26). The case of Kafka, for example, clearly shows that
work does not merely reflect, but actively demystifies, bureaucratized
human relationships. Neither can art be reduced only to a form of
cognition. Behind this conception is the same false idea that the artist is
reflecting reality in images. Rather, art is a particular form of practical
activity that has ideological and cognitive elements but cannot be
reduced to them. Art is a mediation, an active human intervention, that
creatively fashions a new reality.

Pierre Macherey, of the Marxist-structuralist tradition, also addresses
this issue of reflection. Literature is a form of production (Macherey,
1970). An analysis, whether Marxist or sociological, that examines only
the material conditions and class relations of literary production leaves
out an essential element of the social, for within the text the social is not
merely reflected but is actively produced. Ideologies and art are not
confined to ideas or even systems of representation, but are themselves
"objective material *praxes*, with an effective role in the development of
material life" (Macherey, 1976:8).

In this manner Macherey overturns both the mechanical Marxist base-
superstructure argument and the sociological distinction between culture and the social structure (cf. Bell, 1976). Art has a materiality; art and
reality are not two separate domains. Texts are not closed, but express
the unfinished, ongoing social conflicts in life, and offer imaginary

solutions (Macherey, 1976:19). Writing, in its openness, incompleteness, and expression of contradiction, is immanently social, for it is a signifying practice which produces social significance.

Lucien Goldmann's work has been instrumental in introducing the problem of the early Lukacs to French thought since the late 1940s. Goldmann's work focuses on the dialectical totality of art and society. He contrasts the positivist "snapshot" image of the functioning of society with the dialectical method, which is concerned with the "possible," that is, the potentiality of transforming social consciousness and reality (Goldmann, 1976:57, 1969:118–119). From Marx (class consciousness), Weber (ascribed consciousness), and Lukacs (possible consciousness), he develops the concept of "maximum potential consciousness," which focuses not on what a group statically thinks, but on what changes in consciousness are likely to occur in a collectivity within a given structure.

This is precisely why great works of art are treated by Goldmann as privileged objects for sociology. They articulate a maximum structure of possible consciousness. They present a world view of unity and coherence whose negativity and aspiration to transcend the present push a given structure to its furthest limits.

Thus Goldmann reverses the base-superstructure argument and links the status of cultural works to the totality of social life. Positivist sociology sees in a work a reflection of a collective consciousness, while his genetic-structuralist method sees the work itself as "one of its constitutive elements, one of the most important, enabling the members of the group to become aware of what they had been thinking, feeling and doing without having objectively realized its significance" (Goldmann, 1972:247).

Goldmann develops the concept of "transindividual subject." By this he means that a vision of the world is created not by the individual writer but by social groups. The function of creation is to bring to coherence the vision of these groups. Great works thus manifest to a collectivity their aspirations. In *The Hidden Goa* (1964), Goldmann analyzes the work of Racine and Pascal as a creative revelation, a complete structuring of the aspirations of the Jansenist extremists.

With the modern novel and avant-garde literature, however, maximum potential consciousness transcends any given group, for it

... no longer seems to be the imaginary transposition of the conscious structures of a particular group, but seems to express on the contrary (and this may be the case of a very large part of modern art in general) a search for values that no social group defends effectively and that the economic life tends to make implicit in all members of the society (Goldmann, 1975:10).

Thus modern avant-garde literature, in its search to negate the reified structures, goes beyond any particular social group or class. Goldmann points to the current crisis in the concept of class and raises the question of which collectivity can be the agent of change today. His work must therefore be seen as part of an analysis of society as a totality, and cannot be confined to the domain of art, artists, or the superstructure.

SUBJECTIVITY AND CULTURE

A number of recent theorists have raised questions as to the status of the subject in late capitalism (Lacan, 1968; Foucault, 1971; Barthes, 1977). I have previously noted that Benjamin and the surrealists stress breaking with the conventions of the bourgeois individual in order to develop a new public of collective desire. Each of these theorists, in his own terms, believes that the stable sense of self is repressive and part of the entire system of domination in late capitalism. For example, in America, the ideological strength of the concept of the individual, characterized instrumentally as the rational consumer, seems to intensify precisely as the subject is further alienated from historical action. At issue, therefore, is the question: How is it possible to recover a critical interest, in the sense of action that embodies human needs, in the face of increasing domination of the subject?

Toward that end, Julia Kristeva demonstrates that the political practice of the avant-garde is to negate this repressive and ideological unitary subject, to "disrupt the status of the subject, and consequently, the individual, in the bourgeois system" (Lewis, 1974:31).

In this manner, the avant-garde's practice is to do textual work on the subject in order to reveal the ideological and reified nature of both sides of the totality of what were the notions of self/society. As Kristeva puts it:

Through a specific practice which touches upon the very mechanism of language (in Mallarmé, Joyce, Artaud) or the mythic or religious systems of reproduction (Lautreamont, Bataille), the "literary avant-garde" confronts society—even if only on its fringes—with a subject in process, assailing all of the states of a unitary subject. The avant-garde thus assails closed ideological systems (religions), but also social structures of domination (the

state), and accomplishes a revolution . . . [through] this "schizophrenic" process of avant-garde activity (Lewis, 1974:31).

Kristeva's thesis is that this subject in process, or "decentered subject,"
can regain a substantive or practical rationality; it can seek to gratify
human needs beyond a system of means-ends rationality.

In this manner Kristeva analyzes the transgressive nature of the avant-
garde as it resists the logic of capital. Using elements of semiology,
Marxism, and structuralism, her object of study is the phenomenon of
resistance to conventional forms of rationality in poetic practice (Kristeva, 1974). The avant-garde text is difficult precisely in its strangeness,
in its inability to be thought of within the given conceptual system; this
violation lays bare the limits of that system. Hence Kristeva sees poetry
as a production. In an inquiry similar to that of Habermas (1970), she
derives from Marx a concept of production prior to exchange, instrumentality, or meaning; both point to a precommunicative activity based
on Freud's notion of dreamwork.

Kristeva views the specific production of the avant-garde as political:
its practice is the delegitimation of the structure of bourgeois rationality.
Her analysis of Mallarmé argues that his poetic practice pulverizes or
devalues meaning, and moves toward a language of music (Kristeva,
1974:212–13). And further, she states:

> The avant-garde's practice, which in language, is developed as a
> text, contests, in their very economy, the symbolic and/or social
> finitudes and thus rejoins social revolution, this latter being noth-
> ing of the kind if it is not a revolution of the subject (Kristeva,
> 1975:26).

Hence the liberatory practice of the avant-garde, in producing a text,
or writing, that challenges the domination of instrumental rationality,
also contests the repression of the subject or individual in society.

Like Kristeva, Deleuze and Guattari (1977) develop the dialectic of
desire recurring in the midst of domination. They share her position
that the self in late capitalism is a false and repressive unity that serves
the interests of rationalization. They begin with Lukacs's thesis that
capitalism has reduced everything to an undifferentiated flux, a regime
of generalized interchangeability. This pervasive commodity exchange
controls the subject's needs and desires. Through this process splits are
created "between desiring production and social production. Desire is
thrown back upon private life, while sociability recedes into profit
making labor" (Guattari, 1977:79). Work is thus split from desire;
political economy from libidinal economy. But their solution is not, as
it is for Baudrillard, to resist this process, but to push it to its limit.

A liberating practice, therefore, can occur only when human needs are generated beyond the enclosure of the bourgeois self. The self, then, must be decentered, and a strategy to negate the system of instrumental rationalization follows Benjamin's and Adorno's emphasis on the power of the particular, or the fragment, to attack the domination of the whole. In this case the repressive sense of self is fragmented in order to generate "flows of desire." The model for cultural practice is then the schizo-phrenic, as Guattari writes:

> . . . [the] guy who, for whatever reasons, has been touched off by a desiring flow which threatens the social order. There is an immediate intervention to ward off such a menace. The issue is libidinal energy in its process of deterritorialization and not at all the interruption of this process (1977:84).

In this manner the schizophrenic flow attacks the hierarchy, system, and uniformity of instrumental rationality and prizes instead mobility, proliferation, and multiplicity as a means of delegitimating this ration-ality. Flows of desire are thus conceived of as a production in the broadest sense. These material flows cut across all territories, thereby unifying the artifical splits between political economy and libidinal economy, subject and object, base and superstructure, production and representation. Through these flows of desire, then, a critical interest can be regenerated.

Regardless of the details of the positions of these theorists, they each conceive of culture as a material practice that is constituted by and constitutes the social relations of capitalism. The problem of the domination of the subject is confined neither to art nor to the superstruc-ture, but is part of a total analysis that begins with the question of human freedom. These theorists stress the historically changing limita-tions that capitalism places on subjectivity, and they suggest the possibility of cultural production as a liberating practice. And each argues, in his or her own terms, that a liberating practice arises from a critical interest in resisting capitalist rationalization.

CONCLUSION

The various authors whom I have discussed provide a radically different sociology of art from the approaches available in the American litera-ture. Their work leaves several questions unresolved. The danger of Deleuze's and Guattari's position is that their affirmative, antidialectical stance may fall into a kind of positivism. Rather than conceiving of flows of desire as a human practice, they often seem to conceive of them as a spontaneous and ahistorical human nature to which we can return. Sanchez Vazquez's emphasis on art as a creative struggle to achieve non-alienated *praxis* corrects the tendency to see art as a reflection of the social structure, but by raising this to a universal principle, he leaves us with a reified concept of creativity rather than a historically grounded one. The structuralists tend to overemphasize the position of the relative autonomy of culture. Macherey helpfully reminds us that the text is open, incomplete, and contains the contradictions of the social.

This article has focused on themes I believe are most fruitful and most neglected by an empirical sociology of art and by a mechanical Marxism. There are other themes that deserve presentation. For one, the problem of cultural hegemony as developed by Antonio Gramsci (1970) is an important way of relating domination to the total social process; and Pierre Bourdieu's recent work on the role of culture in reproducing capitalist class relations needs attention (Bourdieu and Passeron, 1977).

What, then, could be the alternate perspective of a sociology of art suggested by these authors? A critical sociology of culture must start with a clean break from the positivisms of vulgar Marxisms such as base and superstructure and sociologisms such as reality and reflection. A critique of domination developed from the notion of the reification of the commodity form can be a major focus. In this manner the dialectic of culture is conceived as a resistance to rationalization and,increasingly, as the domain of that rationalization, as occurs in the culture industry (cf. Adorno, 1967). This demands an analysis of society as a totality, a perspective that does not separate social structure from culture, or base from superstructure. Thus, a sociology of culture examines the inscriptions of the social as part of one total field in which the material social relations and contradictions of capitalism are played out and made visible to consciousness. In grappling with the problem of the domination of rationality and its resistances, a critical sociology of culture must reexamine the notion of the individual and society to clarify the historical limits and to define the ideological nature of these two terms.

Since, for all these radical sociologies of art, culture remains an aspect of society rather than something different from it or indifferent to it, their sociologies of art are inevitably politic. From the standpoint of the decentered subject and the possibility of liberation within domination, art now appears as a moment of society's history, and a moment of struggle for political freedom.

NOTES

This is a revision of a paper presented at the Fifth Annual Social Theory and Arts Conference, Syracuse, New York, April 1978. Thanks go to Michael Brown,

Lindsey Churchill, R. P. Cuzzort, George Fischer, Charles Kaplan, Bert Useem, and several anonymous referees for their helpful criticism.

1. There are exceptions to my assertion of the main areas examined in the sociology of art, most notably in the work of Lowenthal (1967), Graña (1964), and Huaco (1965), who are all closer to European critical theory and the rhetorical approaches of Burke (1941) and Duncan (1953). I would argue that, unfortunately, both of these approaches have remained marginal ones. It is beyond the purpose of this paper, however, to examine extensively either the sociology of art or a mechanical Marxism.

REFERENCES

ADORNO, T. W., ELSE FRANKEL-BRUNSWIK, DANIEL J. LEVINSON, and R. NEVITT SANFORD
  1950 The Authoritarian Personality. New York: Harper & Row.
ADORNO, THEODOR
  1967 "A portrait of Walter Benjamin." In Theodor Adorno, Prisms. London: Spearman.
  1973 Philosophy of Modern Music. Translated by Anne G. Mitchell and Wesley V. Blomster. New York: Seabury Press.
ALBRECHT, MILTON, C., JAMES H. BARNETT, and MASON GRIFF
  1970 The Sociology of Art and Literature: A Reader. New York: Praeger.
BARTHES, ROLAND
  1977 Image-Music-Text. Translated Stephen Heath. New York: Hill and Wang.
BAUDRILLARD, JEAN
  1975 The Mirror of Production. Translated by Mark Poster. St. Louis, Mo.: Telos.
  1976 "Toward a critique of the political economy of the sign." Substance 15:111–116.
BELL, DANIEL
  1976 The Cultural Contradictions of Capitalism. New York: Basic Books.
BENJAMIN, WALTER
  1968 Illuminations. Translated by Harry Zohn. Edited by Hannah Arendt. New York: Harcourt, Brace and World.
  1973 Understanding Brecht. Translated by Anna Bostock. London: New Left Books.
BOURDIEU, PIERRE, and JEAN-CLAUDE PASSERON
  1977 Reproduction in Education, Society, and Culture. Translated by Richard Nice. Beverly Hills, Calif.: Sage.
BRECHT, BERTOLT
  1967 Gesammelte Werke, (Werkausgabe), vol. 2. Frankfurt, Suhrkamp.
BURKE, KENNETH
  1941 The Philosophy of Literary Form: Studies in Symbolic Action. Baton Rouge, La.: Louisiana State U. Press.

DELEUZE, GILLES, and FELIX GUATTARI
  1977 Anti-Oedipus: Capitalism and Schizophrenia. Translated by Robert
       Hurley, Mark Seem, and Helen R. Lane. New York: Viking.
DUNCAN, HUGH D.
  1953 Language and Literature in Society. Chicago: University of Chicago
       Press.
EISLER, HANS, and T. W. ADORNO
  1947 Composing for the Films. New York: Oxford University Press.
FOUCAULT, MICHEL
  1973 The Order of Things: An Archaeology of the Human Sciences. New
       York: Random House.
FRANKFURT INSTITUTE FOR SOCIAL RESEARCH
  1972 Aspects of Sociology. Translated by John Viertel. Boston: Beacon Press.
GARFINKEL, HAROLD
  1967 Studies in Ethnomethodology. Englewood Cliffs, N.J.: Prentice-Hall.
GOLDMANN, LUCIEN
  1969 The Human Sciences and Philosophy. Translated by Hayden White.
       London: Cape.
  1972 "Genetic-structuralist method in history of literature." Pp. 243–255 in
       Lang and Williams (eds.), Marxism and Art. New York: McKay.
  1975 Towards a Sociology of the Novel. Translated by Alan Sheridan.
       London: Tavistock.
  1976 Cultural Creation in Modern Society. Translated by Bart Grahl. St.
       Louis, Mo.: Telos.
GRAMSCI, ANTONIO
  1970 Selections from the Prison Notebooks. Translated and Edited by Quintin
       Hoare and Geoffrey Nowell-Smith. London: Lawrence and Wishart.
GRANA, CESAR
  1964 Bohemian versus Bourgeois: French Society and the French Man of
       Letters in the Nineteenth Century. New York: Basic Books.
GUATTARI, FELIX
  1977 "Psycho-analysis and schizo-analysis." Semiotexte 2:77–85.
HABERMAS, JÜRGEN
  1970 "Toward a theory of communicative competence." In Hans Peter
       Dreitzel (ed.), Recent Sociology No. 2: Patterns of Communicative
       Behavior. New York: Macmillan.
  1975 Legitimation Crisis. Translated by Thomas McCarthy. Boston: Beacon
       Press.
HORKHEIMER, MAX, and THEODOR W. ADORNO
  1972 Dialectic of Enlightenment. Translated by John Cumming. New York:
       Seabury Press.
HUACO, GEORGE
  1965 The Sociology of Film Art. New York: Basic Books.
JAMESON, FREDRIC
  1971 Marxism and Form. Princeton: Princeton University Press.

KRISTEVA, JULIA
1974 La Revolution du langage poetique. L'Avant-garde à la fin du XIXe siècle: Lautreamont et Mallarme. Paris: Seuil.
1975 "The subject in signifying practice." Semiotexte 1:19-26.
LACAN, JACQUES
1968 The Language of the Self. Translated by Anthony Wilden. Baltimore: Johns Hopkins Press.
LEFEBVRE, HENRI
1971 Everyday Life in the Modern World. Translated by Sacha Rabinovitch. New York: Harper & Row.
LEWIS, PHILIP E.
1974 "Revolutionary Semiotics." Diacritics 4:28-32.
LOWENTHAL, LEO
1957 Literature and the Image of Man. Boston: Beacon Press.
LUKACS, GEORG
1971 History and Class Consciousness: Studies in Marxist Dialectics. Translated by Rodney Livingstone. Cambridge: MIT Press.
MACHEREY, PIERRE
1970 Pour une theorie de la production littéraire. Paris: Maspero.
1976 "The problem of reflection," Substance 15:6-19.
MARCUSE, HERBERT
1978 The Aesthetic Dimension: Toward a Critique of Marxist Aesthetics. Boston: Beacon Press.
MARX, KARL
1967 Capital: A Critique of Political Economy, vol. I. New York: International Publishers.
PLEKHANOV, GEORGI
1953 Art and Social Life. London: Lawrence and Wishart.
POLONY, CSABA
1974 "Exhaustion of an ideology: bankruptcy of 'modernism.'" Left Curve 2:38-46.
SANCHEZ VAZQUEZ, ADOLFO
1973 Art and Society: Essays in Marxist Aesthetics. Translated by Maro Riofrancos. New York: Monthly Review.
SANGUINETI, EDUARDO
1973 "The sociology of the avant-garde." In E. Burns and T. Burns (eds.), Sociology of Literature and Drama. Baltimore, Md.: Penguin.
WILLENER, ALFRED
1970 The Action Image of Society: On Cultural Politicization. Translated by A. M. Sheridan Smith. New York: Pantheon.
WILLIAMS, RAYMOND
1977 Marxism and Literature. Oxford: Oxford University Press.
WILSON, ROBERT N. (ed.)
1964 The Arts in Society. Englewood Cliffs, N.J.: Prentice-Hall.

3. Ideology—Critique and Social Science: The Use of Discursive Method

SANG JIN HAN

This paper is concerned with the application of discursive method to the problem of ideology.[1] Discursive method refers to discursive analysis and testing as two distinct methodological issues developed in structural semiotics and critical theory. These issues have emerged within the limits of positivism, idealism, and dogmatic versions of Marxism. Specifically, discursive method is critical of the materialist determinism in Marxism and the concept of testing in positivism. The objective and rationale of discursive method lie in producing enlightenment with practical significance. In this paper I would like to explore the rational and practical significance of discursive method by examining how this method, when applied to the problem of ideology, is distinguised from others and what advantages it therefore promises.

I have chosen the problem of ideology for two reasons. First, it is easy to note the existence and importance of this problem in current sociological theory, especially in Europe. Second, the large number of approaches to the problem of ideology have created a situation in which it is difficult, if not impossible, to see what is *not* ideological. Indeed, one can observe that despite, or perhaps because of, all discussions, the final conclusion comes quite close to saying that everything is more or less ideological. Gouldner's recent work (1976) clearly reveals this tendency.

In this paper I shall argue that this tendency can be overcome in the light of the tradition of ideology-critique, which was originally opened up by Marx and can be further strengthened in the framework of discursive science. Ths discursive method advocated here strives for the unity of theory and practice by proposing an undogmatic but critical—a nonpositivistic but scientific—discursive analysis and testing. Discursive analysis establishes ideology as a criticizable distortion, as the denial or absence of material practice (e.g., class domination) in discourse. This analysis, as a theoretical activity with practical intent, can be tested discursively, producing enlightenment with practical significance.

The presentation starts with a brief exposition of Marx's theory of ideology. It shows an internal tension in Marxism deemed relevant for the current diversification of the theory of ideology. This is followed by a criticism of Althusser's Marxism, functionalism, and positivism, and then by an attempt to reconstruct the program of critique in the light of discursive science. Finally, a discursive analysis of ideology is exemplified in relation to state interventionism in late capitalism.

THREE ASPECTS OF THE THEORY OF IDEOLOGY IN MARX

In an attempt to comprehend ideology as "abstraction," Marx (1959:174) denounces German idealism, and especially Hegel's philosophy, as ideological. The critical sense of this polemic may be summed up as follows.[2] A concrete system of thought, including philosophy, possibly can never exist above or outside history, that is to say, it is constituted *and* functions in determinate contexts and levels of social formation. Nevertheless, classical idealism, the ideology Marx attacks, pursues in vain its own unmediated, absolute foundation from within, as exemplified by Hegel's recourse to absolute knowledge. Philosophy is then condemned to delusion. Alienated from the concrete life world, philosophy produces only an empty and illusory knowledge (Marx, 1965:15). This metacritique of ideology is operative when Marx later unveils the ideological layer of commodity relations in capitalism.

It is possible to interpret Marx's *Capital* (1967) as a scientific refutation of bourgeois ideology. The problem of ideology does not appear at the center of this text, but as its subtitle indicates, Marx's whole analysis intends to be a critique of political economy. Marx's strategy in *Capital* is twofold. He situates the theoretical categories of political economy in the historical formation of the modern political economy as socioeconomic organization, and using the systematic confrontation of this theory with its own claims, deflects it into a critique of capitalism.[3] Implied in this strategy is a social criticism mediated by a critique of bourgeois theory. More explicitly, Marx challenges bourgeois theory and reconstructs a set of basic rules of capitalist production in a discursive manner to show that class domination is inscribed in the capitalist mode of production independently of capitalist subjectivity and, based on this theoretical analysis, he refutes the key bourgeois ideology of fair exchange, which is expressed and legitimated by bourgeois theory. Ideology here is viewed as a criticizable, false claim. Marx shows that as rigorous an analysis as possible of the rules of social formation is required for a scientific critique of ideology.

Marx provides an exemplar of the critical analysis of ideology from the metacritical and scientific perspectives, discussed earlier, but he never systematizes the theoretical program of critique, which must include the problem of testing. Moreover, the idea of ideology-critique involves certain assumptions that are incompatible with the materialist determinism also found in Marx's works. It is thus necessary to draw attention to the internal tension in Marx's theory of ideology.

Marx's materialist determinism manifests itself in the statement that ideology is "nothing more than the ideal expression of the . . . material relationship" (1965:39), "the ideological reflexes and echoes" of the material conditions of life (1965:14). Systematizing the materialist position, Marx (1970:21) conjectures that "the changes in the economic foundation lead sooner or later to the transformation of the whole immense superstructure." Ideology is here depicted as functional to the management of production, as something that is functional and thus inescapable, but not as something which is rationally criticizable and thus deconstructable. Furthermore, Marx's materialist strategy tends to erase the specific unity of the ideological reproduction, allowing deduction of revolutionary ideology from economic contradiction (cf. Wellmer, 1971). The inadequacy of this strategy is beyond question today. Instead, it has become quite clear that the critique of ideological integration (legitimation) must precede the consideration of revolutionary praxis.

The rational and practical import of critique, as a threshold to liberation *via* theoretical experience, however, tends to be suffocated by materialist determinism. The enlightenment-oriented, ideology-critical approach clashes with materialist determinism in that the latter, the domain of *praxis*, is simply left to competing ideologies of social groups, while Marxist science is narrowly preoccupied with the laws of the transformation of the economic substructure, thus losing its link to rational *praxis*. This paradox is intrinsic to Marxism and has given rise to the tension within Marxism between discursive and Stalinist approaches to politics.[4]

THE ALTHUSSERIAN PROBLEM

Althusser's theory of ideology may be viewed as innovative and orthodox in the present context. It is innovative because Althusser emphasizes, against dogmatic materialism, the specific unity and effects of the ideological formation. Linear and mechanistic reductionism is replaced by a complex, structural model of analysis which grasps ideology in its relative autonomy with its own "material existence" (Althusser, 1971:166). Yet this theory is also orthodox in the sense that it upholds anew a materialistic determinism with a concept of "structural causality," which is claimed to represent Marx's scientific discovery (Althusser and Balibar, 1970:186). In the latter instance, ideology, though relatively autonomous, is seen as determined by the economy. Althusser (1971:148) thus claims that ideology is a means for the "reproduction of the relations of production" in capitalism.

Althusser's theory of ideology is functionalist, as his own analysis (1971) of the roles of education clearly reveals (for a critique, Hirst, 1976). Ideology is no longer presented in terms of its criticizable distortion, but rather, in terms of its pervasive function in everyday life, which Althusser (1969:231) calls "the practico-social function." Ideology is presented "to such an extent in all the agents' activities that it becomes indistinguishable from their *lived experience*" (Poulantzas, 1975: 206–207), but they are unaware of it because "it act[s] functionally on [them] via a process which escapes them" (Althusser, 1969:233). In short Althusser (1969:235) claims that ideology is "indispensable in any society" as a functional, unconscious, and invariant layer of social life structurally determined by the material conditions of existence.

Althusser tries to rescue materialist determinism with the help of a Marxist functionalism at a substantial cost—the loss of a critical approach which is *de*constructive of ideology and reconstructive of rational *praxis*. If all lived experience is by definition ideological, as Althusser claims, then the possibility of reflexive experience mediated by critique is ruled out.

Althusser's theory of ideology involves two internal flaws, which I will call the Althusserian problem. The first concerns the limit of this theory in its analysis of ideology. Althusser's Marxism commits itself to materialist determinism without formulating a theory of language. Consequently, this theory falls short of providing the proper concepts and tools for the analysis of ideology because, to begin with, ideology is to be seen as a language.[5] The specific unity and effects of the ideological

296 SANG JIN HAN

reproduction to which this theory often alludes can be grasped and analyzed with rigor only in the framework of language, which is unfortunately absent or lacking both in orthodox and Althusser's Marxism. Thus, Althusser's theory, despite its recognition of the relative autonomy of ideology, can neither penetrate the problem of ideology nor work out a viable standard of critique.

The second flaw is a potential dogmatism of Althusser's Marxism, which may be explored in connection with the problem of testing. We may admit, in line with Althusser, that it is a questionable strategy to describe or explain social facts with exclusive reliance on experiential data since, more often than not, the "natural attitude" cannot be treated as a resource of theoretical explanation. But if science is to be conceived as critique in Marx's sense, we must also say that rational reflection on the part of social groups is a condition of testing. Science is part of communication in which the validity of critique is discursively tested, and in which the possibility of *praxis* is discursively formed via enlightenment, which goes beyond the pretheoretical, natural attitude. But Althusser eliminates testing in favor of an objectivistic conception of Marxism. Concerned with structural causality (and to that extent removed from the life world), Althusser puts Marxist science into a position of such exceptional privilege that it stands outside history as the true theory from which the strategy of politics is to be deductively derived (for a critique, Callinicos, 1976). Thus, theory and practice are connected in a way resembling Stalinism by excluding tests of any sort. But what guarantees the truth of Marxist science? Insofar as Althusser cannot answer this question rationally, dogmatic consequences are unavoidable. Despite his recent self-criticism (1974), Althusser does not correct his fundamental epistemological dogmatism. Consequently, Althusser provides only a definition of ideology, but no means of testing.

FUNCTIONALISM AND POSITIVISM

The Althusserian problem is pervasive in today's sociological theories insofar as they adopt relativistic perspectives and avoid a critical approach. Though ethnomethodology is no exception in this regard,[6] I shall confine myself to two important paradigms of sociological theory, namely functionalism and positivism.

Niklas Luhmann presents a functionalist theory which grasps the dynamics of social systems in their process of evolution. Luhmann describes the way in which a system forms and transforms its system boundaries in evolution, with a focus on the self-steering of the system.

Luhmann (Habermas and Luhmann, 1971:13-15) radicalizes the structural-functional approach of Parsons to what may be called a functional-structural approach. One of his key arguments is that the continuity of a system depends on its capacity to reduce environmental complexity and thereby increase its own complexity. A system responds to its environment according to its own rules of selection and exclusion, and in this way institutionalizes ever more diverse and complex, adaptive possibilities without losing its identity (Habermas and Luhmann, 1971:299-302). In Luhmann's theory, therefore—the reduction of environmental complexity as a function of social systems—goes before the structuration of the system. Thus, for example, the political system responds to changing environments by expanding its own complexity, which signals, according to Luhmann and Parsons, an increase in power as a system resource. Furthermore, in Luhmann's view, all social systems are based on the reduction of signification. A system must manage and steer the boundaries between significant and insignificant, between inside and outside, through its function of selection and exclusion of meaning.

Ideology refers to all those animate cultural elements which "can be replaced in their function of orienting and justifying action" (Luhmann, 1970:57). The underlying idea is that a system, through its boundary management of meaning, can modify or change certain attitudes or cultural elements of signification which are not functional enough to carrying out new possibilities of action selected out by the system in the course of evolution. It is clear that the key concern of Luhmann's functionalism is not how to combat ideology but rather, how to plan it more functionally, Luhmann (1969) portrays system performance with such an apologetic intent that the system, if functional enough, procures legitimation through procedural rules and improves ideologies through the reorganization of symbolic means. In so doing, Luhmann's functionalism ignores completely the class nature of system performance and remains silent about the possibility that the ideology-critique. In the tradition of critical rationalism (Weber, Popper, Albert), the problem of ideology hinges on a concept of science that is modest and perhaps less dogmatic than the Marxist one. Topitsch views ideology as a functional invariant of social life, which again, rules out the possibility of a critique. Like Althusser, Luhmann defines all attitudes as ideological, which makes testing impossible.

A positivistically enlightened approach to the problem of ideology at least avoids the dogmatic consequences of Althusser's Marxism and Luhmann's functionalism with a rational, though limited, program of ideology-critique. In the tradition of critical rationalism (Weber, Popper, Albert), the problem of ideology hinges on a concept of science that is modest and perhaps less dogmatic than the Marxist one. Topitsch (1966:40, 34), for example, argues that a system of statements is ideological if it attempts to immunize the underlying value judgment from criticism by presenting itself in such a tautological way that it cannot be empirically tested, or if it deliberately exploits scientific facts to support the concealed value judgment. Here, the problem of ideology is determined by positivist norms such as the dualism of facts and value decisions. In so doing, positivism has surely created a meaningful space for critique, but the rational senses of critique may be limited if the standard of science, against which the problem of ideology is defined, makes it difficult to confront ideology in its own existence.

A fundamental difficulty of positivism is that because of its monistic concept of science (Popper, 1959), positivism is unable to deal with the whole area of practical ideology which remains outside its jurisdiction. Caught in objectivism, positivism has difficulty in recognizing the "science-immanent, technical" interest (Radnitzky, 1970:198), which is independent of the subjective intention of the researcher, but operative in such methodical procedures as deductive construction of causal hypotheses, operationalization, and measurement (Habermas, in Adorno et al., 1976:209). A dogmatic consequence is unavoidable, because science is identified from the outset with positivism, making it difficult to think of a human science with practical intent. For example, it may be that Marxist dialectic, accused of being ideological, can develop a theory as critique that may be testable, provided certain conditions are met and positivist rules of testing are not imposed. But positivism, in fact, privileges itself by firmly denying the possibility of such a human science. Thus, positivism is able to locate ideology in its restrictive framework of value decision but is otherwise unable to tackle it as a normative practical claim, because this claim is not testable in positivism. Though meaningful in many respects, a positivist critique of ideology has little to contribute to the rationalization of practical life.

DISCURSIVE SCIENCE AS AN ALTERNATIVE

Three points have been established in the foregoing discussion. First the privileged concepts of science in Marxism, functionalism, and positivism are all vulnerable to criticism. Their treatments of the problem of ideology are neither as scientific nor as objective as they claim. This shows the need for a radical self-reflexivity of theory. Second, absent or lacking in all of these theories is an ideology-critical approach which intends to be practical. We need an undogmatic approach to the unity of theory and practice in a critical theory of ideology. Finally, ideology is reproduced and maintained as an organic and practical accomplishment of everyday life. Marxism, functionalism, and ethnomethodology are all in agreement on this. Nevertheless, a theory of language, crucial to the analysis and testing of ideology, is absent or lacking in the theories discussed.

In this context the idea of discursive science implies two distinctive methodological innovations. First, with regard to the analysis of ideology, discursive method breaks away from such conventional paradigms as materialist determinism and functionalism, as well as idealism and historicism, reconceptualizing ideology as a form of language which is dispersed in social institutions and characterized by the denial and displacement of the material practices of institutions. With this starting point, discursive science requires a rigorous analysis of the way in which ideology is internally structured and reproduced with its own achievement of denying and legitimizing domination. This innovation may properly be described as discursive analysis. The possibility of a discursive analysis of ideology has been explored from various directions although the specific thrust of the discussion may differ from one to another (Barthes, 1972a; Bourdieu and Passeron, 1977; Baudrillard, 1972; Burton and Carlen, 1977; Chua, 1977; Foucault, 1972; Habermas, 1970).

Some of the requirements of discursive analysis are: (1) that the Marxist concept of social totality be methodologically decomposed into a series of levels and units of social formation so that each level of social formation, such as language, science, the state, socialization, and so forth, can be examined with working concepts and strategies relevent to it; (2) that the analysis be aimed at the reconstruction of the rules of selection and exclusion which are deemed to regulate the functioning of the object in question; and (3) that the analysis be presented in such a way that it makes something appear which remains invisible in the naturelike appearance of the object. A classical example of discursive analysis is Marx's analysis of the rules of capital accumulation and realization, which remained opaque in bourgeois ideology. In the contemporary intellectual situation, discursive analysis may seem to have a close affinity to structuralism. This is well recognized by Barthes (1972b:214–216). But when conceived as critique, discursive analysis must develop its practical intent more explicitly than does structuralism. Discursive analysis must be reflexive enough to be aware of its practical roots and to explore its noncontingent link to social *praxis* though enlightenment. This amounts to saying that discursive analysis needs a discursive program of the unity of theory and practice. Discursive analysis in this sense may be distinguished from structuralism in which such a program remains largely unarticulated. The philosophical self-understanding of discursive analysis has been best expressed in Adorno's concept (1973) of negative dialectic, in which he views dialectic as the critical reconstruction of suppression in history. Viewed in this way, discursive analysis sets distorted social relationships ("the second nature" for Adorno) as the object of analysis and reconstructs the conditions of their formation, tracing their effect in history simultaneously. Such conditions and traces may be invisible to ordinary—pretheoretical—consciousness, but their recognition can have rich practical significance.[8]

This general picture may help us realize the critical sense of the discursive approach to ideology. Adorno (1973:354–355) views ideology as a "natural but perishable" semblance. Commodity fetishism, for example, is "natural because of its inevitable character under the prevailing conditions of production," but it can be practically abolished at the threshold of liberation. To break through the semblance of ideology, however, we need to combat ideology from within, that is, by producing knowledge that shows when and how ideology is reproduced and even perpetuated in the taken-for-granted conceptions of the world. Only this knowledge provides us with the means to combat ideology. It is crucial to examine when, how, and why communication becomes internally deformed thus preventing us from knowing ideological distortion (Habermas, 1970, 1976b). The reconstructive approach to this problem is one of the lasting methodological contributions of structural semiotics (Foucault, Kristeva, Bourdieu) and hermeneutic-critical theory (Habermas, Apel, Lorenzer).

Second, as to the problem of testing, discursive method goes beyond the limits of positivism in which testing is narrowly defined as either an analytic test in terms of deductive logic or an empirical test in terms of observation (Popper, 1959, 1965). Discursive analysis as critique is distinguished from empirical science in that it contains not only a theoretical claim but also a practical-normative claim. As Fahrenbach (1972:55) stated: "Every fundamental social critique, which criticizes the existing system as one which suppresses or hinders the better possibilities of human existence, includes normative and anthropological assumptions and anticipations . . . which require an argumentative development and proof as binding and real possibilities. . . ." While the normative problem of action is only treated discriptively in empirical science (Weber, Durkheim, Parsons), in critique, the "carrying out an analysis itself . . . has normative implications" (Fahrenbach, 1972:49). Discursive analysis is fundamentally normative in the sense that it presents ideology in terms of its distortion, which, once grasped, is subject to rational reflection, and hence, deconstruction. However, since the practical intent of discursive analysis can in no way be adequately tested in the framework of positivism, the concept of testing must be reformulated.[9] This innovative attempt may be described as discursive testing.

The idea of discursive testing, best expressed in Habermas's recent works (1973c, 1975, 1976b), touches the problem of grounding science and, as such, is of general relevance to science. The rationality of empirical science, despite its claimed practical significance (Albert, 1971), is limited in a decisive sense in that empirical science rules out the possibility of a discursive validation of practical claims. This denial is self-deceptive, however, in view of the metatheoretical discovery (cf. Kuhn, 1962; Lecourt, 1975; Habermas, 1971a) that "every theory and every science, in their real existence, already depends on practical assumptions" (Wieland, 1972:530) and that "theory as such already shows practical worth (*Valenz*) even before all application" (Wieland, 1972:530). Yet, the practical-normative basis of science escapes discursive redemption in positivism. Habermas's key argument that the validity claim of norms can also be rationally redeemed in discourse may be seen as an attempted solution to this problem. Habermas (1973c) has specified the formal conditions and rules of such testing in the framework of the logic of discourse. More recently, Habermas (1976b) developed a general theory of communication in which he distinguishes four types of speech-immanent validity claims: intelligibility (*Verständlichkeit*), truth (*Wahrheit*), correctness (*Richtigkeit*), and veracity (*Wahrhaftigkeit*). He argued that, among these, the theoretical claim to truth and the normative claim to correctness are both subject to discursive redemption, yielding two major types of testing: theoretical-empirical and practical.

No less important than a theoretical discourse for testing of ideology is a practical discourse in which "the validity claim of the underlying norms becomes the object of discursive testing" (Habermas, 1976b:253). Open to testing are not only a theoretical analysis but also the normative basis upon which the analysis is carried out, and of which it is conscious. Testing is thus led to "the validity of a normative background of institutions, socioculturally accustomed forms of life" (Habermas, 1976b:240), which are explicitly problematized by critique. Critique, a theoretical activity which grasps the ideological function of the normative layer of social relationships and their supportive theories, contains, at the practical root, a challenge to institutionalized deception and an appeal to emancipatory practice mediated by theoretical experience. The claims of critique are not exhausted in theoretical testing but naturally are extended to practical testing.

The methodological procedures of discursive testing, therefore, can-

302 SANG JIN HAN

not be confined to the controlled observation or its equivalents in positivism. Testing is not made exclusively against the facts which stand outside theory and are measured technically, but free discussion among social groups is a decisive condition of testing. Perhaps the best available, although not completely satisfactory, example of discursive testing is psychoanalysis, which is methodologically significant in the sense that the analysand becomes liberated from unrecognized compulsion when he or she reflexively recognizes the suggested explanation in discourse (Habermas, 1971a:231–233; for the relationship of psychoanalysis to social theory, Habermas, 1973a:9). More generally, the possibility of discursive testing is based on the hermeneutic assumption that the object of study is not merely an object to be explained, but is one that can enter into discourse and thereby rationally recognize or criticize the proposed theory. The eventual goal of discursive testing is, then, the unity of theory and practice. The gap between theory and practice, which Fahrenbach (1972:53–54) correctly mentions, can be reduced, if not eliminated, by discursive testing wherein individuals and groups are involved in unlimited critical discourse, thereby changing their practical consciousness with the experience of self-reflection. The validity of critique may be proved in the last analysis by successful emancipation itself (Wellmer, 1971:41).

DISCURSIVE SCIENCE AND IDEOLOGY-CRITIQUE AS EXEMPLIFIED BY STATE INTERVENTIONISM

Marx was aware of the fact that critical theory can gain material force only when it is represented by social forces. He (1965:69) occasionally pointed out that social revolution is possible only by way of "the alteration of men on a mass scale." But it seems that Marx treated this problem as an immediately political, rather than a discursive, problem. He allowed the reduction of *praxis* to strategy as we find it exemplified in the history of communist revolution. Dogmatic versions of Marxism not only obscure the constitutive link of critique to *praxis*, but are also unable to penetrate the problem of ideology. In this connection discursive method seems useful in reconstructing and radicalizing the ideology-critical approach. Now I would like to explore a discursive analysis of ideology using the example of state interventionism in late capitalism.

It has been recognized that politics is characterized by a dual structure, symbolic and substantive (Edelmann). An unresolved methodological question is how to formulate a theory of the state which shows the class nature of the state in terms of its own activity. Neither Marxism nor bourgeois social science has been prepared to undertake this. In this regard the possibility of a discursive analysis has been forcefully explored by Claus Offe (1974:38–39), who argues, against Marxist reductionism, that the theory of the state must analyze "the internal selectiveness of political institutions" in order to "reconstruct political governance as class rule." The idea of a discursive analysis of state activity is clear when Offe (1974:38) argues that "the class nature of the capitalist state can be reconstructed as a kind of selectiveness which is peculiar to the state itself."

A discursive (not intuitive) presentation of the ideology of state interventionism is possible on the basis of the analysis of state activity in its relationship to accumulation and legitimation. This twofold analysis is necessary because the state is in a position not only to manage accumulation but also to win the recognition of general electorates. On the one hand the state may be viewed as regulated by a set of rationally reconstructable "production rules" (Offe, 1975a:134), by which "the state responds to situations in which labor and/or capital fail to operate in the accumulation process by producing material conditions that allow the continuation of accumulation," that is, "conditions that are essential for the accumulating units but that cannot be achieved by their own activity" (Offe, 1975a:132; O'Connor, 1973). The state may be viewed as regulated by a set of "legitimating rules" by which "the capitalist state manages, through a variety of institutional mechanisms, to convey the image of an organization of power that pursues common and general interests of society as a whole" (Offe, 1975a:127). Productive state activity is obviously bound to collective capitalist interests, which, though not immediately visible, are already presupposed in the given relationship of the state to accumulation, and which Offe (1975a:126–127) reconstructs as exclusion, maintenance, and dependence. This claim may be further substantiated by the analysis of the class-specific selectivity and exclusivity materialized in the structural, social, and controlling state policies,[10] but the rules of legitimation, whether their means are symbolic or material, can be effective only by concealing or displacing the class character of state activity. The ideology of technocracy is an example. Thus, there arises the structural ambivalence that "the state must at the same time practice its class character and keep it concealed" (Offe, 1974:47). Ideology gains specific and systematic import because "the existence of a capitalist state presupposes the systematic denial of its nature as a capitalist state" (Offe, 1975a:127).

This twofold discursive analysis is surely critical of the capitalist state but it avoids the Marxist error of treating the state as nothing more than an instrument of class domination. A cryptic feature of this analysis is its awareness of the situation peculiar to the state in late capitalism, in which a rise of the noncapitalist elements within the state has occurred. The "structural incompatibility" (Offe, 1972:27) appears in the fact that the state is today increasingly involved in concrete use values, exemplified by welfare civil service, education, health, and community planning, that are still managed within the capitalist framework but potentially point to the noncapitalist—decommodified—form of social life. This indicates that there are some objective reasons which permit, though elusively, the state and its agents to interpret state activity as neutral of class domination (cf. Miliband, 1969:72). In this situation, the discursive analysis of the state brings to light a structural tension which arises from the fact that although the state in its socioeconomic intervention has developed a "rudimentary model of organization of social life which is liberated from the commodity form," the state is not yet able "to live up to the promise implicit in that model" because it actually operates under the structural constraints of capitalism which require the state to function as a capitalist state (Offe, 1975b:256). Here, the dialectic of the possibility and the reality becomes particularly acute.

The discursive analysis of the state participates in this dialectic through its search for the theoretical concept of the state liberated from its class nature, and through public enlightenment via discursive testing. To use Foucault's term (1977:208), such an analysis is "a regional system" of the diffused struggle in society against domination. Two hypotheses, recently formulated, are especially meaningful. They are the politicization of late capitalism (Offe, 1973; Habermas, 1975) and the evolution of the normative structures of society in the direction of the erosion of the cultural basis of capitalist relationships (Habermas, 1976a; Baudrillard, 1975; Bell, 1977). According to these hypotheses, the discursive realm of society becomes increasingly reflexive and politicized, resulting in delegitimation and political struggle.[11] Furthermore, these hypotheses strongly support the idea of discursive testing. Discursive testing is as yet not firmly institutionalized, as critics of Habermas have repeatedly pointed out, but the discursive realm of society in which individuals and groups discuss and challenge various instances of reification and domination already points to the idea of discursive testing. Discursive analysis produces critique, relating it to this diffused trend of testing or struggle by social groups, with the strategy toward a progressive emancipation of the discursive layer of society. This strategy is based on the recognition that public enlightenment, which is in principle discursive, and in which individuals and groups form their political will and act for the realization of a better society, is indeed of decisive importance for a progressive movement in history.

CONCLUSION

Discursive method criticizes ideology as a distorted language game. This distortion is constructed analytically by examining the selectivity and exclusivity of institutionalized practice and discourse. Neither Marxism, functionalism, nor positivism is capable of this analysis, discursive analysis can unambiguously disclose the rules, the effects and the problems, of ideology in its own existence. Discursive method also creates the possibility that practical claims, like ideology, can be tested discursively. Because of this methodological superiority, the discursive critique of ideology can realize what remains outside the positivist critique of ideology, that is, comprehensive social rationality.[12] Discursive method advocates the politics of enlightenment[13] and anticipates the unity of theory and practice in a way that is distinctive from Stalinist Marxism and bourgeois technocracy.

NOTES

The author wishes to thank Professors Thomas Burger, Charles Lemert, and Scott McNall for their valuable comments and suggestions on the earlier drafts of this paper.

1. A systematic analysis and justification of the idea of discursive method are beyond the scope of this paper. I am currently undertaking these in my dissertation work "Discursive Method and Social Theory: Selectivity, Discourse, and Crisis."

2. This interpretation has been developed in the Frankfurt School of critical theory, especially in the works of Adorno (1971). Perhaps the metatheory of knowledge, which emphasizes the dialectical interplay between knowledge and social formation, is best systematized in Habermas's metatheoretical work, *Knowledge and Human Interests* (1971a).

3. Alfred Schmidt (1968) has developed this perspective exceedingly well in his attempt to clarify the concept of critique in *Capital.*

4. These two trends may be seen in the history of Marxism as exemplified by the disputes, for example, between Luxemburg and Lenin and between Korsch and Kautsky. More recently, Habermas has opposed a consensus theory of truth to Stalinist Marxism and, in this sense, may be contrasted to Althusser, whose position is close to Stalinism.

5. This recognition is today widely shared by structural semiotics, ethnomethodology, and hermeneutic-critical theory, and much research seems on the way in this direction (cf. Mueller, 1973; Bourdieu and Passeron, 1977). Original attempts to formulate ideology as a language may be found in Habermas (1971a:42, 1971b:287), Barthes (1967:91–93), and Foucault (1972:186).

6. Among the few attempts made so far to explore the connection between

Marxism and ethnomethodology with regard to the problem of ideology, Chua's discussion (1977:30) is most penetrating; he correctly reasons that "ethnomethodology provides no concept of ideology." Insofar as ethnomethodology proceeds within its methodological rules, it cannot develop a critical standard of ideology, although, as Chua implies, it may provide descriptive information which can be ordered into a Marxist theory of ideology.

7. In Luhmann's functionalism discourse is treated as a resource, similar to power and money, which the system can plan functionally. This strategy entails excluding the class perspective from functionalism and neglecting the intrinsic property of testing from the concept of discourse. Luhmann's account of discourse is thus one-sided because it forgets that discourse is also the locus of critique and struggle. Discourse cannot be so functional as Luhmann projects, provided the class nature of the political system is unmasked by such theoretical activity as discursive analysis.

8. The practical significance of discursive analysis is noted by Habermas (1973a:22–24) in the following statement:

> For sciences of the critical type, which, like psychoanalysis, make self-reflection into a method of procedure, reconstruction, of course, appears to have a constitutive significance on the horizontal as well as the vertical level. It is only reliance upon reconstruction which permits the theoretical development of self-reflection. In this way reconstructions therefore attain an indirect relation to the emancipatory interest of knowledge, which enters directly only into the capacity for self-reflection" (p.24).

9. The basic paradigm may be described as discourse as method. Language is the resource of theory construction for psychoanalysis, hermeneutics, ethnomethodology, and structural semiotics, but more decisive than this is the attempt to establish discourse as a medium of testing. Then, the conditions of testing are sought in the formal properties of discourse, that is, the rules of rational argumentation, which are certainly of logical consistency and empirical correspondence.

10. If we examine these policies in their relation to accumulation, it is possible to relate the structural policy to the increase in labor productivity, the social policy to the socialization of labor production, and the controlling policy to the elimination of the factors disruptive to accumulation.

11. State interventionism may be viewed as a kind of system innovation which is both functional and contradictory. It is functional to the management of crisis tendencies but contradictory because the legitimation of the political system as an important condition of the continuity of capitalism is thereby endogenously threatened due to the politicization of late capitalism (Offe, 1972:21–24, 58–63). In his various writings Offe formulates a hypothesis that subversion today proceeds from the marginal to the concentric sectors of the system. In this way Offe avoids functionalism and relocates the problem of contradiction at the political level. As we know, considerable polemics have arisen in this problem area, but one thing is clear: unlike those Marxists who are preoccupied with the contradictory economic consequences of state interventionism, Offe and Habermas are well aware of the specificity of the problem of legitimation.

12. Comprehensive rationality is distinguished from, and perhaps superior to

technical rationality by the way that social groups are involved in the discursive process of will-formation and thereby struggle for the realization of a better society.

13. Habermas (1973a:30–32) defends his universal approach to enlightenment against the sectarian approaches to class struggle on the basis of his previous analysis of the changed conditions of revolution in late capitalism (Habermas, 1973b:70–86).

REFERENCES

ADORNO, T. W.
 1971 Zur Metakritik der Erkenntnistheorie. Suhrkamp.
 1973 Negative Dialectic. New York: Seabury Press.
ADORNO, T. W., H. ALBERT, et al.
 1976 The Positivist Dispute in German Sociology. New York: Harper & Row.
ALBERT, HANS
 1971 Plädoyer für kritischen Rationalismus. Munich: Pipper & Co.
ALTHUSSER, LOUIS
 1969 For Marx. New York: Vintage Books.
 1971 Lenin and Philosophy and Other Essays. New York: Monthly Review.
 1974 Elements d'autocritique. Hachette Literature.
ALTHUSSER, LOUIS, and ETIENNE BALIBAR
 1970 Reading Capital. London: NLB.
BARTHES, ROLAND
 1967 Elements of Semiology. Boston: Beacon Press.
 1972a Mythologies. London: Jonathan Cape.
 1972b Critical Essays. Chicago: Northwestern Univ. Press.
BAUDRILLARD, JEAN
 1972 Pour une critique de l'economie politique du Signe, Paris: Gallimard.
 1975 The Mirror of Production. St. Louis, Mo.: Telos Press.
BELL, DANIEL
 1976 The Cultural Contradictions of Capitalism. New York: Basic Books.
BOURDIEU, PIERRE, and JEAN-CLAUDE PASSERON
 1977 Reproduction in Education, Society and Culture. London: Sage Publications.
BURTON, FRANK, and PAT CARLEN
 1977 "Official discourse." Economy and Society 6:377–407.
CALLINICOS, ALEX
 1976 Althusser's Marxism. London: Pluto Press.
CHUA, BENG-HUAT
 1977 "Delineating a Marxist interest in ethnomethodology." The American Sociologist 12:24–32.
FAHRENBACH, HELMUT
 1972 "Ein programmatischer Aufriss der Problemlage und systematischen Ansatzmöglichkeiten praktischer Philosophie." Pp. 15–56 in Manfred

Riedel (ed.), Rehabilitierung der praktischen Philosphie. Freiburg: Rombach.

FOUCAULT, MICHEL
1972 The Archaeology of Knowledge. New York: Pantheon.

GOULDNER, ALVIN
1976 The Dialectic of Ideology and Technology. New York: Seabury Press.

HABERMAS, JÜRGEN
1970 "Toward a Theory of Communicative Competence." Pp. 114–150 in Hans P. Dreitzel (ed.), Recent Sociology No. 2. New York: Macmillan.
1971a Knowledge and Human Interests. Boston: Beacon Press.
1971b Zur Logik der Sozialwissenschaften. Frankfurt: Suhrkamp.
1973a Theory and Practice. Boston: Beacon Press.
1973b Kultur and Kritik. Frankfurt: Suhrkamp.
1973c "Wahrheitstheorien." Pp. 211–266 in Helmut Fahrenbach (ed.), Wirklichkeit und Reflexion. Neske.
1975 Legitimation Crisis. Boston: Beacon Press.
1976a Zur Rekonstruktion des historischen Materialismus. Frankfurt: Suhrkamp.
1976b "Was heisst universalpragmatik?" Pp. 174–272 in Karl-Otto Apel (ed.), Sprachpragmatik und Philosophie. Frankfurt: Suhrkamp.

HABERMAS, JÜRGEN, and NIKLAS LUHMANN
1971 Theorie der Gesellschaft oder Sozialtechnologie? Frankfurt: Suhrkamp.

HIRST, PAUL
1976 "Althusser's theory of ideology." Economy and Society 5:385–412.

KUHN, THOMAS
1962 The Structure of Scientific Revolution. Chicago: University of Chicago Press.

LECOURT, DOMINIQUE
1975 Marxism and Epistemology. London: NLB.

LORENZER, ALFRED
1974 Die Wahrheit der psychoanalytischen Erkenntnis. Frankfurt: Suhrkamp.

LUHMANN, NIKLAS
1969 Legitimation durch Verfahren. Luchterhand.
1970 Soziologische Aufklärung. Cologne: Westdeutscher Verlag.

MARX, KARL
1959 Economic and Philosophic Manuscripts of 1844. London: Lawrence.
1965 The German Ideology. London: Lawrence.
1967 Capital. New York: International Publishers.
1970 A Contribution to the Critique of Political Economy. New York: International Publishers.

MILIBAND, RALF
1969 The State in Capitalist Society. New York: Basic Books.

MUELLER, CLAUS
1973 The Politics of Communication. London: Oxford University Press.

O'CONNOR, JAMES
1973 The Fiscal Crisis of the State. New York: St. Martin's Press.

OFFE, CLAUS

1972 Strukturprobleme des kapitalistischen Staates. Frankfurt: Suhrkamp.
1973 "Krisen des krisenmanagement." Pp. 196-223 in M. Jänicke (ed.), Herrschaft und Krise, Westdeutscher Verlag.
1974 "Structural problems of the capitalist state." Pp. 31-57 in German Political Studies, Vol. 1. London: Sage Publications.
1975a "The theory of the capitalist state and the problem of policy formation." Pp. 125-144 in Leon Lindberg et al. (eds.), Stress and Contradiction in Modern Capitalism. Lexington, Mass.: Lexington Books.
1975b "Introduction to Part III." Pp. 245-260 in Leon Lindberg et al. (eds.), Stress and Contradiction in Modern Capitalism. Lexington, Mass.: Lexington Books.

POPPER, KARL

1959 The Logic of Scientific Discovery. London: Routledge and Kegan Paul.
1963 Conjectures and Refutation. London: Routledge and Kegan Paul.

POULANTZAS, NICOS

1975 Political Power and Social Classes. London: New Left Books.

RADNITZKY, GERALD

1970 Contemporary Schools of Metascience. Chicago: Regnery.

SCHMIDT, ALRED

1968 "Zum erkenntnisbegriff der kritik der politischen oekonomie." Pp. 30-42 in Eucher and Schmidt (eds.), Kritik der politischen Oekonomie heute 100 Jahre 'Kapital.' Frankfurt.

TOPITSCH, ERNST

1966 Sozialphilosphie zwischen Ideologie und Wissenschaft. Luchterhand.

WELLMER, ALBRECHT

1971 Critical Theory of Society. New York: Seabury Press.

WIELAND, WOLFGANG

1972 "Praktische Philosophie und Wissenschaftstheorie." Pp. 505-534 in M. Riedel (ed.), Rehabilitierung der praktischen Philosophie. Freiburg: Rombach.

4. Critical Theory and the Critique of Conservative Method

JOHN J. SEWART

There has been a general reawakening of interest in historical interpretations of society in contemporary Anglo-American social thought. In particular, Marxism has reemerged as an important social scientific endeavor—partly as a result of problems of social development in the second half of the twentieth century, including changes in the world political situation. At the same time, Marxist thought has developed in very diverse ways; e.g., the various works of Lukács (1971), Gramsci (1971), Korsch (1971) and more recently, the anti-Hegelian-Marxist perspectives of Althusser (1970), Colletti (1973), and Therborn (1976), have attracted much international attention.[1] One of the most important and original strains of neo-Marxism has come from the work of the members of the Frankfurt School, whose intentions were: (1) to distinguish their form of Marxist thought from the mechanistic economic determinism and evolutionism of "official Marxism" of the internationals; (2) to emphasize the significance of cultural factors and of theoretical criticism itself in the development of society; and (3) to mark their affinity with a philosophical, rather than a purely "scientific" and positivist formulation of Marxism. (For an excellent account of the history of the Frankfurt School and an extensive bibliography of the publications of its major figures, see Jay, 1973.) In this paper I will summarize and analyze the core theme in the theoretical program of the

SOURCE: Reprinted from *The American Sociologist* 13 (February 1978):15–22.

School, that is, the establishment of "critical theory," as found in the work of the three original members, Max Horkheimer, Theodor Adorno, and Herbert Marcuse. I will also consider the most prominent "reformulation" of critical theory found in the recent work of Jürgen Habermas, and discuss some critical responses to the theory.

Critical theory is both a critique of society and a critique of the theory of knowledge by which society is known. In order to understand it, I will approach it first as an alternative to positivism in the social sciences and then as a critique of the political organization and culture of advanced industrial society.[2] More pragmatically, critical theory will be considered as a way of escaping technocratic domination and control, and reinstituting reason. The Frankfurt School project for reason is a total intellectual orientation which requires no less than a complete redefinition of: (1) the purpose of social inquiry; (2) the scope of legitimate knowledge of social and political phenomena; (3) the role of theorist; (4) the relation of theory and practice; and, (5) the relationships between facts and values.

POSITIVISM

There is no generally accepted usage of the notion of positivism; scholars of different orientations and in different times have used it to suit their own theoretical requirements and intellectual or ideological predispositions (see Habermas, 1971; Giddens, 1975; Frisby, 1976). In the practice of social science the term has generally been used to refer to the incorporation of natural science methods into that practice. Three assumptions are implied by this notion of positivism: (1) since the methodological procedures of natural science are used as a model, human values enter into the study of social phenomena and conduct only as objects; (2) the goal of social scientific investigation is to construct laws, or lawlike generalizations like those of physics; (3) social science has a technical character, providing knowledge which is solely instrumental. It follows from these assumptions that knowledge is unfinished and relative and, because social scientific knowledge is neutral with respect to values, that the knowledge has no inherent logical implications for policy. The categorical distinction between fact and value prohibits the social theorist from taking a normative position or advocating what "ought to be"; his/her role as a social scientist is confined to formulating and testing propositions about reality, and does not include advocacy or social action.

CRITICAL THEORY

What is missing in such a formulation is attention to "the *critical* role of theory—or perhaps more accurately . . . the problem of the role of critical theory" (Giddens, 1975:18). From a positivist perspective, the task of philosophy is to provide clarity for scientific statements; critical theorists see this as reducing philosophy to methodology. According to the Frankfurt School, this view necessarily enhances a technological system of domination (this point will be developed below). More is involved in this dispute than the issue of proper methodology in the social sciences—the very aim of social science is being questioned. Horkheimer clearly outlined the distinction between critical and traditional theory forty years ago (1937, reprinted in 1972; see also Lukács, 1971, for a similar notion) when he said that for "theory in the traditional sense . . . the social genesis of problems, the real situation in which science is put to use, and the purposes which it is made to serve are all regarded by science as external to itself" (1972:244). He contrasted this with critical theory which "has for its object men as producers of their historical way of life in its totality" (1972:244), and in which "Objects, the kind of perception, the questions asked, and the meaning all bear witness to human activity and the degree of man's power" (1972:244).

Extending his critique of traditional science to bourgeois society, Horkheimer argued that treating the *object* of inquiry as distinct from the subject of inquiry results in a system of technical rationality which effectively blocks rational political practice. Because it restricts the description and categories of science to that which is (the facts), positivism views history as a "natural" process governed by natural laws rather than as a human process capable of being influenced by human activity. (Indeed, Marx's entire critique of bourgeois political economy stands as a methodological reflection upon critical social science, and, as such, has direct relevance for current methodological controversies. (See Marx, 1973:81–111.) Knowledge of social reality becomes "neutral" information which can be integrated into the existing social structure. By separating facts and values and consigning the latter (as *sense*-less) to the arbitrary and subjective realm of politics, positive science becomes incapable of challenging (as science) the existing system, and thereby becomes conservative. Science becomes an activity far removed from the sphere of practical or moral action except in terms of assessing the adequacy of means toward *given* ends. Such a stance, in the words of a contemporary critical theorist, supplies the social engineers of the industrial system with the legitimation of measures in accordance with the dominant value system, which is withdrawn from any effective public discussion: this means—in accordance with the stabilization of the existing social power structure (Wellmer, 1971:21).

Adorno (1976:109), elaborating on the differences between traditional and critical theories, criticizes the former for its approach to problem solution. By criticizing proposed solutions on the basis of *existing* evidence, positivists appear to accept and reify existing social reality. The net consequence of assuming a positivist stance toward society as the object of knowledge is to leave that object unquestioned and to accept its substantive rationality. In a debate with Popper (1969), Adorno (1976) has argued once again that the instrumentalist (positivist) approach to reason artificially separates social scientific knowledge from the object it studies. Marcuse (1964), in a pessimistic analysis of advanced industrial society, states that critical theory is distinguished by refusal to accept the given (i.e., positivist) universe of facts as the final context of validation. Acceptance of knowledge which is derived uncritically from empirical facts allows continuing reproduction of existing relationships in society.

Reification of basic social institutions and of conventional activities is a *logical* and socially crucial consequence of technological practice (postivist social science). A political decision-making apparatus based on such practice (and such social science) will necessarily treat some aspects of the basic structural relationships of the society being studied as *given* (beyond critical or evaluative analysis) (Fay, 1975). In advanced industrial societies, for example, the decision-making process will be constrained by the primary goal of the efficient functioning of the processes of production (for an elaboration of this point see Offe, 1976).

THE SOCIETAL TOTALITY

While, as Horkheimer stated, the "denunciation of what is currently called reason is the greatest service reason can render" (1947:187), critical theory has refused to limit its activity to methodological criticism and clarification. By asserting that traditional scientific methods do not constitute an adequate foundation for valid knowledge, critical theory obviously questions the adequacy and relevance of a traditional experimental method applied to the "testing" of empirical propositions about social phenomena (this is not to argue that the School abstained from empirical research; see below). Critical theory replaces the rejected notion of individual social facts with the concept of societal totalities, observing that empirical experiments which abstract a problematic phenomenon from that totality can never successfully illuminate critical understanding (Frisby, 1972:113; Jay, 1977). I will briefly trace how this totality has been envisioned by members of the Frankfurt School.

From its beginnings, the Frankfurt School has focused on the epistemological and philosophical dimension in Marxism. During the early years (1923-1929), however, under the leadership of the historian Carl Gruenberg, a critique of political economy was central to the concerns and activities of the School. The School's role was seen as integral to problems of the workers' movement—bourgeois science was not regarded as a serious challenge or as of particular interest or concern. The collective goal was the illumination of the objective possibilities for destroying class society.

When Horkheimer became Director in 1930, the orientation of the Frankfurt School changed, in part because of changes in society, in part because of differences in the scholarly orientations of Gruenberg and Horkheimer. Whereas Gruenberg had been a socialist labor historian relatively unconcerned with the philosophical and theoretical bases of Marxism, Horkheimer was a philosopher, concerned with the development of a social philosophy supplemented by empirical investigation. While Horkheimer was a political radical, he had never been a member of a working-class party.

This shift away from the traditional Marxist concern with political economy and proletarian revolution became clear after the School was forced to flee Germany to Geneva in 1933, and to Columbia University in 1934. The principal factor in this shift of emphasis was the disappearance of the revolutionary historical "subject" of traditional Marxism—a militant industrial proletariat. The reorientation was in part an attempt to formulate a perspective which would explain new historical conditions, namely, the consolidation of capitalism and the integration of the proletariat into that consolidated capitalism, phenomena signalled by the rise of the Third Reich, Fascism, and the concommitant decline of the militant labor movement. The change further reflected a philosophical rejection of the economic determinism of orthodox Marxism. The energies of the Frankfurt School were turned increasingly to the study of "mediations" between consciousness and being, psychoanalysis, the structure of authority, the emergence of mass culture, and aesthetic issues.

While Marxist thought continued to be central to the scholarly orientation of the Frankfurt School, during the American years the Frankfurt thinkers were heavily influenced by Freud's work on the mechanisms by which individuals are integrated into society. This attention to Freud was paralleled by a shift toward greater emphasis on understanding modern culture. In particular, the Frankfurt School scholars were interested in applying Freud's insights to analysis of the psychological mechanisms by which authority, repression and domination are internalized and transmitted. Members of the group devised innovative empirical research techniques, and were among the first to apply social-psychological categories to the analysis of working class attitudes, mass society and culture, patterns of authority and family relations, the sources and nature of prejudice, the role of women in modern society, and the genesis and structure of Nazism (see, for example, Neumann, 1944; Fromm, 1968; Adorno *et al.*, 1950; Komarovsky, 1940; Bettelheim and Janowitz, 1950; Lowenthal, 1957). These studies indicate the Frankfurt School's refusal to relegate the cultural superstructure, or societal totality, to a secondary role in the analysis of modern society.

The entire Frankfurt tradition (from Horkheimer to Habermas) has constituted a sustained attack on positivism because it implies a subordination and capitulation to the reality of existing social forms, namely, capitalism. The common interest of scholars in this tradition has been to overcome the "eclipse of moral and political standards" brought about by the instrumental rationality of modern scientific thought. In order to achieve this, the Frankfurt thinkers have attempted to: (1) recover the notion of substantive rationality through a critique of ideology (a critique which permits the illumination of the realities of social life and social structure which are hidden by the distortions of positivistic thought); and, simultaneously (2) provide a "material critique" which will inform revolutionary human activity oriented to the creation of emancipating social conditions, thereby enabling humanity to seek and achieve better lives. In short, critical social theory's purpose is the merger of reason and action, reflection and commitment. To this extent critical theory necessarily has a "practical intent." However, this merger is not free from both theoretical and practical dilemmas, nor do critical theorists themselves agree on how to accomplish the tasks before them. How is critical theory to become a concrete factor in the practical, radical transformation of society? How is it to become more than an empty abstraction which periodically issues condemnations of existing reality? Habermas has given much thought to these issues.

JÜRGEN HABERMAS

Habermas is the most recent and most controversial figure to emerge from the Frankfurt School's "great refusal" to "speak the language of domination." Drawing upon the diverse and opposing traditions of

Marxist-Hegelianism, empiricism, phenomenology, hermeneutics, systems theory, and the modern philosophy of language, Habermas has reformulated the foundations of a critical theory of society in order to develop a more comprehensive alternative to a naturalistic understanding of social inquiry.

Habermas has given new form to the demarcation between traditional and critical theory (see esp. Habermas, 1971). In his discussion of the relationships between cognitive endeavors, and human experience and purpose, Habermas indentifies three different types of knowledge and "knowledge-constitutive interests," i.e., interests which orient humans (unknowingly) in their relations and reflections upon reality: (1) the *emancipatory* interest of the cognitive activities of critical theory; (2) the *technical* cognitive interests of the empirical-analytic mode of thought; and (3) the *practical* interests of the hermeneutic mode of thought. The empirical sciences approach reality from the perspective of technical control and manipulation of objectified processes (as technically exploitable knowledge). Hermeneutic inquiry is oriented toward the basic "practical" interest of human communication between social individuals.

Habermas has withdrawn somewhat from the orthodoxies of earlier Frankfurt thinkers. His critique of empirical analytic reasoning is less sweeping. At the same time, he is more cautious and skeptical than both his predecessors and some of his contemporaries about the emancipatory potential of contemporary Marxism (see Wellmer, 1971, for another contemporary representative of the Frankfurt School). Marcuse, in particular, states that empirical reason is always destructive—not only when it is employed for barbaric ends. To Marcuse, it is not a matter of the object to which empirical reason is applied; empirical reason necessarily and inherently examines its object (society) from an instrumental perspective, which accordingly reduces its object to objectified processes to be controlled, manipulated, and dominated. Social oppression is thus seen as the triumph of instrumental reason (positivism); therefore, social liberation must entail a transformation of scientific reason itself (Marcuse, 1964, 1969b).

Habermas believes that Marcuse has confused the logic by which physical nature can be understood with the logic by which people understand each other. He condemns the original Frankfurt School for falling prey to "speculation" and the "heritage of mysticism" (Habermas, 1971:32–33). Habermas (1970a) singles out Marcuse as a "romantic utopian" calling for a new science and technology to create a "new sensibility" between nature and man. Although Habermas is firm in his critique of domination by technological rationality, he wants to preserve the logic of science as such (as instrumental calculation). He believes that reason should not be *limited* to empirical analytic cognition. Marcuse and Horkheimer, in contrast, want to eliminate positivism as the carrier of a repressive social order.

CRITICAL THEORY AND SOCIAL CHANGE

The relationship between reason and emancipation has direct implications not only for the critical theorist's understanding of the sources of oppressive social relations, but also for the practical task of social change. In 1843 (reprinted in 1975), Marx wrote that a revolutionary theory of society was not yet a "material force" capable of "gripping the masses" and overthrowing the capitalist order. Marxism is still gappling with the problem of how to transform a theory into a concrete historical force, embodied in a self-conscious revolutionary subject (the industrial proletariat). Critical theory must determine the "concrete roads" (Marcuse, 1968) leading its agents of revolutionary praxis to the realization of a just society.

Horkheimer (1972:218, 225), writing during the late nineteen-thirties, apparently accepted the world-historical role ascribed to the proletariat by Marx, although he clearly felt the need to maintain some distance between the proletariat and their scholarly ideologists. In the midst of the turmoil and destruction of the period, Horkheimer's continuing adherence to the classical Marxist model of social change seems somewhat surprising to some critical theorists today. Indeed, Adorno's later work contains a sharply contrasting view of the agent of change (cf. Horkheimer and Adorno, 1972). For Adorno, the proletariat and the possibility of a rational society exist only as "concepts" (Adorno, 1967: 19, 1973:148–151). The task of critical theory is reduced to preserving such notions (or concepts) as justice and freedom, in order to illuminate the extent to which existing reality falls short of these ideals. This model of "immanent criticism" lacks immediate practical consequences for anyone except the critical theorist observing the contradictions of bourgeois society. Marcuse (1969b) also abandons the guiding principle of the unity of theory and practice. He looks beyond the proletariat for a transitional agent (cf. Marcuse, 1972). Recognizing that ". . . . critical theory is left without the rationale for transcending this society" (1964:xiv), Marcuse turns to a new agent for change. He argues for a "new sensibility" and a "new science," to become the imaginative vehicles for the forces of liberation. Marcuse thus fails, as did Adorno, to avoid the trap of empty abstraction.

Habermas is also aware of the problem of connecting critical theory with the actual practice of the human agents of social change. The emancipatory interest of critical theory, according to Habermas, provides all members of society (not only the proletariat) with knowledge of those repressive social conditions which constrain rational autonomous action. The model *critically* adopted by Habermas for the practical realization of critical theory is Freudian psychoanalysis (see Habermas, 1970c, 1971, 1976). Habermas finds within psychoanalysis an emancipatory project of therapy. The analyst gets behind" experiential explanations offered by the patient in order to explain (causally) distorted or repressed meaning patterns that have become inaccessible to the consciousness. The goal is to further self-reflection and self-knowledge in the patient and, ultimately, to explain and remove unnecessary forms of social domination (see McCarthy, 1973). Transferred to the social and political realm, psychoanalysis links causal explanation and subjective interpretation: through undistorted dialogue between participants in an ideal speech situation (mediated by the psychoanalytic method), Habermas claims to have located the ground on which cognition and action can be joined, thus providing critical theory with its practical outlet.

THE PROBLEM OF APPLICATION

Abstractness also plagues implementation of Habermas's project. The process of therapy is accomplished through symbolic communication, in which both parties agree to work toward the emancipation of the patient. But what if the material conditions for this Socratic dialogue are not given? What if there are recalcitrant participants in the discursive process—clearly the rule in human history? As Bernstein (1976:224) has noted, "what seems to be lacking here is any illumination on the problem of human agency and motivation . . . What are the concrete dynamics of this process: Who are or will become its agents?"[3] Emancipation must obviously be more than either a symbolic exercise or the mere recording of distorted communication. We still lack a positive formulation of what it is that enables human beings to overcome repressive social conditions.

Critical theory continues to be perplexed, moreover, by ambiguity regarding its empirical status—what one observer calls its "twilight zone" (Dallmayr, 1976). Is the critique of society based on an understanding of "facts"? Does it take place on the level of some transcendental understanding? Indeed, the very project of bridging the gap between what is and what ought to be necessarily imposes a certain abstractness—an abstractness made even more acute by present social conditions which have increasingly repressed any viable radical political opposition (critical theory's human agency). The concept of the societal totality lacks clear delineation. A fully adequate critical theory, then, has yet to be formulated. However, these fundamental inadequacies are due more to the programmatic character and incomplete development of critical theory, than to doctrinaire assertions claiming a "direct pipeline to reality through science, revelation or metaphysics" (Piccone, 1977:195).

What, then, can critical theory offer sociology today? Despite the above criticisms, sociologists cannot afford to ignore critical theory's questions about the nature and purpose of social inquiry. The insights into the potentially barbaric consequences of scientific rationality are neither capricious nor ideologically motivated. It is vital that sociologists engage in critical self-reflection about what they are actually doing. The critical theorist would argue that there is no such thing as value neutrality or objectivity in sociology, nor should there be. We must examine the relationship between the practice of social scientific research and how our knowledge about social life affects the evolution of that life. Although there are some unresolved (and perhaps unresolvable) difficulties in the application of a critical theory of society, the issues are still significant. Ultimately, critical theory is about the fundamental purpose of knowledge and social theory; and that is its real value for sociology.

NOTES

I wish to acknowledge the assistance of Darlaine Gardetto, Martin Jay, Tom Long, and the editors of *The American Sociologist* at various stages of the manuscript.

1. For a useful account of these various trends within Western Marxism see Howard and Klare (1972). See also Anderson (1976). Much of the debate regarding these authors' contributions to Marxist thought have taken place in the pages of the British journal, *New Left Review*, and also in *Telos* (published at Washington University), and *New German Critique* (published at the University of Wisconsin, Milwaukee).

2. For a discussion of critical theory as contrasted to phenomenology and hermeneutics, see Dallmayr and McCarthy (1977), Giddens (1976, 1977).

3. For some useful discussions regarding this notion of critical theory and its practice, see Jay (1972a, 1972b, 1973), Krahl (1974), Labasz (1975), Piccone (1976, 1977). For criticisms from members of the Althusserian school who identify critical theorists as "historical humanists" who reduce the Marxist "science of political economy" to a "metaphysical humanism," see Althusser (1970), Therborn (1970). Also see Slater (1977), Anderson (1976).

REFERENCES

ADORNO, THEODOR
  1967 Prisms. London: Spearman.
  1973 Negative Dialectics. New York: Seabury.
ADORNO, THEODOR (ed.)
  1976 The Postivist Dispute in German Sociology. London: Heinemann.
ADORNO, THEODOR, et al.
  1950 The Authoritarian Personality. New York: Harper.
ALTHUSSER, LOUIS
  1970 For Marx. New York: Vintage.
ANDERSON, PERRY
  1976 Considerations on Western Marxism. London: New Left Books.
BERNSTEIN, RICHARD
  1976 The Restructuring of Social and Political Theory. New York: Harcourt
        Brace Jovanovich.
BETTELHEIM, BRUNO, and MORRIS JANOWITZ
  1950 Dynamics of Prejudice. New York: Harper & Row.
COLLETTI, LUCIO
  1973 Marxism and Hegel. London: New Left Books.
DALLMAYR, FRED
  1976 "Beyond dogma and despair." American Political Science Review
        70:64–79.
DALLMAYR, FRED, and THOMAS MCCARTHY (eds.)
  1977 Understanding and Social Inquiry. Notre Dame: University of Notre
        Dame Press.
FAY, BRIAN
  1975 Social Theory and Political Practice. London: Allen and Unwin.
FRISBY, DAVID
  1972 "The Popper-Adorno controversy." Philosophy of the Social Sciences
        2:105–119.
  1976 "Introduction." Pp. ix–xliv in T. Adorno (ed.), The Positivist Dispute
        in German Sociology. London: Heinemann.
FROMM, ERIC
  1968 Escape From Freedom. New York: Fawcett.
GIDDENS, ANTHONY
  1975 "Introduction." Pp. 1–22 in A. Giddens (ed.), Positivism and Sociology.
        London: Heinemann.
  1976 New Rules of Sociological Method. London: Hutchinson.
  1977 Studies in Social and Political Theory. London: Hutchinson.
GRAMSCI, ANTONIO
  1971 Selections from the Prison Notebooks of Antonio Gramsci. New York:
        International Publishers.
HABERMAS, JÜRGEN
  1970a Toward A Rational Society. Boston: Beacon.

1970b "Toward a theory of communicative competence." In H. Dreitzel (ed.), Recent Sociology. New York: Macmillan.

1971 Knowledge and Human Interests. Boston: Beacon.

1976 "Some distinctions in universal pragmatics." Theory and Society 3:155–168.

HORKHEIMER, MAX

1947 The Eclipse of Reason. New York: Oxford University Press.

1972 Critical Theory. New York: Herder and Herder.

HORKHEIMER, MAX, and THEODOR ADORNO

1972 Dialectic of Enlightenment. New York: Herder and Herder.

HOWARD, DICK, and KARL KLARE (eds.)

1972 The Unknown Dimension: European Marxism Since Lenin. New York: Basic Books.

JAY, MARTIN

1972a "The Frankfurt School in exile." Perspectives in American History 6:339–385.

1972b "The Frankfurt School's critique of Marxist humanism." Social Research 39:285–305.

1973 The Dialectical Imagination. Boston: Little, Brown.

1977 "The concept of totality in Lukács and Adorno." Telos 32:117–138.

KOMAROVSKY, MIRRA

1940 The Unemployed Man and His Family. New York: The Dryden Press.

KORSCH, Karl

1971 Marxism and Philosophy. New York: Monthly Review Press.

KRAHL, HANS-JUERGEN

1974 "The political contradiction in Adorno's critical theory." Telos 21:164–167.

LUBASZ, HANS

1975 "Review of Jay." History and Theory 14:200–212.

LUKÁCS, GEORG

1971 History and Class Consciousness. Cambridge: MIT Press.

MARCUSE, HERBERT

1964 One Dimensional Man. Boston: Beacon.

1968 Negations. Boston: Beacon.

1969 An Essay on Liberation. Boston: Beacon.

1972 Counterrevolution and Revolt. Boston: Beacon.

MARX, KARL

1973 Grundrisse. New York: Vintage Books.

1975 Karl Marx: Early Writings. New York: Vintage Books.

McCARTHY, THOMAS

1973 "A theory of communicative competence." Philosophy of the Social Sciences 3:135–156.

NEUMANN, FRANZ

1944 Behemoth. New York: Oxford University Press.

322   JOHN J. SEWART

OFFE, CLAUS
  1976 "Problems of legitimation in late capitalism." Pp. 388–421 in P. Conner-
        ton (ed.), Critical Sociology. Harmondsworth: Penguin Books.
PICCONE, PAUL
  1976 "From tragedy to farce: The return of critical theory." New German
        Critique 7:91–104.
  1977 "Internal polemics." Telos 31:178–183, 193–197.
POPPER, KARL
  1969 Conjectures and Refutations. London: Routledge.
SLATER, PHIL
  1977 Origins and Significance of the Frankfurt School. London: Routledge.
THERBORN, GORAN
  1970 "The Frankfurt School." New Left Review 63:65–96.
  1976 Science, Class and Society: On the Formation of Sociology and Histori-
        cal Materialism. London: New Left Books.
WELLMER, ALBRECHT
  1971 Critical Theory of Society. New York: Herder and Herder.

PART VI

THE INDIVIDUAL AND

HUMAN CONSCIOUSNESS

Dickens's discussion of phenomenology, which is rooted in the work of Husserl, is a study of essences, particularly the essence of consciousness. Phenomenology, then, puts essence back into existence and rejects the Kantian perspective, which attributes a dual nature to reality. Husserl, in his attempt to study consciousness and meaning, developed an approach that would allow one to study the nature of things without the burden of the theorist's prejudices. He wanted to move beyond the categories that we use in an unthinking fashion to the true nature of the phenomenon itself. Husserl also moves beyond the Aristotelian form of categorization, and, in this sense, his mode is similar to that which Bell argued for in her discussion of Buddhist sociology. Phenomenology is above all a reflective enterprise which questions experience and traditional methods for studying behavior.

Another promising attempt to study human existence or consciousness is to be found in existential sociology. Like phenomenology, it rejects the standard Aristotelian procedures for categorizing behavior, seeking instead to understand change, flux, and uncertainty. Kotarba, tracing the roots of existential sociology, argues that sociology's emphasis should be on exploring and understanding contrasts in human behavior rather than on reaching prematurely for universals. All facets of human behavior are to be examined in a non-positivistic fashion. Existential sociology carries with it certain assumptions about what should be looked at and how. As Kotarba said, "It is best to study human experience in natural settings," for it is only here that the meanings and feelings which shape everyday behavior come into play. Existential sociologists, perception of self, and how existential sociology can be extended to the study of social institutions are among the other topics explored in Kotarba's paper.

O'Neill's concerns are those of the critical theorist and the phenomenologist. He deals with the difficult problem of the coercive power of language and knowledge. Science is often given as an excuse for doing something rational, thereby discounting everyday, or common-sense, reason as nonrational. Yet institutions shape knowledge and language. Knowledge and language also serve institutions, but because of the process of mystification, ordinary citizens may not understand either the source or the nature of the coercion. Sociology, O'Neill argues, must guard against being an agent of the state, and must understand how its knowledge can be used. O'Neill rejects the Kantian and neo-Kantian division of the world. This is imperative, for not to do so ultimately casts human, nonrational thought into limbo and limits the potential of a critical social science.

Zimmerman introduces ethnomethodological thought by exploring its roots and its methodological assumptions. Though dealing with problems of human consciousness, ethnomethodology is not a carbon copy of phenomenology. It differs from phenomenology primarily, as Zimmerman shows, in its methodology. Its goal is to study general social processes, and not necessarily the individual act. As Zimmerman says, "It is an approach to the study of the fundamental bases of social order. That is, ethnomethodology is concerned with those structures of social interaction which would be invariant to the revolutionary transformation of a society's institutions."

1. Phenomenology

DAVID R. DICKENS

The phenomenology of Edmund Husserl was a philosophical program aimed at disclosing the absolute ground of human knowledge.[1] This quest was based on a search for essences, which were seen as being unbound to the cultural or social sphere and thus not susceptible to the relativism and commonplace prejudices that characterize that realm. Husserl's program, often referred to as pure phenomenology, was not an attempt to describe the objects of the empirical world:

> Phenomenology, insofar as its descriptions encompass the whole *world*, must confine itself to a consideration of the world exclusively *as meant* without invoking as standard of comparison the world "in itself" (Carr, 1924:27).

Husserl was not an idealist, however, as is sometimes argued. Methodologically, he accepted the empiricist claim of Locke, Berkeley, and others, that all genuine knowledge must be derived from experience, more specifically from primary data intuition. "Experience is the consciousness of being with the matters themselves, of seizing upon and having them quite directly" (Husserl, 1970:232). Husserl's concept of experience, to be sure, is much broader than that of the empiricist.[2]

> The fundamental defect of the empiricists' argument lies in this, that the basic requirement of a return to the "facts themselves" is identified or confused with the requirement that all knowledge shall be grounded in experience. . . . Genuine science, and the genuine

325

absence of bias which inwardly distinguishes it, demands as the foundation of all proofs judgments which as such are immediately valid, drawing their validity from primordial dator institutions. . . . Immediate seeing (*sehen*), not merely the sensory seeing of experience, but seeing in general, as primordial dator consciousness of any kind whatsoever, is the ultimate source of justification for all rational statements (Husserl, 1962:74–76).

This broader definition was preferred by Husserl because he wished to allow for the method of ideational intuition. This intuition, or immediate "seeing," could only be accomplished from within the phenomenological reduction, which confines itself to a consideration of the world exclusively as meant.

The task of pure phenomenology, the attempt to clarify the objects of thought through ideational intuition, was begun in the two-volume work *Logical Investigations*. In the first volume, subtitled "Prolegomena to Pure Logic," Husserl attacked psychologism by demonstrating the distinction between the subject matter of psychology and logic. He showed that the function of logic in scientific theory was as a discipline that treats ideal relations among meanings as ideal entities, and not as an empirical discipline concerning mental occurrences where meanings and their relations are exemplified (Carr, 1974). In addition to contributing to what Husserl calls an understanding of "the ideal conditions of the possibility of science or of theory in general," there remains an additional task which only the philosopher can provide:

The philosopher is not content with the fact that we find our way about in the world, that we have laws as formulae which enable us to predict the future course of things, or to reconstruct its past course: he wants to clarify the essence of a thing, an event, . . . (of laws of nature, etc.). . . . And if science constructs theories in the systematic dispatch of its problems, the philosopher inquires into the essence of theory and what makes theory possible, etc. (Husserl, 1970:245).

In this case it now becomes necessary to "scientifically clarify" the ideas which comprise theoretical knowledge such as "concept" and "proposition." In the second volume of *Logical Investigations*, Husserl presents pure phenomenology as the clarifying discipline which "lays bare the sources from which the basic concepts and ideal laws of pure logic 'flow' and back to which they must once more be traced, so as to give them all the 'clearness and distinctness' needed for an understanding, as for an epistemological critique, of pure logic" (Husserl, 1970:249–250).

The philosophical clarification of these fundamental logical notions consists in tracing their origins in a way which is not psychologistic. For Husserl this involves an inquiry into the nature of language because "the objects which pure logic seeks to examine are, in the first instance, given . . . in grammatical clothing" (Husserl, 1970:250). Consistent with his earlier argument, however, this concern with language is not with linguistic expressions as empirical events but with the meanings of these expressions. In language these notions, which pure logic seeks to examine, "come before us embedded in concrete mental states which further function as the meaning–intention or meaning–fulfillment of . . . verbal expressions" (Husserl, 1970:25). As Carr points out, "The meaningful use or the comprehension of language does not create meanings, but it does 'realize' them in human mental life. It is precisely this 'realization' which interests Husserl, the moment in which something not itself belonging to consciousness, or of the nature of consciousness, is nevertheless given to consciousness" (Carr, 1974:12). Thus, Husserl's attempt to search for the absolute grounds or origins of knowledge in the experience of realization or givenness is not an attempt to account for the "being" of objects. What Husserl seeks, as mentioned earlier, is the origin of givenness of objects, either ideal (logic) or real, not the "being" of objects, but their "being for me" (Carr, 1974). This constitutes a vital juncture in Husserl's thought, for the clarification of the purely logical sphere leads to the much broader problem of knowledge in general.

The focus of the *Logical Investigations*, then, expands to include the epistemological as well as the purely logical. The question of the givenness of the objective then includes the physical or empirical, as well as the logical. Husserl finds the solution to this general question in his famous thesis of the intentionality of consciousness. To say that something is given is to say that it fulfills an intention.

> The answer . . . is the intentional or act-character of consciousness, an act of meaning that refers to the object in such and such a way. Such an act is what we live through, or more precisely, an aspect of what we concretely live through when something is given; and it is precisely this aspect that cannot be missing (Carr, 1974:14).

It cannot be stressed enough that this is not a form of idealism. This may be further demonstrated by examining two much-maligned concepts in Husserl's thought, "transcendental" and "constitution." The concept of transcendental refers to the objects of the world, consciousness, and the ego. Concerning the objects of the world (including thought-objects), Husserl writes in the *Cartesian Meditations*, "Neither the world nor any worldly object is a piece of my ego, to be found in my conscious life as a really inherent part of it, as a complex of data of sensation or a complex of acts. This 'transcendence' is part of the intrinsic sense of anything worldly, i.e., its *noninclusion*, in the sense described in the ego or consciousness" (Husserl, 1973:26). The ego is transcendental because of "its essential character of standing in relation to what transcends it" (Carr, 1974:5). Finally, in *Ideas I*, the term "transcendental" is applied to consciousness because of what Husserl calls its "wonderful" capacity to relate to something "that stands over against consciousness itself, something that is other in principle, something not part of it" (Husserl, 1962:285). In short, the world of experience is itself transcendent because it is not included in consciousness (Carr, 1974).

Husserl's nonidealistic conception of phenomenology is further clarified by his concept of constitution. For Husserl constitution does not mean "creation *ex nihilo*," as has been widely misconstrued. Rather, "is constituted" is equivalent to "announces itself." Husserl states, "The recurring expression that in an act 'objects are constituted' always designates the act's character of rendering the object present: not constituting in the actual (everyday) sense."[3] In going from the objectivity of an object to the act which intends it, Husserl has not yet developed the full bases for phenomenology. It is not until the publication of *Ideas I* that Husserl presents those ideas which form the foundation for the phenomenological program for the rest of his life. These include the concept of essence, the theory of noetic–noematic structures, the concept of world, and the *epoché*.[4]

Husserl begins *Ideas I* by illustrating the fundamental difference between phenomenology and psychology. This is important for Husserl in order to dispel any notion that phenomenology's concern with the intentional-act character of consciousness is parallel to psychology's empirical concern with the psychic. Husserl accomplishes this by distinguishing between sciences of essence (phenomenology) and sciences of fact (such as psychology). The distinction between facts and essences deserves special consideration here in light of misunderstandings (Adorno, 1956; Popper, 1968; Psathas and Waksler, 1973). In *Ideas* Husserl states that facts may be generally characterized by their accidental or contingent nature: they could always be other than they are. Husserl lists several more specific characteristics of facts such as "individual form . . . having spatio–temporal existence . . . existing in this time-spot, having this particular duration of its own and a real content which in its essence could just as well have been present in any other time-spot" (Husserl, 1962:46). Essences, in contrast, are not contingent;

rather, they are the necessary prerequisites for the being of object or occurrence.

From this account one might indeed agree with Popper and Adorno that Husserl's conception here is static and dogmatic. To do so, however, would be to confuse the distinction between the nature of facts (their contingency) and their essential structure. The proper characterization of essences is that while they in a sense change as often as do the contingent facts of which they are the structure, everywhere a fact is to be found, it is always and necessarily accompanied or characterized by its essence. For the term "essence" one may substitute the phrase "structure of" to get across the notion that while the fact or phenomena may always be other than it is, whenever "it is," it is characterized by a certain essence or internal structure.

This still does not tell us enough, however, for we also wish to know how essences are discovered in order to fully understand their implication, if any, for sociology. Are essences grasped immediately and all at once, or are they discovered only through a process of constant refinement? It is the first alternative which Husserl's critics have taken him to be advocating and which has led to the discrediting of the notion of essences generally in the social sciences. The critics object on the grounds that such a notion implies that there is no need for further inquiry.

Yet, only a selective reading of Husserl could substantiate this claim in regard to his conception of essences. The most one must concede on this point is that Husserl seems to be ambiguous, at best, in the section on facts and essences in *Ideas*, although even here there is some discussion of the method of free fantasy variation, which is certainly not a one-shot affair.

The clearest and lengthiest presentation of the method of eidetic intuition, however, appears later in Husserl's writing in *Formal and Transcendental Logic*; this is Husserl's most mature statement on the topic of essences, and there can be no doubt here that even if he did hold to an absolutistic view in his earlier work, he repudiated such a view in the later writings. Husserl is quite explicit on this matter:

There is, as we know, an extraordinarily wide-spread interpretation that . . . construes evidence conformable to a naively presupposed truth-in-itself. According to this interpretation, there "must" be an evidence that is an absolute grasping of truth, since otherwise we could neither have nor strive for truth and science. . . .But what if truth is an *idea*, lying at infinity? What if it can be shown, in evidence, that, with respect to world-objectivity in its entirety, this is no accidental matter of fact, resulting from our unfortunately limited human cognitive power, but an *eidetic law?* . . .

It is high time that people got over being dazzled, particularly in philosophy and logic, by the ideal and regulative ideas and methods of the "exact" sciences—as though the in-itself of such sciences were actually an absolute norm for objective being and for truth. Actually, they do not see the woods for the trees . . . to rush ahead and philosophize from on high about such matters is fundamentally wrong; it creates a wrong skeptical relativism and no less wrong logical absolutism, mutual bugbears that knock each other down and come to life again like the figures in a Punch and Judy show (Husserl, 1969:277–278).

Husserl is rarely so explicit or adamant about matters as he is on this point.

If Husserl is not an absolutist or metaphysical realist, then what is his final position regarding the nature and discovery of essences? First, while he clearly makes an important distinction between fact and essence, as mentioned in *Ideas*, this distinction does not negate the fact that there is a "profound reciprocity," as Richard Zanner (1974) calls it, between the two levels. Essences and facts may be viewed as points on a continuum, a continuum, however, which has levels. The continuum and its levels are understood in terms of an increasing completeness. Factual claims about actualities are then seen as furnishing knowledge which is incomplete in light of further possible knowledge about the essence of the claimed state of affairs. Even at the most "complete" level, knowledge is never apodictic but is, rather, complete only to a degree of exemplifying a certain type or *eidos*.

Eidetic inquiry is based on the method of free-fantasy variation, a method put forward by Husserl in various texts (1962, 1969, 1973). The method may be practiced on anything, on an actual ("real") or a possible ("ideal") particular. Any example used must, though, be considered solely as an intentional object or noematic correlate, so that the entire operation takes place within the phenomenological reduction. Accordingly, the variation itself is not empirical but, rather, is totally free of empirical constraints:

It must be understood, not as an empirical variation, but as a variation carried on with the freedom of pure phantasy and with the consciousness of its purely optional character—the consciousness of the "pure" Any Whatever. Thus understood, the variation extends into an open horizon of endlessly manifold free possibilities of more and more variants (Husserl, 1969:247–248).

The concern is to take the particular as an example of some *eidos*. In this inquiry, the variation of the initial example is the performance in which the "eidos" should emerge and by means of which the evidence of the indissoluble eidetic correlation between constitution and constituted should also emerge (Husserl, 1969:267).

This method requires that one attend to the particular individual in terms of a type. By making the type explicit as a type, it becomes possible to allow a specific individual particular to "come to the fore" as the "thing itself," which is then intended as an example of some type or *eidos*.

With a "reduced" example in hand, one may then "freely vary" the example and any other possible example of the kind of which the original example is an instance. Husserl describes this process:

> In such a fully free variation, released from all restrictions to facts accepted beforehand, all the variants (examples) belonging to the openly infinite sphere—which includes the initial example itself, as "optional" and freed of all its factualness—stand in a relationship of synthetic interrelatedness and integral correctness; more particularly, they stand in a continuous and all-inclusive synthesis of "coinciding," what necessarily persists throughout this free and always repeatable variation comes to the fore: the *invariant*, the indissolubly identical in the different and ever again different, the *essence* common to all, the universal essence by which all "imaginable" variants of the example, and all variants of any such variant, are restricted. This invariant is the ontic essential form (a priori form), the *eidos*, corresponding to the example, in place of which any variant of the example could have served equally well (Husserl, 1969:248).

Richard Zaner introduces "kind" as a technical term which denotes *eidos*. This allows him to speak of examples as being examples of a kind.

> Any particular item, it is clear, exemplifies many kinds: or, we can say, any such item is an example of a kind solely by virtue of its having certain features or properties, and it is these which exemplify, whether well or poorly. The kind is presented through or by means of the latter: it "runs through" or "is common to" them (Zaner, 1974:9).

The essence, then is "what is common to a set of individual items," their structural characteristics. The "system of common feature" is the kind itself, the *eidos* (Zaner, 1974:12, 10).

The method of free-fantasy variation requires a number of examples that is, in principle, indefinite, and there is, formally speaking, no criterion for quitting an investigation. All Husserl says on this matter is that the work of free variation will elicit the invariant through "coincidence in conflict." Regardless of one's assessment of Husserl's method, one thing is certain: eidetic claims are essentially tentative or open-ended. The notion of essences as based on absolute apodicticity becomes a chimera, for they are always subject to further confirmation or disconfirmation.

Still, phenomenology as presented in *Ideas* is limited to providing an essential grounding for psychology. Husserl's thought moved out of this rather limited role; because of the issues discussed earlier in *Logical Investigations*. There, phenomenology was concerned with the empirical psychic only insofar as this helped clarify the "purely logical," and more broadly, the givenness of the "objective" in general (Carr, 1974). In bringing out those characteristics of the psychic which are relevant to problems of logic and epistemology in general, phenomenology was going beyond the bounds of psychology alone: "Though the intentional or act-character is an essential element, it is not all there is to consciousness, and Husserl had to then come to grips with the implicit or nonintentional, even if only to clarify the intentional and keep it distinct" (Carr, 1974).

This leads to the highly significant shift in Husserl's thought, from a focus on the logical acts of judging and inferring, to perceiving. Perception now becomes the medium through which to search for the origins of knowledge:

> The object-giving (or dator) intuition of the first, "natural" sphere of knowledge and of all its sciences is natural experience, and the *primordial* dator experience is *perception* in the ordinary sense of the term (Husserl, 1962:45).

This shift opens up a whole new field in Husserl's enterprise, for in perception "it is not only the perceived object that is given: its perceptual background is given with it, a background which in turn presents itself as a mere segment of what can be perceived at all" (Carr, 1974:19). The key aspect of Husserl's examination of perception is that it includes the nonintentional background: "What is actually perceived, and what is more or less clearly co-present and determinate is partly pervaded, partly girt about with a dimly apprehended depth or fringe of indeterminate reality" (Husserl, 1962:92). This "horizon of indeterminate reality" is as essential for the givenness of an object as the intentional act, and Husserl designates this horizon by the concept of "world." The term first appears in *Ideas*, where it is characterized as "the totality of objects that can be known through experience, known in terms of orderly theoretical thought on the basis of direct present experience" (Husserl, 1962:64). It is important to note that the concept of world is first found in the attempt to delineate fully the epistemological origins of knowledge and not as an attempt to be historically or culturally relevant.

Certainly everything about the world is not perceived in the strict manner of sense perception, but everything about the world has some relation to what Carr calls the "spatio-temporal structure of the perceived," and to this extent, is given in a similar manner. Thus the concept of givenness is greatly expanded, and Husserl must expand his investigations accordingly. The givenness of the world cannot be accounted for in the same fashion as the givenness of physical objects, because the world is not an object among other objects; it is the background or horizon of any possible object; and its givenness consists precisely in being a background for something within it (Carr, 1974).

Also, it is not a matter of accounting for the givenness of the world each time a particular object is given because the world must be there, as background, for any and every particular object to be given. Thus the analysis of the intentional act-character of consciousness will not suffice in this case.

There is, however, a peculiar sense in which the world is intended every time a particular object is intended in consciousness, since the world always functions as a background for each particular object. Husserl characterizes this unique way by which consciousness "intends" the world through the use of the terms "attitude," "belief," and "frame of mind." As Carr (1974) points out, these concepts do not refer to intentional acts in the strict sense, but they do indicate something more than mere dispositions, since the attitude is present as background for each particular act. Though there are many possible attitudes, such as the purely practical or theoretical, Husserl refers to a fundamental attitude which underlies all other abstract attitudes, an attitude whose correlate is the world as such; this he refers to as the "natural attitude." Because the world does, in a sense, have a correlate, it, like an intentional act, is intentional. Indeed, Husserl believes that this attitude can even be expressed in a general thesis: "The world exists, is there." As we shall see, Husserl's concept of world, with its corresponding natural attitude, takes on a prominent role in his later writings.

In addition to his reflections concerning the world and the natural attitude, Husserl also further elaborated the notion of intentional object, first mentioned in *Logical Investigations*. He had borrowed the concept of intentionality from his teacher Franz Brentano in order to express the essential character of consciousness as that peculiar relation within an intentional experience between the act of intending (*noesis*) and the intentional object (*noema*). This intentional relation, however, is not so simple as it may initially appear (Carr, 1974). Husserl first maintains that the objective term of the relation is not a "mental" object having some relation to a real object outside consciousness. On the other hand, the intentional relation is not a relation between two elements within consciousness. Rather, what is meant in the experience is the object itself, be it a physical object, a mental object, or even a fictional object such as the god Jupiter:

> This intentional experience may be dismembered as one chooses in descriptive analysis, but the god Jupiter will naturally not be found in it any more than one could discover a tree or a mathematical relation there (Husserl, 1970:558–559).

Husserl must still provide a description of the nature of the intentional object if his account of an intentional experience is not to be incomplete. This brings Husserl to an impasse, which Carr sums up nicely: "The paradox of phenomenology . . . is that it was conceived as a description of the psychic, yet finds itself forced to refer beyond consciousness in order to make its description complete" (Carr, 1974:22).

Husserl solves this seeming paradox by distinguishing between the "object as it is intended (*noema*) and the object (period) which is intended" (Husserl, 1970:576). Each individual act intends an object in a particular way, while the object itself may have other possible determinations which are excluded from consideration. Husserl uses the example of a German emperor. This same person could also be represented as the son of Emperor Friedrich III or as the grandson of Queen Victoria. This distinction does not refer, however, to two different objects, for the object meant and the object as meant are the same, and there is no third entity set up to distinguish between the subject and the object "in itself." What the distinction does introduce is two different ways of considering the object; in one of which, the object as intended or *noema*, involves a reference to some particular act of meaning or intending it (Carr, 1974). Thus the "object-as-intended" is dependent on the act which intends it, which in Husserlian terms is the "simple" dictum that every *noesis* (intentional act) has its corresponding *noema* (intentional object).

By considering an object "as meant," Husserl is taking a stance of neutrality regarding the ontological status of the object since the object "in itself" might not turn out to be exactly as meant. This is the famous notion of an *epochē* (literally meaning "abstention") regarding the nature of an object, also referred to by Husserl as the "neutrality modification" in natural reflection (Husserl, 1962:282).[5] Husserl notes that this comparison between object meant and object as meant and the corresponding neutrality modification are involved in natural or critical reflection. The object as meant is compared with the object meant to see if it corresponds or if the original meaning can be cancelled or modified (Carr, 1974). This, however, always involves an assumption regarding the true status and characteristics of the object in question to which the object as meant can be compared.

A truly radical reflection may then be achieved if the act of meaning involved in the "natural" consideration of the object is itself considered as meant: "We can treat the potential and unexpressed (natural) thesis exactly as we do the thesis of the explicit judgment" (Husserl, 1962:97). This radical reflection, which is later referred to in the *Cartesian Meditations* as the "transcendental-phenomenological reflection," is an attempt to consider every possible object solely according to its status as meant. Thus, unlike natural reflection, radical reflection does not hold up the natural object as a standard for comparison, for its own assumption of authenticity is "bracketed" or "neutralized." Husserl saw this operation of bracketing in Descartes' method of systematic doubt, but he claims that Descartes was still engaging in a form of natural reflection, for the "real" object still functions as the standard against which the meant object is measured.

Through the process of radical reflection, Husserl has finally arrived at the solution to his original problematic, the question of the givenness of the objective. There is a second sense, however, in which this reflection is radical, which concerns the earlier discussion of world. One can reflect on a particular object, in the way discussed earlier, only by ignoring the surrounding world, which is an ever-present background accompanying the object. Insofar as phenomenology goes beyond the intentional act to describe the object of that act "as meant," it is forced to also include the horizon "meant with" the object. Thus in proceeding from the object to its horizon, there is a necessary consideration of the world, although this is also, as in the case of the object, considered strictly "as meant": "phenomenology, insofar as its descriptions encompass the whole world, must confine itself to a consideration of the world exclusively as meant, without invoking as a standard of comparison, the world 'in itself'" (Carr, 1974:27). This extention of the phenomenological *epochē* to the whole world is what Husserl refers to as the phenomenological reduction. David Carr goes so far as to claim that the advent of the phenomenological reduction is consistent with the schema first set down in the *Logical Investigations* (Carr, 1974).

Phenomenology now takes on a new dimension, however, for the world, rather than particular objects, now becomes the focus of attention. Before discussing the implications of this new dimension for Husserl's later "teleological-historical investigations," it is necessary to look at two other earlier developments which are equally important for understanding the later work. Carr (1974) refers to these developments as genetic phenomenology and the phenomenology of intersubjectivity.

Genetic analysis in Husserl's phenomenology is a further expansion of the intentional act conception of consciousness. Genetic analysis refers to the addition of a temporal dimension to the intentional act, and constitutes a further addition to the foreground-background modification presented in *Ideas*. In that modification the notion of world as an indeterminate horizon made the act character conception of consciousness more complex, but the analysis still remained static. The explication of genetic analysis, however, takes off from this static analysis of the background of a particular object. The background is itself only indirectly given, as are the hidden sides of a perceived object, but both are necessary components of the "object-as-meant." The object as perceived is comprised of an act which goes beyond what is directly given (Carr, 1974). This implication gives rise in *Cartesian Meditations* to the insight that "every subjective process has a process 'horizon,'" which changes with the alteration of the nexus of consciousness to which the process belongs and with the alteration of the process itself from phase to phase of its flow" (Husserl, 1973:44). This "process horizon" introduces a temporal dimension as part of the necessary structure of consciousness. In The *Phenomenology of Internal Time-Consciousness*, Husserl delineated the essential way in which the present is given through the nonpresent notions of protention and retention. In the *Cartesian Meditations* Husserl incorporates this insight into his investigations concerning the nature of consciousness itself under the heading "actuality and potentiality of intentional life" (Husserl, 1973:44). According to this conception, the actuality of every present object in consciousness is the realization of a previous potentiality. Furthermore, "not only is this givenness of an object spread out over time, but each temporal phase of its givenness also retains those preceding it and draws them together in its determination of the object. Thus the "object-as-meant" involves an increasing core of actual givenness, along with what Husserl calls the deposit or sediment of the no-longer given but retained" (Carr, 1974:71).

As in the foreground-background analogy of perception, the background, in this case the "temporal background," has some substantive import: the present stands out against a "substratum of sedimented prominences which, as a horizon, accompanies every living present"

(Husserl, 1969:319). With this development the program of phenomenology is further expanded, for we now see "that the givenness of
something objective is not merely the actualization of something which
was *a priori* possible, but follows on and is linked with certain retained
actualities which form a stock of acquisition" (Carr, 1974:74). Not only is
the givenness of the object regarded as temporally constructed, but the
self-constitution of the consciousness itself becomes temporal. Husserl
(1973:66) uses Leibniz's term "monad" to refer to the ego as a "substrate
of habitualities." The importance of this development is that the
phenomenological theory of consciousness now takes on a historical
dimension: "every single process of consciousness, as occurring temporally, has its own 'history'" (Husserl, 1969:316). As Carr points out, the
term "history" here is not used in the usual sense, but the way in which
Husserl does use it here becomes connected with the more common
usage in the later writings. The way in which these two senses are
connected becomes more evident by examining the theory of intersubjectivity.

The theory of intersubjectivity is presented in the Fifth Meditation of
the *Cartesian Meditations,* which is an attempt not to "prove" that
others exist, but to make "phenomenological sense" of the other egos
(Carr, 1974). The objection made by the imaginary critic is that there is
no place in the phenomenological program for the alter ego:

> But what about other egos, who surely are not a mere intending and
> intended in me, merely synthetic unities of possible verification in
> me, but, according to their sense, precisely others (Husserl, 1973:89)?

Husserl proceeds by showing how the experience of others shares
certain features with other forms of experience already discussed earlier
in the *Meditations* and *Ideas.* Most prominently, the experience of others
is in some ways analogous to perception; in other ways it is analogous to
recollection. It is analogous to perception in a way which Husserl calls
"analogizing apprehension." The body of the other is given to me in
experience, not just as a physical object, but as a living body with its
own subjective processes and dispositions, none of which is directly
accessible. Instead, the body of the other is taken as the organ or
expression of consciousness by analogy to my own body and its relation
to my own consciousness. Thus the body of the other is construed as a
living subject, like myself, through this mediated cognition Husserl
calls "appresentation."

> A certain *mediacy of intentionality* must be present here, going out
> from the substratum, "primordial world" and making present to

[my] consciousness a "there too," which nevertheless is not itself there and can never become an "itself-there." We have here, accordingly, a kind of making "co-present," a kind of "appresentation" (Husserl, 1973:109).

Husserl argues that this is also what occurs in ordinary external sense perception as all perception is perspectival.

An appresentation occurs even in external experience, since the strictly seen front of a physical thing always and necessarily appresents a real aspect and prescribes for it a more or less determinate context (Husserl, 1973:109).

What is appresented is always the complement of what is presented in the sense that the presented is what it is only together with the appresented. In the case of perceiving a house while standing in front of it, what we actually perceive is the front of the house, and this is precisely what it is from that vantage point, yet only together with the appresented, the other side and top of the house, is it a house. Thus, "the appresented belongs to the (internal) horizons of what is presented: it is intended in a horizon-consciousness, not an independent act" (Carr, 1974:93). In a similar way the other as conscious ego is given as copresent with the body, as its "other side," so to speak, not as something imagined in a separate act.

Husserl is quick to add that unlike the case of perceiving the other as an ego, there is always the possibility of verifying our sense perception. In the example of perceiving a house, we see only its front side, but we can subsequently verify that it is a "whole house" by walking around it. Husserl feels that although the other's body (the present entails an expression of consciousness that is unique, the analogy to perception, though partial, is helpful in avoiding certain misconceptions of alleged discontinuity between mind and body. Husserl calls these "instructive comparisons."

The second analogy employed by Husserl in the theory of intersubjectivity is the analogy with recollection, which is used to show how one's stream of consciousness might be considered as an object. Recollection is, for Husserl, an act which "renders present something that is not present . . . but is distinguished from acts of phantasy by locating its object in the past, or, more importantly, *my* past" (Carr, 1974:94). It is, in essence, the consciousness not only of something past, but also of this something as having been perceived or otherwise consciously experienced by me. Thus, recollection renders present not only the object of experience, for example, last week's ball game, but a new experience as well, what might be called the recollection-of-last-week's-ball game. Husserl calls this process depresentation, where "the immediate I performs an accomplishment through which it constitutes a variational mode of itself as existing (in the mode of having passed)" (Husserl, 1976:36). A recollection is drawn in depresentation because what is constituted as an experience or "stream of consciousness" is distinct from the stream that constitutes it. This may also involve a different spatial location, such as in Husserl's own example, "Then I was in Paris, now I am in Freiburg." The point is that "one original living present renders another, as past, present to itself, which is similar to what happens in *Fremderfahrung* (experience of the other)" (Carr, 1974:94).

Husserl is again quick to point out the ways in which the analogy to recollection does not apply. First, in recollection the two acts or streams of consciousness are clearly segments of one and the same stream, unlike the case of the other. Second, the recollected act can never be simultaneous with the recollection itself, which is precisely the case in the encounter of ego and alter. Finally, the object of recollection has different kinds of evidence and forms of verification from those pertaining to the experience of another. In recollection it is a matter of reactivation of what had previously been experienced in the present and retained, whereas the case of the other involves an "empathic analogy" through the mediation of the other's body.

More important for sociology, there is another sense in which the comparison to recollection holds, and which leads to a theory of objectivity based on intersubjectivity. In recollection, as stated earlier, there is an inseparable correlation between the experience and the experienced. For example, to recall a musical performance is to recall hearing it, and to recall hearing it is to recall the performance itself, even if indistinctly. In a similar sense, being aware of another person as a stream of experience implies to some extent being aware of what that person experiences (Carr, 1974). When I am face to face with another person, I am aware not only of him but also that I am an object for him and that our surroundings are given to him as they would be to me if I were in his place:

> After all, I do not apperceive the other ego simply as a duplicate of myself and accordingly as having my original sphere or one completely like mine. I do not apperceive him as having, more particularly, the spatial modes of appearance that are mine from here; rather . . . I apperceive him as having spatial modes of appearance like those I should have if I should go over there and be where he is (Husserl, 1973:117).

What is appresented is not only the other consciousness but also his body, my body, and our whole surroundings, as they are appresented for him. From this notion of the alter ego, given by analogy in the experience of the other (*Fremderfahrung*), the other is a stream of experience extending "more or less determinately into the past, together with all its objects" (Husserl, 1973:115):

> It is clear that, with the other ego, there is appresented, in an analogizing modification, everything that belongs to his concretion: first, his primordial world, and then his fully concrete ego. In other words, another monad becomes constituted appresentatively in mine (Husserl, 1973:115).

A full-fledged notion of objectivity is derived from the experience of the other because as monad the other is constituted as having his own world just as I do. The "two own worlds," however, are construed in intersubjective experience as appearances (or modes of givenness) of one and the same world, which is intended by both of us, and, in fact, by everyone.

> The other ego makes constitutionally possible a new infinite domain of what is "other": an *Objective Nature* and a whole Objective world, to which all other Egos and I myself belong. This constitution, arising on the basis of the "pure" others, is essentially such that the "others"-for-me do not remain isolated; on the contrary, an Ego-community, which includes me, becomes constituted as a community, of Egos existing with each other and for each other—ultimately a community of monads which, moreover, constitutes the one identical world (Husserl, 1973:107).

Husserl's intersubjective theory of objectivity may be understood as analogous to his solipsistic theory of ego-constitution: "Just as the latter is given as one by relation to a multiplicity of my acts . . . so the intersubjective object has the same status in relation to a multiplicity of acts by different subjects" (Carr, 1974:96). Husserl also refers to this fusion of my acts and those of others as the "functional community of one perception."

In summary Husserl provides us with a phenomenological account of the alter ego, which, in turn, makes possible a phenomenological account of the objective world:

> I experience the world . . . not as my private synthetic formation because I experience it as given to others as well . . . the intrinsically first other (the first 'non-Ego') is the other Ego. And the other Ego makes constitutionally possible a new infinite domain of what is

"other": an Objective Nature and a whole Objective world, to
which all other Egos and I myself belong (Husserl, 1973:107).

The other consciousness is the "intrinsically first ego" because it is by
being given to him that anything else is objective for me. This, in turn,
is possible only because the consciousness of another is itself given to me
in a peculiar sense.

Husserl's account up to this point remains within the egological
scheme *ego-cogito-cogitatum*. It remains so, however, only by providing
an added dimension to the notion of *cogitatum* (understood as "world"
in the broadest sense): the objective world has been explained by
reference to other subjects who are not in it but are transcendental in
relation to it (Carr, 1974). In this narrow sense the other ego as transcendental is not a part of my world at all, but he and his total contribution
to the make-up of the world do belong within the range of my actual and
possible experience. Though I may distinguish between what is directly
given to me and what is directly given to the other, it is only within my
own experience that I can do this. Thus, while everything in this
framework is understood by reference to ego's actual and possible
experience, the Fifth Meditation introduces an important distinction not
presented in the first four: "The distinction between my actual and
possible experiences in the strict or narrow sense (what Husserl calls the
"sphere of ownness")—those which give an object directly; and those of
my experiences in which what is given is another stream of experience
and through which an object is given indirectly" (Carr, 1974:98).
Accordingly, the reduction to the sphere of ownness is not another
phenomenological reduction; it is simply a focus on the first, narrower
sense of givenness in order to explicate the nature of the second sense:

> The nature of the two reductions is different: the first [the *epoché*]
> consists of a change of attitude in the subject, the second [reduction
> to sphere of ownness] is a restriction of his field of vision (Toulé-
> mont, 1962:40).

Thus, Husserl states at the end of this account that "at no point was
the transcendental attitude, the attitide of the transcendental *epoché*,
abandoned; and our 'theory' of experiencing someone else, our 'theory'
of experiencing others, did not aim at being and was not at liberty to be
anything but explication of the sense 'others,' as it arises from the
constitutive productivity of that experiencing" (Husserl, 1973:148). One
would then more properly speak of Husserl's account as a demonstration rather than as a proof, for the being of the other subject is at issue in
exactly the same way as anything else is at issue for phenomenology: in
the sense of its being-for-me. In the case of the alter ego, Husserl's theory

seeks to show the experiential conditions under which the other exists as a subject.

In Husserl's solution to the problem of solipsism, then, the other ego is not posited outside my own experience; rather, he is brought into the sphere of my own experience through a broadening of the concepts of experience and monad.[6] This broadening has profound implications for Husserl's entire project, for it adds a new dimension, which Husserl calls "intersubjective phenomenology."

A more complete understanding of the transition from "solipsistic" to "intersubjective phenomenology" may be gained by brief reference to Husserl's lectures on internal time-consciousness. In these lectures Husserl shows how a perception of one's own can be considered the functional unity of several temporal phases, not all of which are strictly presentations. In discussing the notion of a perception of a melody, Husserl argues that the presented and the nonpresented are not simultaneous, and that the nonpresented is not appresented in the usual sense but is retained as just past and a protended as about to come. The immediately present, the retained, and the protended together form a functional unity because in consciousness they form the function of a "meaning intention," which is directed toward the whole temporal object, in this case a melody:

> The constituted act, constructed from now consciousness and retentional consciousness, is adequate perception of the temporal Object. This object will indeed include temporal differences, and temporal differences are constituted precisely in such phases, in primal consciousness, retention, and protention (Husserl, 1964:60).

In the same sense the overall perception that constitutes the "whole object" can never be reduced to any of the particular acts of presentation, not even to one that is immediately present. Thus, the perception which is constitutive of the object is comprised of an act that is itself constituted by what Husserl calls the "living present" of each of its temporal phases. This is precisely the sense in which intersubjective objects are constituted in the Fifth Meditation. Husserl refers to this procedure as "oriented constitution": "A constitution that presupposes . . . something 'primordially' and something 'secondarily' constituted" (Husserl, 1973:133–134). The "one perception" of which Husserl speaks is for ego the functional unity of presentation and appresentation. The unified act is constituted for the other also, with the difference that the content of presented and appresented are reversed. From the point of view of either ego or the other, it is the same act which is constituted. Thus, the "one perception" that corresponds to the "whole intersubjective object" can only be considered "our" perception (Carr, 1974). The perception as a constituted act can only rightfully be ascribed to both ego and the other, to the "we," which is the simplest form of what Husserl calls the "communalization of monads": "When two subjects confront one another, and stand in relation to the same objects, they form to that extent, a rudimentary community that can itself be considered as performing an act (*cogitamus*) through 'its' diverse (and in this case simultaneous) presentations" (Husserl, 1973:100–101). This notion forms the basis of Husserl's important philosophical insight that the first form of objectivity is intersubjective in nature.

After the demonstration of transcendental intersubjectivity, the "community" (as Husserl uses the term) replaces individual consciousness as the point of departure for phenomenological investigations; however, Husserl insists that this entire development takes place within the transcendentally reduced sphere of the ego. This is not to say that phenomenological analysis at the intersubjective level is merely a secondary development but, rather, that the intersubjective analysis is a necessary complement to the egological dimension of phenomenology in order to overcome the objection of solipsism. Husserl does say that "the intrinsically first of the philosophical disciplines would be 'solipsistically' reduced egology . . . then only would come intersubjective phenomenology, which is founded on that discipline" (Husserl, 1973:155), but he is speaking of *ordo cognoscendi*, not *ordo essendi*, as is clear from the beginning of the Second Meditation:

Perhaps reduction to the transcendental ego only seems to entail a permanently solipsistic science; whereas the consequential elaboration of this science leads over to a phenomenology of transcendental intersubjectivity and, by means of this, to a universal transcendental philosphy. As a matter of fact, we shall see that, in a certain manner, a transcendental solipsism is only a subordinate stage philosophically; though, as such, it must first be delimited for purposes of method, in order that the problems of transcendental intersubjectivity may be correctly stated and attacked (Husserl, 1973:30–31).

Though the entire account of intersubjectivity for phenomenology remains subjective, the origins of subjectivity are themselves intersubjective. With this turn phenomenology fully escapes from any charges of being solipsistic. We saw earlier that the givenness of the objective includes more than what is immediately and explicity present, that this horizon constitutes an essential part of the particular object given. With the addition of a temporal dimension, the horizon of what is given (*das Mitgemeinte*) was related to the previously and potentially given in the form of a continuum, but now, in the context of the community, *das Mitgemeinte* includes that which is not given directly to me but is intended by me as given to my fellows: "In order to make up or fill in the world, I take over from others what is lacking in my own direct experience. It is through such an act of 'borrowing' that the world-for-us comes to exist for me. This act is, in Husserl's sense, the origin of its givenness" (Carr, 1974:105).

The social dimension in Husserl's thought now becomes paramount, for most of the content of what comprises the world is not traced to an act of direct experience but is instead based on my "borrowing" from the insights of others (Carr, 1974). Thus, Husserl's theory of intersubjectivity is ultimately based on communication.

The communicative aspect is developed in the Fifth Meditation, where Husserl discusses the most basic form of community as a spatial encounter between two persons that involves intersubjective perception: "I am confronted with the reality of a perspective on the surroundings which is not my own, and which, simply by being what it is for me, gives my own view itself the status of a mere perspective. The other's perspective is only indirectly given; yet it is the surroundings for both of us that make up the content of my experience and which are retained and sedimented" (Carr, 1974:105–106). Higher forms of community or society are accordingly more enduring and complex forms of the simple spatial encounter in perception. Of course, the role of language in communication becomes all important in the complex notion of community, but the basic form is still the same; there is a common, surrounding world (*Umwelt*) whose essential characteristic is its shared character.

With the explication of genetic analysis and the theory of intersubjectivity, we are led to the realization of what Carr calls the full-fledged historicity of conscious life. In genetic analysis the nature of consciousness is revealed as a temporal continuum involving a background of "sedimented prominences" and a foreground of "anticipations." The theory of intersubjectivity was first explicated in terms of the static analysis of perception and then combined with the dynamic or genetic analysis to reveal the fully socio-historical character of consciousness: "Individual conscious life may be said to be essentially historical in the sense that every *Erlelonis* (experience) takes place against the background of, and is thus mediated by, a past which is both its own past and a social past. At the same time, the anticipating structure of consciousness is also socially mediated" (Carr, 1974:111).

The substantive implications of this development are demonstrated in the concrete "teleological-historical investigations" of Husserl's last work, *The Crisis of European Sciences and Transcendental Phenomenology*. In this unfinished work the fundamental importance of the socially acquired and unquestioned life-world is described. This taken-for-granted aspect is illustrated by the way in which Galileo's philosophical interpretation of the world became accepted as an ontological belief about the way the world "really is." It is important to note that Husserl's concern is still with the question of the nature of knowledge, and is, again, not an attempt to become historically or culturally relevant.

According to Husserl, Galileo's proposal is that exact and intersubjectively valid knowledge of the real world can be attained by the method of treating everything about the world as an example of a geometrical object or relationship (Carr, 1974). For Galileo this includes things that are not directly measurable, such as Locke's secondary qualities; these may be indirectly accounted for in terms of measurable geometrical correlates. Galileo's geometrization of nature is further completed by Descartes and Leibniz's arithmetization of geometry to yield the complete "mathematization of nature." What interests Husserl is the way in which the abstractions and interpretations involved in the mathematization of nature are forgotten and the thesis becomes an ontological one: "To be is to be measurable in ideal terms as a geometrically determined configuration" (Carr, 1974:124).

In forgetting the abstraction of secondary qualities and the interpretation of considering spatial relations in the world as ideal ones, science ignores the way in which the mathematization of the world is accomplished, and the original world from which it idealizes. This original world is the life-world, the "world of sense-experience," the "intuitively given surrounding world," the prescientific life-world that is the "forgotten meaning-fundament of natural science" (Husserl, 1970: 24,25,43,48). In recalling these abstractions and interpretations, Husserl is not attempting to purge science and philosophy of all historical content, but rather, he is attempting to reveal the taken-for-granted presuppositions of our intellectual tradition. In line with the fullest development of his philosophical program, Husserl unearths the sediments and prejudices (*Vorurteile*) that constitute our present knowledge, and it is precisely this unearthing that constitutes true philosophy and science.

Husserl's fully developed philosophy may be characterized as a philosophical hermeneutic aimed at disclosing the absolute grounds of human knowledge through a bringing to light of the unexpressed presuppositions which characterize that knowledge. Accordingly, the scientific status of phenomenologically informed inquiry is not based on the false guarantee of an absolute zero point as a starting point, but rather, it is the bringing to light of hidden biases and pre-theoretical notions which constitute the objectivity of phenomenology-based inquiry. Because of the essentially historical nature of all understanding, the task of phenomenological clarification is, always, as Richard Zaner (1973) so aptly describes it, one of continuous criticism and re-examination.

NOTES

1. For this account of phenomenology, I am heavily indebted to my teacher, David Carr, and his excellent book, *Phenomenology and the Problem of History* (Evanston: Northwestern University Press, 1974). The reader is urged to read this book, and also Richard Zaner's fine book, *An Invitation to Phenomenology*, for more extensive discussion of the subject.

2. This point is brought out by Christopher Prendergrast in "Phenomenology and Social Theory," a paper presented at the Midwest Sociological Society Meeting in Chicago, Illinois, 1975.

3. From the 1903 and 1907 *Husserl Manuskripte* (unpublished). Quoted in Carr, 1974:15, from Reneé Toulemont, *L'Essence de la societé selon Husserl* (Paris: Presses Universitaires de France, 1962) p. 43, f.n. 2 and 3.

4. *Ideen II* and *Ideen III* are presently being translated into English also, and a new translation of *Ideen I* is underway.

5. In the *Cartesian Meditations*, Husserl distinguishes between natural or critical reflection, and transcendental-phenomenological or radical reflection. In the former "we stand on the footing of the world already given as existing," whereas in "transcendental-phenomenological reflection, we deliver ourselves from this footing, by universal *epoché* with respect to the being or non-being of the world" (Husserl, 1973:34). Accordingly, the *epoché* in natural reflection is not the radical *epoché* which is the hallmark of the phenomenological reduction, but is a step prior to it.

6. As David Carr notes, this places Husserl's project in the Fifth Meditation in a different context from that of the usual problem of solipsism, first presented in Descartes's *Meditations*.

REFERENCES

ADORNO, THEODOR W.
 1956 Zur Metakritik der Erkenntnistheorie. Stuttgart: Volhammer.
CARR, DAVID
 1974 Phenomenology and the Problem of History. Evanston, Ill.: Northwestern University Press.

HUSSERL, EDMUND
1962 Ideas. Translated by W. Boyce-Gibson. New York: Macmillan.
1964 The Phenomenology of Internal Time-Consciousness. Edited by Martin Heidegger, translated by James Churchill. Bloomington: Indiana University Press.
1969 Formal and Transcendental Logic. Translated by Dorion Cairns. The Hague: Martinus Nijhoff.
1970 The Crisis of European Sciences and Transcendental Phenomenology. Translated by David Carr. Evanston, Ill.: Northwestern University Press.
1970 Logical Investigations, 2 vols. Translated by J. N. Findlay. New York: The Humanities Press.
1973 Cartesian Meditations. Translated by Dorion Cairns. The Hague: Martinus Nijhoff.
POPPER, KARL
1968 Conjectures and Refutations. New York: Harpers.
PSATHAS, GEORGE (ed.)
1973 Phenomenological Sociology: Issues and Applications. New York: Wiley-Interscience.
PSATHES, GEORGE, and FRANCES WAKSLER
1973 "Essential features of face-to-face interaction." In Psathes (ed.), Phenomenological Sociology.
TOULEMONT, RENE
1962 L'Essence de la societé selon Husserl. Paris: Presses Universitaires de France.
ZANER, RICHARD
1973 The Way of Phenomenology. New York: Pegasus Press.
1974 "Science and eidos." A paper presented at the Missouri Symposium on Phenomenology and Social Science, Columbia, Missouri.

2. Existential Sociology

JOSEPH A. KOTARBA

Existential sociology, a fairly recent development in the study of everyday life, is part of the broad evolutionary change taking place in Western thought over the past few centuries. Ever since the Copernican revolution supplanted the Aristotelian belief in an inalterable and immutable universe, modern thought has progressed from the search for absolute and eternal ideas to a reconceptualization of reality as change, flux, complexity, and uncertainty. Baumer (1977:20) has referred to this historical trend as the movement from "being to becoming"—that is, to "a mode of thinking that contemplates everything—nature, man, society, history, God himself—*sub specie temporis*, as not merely changing but as forever evolving into something new and different."

In contemporary times, when even the illustrious science of physics accommodates Heisenberg's (1958:81) "uncertainty principles,"[1] the tendency of modern sociology is to view the nature of social life in static, absolute, and causal terms. On the one hand, we have those sociologists who narrowly perceive society in a Durkheimian or systems framework, as a consensual moral order governed by the iron law of "social facts." Essentially, the individual is assumed to be defined and constrained by values or norms.[2] Within the everyday life perspective, absolutist thought appears in the work of those sociologists who seek the invariant properties of cognition or symbol construction by virtue of which, it is asserted, the individual is merely a rational being whose relationship to the world is predetermined by inherent interpretive faculties. As O'Neill (1974:35) states: "Man is nothing else than the way he talks about

348

himself." Accordingly, the sense of social order appears to be derived simply from society's members' rational accounts of their actions. Existential sociology is based upon rejection of simplistic, monocausal, and absolutist explanations of human social orders such as these. In our day-to-day experiences as social actors, as well as in our more programmatic research endeavors, we become aware that the individual is a complex bundle of evaluative, cognitive, and affectiver possibilities.

Social meanings (i.e., values, rules, and norms) are crucial to the construction of social order, but they are problematic in nature and situational in use. This does not mean that we agree with the solipsistic view, held by some microsociologists, that meanings only appear transituational because people talk about them as such (cf. Wieder, 1973), but rather, that social meanings vary empirically in sharedness and effective constraint, for some rules are used as a rational frontwork for behavior, while others, perhaps few in number, are truly core values or key social meanings for most people in our society (see Warren and Johnson, 1972:72–74). Likewise, we have found that the analysis of rational accounts is important—though not sufficient—for understanding highly rationalized, rule-governed, stable, and officially accountable settings like bureaucracies and formal organizations, but is much less important for understanding the problematic, emergent, chaotic, and precognitive experiences that thread their way throughout everyday life, especially in moments of privacy or secrecy.

The uncertainty that natural scientists, philosophers, theologians, and historians have increasingly felt through the past few centuries of modernization is hardly more present or obvious than in American society. We have witnessed increasing fragmentation among groups (ethnic and otherwise), rapid change in the definitions of self and of life's purpose, more independence from absolute rules of morality and conduct, and the frequent creation of new rules and lifestyles. Sociology's emphasis now should be on exploring and understanding the contrasts and innovations in social life instead of prematurely reaching for universals, for as Douglas (forthcoming) notes: "The eventual true explanations of [human processes] will almost certainly be vastly complex and at present our only certainty must be uncertainty."

A working definition of existential sociology must consequently be broad and open-ended. "Existential sociology is defined descriptively as the study of human experience-in-the-world (or existence) in all its forms" (Douglas and Johnson, 1977a: vii).[3] The goal is to arrive at truthful understandings of humans in their total human environment. No facet of human endeavor is excluded *a priori* from consideration, nor is any one human or social contingency held to be singularly determinant of social reality. Underlying all the work, however, is an emphasis on and a deep commitment to understanding how feelings form the foundations of our lives, as well as the intricate social realities we construct.

FEELINGS IN EVERYDAY LIFE

The fact that feelings pervade all aspects of our being probably explains why sociologists for the most part have ignored them as meaningful factors. The structural-functionalists, for example, have assumed that feelings are either epiphenomenal or so universally distributed among people that they are fairly neutral in and of themselves. Values are posited as the crucial determinants of social action, so that feelings are elicited by and are dependent on symbolic definitions of situations. (Merton's theory of anomie [1938] is a good example of this view.) Symbolic interactionists also see feelings as dependent variables, to the point where Becker (1963) can argue that marijuana smoking is not pleasurable unless it is defined by significant others as such. The sociology of emotions, an emerging subspecialty, argues that this class of feelings is also dependent on social elements and that "a systematic sociological theory of emotions requires a sociological model of the conditions that may vary so as to *induce* emotions" (Kemper, 1978:32) (emphasis added).

The existential sociologists contend that these causal explanations of feelings are oversimplified and biased toward rationalism. Feelings form the basis for motivation and interact with thoughts and values in extremely complex ways. Johnson (1975:147) refers to this phenomenon as the "fusion of thinking and feeling." The goal of all human behavior is the accommodation or satisfaction of feelings. This does not mean that people are simply pleasure-seeking creatures. Our point is that social decisions and actions are made primarily in accord with related feelings, and are thus independent of thought to a certain degree. As Douglas (1977:40) indicates, the partial independence of feelings over reason (i.e., rules and values) lies on a continuum. At one end, an individual is a moral absolutist totally committed to social rules out of fear of breaking them. This behavior is most prevalent in homogeneous and morally consensual societies. At the other end, profound situational threats lead an individual to disregard social rules completely if they are perceived as interfering with physical or emotional survival in any way. Most of our experiences lie somewhere in between these two extremes. The crucial question is how often we abide by a rule—or take great pains to avoid getting caught breaking a rule—because we fear the shame or guilt that would accompany the detection of rule-breaking, and not because we feel a moral commitment to the rule. A related question is the degree to which our professed and perceived rationality truly guides our behavior, and to what degree it is used to hide our potentially discreditable feelings of self.

Feelings are more crucial to sociology than ever before. Our society is increasingly marked by the dominance of feelings. This is fairly obvious in the areas of sex, drug use, and violent behavior, but there are less obvious examples. The tremendous growth of the charismatic movement in Christianity and other religions displays the choice of ecstatic, emotional, and even physical religious experience over more traditional, doctrinal, and rational expressions (cf. Lane, 1976). The immense popularity of self-actualization therapies and self-help books also shows a movement away from abstract, moral, and consensual beliefs and rules of personal conduct. In order to explore the complex interplay of feelings and thought in modern society, existential sociology is developing new methodologies geared toward understanding all facets of personal experience.

EXISTENTIAL EPISTEMOLOGY

Existential sociology seeks truthful understandings of human experience primarily, but not exclusively, through direct personal experience (Douglas and Johnson, 1977: vii; Kotarba, 1977). We begin with our own direct experience of self and of everyday life, we also include the experience of others perceived through rigorously defined field research methods, which are designed in light of the types of truth we seek of the social world.

All sciences seek truths about the world, but vary in the types of truths pursued and the choice of means for arriving at them. The development of modern science attempted to replace medieval, metaphysical absolutism with objective knowledge of nature obtained through preestablished methods allowing for verification. Unfortunately, sociology emerged during the nineteenth century at the zenith of classical science, and, following its example, established a science of society that tried to eliminate contamination by subjective and problematic elements of human behavior. Sociologists assumed that the objective features of social life need only be uncovered to disclose the causes of observable behavior (see Hayek, 1955).

The emergence of logical positivism in the early 1940s modified theories of absolute objectivity in light of the new ideas of relativity and uncertainty. In social science, objectivity (the truth about the social world) was now seen as relative to the epistemological assumptions held and the methods used by the researcher. Whether the data received from questionnaires, experimental settings, or demographic sources are "truthful," however, depends less on their "fit" with the real, everyday life experience or perceptions of people than on the internal logic of the methods themselves. Any question of truth and falsity was displaced by a concern with reliability and validity. Perhaps the most glaring example of the separation of methods from questions of truth is positivistic conversation analysis. All accounts are viewed as equally valid data for testing preestablished models of invariant language properties. Whether the account is a reasonable reflection of the speaker's true feelings or perceptions of phenomena, or simply a conscious lie perpetrated on the researcher, is irrelevant; it is just another account.

Existential sociology approaches the problem of truth in social research by first observing how truth is discerned in everyday life. Douglas (1976:4–6) lists four types of truth talked about in everyday life: transcendental, aesthetic, philosophical (or abstract), and everyday (practical) truth. People are ordinarily concerned with the last, because they are forever practically weighing the veracity of statements offered by others. "It is this realm that most concerns us and from which we derive our ideas about truth in social research, though complemented with the abstract ideas that philosophers and scientists have derived from practical forms of everyday life activity" (Douglas, 1976:5). Of all the tests of truth used in everyday life, *direct personal experience* is overwhelmingly the ultimate criterion for judgment. All of us have learned to be wary of relying on the accounts of others because of the possibilities of lying, misinforming, and misunderstanding. Abstract rules of logic are usually reliable, but are instantly waived in the face of direct personal experience to the contrary. Even transcendental truths are situationally doubted (e.g., "How can God do such a thing to me?").

All social research is ultimately grounded by direct personal experience. Our initial knowledge of possible research topics and problems comes from personal experience, and we constantly return to direct personal experience "as the most reliable form of knowledge about the social world" (Douglas, 1976:7). Even the most positivistically oriented, mathematical model-maker sits back and ponders his computer printouts to see if they make sense to him. Existential sociology takes personal experience seriously. Since we are seeking the most reliable knowledge possible of the complex social world, we begin by studying our own experiences as members of partial segments of that world. We supplement, compare, and contrast our own direct experience with that of others obtained through systematic research procedures. Other, less reliable sources of knowledge (i.e., those methods much removed from direct personal experience such as survey research and demographic studies) are situationally useful. They can provide sensitizing information on possible truths in and of the social world. We judge how good they are by how well they meet tests of personal experience.

Direct personal experience is initially relative to topics of inquiry in two ways. First, the researcher may become interested in and informed about a phenomenon because he has experienced that phenomenon naturally in his everyday life. My interest in studying corporal punishment as official deviance, for example, resulted from five years of teaching and administrating in a large public school system (Kotarba, 1978). Second, the researcher can actively seek direct experience of a phenomenon after his initial interest in it is established. The level of involvement depends on the situational contingencies such as the time allowed for the study or the open/secretive nature of the group. Altheide's (1976) study of television newsrooms entailed various degrees of involvement, for example, from informal conversations with newsmakers to spending considerable time with them covering and reporting news stories.

Essentially, the researcher's own direct, personal experience serves four purposes in developing an understanding of social phenomena (Kotarba, 1977:260). First, experience becomes an original source of data. This is especially important for discovering the hidden aspects of human experience, such as physical sensations and deep emotions, that are not always discernable from observations of others, especially "socially dangerous" ones. Second, one's experience provides a basis for comparison with the experience of others. The researcher can use his own experience and perceptions to judge the credibility of accounts given in settings marked by intense conflict and deceit. Third, one's experience generates points of inquiry. Ongoing personal involvement always turns out to be richer than the rationalized presuppositions brought into a setting. Fourth, one's experience facilitates a theoretical understanding of real events. The true participant observer who operates with good faith and realizes, through self-observation and introspection, the complexities he or she faces in making sense of a phenomenon is reluctant to espouse unrealistic and simplistic explanations for other people's behavior.

Although the personal experience of the field researcher can be extremely rich, it is naturally limited in scope. The next best source of knowledge of the social world is the experience of others. Our previous research has shown that, when at all possible, *it is best to study human experience in its natural settings.* We can quite easily learn the most general and abstract symbolic systems held by people through formal interviews and questionnaires, but the social meanings and feelings that actually come into play in shaping everyday life experiences are always situationally invoked, elicited, defined, and grounded. Merleau-Ponty similarly (though philosophically) viewed this situated experience as "being-within-the-world" (1962:452). The individual is of the world due to his corporality, but his world consists of the realm of situations within which he finds himself. Thus, human experience is inherently reflexive, for human beings "are no longer the shapers of the world, but are both shapers and shaped by the surrounding world" (Fontana, 1979). Insisting on the study of human nature in its natural settings, existential sociology also tries to synthesize the fundamental principles of life being developed in a wide spectrum of disciplines such as behavioral biology and ethology (see Griffin, 1976).[4]

Existential field methods are based upon the general finding "that profound conflicts of interest, values, feelings, and actions pervade social life" (Douglas, 1976:55). This view contrasts with the assumption, held by some traditional field researchers, that subjects readily cooperate with interviewers/researchers, understand their questions, and act naturally when observed. Our research has demonstrated that people have many reasons to conceal and even lie about those aspects of their lives that matter most to them (and, consequently, to us as existential sociologists). Thus, the field researcher must take steps to see behind intentional evasions, as well as the unintentional barriers to truth such as misinformation or common self-deceptions.

The first general strategy is to use one's own personal experience in the setting to evaluate members' accounts. This personal criterion can be used with the evaluations of trusted insiders or informants. We have found, moreover, that team field research allows us to appreciate the multiperspectival realities of members in large and conflict-ridden groups and settings (see Douglas, 1976:chapter 9; Adler *et al.*, 1978). A solo field researcher is usually limited to studying small groups or small segments of large groups (see Dalton, 1959, for an exception). A research team, on the other hand, can organize itself according to a systematic division of labor so that all aspects of the setting can be infiltrated, and the individual strengths of each member can be effectively used (e.g., a shy member can concentrate on strict observation and a gregarious member can concentrate on negotiating *entrée*). Finally, amorphous, secret, and covert phenomena—those experiences of everyday life not readily located—can be discovered through a process of defocusing, or as Douglas (1976:195) refers to it, "casting a wide net." The researcher talks to all kinds of people and investigates all kinds of settings where contacts can be made with those who either experience the phenomenon directly or know of others who do. In my research on the chronic pain experience, which only occasionally presents itself in clinical settings, I successfully located a variety of different pain experiences by talking to friends and acquaintances, discussing my research in classes I taught, scouring the newspaper for advertisements by marginal health care practitioners, attending professional health care meetings, discussing injuries and careers with professional baseball players, and enlisting the aid of other resources in the university and the general community (Kotarba, 1979a).

In conclusion, existential sociology's epistemology and research protocol are grounded in what I refer to as methodological honesty.[5] Through intensive involvement with everyday life, existential sociologists understand that people are real and that their experiences are "real." When we look at ourselves and our immediate others (whether friends or subjects), we see complex individuals of flesh and spirit searching for meaning, trying to make sense of often absurd situations, and constantly experiencing and reacting to a multitude of feelings and emotions. We sense a kind of unintentional dishonesty in a researcher who sets aside the complex reality of his own life to do a sociology that concentrates on observing one aspect of human nature and using that data to explain the human being. Within the research setting, moreover, the fusion of thinking and feeling exists not only in our subjects but in ourselves. Therefore, we redefine and seek objectivity by examining how our feelings affect the accomplishment and reporting of field research, and by not naively attempting to minimize the nonrational elements of our experience (see Johnson, 1975:chapter 8; but also Wolff, 1964).[6]

STUDIES IN EXISTENTIAL SOCIOLOGY

As would be expected from this discussion, studies in existential sociology cover a wide range of phenomena, from the Adlers' (1978) small-scale analysis of momentum in sports to Manning's (1977) investigative, historical, and comparative study of the development of the urban police force. The current debate over the merits of doing microsociology versus macrosociology, as well as concern over accommodating the two, are irrelevant to existential sociology and simply distracting to our work. All research accomplished under the aegis of existential sociology is directed toward the ongoing development of an open-ended and cumulative model of the many levels of social orders that comprise the human biosphere. The knowledge we obtain of the human bio-

sphere is cumulative, and thus scientific, because it builds upon fundamental principles of everyday life (e.g., situatedness and problematic-
ness). These fundamental principles, indeed, make meaningful
quantitative prediction unlikely for any but the most stable and most
limited realms of social life, although well-executed quantitative description is useful for learning about those systematic aspects of social
life presently unapproachable by field research methods.

Studies in existential sociology may be analytically divided into three
main areas of concern: the self, deviant behavior, and organizations and
bureaucracies. All such studies are methodologically based upon direct
field research experience. They are written in the language of everyday
life, a style directed at professional and layperson alike. Sounding scientific does not necessarily mean being scientific, as Fontana counsels us:

> But if the sociologists hope, and some of us do, in the wake of the
> great Max Weber, to demystify the world and present its social
> members with analytic insights about the invisible webs that hold
> us together, it is not enough to simply see the world stripped of its
> veils. Sociologists must strip their own language of the veils which
> hide their revelations from the members of society and present their
> sociological understanding with a new kind of sociological imagi-
> nation, one that will guide the sociologist's pen to paint a portrait
> of society which will stir empathy and understanding among
> readers (1977:195–96).[7]

DEFINING THE EXISTENTIAL SELF

The self is a crucial concept in existential sociology, for it provides the
means of summarizing the complex ways human nature is actualized
within the individual (see Kotarba, 1977; Warren and Ponse, 1977). The
existential view of the self differs from other sociological formulations in
that it attempts to account for the individual's total experience of being.
Symbolic interactionists emphasize the socially determined aspect of the
self (i.e., "the looking glass self"). Following Mead (1934), they argue
that the individual's definition of self directly results from interaction
with significant others, based upon and reinforced by a shared universe
of symbols. Goffman's (1959) dramaturgical model emphasizes the self as
the presenter of predefined and learned social roles. Freudian theories,
though correctly reminding us of the unconscious and sexual aspects of
the self, tend to overemphasize pathological and neurotic tendencies (see
Gross, 1978). Ethnomethodology fails to deal with the concept of the

self, for it is viewed as a sociological, not a members', category (Hugh Mehan, in conversation). The ethnomethodologists' narrow concern with invariant properties of cognition has left them insensitive to the fact that real people do, in fact, think and talk about their innermost feelings and self-concepts, as is especially apparent in this age of self-actualization (cf. Henninger, 1977).[8]

While all sociological theories of the self contain partial truths, they tend to oversimplify the complexity of the individual's experience of existence. The more comprehensive existential theory of the self is an emerging theory (Warren and ponse, 1977:288), and the fundamental principles of the self, described in the following paragraphs, display an uncertainty and flux.

The self is embodied. Corporality is the overwhelming fact of human existence. Being-within-the-world means that feelings and primordial perception precede rationality and symbol use, and, in fact, activate them. Prereflective perception (as we will see in our discussion of Merleau-Ponty) is the basis for our awareness of self and of the world, for:

> We do not simply feel, sense, or know our history, our temporality, our Being, our reality; we are bodily immersed in them. The body is the ultimate and primary source of all distances, time, and meanings. The body is the measurement of its world (Fontana and Van de Water, 1977:126).

People affected by chronic pain, for example, are primarily motivated by their constant sensation of physical discomfort and secondarily motivated by the evaluative social meanings of pain received from significant others, such as physicians. Sanctionable definitions of self (e.g., "hypochondriac" and "psychosomatic") are meaningless in the face of perceived physical distress. People who are ordinarily well-socialized into the powerful symbolic universe of American medicine will seek out unusual forms of treatment for their pain (e.g., acupuncture) when bodily perceptions indicate that regular medical interventions are illegitimate to the self (Kotarba, 1975 and 1977).

The self is becoming. Traditional sociological theories of the self view self-image as determined to a large degree by definitions and events occurring in an individual's past life. Their emphasis is on the socially and historically determined aspects of the self. Research has shown that the self is a victim of its past to some degree, but that the spontaneous and creative aspect of the self often characterizes modern man. Many of the traditional American rules of conduct are perceived as illegitimate in the face of changes that occur in our everyday lives. For example the rigid demarcation of family and marital roles appears to be shifting. Modern life in all its forms has been struck by what Douglas (1977:3) refers to as the "revolt of brute being." People are increasingly preoccupied with their innermost feelings and emotions at the expense of rational codes of conduct and thought. The modern individual is often caught in a state of the absurd, in which he is personally responsible for giving meaning to the question, "Who am I?" (see also Lyman and Scott, 1970). The modern self seeks the answer to this question from the future rather than from the often discredited and unworkable definitions of the past. Above all the development of self-image is never complete, for situations and definitions of situations change as quickly as underlying feelings, so that the self is always in a state of becoming.

Warren's extensive research (1974) on male homosexuality illustrates these points. Before defining themselves as homosexuals, the gays were aware of bodily feelings and emotions that were contrary to society's image of sexual normality. At some point gays undergo the process of alteration by which the self is redefined as a member of a new category. Whether or not the homosexual "comes out of the closet," he is aware that his new identity is discreditable, because he has learned throughout his life that society maintains strict definitions of normal and abnormal sexual behavior. Many gays not only come out of the closet but attach their gayness to their most public identities. There are two reasons for doing this. First, joining the gay community relieves the gays of the tension and depression derived from the conflict between their deepest sexual feelings and the normal sex and gender roles they previously felt forced to maintain. Second, their public involvement with other gays provides the nexus for an emerging community that satisfies for them many of the social needs previously obtained from participation in the straight community. The "becoming" process is never complete, however, for the experience of the gay self, like all experiences of self, is complex and to some degree mystifying. Thus, the gays continually strive to become some ideal, future self that they hope will be better adjusted to the conflicts arising from being discredited, as well as more enlightened concerning the always mysterious "causes" of their gayness.[9]

The self is situational. Just as social meanings are invoked, interpreted, and negotiated situationally, the definition of self is always at least partially problematic and partially situational. In some ancient societies, such as early Egypt, the individual probably felt secure being in close identification with a more coherent social world, with strictly demarcated social roles and positions. Among the conflicting realities of modern society, an individual often feels isolated and alienated from the social world and unsure of his own self-identity. As reliance on the belief in a substantial self (i.e., what a person believes he really is at all times and in all places) becomes increasingly untenable, individual definition of self becomes increasingly dependent upon shifting social situations and definitions of situations (see Douglas, 1967:281; Warren and Ponse, 1977:273–75).

Fontana (1977) has studied the problematic meanings of growing old in our society. He has found that unidimensional theories of aging, such as the view that the elderly actively and joyfully disengage themselves from earlier social commitments, are only partially true. Many factors, some of which are situational, contribute to the development of various patterns of growing old. Individuals with strong commitment to the work ethic will replace the loss of old roles (e.g., through retirement) with new, active, and involved roles. The elderly who perceive old age as leisure time are less interested in assuming new roles than in relaxing and enjoying themselves. Others await death, usually because they are either too poor to entertain notions of leisure, or have had previous values shattered by personal crisis. Role transitions are never unproblematic for the elderly as they enter unknown territory, in which the importance of earlier values and goals dwindles. Above all, the definition of an aged self is dependent upon situational contingencies such as health crises, internment in impersonal nursing homes, and the dissolution of family ties.

The self is reflexive. Many factors interact to construct the existential self, among them, learned values and rules, cognitive capabilities, perceptions, feelings, creativity, embodiment, and situational contingencies. The self is the focal point of all aspects of being and is the reflexive center of their interaction. For example, perceptions can affect feelings which in turn affect the evaluation of a rule or the interpretation of an idea. Moreover, the existential self is the focal point for the inherently conflicted and uncertain relationship between the individual and society. Research has shown that perceptions of self inform and are informed by perceptions of social reality. The spontaneous, intentional, and creative facets of the self continuously mediate both realities in the constant search for meaning and direction in life. The influence of power in this negotiation process is a crucial aspect of ongoing research about the self.

Deviant Behavior and Existential Sociology

The study of deviant behavior is central to the goals of existential sociology for two reasons. First, by examining the processes of rule-creation, rule-use, and the social construction of morality, one is better able to understand human social orders. Second, deviant behavior is a realm of existence where fundamental feelings and perceptions clash with rigid and rationalized social rules, often resulting in creative forms of social change.

Traditional theories of deviance display many of the shortcomings of the paradigms from which they are derived, especially a tendency to oversimplify and overrationalize complex social phenomena.[10] For example, the structural-functional analysis of prostitution, a variation of Merton's anomie theory, argues that women enter prostitution as a last resort. Due to a disadvantaged position in life (e.g., lower-class background, minority group status, and physical unattractiveness), they are unable to obtain financial and social success legitimately, and are thus "forced" into prostitution (see Davis, 1955). Conversely, Rasmussen's (1978) focused field research study of massage parlors, probably the most common form of prostitution in America, found that women have various positive reasons for becoming prostitutes. The pay and working conditions are good enough to lead many middle-class college graduates to do sex for play. Another important motive is the desire for the "fast life," or the excitement of working at a job much less boring than the ordinary nine-to-five occupation. The average masseuse-prostitute is normal psychologically and emotionally, and in many cases this current form of "play for pay" reflects her interpretation of liberating changes in attitudes toward sex in our society.

The ongoing trend in our society toward increased concern with and expression of bodily pleasures is the theoretical focus of Douglas and Rasmussen's study (1977) of a nude beach. Since social rules against public nudity are taken for granted in our society, violating such rules is a creative act of deviance that involves searching for new ways of experiencing the self and the world. Nude beachers share their experiences and concerns, and thus form a deviant subculture. When such subcultures gather enough followers and support to become a social movement, they can lead to dramatic changes in social rules.

Traditional sociological perspectives on deviance concentrate on explaining situational rule breaking, street crimes, or delinquency, and assume that lower classes are more deviant than the middle- to upper-classes. Little attention has been given to business and professional types of deviance, because they have been considered less threatening and harmful than lower-class deviance. Existential sociology's goal of studying all aspects of a phenomenon has led to several creative works on widespread, upper-echelon malfeasance (see Douglas and Johnson, 1977b; Johnson and Douglas, 1978). Snow (1978) studied the Arizona land boom to discover the sociopsychological factors underlying fraudulent land sales to unwary buyers. A fear of scarcity permeated the market and led buyers to believe that private desert land with access to water and electricity was bound to skyrocket in value in the future. Many buyers, adhering to the middle-class economic ethos, were easily conned into believing that they were making a shrewd investment, even though they bought land that had a only remote chance of falling into the path of urban growth. Unscrupulous land developers, with the help of ambiguous real estate laws and dishonest public officials, capitalized on these attitudes by engaging in multiple sales of land parcels, reneging on promises to make improvements in subdivisions, and selling land they did not legally own. The mid-1970s economic slump and an extensive media exposure of land fraud helped to replace the boom market mentality with one of caution and restraint.

ORGANIZATIONS AND BUREAUCRACIES

Existential sociology approaches the study of organizations and bureaucracies in much the same way it studies microsociological phenomena. Direct personal experience is the preferred method, but indirect accounts complement limited experience in those settings were entrée is inaccessible. Moreover, many fundamental principles that govern individual interaction also underly more complex organizational phenomena. Altheide and Johnson (1979), for example, have extended the dramaturgical framework of Goffman and others to their analysis of organizations. Both the individual and organization are constantly engaged in impression management, but they differ significantly in the media of communication used to share information. Whereas the individual can manipulate speech, body language, and personal style to accomplish a particular impression, an organization most often relies on official reports, which project a unified image of the organization that contrasts with the complex and often conflicting realities that mark internal operation. The authors define this organizational image-management as bureaucratic propaganda: "Any report produced by an organization for evaluation and other practical purposes, which is targeted for individuals, committees, or publics that are unaware of its promotive character and the editing processes that shaped the report" (Altheide and Johnson, 1979:2). This perspective differs from the traditional social science view that locates propaganda in the attempts of government to influence public attitudes through the mass media. Changes in the structure and public credibility of governments have made this view obsolete. The authors illustrate these points by citing several of their own participant-observation studies of bureaucratic information use, ranging from Altheide's study of television newsrooms (see also Altheide, 1976) to Johnson's analysis of the organizational manipulation of military reports during wartime.

EXISTENTIAL SOCIOLOGY, HISTORY, AND PHILOSOPHY

It is commonly assumed that the sociologies of everyday life are either ahistorical or antihistorical, due in large part to their emphasis on studying interactive social realities (cf. Hexter, 1971; McNall and Johnson, 1975). This criticism is, however, much less valid when applied to existential sociology. Existential sociologists are profoundly critical of the commonplace acceptance of historical records as equal in truth value to everyday experience. Historical documents, like reports written today, are grounded in inherently conflictual situations that lead to deceitful construction of accounts, leaving them much more problematic than the researcher's personal experience. We can never recapture historical experience as it really was.

Nevertheless, existential sociology remains profoundly historical for the simple reason that history is the only source of potential data on the actualization of human nature in innumerable settings over prolonged periods of time. Our point is that history must be interpreted in the light of our awareness of inherent problems with the data, and enriched with the understanding of everyday life that we gain through experience and observation. True understanding of history requires the empathic immersion of the researcher's self into the experience of historical actors, for as Dilthey (1954:3) remarks:

> The genuinely historical is that which engages not merely the powers of mind but those of the heart, of sympathy, of enthusiasm. . . . No concept exhausts the contents of these individual selves. Rather, the variety directly given in them can only be lived, understood, and described.

It is also commonly assumed that existential sociology is simply the empirical application of ideas directly taken from existential philosophy and literature. Though understandable, in light of our chosen designation, this assumption is incorrect. Our insights into and understandings of the social world are derived from our experience and research. We later use philosophical ideas as resources for creating more general, theoretical understandings of our experience (cf. Douglas and Johnson, 1977:vii-ix). The existential philosophers, especially Merleau-Ponty, have been useful in helping sociologists redirect the somewhat over-rationalized focus of phenomenologically oriented social inquiry. Merleau-Ponty appreciated Husserl's concern for methodological purity in science, but felt that the search for true objectivity in asserted invariant properties of the mind was absurd. To "return to the things themselves," Merleau-Ponty (1962:6) argued, one must examine the generic modes of experience that accompany corporeal being-within-the-world—namely, feelings and perceptions. Social meanings exist in the real world and are out there to be discovered, and are not, as Husserl insisted, creations of the individual consciousness (see Brown, 1977:97-100; Fontana and Van de Water, 1977:117-29).

The Scottish moral philosophers—Hume, Smith, James, Stewart, and Ferguson—provide insight into the study of humans and their situated behavior, and have unfortunately been ignored by most sociologists. They reacted against the rationalists of the Enlightenment and argued that reason is always limited by and subordinate to feelings. They felt that human nature is essentially uniform throughout history and based upon inherent drives such as sympathy (i.e., natural sociality). Situated differences in perception lead to variations in historical developments as well as in images of the self. Hume, for example, argued against the prevailing metaphysical belief in an inalterable, substantial self. Smith viewed the self as a fluid "mirror of the world," an idea quite similar to Cooley's "looking glass self." Above all the Scottish moral philosophers insisted that experience is the most reliable source of data on human nature and its situational manifestations (see Schneider, 1967).

CONCLUSION

Existential sociology has emerged as an attempt to understand man and his relationship with the world realistically. The range of substantive interests and theoretical concerns is as broad as modern life is rich, complex, and conflictful. If our efforts appear diffuse and our theoretical statements sound tentative, it is because our goal of understanding existence is comprehensive. We do not propose yet another addition to the growing sectarianism in sociology. We actively seek and invite insightful ideas from all intellectual disciplines and sociological perspectives. The readers should evaluate our work according to two criteria. First, the reader should compare our findings to his or her own experience in the world and common-sense understandings of social life. Second, and most important, the reader should view our work with respect to its practical purpose. The uncertainty and flux prevalent in our society surface in what are commonly referred to as social problems. We hope that the understandings of everyday life emerging from our work can be effectively applied to the solution of those problems.

NOTES

I would like to thank Jack D. Douglas and John M. Johnson for commenting on an earlier draft of this paper.

1. Synder (1978) argues that much of the current uncertainty in modern science and philosophy can be attributed to the movement from holistic to pluralistic philosophies of nature, which is, in part, the result of the exchange of Eastern and Western world views and ideas.

2. Similarly, many forms of Marxism see social life as ruled by the iron laws of history and/or economics.

3. Several other sociologists have used the terms "existential" and "existentialism" in their works. Manning (1973) earlier used the rubric "existential sociology" to encompass all the varieties of everyday life sociology that emerged in reaction to Parsonian functionalism. Throughout this paper I will point out important differences that have developed between existential sociology and the phenomenological and interactionist perspectives on everyday life. Tiryakian (1962) contrasted existential philosophy with Durkheimian sociology, and Craib (1976) attempted to show similarities between the work of Sartre and Weber. As we shall see, existential sociology is based upon the direct study of everyday life and only uses philosophical ideas when they are useful in developing subsequent theoretical statements.

4. Dawkins (1976), for example, argues that cultural transmission is analogous to genetic transmission in that, although basically conservative, it can give rise to creative forms of historical evolution that insure cultural survival.

5. These ideas were refined in conversation with John Johnson and Kathy Ferraro.

6. In general all dissertations and books written on existential sociology include extensive methodological appendices, in which the actual research experience is documented and analyzed. This procedure serves to help recognize the effects of the researcher's personal thoughts and feelings in the field on data collection and use.

7. The use of and respect for everyday language also has theoretical implications. The economists of everyday life (e.g., Menger, 1973) have long realized that macroeconomic patterns evolve directly from patterns of individual economic decision making made in everyday life language forms. The development of economic structures in one's language reflects the development of economic experience in the individual's life.

8. The concept of the self is, however, occasionally mentioned in the literature on phenomenological philosophy (e.g., Berger and Luckmann, 1966; Natanson, 1970). These works concentrate on the cognitive and rational aspects of the self.

9. Other writers have talked about transformation of the self, but have viewed

this process in somewhat simplistic and linear terms. Zurcher (1977), for example, agrees that the individual in modern society can change self-concepts, and he lists four possible self-definitions. However, the existential theory of the self allows for multiple and situational definitions of the self, especially in times of intense personal crisis.

10. I have elsewhere critiqued the traditional theories of deviance in detail (Kotarba, 1979b). I have argued that existing theories of deviance attempt to explain all forms of rule breaking, and therefore, essentially explain very little. We presently have need of more intensive description of deviant behavior and the immediate processes underlying its performance. Only then will we be able to integrate realistically the structural and interactional perspectives that are, at this time, overwhelmingly onesided arguments.

REFERENCES

ADLER, PETER, and PATRICIA A. ADLER
  1978 "The role of momentum in sport." Urban Life 7:153–176.
ADLER, PETER, JOSEPH A. KOTARBA, and PATRICIA A. ADLER
  1978 "Inside the park: field research among professional athletes." Paper presented at the annual meeting of the American Sociological Association, San Francisco.
ALTHEIDE, DAVID L.
  1976 Creating Reality: How TV News Distorts Events. Beverly Hills, Calif.: Sage.
ALTHEIDE, DAVID L., and JOHN M. JOHNSON
  1979 Modern Bureaucratic Propaganda. Boston: Allyn and Bacon.
BAUMER, FRANKLIN L.
  1977 Modern European Thought. New York: Macmillan.
BECKER, HOWARD S.
  1963 Outsiders. New York: The Free Press.
BERGER, PETER L., and THOMAS LUCKMANN
  1966 The Social Construction of Reality: A Treatise in the Sociology of Knowledge. Garden City, N.Y.: Doubleday and Co.
BROWN, RICHARD H.
  1977 "The emergence of existential thought: philosophical perspectives on positivist and humanist forms of social theory." In Jack D. Douglas and John M. Johnson (eds.), Existential Sociology. New York: Cambridge University Press.
CRAIB, IAN
  1976 Existentialism and Sociology: A Study of Jean-Paul Sartre. New York: Cambridge University Press.
DALTON, MELVILLE
  1959 Men Who Manage. New York: Wiley.
DAVIS, KINGSLEY
  1955 "Prostitution." In Robert Merton and Robert Nisbit (eds.), Social Problems. New York: Harcourt, Brace and World.

DAWKINS, RICHARD
1976 The Selfish Gene. New York: Oxford University Press.
DILTHEY, WILLIAM
1954 The Essence of Philosophy. Translated by Stephen A. and William T. Emery. Chapel Hill: University of North Carolina Press.
DOUGLAS, JACK D.
1967 The Social Meanings of Suicide. Princeton, N.J.: Princeton University Press.
1976 Investigative Social Research. Beverly Hills, Calif.: Sage.
1977 "Existential sociology." In Jack D. Douglas and John M. Johnson (eds.), Existential Sociology. New York: Cambridge University Press.
n.d.   "The fundamental processes of cultural conservation, creative deviance, and rule changes." (forthcoming).
DOUGLAS, JACK D., et al.
1979 Introduction to the Sociologies of Everyday Life. Boston: Allyn and Bacon.
DOUGLAS, JACK D., and JOHN M. JOHNSON (eds.)
1977a Existential Sociology: New York: Cambridge University Press.
1977b Official Deviance. Philadelphia: Lippincott.
DOUGLAS, JACK D. and PAUL K. RASMUSSEN, with CAROL ANN FLANAGAN
1977 The Nude Beach. Beverly Hills, Calif.: Sage.
FONTANA, ANDREA
1977 The Last Frontier. Beverly Hills: Sage.
1979 "Toward a complex universe: existential sociology." In Jack D. Douglas, et al. Introduction to the Sociologies of Everyday Life. Boston: Allyn and Bacon.
FONTANA, ANDREA, and RICHARD VAN DE WATER
1977 "The existential thought of Jean-Paul Sartre and Maurice Merleau-Ponty." In Jack D. Douglas and John M. Johnson (eds.), Existential Sociology. New York: Cambridge University Press.
GOFFMAN, ERVING
1959 The Presentation of Self in Everyday Life. Garden City, N.Y.: Doubleday.
GRIFFIN, DONALD R.
1976 The Question of Animal Awareness. New York: Rockefeller University Press.
GROSS, MARTIN L.
1977 The Psychological Society. New York: Random House,.
HAYEK, F. A.
1955 The Counter-Revolution of Science: Studies in the Abuse of Reason. New York: The Free Press.
HEISENBERG, WERNER
1958 Physics and Philosophy. New York: Harper & Row.
HENNINGER, DANIEL
1977 "Why do self-help books sell?" Wall Street Journal. (October 11).
HEXTER, J. H.
1971 Doing History. Bloomington: Indiana University Press.

JOHNSON, JOHN M.
  1975 Doing Field Research. New York: The Free Press.
JOHNSON, JOHN M., and JACK D. DOUGLAS
  1978 Crime at the Top: Deviance in Business and the Professions. Philadel-
        phia: Lippincott.
KEMPER, THEODORE D.
  1978 "Toward a sociology of emotions: some problems and some solutions."
        The American Sociologist 13:30–41.
KOTARBA, JOSEPH A.
  1975 "American acupuncturists: the new entrepreneurs of hope." Urban Life
        4:149–177.
  1977 "The chronic pain experience." In Jack D. Douglas and John M.
        Johnson (eds.), Existential Sociology, New York: Cambridge University
        Press.
  1978 "Masking official violence: corporal punishment in the public schools."
        In John M. Johnson and Jack D. Douglas, Crime at the Top: Deviance in
        Business and the Professions. Philadelphia: Lippincott.
  1979a "Discovering amorphous social experience: the case of chronic pain." In
        William Shaffir, Allan Turowetz, and Robert Stebbins (eds.), Social
        Experience in Field Work. New York: St. Martin's Press.
  1979b "Labelling theory and the everyday world of deviance." In Jack D.
        Douglas et al., Introduction to the Sociologies of Everyday Life. Boston:
        Allyn and Bacon.
LANE, RALPH
  1976 "Catholic charismatic movement." In Charles Y. Glock and Robert N.
        Bellah (eds.), The New Religious Consciousness. Berkeley: The Univer-
        sity of California Press.
LYMAN, STANFORD M. and MARVIN B. SCOTT
  1970 A Sociology of the Absurd. New York: Appleton.
MANNING, PETER K.
  1973 "Existential sociology." The Sociological Quarterly 14:200–225.
  1977 Police Work: The Social Organization of Policing. Cambridge: MIT
        Press.
McNALL, SCOTT G., and JAMES C. M. JOHNSON
  1975 "The new conservatives: ethnomethodologists, phenomenologists, and
        symbolic interactionists." The Insurgent Sociologist 5:49–65.
MEAD, GEORGE H.
  1934 Mind, Self and Society. Chicago: University of Chicago Press.
MERLEAU-PONTY, MAURICE
  1962 The Phenomenology of Perception. London: Routledge and Kegan
        Paul.
MERTON, ROBERT K.
  1938 "Social structure and anomie." American Sociological Review
        3:672–682.
NATANSON, MAURICE
  1970 The Journeying Self: A Study in Philosophy and Social Role. Reading,
        Mass.: Addison-Wesley.

O'NEILL, JOHN
  1974 Making Sense Together. New York: Harper & Row.
RASMUSSEN, PAUL K.
  1978 Massage Parlors. Unpublished Ph.D. dissertation. University of California, San Diego.
SCHNEIDER, LOUIS (ed.)
  1967 The Scottish Moralists on Human Nature and Society. Chicago: University of Chicago Press.
SNOW, ROBERT P.
  1978 "The golden fleece: Arizona land fraud." In John M. Johnson and Jack D. Douglas (eds.), Crime at the Top: Deviance in Business and the Professions. Philadelphia: Lippincott.
SNYDER, PAUL
  1978 Toward One Science. New York: St. Martin's Press.
TIRYAKIAN, EDWARD A.
  1962 Sociologism and Existentialism. Englewood Cliffs, N.J.: Prentice-Hall.
WARREN, CAROL A. B.
  1974 Identity and Community in the Gay World. New York: Wiley.
WARREN, CAROL A. B., and JOHN M. JOHNSON
  1972 "A critique of labelling theory from the phenomenological perspective." In Robert A. Scott and Jack D. Douglas (eds.), Theoretical Perspectives in Deviance. New York: Basic Books.
WARREN, CAROL A. B., and BARBARA PONSE
  1977 "The existential self in the gay world." In Jack D. Douglas and John M. Johnson (eds.) Existential Sociology. New York: Cambridge University Press.
WIEDER, D. LAURENCE
  1973 Language and Social Reality. The Hague: Mouton.
WOLFF, KURT H.
  1964 "Surrender and community study." In Arthur J. Vidich, Joseph Bensman, and Maurice Stein (eds.), Reflections on Community Studies. New York: Wiley.
ZURCHER, LOUIS A.
  1977 The Mutable Self: A Self Concept for Social Change. Beverly Hills, Calif.: Sage.

3. The Mutuality of Accounts: An Essay on Trust

JOHN O'NEILL

I want to draw attention to a central problem—namely, the relationship between scientific knowledge and common-sense knowledge. At the same time, I want to raise the larger question of the political trust invested in the social sciences by democratic societies. In order to bring these issues into focus, I shall raise a question which I refer to as the problem of the mutuality of accounts. I raise this question because I think it requires us to see the everyday practices of common-sense knowledge and the rational procedures of scientific method as interdependent practices. I want to argue that it is false to separate social rationality into rigid categories of common-sense and scientific knowledge, but most important, I believe that we cannot rely upon the presumption of an unexamined subordination of common sense knowledge to scientific knowledge. Today, we must recognize that knowledge, whether in the hands of party bureaucrats or professional experts, is a political trust that must be made accountable, legally and morally speaking, to popular understanding. The issue of which information we should act on is not decidable on the grounds that the procedures of science are superior to those of common-sense and lay practice, merely because the latter do not meet the same standards of rational or methodic accountability. I shall deal first with the purely methodological issue before turning to the problem of the ways in which institutions shape scientific knowledge and public opinion (Habermas, 1970).

COMMON SENSE AND SCIENTIFIC ACCOUNTS

I propose now to contrast "accountable" common sense, or the natural attitude of daily life, and the "accountable" rational procedures of the scientific attitude.[1]

We owe to Schutz (1964) a basic attempt to restore the rationality of everyday life and to show how it could never be replaced by the paradigm of scientific rationality. His argument should not be interpreted as an espousal of irrationalism or as antiscience; it simply advocates a responsible tension in the life of reason that is shared by all, without being peculiar to the calling of science (Weber, 1964). Schutz (1964) points out that in order to interpret human action, to evaluate its empirical adequacy, its delusions and errors, sociologists, of whom Weber and Parsons are the outstanding examples, have conceived of action in terms of the paradigm of instrumentally rational activity, i.e., conduct that for any external observer is directed to the "best" adaptation of given resources to given ends. Before we dismiss people's ordinary, but largely unexamined and untaught, competences as inferior reasoning, we need, Schutz (1964:64–88) argues, to distinguish between various elements of common-sense rationality. We can then see whether they are reducible—or whether they even need to be reduced to the pattern of scientific rationality. We may distinguish the following cases:

1. Where "rational" is synonymous with reasonable, the common-sense use of cookbook knowledge is certainly rational.

2. Rational action may be equated with deliberate action. There are, however, general senses of the notion of deliberation:

    a. Common-sense action is deliberate insofar as it invokes the considerations upon which its practices were originally based.

    b. Common-sense action is deliberate where it sees the applicability of past knowledge to a present situation.

    c. Common-sense action is deliberate in the same sense as is any action that is motivated by some anticipated end.

    d. Common-sense action, by its very nature, is not deliberate in the sense of engaging in an elaborate rehearsal of competing lines of action.

In stricter terms scientifically rational action may be understood as:

1. Planned action
2. Predictable action
3. Logical action
4. Decision-ruled action

The last four items are quite problematic in themselves. We can hardly doubt that everyday life involves planning and predicting. The trouble is that people are committed to schemes and projects that involve long spans of time and encompass roundabout means to their ends. At any time we cannot, as a scientific observer hopes, easily carve out the "unit-acts," i.e., the simple means-end scheme that would account for everyday conduct. By the same token everyday life cannot rely upon the ideals of conceptual clarity and the distinctions espoused by logicians, since people advance ideas and employ talk only within the limits of their own situations. Finally, the concept of action based upon rational choice is applicable to everyday life in that it refers to choices best directed to serve an actor's purposes, provided the actor has given knowledge. But if this means choice guided by the rationality of the knowledge on which the very choice is based, then this is not a practice of everyday life, nor can it provide a methodological principle for the interpretation of everyday conduct. This is because the postulate of rational action presupposes that the observer:

1. Has knowledge of the place of the actor's end in terms of his overall plans, which must also be known to the actor.

2. Knows the relationship of the actor's end with his other ends and its compatibility or incompatibility.

3. Has knowledge of the describable and indescribable consequences that might arise for the actor in achieving his end.

4. Has knowledge independent of the actor of all the technically possible means of achieving his end, as well as of all their mutual interferences.

5. Has knowledge of all the means of accomplishing his end that are actually within the actor's reach.

6. Has knowledge, in view of the social nature of action, of the interpretations and misunderstandings of the actor's conduct by his fellow men.

7. Has knowledge of the ends of the reactions of the other men to the actor.

8. Has knowledge of all the elements (1–5) that the actor attributes to others.

9. Has knowledge of the overall structure of the levels of intimacy and anonymity within which the actor pursues his ends among his fellow men.

Schutz (1964) concludes that the notion of rational action is so idealized that it is not to be found anywhere in the world, and so it cannot be used either to fault everyday standards of practical reasoning or to provide a model for their interpretation. Where, then, do we find use for the notion of the rational actor? Schutz answers that the model of the rational actor is to be regarded as a theoretical construct through which sociologists seek to give to their own knowledge and interest in the analysis of social order the status of scientifically rational knowledge. In other words the postulate of rational action is a maxim of sociological analysis (Garfinkel, 1967:262–283). It requires that the steps to the solution of a sociological problem be constructed in such a way that:

1. They remain in full compatibility with the rules that define scientifically correct decisions of grammar and procedure.

2. All the elements be conceived in full clearness and distinctness.

3. The clarification of the body of knowledge, as well as the rules of investigative and interpretive procedure, be treated as a first-priority project.

4. The projected steps contain only scientifically verifiable assumptions that have to be in full compatibility with the whole of scientific knowledge.

The premise that instrumentally rational action is the dominant sociological frame of reference is thoroughly dependent upon the institutions of exchange, economy, and legal-rational bureaucracy that are the setting of modern society. Furthermore, scientific conduct is, in fact, ruled only by the norms of empirically adequate reasoning. This claim is hotly disputed, however, particularly when we conceive the broad process of scientific imagination and discovery and look closely at the processes of argument and proof in the community of scientists (Phillips, 1972). Thus, we cannot hastily accept the idea that scientific rationality and everyday reasoning are the same. Moreover, since sociology has as its subject matter the everyday self-interpreted conduct of men, and not an external nature that is indifferent to scientific formulations of it, we may find that we have to treat sociological reasoning as yet another practice of rationality. If we are not aware of these differences, we simply conspire with the most general process of rationalization in our lives, namely, that increasing organization and predictability, which Weber himself regarded as the "disenchantment of the world," and the iron cage of bureaucracy. We succumb to the institutions which take the magic out of living, depriving life of its charm and excitement as well as of its ordinary but manageable muddles.

THE POLITICS OF RATIONAL ACCOUNTS

To this point we have examined the presumptions of rationality in the theories and methods through which sociologists seek to produce scientific knowledge of persons and society. We have tried to show the principal differences between modes of rationality that constitute every-day, common-sense knowledge and sociological knowledge of social action. An educated person must learn to bring together the claims of these two rationalities, so that they do not ignore common-sense in favor of science, or indulge a blind faith in the authority of science, ignoring its working difficulties. The issue here, then, is that of the political accountability to which experts must be held, and to which they should be open in order to preserve a democratic community. In complex societies there is a great need for specialized knowledge; usually this can only be acquired by full-time social scientists. Inevitably, professional scientists want to formulate and apply their knowledge to problems of urban development, race, or family disorders, but in a democracy we are committed to the belief that judgment of human conduct is best regarded as a common affair, as in trial by jury. We surrender to experts and elites only at great risk to the republic.

We can perhaps now bring together our earlier discussion of common-sense knowledge and values to show how they bear upon the politics of defining the situation, the goals and means, in which lay populations come to deal with professional social scientists and social planners (Douglas, 1974). A proper respect for the lay community's sense of reasonableness and responsibility would lead to the following observations:

1. The sociologist must in the first instance study lay versions of social problems and remedies.

2. Lay versions of social problems will be found to be highly problematic.

3. The problematic nature of social problems means that basic conflicts will exist between sociological and lay definitions of social problems.

4. In view of these conflicts inherent in lay definitions of social problems and remedies, the sociologist cannot treat his own objective formulation of problems and remedies as completely free of continued discussion and dispute.

The problematic nature of social problems and their remedies is inherent in common-sense sociability. Thus, we tend to locate troubles and remedies as matters of individual responsibility, although we also hold to the view that sociability itself implicates us in chains of events for which we may be held responsible only in a general way. In America this is especially the case, since American freedoms and civil rights were originally built upon the responsibilities of private ownership and decentralized forms of government. As business and government move into centralized and large-scale corporate organizations, America faces the dual problems of the erosion of lay opinion and common-sense morality while struggling to develop responsible central government and corporate business practice. It is, therefore, presumptuous of social scientists to imagine that they can inhabit the middle ground, and from there, hold the nation together. Yet, there is a serious sense in which this is precisely the challenge of the social sciences, provided it can be taken up with humility and consideration for the differences in communities and persons that still exist despite the massive centralizing forces within American society.

SCIENCE AND PUBLIC KNOWLEDGE

We are faced with the enormous task of finding communicative institutions that can mediate the authority of science and technology. These institutions must be geared to the essentially administrative tasks of the state, as well as the ideals of civic understanding and the consensus that motivates democratic societies. This problem is stated in the sharpest terms by Jürgen Habermas (1970:56):

> But if technology proceeds from science, and I mean the technique of influencing human behavior no less than that of dominating nature, then the assimilation of this technology into the practical life-world, bringing the technical control of particular areas within the reaches of the communication of acting men, really requires scientific reflection. The pre-scientific horizon of experience becomes infantile when it naively incorporates contact with the products of the most intensive rationality.

It should be clear, then, that the preceding argument has not distinguished the methodological standing of common sense and scientific reasoning simply to indulge the "infantile disorder" of left-wing phenomenology. The argument is also intended to contribute radically to the place of common-sense communicative competence in the political processes of modern democracy. This is, however, too large a matter to settle, and for the moment what we wish to show are the general outlines of the problem, which we think underlies a shift in perspective that may be addressed as the linguistic turn in the social sciences. This shift represents the combined effect of ordinary language philosophy, particularly after Wittgenstein, phenomenology, hermeneutics and critical theory, especially Habermas's theory of communicative competence (O'Neill, 1976). Leaving aside the intricacies of these developments, what they permit us to do is to formulate the communicative relation between social science and democracy as the proper background for the specific role of sociology's particular ambivalence with regard to the relative claims of scientific and common-sense accounts of persons and society. Within the limits of the present inquiry, we cannot do more than indicate the general features of the communicative approach to political resources and locate the problem of fostering mediating institutions of public discussion called for by the relativization of common-sense and scientific knowledge of social structure and social change:

> Such communication must therefore necessarily be rooted in social interests and in the value-orientations of a given social life-world. In both directions the feedback-monitored communication process is grounded in what Dewey called "value beliefs." That is, it is based on a *historically determined preunderstanding*, governed by social norms, of what is practically necessary in a concrete situation. This preunderstanding is a consciousness that can only be *enlightened hermeneutically*, through articulation in the discourse of citizens in a community. . . .
> Weber's thesis of the neutrality of the sciences with regard to preexisting practical valuations can be convincingly employed against illusionary rationalizations of political problems, against *short-circuiting* the connection between technical expertise and a public that can be influenced by manipulation, and against the distorted response which scientific information meets with in a deformed public realm (Habermas, 1976:69–70).

THE COMMUNICATIVE MODEL OF DEMOCRACY

Without underestimating the complexity of social and political decision making—any more than it should be pessimistically overestimated—we may formulate the problem of the relationship between science and democracy as a communicative task addressed to the mobilization of members' commitment to the goals and institutionalized allocations of scientific and technical resources employed to translate social goals into daily conveniences, rewards, and deterrents. Thus, the legitimacy of a democratic political system consists of the processes that lead to the achievement of the following descriptive states:

1. Its members have access to the information channels whereby social goals are articulated.

2. In varying degrees, its members are aware of and feel entitled to exercise their rights in the translation of subjective needs into specific and local allocations of resources.

3. Its members' troubles with the determinate processes of resource allocation establish prima-facie claims for reforms at level 2 or change of social goals at level 1.

The interrelationship, or loop effect, between these three processes represents the democratic legitimation process as the constitution of a communicative community, in which the channels between scientists and politicians are opened to responses and reformulations directed through the channels of public opinion (O'Neill, 1977).

The validity of a democratic political system rests in the reference of its goals and resource allocations to parliamentary and electoral ratification, which brings political decisions within the social contract. Characteristically, the processes of political legitimation in capitalistic society involve public debate, public information, news media, journalism, and the institutions of public education. These institutions are conceived mostly to reinforce the belief that political life can be exemplary of rational and just conduct, at the same time that the polity accommodates the sheer necessities and incommodities of economic and social life.

The processes of legitimation and delegitimation, however, assume particular features in the present context of state-administered capitalism (Habermas, 1975). In this situation the legitimation process becomes an intrinsic function of political economy and not an epiphenomenal exercise, as Marxists might argue. A large part of the present capitalist economy consists in the activity of state enterprises that do not merely complement or correct the private-market system but which largely determine the parameters of economic activity. Therefore, an essential task of the legitimation process is to secure allegiance to the new schedule of public and private production. A second major feature of this process is the political socialization of large numbers of persons who enjoy goods and services without direct employment in either sector of the economy. In short, employment in the public sector and consumption of health, education, and welfare from that sector without corresponding inputs defines a large population whose loyalty to the political system cannot be identified in terms of previous class and motivational attitudes.

Under these conditions the legitimation problem in which the social sciences are involved acquires the following distinct features:

1. The market system can no longer be legitimated in terms of its power to mobilize the bourgeois ideology of private exchange.

2. The central administrative role of the state in the economy must be legitimated.

3. The administrative role of the state must be maintained independently of the mechanisms of formal participation in democratic politics.

4. The legitimation process requires the mobilization of diffuse mass loyalty without direct participation.

5. The depoliticization of the public realm requires (a) civic privatism, i.e., the pursuit of consumption, leisure, and careers in exchange for political abstinence; (b) the ideological justification of public depoliticization by means of elitist theories of the democratic process or by technocratic and professionalized accounting practices that rationalize administrative power (Habermas, 1975).

The social sciences are engaged at all levels in the administration of the large institutions of industrial democracies. Numerous commentators have drawn attention to the consequent problems of trust and accountability involved in the practice of sociology. Sociologists, like everyone else, have a self-image: they see themselves as inheritors of the Enlightenment legacy of liberal rationalism; they challenge the authority of high places, and the ignorance of the lowly, in order to bring us all into the republic of knowledge and freedom. Sociologists like to think of themselves as a free-floating, intellectual elite, working on behalf of a demystified society in which human energies are committed to reaching their fullest potential. Sociologists claim to challenge the system, to question authority and convention. They are the friends of the poor, the exploited, and of all who suffer social injustice. Yet sociologists, for the most part, live middle-class lives and are dependent upon establishment institutions for their employment and also for the huge sums of money required to conduct their research. These requirements, in fact, penetrate to the very core of the ways in which sociologists *do* sociology. The administrative demands, then, of the social sciences impose the following conditions upon the formulation of sociological knowledge:

1. The rationalization of the administered society requires that scientific discourse be problem-specific and subject to decision making.

2. The very nature of the language and reportage of the social sciences contributes to the administrative effort to manage behavior and institutions according to maximum efficiency standards.

3. The ability of the administered society to command allegiance in exchange for goods and services reduces political participation to the demand for information and to the residual right to withdraw loyalty in elections.

4. The combined effects of these processes (1–3) on the communicative competence of citizens is that discourse about the ideal values of political, economic, and social life is seen as irrelevant to the management of modern states.

To many critics the jargon of the social sciences is a laughable matter. To others, who also recognize it as the pretension of an immature science, there is the more sober conviction that as the social sciences achieve political recognition, their rhetoric will grow more modest:

> The maturity of a science may be measured not only by its power, but by its discrimination in knowing the limits of its power. And if this is so, the layman does not need to worry lest the social sciences, as they become more scientific, will be more likely to usurp political authority. On the contrary, they will stop short of trying to solve completely our major political problems not because they are unlike the natural sciences, but to the extent that they are like them. And the more they get to be like them, the more they will be of a specific service to the policy maker, and the less they will pretend that their methods can measure all relevant aspects of any concrete problem and supply its final answer (Price, 1965:133).

THE LIMITS OF SOCIOLOGICAL KNOWLEDGE

We cannot be sure, however, that the limits of science will be remembered by sociologists as they get closer to the centers of political power. It is likely, too, that politicians will find the rhetoric of a pseudoscientific sociology more congenial than the rigorous language of science. It is, therefore, incumbent upon sociologists to monitor their own rhetoric, to keep what is properly sociological in their speech along with the broader understandings and values of the democratic society to which they owe their existence. Sociologists must strive to increase human understanding and self-control, not for the purpose of making a small part of the earth or one class of persons more precious than others, but in order to mine the inexhaustible resources of humanity. In this task sociology must try to build up sure knowledge that is free from prejudice and jargon. Still, it cannot blindly pursue science's dominion over nature. Sociology has no external referent; it is only another way of addressing people, who do not wait on science, still less on sociology, for their living. Nor are they likely to set aside everything they have found valuable in the plain course of living in favor of a partial speech and minor knowledge. To remember this subjects sociology to a pedagogical rule of limit and dialogue. Sociology should not aspire to domination, or technical control over humans, because the human collectivity is properly motivated only through a consensus of unarticulated affinities and shared deliberations. Such a collectivity does not destructively deny its past ways, nor is it blind to the present, but it does distrust manipulation and is wary of those without local allegiances or any limits.

People are more likely to welcome sociology if it avoids criticizing others as a means of placing itself above others. And perhaps because sociology lacks the elitist tradition of humanist culture and the power and authority of the physical sciences, it may well prove to have an average self-consciousness that resists splitting humans into either scientists or laymen. Ideally, sociology should be a popular science. It may be subverted by its own professional concerns, but this makes sociology no worse than any of the sciences that claim to serve humans. The roots of sociology's problems lie in political economy. We cannot extrapolate the benefits of science, industry, and education from the system of political economy, class, and international stratification in which they are embedded. It is quite easy to devise scientific utopias that are unrelated to the harsh world of political economy. Occasionally, sociology has appeared capable of providing a neutral administrative science of human organization that could cut across these problems, but sociology has had to learn that it cannot work upon society's problems without being part of society—and that this involves the risk of being absorbed into the goods and evils of the very society it seeks to remedy.

NOTE

1. "In exactly the way that persons are members to organized affairs, they are engaged in serious and practical work of detecting, demonstrating, persuading through displays in the ordinary occasions of their interactions the appearances of consistent, coherent, clear, chosen, planful arrangements. In exactly the ways a setting is organized, it *consists* of methods whereby its members are provided with *accounts* of the setting as countable, storyable, proverbial, comparable, picturable, representable—i.e., *accountable events*" (Garfinkel, 1967:34).

REFERENCES

DOUGLAS, JACK D.
　1974 Defining America's Problems. Englewood Cliffs, N.J.: Prentice-Hall.
GARFINKEL, HAROLD
　1967 Studies in Ethnomethodology. Englewood Cliffs, N.J.: Prentice-Hall.
HABERMAS, JÜRGEN
　1970 Toward a Rational Society, Student Protest, Science and Politics. Translated by Jeremy J. Shapiro. Boston: Beacon Press.
　1975 Legitimation Crisis. Translated by Thomas McCarthy. Boston: Beacon Press.
O'NEILL, JOHN
　1974 "Le langage et la decolonisation: Fanon et Freire." Sociologie et Societies 2 (November):53–65.

1976   On Critical Theory. Edited by John O'Neill. New York: Seabury Press.
1977   "Language and the legitimation problem," Sociology 11 (May):351–358.

PHILLIPS, DEREK L.
1972   Wittgenstein and Scientific Method, A Sociological Perspective. Totowa, N.J.: Rowman and Littlefield.

PRICE, DON K.
1965   "The established dissenters." In Science and Culture, A Study of Cohesive and Disjunctive Forces. Edited by Gerald Holton. Boston: Houghton Mifflin.

SCHUTZ, ALFRED
1964   "The problem of rationality in the social world." In Collected Papers, II, Studies in Social Theory. Edited and introduced by Arvid Brodersen. The Hague: Martinus Nijhoff.

WEBER, MAX
1946   "Science as a vocation," In From Max Weber: Essays in Sociology. Translated and edited by H. H. Gerth and C. Wright Mills. New York: Oxford University Press.

4. Ethnomethodology

DON H. ZIMMERMAN

Ethnomethodology, like sociology itself, encompasses a number of more or less distinct and sometimes incompatible lines of inquiry. The term is often applied to the work of persons who, if consulted on the matter, might choose other designations, e.g., phenomenological sociology or conversation analysis. Unfortunately, few commentators seem to appreciate the increasing diversity among ethnomethodologists, with respect to choice of both problem and method (Mehan and Wood, 1976).

Garfinkel (1974:18) asserts that the term has become a shibboleth, and elsewhere (Hinkle, *et al.*, 1977:9-17) intimates that attempts to clarify the "program" and define the boundaries of ethnomethodology have deflected attention from serious research. While it is difficult to contest the importance of doing research rather than talking about it,[1] there is nevertheless the problem of providing access to the area for those interested in it. Moreover, since ethnomethodology has been the target of a number of critiques (cf. Armstrong, 1977) that may be more familiar than the primary literature in the area, passing attention to certain of these criticisms is necessary in order to furnish a more reliable guide to understanding and appraising ethnomethodological inquiry.

The aim of this paper, therefore, is not to define ethnomethodology, or to provide an authoritative reply to its critics. Instead, this brief essay will attempt to make certain strands of ethnomethodological thought intelligible to a general audience, thereby perhaps, to open this growing

SOURCE: Reprinted from *The American Sociologist* 13 (February 1978):6-15.

tradition to those who are interested and who may find it useful in their own work. Discussion will focus, in turn, on phenomenological sociology, the issue of reductionism, the concept of "natural language," the relationship between context and particular in ethnomethodological work, and, in conclusion, on the relationship between ethnomethodology and other concerns in sociology.

PHENOMENOLOGICAL SOCIOLOGY: INTELLECTUAL HERITAGE AND INTELLECTUAL CONTENT

Critics frequently assume that ethnomethodology is a phenomenological sociology. This often leads to critiques of phenomenology rather than critiques of ethnomethodology, and thus to obfuscation of more pertinent issues. Critical surveys such as Attewell (1974), Goldthorpe (1973), and Mayrl (1973), all proceed on the assumption that ethnomethodology is a phenomenological sociology. Mayrl (1973:15) flatly asserts that "ethnomethodology represents an attempt to develop a systematic program of research based upon phenomenological premises." He writes:

> [Ethnomethodology's] theoretical thrust is entirely consistent with Schutz's postulate of subjective interpretation and its use of meaning in no way contradicts the concept of that phenomenon as a quality of individual subjectivity . . . their methodological stance leads quite logically to idealism and ultimately solipsism . . ." [2] (p. 27).

The work of phenomenologists, and in particular that of Schutz (1962, 1964, 1966, 1967, 1970a, 1970b), has indeed figured prominently in the development of ethnomethodology. However, Giddens (1976a), in discussing critics of Durkheim, makes a relevant and very important point:

> We may, and ordinarily must, distinguish between the intellectual antecedents of a man's thought, the tradition he draws upon in framing his views, and the intellectual *content* of his work, what he makes of the ideas he takes from the tradition (pp. 710–711).

In the present context, the question is: What has happened to phenomenological ideas in the transformation from Schutz to Garfinkel, Sacks, and other ethnomethodologists?

First of all, there are many enterprises that could be called phenomenological in some sense of the word, such as Weber's emphasis on the importance of the meaning of behavior to the actor. Others claim to use a phenomenological method, and of these, some—as shown by Heap and Roth (1973) (but see also Wieder in Hinkle *et al.*, 1977:105)—are misguided or naive. Others are more sophisticated; for example, the work of Bittner (1973) and Wieder (1974, 1977). Work in this last vein might properly be called "phenomenological sociology," for it proceeds from a thorough grasp of technical phenomenology and seeks to develop an approach to studying society that is informed by phenomenological concepts and methods. Wieder (Hinkle *et al.*, 1977:4–5) argues, for example, that:

> The import of the phenomenological method . . . is to give direct access to the world of immediate experience in terms of intending (the acts of consciousness) and the objects intended . . . through these acts. As I see it, it would be the task of a phenomenological sociology to describe and explicate such intended objects as the . . . experience ordinarily referred to by way of the concepts social role, norm, institution, cultural object, the other person, motives, language, and the like. Furthermore, such a discipline would describe that which is distinctive about the intentional acts which present these objects to consciousness.

While ethnomethodology might be called "phenomenological" in the weak sense that the work of Schutz and other phenomenologists was a significant antecedent (cf. Heap and Roth, 1973), and while some ethnomethodologists may find the writings of phenomenologists relevant to their work, treating ethnomethodology as a whole as a phenomenological sociology risks a number of errors, among them the assumption that ethnomethodology necessarily employs phenomenological methods, or that its varieties are united, as Coser (1975:698) put it, by a "celebration . . . of the transcendental ego." (It should be noted that the latter characterization does not even pertain to phenomenological sociology.)

One particularly grotesque consequence of viewing ethnomethodology in this way is the treatment accorded the work of Sacks and his associates. Their work, while heavily influenced by Garfinkel, bears the mark of linguistic and anthropological thinkers (for example, Chomsky, 1959, 1965; Goodenough, 1965) and linguistic philosophers (such as the later Wittgenstein, 1953; Austin, 1961, 1965) rather than specifically phenomenological sources. For example, Attewell (1974) tells us that Sacks' enterprise involves recourse to the realm of the "transcendental ego"; according to Mayrl (1973), Sacks was engaged in furnishing an "eidetic description of eidetic description," whatever that is supposed to mean. Even a casual reading of Sacks' work would dispel such claims.

In the development of ethnomethodology, ideas originally inspired by deep familiarity with the work of Schutz and others have undergone major changes, e.g., Garfinkel's (1967:262-283) transformation of Schutz' (1964) analysis of rationality into an empirical sociological problem. His appropriation of Schutz' (1964:3-96; 207-259) description of the "natural attitude" for the study of common sense understanding of social action (1967:35-75) might also be noted. Strictly speaking, the term "phenomenological" is inappropriate as a blanket characterization of the working tools, methods and problems of ethnomethodology, if for no other reason than that it blurs the distinction between intellectual heritage and intellectual content.

REDUCTIONISM

A critic might argue that even allowing some degree of "discontinuity" with the phenomenological tradition, and granting the distinctions between various phenomenological sociologies or among ethnomethodologists, ethnomethodology nevertheless remains, in general, a form of subjectivism in social science, and can be read as denying the possibility of a science of society. This is so, the argument might go, because ethnomethodology denies that social facts are exterior and constraining, or alternately, that society as an objective entity conditions social life at the everyday level; hence, individual members of society, operating in a context of few if any constraints, simply decide how the world should be as a matter of mere preference. Moreover, since ethnomethodology treats "meanings" as indexical rather than transituationally stable, as implied in the notion of "cognitive consensus" (cf. Wilson, 1970; Parsons, 1951), it denies the intersubjective character of culture, and is reduced to cataloguing particular meanings on an ad hoc basis, a phenomenologically inspired but sociologically aimless empiricism.

This characterization of ethnomethodology is an example of the old controversy between "holism" and "individualism" in history and social science, used here in the sense of the opposition between "society" and "individual." Even if it is conceded that ethnomethodology is not concerned with the constitution of the social world in the individual consciousness, it could still be charged that "society," i.e., the institutional order, is being reduced to the various understandings, perceptions, beliefs, lay-theories, attitudes and the like employed or invoked on concrete occasions by individual members of society. That is, society is "reduced" to a "mind-originated" and "mind-dependent" phenomenon, as, for example, in the case of dreams (Jarvie, 1972:153–154). From this perspective, ethnomethodology is either a form of radical subjectivism or, what is little better, a species of psychologism. In fact it is neither, as the following considerations suggest.

How are such objects as "individuals" referred to in the context of ethnomethodological writings? In some cases they are called "actors," but the more theoretically relevant term is "member-of-society" or simply "member." The term "member" has shifted in meaning over time. The earlier more Parsonian usage took the form of "collectivity member" (cf. Garfinkel, 1967:76; Parsons, 1951:41–98). More recently the notion refers not to persons as such but to "mastery of the natural language" (Garfinkel and Sacks, 1970:342). "Natural language" should not be construed in a narrow sense, e.g., as the syntax and semantics of, say, a specific language; rather, the notion refers to a system of practices

> that permit speakers and auditors to hear, and in other ways to witness, the objective production and objective display of common sense knowledge, and of practical circumstances, practical actions and practical sociological reasoning . . . (Garfinkel and Sacks, 1970:342).

For present purposes, what is important about these two ways of regarding individuals—the first in terms of obligations and constraints imposed by collectivity membership, the second in terms of constraints imposed on speaker-hearers by the properties and practices of natural language—is that reference to an individual necessarily implies a supra-individual system, a form or forms of social organization in terms of which the notion "individual" becomes intelligible. Such a system is clearly *inter*subjective. It involves shared skills or procedures by which particular events are organized into instances of an external social order. In this sense, "members" (or alternatively, speaker-hearers) are *agents* of the system in question. That is, the activities of individuals are of interest only insofar as their activities exhibit the workings of the system. In this restricted sense Giddens (1976b:5) is correct when he proposes that ethnomethodology places

> *the notion of agency* once more in the forefront of sociological theory . . . the thesis that human society as produced by human individuals is a creative and skilled production, that the sustaining of even the most trivial kind of encounter between individuals . . . is a creative phenomenon of the same order as the speaking of a language is a creative phenomenon.

The notion of "creativity" should not, however, be confused with free will or like notions which imply that persons "freely" create—out of the whole cloth—the society that encompasses them. Instead, this is creativity in Chomsky's (1959) sense, when he speaks of the creative character of linguistic competence, i.e., the ability of speaker-hearers to produce and recognize an indefinitely large number of novel sentences through the use of a finite set of elements and rules for their combinations. Creativity, however, is both possible and occurs within the context of the constraints such rules provide. To adopt such a view of "agency" and of "creativity" does not deny the consciousness of the individual, or transform the person into a mere automaton, but instead *specifies* a particular kind of interest in the activities, capacities, and perceptions that characterize individuals.

Mandelbaum (1959) has suggested a criterion of irreducibility, i.e., a means of testing the claim of methodological individualism that all societal level concepts can be translated into concepts referring to the properties of individuals. Mandelbaum's criterion asks whether or not

> . . . those concepts which are used to refer to the forms of organiza-
> tion of a society [can] be reduced without remainder to concepts
> which only refer to the thoughts and actions of specific individuals
> (p. 479).

It is Mandelbaum's view that many forms of behavior in society cannot be reduced to the properties of individuals "without remainder," i.e., without presupposing or making reference to an institutional order in terms of which the meaning of the behavior is defined. For example, the concept of "natural language" cannot be reduced to individual terms "without remainder," any more than the more restricted term "English language" could be so reduced. "Natural language" is, in some sense, a societal level concept, or at least a supra-individual notion. An often neglected implication of Mandelbaum's argument is that in many respects the properties of "individuals" themselves are not readily defined wtihout reference to societal or supra-individual notions. For example, how can reference be made to an individual's "thoughts" without presupposing some language in which thoughts are thought— or at least expressed. In any event, it does not follow that by rejecting an absolute transcendance of "society" over "individual" ethnomethodology necessarily embraces a radical subjectivism—any more than having phenomenological antecedents necessarily entails a phenomenological commitment.

Natural Language

It was suggested earlier that "natural language" is not defined by reference to linguistic categories such as syntax and semantics, although those aspects of language structure are potentially relevant to any research into the properties of "natural language." However, linguistic units such as "sentence," when studied in isolation from their pragmatic contexts, suppress what is of prime interest here: the use of natural language expressions in interactive situations. Indeed, an actual utterance cannot properly be viewed only as a more or less flawed production by a speaker employing his or her grasp of the rules of sentence construction. Instead it must be seen as an *interactional object*, subject not only to syntactic and semantic constraints in the narrow sense, but also to the properties of speaker-hearer interaction (cf. Goodwin, 1975) and, among other things, to the constraint of turn-taking and to repair-systems for conversation interaction as formulated by Sacks, Schegloff and Jefferson (1974). Giddens (1976b), a non-ethnomethodologist, suggests that ethnomethodology has called attention to

> the significance of language as a medium of practical activity . . . [This notion] deviates rather basically from the [idea of] the language as a series of signs or symbols. . . . The significance of [this] new view of language is that language is a practical medium of the accomplishment of practical social tasks, that is, that language is a mode of doing things (p. 6).

Ethnomethodology is not, of course, unique in the view that "language is a mode of doing things" (cf. Wittgenstein, 1953; Austin, 1961, 1965). Sociolinguistics, and in particular, the approach called the "ethnography of speaking" (see, for example, Bauman and Sherzer, 1975; Gumperz and Hymes, 1964; Hymes, 1962, 1974; Philips, 1976), share with ethnomethodology a concern with language-in-use as a social and interactional object to be observed *in situ* and described in its own right rather than merely as a resource for studying social life. Natural language is, in this view, basically social. Ethnomethodology differs from other approaches to language in society in the conception of natural language as a system which is (1) prior to and independent of any particular speaker, that is, external, and (2) less preferential than obligatory, that is, constraining. As a system, natural language exhibits the properties of the Durkheimian social fact, although such properties are themselves the accomplishment of members using the system on actual occasions of interaction. Moreover, in contrast to the emphasis on social variation characteristic of the ethnography of speaking (e.g., Bauman and Sherzer, 1975; Hymes, 1974; Philips, 1976), natural language is considered to be a widespread general and abstract system which operates on any local context to order the particulars of talk and action into patterns which reflect both the "immediate" social reality and a "transcendent" social reality beyond that local context (Zimmerman and Pollner, 1970).

In particular, the study of "natural language" involves the systematics of producing utterances, expressions, gestures, and so forth, which (a) achieve a particular meaning or delineated range of alternative meanings in some local environment; (b) contribute to, establish, negotiate or expose a "definition or definitions of the situation"; or (c) express and warrant assertions or statements concerning one's or the other's "state of mind," "motive," "feeling," what's right or what's wrong with the world, and so on. These are seen as situated accomplishments of the use of "natural lanauge" (cf. Garfinkel and Sacks, 1970) and are of interest only insofar as they lead to a fuller understanding of how the system which produced them works. Of course, a focus on the properties of "natural language" does not entail limiting inquiry to what members "know explicitly" about their own activities and the conditions of their interaction, any more than the linguist's informant can produce a linguistically acceptable grammar of his or her language.

CONTEXTS AND PARTICULARS

Another important issue must be addressed: ethnomethodology's insistence on the "situated," "contextual," or "embedded" character of social activity—including within the domain of the latter term the activity of describing social activity. Ethnomethodology proposes that the properties of social life which seem objective, factual, and transituational, are actually managed accomplishments or achievements of local processes. Some critics (cf. Coser, 1975) apparently consider this sufficient to claim that ethnomethodology is primarily concerned with a theoretical description of particular meanings, and that it eschews—or even denies the possibility of—generalizing beyond such narrow and particular events. Doubtless, persons calling themselves ethnomethodologists could be found who take such a view. Nevertheless, a generalizing intent lies behind the ethnomethodological concern for the particular-in-context. Ethnomethodology studies on-going social activity in order to discover the properties of the social organization of natural language which provide for the accomplishment of definite meanings, convergent definitions, warranted accounts, all in the lively context of their occurrence. Obviously, to extract an event such as a member's statement from the locally organized context in which it occurs, without knowledge of the principles of that local organization, runs the risk of fundamentally distorting the information carefully garnered through coding procedures or other research tools.

An example modeled after Cicourel (1973:11-41) may serve to illustrate these remarks in a limited way. Sociologists employ the concepts of status and role to refer to more or less institutionalized patterns· of conduct. As Cicourel (1973:11-24) observes, a distinction is often made between these concepts, status being considered the more institutionalized of the two. Simply stated, however, status and role entail rules of conduct which define appropriate conduct in specified situations; they are independent of particular incumbents; and, to the extent that they are deemed effective guides for conduct, they are coercive. Roles must be brought to bear in actual situations, i.e., they must enter in some way into the activity of persons subject to them. The general pattern of action indicated by the role must be employed by an actor in some setting: it must be fitted to the setting, called into play at the appropriate time, interpreted in light of past and present events and the reactions of other participants, and so forth. Role, of course, is not only a prescription for conduct; it is also a scheme of interpretaton. Our own and others' activities are recognized, evaluated, praised and criticized in terms of roles. Moreover, social actors are subject to a multiplicity of role demands, and hence, must be thought of as entering into a sequence of roles, presumably organized in terms of particular local settings.

It would surely be odd if a society were designed so that its institutions were partly constructed of role-relationships, but lacked any systematic mechanism for articulating societal roles within the features of various interactional settings (cf. Cicourel, 1973:33-39; Wieder, 1974; Sacks *et al.*, 1974; West and Zimmerman, 1977; Zimmerman and West, 1975, 1977). It would be stranger still if this articulation were itself not socially organized. Strangest of all would be a state of affairs in which the instantiation of a role in an actual situation had no bearing on the understanding of roles in general, or the sense of "objectivity" and transcendence of the role. Ethnomethodology posits a reflexive or, perhaps, a dialectical relationship. A widespread, abstract, and general form of social organization—the constituent practices of "natural language" (Garfinkel and Sacks, 1970)—is available as a resource for the accomplishment of society *and* biography in local contexts; individuals ("members"), as agents of this massive, socially organized system, do employ those resources; and the activities summarized here are public, observable, controllable events which require no empirically uncontrolled reference to "mind" nor any special modes of access to the private or subjective.

CONCLUDING REMARKS

In this paper I have outlined a particular way of understanding certain aspects of ethnomethodology, which other ethnomethodologists may not share. The requirement of brevity, moreover, brings with it an inevitable sketchiness that can also mean distortion. Yet, my aim is not to preserve the purity of the enterprise, and with it, the choosing up of sides. Just as ethnomethodology has used phenomenological writings without necessarily committing itself to the intellectual problems and disciplinary constraints of phenomenology, so too the work of ethnomethodology could be used by other approaches without limiting them to its particulars. As Garfinkel has suggested (Hinkle, *et al.*, 1977:10–13) there is an important difference between the pursuit of problems within a tradition of thought (where the problems will have their own, distinct, local complexion), and the use of a tradition to reflect upon, speculate about, and imaginatively play with research issues that have an altogether different frame and countenance. This is not a license for the wholesale distortion of any body of work. The pertinent distinction is between scholarly accuracy in dealing with ideas in their intellectual context and insistence on doctrinal purity. The former may be applauded, the latter can be done without.

Which brings me to my last point. Ethnomethodology is not a comprehensive theory of society as the latter term is understood. It is an approach to the study of the fundamental bases of social order. That is, ethnomethodology is concerned with those structures of social interaction which would be invariant to the revolutionary transformation of a society's institutions. Thus, it has not directly concerned itself with such issues as power, the distribution of resources in society, or the historical shape of institutions. Nevertheless, the possible interchange between ethnomethodology and more "macrosociological" concerns is being explored more and more (cf. Chua, 1977; Collins, 1975; Mehan and Wood, 1975: 205–224; Molotch and Lester, 1974; Smith, 1974a, 1974b, 1975; West and Zimmerman, 1977; Zimmerman and West, 1975, 1977). Whether or not cross-fertilization is possible between, for example, recent Marxist approaches to sociology (cf. Appelbaum, in press, and in this book) and ethnomethodology is an open question, and an intriguing possibility.

NOTES

Revised version of a paper presented at the 1976 Pacific Sociological Association Annual Meeting, San Diego. I would like to thank Douglas Maynard, Candace West, Thomas P. Wilson and four anonymous readers for their many helpful comments and suggestions.

1. Whether or not the energies of ethnomethodologists have been largely devoted to programmatic statements is open to question. While Garfinkel's (1967) classic statement contains definite programmatic elements, *Studies in Ethnomethodology* is a collection of empirical studies over the course of which Garfinkel developed his conception of ethnomethodology. Sacks (1963) published only one frankly programmatic statement. There are, of course, publications which can be viewed in this way, e.g., Zimmerman and Pollner (1970) or even Cicourel (1964). There is at the present time one book which might be viewed as a text (Mehan and Wood, 1975). While other empirical and theoretical works may contain programmatic remarks, it seems evident that the bulk of published work by persons who could be identified as ethnomethodologists of one stripe or another (as opposed to commentaries on ethnomethodology provided largely by critics) consist of actual empirical research (e.g., Bittner, 1967a, 1967b; Cicourel, 1968, 1973; Cicourel *et al.*, 1974; Emerson and Pollner, 1976, in press; Jefferson, 1972, 1973; Jefferson and Schenkein, 1977; Garfinkel and Sacks, 1970; McHugh, 1968; Pollner, 1974, 1975, in press; Schegloff, 1968; Schegloff and Sacks, 1973; Sacks, 1972a, 1972b, 1972c, 1973, 1974, 1975; Sacks, Schegloff and Jefferson, 1974; Sudnow, 1965, 1969, 1972; Wieder, 1970, 1974; Zimmerman, 1969, 1970a, 1970b; Zimmerman and Wieder, in press).

2. I do not intend to imply that, if ethnomethodology were phenomenological through and through, these critiques would be correct. It is not clear, for example, that a phenomenological stance leads inevitably to solipsism (cf. Bittner, 1973; Wieder, 1977).

REFERENCES

APPELBAUM, RICHARD
   1978 "Marx's theory of the falling rate of profit: Towards a dialectical analysis of structural social change." American Sociological Review 43:81–93.
ARMSTRONG, EDWARD G.
   1977 "Phenomenologophobia." Paper presented at the Annual Meeting of the American Sociological Association, Chicago.
ATTEWELL, PAUL
   1974 "Ethnomethodology since Garfinkel." Theory and Society 1:179–210.

AUSTIN, J. L.
  1961 Philosophical Papers. J. O. Urmson and G. L. Warnock (eds.). London: Oxford University Press.
  1965 How to Do Things with Words. J. O. Urmson (ed.). London: Oxford University Press.
BAUMAN, RICHARD, and JOEL SHERZER
  1975 "The ethnography of speaking." Pp. 95–119 in B. J. Siegel (ed.), Annual Review of Anthropology, Volume 4. Palo Alto, Calif.: Annual Reviews Inc.
BITTNER, EGON
  1967a "The police on skid row." American Sociological Review 32:699–715.
  1967b "Police apprehension of mentally ill persons." Social Problems 14:278–292.
  1973 "Objectivity and realism." Pp. 109–125 in George Psathas (ed.), Phenomenological Sociology: Issues and Approaches. New York: Wiley.
CHUA, BENG-HUAT
  1977 "Delineating a Marxist interest in ethnomethodology." The American Sociologist 12:24–32.
CHOMSKY, NOAM
  1959 Syntactic Structures. The Hague: Mouton.
  1965 Aspects of the Theory of Syntax. Cambridge: The M.I.T. Press.
CICOUREL, AARON V.
  1964 Method and Measurement in Sociology. New York: The Free Press.
  1968 The Social Organization of Juvenile Justice. New York: Wiley.
  1973 Theory and Method in a Study of Argentine Fertility. New York: Wiley.
  1974 Cognitive Sociology. New York: The Free Press.
CICOUREL, A. V., K. H. JENNINGS, S. H. M. JENNINGS, K. C. W. LEITER, R. MACKAY, H. MEHAN, and D. R. ROTH
  1974 Language Use and School Performance. New York: Academic Press.
COLLINS, RANDALL
  1975 Conflict Sociology: Toward an Explanatory Social Science. New York: Academic Press.
COSER, LEWIS A.
  1975 "Presidential Address: Two methods in search of a substance." American Sociological Review 40:691–700.
EMERSON, ROBERT M., and MELVIN POLLNER
  1976 "Dirty work designations: Their features and consequences in a psychiatric setting." Social Problems 23:243–254.
  In   "Policies and practices of psychiatric case selection." Sociology of Work
  press and Occupations.
GARFINKEL, HAROLD
  1967 Studies in Ethnomethodology. Englewood Cliffs, N.J.: Prentice-Hall.
  1974 "The origins of the term 'ethnomethodology.'" Pp. 15–18 in Roy Turner (ed.), Ethnomethodology. Baltimore: Penguin.

GARFINKEL, HAROLD, and HARVEY SACKS
  1970 "On formal structures of practical actions." Pp. 337–366 in J. C. McKinney and Edward A. Tiryakian (eds.), Theoretical Sociology: Perspectives and Developments. New York: Appleton, Century-Crofts.
GIDDENS, ANTHONY
  1976a "Classical social theory and modern sociology." American Journal of Sociology 81:703–729.
  1976b Address to the American Sociological Association, excerpt in Phenomenological Sociology Newsletter 4:5–8.
GOLDTHORPE, JOHN H.
  1973 "A revolution in sociology?" A review of J. Douglas (ed.), Understanding Everyday Life; and P. Filmer et al. (eds.), "New directions in sociological theory." Sociology 7:449–462.
GOODENOUGH, WARD H.
  1965 "Rethinking 'status' and 'role': Toward a general model of the cultural organization of social relationships." Pp. 1–22 in M. Banton (ed.), The Relevance of Models of Anthropology. London: Tavistock.
GOODWIN, CHARLES
  1975 "The interactive construction of the sentence within the turn at talk in natural conversation." Paper presented at the Annual Meetings of the American Anthropological Association. San Francisco.
GUMPERZ, JOHN J., and DELL HYMES (eds.)
  1964 The Ethnography of Communication. Special Issues of American Anthropologist 66, no. 6, part 2.
HEAP, JAMES L., and PHILLIP A. ROTH
  1973 "On phenomenological sociology." American Sociological Review 38:354–367.
HINKLE, G., H. GARFINKEL, J. HEAP, J. O'NEILL, G. PSATHAS, E. ROSE, E. TIRYAKIAN, D. L. WIEDER and H. WAGNER
  1977 "When is phenomenology sociological?" Pp. 1–39 in Myrtle Korenbaum (ed.), The Annals of Phenomenological Sociology II. Dayton, Ohio: Wright State University.
HYMES, DELL
  1962 "The ethnography of speaking." Pp. 13–53 in T. Gladwin (ed.), Anthropology and Human Behavior. Washington, D.C.: Anthropological Society of Washington.
  1974 Foundations in Sociolinguistics: An Ethnographic Approach. Philadelphia: University of Pennsylvania Press.
JARVIE, I. C.
  1972 Concepts and Society. London: Routledge and Kegan Paul.
JEFFERSON, GAIL
  1972 "Side sequences." Pp. 294–338 in D. Sudnow (ed.), Studies in Social Interaction. New York: The Free Press.
  1973 "A case of precision timing in ordinary conversation: Overlapped tag-positioned address terms in closing sequences." Semiotica 9:47–96.

394   DON H. ZIMMERMAN

JEFFERSON, GAIL, and J. SCHENKEIN
1977 "Some sequential negotiations in conversation: Unexpanded and expanded versions of projected action sequences." Sociology 11:87-103.
MANDELBAUM, MAURICE
1959 "Societal facts." Pp. 476-513 in Patrick Gardiner (ed.), Theories of
History. New York: The Free Press.
MAYRL, WILLIAM W.
1973 "Ethnomethodology: Sociology without society." Catalyst 7:15-28.
McHUGH, PETER
1968 Defining the Situation. Indianapolis: Bobbs-Merrill.
MEHAN, HUGH, and HOUSTON WOOD
1975 The Reality of Ethnomethodology. New York: Wiley Interscience.
1976 "De-secting ethnomethodology." The American Sociologist 11:13-21.
MOLOTCH, HARVEY, and MARILYN LESTER
1974 "News as purposive behavior." American Sociological Review
39:101-112.
PARSONS, TALCOTT
1951 The Social System. Glencoe, Ill.: The Free Press.
PHILIPS, SUSAN U.
1976 "Some sources of cultural variability in the regulation of talk." Language in Society 5:81-95.
POLLNER, MELVIN
1974 "Mundane reasoning." Philosophy of the Social Sciences, 4:35-54.
1975 "The very coinage of your brain: The anatomy of reality disjunction."
Philosophy of the Social Sciences 5:411-430.
In   "Explicative transactions: Making and managing meanings in traffic
press court." To appear in George Psathas (ed.), Studies in Language
Analysis: Ethnomethodological Approaches. New York: Irvington Press.
SACKS, HARVEY
1963 "Sociological description." Berkeley Journal of Sociology 8:1-17.
1972a "On the analyzability of stories by children." Pp. 325-345 in J. Gumperz
and D. Hymes (eds.) Directions in Sociolinguistics. New York: Holt,
Rinehart and Winston.
1972b "An initial investigation of the usability of conversational data for doing
sociology." Pp. 31-63 in David Sudnow (ed.), Studies in Social Interaction. New York: The Free Press.
1972c "Notes on the police assessment of moral character." Pp. 280-293 in
David Sudnow (ed.), Studies in Social Interaction. New York: The Free
Press.
1973 "On some puns with some intimations." Pp. 135-144 in Roger Shuy
(ed.), Monograph #25, Linguistics and Language Science. Washington,
D.C.: Georgetown University Press.
1974 "An analysis of a joke's telling in conversation." Pp. 337-353 in Richard
Bauman and Joel Sherzer (eds.), Explorations in the Ethnography of
Speaking. New York: Cambridge University Press.

1975 "Everybody has to lie." Pp. 57–80 in Mary Sanchez and Ben Blount (eds.), Sociocultural Dimensions of Language Use. New York: Academic Press.

SACKS, H., E. SCHEGLOFF, and G. JEFFERSON

1974 "A simplest systematics for the organization of turn-taking for conversation." Language 50:696–735.

SCHEGLOFF, EMANUEL

1968 "Sequencing in conversational openings." American Anthropologist 70:1075–1095.

SCHEGLOFF, EMANUEL and HARVEY SACKS

1973 "Opening up closings." Semiotica 8:289–327.

SCHUTZ, ALFRED

1962 Collected Papers I: The Problem of Social Reality. The Hague: Martinus Nijhoff.

1964 Collected Papers II: Studies in Social Theory. The Hague: Martinus Nijhoff.

1966 Collected Papers III: Studies in Phenomenological Philosophy. The Hague: Martinus Nijhoff.

1967 The Phenomenology of the Social World. Evanston, Ill.: Northwestern University Press.

1970a On Phenomenology and Social Relations. Chicago: University of Chicago Press.

1970b Reflections on the Problem of Relevance. New Haven: Yale University Press.

SMITH, DOROTHY

1974a "Social construction of documentary reality." Sociological Inquiry 44:257–267.

1974b "The ideological practice of sociology." Catalyst 8:39–54.

1975 "What it might mean to do a Canadian sociology: The everyday world as problematic." Canadian Journal of Sociology 1:363–376.

SUDNOW, DAVID

1965 "Normal crimes." Social Problems 12:255–276.

1969 Passing On. Englewood Cliffs, New Jersey: Prentice-Hall.

1972 "Temporal parameters of interpersonal observation." Pp. 259–279 in David Sudnow (ed.), Studies in Social Interaction. New York: The Free Press.

WEST, CANDACE, and DON H. ZIMMERMAN

1977 "Women's place in everyday talk: Reflections on parent-child interaction." Social Problems 24:521–529.

WIEDER, D. LAWRENCE

1970 "On meaning by rule." Pp. 107–135 in J. Douglas (ed.), Understanding Everyday Life. Chicago: Aldine.

1974 Language and Social Reality. The Hague: Mouton.

1977 "Sociology and the problem of intersubjectivity." Paper presented at the Annual Meetings of the American Sociological Association, Chicago.

WITTGENSTEIN, LUDWIG

1953 Philosophical Investigations. London: Basil Blackwell and Mott.

WILSON, THOMAS P.
  1970 "Conceptions of interaction and forms of sociological explanation."
       American Sociological Review 35:697-710.
ZIMMERMAN, DON H.
  1969 "Tasks and troubles: The practical bases of work activities in a public
       assistance organization." Pp. 237-266 in Donald A. Hansen (ed.), Ex-
       plorations in Sociology and Counseling. Boston: Houghton-Mifflin.
  1970a "Record keeping and the intake process in a public welfare agency." Pp.
       311-354 in Stanton Wheeler (ed.), On Record. New York: Basic Books.
  1970b "The practicalities of rule use." Pp. 221-238 in J. Douglas (ed.), Under-
       standing Everyday Life. Chicago: Aldine.
ZIMMERMAN, DON H., and MELVIN POLLNER
  1970 "The everyday world as a phenomenon." Pp. 80-104 in J. Douglas (ed.),
       Understanding Everyday Life. Chicago: Aldine.
ZIMMERMAN, DON H., and CANDACE WEST
  1975 "Sex roles, interruptions and silences in conversations." Pp. 105-129 in
       B. Thorne and N. Henley (eds.), Language and Sex: Difference and
       Dominance. Rowley, Massachusetts: Newbury House.
  1977 "Doing gender." Paper presented at the Annual Meeting of the American
       Sociological Association, Chicago.
ZIMMERMAN, DON H., and D. LAWRENCE WIEDER
  In   "You can't help but get stoned: Notes on the social organization of
  press marijuana smoking." Social Problems.

PART VII
BIOLOGY AND HUMAN
BEHAVIOR

To this point, this collection of essays has dealt with the question of how to think of human behavior. Here we find what is almost a counter perspective in sociology—the claim that certain elements of human behavior are best understood in terms of biological predispositions. There has been an inordinate amount of resistance to biological explanations of human behavior in the social sciences, partly because the social sciences evolved in opposition to biological reductionism and were founded on the assumption that human beings were best understood socially. There have also been objections to biological explanations as inherently racist and/or sexist, since they preclude the possibility of human change based on education and socialization. The images of the early sociologists such as Ward were such that biological considerations were paid little attention. The articles in this section proceed with caution and note which information from the biological sciences should be considered in developing models and explanations of human behavior.

Feinman describes the main features of biosociology: an evolutionary model coupled with a view that humankind is not completely mutuable and an assumption that some human behavior is best explained genetically. The topics that sociobiologists usually deal with in relating human behavior to studies of animal behavior are fitness, kin selection, and altruism. Feinman examines some of the claims of the new biosociological theories, and finds many of them wanting. He cautions us, however, against rejecting biological explanations out of hand.

Greene, Morgan, and Barash cover wider ground than Feinman does, for their goal is somewhat different. They wish to argue for a synthesis of theories from evolutionary biology and the social sciences. In a concise fashion they deal with concepts central to evolutionary theory and sociobiology such as selection and its types, heritability, heterosis (or heterozygote advantage), genetic drift, kin selection, and altruism. The relevance of these topics to human behavior is explained by an examination of the works of some contemporary sociobiologists. Their caveat is an important one, for they say that "a concern with evolutionary biology does *not* ignore the undoubted role of such environmental factors as early experience, social learning, and/or cultural tradition."

Kemper is clearly aware of the problems involved in applying biological explanations to the study of emotions, and he combines a sociological model with an understanding of biology. In order to study emotions empirically, he proposes a model with two dimensions, consisting of power and status, the differential possession of which is seen as giving rise to such things as guilt, shame, anxiety, depression, and anger. By approaching the study of emotions in this way, he is able to shed light on the psychophysiological controversy as to whether or not emotions have a specific neurochemical basis or whether emotions have a common physiological substrate. He concludes that a sociological analysis supports the specificity theory, and, in a complementary fashion, that the specificity theory supports a psychophysiological argument for the power-status model.

The article by Shott is quite different from Kemper's. She writes of a symbolic-interactionist analysis of emotions. There are, however, good reasons for placing her article in this section. As Kemper's essay makes clear, it is not easy to place emotional behavior. We know that the social world produces emotional responses, but we do not as sociologists always know what to do about biological responses to social behavior. For this reason, it is well to consider Shott's article in conjunction with Kemper's. Shott attempts to call sociologists' attention to the necessity of studying emotional behavior. She systematically discusses how certain concepts, e.g., envy, jealousy, and rage, have been handled while demonstrating that sociologists have something to contribute to the study of emotion, whether one concentrates on biology or sociology.

1. Biosociological Approaches to Social Behavior

SAUL FEINMAN

General theories of behavior are characterized by attempts to answer the following basic question; if an individual is located in an environment with a particular set of physical and social attributes, and is faced with a situation to which he can respond by one of two or more alternative behaviors, which behavioral path will he pursue? The varying answers to this question constitute a wide range of models of behavior. Biosociology is one such general theory.[1] This paper aims to provide a general outline of the basic concepts and hypotheses of this theory, some examples of empirical applications, and an examination of potential value of biosociology to the study of human social behavior and societies.

BASIC PROCESSES IN THE EVOLUTION OF SOCIAL BEHAVIOR

Assume that an individual lives in an environment and is confronted with a situation that requires a behavioral response. Also assume that there are two or more possible responses to that situation, and the individual's choice of response is under obligate or facultative genetic influence. Genetic control of human social behavior is not usually conceived of as being obligate and response specific, but rather, is believed to be facultative and oriented toward general mechanisms for response (Chagnon and Irons, forthcoming). Nevertheless, many biosociological analyses of human social behavior (e.g., Trivers, 1971) conventionally refer to genes for specific behavioral responses. This convention will be accepted here with the understanding that its use is but a convenient shorthand. The issue of the genetics of human social behavior will be considered in a later section of the paper.

Imagine that one behavioral response is more adaptive than the others in this situation. Individuals who have a gene for the more adaptive response will, as a consequence of their action, produce relatively more adult offspring equivalents (West Eberhard, 1975). These are any of an individual's offspring who survive to sexual maturity or the offspring of an individual's relatives who survive to sexual maturity, devalued proportionately by the relatedness of the offspring to the individual. Adaptive behavior is any behavior that increases the relative proportion of adult offspring equivalents produced by an individual. An adaptive behavior may contribute directly to the reproductive or rearing behavior of the actor, or it may affect these behaviors indirectly by aiding in the acquisition of material resources, improvement of physical condition, or development of social skills helpful in mate selection success. According to biosociological theory, if you want to understand a behavior and predict whether it will be perpetuated, you must consider its contribution to reproductive and rearing success.

Some theorists (e.g., Lenski and Lenski, 1978) have suggested that behavior which aids species or population continuance is adaptive. Biosociological theory postulates that adaptation and selection are relevant to the individual rather than to the group or species. While some have favored group-selection approaches (Wynne-Edwards, 1962), most evolutionary biologists and biosociologists do not believe that such selection is significant (G. C. Williams, 1966; Hamilton, 1964; Barash, 1977; Dawkins, 1976).

Although it is acceptable to argue that selection favors individuals whose behavior is fairly adaptive, biosociologists believe the individual acts as if he is a receptacle for genes that provide instructions for his behavior (Cloak, 1975; Dawkins, 1976). As Wilson (1975) has suggested, the organism is the gene's way of producing more genes. Genes that provide for greater reproductive and rearing success of their host organisms produce relatively more identical genes in the future. Since a gene cannot replicate itself without supporting the survival of organisms that harbor it, the distinction between gene selection and individual selection becomes unimportant in many discussions of selection[2] and much biosociological analysis is phrased in the language of individual selection. As long as we remember that the gene is what is being selected, and that gene frequencies in the gene pool evolve, then the use of individual selection language is acceptable.

The process by which some genes and individuals come to be more highly represented through the production of a higher proportion of adult offspring equivalents is known as natural selection. The process is characterized by an interaction between behavioral responses and environmental parameters in which some alleles for behavior, as well as any other traits, come to be more highly represented in future generations. It is crucial that we conceive of the success of a behavior as lying in its contribution to reproductive and rearing effectiveness, specifically. The survival and condition of the organism is not of consequence, except as it influences the production of adult offspring equivalents.

Natural selection consists of two components: individual (personal, classical Darwinian) selection and kin selection. Individual selection is the type of natural selection by which genetic alleles change in frequency in a population owing to the effects on the personal production of adult offspring by the individual itself (West Eberhard, 1975). The outcome of individual selection is the individual fitness of the organism. Individual fitness is defined as the number of adult offspring produced by the organism that survive to maturity. If one individual reproduces while another remains childless, the first will have higher individual fitness. The genes of the first will be more highly selected through the process of individual selection. It is stipulated that fitness be measured in units of adult offspring, because an offspring that dies prior to sexual maturation will not be able to contribute to future genetic representation. High rates of fertility and a high investment in few offspring increase the number of adult offspring produced.

Kin selection refers to the type of natural selection by which genetic alleles change in frequency in a population owing to the effects on the production of adult offspring by relatives of the individual. The outcome of kin selection is the kin component fitness of the individual. If one individual acts so as to help his sister produce offspring and rear them to maturity, he will have a higher kin component fitness than will another individual who does not engage in such facilitative action.[3]

The sum of individual and kin component fitnesses is called inclusive fitness. Inclusive fitness is operationalized in units of adult offspring equivalents. To gain one offspring equivalent, an individual can produce one direct offspring who survives to adulthood, or he can aid his full sibling in producing two offspring. Since one's offspring are related to oneself with a genetic relatedness coefficient of one-half, an offspring equivalent is an individual whose relatedness to oneself is one-half.

Thus, if ego acts so as to enable his mother to produce a child who is ego's full sibling, ego has added one offspring equivalent, since full siblings are related by one-half. This would constitute a gain to his kin component fitness, while production of his own offspring would be a gain to individual fitness. If the individual enabled his sister to produce one offspring, he would gain one-half offspring equivalents in his kin fitness, since one's full sister's offspring are related to oneself by a coefficient of one-fourth.

In sum the ultimate success of a gene for behavior lies in its ability to facilitate the production of more genes of its own type. Such production can either be through the individual directly or through the individual's facilitation of the reproductive and rearing success of his relatives. Thus, an individual who engages in behavior which results in a high number of adult offspring equivalents due to investment in his own offspring and/or those of his relatives, particularly close relatives, will have relatively high inclusive fitness. The adaptiveness of a behavior is judged on the standard of adult offspring equivalent production. Behaviors that result in high adult offspring equivalent production, i.e., high inclusive fitness, will be selected in evolution.

MECHANISMS AND CAUSES OF BEHAVIOR

Orians (1962) distinguished between ultimate and proximate causes of behavior. Proximate causes are those that are more immediate factors responsible for a response (Barash, 1977). Ultimate causation refers to inclusive fitness advantages of behavior which confer selective advantage on a particular proximate cause (Barash, 1977). Biosociologists are most interested in specifying ultimate causation, i.e., the inclusive fitness effects of behavioral variation. The delineation of the immediate causes by which the ultimate advantage is achieved is a secondary goal. This approach has important implications for the type of data that one seeks. While many sociologists immersed in the *verstehen* and symbolic interactionist traditions are likely to take meaning systems as a basic object of study, and are likely to seek explanation of behavior in such subjective understanding, biosociologists usually reject meanings and utterances as ultimate explanations of behavior (Kurland, forthcoming). As is characteristic of many cultural ecologists (Harris, 1977), biosociologists are likely to argue that individuals are often not reliable sources of the ultimate explanations for their own behavior. Rather than search for significant explanations in participants' understandings of their behavior, the biosociologist evaluates the functions for inclusive fitness that the behavior confers in a particular environment.

The view of behavior as being selected for or against on the basis of its contribution to reproductive and rearing success suggests that researchers must be concerned with such consequences of all behavior. The more directly related behavior is to reproduction and rearing, the greater the interest a biosociologist would have in it. The centrality of reproductive and rearing behaviors and the practice of evaluating the inclusive fitness consequences of behaviors are central characteristics of biosociology. Thus, a biosociological analysis of phenomena such as territoriality, mating systems, acquisition and accumulation of wealth, and warfare would aim to describe the inclusive fitness advantages of these behaviors for individuals in particular environments. Other consequences of these same phenomena are of secondary importance.

THE BIOSOCIOLOGICAL MODEL OF MAN

Humans and animals generally are viewed as individuals whose genes are being selected on the basis of inclusive fitness. Some theorists (Barash, 1977; Chagnon and Irons, forthcoming) have suggested what has come to be called the central theorem of biosociology: actors can be seen as behaving as if they are seeking strategies to enhance inclusive fitness. The notion of the individual as a strategist is similar to the exchange theory conceptualization of rational actors. The major difference is that while the reward structure of exchange actors is considered to be variable, biosociological actors are seen as seeking a specific goal: inclusive fitness.

The central theorem may be incomplete and should be modified. If we view all actors as being selfish and strategic, rather than restricting this designation to successful actors, we are likely to seek—and fallaciously find—adaptiveness in all behavior. Chagnon and Irons (forthcoming) use the central theorem conceptualization of actors to argue that the significant question for researchers is to explain variation in behaviors as adaptive responses to variations in the individual's environment. Such an approach ignores the fact that some behaviors are maladaptive or neutral and will not be selected over time. The central theorem should be modified to read: successful actors may be seen as behaving as if they are seeking strategies to enhance inclusive fitness. This modification allows for a judgment of the adaptiveness of each behavior and prevents the automatic perception of adaptiveness in all behaviors.

Thus the biosociological model allows for individuals who are truly altruistic, nonstrategic, and who attempt to maximize rewards other than, and even antagonistic to, inclusive fitness. The model also suggests that these individuals will be selected against, and that these tendencies will not be continued.

In diploid species, such as humans, individuals other than identical twins have a relatedness of no more than one-half (assuming negligible inbreeding). Social life, therefore, is likely to be characterized by conflict among individuals selfishly pursuing their own different genetic interests (Alexander, 1974). Actors are conceived of as truly selfish, although their behaviors may be either selfish or altruistic in appearance, and cooperation among individuals can be considered as one of a variety of selfish strategies. Conflict between individuals, even those of close relatedness, e.g., parent-offspring conflict and sibling rivalry, is a process within which some individuals gain inclusive fitness while others lose.

SOME APPLICATIONS OF BIOSOCIOLOGICAL THEORY: ALTRUISM, TREATMENT OF THE AGED, AND LINEAGE SYSTEMS

Biosociologists define altruism as behavior which confers an individual fitness gain on the recipient and an individual fitness loss on the altruist. Under what conditions would it be advantageous for an individual to be altruistic? If the recipient were a close relative, or if one altruistic act helped many more distant relatives, the loss to the individual fitness of the donor could be compensated by the gain in kin-component fitness. It is the overall fitness effect of the behavior that affects its selection. All other things being equal, we would expect individuals to prefer to be altruistic toward close relatives than toward distant relatives or nonrelatives. There is some support for this idea in the literature (S. Feinman, 1977; Sahlins, 1972; Damas, 1972; Turnbull, 1966), but there is also the finding that some social groups in which individuals share with each other little concern for reciprocity are characterized by low biological relatedness (Sahlins, 1976).

This raises the question of when it is advantageous for individuals to be altruistic toward recipients who are of very low relatedness. Trivers (1971) has suggested that such altruism is selected for when it is reciprocated. Human societies, particularly early hunter-gatherer groups, are seen as possessing conditions that are conducive to such patterns of altruism: long-lived individuals, low population dispersal rates, and weak-to-moderate dominance hierarchies. Under such conditions altruistic acts are most likely to be reciprocated at a later time. If the cost of the altruistic act is relatively low to the donor, and if it has a particularly high benefit to the recipient, such patterns will be further strengthened.

The successful selfish altruist considers not only the relatedness of the recipient to himself and the likelihood of reciprocity when helping nonkin, but also the reproductive value of those kin who are helped. Of what good is it to help a close relative who is not likely to produce many offspring, i.e., who has low reproductive value? While being altruistic to one's elderly mother and one's full sibling are both acts which benefit kin with a relatedness coefficient of one-half to ego, the former act is less likely to be adaptive. An elderly woman is less likely than is a sibling to produce new offspring, i.e., the reproductive value of the sibling is higher. Consequently, the individual would do better to invest altruistically in a full sib, or even in a half-sib, than in an elderly parent.

Such an analysis predicts that individuals will be likely to mistreat old people, particularly in times of resource shortage. Consideration of the notion of reciprocal altruism further suggests that old persons will be treated altruistically when they can confer benefit on the fitness of the altruist by helping him rear his own children or by helping rear his relatives' offspring (S. Feinman, 1977). If old people help in resource gathering or production of material culture, they are more likely to be treated well. Once the old persons are incapable of providing these services, however, or when external conditions make these services too expensive, the aged are likely to be eliminated from the social group. A recent cross-cultural investigation of the role and treatment of old people in nonindustrial society (Glascock and S. L. Feinman, 1978) suggests that many societies do follow these predicted patterns, and that old people are likely to resist their negative treatment. In times of shortage this lack of resistance would benefit the old person's inclusive fitness. A bisociological theory of altruism sees such behavior as selfish. "True" altruism would be selected against, because it would decrease inclusive fitness.

Another example of biosociological application concerns the conditions under which matrilineality—rather than patrilineality—will develop. In both types of lineage systems, mothers invest in their offspring. The key difference lies in the behavior of males. In patrilineal societies males invest primarily in their wives' offspring; in matrilineal societies they invest more in their sisters' offspring, resulting in the social institution of the avunculate. Kurland (forthcoming) has argued that the relative amounts of investment a male will make in his wife's offspring and his sister's offspring depends on his estimate of paternity certainty. If paternity certainty is low (Kurland estimates a threshold of one-third), a male is likely to invest in his sister's children. Even if his sister is only a half-sibling (the coefficient of relatedness $r = \frac{1}{4}$), her offspring will still be related to him ($r = \frac{1}{8}$). If he is not the biological father, his wife's children are not related to him ($r = 0$).[4] But, if paternity certainty is high, the offspring of his full sister are related to him with a lower coefficient (one-fourth) than his wife's offspring (one-half). Kurland presents data which suggest that female promiscuity is higher in matrilineal societies. Female promiscuity decreases paternity certainty. While this hypothesis would be better tested through the use of a systematically selected sample of human societies, the preliminary evidence is reinforcing.

Similar analyses can be made concerning adultery, rape, limitation of offspring, parent-offspring conflict, incest avoidance, and nonkin adoption. At this time little data exist on the fit of human social behavior with biosociological theory. Limited evidence is available concerning food sharing (S. Feinman, 1977), the positive effects of economic success and social status on fitness (Irons, forthcoming/a), the selective defense of close kin during physically aggressive encounters (Chagnon and Bugos, forthcoming), residence choice (Irons, 1975), territorial behavior (Dyson-Hudson and Alden-Smith, 1978), primitive warfare (Durham, 1976a), and the distribution of interpersonal investments (Irons, forthcoming/b). Thus far, virtually all human applications of biosociological theory have been directed to preindustrial societies.

The best analysis of the present confirmation status of biosociological theory has been provided by Barkow (1978) who suggested that the current studies represent the beginning of investigation into this theory and not the final statement of the usefulness of such theory. Any attempt to evaluate the usefulness of biosociological theory at the present time would be premature. At present biosociology basically offers a generation of explanations and predictions, which with appropriate data collection,[5] can be precisely tested. Such theory has been found to be very useful in the understanding of social behavior of other animal species (Wilson, 1975; West Eberhard, 1975; Alexander, 1974; Orians, 1969; Trivers, 1972, 1974). Its usefulness for humans is yet to be adequately considered.

GENETICS, CULTURE, AND LEARNING

Since biological evolution proceeds by the modification of gene frequencies, the applicability of evolutionary theories to human social behavior would appear to depend on the existence of at least some genetic influence. Some theorists have suggested that while much human social behavior is caused by culturally learned instructions, the basis of human plasticity, learning ability, and the capacity for culture and symbol creation is largely genetic (Wilson, 1975; Chagnon and Irons, forthcoming; Durham, 1976b, forthcoming). Others have suggested the more intriguing and controversial idea that in addition to general dispositions for culture and learning, capacities for learning some behaviors more easily than others have evolved for behaviors which are more adaptive (Washburn, Jay, and Lancaster, 1965; Barkow, 1978). While there is little conclusive evidence one way or the other regarding such claims, the fact that culture is a species-level characteristic, coupled with the fact that some behaviors do appear to be easy to acquire and difficult to extin--guish, e.g., group identity and aggression, indicate that these ideas are viable.

Still other thinkers have suggested that culture consists of instructions which direct behavior from without, much as genes instruct from within an organism. Unlike genetic evolution, cultural instructions are conceived of as evolving without necessarily conferring adaptive advantage upon their hosts (Cloak, 1975; B. J. Williams, 1978; Dawkins, 1976). If cultural instructions can "gain fitness" through dissemination to nonbiological relatives of their hosts, cultural evolution can proceed away from or antagonistic to genetic evolution.

On the other hand Durham (1976b, forthcoming) has argued that culturally acquired behaviors are selected for by natural selection. Cultural, as well as genetic, instructions that bestow inclusive fitness advantage upon their hosts are perpetuated. If this is indeed the case, then whether human social behaviors are genetically based—obligately or facultatively—or are culturally acquired has little implication for the applicability of biosociological theory to humans. It would appear, though, that one requirement that must be met in order for Durham's coevolutionary theory to be viable is that the transmission of cultural instructions must proceed along kin-based lines. Otherwise, biosociological predictions that concern preferential selection and aid of biological relatives (nepotism) are not meaningful.

Evidence often does not deny a genetic influence on human social behavior, e.g., infants' responses to strangers (Lewis and Rosenblum, 1974), smiling (Freedman, 1965), incest avoidance (Parker, 1976). But methodological flaws in twin study design (Scarr, 1968; Bronfenbrenner, 1975) and ethical restrictions on experimentation with human subjects[6] have inhibited the development of more definitive evidence.

The long-range solution of this set of issues is the delineation of the genetic and environmental influences on behavior, including the specification of which behaviors, if any, are more or less easily learned

(Barkow, 1978). Empirical investigation of the relative merits and applicability of the coevolutionary model (Durham, 1976b) and the cultural selection—genetic selection antagonism model (Dawkins, 1976; Cloak, 1975) would also contribute to the usefulness of the biosociological theory for human behavior.

Some theorists (Chagnon and Irons, forthcoming; DeVore [in Morris, 1977]) have argued that even if the genetic influence of behavior is found to be very low in humans, biosociological theory would still be relevant. Whatever the merits of this argument, it does suggest an interesting solution. It may be profitable to modify the basic propositions of the theory by adding an "as if" element. Individuals can be postulated to respond *as if* their behavior is genetically based and *as if* they are being selected on the basis of inclusive fitness maximization. Other sociological theories, e.g., social exchange theory and models of social influence, have effectively used "as if" assumptions. It is quite possible that a biosociological theory which predicted behavior *as if* such behavior were genetically controlled would be viable.

IS BIOSOCIOLOGICAL THEORY RELEVANT
TO MODERN SOCIETIES?

It has been suggested that human behavior in industrial societies is better adapted to past environments than to the present (Rossi, 1977; Hamburg, 1968; Tiger & Fox, 1971). Perhaps human cultures have changed faster than human genetics since the Neolithic Revolution, especially since the Industrial Revolution. This may have rendered genetic systems maladaptive in industrial societies. If we want to understand the adaptiveness of a given behavior, perhaps we should evaluate it within the context of the "environment of evolutionary adaptiveness" (Bowlby, 1969)—the hunter-gatherer setting in which early humans evolved.

I would argue that such objections are inappropriate. Researchers often look at behavior and fail to find adaptiveness for it in its current environment. In order to find adaptiveness, they consider it in the context of a past environment in which it could have been better adapted. An alternative approach would be to judge the behavior to be maladaptive and to predict that it is likely to be extinguished in the current environment. As environments change, the nature of adaptive behavior changes, thus modifying the composition of the gene pool and/or the culture pool frequencies for behavior. It is the focus on the adaptiveness of all existing behaviors, and the corresponding lack of focus on the possibility that some current behaviors are maladaptive, that lead to the conclusion that biosociological theory is not appropriate for the analysis of modern social life.

Consider the following examples. Let us assume that in early hominid groups, kin relatedness was high and dispersal rates were low (Hamilton, 1975). If an individual sacrificed his life for the lives of many kinsmen who had high reproductive value, he would benefit his inclusive fitness. A proximate mechanism by which an individual defined persons with whom he frequently associated as kinsmen would lead to such behavior and would be adaptive.

But what would happen if the social environment changed so that groups and relationships became secondary, kin relatedness within groups decreased, and dispersal increased? This set of modifications would seem to characterize the transition from preindustrial to industrial societies. If the individual used this proximate mechanism to define kin in the new environment, he would sacrifice his own individual fitness, but would gain nothing in return in kin component fitness because he would have given up his own life to save nonrelatives. While we can understand modern behavior by means of reference to its adaptiveness in an earlier environment, we can also argue that such behavior is maladaptive to the inclusive fitness of the individual in the current environment. Data indicate that soldiers who commit grenade self-sacrifice, i.e., throw themselves on live grenades in order to save the lives of their unit members, are more likely to have been well integrated into the military group. Soldiers who are newly arrived or just about to leave the group are less likely to sacrifice their own lives (Blake, 1978). If the group members had been relatives of the altruist, he would have lost individual fitness but gained kin component fitness. Since group members in industrial societies are more likely to be nonrelatives, the altruist loses not only individual fitness, but also kin component fitness, and although the response would have been more adaptive in earlier human groups, it must be judged to be maladaptive in its present context.

In sum, the possibility that some behaviors are better adjusted to the Pleistocene era than to our current one should not lead to the conclusion that biosociological theory is less applicable to the present than the past. Such a conclusion occurs only if we assume that because a behavior exists, it must be adaptive. If we assume that some behaviors will be maladaptive or will have no effect, then modern industrial societies certainly can be included in biosociological analysis.[7]

NOTES

The author would like to thank the following people for their valuable comments and suggestions concerning an earlier draft of this paper: David

Barash, Lee Ellis, Susan Feinman, Mark Granovetter, Marshall Jones, Garth Massey, and Allan Mazur.

1. Other terms—sociobiology, biosocial anthropology—also refer to the same common body of theory. While biosociology is often also used to refer to physiological sociology, this paper considers only what may be called the evolutionary sociological part of biosociology. This restriction is not meant to suggest that work in physiological sociology (Barchas, 1976; Mazur, et al., no date) is unimportant.

2. While a gene may be advantaged by sacrificing one host to help others, it is not to its advantage to sacrifice all hosts.

3. One could also help one's brother. In societies in which males are unsure of the paternity of their wives' children, it would be more advantageous for men and women to invest in their sister's rather than their brother's children.

4. More accuracy is achieved by indicating lack of relatedness than by saying that the relatedness of ego to the other person is equal to, or less than, the average relatedness within the group.

5. One problem that exists in testing biosociological theory is the inapplicability of data collected within earlier paradigms. Much new data collection will apparently be required for consideration of biosociological theories.

6. I would not suggest that such ethical restrictions be lifted, even though these restrictions act to limit our understanding of genetic influences on humans.

7. Although the terms "adaptive" and "maladaptive" have been expressed as categorical levels of adaptiveness throughout this article, they are more appropriatly considered as points along a continuum of adaptiveness. The terminology used in this presentation was selected because it appeared to be effective heuristically.

REFERENCES

ALEXANDER, R. D.
1974 "The evolution of social behavior." Annual Review of Ecology and Systematics 5:325-383.
BARASH, D. P.
1977 Sociobiology and Behavior. New York: Elsevier.
BARCHAS, P. R.
1976 "Physiological sociology: Interface of sociological and biological processes." Annual Review of Sociology 2:299-333.
BARKOW, J. H.
1978 "Culture and sociobiology." American Anthropologist 80:5-20.
BLAKE, J. A.
1978 "Altruistic suicide and its relation to career phase of the American combat soldier in Vietnam." Unpublished paper. Virginia Polytechnic Institute and State University.
BOWLBY, J.
1969 Attachment. New York: Basic Books.

BRONFENBREENER, U.
1975 "Is 80% of intelligence genetically determined?" Pp. 91-100 in U. Bronfenbrenner and M. A. Mahoney (eds.), Influences on Human Development, 2nd ed. Hinsdale, Ill.: Dryden.

CHAGNON, N. A., and P. E. BUGOS, JR.
forth "Kin selection and conflict: An analysis of a Yanomamo ax fight." In
com- N. A. Chagnon and W. Irons (eds.), Sociobiology and the Social Sci-
ing ences. Scituate, Mass.: Duxbury.

CHAGNON, N. A., and W. IRONS
forth "Genetic selection and behavioral plasticity." In N. A. Chagnon and
com- W. Irons (eds.), Sociobiology and the Social Sciences. Scituate, Mass.:
ing Duxbury.

CLOAK, F. T., JR.
1975 "Is a cultural ethology possible?" Human Ecology 3:161-182.

DAMAS, D.
1972 "Central Eskimo systems of food sharing." Ethnology 11:220-240.

DAWKINS, R.
1976 The Selfish Gene. New York: Oxford University Press.

DURHAM, W. H.
1976a "Resource competition and human aggression, Part I: A review of primitive war." Quarterly Review of Biology 51:385-415.
1975b "The adaptive significance of cultural behavior." Human Ecology 2:89-121.
forth "Toward a coevolutionary theory of human biology and culture. In
com- N. A. Chagnon and W. Irons (eds.), Sociobiology and the Social Sciences.
ing Scituate, Mass.: Duxbury.

DYSON-HUDSON, R., and E. ALDEN-SMITH
1978 "Human territoriality: An ecological reassessment." American Anthropologist 80:21-41.

FEINMAN, S.
1977 "Food sharing: An evolutionary perspective." Paper presented at the American Sociological Association Meeting, Chicago.

FREEDMAN, D.
1965 "Hereditary control of early social behavior." Pp. 149-159 in B. M. Foss (ed.), Determinants of Infant Behavior, vol. III. London: Methuen.

GLASCOCK, A. P., and S. L. Feinman
1978 "A cross-cultural analysis of the determinants of old age." Paper presented at the American Anthropological Association Meeting, Los Angeles.

HAMBURG, D. A.
1968 "Evolution of emotional response: Evidence from recent research on nonhuman primates." Science and Psychoanalysis 12:39-53.

HAMILTON, W. D.
1964 "The genetical evolution of social behavior, vols. I and II." Journal of Theoretical Biology 7:1-52.

1975   "Innate social aptitudes of man: An approach from evolutionary genetics." Pp. 135-155 in R. Fox (ed.), Biosocial Anthropology. London: Malaby.

HARRIS, M.
1977   Cannibals and Kings: The Origins of Cultures. New York: Random House.

IRONS, W.
1975   "Residence choice and biological fitness." Paper presented at the American Anthropological Association Meeting, San Francisco.
forth   "Economic and reproductive success." In N. A. Chagnon and W.
com-   Irons (eds.), Sociobiology and the Social Sciences. Scituate, Mass.:
ing/a   Duxbury.
forth   "Nepotism and primary social ties." In N. A. Chagnon and
com-   W. Irons (eds.), Sociobiology and the Social Sciences. Scituate, Mass.:
ing/b   Duxbury.

KURLAND, J. A.
forth   "Matrilines: The Primate sisterhood and the human avunculate." In
com-   I. DeVore (ed.), Sociobiology and the Social Sciences. Chicago: Aldine-
ing   Atherton.

LENSKI, G., and J. LENSKI
1978   Human Societies, 3rd ed. New York: McGraw-Hill.

LEWIS, M., and L. A. Rosenblum
1974   "Introduction." Pp. 1-10 in M. Lewis and L. A. Rosenblum (eds.), The Origins of Fear. New York: Wiley.

MAZUR, A., M. FARPEL, J. HELLER, R. LEEN, C. RILEY, and E. ROSA
n.d.   "Physiological aspects of social staring." Unpublished paper. Syracuse University.

MORRIS, S.
1977   "The new science of genetic self-interest." Psychology Today 10 (February):42-51, 84-88.

ORIANS, G. H.
1962   "Natural selection and ecological theory." American Naturalist 96:257-264.
1969   "On the evolution of mating systems in birds and mammals." American Naturalist 103:589-603.

PARKER, S.
1976   "The precultural basis of the incest taboo: Toward a biosocial theory." American Anthropologist 78:285-305.

ROSSI, A. S.
1977   "A biosocial perspective on parenting." Daedalus 106(2):1-31.

SAHLINS, M.
1972   "On the sociology of primitive exchange." Pp. 185-275 in M. Sahlins, Stone Age Economics. Chicago: Aldine.
1976   The Use and Abuse of Biology: An Anthropological Critique of Sociobiology. Ann Arbor: University of Michigan Press.

SCARR, S.
  1968 "Environmental bias in twin studies." Pp. 205-213 in S. G. Vandenberg
        (ed.), Progress in Human Behavior Genetics. Baltimore: Johns Hopkins
        Press.
TIGER, L., and R. FOX
  1971 The Imperial Animal. New York: Holt, Rinehart and Winston.
TRIVERS, R. L.
  1971 "The evolution of reciprocal altruism." Quarterly Review of Biology
        47:35-57.
  1972 "Parental investment and sexual selection." Pp. 136-179 in B. Campbell
        (ed.), Sexual Selection and the Descent of Man, 1871-1971. Chicago:
        Aldine.
  1974 "Parent-offspring conflict." American Zoologist 14:249-264.
TURNBULL, C. M.
  1966 Wayward Servants. London: Eyre & Spottiswoode.
WASHBURN, S. L., P. C. JAY, and B. LANCASTER
  1965 "Field studies of old world monkeys and man." Science 150:1541-1547.
WEST EBERHARD, M. J.
  1975 "The evolution of social behavior by kin selection." Quarterly Review of
        Biology 50:1-33.
WILLIAMS, B. J.
  1978 "Kin selection, fitness, and cultural evolution." Paper presented at the
        American Association for the Advancement of Science Meeting, Wash-
        ington, D.C.
WILLIAMS, G. C.
  1966 Adaptation and Natural Selection: A Critique of Some Recent Evolu-
        tionary Theory. Princeton, N.J.: Princeton University Press.
WILSON, E. O.
  1975 Sociobiology: The New Synthesis. Cambridge, Mass.: Harvard Univer-
        sity Press.
WYNNE-EDWARDS, V. C.
  1962 Animal Dispersion in Relation to Social Behavior. New York: Hafner.

2. Sociobiology

PENELOPE J. GREENE, CHARLES J.
MORGAN, and DAVID P. BARASH

In the beginning, with Comte and Spencer, there was evolutionary thought in sociology, but these early formulations were confused and of limited predictive value. They were selected against. The frequency of evolutionary thought in sociology dropped to mutational equilibrium and often proved to be developmentally lethal. But biology and evolution are again being considered seriously by social scientists (e.g., the collection edited by Fox, 1975; van den Berghe, 1974; Campbell, 1975; and subsequent comments). Advances in evolutionary biology have facilitated this renewed interest. Wilson (1975:547) has suggested that "anthropology and sociology together constitute the sociobiology of a single primate species"; this attempt to treat human social behavior in sociobiological terms has generated considerable controversy (see Wade, 1976, for a review), and the purpose of this article is to outline the relevant sociobiological theory, to review and suggest applications to the study of human social behavior, and, incidentally, to answer some of the objections that are frequently raised.

Having originated in ethology, population genetics, and theoretical ecology, sociobiology is a new discipline that applies evolutionary biology to the analysis of social behavior (Wilson, 1975). Sociobiology sees selection as taking place overwhelmingly at the individual level rather than at the group level (see Maynard Smith, 1976a, for a review). Changes in groups result from changes in individuals. Further, there is no implication that evolutionary change is good. It occurs, rather, because of some situational reproductive advantage: environmental change can alter the direction of evolutionary change. Cooperation and altruism are central to human social behavior, and rather than bemoaning them as factors that slow evolutionary progress (as did the Social Darwinists), sociobiology incorporates them into the framework of a unified theory. Such concepts are explicitly defined in terms of their reproductive consequences, and they make no assumptions about the cognitive or motivational states of the organism. Altruism, for example, is defined as behavior which benefits another animal at some apparent personal cost to the actor, where cost and benefit are measured in terms of reproductive success.

EVOLUTIONARY MECHANISMS AND SOCIOBIOLOGICAL THEORY

Selection

Sociobiologists view behavior as the ultimate product of evolution by natural selection. In order for this view to be credible as an explanation of human social behavior, one has first to explicate the mechanisms of natural selection and the sense in which behavior is the "result" of evolution. The theory of evolution is simple, but deceptively so, and it is often misunderstood. Darwin's enormous contribution was the elucidation of a mechanism by which evolution might take place. That mechanism is natural selection, and the basic points—a mixture of natural history and logic—follow:

1. Living organisms possess an inherent capacity to overreproduce.
2. Natural populations tend to remain numerically stable over time. The balance of nature is real.
3. This balance derives from the competition of individuals, which insures that some are more successful reproductively than others.
4. Individuals differ from each other in their competitive prowess, and to some extent, these differences are inheritable by their offspring.
5. Ultimately, the genetic composition of a population changes, reflecting the characteristics of the more successful individuals who have left more offspring.

Over time, the genes carried by the more successful individuals become more common in the gene pool of the population. It is this change in gene frequency that *is* evolution. If one considers the distribution of any trait in any species, evolutionary change occurs when that distribution is altered by virtue of differential reproductive success among members from one generation to the next. It requires (a)

differential reproductive success among individuals and (b) some correspondence between the overt manifestation of a particular trait (pheno-
type) and its underlying genetic representation (genotype).

There are three types of selection which are of particular importance.

Directional Selection: Consider a trait with a normal distribution. If
individuals removed from the mean in one particular direction are
relatively more successful in producing offspring, then the distribution
of the trait will shift in that direction over generations (see Figure 1).

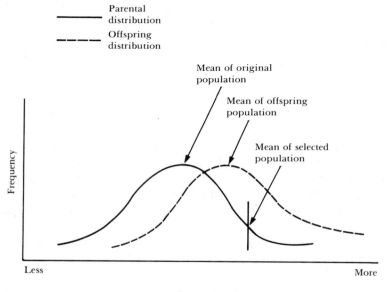

Figure 1

Directional selection corresponds to the usual conception of evolutionary change. For example the progressive increase in brain size among
ancestors of *Homo sapiens* bespeaks directional selection.

Stabilizing selection: Reproductive success, the criterion of natural
selection, may be inversely proportional to the distance from the mean,
so that individuals are less successful as they deviate (see Figure 2).
Selection against the deviants tends to maintain the mean, while
decreasing or maintaining the variance within a population, but the
variability is never entirely eliminated, and is produced anew each
generation by mutation and sexual recombination. Stabilizing selection
is probably a common form of natural selection but it is rarely recognized because its effects are so undramatic.

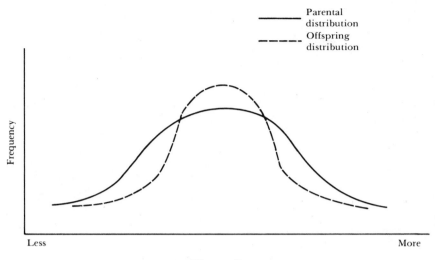

Figure 2

Disruptive selection: It may be that the population distribution shifts in two or more directions, resulting in the polymorphism (see Figure 3). For example the colors of certain insect pupae are characterized by a hue that is either green *or* brown; few individuals exist with intermediate colors. Under given conditions either of the two or more forms of the trait may be adaptive, and the fitness conveyed by the morphs (alternate forms of the trait) may be partly dependent upon their relative frequencies in the population.

Heritability

Evolution by natural selection also requires that, to some extent, the relevant traits be inherited by offspring. For simplicity, consider directional selection: Let S (the selection differential) represent the difference between the mean of the initial generation with respect to a particular trait and the mean of those individuals chosen to be parents of the next generation, and let R (the response to selection) represent the difference between the mean of the initial generation and the mean of the first offspring generation (see Figure 4). In this case $R/S = h^2$ is a measure of the responsiveness of the trait to selection, i.e., its heritability. Heritability in this sense is a special case of the more general and familiar "regression toward the mean." Heritability, h^2, is the same as the

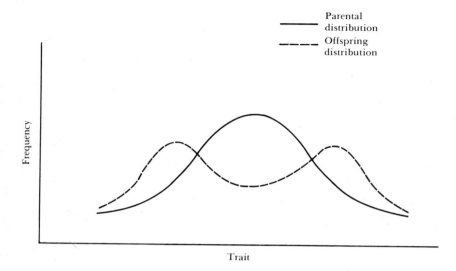

Figure 3

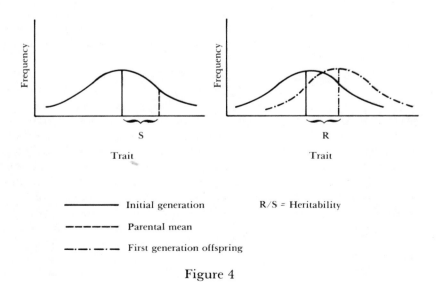

Figure 4

regression slope when offspring is regressed on midparent (a parental average). The important point here is that behaviors have been shown to have heritabilities greater than zero. Behavioral genetics is a growing area of research; for a recent introduction, see Ehrman and Parsons (1976).

These forms of selection hold for quantitative characters, that is, characters that can vary quantitatively along some continuum because they are polygenic (genes at two or more loci contribute to the effect). Qualitative characters, on the other hand, are usually controlled by one locus only, and the character is normally either present or absent. The modern synthetic theory of evolution (Huxley, 1942) was developed in the early twentieth century from the rediscovery of Mendelian genetics and its amalgamation with Darwinian theory through the development of population genetics (Fisher, 1930; Haldane, 1932; Wright, 1931). For a concise introduction to population genetics, see Wilson and Bossert (1971).

Heterosis

Another mechanism that could maintain genetic variation is heterozygote advantage, or heterosis. In a sexually reproducing species, an individual receives one allele (alternate form of a gene) from a parent. Heterozygotes, with respect to a specific locus, are organisms which have two different alleles, for example, Aa. Homozygotes have identical alleles at the locus in question, i.e., AA or aa. If the heterozygote is more successful than either homozygote in a particular environment, both alleles will be maintained in the population. An illustrative example in humans is sickle cell anemia. Individuals who have the disease are homozygous (let us call them AA) and are characterized by severe and frequently lethal blood disorders. Those individuals who are homozygous for not having the trait (that is, aa) are, in fact, more successful in most environments. Thus one would expect the A allele to decrease in frequency through directional selection. In areas where malaria is prevalent, however, it turns out that individuals who are heterozygous with respect to sickle cell anemia (that is, Aa) are more successful than either of the homozygotes. They do not suffer the debilitating affects of the anemia; in addition, they are less susceptible to the effects of malaria than the aa individual. Thus, even if *all* AA and aa individuals died without reproducing, both the A and a alleles would be maintained in the population by heterozygous individuals. That is, heterozygous couples (Aa with Aa) will have offspring with the following genotypes:

AA, Aa, aA, and aa. Half of these would be viable, and half of their offspring would, in turn, be viable heterozygotes.

Evolutionarily Stable Strategies

Diversity may exist as a result of polymorphisms which are maintained in stable proportions. Maynard Smith and Price (1973) and Maynard Smith (1976b) use game theory to analyze ritualized combat and sex ratios, for example. Imagine a population of animals, each of which fights for mates and food; any behavioral strategy will have expected costs and benefits. An animal that always fights to the death may eliminate its competitor but risks injury or death. An animal that always runs away when attacked never wins anything. A third animal that attacks once and runs away if its opponent stands its ground will always lose to an animal pursuing the first strategy, and will always win against an animal pursuing the second. The fitness of each strategy varies with the distribution of the different strategies. If there are a lot of cowards, the bluffer has an advantage. Under given conditions the behavioral types will be distributed in relatively stable proportions, or the animals may play each strategy randomly, but in those same proportions. This is called an Evolutionarily Stable Strategy (ESS), and it is thought to be responsible for much of the variability present in natural populations.

Genetic Drift

Genetic drift has been defined as "the alteration of gene frequencies through sampling error" (Wilson, 1975:64). The effects of sampling errors are, of course, most pronounced when the sample is small. Thus, genetic drift is most likely to disturb a small population in such a way that a particular allele may, by chance alone, not be passed from the parental to the offspring generation. Once this occurs, the change is irreversible, except for mutation gene exchange with another group which has not lost the allele. The equivalent random process with respect to behavior and social organization has been labeled social drift. Just as all phenotypes derive from a genetic and an environmental component, so, too, can social drift be attributed to a combination of genetics (genetic drift) and divergent experience (tradition drift: Wilson, 1975:13).

   Wright (1968) suggested that the most rapid acquisition of adaptation is likely to occur in small, relatively isolated populations within which *both* natural selection and genetic drift are operating. He developed an heuristic device called the "adaptive landscape" which is useful in

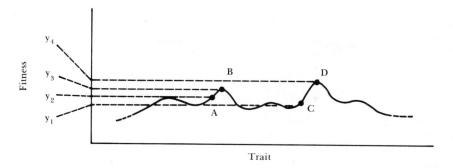

Figure 5

considering this acquisition. To understand it, visualize a landscape based upon one trait (see Figure 5), though the model clearly can be expanded to any space for any number of traits. The level of adaptation is the height on the curve. If a set of individuals has a level of a trait with a fitness of y_2 in a particular environment (e.g., point A), and if only natural selection is operating, then this set of individuals can increase its fitness (e.g., through directional selection) up to a limit of y_3, the local maximum of the curve. It *cannot* in such a case reach y_4 through selection alone because this would first require a decrease in fitness. If the population size is small, however, the random process of drift may operate so that a less fit level temporarily predominates (e.g., progression from B to C). It would be through a combination of drift and selection, then, that other local maxima (e.g., D) could be reached.

This model is especially helpful in addressing one objection that is frequently directed at the sociobiological perspective, namely, that such a perspective supports the status quo by assuming that groups are optimally adapted. This is certainly not implied by an evolutionary approach. Except for random drift or environmental change, individuals may be approaching or even stranded at, one level of adaptation with no hope of reaching a "better" level, but drift and/or environmental change, be it natural or artificial, can facilitate rather dramatic changes. Thus, the charge that sociobiology supports the notion that "the way things are is the way they must necessarily be" (Alper et al., 1976:426) is inappropriate. Mechanisms for change do exist.

Kin Selection and Reciprocal Altruism

Altruism was a paradox for evolutionary theory because it seemingly required a decrease in the reproductive success of the individual concerned. If a particular gene, or set of genes, increased the probability that its carrier will behave in such a manner as to decrease its representation in succeeding generations, then how could it evolve?

One of the exciting breakthroughs in theoretical population genetics was the recognition that natural selection, operating on individuals, can explain the evolution of apparent altruism (Hamilton, 1964; Fisher, 1930; Haldane, 1932). Indeed, Hamilton's insights and their enormous implications for the evolutionary analysis of social behavior (see especially Hamilton, 1975) have provided much of the intellectual impetus for sociobiology. Basically, Hamilton recognized that parental care of offspring is but a special case of a more general phenomenon: concern for relatives. This evolutionary mechanism has been termed "kin selection" (Maynard Smith, 1964), and provides a reasonable explanation for the behavior of those group members who assist other group members in securing relatively scare resources (e.g., food, protection) at some apparent personal cost. Since natural selection operates through the representation of genes in succeeding generations, any one individual can pass on its own genes either by raising offspring or by helping a relative (with whom some genes are shared by common descent) to reproduce. Thus, if two individuals are sufficiently related, then one individual may best further its own ultimate reproductive success by helping the other, even at some apparent immediate cost. More precisely, altruism via kin selection should evolve in this manner if $K > 1/r$, where K equals the ratio of benefit to the altruist's relatives as a result of the behavior in question to the cost suffered by the altruist, and where r equals the coefficient of the relationship between the altruist and beneficiary. In this formulation benefit and cost are measured in terms of units of fitness. The coefficient of relationship, r, is measured by the proportion of genes shared by virtue of common descent. For example, in a sexually reproducing, diploid species, each parent shares one-half of its genes with each offspring. Similarly, adults share one-fourth of their genes with grandchildren, full siblings share one-half and cousins share one-eighth.

This theory represents an important extension of evolutionary thought in that it substitutes inclusive fitness for simple Darwinian fitness as the ultimate arbiter of adaptive significance. Whereas Darwinian fitness is concerned only with the production of successful offspring, inclusive fitness recognizes the importance of all relatives, devalued in proportion as these relatives are genetically more distant. In fact an evolutionary approach to altruism does not necessarily require relatedness among the individuals concerned. Under certain conditions, which are perhaps most likely to occur in humans (e.g., individual recognition, repeated interactions, memory), altruism can be selected between unrelated individuals, provided there is a sufficiently high probability of reciprocity (Trivers, 1971). Limitations of space have made the preceding a rather cursory treatment. Excellent introductions to evolution can be found in Maynard Smith (1975), Stebbins (1971) and Dobzhansky (1970), among others.

Relevance to Behavior

Sociobiologists are mostly concerned with one basic question: why does animal x perform behavior y? Answers to this question can focus upon one or both of the two types of factors which influence behavior: proximate and ultimate factors. Proximate factors are the immediate mechanisms that are responsible for a behavior. For example consider why red-winged blackbirds migrate. They may do so in response to changes in climate, changes in day length, individual weight gain, and/or hormonal changes. The social sciences have traditionally dealt almost exclusively with proximate factors by studying internal mechanisms, external stimuli, and the ontogeny of behavior within individuals. Yet reconsider why red-winged blackbirds migrate. Regardless of the hormonal or neutral mechanisms, why do they do it at all? Ultimate factors are the evolutionary mechanisms which differentiate the comparative reproductive success of those which do or do not behave in a particular fashion. In this case one bird that migrated was more successful reproductively, e.g., they were better able to survive the winter in a warmer climate.

In order for evolution to operate upon any trait, there must be some correspondence—however slight—between that trait and the genetic makeup of the individuals involved. Social scientists, in particular, are inclined to reject this notion, and indeed, sociology, anthropology, and psychology are all strongly committed to environmental determinism of behavior. There can be no doubt that experience is a major determinant of human behavior, but this does not necessitate rejection of genetic predispositions as well.

Experimental and Field Evidence

There are no experimental data concerning genetically mediated behavior tendencies in humans because of the ethical constraints upon such manipulations of our own species. However, abundant evidence exists for genetic influences on behavior in other animals, ranging from single-gene effects (Bastock, 1956; Rothenbuhler, 1967) to extensive hybridization studies (Clark *et al.*, 1954; Sharpe and Johnsgard, 1965). For example two species of African parrots differ in the way they carry nesting materials: members of one species use their beaks exclusively, whereas members of the other tuck the materials into their rump feathers. A genetic component for this behavior is strongly suggested by the actions of cross-species hybrids. These animals show intermediate behaviors which are particularly inefficient and confused (Dilger, 1962). Artificial selection, in which human experimenters determine which individuals shall be reproductively favored (e.g., in animal and plant breeding), has been found effective in modifying the distribution of behavioral traits, in studies ranging from mating speed and directional preference in fruit flies (Manning, 1965; Hirsch and Erlenmeyer-Kimling, 1962) to aggressiveness in chickens (Cook *et al.*, 1972). A classic study of selection for maze-bright and maze-dull rats succeeded in deriving statistically distinct strains within only two generations (Tolman, 1924), and these differences remained after many generations with no further experimental manipulations (Searle, 1949). Field studies of baboons (e.g., Kummer, 1971) have revealed behavioral repertoires which reflect genetic and environmental factors. Packer (1977) reports instances of reciprocal altruism in the olive baboon. Finally, comparisons between olive baboons and chimpanzees indicate that social behavior reflects the underlying genetic relationships (J. Maynard Smith, personal communication). Olive baboons are matrilocal, and the young males invariably disperse; thus males in any single troop are not closely related, and they are, in fact, highly aggressive and competitive. Chimpanzees, on the other hand, are patrilocal—it is the females who disperse. Males in any one chimpanzee troop are thus very closely related, and, predictably, they are gregarious and cooperative.

SOCIOLOGICAL ISSUES

Applications of sociobiological theory to humans are recent. Basically, society is viewed as arising from the interactions among individuals, and the behavior of individuals is viewed as having been shaped by natural selection. Precisely how much of the subject matter of traditional sociology is reducible in this fashion is not yet clear, but theoretical treatments and empirical studies now strongly suggest that at least some parts of our social structure are suitable for this type of analysis.

Kinship Structure

Kin-selection theory leads one to predict that our interactions with genetically related individuals are a crucial part of social behavior. It is, thus, not surprising that all cultures are characterized by some form of kinship system. The problem, however, as Sahlins (1977) has pointed out, is that human kinship groups contain a strong element of social definition, and have the effect of separating some biologically related individuals while lumping together others who are biologically unrelated. Yet no other result is possible unless humans give up pair bonding or practice systematic inbreeding, which would itself be selected against. Inbreeding, the mating of close kin, frequently has deleterious effects upon the offspring (Maynard Smith, 1975:146). Note here that men and women who grew up together in the same peer group on Israeli kibbutzim systematically avoid marriage and heterosexual activity with each other, even though there is no social sanction against it (Shepher, 1971). This is probably an expression of an evolved incest-avoidance mechanism.

In the kibbutzim children this predisposition may be biologically inappropriate since the situation is unusual; nevertheless the predicted behaviors continue. In any case the critical question in assessing the applicability of kin selection theory to humans is *not* whether social terminology *precisely* reflects biological relationships, but whether human activity is, in fact, structured in such a way that kin selection might be operating. For instance Morgan (forthcoming) has found that in the four most active whaling boats in an Eskimo village, the captain-to-crew coefficients of relationship were as high as .50. Further, even the kinship terminology itself may reflect actual patterns of genetic relatedness (Greene, unpublished manuscript). Hartung (1976) discusses the relevance of biology to inheritance patterns, concluding that since male offspring are high risk and high benefit from the parents' point of view, under conditions of polygyny, wealth is most effective when transmitted through the male line. Finally, Alexander (1974), Kurland (1977), and Greene (unpublished manuscript) discuss the implications of female promiscuity, which affects the *average* certainty of paternity, with respect to social structure, especially with respect to instances of the avunculate.

For the social scientist kin selection is particularly important in that it provides a unified, coherent theory for the biology of nepotism—an apparently universal human trait. It also offers a whole new perspective on human mating systems. Furthermore these evolutionary considerations suggest some possible insight into the biology of female-male differences (Trivers, 1972), parent-offspring conflict (Trivers, 1974), sibling rivalry (Barash, Holmes, and Greene, 1978), and xenophobia (Hamilton, 1975).

Norms

The classic sociological view holds that norms are properties of social groups, and that they exist in the interests of the group to constrain the selfish, biologically motivated behavior of individuals (see Campbell, 1975, and Greene and Barash, 1976, for opposing views). But it must be that individuals themselves hold the norms, rather than the groups. The question, then, becomes one of how it is in the interests of the individual to hold to the norms.

Consider the norms of reciprocity and beneficence, which Gouldner (1973) has suggested characterize human groups everywhere. Trivers' reciprocal altruism (1971) provides a model to account for behavior which benefits those who help us, or are likely to help us, again considering the ultimate reproductive success of the individual.

The norms are seen as existing in the interests of those who hold them. If individuals of different groups hold different norms, there may be a genuine conflict between them. Since the norms are not seen as reflecting the interests of the group, there is no implication that they represent some sort of evolutionary optimum for the society.

SUMMARY

The past few years have seen a dramatic increase in the number of sociological works which have incorporated various aspects of biology and evolutionary theory. Two recent collections (Fox, 1975; Bateson and Hinde, 1976) characterize the potential integration of these fields. Tiger (1975) reviews studies which have included somatic factors (particularly hormones) as correlates of behavior. Blurton Jones (1976) considers cultural inheritance from an evolutionary perspective (see also Dawkins's [1976] treatment of "memes" as the unit of cultural transmission). The approaches used by Clutton-Brock and Harvey (1976, 1977) in their analyses of primate societies may prove especially fruitful in generating hypotheses about the evolutionary history of human social structure. They discuss correlations among a wide variety of variables such as population density, diet, sexual dimorphism, pair bonding, group size, and breeding patterns. For example polygyny is correlated with a high degree of sexual dimorphism.

We wish to end with a few caveats. First, such terms as "altruism," when used by sociobiologists, carry no implication as to the cognitive or motivational state of the individuals concerned. The behavior is identified strictly in terms of its consequences for the distribution of genes in succeeding generations. Second, a concern with evolutionary biology does *not* ignore the undoubted role of such environmental factors as early experience, social learning, and/or cultural tradition. In fact tradition can be viewed as reflecting underlying biological adaptive strategies (Greene and Barash, 1976). A final example is offered by Rozin (1976:66), wherein he concludes that "the avoidance of milk institutionalized in Chinese cuisine is no doubt in part a cultural adaptation to high-lactose intolerance."

Cross fertilization between evolutionary biology and the social sciences may well result in hybrid vigor. In any case it certainly seems worth pursuing with an open mind and as much understanding as possible.

NOTE

Special thanks to Paul Harvey for helpful comments on an earlier version of this paper.

REFERENCES

ALEXANDER, R. D.
1974 "The evolution of social behavior." Annual Review of Ecology and Systematics 5:325-383.
ALPER, S. J. BECKWITH, S. L. CHOROVER, J. HUNT, H. INONYE, T. JUDD, R. V. LANGE, and P. STERNBERG
1976 "The implications of sociobiology." Science 192:424-427.
BARASH, D. P., W. G. HOLMES, and P. J. GREENE
1977 "Exact versus probabilistic coefficients of relationship: Some implications for sociobiology." American Naturalist 112:355-363.
BASTOCK, M.
1956 "A gene mutation which changes a behaviour." Evolution 10:421-439.
BATESON, P. P. G., and R. A. HINDE (eds.)
1976 Growing Points in Ethology. Cambridge: Cambridge University Press.
VAN DEN BERGHE, P. L.
1974 "Bringing beasts back in: Towards a biosocial theory of aggression." American Sociological Review 39:777-788.

BLURTON JONES, N.
  1976 "Growing points in human ethology: Another link between ethology and the social sciences?" In P. P. G. Bateson and R. A. Hinde (eds.), Growing Points in Ethology. Cambridge: Cambridge University Press.
CAMPBELL, D. T.
  1975 "On the conflicts between biological and social evolution and between psychology and moral tradition." American Psychologist 30:1103-1126.
CLARK, E., L. R. ARONSON, and M. GORDON
  1954 "Mating behaviour patterns in two sympatric species of xiphophorin fishes: Their inheritance and significance in sexual isolation." Bulletin of the American Museum of Natural History 103:135-226.
CLUTTON-BROCK, T. H., and PAUL H. HARVEY
  1976 "Evolutionary rules and primate societies." In P. P. G. Bateson and R. A. Hinde (eds.), Growing Points in Ethology. Cambridge: Cambridge University Press.
  1977a Primate ecology and social organisation. Journal of Zoology 183:1-39.
  1977b Readings in Sociobiology. San Francisco: Freemans.
COOK, W. T., P. SIEGEL, and K. HINKELMANN
  1972 "Genetic analyses of male mating behaviour in chickens: Crosses among selected and control lines." Behaviour Genetics 2:289-300.
DAWKINS, RICHARD
  1976 The Selfish Gene. Oxford: Oxford University Press.
DILGER, W. C.
  1962 "The behaviour of lovebirds." Scientific American 206:88-98.
DOBZHANSKY, T.
  1970 Genetics of the Evolutionary Process. New York: Columbia University Press.
EHRMAN, L., and P. A. PARSONS
  1976 The Genetics of Behaviour. Sunderland, Mass.: Sinauer Associates.
FISHER, R. A.
  1930 The Genetical Theory of Natural Selection. Oxford: Clarendon Press.
FOX, ROBIN (ed.)
  1975 Biosocial Anthropology. London: Malaby Press.
GOULDNER, H. W.
  1973 For Sociology: Renewal and Critique in Sociology Today. London: Allen Love.
GREENE, P. J.
  1978 "Promiscuity, paternity and culture." American Ethnologist 19:151-159.
GREENE, P. J., and D. P. BARASH
  1976 "Genetic basis of behaviour—especially of altruism." American Psychologist 31 (May):359-61.
HALDANE, J. B. S.
  1932 The Causes of Evolution. Ithaca: Cornell University Press. (1966)
HAMILTON, W. D.
  1964 "The genetical theory of social behaviour," parts I and II. Journal of Theoretical Biology 7:1-52.

1975 "Innate social aptitudes of man: An approach from evolutionary genetics." In R. Fox (ed.), Biosocial Anthropology. London: Malaby Press.

HARTUNG
1976 "On natural selection and the inheritance of wealth." Current Anthropology 17:607–613.

HIRSCH, J., and L. ERLENMEYER-KIMLING
1962 "Individual differences in behaviour and their genetic basis." In E. L. Bliss (ed.), Roots of Behaviour. New York: Harper & Row.

KUMMER, H.
1971 Primate Societies: Group Techniques of Ecological Adaptation. Chicago: Aldine-Atherton.

KURLAND, J. A.
1977 "Matrilines: the primate sisterhood and the human avunculate." Unpublished manuscript.

MANNING, A.
1963 "Selection for mating speed in Drosophila melanogaster based on the behaviour of one sex." Animal Behaviour 11:116–120.

MAYNARD SMITH, J.
1964 "Group selection and kin selection." Nature 201:1145–1147.
1975 The Theory of Evolution. Baltimore: Penguin Books.
1976a "Group selection." Quarterly Review of Biology 51 (June).
1976b "Evolution and the theory of games." American Scientist 64:41–45.

MAYNARD SMITH, J., and G. R. PRICE
1973 "The logic of animal conflict." Nature 246:15–18.

MORGAN, C. J.
1978 "Eskimo hunting groups and the possibility of kin selection in humans." Pacific Sociological Association meetings, Spokane, Wash.

PACKER
1977 "Reciprocal altruism in Papio anubis." Nature 265:441–443.

ROTHENBUHLER, W. C.
1967 "Genetic and evolutionary considerations of social behaviour of honeybees and some related insects." Pp. 61–111 in J. Hirsch (ed.), Behaviour-Genetic Analysis. New York: McGraw-Hill.

ROZIN
1976 "The selection of food by rats, humans, and other animals." Advances in the Study of Behavior 6:21–76.

SAHLINS, M.
1976 Use and Abuse of Biology: An Anthropological Critique of Sociobiology. Ann Arbor: University of Michigan.

SEARLE, L. V.
1949 "The organization of hereditary maze-brightness and maze-dullness." Genetic Psychology Monographs 39:279ff.

SHARPE, R. S., and P. A. JOHNSGARD
1966 "Inheritance of behavioural characters in F$_2$ mallard x pintail (Anas platyrhynehos L. x Anas acuta L.) hybrids." Behaviour 27:259–272.

SHEPHER, J.
  1971 "Mate selection among second generation kibbutz adolescents and adults: Incest avoidance and negative imprinting." Archives of Sexual Behavior 1:293–307.
STEBBINS, G. LEDYARD
  1971 Processes of Organic Evolution, 2nd ed. Englewood Cliffs, N.J.: Prentice-Hall.
TIGER, LIONEL
  1975 "Somatic factors and social behaviour." In R. Fox (ed.), Biosocial Anthropology. London: Malaby Press.
TOLMAN, E. C.
  1924 "The inheritance of maze-learning ability in rats." Journal of Comparative Psychology 4:1–18.
TRIVERS, R. L.
  1971 "The evolution of reciprocal altruism." Quarterly Review of Biology 46:35–57.
  1972 "Parental investment and sexual selection." In B. Campbell (ed.), Sexual Selection and the Descent of Man, 1871–1971. Chicago: Aldine.
  1974 "Parent-offspring conflict." American Zoologist 14:249–264.
WADE, N.
  1976 "Sociobiology: Troubled birth for a new discipline." Science 191:1151–1155.
WILSON, E. O.
  1975 Sociobiology: The New Synthesis. Cambridge: Harvard University Press.
WILSON, E. O., and W. H. BOSSERT
  1971 A Primer of Population Biology. Stamford, Conn.: Sinauer Association.
WRIGHT, S.
  1931 "Evolution in Mendelian populations." Genetics 16:97–158.
  1968 Evolution and the Genetics of Populations, Vol. 1. Genetic and Biometric Foundations. Chicago: University of Chicago Press.

3. A Sociology of Emotions: Some Problems and Some Solutions

THEODORE D. KEMPER

Durkheim's *Sucide* was a tour de force that showed how sociology could explain phenomena seemingly far distant from it. What could be more private than the inner turmoil, personal despair, or impassioned madness that leads a person to take his or her own life? Surely sociology could have nothing to contribute here. Yet, by his analysis of the *social* forms of suicide, Durkheim illuminated conditions external to the individual that determine the passion for self-extinction.

The study of the emotions is a similar case. Here again the phenomena are private, buried even more deeply in the organism than the reasons for suicide, since the emotions are by general agreement phenomena of the autonomic nervous system, beyond the conscious control of the actor. Thus, emotions appear doubly removed from the social realm. Whereas the actor himself must participate in his own suicide, he has no control at all in the earliest stages of emotional arousal. What, then, is sociology's role in the study of emotions?

My purpose here is to discuss some problems and solutions in developing a sociological theory of emotions. First, I shall sketch briefly some of the current approaches to the study of emotions in psychology. Second, I shall propose a general model of social relations that can be used to gain insight into the problem of emotions. Next I shall apply the model to the systematic analysis of five distressful emotions: guilt, shame, anxiety, depression, and anger. Finally, I shall discuss the

SOURCE: Reprinted from *The American Sociologist* 13 (February 1978):30–41.

empirical grounds for a theoretical link between sociology and psycho-physiology.[1]

THE STUDY OF EMOTIONS

The systematic study of emotions is mainly in the hands of psychologists. I shall briefly review five traditions of research on emotions in psychology in order to clarify the basis for a sociological contribution. First, many investigations have been devoted to discovering and classifying the sheer number of emotions. This is an old quest and includes the speculations of many philosophers beginning at least as far back as Aristotle (for a useful review of the philosophic tradition see Gardiner, *et al.*, 1937). In the present era of "scientific psychology," the question has been pursued theoretically as an aspect of instinct theory (McDougall, 1933), psychoanalytic theory (Stanley-Jones, 1970), and biological adaptation theory (Plutchick, 1962). Empirically, a popular approach involves the study of facial expressions, often by the method of asking research subjects to sort photographs of individuals with different expressions (Osgood, 1966; Ekman, *et al.*, 1972). The results of these studies are mixed; different investigators report different numbers of emotions. The sociologist's response must be to ignore the question of how many emotions there are, and to concentrate on the number of different social conditions—whether as cues, socialization parameters, interactional and relational outcomes, and so on—that trigger emotions.

A second approach to emotions in psychology uses phylogenetic and innate theories deriving from the work of Darwin (1873), who saw evolutionary continuity in the emotions of animals and human beings. A strong Darwinian influence pervades much of the study of emotions today; in fact, the evolutionary, adaptive perspective has no serious challengers (see Plutchik, 1962; Lazarus and Averill, 1972; and Hamburg, *et al.*, 1975). An important debate in this tradition is whether emotions are innate (e.g., Lorenz, 1966; Wilson, 1975), or learned (e.g., Berkowitz, 1962; Staub, 1971). Regardless of the outcome of the nature vs. nurture argument, the sociological position is secure: either we investigate the social cues that trigger innate emotions, or we investigate the socialization conditions that instill emotions.

A third approach to the study of emotions examines the psycho-physiological—brain and autonomic nervous system—causes, concomitants, and sequels of emotion. While this approach would seem to hold the least interest for sociologists since it depends on the technical lore of physiology—a discipline far removed from sociology—there is a body of work in psychophysiology that remarkably invites, *and repays,* close attention by sociology. I shall devote the last section of this paper to a consideration of one of the pertinent questions in this area.

Cognitively-oriented psychologists take a fourth approach to emotions. They acknowledge the presence of an external world—often social in nature—which inaugurates the cognitive processes of "appraisal" or "comparison" that lead to felt emotions (Arnold, 1960; Schachter and Singer, 1962; Lazarus, 1975). But cognitive theorists pay relatively little attention to the dimensional or conceptual nature of the social world, since their concern is with the psychological process. Hence, sociologists can make a vital contribution here. They can provide a conceptual model of the social settings that cue the specific appraisals and comparisons which, according to the cognitive theorists, precede emotions.

Learning theories comprise a fifth distinctive approach to the emotions in psychology. This approach is closest to a situational or sociological analysis. In most learning theories, environmental events are understood to consist of rewards and punishments (or reinforcements). According to Gray (1971:9), "the common element binding the emotions into a class is that they all represent some kind of reaction to a 'reinforcing event' or to signals of impending reinforcing events." Lazarus (1968), for example, proposes that anxiety is the consequence of noxious or threatening stimuli, while depression is a reaction to a real or potential deprivation of positive reinforcements. Similarly, Gewirtz (1969) discusses depressed mood as a response to the absence of environmental reinforcers that ordinarily elicit pleasurable behavior.

The learning theory approach points clearly to a *social* context for emotions, since it is mainly other actors who provide the positive and negative reinforcements in the course of interaction. The learning theorists, perhaps unknowingly, have taken to heart Durkheim's (1938:10) definition of a "social fact": it is "external" to the individual and it "constrains" him. Indeed, any individual's reinforcement contingencies are the social facts that elicit the autonomic-motoric-cognitive responses we call emotions. Sociologists, however, are not learning theorists, and need to work with a somewhat more concretely and socially specified set of concepts than merely rewards and punishments. In the following section I shall present what I believe may be a sufficient set of "social facts" to inaugurate a broad sociological approach to the question of emotions.

While there are many theories of emotions, none is specifically sociological. This is not to say that sociologists have entirely neglected emotions. Cooley (1902) identified a particular emotion (the "my feeling") as a fundamental part of the experience of the self. Marx (1964) discussed the "mortification" of alienated labor. Durkheim (1915; 1951) analyzed the religious emotion, and the despair and elation that may both lead to suicide. Weber (1946:215–216) dissected the bureaucratic administrative style: "Its specific nature, which is welcomed by capitalism, develops the more perfectly the more the bureaucracy is 'dehumanized,' the more completely it succeeds in eliminating from official business love, hatred, and all purely personal, irrational, and emotional elements." Indeed one of Weber's four types of social action is the "affectual," or emotional (Weber, 1947:115).

Contemporary sociologists have also touched on emotions: there is Reisman *et al.*'s (1950) delineation of typical emotions for their several character types—shame for the "tradition-directed," guilt for the "inner-directed," and anxiety for the "other-directed"; Homans' (1961:75) concern with guilt or anger when the principle of "distributive justice" is violated in social exchange; Gross and Stone's (1964) empirical investigation of embarrassment; Goffman's (1967) analysis of "face" and shame in interaction; Garfinkel's (1967:50–51) conclusions concerning anger and embarassment when interaction takes an untoward course. Not surprisingly, sociologists discuss emotions most often within the context or as the results of particular social conditions—for example, types of division of labor or of social relations. These are the social cues or reinforcement contingencies that evoke emotions. Therefore, a systematic sociological theory of emotions requires a sociological model of the conditions that may vary so as to induce emotions. I believe there is empirical support for a certain model of social relations which offers a basis for a sociological theory of emotions. I turn to this now.

A MODEL OF SOCIAL RELATIONS

The most important premise of any sociological theory of emotions must be that *an extremely large class of human emotions results from real, anticipated, imagined, or recollected outcomes of social relationships:* she says she does not love me; he says I did a good job; I claimed to be honest, but was caught in a lie; he obligated himself to me, but then reneged; and so forth. These are outcomes of social relationships that ought to stimulate emotion. It follows that we would understand the production of emotions better if we understood social relationships better. I shall suggest now a taxonomy of social relationships which can constitute a systematic specification of the situational matrix which produces emotion.

Many recent studies have sought to identify the basic dimensions of relational behavior or personality in the social setting (many studies in this literature are examined in Kemper [1973, 1978], including Carter [1954], Schutz [1958], Lorr and McNair [1963], Borgatta [1964], Longabaugh [1966], and Benjamin [1974]). The usual technique is to factor analyze a set of scores of behavioral or personality items. While there is relatively little agreement on the total number of dimensions of social behavior or personality in the social context, two clearly relational factors have always emerged.

Despite different names and nuances assigned to the factors, the items point to two underlying relational themes: *control of one actor by another* and *degree of positive social relations*. Elsewhere (Kemper, 1972, 1973, 1974), I have labeled these two dimensions *power* and the giving of *status*.

Generally, the *power* dimension of relationship encompasses such acts as coercing, forcing, threatening, punishing, dominating, and so on. This relational understanding of power is close to Weber's notion of 'overcoming the resistance' of the other (Weber, 1946:180). It should be apparent that actors do not *ordinarily* use power unless the other resists giving what is wanted or could conceivably resist in the future. What is wanted, of course, are various benefits, rewards, and privileges. Power is a dimension of relationship in which, as Weber (1946) suggests, benefits are obtained from others who do not confer them willingly.

The *status* dimension of relationship, on the other hand, accounts for the voluntary, uncoerced giving of benefits, rewards, and privileges. Thus, one actor willingly complies with, approves of, gives money, praise, emotional support, friendship, or even love, to an other because that actor wants to do so. The benefits and rewards are freely offered without the use of power.

Because of the large number of studies which have reported the power and status dimensions as central to relational behavior, I shall use these dimensions to generate a set of relational structures and outcomes that might produce certain distressful emotions.

Toward a Sociological Theory of Distressful Emotions

Each actor (in a dyadic setting) has a varying amount of power over the other. Each actor also receives a varying amount of status from the other. An actor can sense or feel that he has, or has used, an *excess* of power in his relations with the other, or that he has acquired or claimed an *excess* of status. An actor can also sense or feel that he has *insufficient* power or

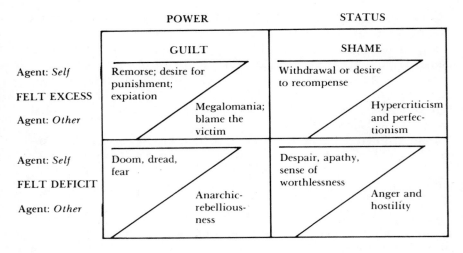

Figure 1

receives *insufficient* status from the other. These make a set of four relational possibilities from the perspective of the given actor (see Figure 1). The actor may feel excess or insufficiency of power and/or status as a result of comparing his actions with internalized social norms, idiosyncratic sentiments acquired in the course of a lifetime, persuasive labeling by others (Scheff, 1963), misperception or distortion of communications from others, and so on.

I introduce now the concept of *agency*, which entails the actor's sense of who is responsible for the excess or insufficiency of power and/or status (cf. Pastore, 1952). I propose that when *self* is viewed as agent, the emotion will be *introjected* and *intropunitive*. When *other* is viewed as agent, the emotion will be *extrojected* and *extropunitive*. When the actor's sense of agency and responsibility oscillates between self and other, the felt relational excess or deficit will produce *compound*, or *mixed* emotions.

Taking into account the several conceptual distinctions presented— felt excess or insufficiency of power and/or status, and self-or-other as responsible agent—I propose particular emotions for each of the relational conditions. These are shown in the figure and I shall discuss them in turn.[2]

(1) *Guilt*: When an individual senses that he has used excessive power against another he will feel the emotion of guilt. Ausubel (1955) defines guilt as "a special kind of negative self-evaluation which occurs when an individual acknowledges that his behavior is at variance with a given

moral value to which he feels obligated to conform" (1955:379). Moral values overwhelmingly refer to relational conduct: the Decalogue, the Sermon on the Mount, the teachings of the Buddha. Transgressions of moral values—murder, assault, theft, lies, etc.—can be seen as violations of standards relating to the use of *power* in social relationships.

When *self* is seen as the responsible agent, the guilt feelings are introjected and the emotion of guilt will be felt as regret, remorse, and a desire for relief of the psychic pain, possibly through some form of *expiation* (cf. Galtung, 1958). The clinical literature is filled with cases in which feelings of guilt are introjected and patients express the need to be punished for their real or imagined transgressions (Sarnoff, 1962; Lewis, 1971).

If, on the other hand, guilt feelings are extrojected through viewing the *other* as the responsible agent, the punitive orientation is turned away from the self and the result will be a form of *megalomania*. This is a more or less delusionary view of the self in grandiose terms, based principally on the sense of self as a mighty power who has the right to determine the fates of others—even, apparently, whether they will live or die. Megalomania mediates guilt by casting the responsibility for the use of excess power upon the other, thus blaming the victim (Ryan, 1971). But the act of blaming the victim and the self-aggrandizement that goes with it are responses to having used excess power in the first place, and are modes of handling the discomfort of guilt. They are responses of guilt just as is the conventional introjected mode where the discomfort is mediated by acceptance of punishment.[3]

(2) *Shame*: Shame is the emotion experienced when an actor believes that he has claimed and/or received more status than he deserves. Status, as defined above, is the amount of reward, recognition, and gratification which others give to the actor *voluntarily*, without his coercion. Status is ordinarily given for competence or achievement in the division of labor, or for competence in social relationships. Thus, when an actor claims more competence than he has, or is offered and accepts more status than he deserves, he feels shame.

Even momentary lapses of competence make us subject to shame, although it is usually called embarrassment (Ausubel, 1955; Weinberg, 1968; Modigliani, 1968). Whether momentary or longlasting, the experience is one of "self-depreciation vis-a-vis the group" (Ausubel, 1955:382) or "loss of self-esteem" (Modigliani, 1968:315).

When the actor views *self* as the agent of the failed status-claim, the shame will be introjected, and there will either be a withdrawal from interaction—the "retreatist" alternative (Merton, 1957)—or a desire to *recompense* those who were induced to give status under false pretenses.

Thus, the embezzler promises to repay, the coward places himself in the most perilous position, each in order to revalidate his status.

Alternatively, when the *other* is seen as agent, the shame is extrojected. This occurs often when the other is the agent of exposure of the status discrepancy, as in a joke told at the actor's expense, or the revelation of a peccadillo. Extropunitive versions of shame turn the searchlight for incompetence on others. This gives rise, I suggest, to a *hypercritical-perfectionism* directed toward the other which reequilibrates the status system, though at a lower level for both self and other. In effect, the actor says, "If I did not deserve the status I received, neither do you!" Thibaut and Kelly (1959:234) see this mode of status reduction as a general solution for persons of low status: ". . . we would expect him [the low status person] to try to improve his level of outcomes or, what could have the same effect, to reduce the outcomes of those better off than he is." Of course, the latter alternative would appeal to those who feel others are responsible for their loss of face.

In ordinary discourse there is frequent confusion between guilt and shame, and some authors even question whether there is a difference between the two (e.g., Bandura and Walters, 1963). The relational perspective used here maintains the analytical and empirical distinctiveness of the two emotions (cf. Lynd, 1958:20–26).

(3) *Anxiety:* When there is an imbalance in the power relationship between actors, the one with relatively less power is vulnerable to the encroachments of the other, and the anticipation that the other will use power is the core of anxiety. Whether or not the anxiety is of pathological intensity and related to repressed experiences, the relational context is one of power relations. Weems and Wolowitz (1969:191) found that "self-perceived power deficit is a demonstrably prominent factor in the dynamics of . . . paranoids," for whom anxiety is a principal symptom. Lemert's (1962) description of the development of paranoia also reveals how the social environment exerts considerable power behavior—acting in secret, isolating the actor, excluding him, and so forth—which fosters in the actor the sense that others are acting against him.

The role of power in the development of anxiety was recognized by Freud (1966:394):

> On what occasions anxiety appears . . . will of course depend to a large extent on the state of the person's knowledge and on his sense of *power* vis-a-vis the external world (emphasis added).

The important "external world" for most human actors is, of course, the social world, and power is held in relation to other actors.

When *self* is seen as responsible for the power deficit, the actor has insufficient power to deter the other and focuses on his own incapacities and deficiencies. Anxiety will be introjected and the power deficit will bring about the classic sense of dread and impending doom often associated with anxiety (cf. Portnoy, 1959:308). The actor feels helpless to prevent the oncoming blow.

When *other* is seen as responsible for the power deficit, the anxiety is extrojected and the response takes a different form. The actor focuses on the other as agent and assigns the other the intent and will to overcome him and benefit thereby. This leads to resistance and an effort to destroy the other's power or the bases of that power—a form of *rebelliousness* or *anarchy*. Brehm (1966) indicates a strong counter-power reaction to an other's efforts to control the actor's previously "free" movements. Stokols (1975) also differentiates between "subjugation" (introjected form) and "rebellion" (extrojected form) as responses to power imbalances in favor of the other.

(4) *Depression:* Depression results from a deficit of status, i.e., an insufficiency of reward and gratification given voluntarily by others. This may be due to rejection by a loved one, loss of a loved one, rejection of one's work, etc. Each of these losses or rejections has the implication that the expected, hoped for, or customary gratifications which the other(s) could provide are not, or will not be forthcoming (cf. Lazarus, 1968; Gewirtz, 1969).

In the intropunitive type of depression, where *self* is seen as the agent of the status deficit, there is the classic syndrome of withdrawal, *despair*, apathy, feelings of worthlessness, and, at the extreme, suicide.

In the extropunitive response to insufficient status, where *other* is seen as the agent, anger and hostility are directed against the other, and often generalized against all possible others who may potentially have status to withhold. In the apathy-despair response in depression there is a sensed justice in the judgment of others; in the hostile response, their judgment to withhold status is rejected as unjust.

The relational view of depression differs from the Freudian view by treating depression not as a result of hostility turned inward, but as a result of deprivation of gratifications received from others. Depression is simply hunger for what others have to offer and have not given, or have withdrawn.

I have proposed that guilt, shame, anxiety, depression, and anger stem from certain felt excesses or deficiencies in either power or status, in conjunction with judgments concerning agency.[4] It is also obvious that there are connections between these distressful emotions. Fairbairn (1952), a psychiatrist, reports that as the schizophrenic patient's ego begins to reintegrate, the patient shifts from a paranoid-schizoid position into depression. In the relational terms sketched here, this implies a shift from problems of *power* to problems of *status*, from the problem of how to avoid destruction to the problem of how to acquire gratification.

Fairbairn's point, however, encourages a far-reaching surmise, namely that, very broadly speaking, the disorders labeled schizophrenia are essentially disorders associated with power relations and the disorders involving depression are disorders of status. This is not to say that power disorders and status disorders are mutually exclusive. In fact, they readily interpenetrate, not only because social relationships are comprised of both power and status dimensions, but also because when there is a breakdown in one relational dimension, it is likely the other dimension will suffer as well. If one feels guilt, it is easy also to feel shame (due to a failure to validate the virtuous self presented to others), anxiety (due to fear of retribution for the initial trespass which inspired the guilt) and depression (due to real or imagined status-loss which may be the punishment for the transgression).

It should be obvious that these conclusions concerning guilt, shame, anxiety, depression, and anger, and the relational roots of the two major categories of psychosis—schizophrenia and depressive disorders—are possible only from a sociological stance: emotions flow from real, anticipated, imagined, or recollected outcomes of *social relations*. It should also be apparent that the sociologist must have some model of social relations with which to explicate or predict emotions. I have proposed a model involving the two dimensions of power and status. Other researchers may prefer a different nomenclature for the underlying concepts, but I believe that the power and status concepts are so fundamental for the analysis of emotions that they will be retained by whatever name.

I turn now to an important psychophysiological problem in the study of emotions which quite unexpectedly was clarified when the power-status relational dimensions were applied. Even more unexpectedly, the solution lent persuasive support to the theoretical soundness of the relational dimensions themselves.

TOWARD A SOCIOPHYSIOLOGY OF EMOTIONS

Emotions are physiologically rooted in the organism. Ordinarily this would turn sociological attention away from the phenomena, for sociologists seldom "do sociology" and know physiology too. Yet I want to report a startling and welcome result that gives support to the power-status formulation at the sociological level while it clarifies a longstanding problem at the psychophysiological level. There is too little space available to cover the question extensively, but I shall summarize the basic facts (see Kemper, 1978, for an extensive discussion of these materials).

The autonomic basis for emotions is in the *sympathetic* and the *parasympathetic* branches of the nervous system. These operate together to maintain a *more* or *less* homeostatic state along the emotional front. The sympathetic system is generally associated with emotions of arousal such as anger and fear, while the parasympathetic is generally associated with emotions of pleasure and satisfaction. Each system is connected with the peripheral organs—heart, stomach, blood vessels, lungs, pupils, etc.—that contribute the physical signs of emotion. Each system operates more or less to modulate the other when it reaches a level of activation that threatens either to "blow up" the organism from over-arousal or to "wind it down" from excess of calm, responseless, contentment (see Lex, 1974, for a short cogent discussion of the interaction of the two systems in the case of "voodoo" death).

A very considerable body of research (Funkenstein, 1955, reports the fundamental developments) supports the following hypothesis: when an individual experiences what is generally agreed to be the emotion of anger, a particular neurochemical called norepinephrine (or noradrenaline) is released in the body. On the other hand, when the individual experiences what is commonly understood to be fear or anxiety, a hormone called epinephrine (or, more commonly, adrenaline) is released. Of the utmost importance for this discussion is that *no other hormones or neurochemicals have been found to be so specifically related to particular emotions.* This extremely important body of experimental research, developed in the 1950s and early 1960s, permits the following heuristic conclusion.

Since deficit of own power (or excess of other's power) is the social relational condition for fear or anxiety, and since loss of customary, expected, or deserved status (other as agent) is the basic relational condition for anger, it seems entirely compatible to suppose that specific social relational conditions are accompanied by specific physiological reactions, with the felt emotions as the psychological mediators between the two. Furthermore, the fact that only two neurochemical substances appear to differentiate the power emotion (fear) from the status-loss emotion (anger), suggests that two may be a correct estimate of the number of separate dimensions of relationship. Though it may be only coincidental to find two social relational dimensions and two neuro-chemicals of specific emotions, there is much to be gained from viewing the two findings as mutually supportive. It makes sense, I believe (and a close analysis of the problem of emotions demands it), that there be some kind of integration between the social relations we enact and the cognitive-somatic-autonomic accompaniments of the interaction. If there is not, there is no sense to studies of "social stress," or to the social facet of psychosomatic medicine.

Yet it isn't quite this simple. I will take up two additional considerations. First, I have said nothing about positive emotions, which seem to have something to do with the parasympathetic nervous system where neither norepinephrine nor epinephrine are found. Indeed, the major neurochemical in the parasympathetic system is *acetylcholine.* This substance seems to be involved with consummatory responses, contentment, mild satisfaction, and a sense of well-being. *Relationally* that would mean that felt levels of *both* power and status are *adequate*— neither excessive, producing either guilt or shame; nor insufficient, producing either fear or anger. Thus, the conclusion now reads: the parasympathetic nervous system dominates when both power and status are sufficient and no specially compelling emotions are felt; the sympathetic nervous system dominates when power and/or status are disturbed from satisfactory levels, with norepinephrine as the organismic correlate of status loss (anger) and epinephrine as the organismic correlate of power-insufficiency (fear).[5] Thus, the additional consideration of relatively calm positive feelings does not disturb the initial formulation, in which specific neurochemical substances correspond to specific social relational conditions.

A second consideration in regard to the sociophysiological integration I have proposed is that the specificity theory in psychophysiology, first proposed by William James (1893), has many opponents. They deny the specificity of physiological response that I have detailed above (Cannon, 1929). They claim that a common physiological substrate underlies all emotions and that the differentiation of emotions is based on other grounds. Schachter and Singer (1962) present a particularly persuasive formulation for sociologists. They argue that the individual looks to the social environment to see "what is happening," so to speak, engaging in "social comparison" as defined by Festinger (1954). In a quite ingenious experiment that has become a classic, Schachter and Singer (1962) appeared to establish that emotions as different as anger and euphoria can both be associated with epinephrine, the substance which had been found in previous research to be associated only with fear. Thus, with one seemingly "crucial" experiment Schachter and Singer appeared to demolish the entire structure of specificity theory, and the specificity viewpoint is hardly pursued today in psychophysiology (Levi, 1972, and Frankenhaeuser, 1971, also report research that seems to support the antispecificity perspective).

But there is one problem with this antispecificity research: a *sociological* analysis of the experimental conditions in each of the studies reveals that, where measured, norepinephrine flowed when relational conditions reflected status-withdrawal and, by inference, anger; and that, where measured, epinephrine was secreted when relational conditions reflected insufficient power of self, or excess power of other and, by inference, fear or anxiety. Where the neurochemical secretions themselves were not measured, a straightforward analysis of the power-status *relational structure* of the experimental design reveals that relational conditions appropriate to evoke emotions of fear or anger, or their common behavioral manifestations, were present. The antispecificity experimenters are aware in only the most vague way of the relational nature of their experimental designs, thereby completely ignoring the quite obvious evidence for specificity in their own data. Ironically, since those psychophysiologists who espouse specificity theory are also not sociologists, they too have failed to see that the sociological structure of their opponents experiments invalidated the conclusions drawn from them.

From a strictly sociological viewpoint, it does not matter whether specificity theory is correct or not. Sociologists must still detail the range and extent of systematic variability of social conditions that are associated with the production of emotions. But there is an importance and elegance to the integration of sociological relational theory with psychophysiological specificity theory that warrants its vigorous investigation. Sociology made an unexpected eleventh-hour save of specificity theory. At the same time, the psychophysiological evidence for specificity lends unexpected support to sociology's two relational dimensions. Psychophysiologists—with the assistance of sociologists who are sensitive to the social relational aspects of experimental paradigms—must devise new experiments to test specificity and to establish it now more positively. This work must proceed on the basis of an informed integration of three disciplines: physiology, psychology, and sociology. No one or two of them can solve the problem alone.

CONCLUSION

In an extremely brief space I have tried to present an overview of the field of emotions as currently practiced by psychologists, as well as some sociological contributions to the study of emotions. This by no means exhausts the domain of sociological interest in the field. Indeed, the emotions—as the basis of motivation and wide spans of human action—

444   THEODORE D. KEMPER

are ever present, though they may be repressed or suppressed, or institutionalized away (as in Weber's "disenchantment of the world" by the ethos of rationalization). Emotions maintain, alter, and sometimes destroy many social processes: marriage and family relations; relationships across authority levels in work settings (Myers, 1977), competition and conflict between social groups such as classes, ethnic groups, or athletic teams; collective behavior phenomena, whether a reported invasion from Mars (Cantril, 1940), racial conflict (Ransford, 1968), a stock market panic (Weber, 1947:92), or economic boom or bust (Durkheim, 1951; Bensman and Vidich, 1962). In a very suggestive analysis, Collins (1975) proposes that group emotions are manipulated by social hierarchies so as to legitimate the distribution of benefits and control in the social order. Sociological analysis of emotions, so long in emerging as a systematic study, may yet establish sociology more firmly both as science and as informed interpreter of social life.

NOTES

1. In Kemper (1978) I treat a large number of questions relating to a sociology of emotions. The brief space of this paper does not permit more than a very few topics to be considered.

2. The emotions treated here as consequences of certain felt patterns of power-status outcomes are distressful or "negative." Positive emotions—such as security and happiness—are also consequences of felt outcomes of power-status relations (see Kemper, 1978, for discussion of these).

3. Although the four cells of Figure 1 are designated by ordinary emotional labels—guilt, shame, etc.—the introjected and extrojected portions of each cell are variously moods, coping behaviors, character traits, and so on. This points up the oft-noted lack of a mutually exclusive set of labels of a single modality which can be mapped onto the autonomic-motoric-cognitive states that comprise emotions (cf. Young, 1961:352–353; Osgood, 1966:29; Lazarus and Averill, 1972:244). Another aspect of this problem concerns the differential naming of different points of intensity of single emotions: for example, concern, apprehension, fear, anxiety, dread—each a different level of intensity of one emotion. I have chosen emotional labels according to the levels of intensity conventionally discussed in the literature. Intensity of emotion is largely a function of the felt intensity of the outcomes of power-status relations.

4. I have not identified all possible sources of the five distressful emotions, but have indicated the social relational outcomes that would cue them.

5. Gellhorn and Loufbourrow (1963) and Gellhorn (1967) are important interpreters of the "interaction effects" of the sympathetic and parasympathetic systems in the production of emotions.

REFERENCES

AUSUBEL, DAVID P.
  1955 "Relationships between shame and guilt in the socializing process."
    Psychological Review 62:378-390.
BANDURA, ALBERT, and RICHARD H. WALTERS
  1967 Social Learning and Personality Development. New York: Holt, Rine-
    hart and Winston.
BENJAMIN, LORNA
  1974 "Structural analysis of social behavior." Psychological Review
    81:392-425.
BENSMAN, JOSEPH, and ARTHUR VIDICH
  1962 "Business cycles, class, and personality." Psychoanalysis and Psychoana-
    lytic Review 49:30-52.
BERKOWITZ, LEONARD
  1962 Aggression: A Social Psychological Analysis. New York: McGraw-Hill.
BORGATTA, EDGAR F.
  1964 "The structure of personality characteristics." Behavioral Science
    9:8-17.
BREHM, JACK W.
  1966 A Theory of Reactance. New York: Academic.
CANNON, WALTER B.
  1929 Bodily Changes in Pain, Hunger, Fear, and Rage. 2nd ed. New York:
    Ronald.
CANTRIL, HADLEY
  1940 The Invasion from Mars. Princeton: Princeton University Press.
CARTER, LAUNOR F.
  1954 "Evaluating the performance of individuals as members of small
    groups." Personnel Psychology 7:477-484.
COLLINS, RANDALL
  1975 Conflict Sociology. New York: Academic.
COOLEY, CHARLES H.
  1902 Human Nature and the Social Order. New York: Scribners.
DARWIN, CHARLES
  1873 The Expression of Emotions in Man and Animals. New York: Appleton.
DURKHEIM, EMILE
  1915 Elementary Forms of the Religious Life. London: Allen and Unwin.
  1938 The Rules of Sociological Method. Chicago: University of Chicago.
  1951 Suicide. Glencoe, Ill.: Free Press.
EKMAN, PAUL, WALLACE V. FRIESEN, and PHOEBE ELLSWORTH
  1972 Emotion in the Human Face. New York: Pergamon.
FAIRBAIRN, W. RONALD D.
  1952 Psychoanalytic Studies of the Personality. London: Tavistock Publica-
    tions.
FESTINGER, LAWRENCE
  1954 "A theory of social comparison processes." Human Relations 7:117-140.

446 THEODORE D. KEMPER

FRANKENHAEUSER, MARIANNE
1971 "Experimental approaches to the study of human behavior as related to neuroendocrine function." Pp. 22–35 in Lennart Levi (ed.), Society, Stress, and Disease, Vol. 1: The Psychosocial Environment and Psychosomatic Diseases. New York: Oxford.

FREUD, SIGMUND
1966 The Complete Introductory Lectures on Psychoanalysis. Translated and Edited by James Strachey. New York: W. W. Norton.

FUNKENSTEIN, DANIEL
1955 "The physiology of fear and anger." Scientific American 192:74–80.

GALTUNG, JOHAN
1958 "The social functions of a prison." Social Problems 6:127–40.

GARDINER, H. M., RUTH C. METCALF, and JOHN G. BEEBE-CENTER
1970 Feelings and Emotion. Westport, Conn.: Greenwood. First published in 1937.

GARFINKEL, HAROLD
1967 Studies in Ethnomethodology. Englewood Cliffs, New Jersey: Prentice-Hall.

GELLHORN, ERNEST
1967 Principles of Autonomic-Somatic Integration. Minneapolis: University of Minnesota Press.

GELLHORN, ERNEST, and G. N. LOUFBOURROW
1963 Emotions and Emotional Disorders: A Neurophysiological Study. New York: Harper & Row.

GEWIRTZ, JACOB L.
1969 "Mechanisms of social learning: Some roles of stimulation and behavior in early human development." Pp. 57–212 in David Goslin (ed.), Handbook of Socialization Theory and Research. Chicago: Rand-McNally.

GOFFMAN, ERVING
1967 "Embarrassment and social organization." American Journal of Sociology 62:264–274.

GRAY, JEFFREY A.
1971 The Psychology of Fear and Stress. New York: McGraw-Hill.

GROSS, EDWARD, and GREGORY P. STONE
1964 "Embarrassment and the analysis of role requirements." American Journal of Sociology 70:1–15.

HAMBURG, DAVID A., BEATRICE A. HAMBURG, and JACK D. BARCHAS
1975 "Anger and depression in perspective of behavioral biology." Pp. 235–278 in Lennart Levi (ed.), Emotions: Their Parameters and Measurement. New York: Raven.

HOMANS, GEORGE C.
1961 Social Behavior: Its Elementary Forms. New York: Harcourt, Brace, World.

JAMES, WILLIAM
1893 Principles of Psychology. New York: Holt.

KEMPER, THEODORE D.
  1972 "Power, status, and love." Pp. 180–203 in David R. Heise (ed.), Personality and Socialization. Chicago; Rand-McNally.
  1973 "The fundamental dimensions of social relationship: A theoretical statement." Acta Sociologica 16:41–58.
  1974 "On the nature and purpose of ascription." American Sociological Review 39 844–853.
  1978 A Social Interactional Theory of Emotions. New York: Wiley.
LAZARUS, ARNOLD A.
  1968 "Learning theory and the treatment of depression." Behavior Research and Therapy 6:83–89.
LAZARUS, RICHARD S.
  1975 "The self-regulation of emotion." Pp. 47–67 in Lennart Levi (ed.), Emotions: Their Parameters and Measurement. New York: Raven.
LAZARUS, RICHARD S., and JAMES S. AVERILL
  1972 "Emotion and cognition with special reference to anxiety." Pp. 242–290 Charles D. Spielberger (ed.), Anxiety: Current Trends in Theory and Research, Vol. 2. New York: Academic.
LEMERT, EDWIN M.
  1962 "Paranoia and the dynamics of exclusion." Sociometry 25:2–20.
LEVI, LENNART
  1972 "Stress and distress in response to psychosocial stimuli: Laboratory and real life studies in sympathoadrenomedullary and related reactions." Acta Medica Scandinavica. Supplementum 528. Stockholm: Almquist and Wiksell.
LEWIS, HELEN B.
  1971 Shame and Guilt in Neurosis. New York: International University Press.
LEX, BARBARA W.
  1974 "Voodoo death: New thoughts on an old explanation." American Anthropologist 76:818–823.
LONGABAUGH, RICHARD
  1966 "The structure of interpersonal behavior." Sociometry 29:441–460.
LORENZ, KONRAD
  1966 On Aggression. New York: Harper.
LORR, MAURICE, and DOUGLAS M. McNAIR
  1963 "An interpersonal behavior circle." Journal of Abnormal and Social Psychology 67:69–75.
LYND, HELEN M.
  1958 On Shame and the Search for Identity. London: Routledge and Kegan Paul.
MARX, KARL
  1964 Early Writings. Translated and edited by T. B. Bottomore. New York: McGraw-Hill.
McDOUGALL, WILLIAM
  1933 The Energies of Men. New York: Scribners.

448   THEODORE D. KEMPER

MERTON, ROBERT K.
  1957 "Social structure and anomie." Pp. 131-60 in Robert K. Merton, Social Theory and Social Structure. New York: Free Press.
MODIGLIANI, ANDRE
  1968 "Embarrassment and embarrassability." Sociometry 31:313-326.
MYERS, ROBERT J.
  1977 Fear, Anger, and Depression: A Study of the Emotional Consequences of Power. Unpublished Ph.D. Dissertation. St. John's University, New York.
OSGOOD, CHARLES E.
  1966 "Dimensionality of the semantic space for communication via facial expressions." Scandanavian Journal of Psychology 7:1-30.
PASTORE, NICHOLAS
  1952 "The role of arbitrariness in the frustration-aggression hypothesis." Journal of Abnormal and Social Psychology 47:728-31.
PLUTCHIK, ROBERT
  1962 The Emotions: Facts, Theories and a New Model. New York: Random House.
PORTNOY, ISIDORE
  1959 "The anxiety states." Pp. 307-323 in Silvano Arieti (ed.), American Handbook of Psychiatry, Vol. 1. New York: Basic Books.
RANSFORD, H. EDWARD
  1968 "Isolation, powerlessness, and violence: A study of attitudes and participation in the Watts riot." American Journal of Sociology 73:581-591.
RIESMAN, DAVID, NATHAN GLAZER, and REUEL DENNY
  1950 The Lonely Crowd. New Haven, Conn.: Yale University Press.
RYAN, WILLIAM
  1971 Blaming the Victim. New York: Pantheon Books.
SARNOFF, IRVING
  1962 Personality Dynamics and Development. New York: Wiley.
SCHACHTER, STANLEY, and JEROME SINGER
  1962 "Cognitive, social, and physiological determinants of emotional state." Psychological Review 69:379-399.
SCHEFF, THOMAS J.
  1963 "The role of the mentally ill and the dynamics of mental disorder: A research framework." Sociometry 26:436-453.
SCHUTZ, WILLIAM C.
  1958 FIRO: A Three Dimensional Theory of Interpersonal Behavior. New York: Holt, Rinehart and Winston.
STANLEY-JONES, D.
  1970 "The biological origins of love and hate." Pp. 25-37 in Magda B. Arnold (ed.), Feelings and Emotions. New York: Academic.
STAUB, ERVIN
  1971 "The learning and unlearning of aggression." Pp. 93-124 in Jerome L. Singer (ed.), The Control of Aggression and Violence. New York: Academic.

STOKOLS, DANIEL
  1975 "Toward a psychological theory of alienation." Psychological Review
        82:26–44.
THIBAUT, JOHN W., and HAROLD H. KELLEY
  1959 The Social Psychology of Groups. New York: John Wiley.
WEBER, MAX
  1946 From Max Weber: Essays in Sociology. New York: Oxford University
        Press.
  1947 The Theory of Social and Economic Organization. New York: Oxford
        University Press.
WEEMS, LUTHER B., JR., and HOWARD M. WOLOWITZ
  1969 "The relevance of power themes among males, Negro and white para-
        noid and nonparanoid schizophrenics." The International Journal of
        Social Psychiatry 15:189–96.
WEINBERG, MARTIN S.
  1968 "Embarrassment: Its variable and invariable aspects." Social Forces
        46:382–388.
WILSON, EDWARD C.
  1975 Sociobiology: The New Synthesis. Cambridge, Mass.: Harvard.
YOUNG, PAUL T.
  1961 Motivation and Emotion. New York: Wiley.

4. The Sociology of Emotion: Some Starting Points

SUSAN SHOTT

Curiously, little systematic discussion of emotion has been attempted by contemporary sociologists, perhaps because feelings are often considered either irrelevant to sociological concerns or not amenable to sociological analysis. Yet many of the classical sociological theorists (particularly Comte, Cooley, Durkheim, Simmel, and Adam Smith) gave considerable attention to emotions, viewing them as inextricably bound to social life, and several sociologists have recently argued for the sociological significance of feelings. Hochschild (1975), for example, has described the impact of "feeling rules" on emotions, while Kemper presents a theory of "distressful emotions" in this volume. In addition, there exists a fairly substantial literature on specific emotions (written primarily by nonsociologists), which is clearly relevant to a number of sociological issues.

The purpose of this paper is to indicate the sociological significance of emotion by briefly reviewing some of these classical and contemporary studies of feeling and by presenting a symbolic interactionist analysis of the diffusion of collective affect and its importance for social solidarity. While my review will by no means be complete (since space limitations prohibit an exhaustive review), I shall touch upon several areas of particular interest to sociologists: these are the role of various emotions in social control, socialization, and social cohesion and conflict; the cultural and structural patterning of feelings; and the construction of emotion by the actor. In my discussion of collective feeling, I shall attempt to synthesize work by Durkheim (1965) and Mead (1934).

In the review and the analysis of collective emotion that follows it, I hope to suggest some starting points for a sociology of emotion and thereby show that feelings are both amenable and relevant to sociological analysis. Indeed the case for sociological investigations of emotion can be stated even more strongly; I shall argue that the sociological study of feeling is necessary for a full understanding of social conduct and that the explication of many aspects of emotion requires a sociological perspective.

EMOTION AND SOCIAL CONDUCT

Of the many aspects of social conduct influenced by emotion, social control is perhaps the most obviously affected by feelings, particularly shame, guilt, embarrassment, and empathy. Ausubel (1955:382) has suggested that shame is evoked by "an actual or presumed negative judgment of [oneself] resulting in self-depreciation vis-à-vis the group," while guilt accompanies the acknowledgement that one's actions are "at variance with a given moral value to which [one] feels obligated to conform." Embarrassment, according to Goffman (1967:97ff.), results when expectations concerning the appropriate presentations of self for a social encounter are unfulfilled.[1] Because these sentiments can be felt even in the absence of any public knowledge of one's actual or presumed misdeeds (Piers and Singer, 1953:51; Riezler, 1943:457; Modigliani, 1971), they often check and punish deviant behavior when no external sanctions are possible. Gross and Stone (1964:13-15) suggest that deliberate embarrassment may even be used to establish and maintain power relationships. Embarrassment and guilt, moreover, tend to prompt altruistic behavior, perhaps in order to repair a damaged self-conception (in the case of guilt) or to patch up a bungled presentation of self (in the case of embarrassment). (See Apsler, 1975, on embarrassment; and Berscheid and Walster, 1967; Brock and Becker, 1966; Carlsmith and Gross, 1969; Darlington and Macker, 1966; Freedman, Wallington, and Bless, 1967; and Regan, Williams, and Sparling, 1972, on guilt.) Emotional empathy, which consists of feeling the emotion one observes in another or the emotion one would feel in another's situation, is yet another affective motivator of altruistic conduct, as Aderman and Berkowitz (1970), Aronfreed (1968:137-159), Krebs (1975), and Midlarsky and Bryan (1967) have found.

Hence, these sentiments facilitate social control by prompting altruistic behavior or inhibiting deviant conduct, thereby encouraging the self-control that constitutes much of social control. Emotion also appears to be crucial for the socialization process that makes the individual capable of such self-control, a point elaborated on by Comte (1875:155ff.), in his discussion of the family, and by Cooley (1962:23ff.), in his analysis of primary groups. Parsons (1970:29, 70) has argued that the generalized emotional attachment of the child to its parents is essential for its identification with them and thus for the "internalization of common culture." Collins (1975:268–270) presents a somewhat similar analysis, focusing on the use of parental love-deprivation for engendering "strong emotional controls." Some evidence for the efficacy of love-deprivation in the development of conscience has been presented by Aronfreed (1968:322), Sears, Maccoby, and Levin (1957:387–392), and Whiting and Child (1953:244–246), and two early studies of institutionalized children found that these children, who lacked the usual close emotional ties, displayed severely retarded social development (Goldfarb, 1945; Spitz, 1945). Thus, some sort of positive affective bond appears to be necessary, as a rule, for complete socialization, and particularly, for moral development.

Much of social solidarity also rests on emotion. Gratitude, for example, has been insightfully described by Simmel (1950:396) as one of "those 'microscopic,' but infinitely tough, threads which tie one element of society to another, and thus eventually all of them together in a stable collective life." For gratitude enforces reciprocity and maintains the bond of interaction when legal requirements do not apply; moreover, it serves as the "moral memory" of humankind, recalling the meaning and consequences of an act of exchange (Simmel, 1950:389). Humor, also, can be a powerful means of cohesion, as a number of writers have noted (e.g., Bales, 1951:9; Blau, 1963:110; Jones and Liverpool, 1976; and Martineau, 1972). Radcliffe-Brown (1965:90 ff.) has argued that joking relationships, which allow or require people to humorously poke fun at each other, help sustain relationships that combine social disjunction (which produces divergent interests) and social conjunction (which necessitates avoidance of overt conflict). Another affective source of social solidarity is the emotion induced by collective ritual, as Durkheim (1965) has suggested in an analysis that will be discussed in the section on collective emotion.

Emotions may, of course, engender conflict as well as cohesion, as Weber's analysis of charisma indicates. Because charismatic authority rests on intense devotion and trust directed toward a person or group of persons, it makes a "sovereign break" with tradition. Those subject to such authority are, therefore, a potent force for revolutionary change and conflict in the larger society (Weber, 1968:24). Envy, also, can be an affective instigator of conflict. Directed toward the owner of an asset legitimately denied to the envious person, envy differs from jealousy, which arises when a person's legitimate claim to a desired object is threatened (Simmel, 1955:52). Foster (1972:168 ff.) has extensively analyzed the role of envy in stratification systems, arguing that envy characterizes societies organized by the rules of a zero-sum game. When successes are seen as the losses of the less fortunate, envy may motivate aggression, such as attempted witchcraft, toward those who are success-ful (Foster, 1972; Schoeck, 1966:32). Envy is thus quite unlike jealousy, which is manifested in accordance with the normative and institutional structure of society, as Davis (1949:175) notes. Hence, while jealousy is certainly a source of conflict, it is a conservative force that protects "the fundamental institutions of property" (particularly sexual "property") from trespass by those who envy (Davis, 1949:185).

As all of these writers have suggested, feelings do have substantial impact on several areas traditionally within the purview of sociologists. To exclude emotions from sociological consideration, then, must neces-sarily limit our understanding of social conduct. It is equally necessary, however, to apply a sociological perspective to feelings if we wish to explicate emotion. For feelings, no less than those aspects of behavior more systematically studied by sociologists, are profoundly affected by society.

THE SOCIALIZATION AND CONSTRUCTION OF SENTIMENT

Averill (1976:92) has argued convincingly that "emotions are social constructions. . . . They are fashioned, organized, brought about—in short, *constructed*—according to rules of culture" (emphasis in origi-nal). Hochschild (1975:289-290) makes a similar point, suggesting that "feeling rules" prescribe or discourage certain emotions in a given situation and often prompt people to do "emotion work" in an attempt to arouse the "appropriate" sentiments. Because the experience and expression of emotion are socialized, they vary across cultures. Even a casual survey of the anthropological literature turns up instances of this. Chagnon (1968), for example, has described the manner in which aggressive feelings, particularly rage, and their violent expression are encouraged among the Yąnomamö. Dentan (1968) has found quite a different sort of affective socialization among the Semai, who discourage anger while encouraging fearfulness. And, finally, Hildred Geertz (1959:226, 239) has discussed "emotional specialization" in Java, where children learn to feel and express deep respect while keeping the expression of other emotions under careful control. Thus, different societies often develop different affective "vocabularies of motive" (cf. Mills, 1940).

It also seems likely, as Hochschild (1975:283, 294) argues, that certain emotions and affective styles are, like many other aspects of behavior, differentially distributed within societies, due to varying norms and the dissimilar experiences that usually result from different positions in the social structure. Envy, of course, is one such sentiment; we would expect it to be most frequently felt and expressed by those classes with fewer resources. Other sociologists have suggested that historical changes in affective experience and expression may take place within a society. Tönnies (1957:159–161), for example, held that shame, the representative of morality in *Gemeinschaft* society, is entirely out of place, and hence, is rarely felt in the modern *Gesellschaft* society. Similarly, Riesman (1961) argues that shame has been replaced by guilt, and guilt by anxiety, as the primary affective sanction in American society.

At a more microsociological level, emotions are shaped by the actor's definitions of the situation, which of course, are influenced by social norms. At the very least we would expect an actor's interpretation of a situation to include an assessment of its affective significance and thus to influence whether one becomes emotionally aroused. Emotions may well be especially susceptible to shaping by definitions and situational cues, if Cannon (1927) and Brown (1965:629) are correct in arguing that similar visceral states accompany many emotional and even nonemotional states. As I have argued elsewhere (Shott, forthcoming), actors appear to construct their feelings in a process affected by situational and internal cues. Schachter and Singer (1962) have offered some evidence for this view; they found that the state of physiological arousal induced by epinephrine was interpreted quite differently—as anger or euphoria—by subjects in different experimental conditions.[2] Other research bearing on the construction of emotions has been presented by Nisbett and Schachter (1966), Schachter (1971), Schachter and Wheeler (1962), Valins (1966, 1974), and Barefoot and Straub (1971). The nature of the relationship between physiological arousal, situational cues, and definitions is certainly an area that requires further research; it is also an area that sociologists may be able to study profitably, since they have often focused before on the interrelationship of norms and situational cues, definitions, and individual conduct.

Hence, it appears that sociologists do have a great deal to contribute to the study of emotion. Certainly, the variability in affective experience and expression across cultures remains inexplicable without the application of a sociological perspective. The study of subcultural and historical variation in emotional experience and style, like the study of any other kind of subcultural or historical variation, also requires a sociological viewpoint, and investigations of the construction of emotion may benefit from a sociological approach. In the next section I hope to show the utility of a sociological perspective for the analysis of collective affect as well.

COLLECTIVE EMOTION AND COMMITMENT

Durkheim (1965) has presented an analysis of collective emotion and solidarity which, like the other analyses of emotion reviewed here, can be further refined and formalized as an initial step toward empirical testing. In attempting such a tentative formalization from a symbolic interactionist perspective, I shall focus on two areas: the impact of collective feeling on commitment and the diffusion of collective emotion.

For Durkheim the powerful collective emotions often evoked by collective ritual are an important means of increasing social cohesion. Such collective feeling is an extraordinary state of exaltation, since emotions are sympathetically reflected and intensified by participants in the ritual. Thus animated, people become capable of collective actions and feelings too overwhelming for them to accomplish as individuals (Durkheim, 1965:240, 247). They are seized by a force beyond them, compelled to recognize the potency of society, and thereby to feel at one with it. After the ritual assembly ends, however, this transcendent feeling of fusion is "covered over little by little by the rising flood of daily experiences" (Durkheim, 1965:387). To revive it, to bring it forcefully back into consciousness, another collective ritual again draws people together. A cycle of collective emotion, rising and falling, is thus perpetuated through recurrent rituals, and contributes substantially to enduring social bonds.

Although Durkheim's analysis is quite insightful, there are two links in his argument that require further elaboration. One is his too-brief description of the means by which the transcendent feelings of exaltation he describes come about. (Durkheim states only that collective feelings are sympathetically reflected and magnified.) The other incomplete link is his analysis of the mechanisms underlying the arousal, contagion, and intensification of collective emotion, since these are left largely unspecified. In my view a symbolic interactionist perspective is quite useful for filling in these gaps. I shall summarize Mead's discussion of affective exaltation and use general symbolic interactionist principles to analyze the diffusion of collective emotion. I shall then schematically present an expanded version of Durkheim's argument that includes these elaborations.

Mead (1934:175, 273) argues that the sort of affective exaltation described by Durkheim results from a fusion within the individual of the "I" ("the response of the organism to the attitudes of . . . others") and the "me" ("the organized set of attitudes of others which one himself [herself] assumes"). In other words this intense exaltation occurs when the individual no longer has the usual awareness of social control because he feels that his "interest is the interest of all" (Mead, 1934:274). This "complete identification of individuals" involves "the successful completion of the social process," for then the individual wishes fully to do what is socially required (Mead, 1934:274-275). Like Durkheim, Mead suggests somewhat less explicitly that this kind of experience contributes to social cohesion.

Examining the diffusion of collective affect from a symbolic interactionist view, we would expect to find that:

1. Group norms exist in a collective group and influence (without determining) individual interpretations and conduct (Blumer, 1969), *including physiological arousal and definitions of such arousal.*

2. The actor is influenced by internal states and impulses (which are) taken into account in his definitions and interpretations) as well as less external events and stimuli (Hewitt, 1976:47; Mead, 1938:3-8, 23-25).

3. Certain symbols have, for most people, an emotional significance that is *learned.*

Somewhat ironically, Blumer (1969) does not apply to collective emotion the symbolic interactionist principles he has used so effectively to examine other aspects of behavior. Viewing the affective aspects of attitudes as the result of "nonsymbolic interaction," Blumer (1936:518-519; 1969:81) has argued that the rapid transmission and intensification of collective feelings occurs because individuals in a collective group respond directly to gestures rather than interpreting them.[3] I wish to argue that symbolic interactionist theory does apply to feelings and that the interpretive processes in an emotionally aroused collective group are essentially the same as those in everyday life. In fact these processes may constitute the means by which collective feelings are shared and intensified. Because individuals at many collective gatherings receive a restricted flow of information (often further restricted by a common focus of attention), they rely more on group norms and definitions; and thus, interpretations that accord with those norms and definitions become more likely (see Heirich, 1968:414, for a similar analysis). Thus, participants in a collective gathering are likely to interpret the generalized excitement and intense interest often felt on such occasions as the emotions suggested by the group's norms. In addition such gatherings usually focus attention on speeches, songs, chants, and other symbols to which most participants have learned to respond with certain feelings. These sorts of processes, then, may be the means by which the diffusion and intensification of collective sentiments take place.

Incorporating these modifications into Durkheim's analysis, we can

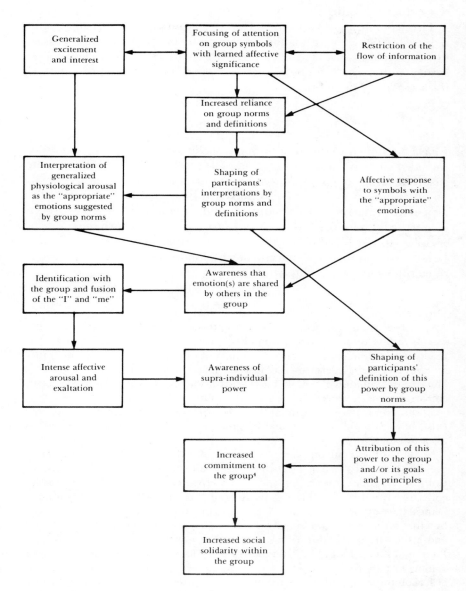

Figure 1

schematically represent the modified argument, which extends to collective gatherings other than collective rituals, as in Figure 1.

This formalization is simply a tentative outline, of course, and would require further elaboration and refinement for empirical testing. I hope, however, that it serves to indicate how the analyses of emotion discussed earlier in this paper can be further developed and used as starting points for a sociology of emotion.

CONCLUSION

I have attempted to touch upon some of the major areas that weould be included in a sociology of emotion. The works discussed here indicate that a sociology of emotion need not start from scratch, although it will be necessary, in many areas, to make explicit what has been implicit, articulate what has been disjointed, and to emphasize what has been submerged. I have tried to show that this task is well worth the efforts of sociologists. By building on the works described here, sociologists may be able to illuminate the shaping of emotion by society and the influence of emotion on social conduct.

NOTES

1. Hence, embarrassment can be distinguished from shame by the fact that shame results from the realization that others or oneself consider one's self inadequate, while embarrassment accompanies the recognition that one's presentation of self is deficient. Because an inadequate self usually produces a bungled presentation of self, shame is generally accompanied by embarrassment; embarrassment, however, is not generally followed by shame.

2. Disagreement over the interpretation of Schachter's and Singer's study does exist, however, and the reader has no doubt noticed that Kemper's view differs from mine.

3. Many other contemporary discussions of collective behavior also describe the diffusion of collective affect as an essentially automatic, irrational process. Collins (1975:152), for example, in his derivation of Durkheim's theory of collective ritual and solidarity, postulates: "All animals [including human beings] have *automatic* emotional responses to certain gestures and sounds made by other animals" (emphasis added). This view, in my judgment, is incorrect and results from a failure to see emotions as essentially social products. (See Lang and Lang, 1961:215ff., and Swanson, 1970:137ff., for similar criticisms of Blumer's analysis.)

4. Commitment will be defined, in Kanter's words, (1972:66) as "the willingness of people to do what will help maintain the group because it provides what they need. . . . [C]ommitment means the attachment of the self to the requirements of social relations that are seen as self-expressive."

REFERENCES

ADERMAN, DAVID, and LEONARD BERKOWITZ
  1970 "Observational set, empathy, and helping." Journal of Personality and
    Social Psychology 14:141–48.
ARONFREED, JUSTIN
  1968 Conduct and Conscience. New York: Academic Press.
AUSUBEL, DAVID P.
  1955 "Relationships between shame and guilt in the socializing process."
    Psychological Review 62:378–90.
AVERILL, JAMES M.
  1976 "Emotion and anxiety." Pp. 87–130 in Marvin Zuckerman and Charles
    D. Spielberger (eds.), Emotions and Anxiety. Hillsdale: Erlbaum.
BALES, ROBERT F.
  1951 Interaction Process Analysis. Reading, Mass.: Addison-Wesley.
BAREFOOT, JOHN C., and RONALD B. STRAUB
  1971 "Opportunity for information search and the effect of false heart-rate
    feedback." Journal of Personality and Social Psychology 17:154–57.
BERSCHEID, ELLEN, and ELAINE WALSTER
  1967 "When does a harm-doer compensate a victim?" Journal of Personality
    and Social Psychology 6:435–41.
BLAU, PETER M.
  1963 The Dynamics of Bureaucracy, rev. ed. Chicago: University of Chicago
    Press.
BLUMER, HERBERT
  1936 "Social attitudes and nonsymbolic interaction." Journal of Educational
    Psychology 9:515–23.
  1969 "The field of collective behavior." Pp. 64–121 in Alfred McClung Lee
    (ed.), Principles of Sociology. New York: Barnes and Noble.
BROCK, TIMOTHY C., and LEE A. BECKER
  1966 "'Debriefing' and susceptibility to subsequent experimental manipula-
    tions." Journal of Experimental and Social Psychology 2:314–23.
BROWN, ROGER
  1965 Social Psychology. New York: Free Press.
CANNON, WALTER B.
  1927 "The James-Lange theory of emotion." American Journal of Psychol-
    ogy, 39:106–24.
CARLSMITH, J. MERRILL, and ALAN E. GROSS
  1969 "Some effects of guilt on compliance." Journal of Personality and Social
    Psychology 11:232–39.
CHAGNON, NAPOLEON A.
  1968 Yąnomamö. New York: Holt, Rinehart and Winston.
COMTE, AUGUSTE
  1875 System of Positive Polity, vol. 2. London: Longmans, Green.
COLLINS, RANDALL
  1975 Conflict Sociology. New York: Academic Press.

COOLEY, CHARLES HORTON
1962 Social Organization. New York: Schocken Books.
DARLINGTON, RICHARD B., and CLIFFORD E. MACKER
1966 "Displacement of guilt-produced altruistic behavior." Journal of Personality and Social Psychology 17:208–13.
DAVIS, KINGSLEY.
1949 Human Society. New York: Macmillan.
DENTAN, ROBERT KNOX
1968 The Semai. New York: Holt, Rinehart and Winston.
DURKHEIM, EMILE
1965 The Elementary Forms of the Religious Life. New York: Free Press.
FOSTER, GEORGE M.
1972 "The anatomy of envy." Current Anthropology 13:165–202.
FREEDMAN, JONATHON L., SUE ANN WALLINGTON, and EVELYN BLESS
1967 "Compliance without pressure." Journal of Personality and Social Psychology 7:117–24.
GEERTZ, HILDRED
1959 "The vocabulary of emotion." Psychiatry 22:225–37.
GOFFMAN, ERVING
1967 Interaction Ritual. Garden City, N.Y.: Anchor Books.
GOLDFARB, WILLIAM
1945 "Psychological privation in infancy and subsequent adjustment." American Journal of Orthopsychiatry 15:247–55.
GROSS, EDWARD, and GREGORY P. STONE
1964 "Embarrassment and the analysis of role requirements." American Journal of Sociology 70:1–15.
HEIRICH, MAX
1968 The Spiral of Conflict. New York: Columbia University Press.
HEWITT, JOHN P.
1976 Self and Society. Boston: Allyn and Bacon.
HOCHSCHILD, ARLIE RUSSELL
1975 "The sociology of feeling and emotion." Pp. 280–307 in Marcia Millman and Rosabeth Moss Kanter (eds.), Another Voice. Garden City, N.Y.: Anchor Books.
JONES, JAMES M., and HOLLIS V. LIVERPOOL
1976 "Calypso humor in Trinidad." Pp. 259–86 in Tony Chapman and Hugh Foot (eds.), Humor and Laughter. New York: Wiley.
KANTER, ROSABETH MOSS
1972 Commitment and Community. Cambridge: Harvard University Press.
KREBS, DENNIS
1975 "Empathy and altruism." Journal of Personality and Social Psychology 32:1134–46.
LANG, KURT, and GLADYS ENGEL LANG
1961 Collective Dynamics. New York: Crowell.

MARTINEAU, WILLIAM H.
1972 "A model of the social functions of humor." Pp. 101-25 in Jeffry H.
       Goldstein and Paul E. McGree (eds.), The Psychology of Humor. New
       York: Academic Press.
MEAD, GEORGE HERBERT
1934 Mind, Self, and Society. Chicago: University of Chicago Press.
1938 The Philosophy of the Act. Chicago: University of Chicago Press.
MIDLARSKY, ELIZABETH, and JAMES H. BRYAN
1967 "Training charity in children." Journal of Personality and Social
       Psychology 5:408-15.
MILLS, C. WRIGHT
1940 "Situated actions and vocabularies of motive." American Sociological
       Review 5:904-13.
MODIGLIANI, ANDRE
1971 "Embarrassment, facework, and eye contact." Journal of Personality and
       Social Psychology 17:15-25.
NISBETT, RICHARD E., and STANLEY SCHACHTER
1966 "Cognitive manipulation of pain." Journal of Experimental and Social
       Psychology 2:227-36.
PARSONS, TALCOTT
1970 Social Structure and Personality. New York: Free Press.
PIERS, GERHART, and MILTON B. SINGER
1953 Shame and Guilt. Springfield: Thomas.
RADCLIFFE-BROWN, A. R.
1965 Structure and Function in Primitive Society. New York: Free Press.
REGAN, DENNIS T., MARGO WILLIAMS, and SONDRA SPARLING
1972 "Voluntary expiation of guilt." Journal of Personality and Social
       Psychology 24:42-45.
RIESMAN, DAVID, NATHAN GLAZER, and RUELL DENNY
1961 The Lonely Crowd, abridged ed. New Haven, Conn.: Yale University
       Press.
RIEZLER, KURT
1943 "Comment on the social psychology of shame." American Journal of
       Sociology 48:457-65.
SCHACHTER, STANLEY
1971 Emotion, Obesity, and Crime. New York: Academic Press.
SCHACHTER, STANLEY, and LADD WHEELER
1962 "Epinephrine, chlorpromazine, and amusement." Journal of Abnormal
       and Social Psychology 65:121-28.
SCHOECK, HELMUT
1966 Envy. New York: Harcourt, Brace and World.
SEARS, ROBERT R., ELEANOR J. MACCOBY, and HARRY LEVIN
1957 Patterns of Child Rearing. Stanford, Calif.: Stanford University Press.
SHOTT, SUSAN
forth- "Emotion and Social Life." American Journal of Sociology.
coming

SIMMEL, GEORG
  1950 The Sociology of Georg Simmel. Glencoe, Ill.: Free Press.
  1955 Conflict and the Web of Group Affiliations. Glencoe, Ill.: Free Press.
SPITZ, RENE A.
  1945 "Hospitalism." Psychoanalytic Study of the Child 1:53–74.
SWANSON, GUY E.
  1970 "Toward corporate action." Pp. 124–44 in Tamotsu Shibutani (ed.),
        Human Nature and Collective Behavior. Englewood Cliffs, N.J.:
        Prentice-Hall.
TÖNNIES, FERDINAND
  1957 Community and Society. New York: Harper & Row.
VALINS, STUART
  1966 "Cognitive effects of false heart-rate feedback." Journal of Personality
        and Social Psychology 4:400–8.
  1974 "Persistent effects of information about internal reactions." Pp. 116–24
        in Harvey London and Richard E. Nisbett (eds.), Thought and Feeling.
        Chicago: Aldine.
WEBER, MAX
  1968 On Charisma and Institution Building. Chicago: University of Chicago
        Press.
WHITING, JOHN W. M., and IRVIN L. CHILD
  1953 Child Training and Personality. New Haven: Yale University Press.

PART VIII
SOCIETY AND THE
ENVIRONMENT

We often forget that people live in a society, an area with unique physical and political characteristics. Environment, taken as a whole or as a part of a whole, must be taken into account.

Working from the assumption that the whole ecosystem must be considered in order to understand human behavior, Catton and Dunlap articulate the premises of the Human Exceptionalism Paradigm (HEP), which has dominated the environmental discipline. Briefly, this model sees humans as unique among earth's creatures, with a culture that can change infinitely and more rapidly than biological traits. Further, it sees most human differences as the result of socialization, not biology, and therefore, subject to change and inevitable progress. Counterposed to this view, is the New Environmental Paradigm (NEP), which sees humans as but one species among many involved in intricate linkages of cause and effect and bounded by a finite world with definite limits on economic, social, and political growth. The applicability of this model to diverse areas of social research is explored.

Living in a modern American city means that one is involved in a struggle for resources—personal resources and resources to maintain the city. The modern city is a microcosm of the political and economic life of the nation-state, and the same techniques which are useful for understanding the behavior of today's nation-states can be applied to a study of the city. Goering demonstrates how some of the older theories that sociologists have for studying modern urban processes are inappropriate because they cannot deal with such things as conflict, economic competition, or the destruction of neighborhoods for profit. A Marxian model has more utility, for it conceives of the city as a marketplace.

In the final selection, London ends on a positive note. Marcosociology and ecology are indivisible. Ecology is macrosociological, and macrosociology is ecological. To get to this point, London examines the contributions of general social theory to ecology, and those of ecology to social theory. He deals with criticisms that have been raised and shows how an ecological theory is not conservative, static, or incapable of dealing with change. Drawing on Dotson's elementary theory of organization, London shows that what human ecologists set as their task provides a basis for a generalized theory of human behavior.

1. Environmental Sociology: A New Paradigm

WILLIAM R. CATTON, JR. and
RILEY E. DUNLAP

Sociology appears to have reached an impasse. Efforts of sociologists to assimilate into their favorite theories some of the astounding events that have shaped human societies within the last generation have sometimes contributed more to the fragmentation of the sociological community than to the convincing explanation of social facts. But as Thomas Kuhn (1962:76) has shown, such an impasse often signifies "that an occasion for retooling has arrived."

The rise of environmental problems, and especially apprehensions about "limits to growth," signalled sharp departures from the exuberant expectations most sociologists had shared with the general public. Environmental problems and constraints contributed to the general uneasiness in American society brought about by events in the sixties. Sociologists, no less than other thinking people, are still grappling with the dramatic shift from the calmer fifties, when the American dreams of social progress, upward mobility, and societal stability seemed secure.

In 1976 the American Sociological Association, following precedents set a few years earlier in the Rural Sociological Society and in the Society for the Study of Social Problems, established a new "Section on Environmental Sociology."[1] In this paper we shall try to account for the development of environmental sociology by showing how it represents an attempt to understand recent societal changes that are difficult to

SOURCE: Reprinted from *The American Sociologist* 13 (February 1978):41–49.

comprehend from traditional sociological perspectives. We contend that, rather than simply representing the rise of another speciality within the discipline, the emergence of environmental sociology reflects the development of a new paradigm, and that this paradigm may help to extricate us from the impasse referred to above.

The "New Environmental Paradigm" (NEP) implicit in environmental sociology is, of course, only one among several current candidates to replace or amend the increasingly obsolescent set of "domain assumptions" which have defined the nature of social reality for most sociologists. Environmental sociologists, no less than the advocates of the very different alternatives Gouldner (1970) has described, are attempting to come to grips with a changed "sense of what is real." Further, we believe the NEP may contribute to a better understanding of contemporary and future social conditions than is possible with previous sociological perspectives. To illustrate the power of this paradigm to shed new light on important sociological issues, we shall briefly describe some recent NEP-based examinations of problems in stratification. But first we must contrast the old and new sets of assumptions.

THE "HUMAN EXCEPTIONALISM PARADIGM"

The numerous competing theoretical perspectives in contemporary sociology—e.g., functionalism, symbolic interactionism, ethnomethodology, conflict theory, Marxism, and so forth—are prone to exaggerate their differences from each other. They purport to be paradigms in their own right, and are often taken as such (see e.g., Denisoff, *et al.*, 1974, and Ritzer, 1975). But they have also been construed simply as competing "preparadigmatic" perspectives (Friedrichs, 1972). We maintain that their apparent diversity is not as important as the fundamental anthropocentrism underlying *all* of them.

This mutual anthropocentrism is part of a basic sociological worldview (Klausner, 1971:10–11). We call *that* worldview the "Human Exceptionalism Paradigm" (HEP). We contend that acceptance of the assumptions of the HEP has made it difficult for most sociologists, regardless of their preferred orientation, to deal meaningfully with the social implications of ecological problems and constraints. Thus, the HEP has become increasingly obstructive of sociological efforts to comprehend contemporary and future social experience.

The HEP comprises several assumptions that have either been challenged by recent additions to knowledge, or have had their optimistic implications contradicted by events of the seventies. Accepted explicitly or implicitly by all existing theoretical persuasions, they include:

1. Humans are unique among the earth's creatures, for they have culture.

2. Culture can vary almost infintely and can change much more rapidly than biological traits.

3. Thus, many human differences are socially induced rather than inborn, they can be socially altered, and inconvenient differences can be eliminated.

4. Thus, also, cultural accumulation means that progress can continue without limit, making all social problems ultimately soluble.

Sociological acceptance of such an optimistic worldview was no doubt fostered by prevalence of the doctrine of progress in Western culture, where academic sociology was spawned and nurtured. It was under the American branch of Western culture that sociology flourished most fully, and it has been clear to foreign analysts of American life, from Tocqueville to Laski, that most Americans (until recently) ardently believed that the present was better than the past and the future would improve upon the present. Sociologists could easily share that conviction when natural resources were still so plentiful that limits to progress remained unseen. The historian, David Potter (1954:141), tried to alert his colleagues to some of the unstated and unexamined assumptions shaping their studies; his words have equal relevance for sociologists: "The factor of abundance, which we first discovered as an environmental condition and which we then converted by technological change into a cultural as well as a physical force, has . . . influenced all aspects of American life in a fundamental way."[2]

Not only have sociologists been too unmindful of the fact that our society derived special qualities from past abundance; the heritage of abundance has made it difficult for most sociologists to perceive the possibility of an era of uncontrived scarcity. For example, ecological concepts such as "carrying capacity" are alien to the vocabularies of most sociologists (Catton, 1976a; 1976b), yet disregard for this concept has been tantamount to assuming an environment's carrying capacity is always enlargeable as needed—thus denying the possibility of scarcity.

Neglect of the ecosystem-dependence of human society has been evident in sociological literature on economic development (e.g., Horowitz, 1972), which has simply not recognized biogeochemical limits to material progress. And renewed sociological attention to a theory of societal evolution (e.g., Parsons, 1977) has seldom paid much attention to the resource base that is subjected to "more efficient" exploitation as societies become more differentiated internally and are thereby "adaptively upgraded." In such literature, the word "environment" refers almost entirely to a society's "symbolic environment" (cultural systems) or "social environment" (environing social systems).[3]

It is the habit of neglecting laws of other sciences (such as the Principle of Entropy and the Law of Conservation of Energy)[4]—as if human actions were unaffected by them—that enables so distinguished a sociologist as Daniel Bell (1973:465) to assert that the question before humanity is "not subsistence but standard of living, not biology, but sociology," to insist that basic needs "are satiable, and the possibility of abundance is real," to impute "apocalyptic hysteria" to "the ecology movement," and to regard it as trite rather than questionable to expect "compound interest" growth to continue for another hundred years. Likewise, this neglect permits Amos Hawley (1975:8-9) to write that "there are no known limits to the improvement of technology" and the population pressure on nonagricultural resources is neither "currently being felt or likely to be felt in the early future." Such views reflect a staunch commitment to the HEP.

Environmental Sociology and the "New Environmental Paradigm"

When public apprehension began to be aroused concerning newly visible environmental problems, the scientists who functioned as opinion leaders were not sociologists. They included such individuals as Rachel Carson, Barry Commoner, Paul Ehrlich and Garrett Hardin— biologists. Leadership in highlighting the precariousness of the human condition was mostly forfeited by sociologists, because until recently, most of us had been socialized into a worldview that makes it difficult to recognize the reality and full significance of the environmental problems and constraints we now confront. Due to our acceptance of the HEP, our discipline has focused on humans to the neglect of habitat; consideration of our *social* environment has crowded out consideration of our physical circumstances (Michelson, 1976:17). Further, we have had unreserved faith that equilibrium between population and resources could and would be reached in noncatastrophic ways, since technology and organization would mediate the relations between a growing population and its earthly habitat (see, e.g., Hawley, 1975).

But, stimulated by troubling events, some sociologists began to read such works as Carson (1962), Commoner (1971), Ehrlich and Ehrlich (1970), and Hardin (1968), and began to shed the blinders of the HEP. As long-held assumptions began to lose their power over our perceptions, we began to recognize that the reality of ecological constraints posed serious problems for human societies *and* for the discipline of sociology (see, e.g., Burch, 1971). It began to appear that, in order to make sense of the world, it was necessary to rethink the traditional Durkheimian norm of sociological purity—i.e., that social facts can be explained *only* by linking them to other *social* facts. The gradual result of such rethinking has been the development of environmental sociology.

Environmental sociology is clearly still in its formative years. At the turn of the decade rising concern with "environment" as a social problem led to numerous studies of public attitudes toward environmental issues and of the "Environmental Movement" (see Albrecht and Mauss, 1975). A coalition gradually developed between sociologists with such interests and sociologists with a range of other concerns—including rather established interests such as the "built" environment, natural hazards, resource management and outdoor recreation, as well as newer interests such as "social impact assessment" (mandated by the National Environmental Policy Act of 1969). After the energy crisis of 1973, numerous sociologists (including many with prior interests in one or more of the above areas) began to investigate the effects of energy shortages in particular, and resource constraints in general, on society: the stratification system, the political order, the family, and so on. (For an indication of the range of interests held by environmental sociologists see Dunlap, 1975, and Manderscheid, 1977; for reviews of the literature see Dunlap and Catton, forthcoming, and Humphrey and Buttel, 1976.)

These diverse interests are linked into an increasingly distinguishable specialty known as environmental sociology by the acceptance of "environmental" variables as meaningful for sociological investigation. Conceptions of "environment" range from the "manmade" (or "built") environment to the "natural" environment, with an array of "human-altered" environments—e.g., air, water, noise and visual pollution—in between. In fact, *the study of interaction between the environment and society is the core of environmental sociology*, as advocated several years ago by Schnaiberg (1972).[5] This involves studying the effects of the environment on society (e.g., resource abundance or scarcity on stratification) and the effects of society on the environment (e.g., the contributions of differing economic systems to environmental degradation).[6]

The study of such interaction rests on the recognition that sociologists can no longer afford to ignore the environment in their investigations, and this in turn appears to depend on at least tacit acceptance of a set of assumptions quite different from those of the HEP. From the writings of several environmental sociologists (e.g., Anderson, 1976; Burch, 1971, 1976; Buttel, 1976; Catton, 1976a, 1976b; Morrison, 1976; Schnaiberg, 1972, 1975) it is possible to extract a set of assumptions about the nature of social reality which stand in stark contrast to the HEP. We call this set of assumptions the "New Environmental Paradigm" or NEP (see Dunlap and Van Liere, 1977 for a broader usage of the term, referring to emerging public beliefs):

1. Human beings are but one species among the many that are interdependently involved in the biotic communities that shape our social life.

2. Intricate linkages of cause and effect and feedback in the web of nature produce many unintended consequences from purposive human action.

3. The world is finite, so there are potent physical and biological limits constraining economic growth, social progress, and other societal phenomena.

ENVIRONMENTAL FACTS AND SOCIAL FACTS

Sociologists who adhere to the NEP readily accept as factual the opening sentences of the lead article (by a perceptive economist) in a recent issue of *Social Science Quarterly* devoted to "Society and Scarcity": "We have inherited, occupy, and will bequeath a world of scarcity: resources are not adequate to provide all of everything we want. It is a world, therefore, of limitations, constraints, and conflict, requiring the bearing of costs and calling for communal coordination" (Allen, 1976:263). Persistent adherents of the HEP, on the other hand, accustomed to relying on endless and generally benign technological and organizational breakthroughs, could be expected to discount such a statement as a mere manifestation of the naive presumption that the "state of the arts" is fixed (see, e.g., Hawley, 1975:6-7).

Likewise, sociologists who have been converted to the assumptions of the NEP have no difficulty appreciating the sociological relevance of the following fact: the $36 billion it now costs annually to import oil to supplement depleted American supplies is partially defrayed by exporting $23 billion worth of agricultural products—grown at the cost of enormous soil erosion (van Bavel, 1977). Environmental sociologists expect momentous social change if soil or oil, or both are depleted. But sociologists still bound by the HEP would probably ignore such topics, holding that oil and soil are irrelevant variables for sociologists. However, we believe that only by taking into account such factors as declining energy resources can sociologists continue to understand and explain "social facts." We will attempt to demonstrate this by examining some work by NEP-oriented sociologists in one of the areas they have begun to examine—social stratification.

USEFULNESS OF THE NEP: RECENT WORK IN SOCIAL STRATIFICATION

The bulk of existing work in stratification appears to rest on the Human Exceptionalism Paradigm, as it "... does not adequately consider the context of resource constraints or lack thereof in which the stratification system operates ..." (Morrison, 1973:83). We will therefore describe recent work in the area by environmental sociologists, in an effort to illustrate the insights into stratification processes provided by the NEP. We will limit the discussion to three topics: the current decline in living conditions experienced by many Americans; contemporary and likely future cleavages in our stratification system; and the problematic prospects for ending self-perpetuating poverty.

Recent decline in standard of living: A majority of Americans are concerned about their economic situation (Strumpel, 1976:23), and in *Food, Shelter and the American Dream*, Aronowitz (1974) exemplifies the growing awareness that *something* is not going according to expectation—that old ideals of societal progress, increasing prosperity and material comfort, and individual and intergenerational mobility for *all* segments of society are *not* being realized (also see Anderson, 1976:1–3). Yet, even a "critical sociologist" such as Aronowitz seems impeded by the HEP in attempting to understand these changes. He views recent shortages in food, gasoline, heating oil, and so on, entirely as the result of "manipulations" by large national and supranational corporations, and is skeptical of the idea that resource scarcities may be real. Thus, his solution to the decline in the American standard of living would apparently be solely political—reduce the power of large corporations.

Although many environmental sociologists would not deny that oil companies have benefited from energy shortages, their acceptance of the NEP leads to a different explanation of recent economic trends. Schnaiberg (1975:6–8), for instance, has explicated a very useful "societal-environmental dialectic." Given the *thesis* that "economic expansion is a social desideratum" and the *antithesis* that "ecological disruption is a necessary consequence of economic expansion," a dialectic emerges with the acceptance of the proposition that "ecological disruption is harmful to human society." Schnaiberg notes three alternative *syntheses* of the dialectic: (1) an *economic synthesis* which ignores ecological disruptions and attempts to maximize growth; (2) a *managed scarcity synthesis*[7] which deals with the most obvious and pernicious consequences of resource-utilization by imposing controls over selected industries and resources; and (3) an *ecological synthesis* in which "substantial control over both production and effective demand for goods" is used to minimize ecological disruptions and maintain a "sustained yield" of resources. Schnaiberg (1975:9–10) argues that the synthesis adopted will be influenced by the basic economic structure of a society, with "regressive" (inequality-magnifying) societies most likely to maintain the "economic" synthesis and "progressive" (equality-fostering) societies least resistive to the "ecological" synthesis.[8] Not surprisingly, therefore, the U.S., with its "non-redistributive" economy, has increasingly opted for "managed scarcity" as the solution to environmental and resource problems.[9]

Managed scarcity involves, for example, combating ecological disruptions by forcing industries to abate pollution, with resultant costs passed along to consumers via higher prices, and combating resource shortage via higher taxes (and thus higher consumer prices) on the scarce resources. There is growing recognition of the highly regressive impacts of both mechanisms (Morrison, 1977; Schnaiberg, 1975), and thus governmental reliance on "managed scarcity" to cope with pollution and resource shortages at least partly accounts for the worsening economic plight of the middle-, working, and especially lower-classes— a plight in which adequate food and shelter are often difficult to obtain. Unfortunately, these economic woes cannot simply be corrected by returning to the economic synthesis. The serious health threats posed by pollutants, the potentially devastating changes in the ecosystem wrought by unbridled economic and technological growth (e.g., destruction of the protective ozone layer, alteration of atmospheric temperature), and the undeniable reality of impending shortages in crucial resources such as oil, all make reversion to the traditional economic synthesis impossible in the long run (see, e.g., Anderson, 1976; Miller, 1972). Of course, as Morrison (1976) has noted, the pressures to return to this synthesis are great, and understanding them provides insights into contemporary and future economic cleavages.

Cleavages within the stratification system: Schnaiberg's ecological synthesis amounts to what others have termed a "stationary" or "steady-state" society, and it is widely agreed that such a society would need to be far more egalitarian than the contemporary U.S. (Anderson, 1976:58–61; Daly, 1973:168–170).[10] Achieving the necessary redistribution would be very difficult, and opposition to it would be likely to result in serious, but unstable cleavages within the stratification system. In the long run, as environmental constraints become more obvious, ecologically aware "haves" are likely to opt for increased emphasis on managed scarcity to cope with them. The results would be disastrous for the "have nots," as slowed growth and higher prices would reverse the traditional trend in the U.S. in which *all* segments of society have improved their material condition—not because they obtained a larger slice of the "pie," but because the pie kept growing (Anderson, 1976:28–33; Morrison, 1976). Slowed growth *without* increased redistribution will result in real (as well as relative) deprivation among the "have nots," making class conflict more likely than ever before.[11] As Morrison (1976:299) notes, "Class antagonisms that are soothed by general economic growth tend to emerge as more genuine class conflicts when growth slows or ceases." Thus, in the long run the NEP suggests that Marx's predictions about class conflict may become more accurate, although for reasons Marx could not have foreseen.

In the short run, however, a very different possibility seems likely. The societal pressures resulting from managed scarcity are such that large portions of *both* "haves" and "have nots" will push for a reversion to the economic (growth) synthesis. In fact, Morrison (1973) has predicted the emergence of a Dahrendorfian (i.e., non-Marxian) cleavage: "growthists vs. nongrowthists," with *all* those highly dependent upon industrial growth (workers *and* owners) coalescing to oppose environmentalists (who typically hold positions—in the professions, government, education, for example—less directly dependent on growth). The staunch labor union support for growth, and the successful efforts of industry to win the support of labor and the poor in battles against environmentalists, both suggest the emergence of this coalition. Somewhat ironically, therefore, support for continued economic growth has united capitalists and the "left" (used broadly to include most labor unions, advocates for the poor, and academic Marxists). Not only does this support reveal the extent to which most of the left has abandoned hopes for real *redistribution* in favor of getting a "fair share" of a growing pie, but it also reveals a misunderstanding of the distribution of costs and benefits of traditional economic growth.

The "Culture of Poverty" solidified: Sociologists guided by the NEP have not only questioned the supposed universal benefits of growth, but they consistently point to the generally neglected "costs" of growth— costs which tend to be very regressive (Anderson, 1976:30–31; Schnaiberg, 1975:19). Thus, it is increasingly recognized that the workplace and inner city often constitute serious health hazards, and that there is generally a strong inverse relationship between SES and exposure to environmental pollution (Schnaiberg, 1975:19). Further, in his study of the SES-air pollution relationship, Burch (1976:314) has gone so far as to suggest that, "Each of these pollutants when ingested at certain modest levels over continuing periods, is likely to be an important influence upon one's ability to persist in the struggle for improvement of social position . . . These exposures, like nutritional deficiencies, seem one mechanism by which class inequalities are reinforced." This leads him to suggest that efforts to eradicate poverty which do not take into account the debilitating impact of environmental insults are likely to fail.

CONCLUSION

We have attempted to illustrate the utility of the NEP by focusing on issues concerning stratification, for we believe this is one of many aspects of society that will be significantly affected by ecological constraints. As noted above, in the short run we expect tremendous pressure for reverting to the economic growth synthesis, for such a strategy seeks to alleviate societal tensions at the expense of the environment. Of course, the NEP implies that such a strategy cannot continue indefinitely (and the evidence seems to support this—see, e.g., Miller, 1972). Thus we are faced with the necessity of choosing between managed scarcity and an ecological synthesis.[12] The deleterious effects of the former are already becoming obvious; they help account for the trends described by Aronowitz and others. However, the achievement of a truly ecological synthesis will require achieving a steady-state society, a very difficult goal. As students of social organization, sociologists should play a vital role in delineating the characteristics of such a society, feasible procedures for attaining it, and their probable social costs. (See Anderson, 1976 for a preliminary effort.) Until sociology extricates itself from the Human Exceptionalism Paradigm, however, such a task will be impossible.

NOTES

The authors contributed equally to the preparation of this paper, and are listed alphabetically. At various times we have had the benefit of stimulating discussions, for which we are grateful, with the following colleagues or graduate students: Don A. Dillman, Viktor Gecas, Dennis L. Peck, Kenneth R. Tremblay, Jr., Kent D. Van Liere, John M. Wardwell, and Robert L. Wisniewski. We are especially indebted to Don Dillman for his critical reading of an earlier draft of this paper. Dunlap's contribution to the paper was supported by Project 0158, Department of Rural Sociology, Washington State University, and this is Scientific Paper No. 4933, College of Agriculture Research Center, Washington State University, Pullman, WA 99164.

1. In the late sixties a Natural Resources Research Group was formed in the RSS, and in 1973 SSSP established an Environmental Problems Division.

2. For an early warning that this exuberance-producing force could be temporary, see Sumner (1896). Few twentieth century sociologists have taken the warning seriously.

3. Even sociological human ecologists have limited their attention primarily to the *social* or *spatial* environment, rather than the *physical* environment (see Michelson, 1976:17–23), reflecting their adherence to the HEP.

4. See Miller (1972) for a lucid discussion of these laws.

5. This does not mean that environmental sociologists focus only on bi-variate relationships between social and environmental variables, as illustrated by Schnaiberg's (1975) "societal-environmental dialectic" (to be discussed below).

6. For an alternative and narrower view of the domain of environmental sociology see Zeisel (1975: Chap. 1).

7. Schnaiberg's term was "planned scarcity," but because adherents of the HEP might suppose that phrase referred to scarcity *caused* by planners—rather than scarcities (and their costs) *allocated* by planners—we prefer to speak of "managed scarcity."

8. Thus, e.g., among industrialized nations Sweden appears to have come closest to the ecological synthesis, while China represents the closest approximation to it by any developing nation (Anderson, 1976:242–251). In contrast, highly regressive developing nations such as Brazil seem strongly committed to the economic synthesis.

9. The U.S. economy is "non-redistributive" because overall patterns of inequality (i.e., relative shares of wealth) have been altered very little by growth, even though all strata have improved their lot via growth (Schnaiberg, 1975:9; Zeitlin, 1977; Part 2).

10. For example, wasteful consumption due to excess wealth and economic growth stemming from the investment of excess capital (for profit) would need to be halted, as would pressure for economic growth stemming from the unmet needs of the lower strata (see, e.g., Anderson, 1976:58–61; Daly, 1973:168–171).

11. Managed scarcity and slowed growth are also likely to exacerbate tensions between developed and developing nations. This leads NEP-oriented sociologists (e.g., Anderson, 1976:258–269; Morrison, 1976) to see the future of international development quite differently than sociologists bound by the HEP (see, e.g., Horowitz, 1972).

12. A point implicit in our discussion is worth making explicit: the NEP suggests that resource scarcities are unavoidable, but—as Schnaiberg's work indicates—societies may react to them in a variety of ways. Thus, as Schnaiberg (1975:17) suggests, sociologists should begin to examine the social impacts (especially distributional impacts) of *alternative* responses to scarcity.

REFERENCES

ALBRECHT, STAN L., and ARMAND L. MAUSS
 1975 "The environment as a social problem." Pp. 556–605 in A. L. Mauss, Social Problems as Social Movements. Philadelphia: Lippincott.

ALLEN, WILLIAM R.
  1976 "Scarcity and order: The Hobbesian problem and the Humean resolution." Social Science Quarterly 57:263–275.
ANDERSON, CHARLES H.
  1976 The Sociology of Survival: Social Problems of Growth. Homewood, Ill.: Dorsey.
ARONOWITZ, STANLEY
  1974 Food, Shelter and the American Dream. New York: Seabury Press.
BELL, DANIEL
  1973 The Coming of Post-Industrial Society. New York: Basic Books.
BURCH, WILLIAM R., JR.
  1971 Daydreams and Nightmares: A Sociological Essay on the American Environment. New York: Harper and Row.
  1976 "The peregrine falcon and the urban poor: Some sociological interrelations." Pp. 308–316 in P. J. Richerson and J. McEvoy III (eds.), in Human Ecology: An Environmental Approach. North Scituate, Mass.: Duxbury.
BUTTEL, FREDERICK H.
  1976 "Social science and the environment: Competing theories." Social Science Quarterly 57:307–323.
CARSON, RACHEL
  1962 Silent Spring. Boston: Houghton-Mifflin.
CATTON, WILLIAM R., JR.
  1976a "Toward prevention of obsolescence in sociology." Sociological Focus 9:89–98.
  1976b "Why the future isn't what it used to be (and how it could be made worse than it has to be)." Social Science Quarterly 57:276–291.
COMMONER, BARRY
  1971 The Closing Circle. New York: Knopf.
DALY, HERMAN E.
  1973 "The steady-state economy: Toward a political economy of biophysical equilibrium and moral growth." Pp. 149–174 in H. E. Daly (ed.), Toward a Steady-State Economy. San Francisco: W. H. Freeman.
DENISOFF, R. SERGE, OREL CALLAHAN, and MARK H. LEVINE (eds.)
  1974 Theories and Paradigms in Contemporary Sociology. Itasca, Ill.: Peacock.
DUNLAP, RILEY E. (ed.)
  1975 Directory of Environmental Sociologists. Pullman: Washington State University, College of Agriculture Research Center, Circular No. 586.
DUNLAP, RILEY E., and WILLIAM R. CATTON, JR.
  forth- "Environmental sociology." Annual Review of Sociology. Palo Alto,
  coming Calif.: Annual Reviews, Inc.
DUNLAP, RILEY E., and KENT D. VAN LIERE
  1977 "The new environmental paradigm': A proposed measuring instrument and preliminary results." Paper presented at the Annual Meeting of the American Sociological Association, Chicago.

EHRLICH, PAUL R., and ANNE H. EHRLICH
1970 Population, Resources, Environment. San Francisco: W. H. Freeman.
FRIEDRICHS, ROBERT W.
1972 A Sociology of Sociology. New York: Free Press.
GOULDNER, ALVIN W.
1970 The Coming Crisis of Western Sociology. New York: Basic Books.
HARDIN, GARRETT
1968 "The tragedy of the commons." Science 162:1243–1248.
HAWLEY, AMOS H. (ed.)
1975 Man and Environment. New York: New York Times Company.
HOROWITZ, IRVING L.
1972 Three Worlds of Development: The Theory and Practice of International
       Stratification. 2nd ed. New York: Oxford University Press.
HUMPHREY, CRAIG R., and FREDERICK H. BUTTEL
1976 "New directions in environmental sociology." Paper presented at the
       Annual Meeting of the Society for the Study of Social Problems, New
       York.
KLAUSNER, SAMUEL Z.
1971 On Man in His Environment. San Francisco: Jossey-Bass.
KUHN, THOMAS S.
1962 The Structure of Scientific Revolutions. Chicago: University of Chicago
       Press.
MANDERSCHEID, RONALD W. (ed.)
1977 Annotated Directory of Members: Ad Hoc Committee on Housing and
       Physical Environment. Adelphi, Maryland: Mental Health Study Center,
       NIMH.
MICHELSON, WILLIAM H.
1976 Man and His Urban Environment. 2nd ed. Reading, Mass.: Addison-
       Wesley.
MILLER, G. TYLER, JR.
1972 Replenish the Earth: A Primer in Human Ecology. Belmont, Calif.:
       Wadsworth.
MORRISON, DENTON E.
1973 "The environmental movement: Conflict dynamics." Journal of Volun-
       tary Action Research 2:74–85.
1976 "Growth, environment, equity and scarcity." Social Science Quarterly
       57:292–306.
1977 "Equity impacts of some major energy alternatives." Paper presented at
       the Annual Meeting of the American Sociological Association, Chicago.
PARSONS, TALCOTT
1977 The Evolution of Societies (ed. by Jackson Toby). Englewood Cliffs,
       N.J.: Prentice-Hall.
POTTER, DAVID M.
1954 People of Plenty. Chicago: University of Chicago Press.
RITZER, GEORGE
1975 Sociology: A Multiple Paradigm Science. Boston: Allyn and Bacon.

SCHNAIBERG, ALLAN
   1972 "Environmental sociology and the division of labor." Department of
         Sociology, Northwestern University, mimeograph.
   1975 "Social syntheses of the societal-environmental dialectic: The role of
         distributional impacts." Social Science Quarterly 56:5-20.
STRUMPEL, BURKHARD (ed.)
   1976 Economic Means for Human Needs. Ann Arbor: Institute for Social
         Research, University of Michigan.
SUMNER, WILLIAM GRAHAM
   1896 "Earth hunger or the philosophy of land grabbing." Pp. 31-64 in A. G.
         Keller (ed.), Earth Hunger and Other Essays. New Haven: Yale Univer-
         sity Press, 1913.
VAN BAVEL, CORNELIUS H. M.
   1977 "Soil and oil." Science 197:213.
ZEISEL, JOHN
   1975 Sociology and Architectural Design. New York: Russell Sage Founda-
         tion.
ZEITLIN, MAURICE (ed.)
   1977 American Society, Inc. 2nd ed. Chicago: Rand McNally.

2. The Marxist Perspective and Urban Sociology

JOHN M. GOERING

American urban scholars are increasingly willing to admit that the traditional model of social ecology does not apply to many of the characteristics and problems of cities. Several years ago Jessie Bernard (1973:13) argued that the ecological and capitalist paradigms:

> . . . do not tell us how cities function; we are at a loss to interpret the nature and operation of power in the community; old criteria of social class no longer fit the current scene. Events, in brief, have overtaken old paradigms and research as usual will not do what has to be done . . .

This paradigm crisis is partly the result of the inability of older theoretical approaches to explain such things as the fiscal insolvency and population decline of most large Western cities. In fact they have failed to explain most of the critical events in American cities over the last two decades (Aiken and Castells, 1977).

The inadequacy of older perspectives has become even more apparent because of the recent challenges by Marxist urbanists to the dominance of the ecologically oriented Chicago school paradigm. Marxist urban theory uses many of the assumptions and strengths of traditional Marxian analysis to understand and reinterpret urban phenomenon. This new perspective has made it more apparent that a whole series of questions was foreclosed by the social-ecological approach to the city. Urban social scientists can now more clearly understand the limitations and contributions of earlier views. The following sections outline the characteristics of the Marxist urbanists and the social ecologists and draw out some of the implications of choosing one paradigm over the other.

SOCIAL ECOLOGY

The perspective of social ecologists was developed over fifty years ago, when a unique combination of social problems, desire for reform, and private funding combined to provide the basis for a perspective on population change in cities (Carey, 1975; Short, 1971). Most of these efforts were initially concentrated on explaining some of the patterns of the seemingly chaotic character of urban life in the 1920s and 1930s. Social ecologists sought to understand the conditions and possible effects of the rapid growth of large American cities by focusing on what they felt were many of the natural, ethnic features of city life (Park, 1952; Wirth, 1938).

The interest of social ecologists in the distribution, decentralization, and culture of urban populations has continued up to the present, offering additional data and insights into the microcosm of urban life (Hawley, 1950; Suttles, 1968, 1972; Hunter, 1974; Kornblum, 1974; Berry and Kasarda, 1977). Several themes have run throughout the intellectual development of this perspective. One is the view of the city as an integrated system of population groups, functions, and neighborhood life. Another is the interest in the populations of urban areas. Ecologists are masters of demographic statistics that depict the changing character of communities. These statistics, however, often take on a life of their own, for the rules of demographic conduct appear to be the main determinants of the pattern of urban life. Patterns of population density, segregation, growth, migration, and deconcentration often appear as autonomous processes, generating their own dynamics and effects.

One of the best and oldest examples of the social dynamics of population movement is the ecologist's explanation of the patterns of population expansion within cities. Cities develop, in this view, as a configuration of stable natural areas, or neighborhoods, that are tied into a model of geographic and social mobility. Newcomers enter the city, settle in its core, which is a low-income ghetto and then they gradually spread toward the suburban periphery. This was a model that crystalized the association between suburbanization and social mobility.

The core area is always one of transition; in it industry and commerce operate and expand; the poor are displaced; and some undesirables—

such as prostitutes—are moved into the next ring of residence. It was also a model of gradual displacement, rooted in assumptions about the health and vitality of the city's economic base, private property, housing, and in the belief that ethnically homogeneous neighborhoods were a natural and useful part of the urban scene.

The process by which urban populations were reshuffled into decentralized, middle-class, residential areas consisted of four steps. The founding father of many of these ideas, Ernest Burgess (1928:12), explains the steps:

> These population movements, from the center toward the periphery of the city as the resultant of outward pressure and local community, take the form of successive waves of invasion. Succession as a process has been studied and its main course charted as (1) invasion, beginning often as an unnoticed or gradual penetration, followed by (2) reaction, or the resistance, mild or violent, of the inhabitants of the community, ultimately resulting in (3) the influx of newcomers and the rapid abandonment of the area by its old-time residents, and (4) climax or the achievements of a new equilibrium of community stability.

Invasion, resistance, flight, and stability, then are the steps by which older populations are displaced from the center to the periphery by the arriving immigrants.

Invasion, like other stages, appears to the ecologist as a relatively impersonal and inevitable process in which significant numbers of new residents force their way, by sheer weight of numbers, into a neighborhood. Population pressure appears as the cause of this process as well as the result. There appear to be no structural or institutional choices or breaks in this process. There is, consequently, little sense that there may be noticeably different rates, volumes, or control over the initial stage of population movement.

The result, abandonment, also appears inevitable and desirable. Resistance is presumably only a temporary, even superficial, response to the overwhelming necessities of this model. Finally, everything settles into what may be the norm—stability—although there is no clear way to define the meaning of stability except insofar as the model temporarily "rests" between waves of newcomers who will again begin the chain reaction of ecological succession.

The city appears to operate by laws of its own, tied to the inevitable logic of population movement. Groups may compete for certain space, but the pressure of market-related forces will gradually produce a centrifugal drift. The city is portrayed as a mosaic of ethnic and social

enclaves, which apparently emerge from the interaction of heterogeneous populations, space, and the forces of competition and expansion.
These enclaves are an essential respite from the tendencies toward
impersonality, crime, disorder, and rootlessness that would otherwise
result from the size and complexity of urban life.

The dynamics of population expansion, as well as the characteristics
of population groups, are central to the armament of ecological analysis.
It is all too easy, however, for population data, gathered from census
returns, to be fallacious. Items such as income, age, race, and family size
are then said "to account for the social organization of the local
community and in particular for the balance between change and
stability" (Janowitz and Street, 1970:102). Too little account is paid to
other demonstrably relevant factors, and too little attention is paid to the
logical or theoretical character of these descriptions, though as descriptions, they are extremely useful.

Another logically necessary part of the ecologists' view of the city is
technology, particularly transportation innovations. The automobile,
for example, is said to have had a revolutionary effect on the structure of
the metropolis (Kasarda, 1978:30). Technological developments appear
as nonanthropomorphic instruments arising out of an unexamined set
of needs and interests, and creating a supposedly decisive, positive
effect in redistributing population. This is not a process of innovation which seems to have historically specific roots, exceptions, social
costs, or even unanticipated effects. Changes in productive technology
are also seen as more or less impersonal changes, which result from the
needs of the market for either greater efficiency or more space (Kasarda,
1978:36-37).

> Old central-city manufacturing facilities had been constructed as
> multi-story, loftlike structures that are not adaptable to much of
> today's mass production technology. The assembly line, in particu-
> lar, has large horizontal space requirements that are more difficult
> and more costly to obtain in the central city than in the suburban
> rings.

This analysis blithely ignores the role of industrial strikes, rioting, labor
unions, taxes, and the powerful role of nonindustrial economic interests
in forcing factories out of the city (Fitch, 1977). It also ignores the fact
that many of these plants still remain behind in inner cities, seemingly
in defiance of the technological imperatives attributed to their operations.

The role of technology in shaping the growth of cities is more of an
assertion than an item of fundamental empirical interest for ecologists.

It appears as a relatively convenient and simplified construct that is used to interpret many of the variations and exceptions to the rule of concentric growth. It does not fundamentally alter the ecologist's interest in the conditions for population growth and stability in cities.

Newer ecologists, like their predecessors, focus considerable attention on the composition, persistence, and culture of local community life. For them most of the questions about how cities operate—or fail to operate—are answerable only through an examination of the organization and integration of the residents of cities.

The ecologist attempts to understand the city by examining the attachments and reactions of individuals to the scale and complexity of urban life. The "critical mass" of people found in cities, as opposed to those in rural areas, presumably generates unique, positive interests and institutions. Organized and disorganized subcultures are also formed out of the critical fusion of personal contacts, encounters, and even from the "recoil" which occurs in cities (Fischer, 1976:38). Many of these urban communities apparently form in reaction to the scale and mass of city life. Community life persists as a necessary and stable antidote to the disruption between work and residence and to the fear of living without the defenses of neighborhood life.

The stability of urban life is not, however, solely or even distinctively a matter of individual, social-psychological encounters. The roots of this stability and persistence are in the socio-spatial mechanisms by which individuals and groups create a safe, sensible local moral order. Mechanisms of segmentation, negotiation, symbolic attachment, and limited liability establish the basis for order and stability in an otherwise frightening and chaotic environment. These territorial enclaves no longer serve everyday needs, but are a response to the intersection of territorial rights, principles of local accountability, ethnicity, age, and family relationships (Hunter, 1974).

The city is divided into enclaves in which the main purpose of local life is security, and to a lesser degree, accountability. The defended community becomes the basic building block of the city.

> Functionally, the defended neighborhood can be conceived of as the smallest spatial unit within which co-residents assume a relative degree of security on the streets as compared to local areas. The defended neighborhood,, then, is an area within which people retreat to avoid a quantum jump or injury they must take in moving about outside that area (Suttles, 1972:57).

The general apprehensiveness of the rich and the poor is presumably reduced or eliminated through the symbolic, territorial, and tangible defenses of the local area (Suttles, 1972:34). Little or no attention is paid to the analogous defenses offered by professional associations, labor unions, churches, and the family itself. This model of urban life seems logically connected to earlier social ecological conceptions of the city, in which fear and lack of meaning are an inherent derivative of the size of population. The ultimate destruction of the city, and the disgorging of its population, would surely result from the decline in symbolic attachment and ethnic defenses. This model justifies the protection of turf and the reinforcement of ethnically homogeneous neighborhoods as the correct method for solving the city's problems.

The tangibility of local defenses is reinforced through an emphasis by ecologists on the role of voluntary associations in maintaining the integrity and vitality of the local community (Janowitz and Street, 1978). These local associations operate to socialize new neighbors and children, "to give content to the idea of collective responsibility among neighbors," to resolve conflicts of interest, and to develop presumably more "effective modes of political participation" (Janowitz and Street, 1978:118). Their entire purpose seems to be to integrate and manage conflict within the urban context. Ecologists do not know, however, why integration and not conflict and socialization and not protest are the primary goals of these local associations. In the absence of careful research on these associations, it is not clear just how effective they are either in local life or in the overall political structure of the city. Many militant community organizations operating in cities will never become part of traditional political mechanisms. The conflict of interest between bankers and politicians over an issue such as red-lining, for example, leaves one feeling that the local associations have important and alternative roles to play. Some of these alternatives have gained the interest of Marxist urbanists.

The social-ecological view of the city is basically a view from the bottom. Its analytical base is the perspective of everyday life and its needs for integration and coherence. It is a view which virtually ignores the hierarchical complexities of local, metropolitan, and national life and substitutes the problem of parochialism. It promotes more order than conflict, and more integration than exploitation. It generally ignores the problem of composing discrete territorial units into a functioning whole, and substitutes instead an understanding of the demographics of metropolitan life for a more definitive theoretical statement about the dynamics of metropolitan change. It tries to understand the enormous complexities of urban life by describing the appearance of locally significant attachments and events.

The neighborhood and the city are described, understood, and improved as things unto themselves. This is a view of the ordinariness of life, which its holders and beholders see little reason to change. Change, if and when it occurs, is ultimately unwelcome and externally generated. Left alone, neighborhoods and the community presumably find their own solutions to their problems. Conflict, disorder, and rootlessness are, in this way of viewing the urban world, both incidental and external to the character of local life. No threat or condition is envisaged which could overwhelm the intransigence of the defended neighborhood.

There are, however, easily imagined circumstances in which a local community, no matter how well built its defenses or how well developed its symbolic integrity, can be overwhelmed by forces totally outside its control. Natural disasters, economic upheavals, war, and the asymetrical use of power are obvious instances of overwhelming events. There are also internally generated conflicts over such questions as race and housing. These can fracture the fragile texture of cohesion and integration. Local areas, the Marxist urbanists hypothesize, are vulnerable in a host of ways that need to be examined in order to understand when the processes of local defense may or may not be effective.

Doubts, questions, and missed opportunities are inherent in the ecological view of the city. It has contributed mightily to the analysis of demographic and microlevel processes, while leaving unexamined other critical questions. Marxist urbanists have, over the last several years, begun to criticize the social ecological viewpoint, as well as to offer their own alternative view of the endemic features of metropolitan society.

THE MARXIST PERSPECTIVE

Since the late 1960s, American and European urbanists have tried to develop an alternative view to the social-ecological perspective (Harvey, 1973; O'Connor, 1973; Pickvance, 1976; Castells, 1977; Tabb and Sawyers, 1978). These attempts to find a new perspective have used much of the empirical research of ecologists, as well as the extensive criticisms that others have directed at the social ecological perspective over the last decades (Alihan, 1938; Sjoberg, 1959; Beshers, 1962; Gans, 1970). A new perspective, based on the conviction that older models are increasingly inapplicable and unhelpful (Castells, 1977:4), has gradually emerged, although it is not yet ready to be presented as a final, polished theory.

The opening theme in this perspective is that most of the characteristics and crises of our times are mislabeled as urban crises (Castells, 1976). Cities are not the source of most of their problems. The characteristics which ecologists view as urban, the Marxists argue, are either created or conditioned by the broader social class character and contradictions of the whole society. Alienation, conflict, and disorder are not inherent in urban life, but are, rather, the endemic features of class relationships and antagonisms. Autonomy, or even quasi-autonomy, is not a product of spatial negotiations and practices internal to a neighborhood, but is a fragile tie to the economic and political exchanges at the regional and national level.

To ecologists the city is a place for understanding how space, people, time, and business are balanced in a system which is basically equitable and homeostatic. To Marxists the city is only one of many suitable contexts in which one can examine the process of the accumulation, circulation, and management of capital. The principal elements for examination are the investment needs of business tied to certain technological imperatives, the centrality of the accumulation of profit, and the social costs associated with the reproduction of a labor force. The chief theoretical and practical objective of Marxist urbanists is to understand the laws for the creation and transformation of social space as they are tied to the character of economic, political, and class relationships. Space is not an environmental given, but is created, used, and abandoned to meet the changing needs of industrial, commercial, and property capital, as well as to satisfy the needs for collective services of residents.

Central to the Marxist argument is the belief that the political and planning agencies of the state primarily function to stimulate or restrain the shortcomings of the system's economic operations. The accumulation needs of business often create conditions of instability that political institutions attempt to moderate or regulate in order to insure stability. They may not succeed in this objective and in their turn, may create additional instability and conflict. The tendency is for political and economic institutions to co-maintain the basic pattern of class interests and divisions. Reform, if and when it occurs, serves only to reduce the cyclical volatility or crises in the system without altering the basic pattern of private sector profits and rights.

Marxists are particularly interested in the trend for businesses and industry to relocate outside cities. Large segments of the economy, typified by business and industry, simply no longer need the city. New patterns of regional and international economic exchanges have drastically reduced the need for centralized urban labor, materials, and markets. As businesses and industry depart, they create labor surpluses and leave an abundance of poorly paid, unskilled jobs. They also leave behind an increasingly depleted tax base and a labor force with an insecure economic future.

. . . with the developing of modern one story plants . . . and the use of trucking and air freight . . . manufacturing and warehouse and other facilities and the better-paid monopoly sector working-class jobs . . . move to the periphery. What is left is small-scale manufacturing, retail trade, and food and other competitive sector services, where productivity and wages are relatively low. In effect, except for downtown bank and corporate activity, the city becomes the competitive sector—a reservoir of cheap labor (O'Connor, 1973:127).

The power of the economic sector to pick up and move, virtually at will, leaves cities crucially vulnerable. The loss of jobs need not always bring with it the loss of population, but it does compromise the fiscal stability of cities.

The suburbanization of industry, and consequent population decentralization, are not then the result of the acting out of impersonal market forces, but are, rather, a dislocation of the industrial sectors of the economy as they seek the specific advantages of suburbia and an escape from the strikes and taxes to which they are subjected in the city (Gordon, 1978). Economic decentralization represents a new stage in the management of economic and spatial relationships by sectors of the capital economy.

The second dimension of the political economy of urban dynamics is the forces for the management and the transformation of property capital. Property capital consists of the accumulation of profit based on the development and management of land, rents, and housing. It is the sector of the urban political economy in which instruments of finance, which include banking, mortgage lending, and other public and private large-scale property developers, are most central and powerful.

The role of property capital is based on the private ownership of land as a condition for the existence of capital, the accumulation of profit, and the location of economic and residential activities. The private ownership of urban land and property permits the accumulation of tracts of land as a basis for the development or expansion of other economic activities. Land developers play a crucial role in acquiring large tracts of land, thereby facilitating the settlement of large industrial or corporate enterprises, suburban housing tracts, retail shopping plazas, and new towns. Land, when combined with a good location, becomes a critical ingredient in the pattern and rate of economic growth and population expansion.

The development of land and of housing construction is based upon the availability of finance capital or mortgages. Since 1900, mortgage lenders have played an increasingly important role in supplying the funds to the housing industry. Financial institutions have become a dominant force in housing, playing a decisive role in determining "who lives where, how much new housing gets built, and whether neighborhoods survive" (Stone, 1978:190).

The support of banks and mortgage lenders severely affected by the cyclical instability of capital growth, resulted in growth spurts and shortages of new housing which caused the federal government during the 1930s to begin to play a role in regulating economic growth. Since its first efforts at intervention into the housing market, the primary objective of government has been to "encourage a stable and high level of housing production, coupled with stability of employment and production in the construction industry" (Solomon, 1977:147). Federal housing policy supports the development of housing construction with specific incentives, objectives, and effects.

The first effect of federal policy has been to clear land of its earlier uses and tenants and to replace it with more profitable activities. There is little evidence that state intervention in the housing market has ever substantially benefited the poor or working class residents of older urban neighborhoods. It has generally forced them to relocate to other, often suburban areas, and increased the demand for older housing. Low-income families are relocated not in accordance with the ecologist's view of unaided social mobility, but as part of a policy of urban redevelopment that facilitated the accumulation of profit by developers and the subsidized access to newer housing by better-off households. The effect was to create the development and stabilization of land use for the rich while destabilizing the land-use patterns of substantial numbers of the poor. The basic tendency of federal renewal policies has been to reinforce the inequality of the status quo.

Government acts to generate or insure stable profits for land and real estate developers and for the construction industry. It acts to stabilize the concept and profitability of suburban home ownership and indirectly to weaken the fiscal health of the inner-city housing market. As a result, cities such as New York and Chicago are left with an aging and deteriorated housing stock and few of the resources necessary to repair it.

From the view of the political economist, the city is not a mosaic of relatively self-sustaining ethnic and racial communities; it is a fragile bundle of economic and housing options which have been severely eroded over the last few decades. The stability that exists is the result of the decisions by the various sectors of the private market to transform and accumulate profit under fixed conditions, which has resulted in decentralization and expansion at the outer rings of the circle while drawing population, profits, and taxes out of the city.

The creation, management, and transformation of urban space is not without evidence of crises and contradictions. The techniques of urban planning do not always succeed, nor do they always develop solely in response to the interests of the dominant class. Political economists argue that the transformation of space is accomplished through the tension, or dialectic, of forces associated with class struggle.

The clearest example of such struggles are the urban social movements that have emerged in cities throughout the world to assert the rights or needs of the underdogs. The aim of these urban movements is to produce "a qualitatively new effect on the social structure" by transforming or modifying the system of power relations (Castells, 1977:262–263). The movement toward grass-roots political mobilization and struggle can be either a part of the movement toward urban reform or toward a more basic change in the relationship between classes.

It is difficult to determine whether an issue reflects a basic structural problem, and to define the meaning of a true qualitative change. Neither reform nor revolution, these urban social movements represent a variety of strategies, agents, and interests aimed at altering the methods by which collective goods are distributed.

> Urban social movements . . . have their birth and development in everyday facts, posing new problems and issuing new challenges, in a cry of life and conflict that drowns the technocratic myths of urban rationality. A cry that is a strong reminder that urban power, too, lies in the streets (Castells, 1977:464).

An intense optimism is associated with the feeling that power and change can come from the streets. Much of this optimism stems from the changes associated with the protests of workers, students, and blacks during the late 1960s in the United States, France, and other countries. Such movements may never reappear, as cynicism, success, or repression eliminate the agents for change. Yet Marxist attention to the basic roots or reasons for those protests suggests they may not have been so historically specific, and that the conditions for mass movements in cities may again reemerge.

Considerable theoretical and empirical ambiguity exists in the Marxist analysis of urban social movements. Protest organizations take on many forms and often act with little coherent purpose or radical intent. Though the United States may be the last capitalist country in which to expect class mobilization and struggle, the Marxists point to the possible evidence of protest against inequities as evidence that conflicts of interest may be inherent in the dynamics of allocation of resources and the management of social space.

CONCLUSION

Marxists have introduced an admittedly embryonic, tentative set of questions and propositions which challenge and redirect many of our ways of understanding cities. Population, space, and urban culture are replaced in their central role in social ecological explanations with a focus on a system of forces largely determined by the separate but supporting movements of industrial, corporate, and property capital in conjunction with governmental practices. The basic structural characteristics of cities are tied to the policies and contradictions of public and private actions.

Cities are left to manage scarce resources and an increasingly mobile populace that is also seeking change and improvements. Mobilization and conflict, rather than integration and order, are the logical consequences of such an urban system. Marxist urbanists are less concerned with the conditions for the persistence of communities and the patterns of segregation than they are with the conditions for the successful mobilization of protest against the system of class oppression and manipulation. They see a variety of urban interests struggling for the maintenance of the conditions for profit versus the conditions for equitable survival. This tension is at the root of the political economy of local areas.

Most Marxists recognize that there must be a continued refinement and critique of the applicability of Marxian problematics for understanding the urban condition. There is, in fact, almost as much debate and disagreement among Marxists as there is between Marxists and non-Marxists. Discussion will probably continue to focus on at least three areas. The first is the comparison of urban dynamics in socialist and non-socialist countries. The similarities in urban dynamics are striking enough to warrant extensive comparative examination (Szelenyi, 1978). A second area of refinement will be the clarification of the distinctiveness of the Marxian viewpoint. For example, Weber's concern with political economic factors and urban development offers a potentially interesting, but as yet undeveloped, additional view on urban political economy, which may parallel some of the issues raised by Marxian political economists (Bensman, 1978). Finally, there will probably continue to be discussion of political mobilization and urban change. The degree to which urban social movements represent simply another kind of interest group vying for influence or a new social form challenging state and private sector practices is a central theoretical and empirical question that needs to be addressed.

Almost as many questions are raised about the Marxian urban perspective as about the non-Marxian paradigm, but when the questions, strengths, and limitations of each model are more clearly visible, in the light of the comparison, a clearer choice can be made. Beyond simply providing a choice of viewpoints, however, the Marxists have exposed a new set of questions that had previously been blurred or concealed from view.

REFERENCES

AIKEN, MICHAEL, and MANUEL CASTELLS
  1977 "Introduction." Comparative Urban Research.
ALIHAN, MILLA
  1938 Social Ecology: A Critical Analysis. New York: Columbia University Press.
BENSMAN, JOSEPH
  1978 "Marxism as a foundation for urban sociology." Comparative Urban Research, forthcoming.
BERNARD, JESSIE
  1973 The Sociology of Community. Glenview, Ill.: Scott, Foresman.
BERRY, BRIAN, and J. D. KASARDA
  1977 Contemporary Urban Ecology. New York: Macmillan.
BESHERS, JAMES
  1962 Urban Social Structure. New York: Free Press.
BURGESS, ERNEST W.
  1928 "Residential segregation in American cities." The Annals 140:105–115.
CAREY, JAMES T.
  1975 Sociology and Public Affairs: The Chicago School. Beverly Hills, Calif.: Sage.
CASTELLS, MANUEL
  1976 "Is there an urban sociology?" Pp. 383–390 in C. Pickvance, Urban Sociology: Critical Essays. New York: St. Martin's Press.
CASTELLS, MANUEL
  1977 The Urban Question: A Marxist Approach. Cambridge: MIT Press.
FISCHER, CLAUDE
  1976 The Urban Experience. New York: Harcourt Brace Jovanovich.
FITCH, ROBERT
  1977 "Planning New York." Pp. 246–284 in R. Alcaly and D. Mermelstein (eds.), The Fiscal Crisis of American Cities. New York: Vintage.
GANS, HERBERT
  1970 "Urbanism and suburbanism as ways of life: a re-evaluation of definitions." Pp. 70–82 in R. Gutman and D. Popenoe (eds.), Neighborhood,

City, and Metropolis: An Integrated Reader in Urban Sociology. New York: Random House.

GORDON, DAVID M.
1978 "Capitalist development and the history of American cities." Pp. 43–51 in W. Tabb and L. Sawyers (eds.), Marxism and the Metropolis. New York: Oxford.

HARVEY, DAVID
1973 Social Justice and the City. Baltimore: Johns Hopkins Press.

HAWLEY, AMOS
1974 Human Ecology: A Theory of Community Structure. New York: The Ronald Press.

HUNTER, ALBERT
1974 Symbolic Communities: Persistence and Change in Chicago's Local Communities. Chicago: University of Chicago.

JANOWITZ, MORRIS, and DAVID STREET
1978 "Changing social order of the metropolitan area." Pp. 90–128 in D. Street (ed.), Handbook of Contemporary Urban Life. San Francisco: Jossey Bass.

KASARDA, JOHN D.
1978 "Urbanization, community, and the metropolitan problem." Pp. 27–57 in D. Street (ed.), Handbook of Contemporary Urban Life. San Francisco: Jossey Bass.

KORNBLUM, WILLIAM
1974 Blue Collar Community. Chicago: University of Chicago Press.

O'CONNOR, JAMES
1973 The Fiscal Crisis of the State. New York: St. Martin's Press.

PARK, ROBERT
1952 Human Communities. Glencoe, Ill.: The Free Press.

PICKVANCE, CHRIS
1976 Urban Sociology: Critical Essays. New York: St. Martin's Press.

SHORT, JAMES
1971 The Social Fabric of the Metropolis. Chicago: University of Chicago Press.

SJOBERG, GIDEON
1959 "Comparative urban sociology." Pp. 334–359 in R. K. Merton, et al. (eds.), Sociology Today: Problems and Perspectives. New York: Basic Books.

SOLOMON, ARTHUR P.
1977 "A national policy and budgetary framework for housing and community development." Journal of the American Real Estate and Urban Economics Association 5:147–170.

STONE, MICHAEL E.
1978 "Housing, mortgage lending, and the contradictions of capitalism." Pp. 179–207 in W. Tabb and L. Sawyers (eds.), Marxism and the Metropolis. New York: Oxford.

SUTTLES, GERALD
  1968 The Social Order of the Slum: Ethnicity and Territory in the Inner City. Chicago: University of Chicago Press.
  1972 The Social Construction of Communities. Chicago: University of Chicago Press.
SZELENYI, IVAN
forth- "Class analysis and beyond: further dilemmas for the new urban sociol-
com-   ogy." Comparative Urban Research.
ing
TABB, WILLIAM, and LARRY SAWYERS
  1978 Marxism and the Metropolis: New Perspectives in Urban Political Economy. New York: Oxford.
WIRTH, LOUIS
  1938 The Ghetto. Chicago: University of Chicago Press.

3. Ecology as Macrosociology: A New Look at an Old Perspective

BRUCE LONDON

It is generally assumed that the present unhealthy state of the field of human ecology derives largely from a lack of systematic theory (cf. Gibbs and Martin, 1959; Martin, p.c.; Micklin, 1973:xiv). Efforts to provide it have rarely been forthcoming, however, due to a certain recurrent disenchantment with human ecology, and to the pervasive impression that the field is functionalist (Beshers, 1962), ideological (Castells, 1968; Pickvance, 1975), or economically and environmentally deterministic (Smith and Evers, 1977). Additional critiques were noted in the published debate over the role of human ecology in sociology (cf. Hollingshead, 1948:141; Quinn, 1948:146–147; Schnore, 1961).

This article is an attempt to reassess the contributions of sociological theory to human ecology and to take the initial steps toward creating a more systematically theoretical human ecology. In addition, this attempt may yield certain implications concerning the contributions of human ecology to sociological theory, especially in terms of a partial critique and synthesis of the well-worn consensus-conflict debate. These efforts are possible precisely because human ecology and sociological theory are inextricably and reciprocally related.

ECOLOGY AS MACROSOCIOLOGY: A PERSPECTIVE

The literature on human ecology—especially the work of ecology's most prestigious and supportive advocates such as Duncan (1959; 1961;

1964), Duncan and Schnore (1959), Gibbs and Martin (1959), Hawley (1944; 1950; 1968; 1971), Schnore (1958; 1961), and Steward (1955)—is replete with statements to the effect that although human ecology deals with some of the central problems of sociology, it does not represent the sum and substance of sociology. It is, in short, merely one nonexhaustive attempt to deal with certain macrosociological issues. In this regard the ecological perspective is variously seen to be most profitably employed in the study of culture as a dependent variable (Steward, 1955); in seeking partial solutions to questions about the problems of order, solidarity, relativism, and change (Duncan, 1959:683); in the study of the community (Hawley, 1944; 1950); social systems (Duncan, 1964; Hawley, 1968); or sustenance organization (Gibbs and Martin, 1959); as forms of social organization; or in the study of certain "inclusive forms of organization" such as stratification, bureaucracy, and the urban community (Duncan and Schnore, 1959).

These points of view place undue and perhaps artificial limitations on the potential of ecology as a macrotheoretical perspective on the core problem of sociology—namely, the study of the process of social organization. Indeed, there seems to be a considerable amount of ambivalence on the part of these authorities themselves regarding the scope of human ecology. In a very early statement, Hawley noted the possibilities of an ecological approach to the macroscopic study of human social life. He felt that this potential, as manifested in the theoretical development of the field, had been relegated to a secondary role, with most researchers focusing on empirical studies rather than aiming at "exploring the full implications of ecology as applied to man" (1944:399). His purpose was to correct these deficiencies by moving toward a reorientation of the field. In his later, classic work (1950:177), he indicated his awareness of ecology's macrotheoretical potential by noting that "ecology seeks to discover and describe the pattern or patterns that human organization assumes." He nonetheless persisted in restricting his attention to the community, which offers a small, convenient unit for investigation.

In a more recent statement (Hawley, 1968), this ambivalence persists. Hawley noted, on the one hand, that "human ecology . . . is concerned with the general problem of organization . . . with sociological problems in their fullest breadth. It overlaps, therefore, all the spheres of learning that concern the social life of man" (1968:329–330). He even went so far as to suggest that his earlier focus on the community was restrictive, and that the more neutral and inclusive term "social system" is preferred (1968:331). On the other hand, in his concluding paragraphs, he strongly reemphasized "the limits of human ecology" (1968:336–337):

As with most approaches in social science, human ecology has
limited objectives. It seeks knowledge about the structure of a social
system and the manner in which the structure develops. Hence, it is
not prepared to provide explanations for all of the manifold
interactions, frictions, and collisions that occur within the bounds
of a social system . . . Human ecology is not qualified to deal with
the normative order in a social system.

Duncan (1959:680–81), too, hinted at ecology's potential inclusiveness
in his discussion of "the natural history of man approach" as a
comprehensive picture of man-environment relationships. But, again,
his focus was on human ecology in Hawley's earlier restricted sense.
Duncan and Schnore (1959:133) carried the analysis one step further by
pointing out that Hawley's focus on the community level of organization was a temporary expedient and that "there is nothing in the basic
framework of ecology that precludes its attention to more inclusive
forms of organization". Note, however, that the stress here is on
applying the ecological perspective to the study of forms of organization
other than the community, and not on specifying ecology's potential for
the study of social organization as a generic process. Schnore (1958:1061)
took a step in this direction by pointing out that ecologists since
Durkheim have viewed social organization as their dependent variable
(1958:629), and that human ecology, far from being marginal to sociology, is one effort to deal with the study of social organization
(1961:128–129); however, he did not see it as the "most profitable" way to
do so.

Gibbs and Martin (1959) elaborated a stance similar to that of Schnore.
They saw social organization or, in their terms, "sustenance organization" as the subject matter (i.e., dependent variable) of human ecology
(1959:43), but suggested that attention should be restricted to variability
in the form or characteristics of sustenance organizations as entities
(1959:44, 48–49). As in most of the major theoretical statements reviewed,
the limiting emphasis is on form rather than on process. In this regard
Micklin (1973:5) noted that all of these writers "generally fail to specify
the dynamics of the adjustment process." In his own theoretical discussion, Micklin (1973:6) emphasized "the process of collective adaptation"
as the focus of human ecology, with the central argument of his
conceptualization being that "the key to understanding ecological
relationships is social organization" (1973:9). He then reduced social
organization to four components or "mechanisms" of adaptation (i.e.,
engineering, symbolic, regulatory, and distributional), which function
to determine "levels of ecological adaptation" (i.e., quantitative sur-

vival, qualitative survival, and the overall balance of man and nature) (1973:9–13). In so doing, Micklin has rendered social organization an independent variable, and the outcomes of organizational processes have become his dependent variables.

The lesson in all this ambivalence is that no logical or theoretical need exists to limit ecology to the study of anything less than social organization broadly conceived. Indeed, any attempt to understand the process of social organization must be ecological in nature. In his explicit discussion of the limitations of human ecology, Hawley (1950:73) indicated the most probable reason that this macroscopic application had not been forthcoming at midcentury. For Hawley human ecology yields insights into the development of the human community as an organization of functional relationships. Collective life as a whole (i.e., the total process of social organization), however, involves psychological and moral, as well as functional, integration. Although these types of integration should be regarded as complementary, human ecology as traditionally conceived is only capable of dealing with functional integration—with "the question of how men relate themselves to one another in order to live in their habitats" (1950:74).

This view, clearly limiting human ecology to the study of biotic, subsocial, or functional phenomena, can be traced back at least to Park's distinction (1936; 1952) between moral and ecological orders. It is an important component of nearly all neo-classical or materialist (Bailey and Mulcahy, 1972; Sjoberg, 1965; Willhelm, 1962; 1964) ecological theories, including the works of Hawley, Duncan, Schnore, Gibbs and Martin; manifested in their writings is the widespread acceptance of the notion that ecology is truly sociological because of its emphasis on aggregates rather than on individuals. It has been suggested (Kasarda, 1974b:18; Berry and Kasarda, 1977:17) that this emphasis was largely a polemical reaction to the pervasive social-psychological thrust of American sociology at midcentury; it probably also reflects the sensitivity of ecologists to the well-known critiques of "the ecological fallacy" (Robinson, 1950). "It was thus almost overdetermined that a series of papers would be written by students of human ecology to remind the sociological audience that all principles of social organization could not be reduced to individualistic concepts" (Berry and Kasarda, 1977:17).

Stated in these terms, human ecology is *not* a synthetic, macroscopic theoretical perspective on the total process of social organization; no formulation that explicitly omits the normative and the social-psychological could hope to be. Consequently, although the study of functionally integrated forms of social organization should yield insights into social organization as a generic process, this most macroscopic level of investigation is left beyond the ken of a traditionally circumscribed human ecology.

We take the position that the processes of psychological and moral integration, (Hawley, 1950), or, more generally, the voluntaristic or sociocultural phenomena that most neoclassical, materialist ecologists view as not amenable to analysis in ecological terms, cannot themselves be fully understood outside of an ecological perspective. This, of course, requires rather drastic revision of what is generally meant by the term "human ecology."

We turn first to a discussion of the process of social organization, which, in effect, emphasizes the complementarity of various types of integration. Subsequently, we will focus on the fundamentally ecological nature of this perspective.

CONTEXT: AN ELEMENTARY THEORY OF SOCIAL ORGANIZATION

Dotson[1] has argued that we now have in the literature of sociology the basic components of an elementary theory of social organization. We do not have, nor are we likely to get, a truly rigorous general theory of social organization, precisely because sociological theory, like all bodies of knowledge, is a historical, collective, and continuously developing inventory of ideas. (This emergent theoretical inventory does provide us with some fundamental insights into the nature of social organization by focusing our attention on the recognizable elements of this very complex phenomenon.)

From the perspective of Dotson's elementary theory of social organization, there are three analytically distinguishable components of society or social organization: (1) a cultural component, (2) a social component, and (3) an individual component. Culture refers to shared behavior, but, to extrapolate from an argument made by Bateson (1947), much human behavior can be reduced analytically to ideas. People are capable of symbolization and of the communication of symbolized ideas. As individuals interact with each other, they generate ideas about these collective endeavors which they share with their fellow participants. In this communication or sharing of ideas lies the creation of a culture (Olsen, 1968). In terms of content the cultural component consists of a shared mentality comprised of a collection of shared symbols and ideas.

The cultural component is often confused with the social component, because both are collective phenomena. This basic confusion usually arises when something that is, in fact, cultural is thought of as social.

For example the normative ideas that define, direct, or guide the ideal patterns for social relationships are cultural phenomena, yet they are often mistakenly described as social phenomena. What, then, is Doston's social component, and how do we distinguish it from the cultural component?

The social component is the active, concrete, experiential process of interaction between and among people or groups: As compared to the cultural component, this is a decidedly nonnormative element. Although a considerable portion of all behavior can be understood as guided by normative ideas, an analytically distinct aspect of behavior does exist. It is determined by the uniqueness of a given interaction situation, and it cannot be reduced to abstract ideas. Norms may define the ideal patterns for social relationships, but what actually happens when people interact is often very different from the ideal normative definition.

Less obvious is the fact that no conception of society, however elementary, would be complete if we left out the real[2] people who are doing the interacting. This, according to Dotson, is the individual component. We must be careful, however, to conceptualize the individual in an organismic or biological sense rather than as a personality in the most common social-psychological usage. The individual here serves as a kind of physiological mechanism for the various sociocultural processes, as a biological means to actualize what, in Dotson's social and cultural components, are nontangible entities. Viewed as an elementary component in Dotson's theory of social organization, the individual is not equated with personality, precisely because personalities are comprised of *all three* of these elementary components.

Social organization, then, is logically reducible to a cultural content, a social context, and individual actors. All three elements can be demonstrated analytically to exert independent influences on what people do. An awareness of the potential influence of each component is necessary to an understanding of the total human situation, precisely because each is qualitatively different from the other. Culture is reducible to ideas, the social component to concrete interaction, and the individual to the biological means of putting the entire process in motion. In this light the elements become mutually exclusive. Empirically, however, the three totally interpenetrate each other (Olsen, 1968).

A truly rigorous theory of the process of social organization would fully articulate these components; this, however, has never been done. The task is simply too complex for anyone merely sketching a brief and elementary theory. Still, elementary need not mean simplistic. Rather, a theory is necessarily elementary because any attempt to analyze society without first isolating its basic components precludes explanation. The common failure to distinguish between cultural and social components, for example, leaves one or the other element unanalyzed, and is, therefore, not only a potential source of confusion, but also of conflicting, irreconcilable points of view. To elaborate briefly, much of the sterile debate over functionalism may be traced to a failure to make this distinction. Functionalism tends to overemphasize the salience of the cultural component by suggesting that normative homogeneity, as the dominant force in societies, automatically yields consensus. Conversely, critics of functionalism tend to overemphasize the social component by suggesting that the interaction between or among groups located at different positions in the societal hierarchy is characterized by conflict, and that the latter is the basic dynamic of society. The tendency in previous literature has been to view these phenomena categorically, i.e., so that either consensus or conflict predominates (Lenski 1966:20), whereas an elementary theory would emphasize their complementarity. We will elaborate upon these points below in our discussion of ecology's synthetic potential.

Although the different terminologies still require some sorting out, it can now be seen that Dotson's elementary theory of social organization is the perspective to which we alluded above, since it attempts to show the complementarity of moral, psychological, and functional integration. To emphasize the fundamentally ecological nature of this theory, we must now turn to a discussion of some of the key insights of human ecology.

THE DEFINING CHARACTERISTICS OF HUMAN ECOLOGY

General ecology is usually defined as the study of "the relationship of organisms or groups of organisms to their environment" (Hawley, 1950:3). In human ecology, the organisms referred to are obviously people. This simple fact makes necessary a somewhat more subtle specification of the human ecological referent of environment. For a truly human ecology environment must be defined broadly to include "other people" or human groups, as well as the physical-biological (nonhuman) realm.

These rather familiar definitional considerations have certain implications for other foci of human ecology. For example the study of man-environment relationships implies a concern with the dependence of the organism on the environment and, therefore, with the process of the organism's adaptation to that environment. (This emphasis in no way denies the fact that organisms usually modify their environments in significant ways). This concern, in conjunction with the fact that ecology's unit of analysis has traditionally been some sort of aggregate, yields an elaboration of the meaning of the phrase "man-environment relationships": ecology is the study of the process of adaptation of an aggregate or population of living units to their environment. Adaptation is thus a collective process. In the last analysis, human ecology focuses on "objective relations among interdependent living units" (Duncan, 1961:142), or on "human interdependencies," "the interrelations among men," and, ultimately, "the process and organization of relations" (Hawley, 1950:72). Human aggregates are of necessity adaptive mechanisms: organization is the means of their adaptation to the environment.

Such a focus on aggregates as the ecological units of analysis should not ignore the fact that populations are comprised of real interacting human beings. As noted earlier, neoclassical, materialist human ecologists have been overly sensitive on this point ever since Robinson (1950) illustrated that ecological correlations do not necessarily yield appropriate inferences about individual behavior (for a very recent statement, see Firebaugh, 1978). They have tended to avoid scrupulously the analysis of individual behavior. While this may be both practical from a methodological point-of-view and consistent with a belief in an academic division of labor, it is limiting theoretically, especially in terms of developing a truly macroscopic, ecological theory of social organization. We opt, therefore, to attempt to include the individual in our analysis.

Along with our recognition of the elementary importance of individuals, we must note that interaction, in its most basic conceptualization, implies proximity or contact—i.e., a spatial locus. The first generation of empirically oriented human ecologists seized upon this point and never let it go. The result was such an overemphasis on space that the mapping of urban functions has often been mistaken for the discipline of human ecology itself (Hawley, 1944). This criticism notwithstanding, ecology's most fundamental contribution to macrosociology lies in its strong empirical grounding—in its distinctive focus on what happens when real people interact in space and time.

These points lay the groundwork for the inclusion of the individual in ecological analysis. In addition to the fact that the interaction of individuals implies locations in space and efforts at overcoming "the friction of space" (Hawley, 1950), human interaction also implies the use of symbolic communication to facilitate social relationships (Beshers, 1962:111; Olsen, 1968). The persistence of social relationships over time among the members of a spatially delimited aggregate often leads to the formation of an identifiable group. Symbolic communication among group members may bring about shared ideas or impose a collective meaning upon individual behavior. These microlevel phenomena have not been ignored by all human ecologists. Indeed, insights of this sort are common to the writings of sociocultural or voluntaristic human ecologists (cf. Bailey and Mulcahy, 1972; Cohen, 1976; Firey, 1945; 1947; Insel and Moos, 1974; Klausner, 1971; Kunkel, 1967; Michaels, 1974; Michaelson, 1976; Willhelm, 1962; 1964). Even Duncan (1964:77), who is usually considered a rather strict materialist, emphasizes that "human culture and social organization develop ecologically" and that "you cannot throw away what is most distinctively human— communication with symbols, custom, and the artificial or cultural transformations man makes in his environment—and treat the residue as the ecology of the species."

In short a dialectical relationship exists between symbolic communication and group formation. On the one hand symbolic interaction may give meaning to group membership or allow individuals to identify themselves as part of a consciously defined collectivity. In Hawley's terms "psychological integration" is one possible result of interaction in space and through time. On the other hand the meanings imposed upon behavior by the group may assume a normative cast and become a cultural component that ideally guides member behavior. Again in Hawley's terms "moral integration" may be the result.

This dialectic would seem to be the basis for two of the key assumptions of human ecology: "that at least some spatially delimited population aggregates have unit character" and "that there are significant properties of such an aggregate which differ from the properties of its component elements" (Duncan, 1959:681).[3] Thus, although analytically separable, interaction in space and psychological and moral integration (the creation of culture) are empirically interdependent.

This sort of interaction within groups having a unit character is, however, only one type of contact in space. Ecology is well equipped to deal with another type of interaction, namely, contact between and among groups (Richerson and McEvoy, 1976:3). These relationships are implicit in Hawley's (1950:36–41) discussion of "symbiosis" ("a mutual dependence between unlike organisms") and "commensalism" ("a second and equally important relation . . . between similar creatures"). While interaction within groups gives the aggregate a certain degree of cultural homogeneity, interaction between such groups creates situations characterized by cultural heterogeneity.[4] The ecologist's perspective lends the ability to deal with both intra- and intergroup interactions, and with the obviously diverse results of all such interactions. This is an important theoretical merit, but also one that requires some elaboration, especially as it relates to the view that ecology is theoretically synthetic.

As noted earlier, human ecology is often seen as a form of functionalism (Beshers, 1962; Logan, p.c.). Criticisms of functionalism have been numerous, and the debate over functionalism (Demerath and Peterson, 1967) has been "one of the principal substantive issues in the recent literature of social theory" (Cohen, 1968:166). Stephan (1970:225) argues that this issue is not foreign to human ecological writings:

> In human ecology the issue has appeared, for example, in Park's distinction (1936:13) between the biotic (competitive) and cultural (consensus) levels of human social organization; in the emphasis placed by Form (1954), Hollingshead (1947), and Long (1958) on the distinctive interest groups, sub-cultures, and sub-community structures operating within an overall social system; and in the emphasis placed by Hawley (1950:209) on the integrative relationships of symbiosis and commensalism. . . . The question of cooperation or competition becomes an empirical problem. Competitive, complementary, predatory, parasitic, and even indifferent relations are all theoretically possible in an ecological community.

Some contemporary ecologists, building on the work of earlier theorists, have recently taken additional steps toward a denial of the strict functionalist label and also toward effecting a synthesis of the consensus and conflict perspectives by explicitly illustrating that ecological theory can account for conflict and change as well as for functional integration and equilibrium (Cohen, 1976; Micklin, 1973; Richerson and McEvoy, 1976; Stephan, 1970).

Richerson and McEvoy (1976:4), for example, note that "for the most part students of human systems have viewed functionalism and conflict theory as contradictory and competing explanatory frameworks." They feel, to the contrary, "that conflict and functional interpretations can be integrated" and "that a tentative synthesis can be made." A number of ecology's key concepts are cited to illustrate the argument:

> Natural selection and succession are fundamentally similar to conflict theory, whereas the ecosystem concept is very much like functionalism. Natural selection and succession [and, perhaps, invasion, dominance, and parasitism] stress competitive and exploitative interactions between individuals and species, much as conflict theory stresses the competitive and exploitative relations among social classes or groups. . . . But ecologists studying ecosystems

stress [cooperation and] the negative feedback mechanisms regulating the contribution of component species to the necessary organized processing of matter and energy. Likewise, functionalists in
social science relate the existence of social and cultural entities to
the operational necessities for the continued existence of societies as
a whole.

In general, little time is wasted by ecologists on the debate over
whether or not society is somehow dominated by consensus or conflict.
They escape this sort of misplaced effort because each and every one of
ecology's key terms describes one or another result of what happens
when real people interact, whether that interaction is taking place
between members of the same aggregate or between two different
aggregates. In either case the ecologist realizes that the occupants of such
contacting niches (or positions or social strata) may or may not have
different needs and interests (or orientations or definitions of the situation) (Cohen, 1976:58). It is simply an ecological fact of life that all such
interactions can yield either consensus or conflict, depending largely
upon the environment in which the interaction is taking place. Ecology's dual emphasis on cooperation and competition reflects this awareness.

This ability to encompass both poles in the consensus-conflict debate
is one pertinent indication of ecology's synthetic nature, as well as a
parallel between ecological theory and Dotson's elementary theory,
which is itself a synthetic formulation. Couching this ecological synthesis in elementary terms, one finds that when any number of aggregates,
each possessing distinctive cultural contents, are trying to accomplish
the same thing in the same environment, the potential exists for either a
cooperative effort at mutual adaptation or a conflictive resolution of the
adaptive problem (cf. Hawley, 1950:30).

Whether a population adjusting to its environment is marked by a
predominance of consensual or conflictive interactions, the fact remains
that adaptation is explicitly recognized to be a continuous, dynamic
process (Hawley, 1950:17). Ecology thus accepts the ubiquity of change
(Dahrendorf, 1959:162), and herein lies a second indication of ecology's
synthetic nature—the ecologist's ability to handle change in a manner
that functionalist consensus theory is supposedly unable to do, while
still recognizing the existence of continuity (e.g., in the form of persisting successful adaptations). In addition to merely accepting the ubiquity
of change, many sociologists espousing human ecology also seek to
explain this phenomenon by integrating ecological theory with the
neoevolutionsism of such twentieth-century anthropologists as White
(1949), Steward (1955), and especially Sahlins and Service (1960) (see, for

example, Duncan, 1964:45ff.; Hawley, 1950:72). In describing an ecological-evolutionary approach to the macroscopic study of human societies, Lenski and Lenski (1974:8) argue that those adaptive mechanisms upon which ecology focuses can only be fully understood in evolutionary terms (cf. Catton, 1968).

One final indication of ecology's synthetic nature is its ability to deal with some aspects of the phenomenon of power in a manner which is, again, supposedly beyond the scope of a strictly functionalist consensus theory. Duncan and Schnore (1959:139) note the striking formal similarities between the concept of power and the ecological use of dominance: "Both concepts point to the ability for one cluster of activities or niches to set the conditions under which others must function." Hawley (1950:220–221) is clearly aware that competitive "inter-unit relations" result in the emergence of a hierarchy of power: "Inequality is an inevitable accompaniment of functional differentiation." One way of describing such differentiation is in terms of the possession of variable resources. Resources, in this sense, must be defined broadly to include any aspect of a group's cultural content which enhances its competitive bargaining position vis-à-vis another group. A group's resources evolve historically and range from natural environmental advantages to sheer population numbers, from technological capabilities to instrumental forms of social organization (Duncan, 1959). It is the variable cultural resources possessed by each group in an interactive situation that serve as the bases of resulting dominance-subdominance relationships.

Dotson and Dotson (1968:1–10, 341–343, 380–409) elaborate upon this conception of power, drawing on insights of an explicitly ecological nature originally provided by Robert E. Park (1936:1952). A normative-functionalist interpretation of social behavior based upon the concept of culture seeks to describe societies holistically. In doing so, it overemphasizes the degree of consensus prevailing in a society and underemphasizes the Machiavellian nature of the struggle for power between competing groups. Although formulated long before these issues were to become prominent, Park's ecological theory serves to balance these views by distinguishing a moral order, based on normative consensus, from an ecological order, which emphasizes that portion of social behavior which lies beyond normative awareness and control (Dotson and Dotson, 1968:342, 389–90) and is grounded in interaction among groups. The norms which guide behavior in one situation are not necessarily applicable in another. Any group enters into any social situation with its own historically evolved cultural baggage. If the contact involves interaction with new groups, who have their own distinctive norms and resources, behavior will necessarily be non-normative, in the absence of rules or ideas concerning how to behave in the new situation. It follows that the results of such interaction are largely unplanned or unintended. In such virgin interactions, groups confront each other in competition and conflict, "each equipped from the past with the cultural means for the struggle" (Dotson and Dotson, 1968:341).

These means are not likely to be equal and "inequality of position and status is the inevitable result" (Dotson and Dotson, 1968:341). Culture is thus instrumental, and "cultural means provide the foundation to power" (Dotson and Dotson, 1968:341).

It is important in this discussion of the cultural means of power to emphasize that cultural contents change to facilitate accommodation to new contexts. Culture is an adaptive mechanism that largely determines how a group will accommodate itself—as dominant or subordinate—to new social environments. This process of positioning within a power hierarchy is only initially non-normative, and continued interaction between the groups may bring conscious awareness and, hence, "normative moral definition" to the relationships.

> Seen in this perspective, society appears not as a static structure of norms but as a dynamic "emergent"—partly conscious and partly unconscious, partly normative and partly non-normative. *A product of continuous interaction*, its future forms are never fully prefigured in the normative context of any one of its constituent groups at any given historical present (Dotson and Dotson, 1968:342. Emphasis added.).

This fundamentally ecological focus on the interactions of real people in space and time enables the analytical separation of culture and society, or normative and non-normative, of moral and ecological. This provides this perspective with its potential for inclusiveness.

The Ecological Aspects of Dotson's Elementary Theory

Several similarities between Dotson's elementary theory of social organization and the defining characteristics of human ecology should by now be evident.[5] His individual component is ecological in its emphasis on real people as biological actors. His social component consists of real people in space and over time. And his cultural component becomes ecological in its awareness that the interaction of real people in space and time gives aggregates a unit character (proximate normative homogeneity), and in that this normative content, (as manifested in forms of social organization and ideas), serves as an adaptive mechanism in social environments.

If our elementary theory is fundamentally ecological, why is human ecology rarely perceived to be macrosociologically inclusive?[6] Contemporary discussions of human ecology usually equate the field with Duncan's (1959) ecological complex (cf. Schnore, 1961:137). An ecological frame of reference is seen to include the four reciprocally interrelated variables of population, (social) organization, environment, and technology (i.e., POET).[7] An ecological complex stresses the causal efficacy of each of these variables in producing changes in the others. Much of the recent empirical research by human ecologists focuses on the testing of hypotheses generated by the ecological complex or on assessing the relationships among various indicators of each rubric (cf. Bidwell and Kasarda, 1975; Clemente and Sturgis, 1972; Frisbie and Poston, 1975; Kasarda, 1971; 1972a; 1972b; 1974a; Sly, 1972; Sly and Tayman, 1977). In addition prominent textbook treatments of human ecology tend to emphasize some or all of the variables in Duncan's ecological complex (cf. Berry and Kasarda, 1977:14–15; Gist and Fava, 1974:151–161; Micklin, 1973).

It may well be, however, that this common view that "ecology is POET" is a key factor in preventing the development of human ecology as a macroscopic perspective on social organization. The focus on POET may be the reason behind critiques that describe ecology as external and descriptive (cf. Willhelm, 1962:20, 25–26; 1964:242–243, 246). As a heuristic device, POET can only be descriptive, because it is not elementary in the sense that its terms are not well-defined. At the very least a coherent synthesis of the ecological complex with our elementary theory is required. In other words the macrosociological promise of human ecology lies not in the variables of the ecological complex themselves, but in the defining characteristics of each of these variables. In our reformulation populations become aggregates of real interacting people. Environment is defined broadly to include both natural and social milieus. Technology is clearly recognized as a critical part of an aggregate's cultural means. Finally, organization is seen as the adaptive mechanism that aggregates may use to cooperate or compete with other populations in their total environments.

In summary the linking of human ecology and the elementary theory of social organization draws upon certain complementary strengths of each. Both are initially similar in their eclectic, synthetic, or comprehensive potentials. Human ecology contributes its strong empirical grounding and its emphasis on the fact that interaction takes place within a total environment. Elementary theory contributes its simplicity, a scientific virtue of the highest order, and its heuristic potential.

As a final observation, we might suggest that any macrosociological theory of social organization in its broadest sense must incorporate certain key insights that are decidedly ecological. Human ecology cannot be a separate type of macrosociology, but rather, ecological principles are a theoretical foundation upon which a macroscopic theory of social organization must be built. This is the basis for the argument that macrosociology and ecology are indivisible—that ecology is macrosociological and that macrosociology is ecological.

NOTES

I am indebted to Professor Floyd Dotson for sharing his ideas with me and stimulating my work. I wish, too, to thank Professors Amos Hawley, Walter Martin, and Leo F. Schnore for their helpful comments on earlier drafts of this paper. Any remaining errors are the responsibility of the author.

1. This theory is presented by Professor Floyd Dotson in his graduate seminars. Although developed independently, it bears a strong resemblance to the statement presented by Olsen (1968). Both formulations are drawn upon heavily in the present statement. Any errors in their presentation are those of the author.

2. Use of the term "real" is not meant to imply that we may conceive of "unreal" people. Rather, it is used to emphasize a point often forgotten by contemporary sociologists, namely, "The first premise of all human history is . . . the existence of living human individuals. . . . Men are the producers of their conceptions, ideas, etc.—real, active men." (Marx and Engels, 1970:42, 47). This usage dramatically reminds us of the need for an empirically grounded human ecology (Micklin, 1973:xv).

3. Note that human ecology's unit of analysis is a concrete population of real, interacting individuals—a lesson that may well have been learned from Marx and Engels (1970:42, 47). Yet, from this starting point we derive the second ecological assumption of a very Durkheimian "reality of the social." Any macroconceptualization must encompass both individual and aggregate phenomena.

4. That interaction *within* homogeneous cultures and interaction *between* homogeneous cultures are the two ideal-typical poles of an interactional continuum, rather than all-inclusive categories, can be illustrated by Shils's (1961; 1968) "center-periphery" distinction. Cultural heterogeneity of a sort is often a characteristic of those supposedly homogeneous units we often loosely refer to as cultures, societies, or nation-states. There can be any number of diverse groups, each having unit character, interacting within such a homogeneous macroaggregate as a society. "Center" refers to those groups within a society which maintain a position of dominance, while "periphery" refers to those groups in the same society which are in various ways subordinate to the center. Thus, homogeneity and heterogeneity are, in these terms, relative to the specific level and type of interacting units being observed.

5. Ecological principles were clearly instrumental in Dotson's formulation of

the elementary theory, but perhaps that is just the point: the macrosociological elementary view could not have been formulated without certain key ecological insights.

6. We should note here that many human ecologists perceive their work to be macrosociological. Schnore (1961:139), for example, suggests "that 'human ecology' might be best regarded as a type of 'macrosociology,'" and Berry and Kasarda (1977:17) note that "earlier human ecologists have argued . . . that one can study many observable patterns of organized activities without necessarily referring to the subjective feelings of individual actors. This, of course, is the essence of a macrosocial approach."

The author feels, however, that this is not the only way to define macrosociology. By macrosociological inclusivity, he means the integration of macro- and microlevels of analysis. As Collins (1975:14) notes, "The strategic problem in building a scientific sociology is to integrate macro- and microlevels of analysis. The microlevels must provide the detailed mechanisms through which the processes summarized on the macro-levels may be explained. . . . The justification for such an integration is pragmatic; only in this way can a satisfactory explanatory theory be created."

7. Variations on the Duncan schema have included (1) "POETS" (Gist and Fava, 1964:97–105; 1974:151–161), based ultimately on Firey's insight (1947) that the causal influence of sociocultural factors must be taken into consideration and (2) "PILOT", which reflects a similar attempt by Schrag (1968) to include normative phenomena in the model.

REFERENCES

BAILEY, KENNETH D., and PATRICK MULCAHY
  1972 "Sociocultural versus neoclassical ecology: a contribution to the problem of scope in sociology." Sociological Quarterly 13:37–48.
BATESON, GREGORY
  1947 "Sex and culture." Annals of the New York Academy of Sciences 47:647–660.
BERRY, BRIAN J. L., and JOHN D. KASARDA
  1977 Contemporary Urban Ecology. New York: Macmillan.
BESHERS, JAMES M.
  1962 Urban Social Structure. New York: Free Press.
BIDWELL, CHARLES E., and JOHN D. KASARDA
  1975 "School district organization and student achievement." American Sociological Review 40:55–70.
CASTELLS, MANUEL
  1968 The Urban Question: A Marxist Approach. London: Edward Arnold Press.
CATTON, WILLIAM R., JR.
  1967 "Flaws in the structure and functioning of functional analysis." Pacific Sociological Review 10:3–12.

CLEMENTE, FRANK, and RICHARD B. STURGIS
   1972 "The division of labor in America: An ecological analysis." Social Forces
        51:176-82.
COHEN, ERIK
   1976 "Environmental orientations: A multidimensional approach to social
        ecology." Current Anthropology 17:49-70.
COHEN, PERCY S.
   1968 Modern Social Theory. New York: Basic Books.
COLLINS, RANDALL
   1975 Conflict Sociology: Toward an Explanatory Science. New York: Aca-
        demic Press.
DAHRENDORF, RALF
   1959 Class and Class Conflict in Industrial Society. Stanford, Calif.: Stanford
        University Press.
DEMERATH, N. J., III, and RICHARD A. PETERSON (eds.)
   1967 System, Change, and Conflict. New York: Free Press.
DOTSON, FLOYD, and LILLIAN O. DOTSON
   1968 The Indian Minority of Zambia, Rhodesia, and Malawi. New Haven:
        Yale University Press.
DUNCAN, OTIS D.
   1959 "Human ecology and population studies." Pp. 678-716 in P. M. Hauser
        and L. F. Schnore (eds.), The Study of Population. Chicago: University
        of Chicago Press.
   1961 "From social system to ecosystem." Sociological Inquiry 31:140-149.
   1964 "Social organization and the ecosystem." Pp. 36-82 in R. E. L. Faris
        (ed.), Handbook of Modern Sociology. Chicago: Rand McNally.
DUNCAN, OTIS D., and LEO F. SCHNORE
   1959 "Cultural, behavioral, and ecological perspectives in the study of social
        organization." American Journal of Sociology 65:132-146.
FIREBAUGH, GLENN
   1978 "A rule for inferring individual-level relationships from aggregate data."
        American Sociological Review 43:557-572.
FIREY, WALTER
   1945 "Sentiment and symbolism as ecological variables." American Sociologi-
        cal Review 10:140-148.
   1947 Land Use in Central Boston. Cambridge, Mass.: Harvard University
        Press.
FORM, WILLIAM H.
   1954 "The place of social structure in the determination of land use: Some
        implications for a theory of human ecology." Social Forces 32:317-23.
FRISBIE, W. PARKER, and DUDLEY L. POSTON
   1975 "Components of sustenance organization and non-metropolitan popula-
        tion change: A human ecological investigation." American Sociological
        Review 40:773-84.
GIBBS, JACK P., and WALTER T. MARTIN
   1959 "Toward a theoretical system of human ecology." Pacific Sociological
        Review 2:29-36.

GIST, NOEL P., and SYLVIA F. FAVA
  1964 Urban Society, 5th ed. New York: Thomas Y. Crowell.
  1974 Urban Society, 6th ed. New York: Thomas Y. Crowell.
HAWLEY, AMOS H.
  1944 "Ecology and human ecology." Social Forces 22:398-405.
  1950 Human Ecology: A Theory of Community Structure. New York: Ronald Press.
  1968 "Human ecology." Pp. 328-337 in D. Sills (ed.), International Encyclopedia of the Social Sciences. New York: Crowell, Collier, and Macmillan.
  1971 Urban Society: An Ecological Approach. New York: Ronald Press.
HOLLINGSHEAD, AUGUST B.
  1947 "A re-examination of ecological theory." Sociology and Social Research 1:194-204.
  1948 "Community research: Development and present condition." American Sociological Review 13:136-146.
INSEL, PAUL M., and RUDOLF H. MOOS
  1974 "Psychological environments: Expanding the scope of human ecology." American Psychologist March:179-188.
KASARDA, JOHN D.
  1971 "Economic structure and fertility: A comparative analysis." Demography 8:307-317.
  1972a "The impact of suburban population growth on central city service functions." American Journal of Sociology 77:1111-24.
  1972b "The theory of ecological expansion: An empirical test." Social Forces 51:165-175.
  1974a "The structural implications of social system size: A three-level analysis." American Sociological Review 39:19-28.
  1974b The Ecological Approach in Sociology. Unpublished manuscript. Department of Sociology, University of Chicago.
KLAUSNER, SAMUEL A.
  1971 On Man in His Environment. San Francisco: Jossey-Bass.
KUNKEL, JOHN H.
  1967 "Some behavioral aspects of the ecological approach to social organization." American Journal of Sociology 73:12-29.
LENSKI, GERHARD E.
  1966 Power and Privilege: A Theory of Social Stratification. New York: McGraw-Hill.
LENSKI, GERHARD E., and JEAN LENSKI
  1974 Human Societies: An Introduction to Macrosociology. New York: McGraw-Hill.
LOGAN, JOHN R.
  n.d. Personal communication.
LONG, NORTON E.
  1958 "The local community as an ecology of games." American Journal of Sociology 64:251-261.

MARTIN, WALTER T.
  n.d.   Personal communication.
MARX, KARL, and FRIEDRICH ENGELS
  1970   The German Ideology. New York: International Publishers.
MICHAELS, JAMES W.
  1974   "On the relation between human ecology and behavioral social psychol-
         ogy." Social Forces 52:313–21.
MICHELSON, WILLIAM H.
  1976   "What human ecology left behind in the dust." Pp. 3–32 in William H.
         Michelson (ed.), Man and His Urban Environment: A Sociological
         Approach. Reading, Mass.: Addison-Wesley.
MICKLIN, MICHAEL
  1973   Population, Environment, and Social Organization: Current Issues in
         Human Ecology. Hinsdale, Ill.: Dryden Press.
OLSEN, MARVIN E.
  1968   The Process of Social Organization. New York: Holt, Rinehart and
         Winston.
PARK, ROBERT E.
  1936   "Human ecology." American Journal of Sociology 42:1–15.
  1952   Human Communities: The City and Human Ecology. Glencoe, Ill.: Free
         Press.
PICKVANCE, C. G.
  1975   "Review essay: Toward a reconstruction of urban sociology." American
         Journal of Sociology 80:1003–1008.
RICHERSON, PETER J., and JAMES McEVOY, III
  1976   Human Ecology: An Environmental Approach. Scituate, Mass.: Dux-
         bury.
ROBINSON, W. S.
  1950   "Ecological Correlations and the behavior of individuals." American
         Sociological Review 15:351–357.
SAHLINS, MARSHALL D., and ELMAN R. SERVICE
  1960   Evolution and Culture. Ann Arbor: University of Michigan Press.
SCHNORE, LEO F.
  1958   "Social morphology and human ecology." American Journal of Sociol-
         ogy 63:620–634.
  1961   "The myth of human ecology." Sociological Inquiry 31:128–139.
SCHRAG, CLARENCE C.
  1968   "The 'pilot' variables: An illustration." Pp. 119–123 in G. A. Lundberg
         et al., Sociology, 4th ed. New York: Harper & Row.
SHILS, EDWARD
  1961   "Centre and periphery." Pp. 117–130 in The Logic of Personal Knowl-
         edge: Essays Presented to Michael Polanyi. Glencoe, Ill.: Free Press.
  1968   "Society and societies: The macro-sociological view." Pp. 287–303 in T.
         Parsons (ed.), American Sociology: Perspectives, Problems, Methods.
         New York: Basic Books.

SJOBERG, GIDEON
  1965 "Theory and research in urban sociology." Pp. 157–190 in P. M. Hauser and L. F. Schnore (eds.), The Study of Urbanization. New York: Wiley.
SLY, DAVID F.
  1972 "Migration and the ecological complex." American Sociological Review 37:615–28.
SLY, DAVID F., and JEFF TAYMAN
  1977 "Ecological approach to migration re-examined." American Sociological Review 42:783–795.
SMITH, JOEL and MARK EVERS
  1977 Ecology and Demography. Dubuque, Iowa: William C. Brown.
STEPHAN, G. EDWARD
  1970 "The concept of community in human ecology." Pacific Sociological Review Fall:218–228.
STEWARD, JULIAN H.
  1955 Theory of Culture Change. Urbana: University of Illinois Press.
QUINN, JAMES A.
  1948 "Discussion." American Sociological Review 13:146–148.
WHITE, LESLIE A.
  1949 The Science of Culture. New York: Farrar, Straus and Giroux.
WILLHELM, SIDNEY M.
  1962 Urban Zoning and Land-Use Theory. New York: Free Press.
  1964 "The concept of the 'ecological complex': A critique." American Journal of Economics and Sociology 23:241–248.

PART IX
ANNOTATED
BIBLIOGRAPHY

INTRODUCTION:
Alternative Theoretical Perspectives in Modern Sociology

BENTON, TED

1977 Philosophical Foundations of the Three Sociologies. London: Routledge and Kegan Paul. Benton, a philosopher, is dealing with the sociology of sociology. His first two sociologies are seen as competing paradigms: positivism, which sees sociology as similar to the natural sciences, and humanism, which flows from Kant's mind/body distinction. He feels that these approaches are too narrow and proposes a third, materialism, which involves a refection of the positivistic notion that there is a universal scientific method, without surrendering to the humanistic rejection of any notion of the unity of science.

CLEÇAK, PETER

1974 Radical Paradoxes: Dilemmas of the American Left: 1945–1970. New York: Harper Torchbooks. Clecak's reason for writing this book was to clarify his thinking about the problem of powerlessness and the seemingly permanent separation of power and goodness in America. The social theories advanced during the 1960s often seem inadequate. In a careful and thoughtful analysis, Clecak examines the work of such men as C. Wright Mills, Paul Baran, Paul Sweezy, and Herbert Marcuse in an attempt to show the radical paradoxes that lay at the heart of their work.

FAY, BRIAN

1975 Social Theory and Social Practice. London: George Allen and Unwin. In this brief work Fay provides a summary and critique of positivist social science and technological politics. An alternative view, an interpretive social science, is advanced, and the future of a critical social science is examined.

GIDDENS, ANTHONY

1971 Capitalism and Modern Social Theory: An Analysis of the Writings of Marx, Durkheim and Max Weber. Cambridge: Cambridge University Press. Giddens believes that modern social theory stands in need of revision and that it must begin with an examination of the works of those whose thoughts infuse today's theories. With that in mind, he provides a concise overview and interpretation of the works of Marx, Durkheim, and Weber. Finally, the divergence of Marx's views from those of Durkheim and Weber are treated at length.

HINKLE, GISELA J.
1978 "Seeing trends in recent sociological theory." The Wisconsin Sociologist 15 (Spring/Summer):63–74. The author reviews a considerable amount of literature and treats, in a most coherent fashion, the topic of where sociological theory is going. She outlines seven different developments.

MORRIS, MONICA B.
1977 An Excursion into Creative Sociology. New York: Columbia University Press. Creative sociology, for Morris, includes ethnomethodology, symbolic interaction, neo-symbolic interaction, phenomenology, and existentialism. She manages in a straightforward and simple fashion to present the essentials of each of these forms of creative sociology, and relates many of their ideas to themes in contemporary drama and fiction.

NISBET, ROBERT
1976 Sociology as an Art Form. New York: Oxford University Press. Nisbet begins his short work with an observation that has impressed him throughout his career: that the great themes which have provided continuing challenge and theoretical foundation for sociologists have never been reached through anything resembling the scientific method. For Nisbet a good theory is like good art; it must allow us to both understand reality, and to present it. The work of a number of classical social theorists are examined in light of these concerns.

TURNER, JONATHAN H.
1978 The Structure of Sociological Theory. Homewood, Ill.: Dorsey. This is a basic text for the study of social theory, but it covers a wide range of topics, includes a considerable amount of information about contemporary social theories and critiques, most of them in a sensible fashion.

WARSHAY, LEON H.
1975 The Current State of Sociological Theory. New York: McKay. While covering a wide range of current theories, Warshay notes which are presently dominant and why. This is an empirical study of social theory, its current trends, and the methodological and political issues. The book also points to areas of convergence among concepts and pragmatic research and theory building.

ZEITLIN, IRVING M.
1973 Rethinking Sociology: A Critique of Contemporary Theory. Englewood Cliffs, N.J.: Prentice-Hall. Zeitlin examines five main schools of sociology—functionalism, social exchange theory, conflict theory, phenomenology and ethnomethodology, and symbolic interactionism—and points to their problems, ambiguities, and defects. He then provides a synthesis in the form of a Marx–Weber model.

PART I. WORLD VIEWS

1. Michael Burawoy, "Contemporary Currents in Marxist Theory."

AMIN, SAMIR
1976 Unequal Development: An Essay on the Social Formations of Peripheral

Capitalism. New York: Monthly Review Press. A global reformulation and incorporation of existing theories of development and underdevelopment.

BRAVERMAN, HARRY
1974 Labor and Monopoly Capital. New York: Monthly Review Press. A theory of the development of the labor process under capitalism with an analysis of the implications for changes in class structure.

GENOVESE, EUGENE
1976 Roll, Jordan, Roll: The World the Slaves Made. New York: Pantheon. An account of resistance and domination in the ante-bellum South; it draws on Gramsci and Thompson.

GRAMSCI, ANTONIO
1971 Selections from Prison Notebooks. New York: International Publishers. A theoretical elaboration of the interrelationship of politics and ideology as they developed in different capitalist countries during the early part of the twentieth century.

HILTON, RODNEY (ed.)
1976 The Transition from Feudalism to Capitalism. London: New Left Books. A collection of essays which bring together the views of a number of famous Marxist historians on the transition from feudalism to capitalism.

MARCUSE, HERBERT
1955 Eros and Civilization. Boston: Beacon Press. The incorporation of a Freudian psychology within a Marxist framework.

O'CONNOR, JAMES
1973 The Fiscal Crisis of the State. New York: St. Martin's Press. A theory of how the competing imperatives of accumulation and legitimation are manifested as crises in the political arena.

POULANTZAS, NICOS
1973 Political Power and Social Classes. London: New Left Books. A reformulation of Marxist theories of the state stressing the relative autonomy of state institutions.

SWEEZY, PAUL
1942 The Theory of Capitalist Development. New York: Monthly Review Press. A lucid and comprehensive account of the classic debates in Marxist economics.

THOMPSON, EDWARD
1963 The Making of the English Working Class. London: Victor Gollancz. A classic and influential account of the struggles that led to the formation of class consciousness within the English working class between 1780 and 1830.

2. Immanuel Wallerstein, "A World-System Perspective on the Social Sciences."

AMIN, SAMIR
1974 Accumulation on a World Scale, 2nd volume. New York: Monthly Review Press. Critique of developmentalist theories, to be replaced by a

theory of accumulation at a world scale. Periodization of stages of unequal international specialization.

BRAUDEL, FERNAND

1973 Capitalism and Material Life: 1400-1800. Translated by Miriam Kochan. New York: Harper Colophon. This is a masterly study of what the world was like materially during the period referred to in the title. Braudel manages to recreate the daily existence for a variety of social classes by looking at their consumption of food, their clothing, housing, technology, and the types of communities they lived in.

1972 "History and the Social Science," in Peter Burke (ed.) Economy and Society in Early Modern Europe. London: Routledge & Kegan Paul. The plurality of social times, and the links between history and the social sciences.

CIPOLLA, CARLO M.

1976 Before the Industrial Revolution: European Society and Economy, 1000-1700. New York: Norton. This work, by the eminent historian Cipolla, is a blend of economic theory and economic history. The workings of the social and economic system of preindustrial Europe through the interaction of supply and demand are explained. The author considers demographic variables, the distribution of wealth, the nature of the productive apparatus, and the overall level of productivity throughout the society. The emergence of the modern system, and what caused it, are then treated.

DOBB, MAURICE

1946 Studies in the Development of Capitalism. London: Routledge and Kegan Paul. Working out of a Marxist tradition, Dobb argues that the transition from feudalism to capitalism took place because of an alteration in the mode of production. This occurred because of the contradictions inherent in feudalism. He notes these contradictions and examines in detail the demographic factors (including increasing population) that were involved in the changes.

DUPLESSIS, ROBERT S.

1976 "From demesne to world-system: a critical review of the literature on the transition from feudalism to capitalism." Radical History Review 3 (September):3-41. This is an excellent review of the essential materials and arguments concerning the rise of the modern capitalist state. In particular the article evaluates the theories of Dobb and Wallerstein and concludes that Dobb's analysis might be the most fruitful one for understanding the sixteenth century.

EMMANUEL, ARGHIRI

1972 Unequal Exchange. New York: Monthly Review Press. Critique of Ricardo's theory of comparative costs. Asserts the existence of a transfer of surplus-value via international trade called "unequal exchange."

FRANK, ANDRE GUNDER

1978 World Accumulation, 1492-1789. New York: Monthly Review Press. Analysis of history of capitalist world from 1492-1789, emphasizing the process by which the (West) European powers created underdevelopment in overseas colonies.

HARDY, JAMES D.

1974 Prologue to Modernity: Early Modern Europe. New York: Wiley. In order to understand the vast number of transformations that conjoined to produce a world order, it is necessary to examine historical materials covering a wide range of topics and extending over several centuries. Hardy's well-written and delightful book is an excellent place to begin, for he manages to deal with the work of a number of scholars and produce an understandable introduction to precapitalist Europe.

HILTON, RODNEY (ed.)

1976 The Transition from Feudalism to Capitalism. London: New Left Books. This is a collection of classic essays, dealing with the rise of capitalism, that was first published in Science and Society in the early 1950s. They cover the significant issues and deal with the all-important question of what caused the move to capitalism, e.g., trade or alterations in the mode of production.

HOBSBAWM, E. J.

1972 "From social history to the history of society." In F. Gilbert and S. R. Graubard (eds.), Historical Studies Today. New York: W. W. Norton. Limitations of social history as a field.

1965 "The crisis of the seventeenth century." In Trevor Aston (ed.), Crisis in Europe: 1560–1660. New York: Basic Books. After a short period of prosperity during the sixteenth century, Europe experienced rapid price rises, economic decay, and political turmoil. Hobsbawm's examination of the nature of these crises is particularly instructive for understanding how a nascent capitalist system operated. There is an excellent discussion of the origins of the Industrial Revolution and the central role of the Dutch.

LENIN, V. I.

1934 Imperialism: The Highest State of Capitalism. New York: International Publishers. No study of the development of world systems would be complete without an examination of Lenin's classic work. It was written as an economic analysis and as a justification for his intended political program. Imperialism is seen as a special stage of capitalism with five essential features. Among these features were a concentration of capital and production by a few countries, a merging of bank and finance capital, and a division of the world into economic regions by the advanced industrial powers.

PARRY, J. H.

1966 The Establishment of the European Hegemony: 1415–1715. New York: Harper Torchbooks. Parry begins his study by noting that one of the most striking features of the last two hundred years has been the dominant influence exerted by Europeans outside Europe. How this domination, which was begun in the fifteenth century and firmly established in the sixteenth and seventeenth centuries, developed is the focus of the book. Parry does an excellent job of describing the conditions for and drawing out the implications of the rise of the central state.

POLANYI, KARL

1977 "The economistic fallacy." Review 1 (Summer):9–18. (Also ch. I of The Livelihood of Man. New York: Academic Press, 1978). Criticism of theories of classical economics which see the marketing mind as natural rather than as a socially-created phenomenon which is historically rare.

WALLERSTEIN, IMMANUEL

1974a The Modern World System: Capitalist Agriculture and the Origins of the European World-Economy in the Sixteenth Century. New York: Academic Press. Wallerstein discusses the rise of capitalism, and the contributing factors during the sixteenth century in Europe. He shows how a world-wide division of labor developed, how certain states dominated at the expense of a peripheral group, and how this produced the system that we are familiar with today. An excellent bibliography is provided for those interested in the subject of the origins of capitalism.

1974b "The rise and future demise of the world capitalist system: concepts for comparative analysis." Comparative Studies in Society and History, 16, 4 (September). Reinterpretation of some classic debates in light of assertion of existence of an historically specific totality which is the capitalist world-economy.

1976 "Modernization: requiescat in pace." In Lewis A. Coser and Otto N. Larsen (eds.), The Uses of Controversy in Sociology. New York: Free Press. Critique of modernization theories in terms of inability to address some major issues; agenda for research.

PART II. COUNTERPERSPECTIVES

1. Inge Powell Bell, "Buddhist Sociology: Some Thoughts on the Convergence of Sociology and the Eastern Paths of Liberation."

BERGER, PETER L.

1965 Invitation to Sociology: A Humanist Perspective. Garden City, N.Y.: Doubleday Anchor. An exposition of the sociological approach which comes closest to a Buddist understanding of social reality.

FROMM, ERICH, D. T. SUZUKI, and REINDARD DE MARTINO

1960 Zen Buddism and Psychoanalysis. New York: Harper. A discussion of the similarities and differences between Western psychology and the psychology of Buddism.

GOULDNER, ALVIN W.

1970 The Coming Crisis of Western Sociology. New York: Basic Books. A radical critique of sociology and its inability to become an effective agent of social change.

HERRIGEL, EUGENE

1971 Zen in the Art of Archery. New York: Vintage, Random House. A simple, beautifully written account of a Western scholar's experience in penetrating Buddhism by way of learning the Japanese-Buddhist practice of archery.

KRISHNAMURTI, J.

1969   Freedom from the Known. New York: Harper & Row. One may begin anywhere in Krishnamurti's works for probably the most lucid statement of Eastern thought as antiphilosophy.

MASLOW, ABRAHAM

1962   Toward a Psychology of Being. Princeton, N.J.: Van Nostrand. A rare attempt in Western psychology to explore beyond "normal functioning" to the heights of creative emotional maturity.

MILLS, C. WRIGHT

1959   The Sociological Imagination. Oxford: Oxford University Press. A great radical critique of the effectiveness of western sociology.

POWELL, ROBERT

1967   Crisis in Consciousness. Greenwood, S.C.: Attic Press. Powell is the best explicator of Krishnamurti's thought, and may provide an approach for those who find the master's work too difficult on first acquaintance.

TRUNGPA, CHOGYARU

1973   Cutting Through Spiritual Materialism. Berkeley, Calif.: Chambhala Publications. The nature of the Buddhist spiritual path is here clearly illuminated by a discussion of its pitfalls.

TRUNGPA, CHOGYARU

1969   Meditation in Action. Berkeley, Calif.: Chambhala Publications. A brief, lucid discussion of the role of meditation in Tibetan Buddhist practice.

WATTS, ALAN W.

1961   Psychotherapy East and West. New York: Ballantine. Perhaps the best introduction for a Westerner, this work compares the healing practices of Western and Eastern psychology.

2. Marcia Texler Segal and Catherine White Berheide, "Towards a Women's Perspective in Sociology: Directions and Prospects."

COLLINS, RANDALL

1975   Conflict Sociology. New York: Academic Press. An innovative approach which synthesizes various currents in contemporary sociology. An attempt is made to specify conditions under which females and males will have more or less power vis-a-vis each other. The same principles which guide explanations of class stratification and organizational behavior are applied to stratification by kin group, sex, and age.

GLAZER, NONA, and HELEN YOUNGELSON WAEHRER (eds.)

1977   Woman in a Man-Made World: A Socioeconomic Handbook. Chicago: Rand McNally. Edited by a sociologist and an economist, this collection includes some classics, and some hard data on the socioeconomic position of women, along with contemporary theoretical discussions, review essays, and recent empirical research. Some of the selections are excerpted from longer works. Editorial introductions to each section tie the material together.

HUBER, JOAN (ed.)
1973 Changing Women in a Changing Society. Chicago: University of Chicago Press. Originally a special issue of the American Journal of Sociology, this volume contains critical essays, empirical research, and important statements by senior female sociologists indicating that within the discipline, as well as the society, the personal is political and sociological.

LIPMAN-BLUMEN, JEAN
1976 "Toward a homosocial theory of sex roles: an explanation of the sex segregation of social institutions." Signs 1:15–32. An attempt at middle-range theory building. This article offers an alternative explanation for male bonding as viewed from a woman's sociological perspective.

MILLETT, KATE
1970 Sexual Politics. Garden City, N.Y.: Doubleday. A critical examination of the scholarship and literature of the nineteenth and twentieth century from a feminist perspective.

MILLMAN, MARCIA, and ROSABETH MOSS KANTER (eds.)
1975 Another Voice. Garden City, N.Y.: Anchor. Subtitled "Feminist Perspectives on Social Life and Social Science," this volume includes a dozen critical essays each on a specific area within sociology. Areas which have been generally neglected, such as the sociology of feeling and emotion, as well as those such as deviance, urban sociology, and organizations which have neglected to consider women, are covered.

ROSOLDO, MICHELLE ZIMBALIST, and LOUISE LAMPHERE (eds.)
1974 Woman, Culture and Society. Stanford, Calif.: Stanford University Press. An anthology with a cross-cultural focus, this volume includes provocative theoretical essays and research guided by the women's perspective. Both Marxist and non-Marxist theoretical essays are included. The research settings range from U.S. urban ghettos to Guatemalan villages.

ROSSI, ALICE S.
1977 "A biosocial perspective on parenting." Daedalus 106 (2):1–31. A controversial article which argues for more recognition of the biological base of social life. Current biological research is described, and the suggestion is made that sociologists reject biological variables because they have an outdated view of biology.

SZYMANSKI, ALBERT
1976 "The socialization of women's oppression: a Marxist theory of the changing position of women in advanced capitalist society." The Insurgent Sociologist 6(2):30–58. An updated Marxist approach, which argues that capitalism now has greater need for women as wage laborers than as houseworkers. Includes discussion of women from differing economic classes and the women's movement.

WALUM, LAUREL RICHARDSON

1977 The Dynamics of Sex and Gender: A Sociological Perspective. Chicago: Rand McNally. A well-written basic text which incorporates scholarship from various disciplines from biology to law bringing them to bear on how cultural patterns of sexual inequality are established and maintained.

3. Thomas Ford Hoult, "The Humanist Perspective."

BERGER, PETER L.

1963 Invitation to Sociology: A Humanistic Perspective. Garden City, N.Y.: Anchor Books. A brief and engaging paperback, wherein Professor Berger clarifies both the need for, and the dimensions of, the humanistic view in sociology.

COMMONER, BARRY

1976 The Poverty of Power: Energy and the Economic Crisis. New York: Knopf. Environmentalist Barry Commoner, a master teacher, demonstrates the depth of our ecological and political-economic crisis and how we can avert disaster.

DOMHOFF, G. WILLIAM

1970 The Higher Circles: The Governing Class in America. New York: Random House. This book, along with that by Wise (noted below), is suggested because it indicates so clearly that improvement for the general run of humankind cannot occur if individuals alone are changed—the change must be structural and institutional as well.

FRIEDRICHS, ROBERT W.

1970 A Sociology of Sociology. New York: The Free Press. In this prize-winning book, Professor Friedrichs demonstrates how readily conventional "value-free" sociology becomes a "hand-maiden to the establishment."

GOULDNER, ALVIN

1962 "Anti-minotaur: the myth of a value-free sociology." Social Problems 9 (Winter):199–213. In this brief account Professor Gouldner laid the groundwork for what he later termed "reflexive sociology," a close cousin of the humanistic approach to social study.

LEE, ALFRED MCCLUNG

1978 Sociology for Whom? New York: Oxford University Press. Professor Lee, the first humanist to be elected president of the American Sociological Association, is widely noted as a consciousness-raiser for social scientists. In this brief volume Lee demonstrates how sociology can be a major tool for building a more humane society.

MACRAE, DUNCAN, JR.

1976 The Social Function of Social Science. New Haven: Yale University Press. In this major work Professor MacRae summarizes his long-term concern with the place of ethics in social science.

MERCER, JANE R.
 1973 Labeling the Mentally Retarded: Clinical and Social System Perspectives on Mental Retardation. Berkeley, Calif.: University of California Press. Using a study of children in Riverside, California, as her vehicle, Mercer demonstrates the determining effect that society has on individual personality development, thus undermining the claims of those who say that with the exercise of "free will" each person can be "captain" of his or her own fate.

PLATT, JOHN
 1972 "Beyond freedom and dignity, a revolutionary manifesto." The Center Magazine 5 (March/April):34–52. Here is another commentary on the "free-will" beliefs of some humanists, as expressed at a conference sponsored by the Center for the Study of Democratic Institutions.

WISE, DAVID
 1976 The American Police State: The Government Against the People. New York: Random House. This book, along with that by Domhoff (noted earlier) shows that individuals cannot save themselves alone. The clear implication of Wise's work is that progressive social change must be primarily political and economic rather than individualistic.

4. Charles Lemert, "Structuralist Semiotics and the Decentering of Sociology."

ALTHUSSER, LOUIS, and ETIENNE BALIBAR
 1970 Reading Capital. New York: Vintage Books. A principal source for the application of Althusser's semiotic reading theory to Marx's Capital. Part One includes a clear presentation of the method of symptomatic reading.

BARTHES, ROLAND
 1970 Elements of Semiology. Boston: Beacon Press. Published along with Barthes's famous essay, "Writing Degree Zero," this is still the most useful guide to classical structuralist semiotics. The writing is highly condensed at times, but, relative to many French authors, Barthes is quite clear to English readers.

CULLER, JONATHAN
 1975 Structuralist Poetics. Ithaca, N.Y.: Cornell University Press. An excellent analytic study of structuralist semiotics from Saussure through Tel Quel. Though controversial because of its attempt to combine Chomsky's idea of linguistic competence with structuralism's more contextual approach, this book is a superior secondary source.

DERRIDA, JACQUES
 1977 Of Grammatology. Baltimore: Johns Hopkins University Press. Though difficult due to the complexity of Derrida's literary and philosophical method, this is an indispensible source for Derrida's important theory of

textuality and writing, and includes his critiques of phonocentrism; Levi-Strauss, Rousseau, and Saussure.

DIACRITICS

1970 [Journal founded in 1970 by the Department of Romance Studies at Cornell University.] Baltimore: Johns Hopkins University Press. A high-quality journal featuring expositions, translations, and critiques of European (especially French) literary and social theorists. In addition, texts by important non-European theorists and critics (e.g., Harold Bloom, Hayden White, Edward Said, Fredric Jameson) have appeared. Invaluable.

ECO, UMBERTO

1976 A Theory of Semiotics. Bloomington, Ind.: Indiana University Press. The most complete recent theoretical statement of structuralist-oriented semiotics. A clearly written and well-outlined formal statement of special interest to sociologists because of its theory of the relationship between codes and culture.

FOUCAULT, MICHEL

1972 Archaeology of Knowledge. New York: Random House. Foucault's systematic statement of his archaeological method of discursive analysis. Includes "The Discourse on Language" (Foucault's inaugural lesson for the *College de France*), which is an excellent starting point for serious readers of Foucault's method.

LACAN, JACQUE

1977 Ecrits: A Selection. New York: Norton. Lacan is one of the most important sources for recent French social thought, including semiotics. This collection is difficult reading, but is obligatory for a complete understanding of the tradition. Lacan has influenced Althusser and Kristeva, among others.

MACKSEY RICHARD, and EUGENIO DONATO (eds.)

1970 The Structuralist Controversy. Baltimore: Johns Hopkins University Press. This collection of papers, delivered by French and American structuralists at Johns Hopkins in 1966, remains an important primary source in spite of its age. Includes important essays by Derrida, Barthes, Todorov, Girard, and Lacan. The best by far of the English-language collections.

SAUSSURE, FERDINAND

1966 Course in General Linguistics. New York: McGraw Hill. The classical source. Should be read historically and critically. The principle context against which much of modern structuralist semiotics has developed.

PART III. FORMAL THEORY

1. Richard Ball, "Sociology and General Systems Theory."

BERRIEN, F. KENNETH

1968 General and Social Systems. New Brunswick, N.J.: Rutgers University Press. Included here is an excellent discussion of the concept of boundaries as filters, of the processes of system interfacing, and of the relationships between subsystems and supersystems. A great deal of attention is given to the distinction between maintenance inputs and signal inputs and the possibility of a computation of necessary balance. System variability and adaptation is examined with a stress upon the importance of system flexibility. A discussion is included of various principles of system growth, including the processes of nucleation and nonproportional change. Attention is given to different conflict processes. The substantive application of systems concepts is devoted to the social psychology of groups and organizations.

BOGUSLAW, ROBERT

1965 The New Utopians. Englewood Cliffs, N.J.: Prentice-Hall. This is an excellent cautionary statement, which should temper the enthusiasm of systems thinkers and induce some humility. The book is an examination of the utopianism which the author finds at the root of contemporary systems engineering and operations research, including a dangerous impatience with human error and a tendency to stress total system design through a formalist, heuristic, operating unit, or an ad hoc approach, each of which has a neglected background in the utopian thought of the past. Linear programming models, game theory models, rigorously rational models, ritual modeling, and recondite modeling are taken to exemplify formalism and are subjected to a probing critique. Command and prohibition heuristics, relativist heuristics, instrumental heuristics, and value heuristics are contrasted. Operating unit designs are critiqued, with special emphasis given to Skinner's Walden Two. Mercantilism, the doctrine of laissez faire, evolutionary design, and existentialist design are examined as examples of the ad hoc approach. The author emphasizes the extent to which the basic question of the source of social unity—consensus or coercion—is ignored by the new utopians.

BOULDING, KENNETH E.

1961 The Image. Ann Arbor: The University of Michigan Press. Boulding proposes a new science of "eiconics," which deals with the issue of images and their relationship to particular systems. The behavior of any system, he asserts, depends upon an information-processing filter, which he calls the image. The meaning of a message is defined as the change produced in this image. Values represent the rating assigned to various aspects of the image. So-called facts are treated as messages filtered through a changeable value system. The key to the effectiveness of any image, whether it is functioning with respect to biological or sociocultural systems, lies in its capability to process information. Various levels of systems are discussed, including mechanical, biological, and socio-cultural. Analogies are drawn from the operation of DNA, the theories of the gestalt psychologists, the sociology of knowledge, the theories of George Herbert Mead, and the tradition of psychoanalysis.

BUCKLEY, WALTER

1967   Sociology and Modern Systems Theory. Englewood Cliffs, N. J.: Prentice-Hall. This book contains a comparison of the mechanical, organic, and process models, along with a discussion of basic concepts derived from general systems theory, which gives considerable emphasis to the question of open systems and morphogenesis. An examination of the genesis of organization, with examples, is drawn from exchange theory, Newcomb's A-B-X model, Secord and Backman's interpersonal theory of personality, and Ackoff's behavioral theory of communication. Attention is given to institutionalization as a social process with a focus upon the relationship of this process to collective behavior, exchange, and negotiation. Both Homan's and Blau's perspectives on institutionalization are considered in this light. Various models for the process, including the concepts of role making, negotiated order, and resolution of role strain, are discussed. Finally, the key issue of social control is explored through a detailed consideration of the questions of social deviance and social power. The volume is particularly strong in its critique of leading sociological theories.

CHURCHMAN, C. WEST

1968   The Systems Approach. New York: Dell. The idea of systems thinking is proposed, and attention is directed to the ongoing debate among the advocates of a criterion of efficiency and those who stress scientific adequacy, humanistic concerns, or the resistance to planning itself. Each of these positions is examined. A major transportation problem is used as an illustration. System description is considered in terms of measures of performance environments, resources, components, and management. Program budgeting and management information systems are described. Attention is given to the problem of organizing a system for purposes of planning. The place of human values and behavior is closely examined. The emphasis throughout is upon management applications, but the author is at pains to stress the limitations of any one perspective.

LASZLO, ERVIN

1972   Introduction to Systems Philosophy. New York: Harper & Row. This work attempts to sketch the direction of movement from analytic to synthetic philosophy. The concept of a natural system is developed and applied to the physical, biological, and social sciences. The concept of the cognitive system is developed and applied to psychological processes. Through an approach termed "biperspectivism," natural and cognitive systems are linked in an effort to demonstrate the artificiality of dualism. Hierarchical relationships between systems are examined with a criticism of reductionism. An emphasis upon the distinction between systems is based on self-stablizing controls operating through error-reducing negative feedback and systems involving deviation amplification based on positive feedback. The concepts of homeostasis and homeorhesis are contrasted, and different forms of equilibrium described. There is a discussion of the relationship between knower and known implied in systems philosophy and the implications for criteria by which values may be ordered within systems.

LOCKLAND, GEORGE T.

1973 Grow or Die. New York: Dell. Here is a comparison of work from the hybrid sciences of cybernetics, general systems, biochemistry, biophysics, and molecular genetics, all of which are designed to explore the phenomenon of growth and transformation. Patterns of accretive, replicative, and mutual growth are distinguished. Growth is treated as the joining of larger amounts of information into meaningful units. Growth processes are conceived of as consisting of a pattern of searching followed by screening, digestion, synthesis of digested material, use, assimilation of environmental responses to activity, and regulation based on the foregoing. Syntrophy and entrophy are treated as complementary processes of recombination and decomposition. Feedforward processes are distinguished from feedback processes. The principle of redundancy is employed to explain the relative rigidity of lower level systems. Self-catalyzing processes are outlined and growth phases are summarized in terms of sigmoid curves. Comparisons are made among biological, psychological, and social systems.

MICHAEL, DONALD N.

1973 On Learning to Plan—And Planning to Learn. San Francisco: Jossey-Bass. This volume represents an approach to social planning through a basically sociopsychological perspective. The particular perspective is, however, very close to a general systems theory approach. One of the major strengths of the book is the wealth of documentation and the breadth of citation. There is considerable discussion of the concept of environmental turbulence and its relationship to planning. Long-range social planning is conceived of as a societal learning process. The problem of uncertainty is investigated with an emphasis upon acceptance and error-embracing activity. The requirements for systemic feedback are emphasized, and there is a powerful discussion of institutionalized obstacles to such feedback. Restructuring capability and boundary spanning are studied as processes necessary to information-sharing in complex systems. Attention is given to the incorporation of human values into the systems-planning process. Problems of bureaucracy are illuminated through a systems perspective, which stresses the problem of the institutionalization of selective perception, avoidance of goal examination in favor of expediency, and resistance to any holistic approach.

SUTHERLAND, JOHN W.

1973 A General Systems Philosophy for the Social and Behavioral Sciences. New York: Braziller. The basic assumptions of general systems theory is contrasted with the rationalistic, positivistic, and phenomonological approaches. There is a criticism of scientism and ill-considered application of reductionism, analogic inventions, and expediency. The importance of instrumental congruence and analytical congruence is stressed. System-theory approaches on the various levels, including the state-variable level, the parametric level, the relational level, and the coefficient level are distinguished. There is a heavy stress on the need for an interdisciplinary approach which will unite the social and behavioral sciences and the demand for models which will reflect the actual complexity of events rather than a concentration upon narrow segments of reality.

VON BERTALANFFY, LUDWIG
1967   Robots, Men and Minds. New York: Braziller. This volume provides a glimpse into the development of the author's general perspective and a sense of the humanistic concern behind it in a way which may be less easily grasped in the context of his more complicated treatises. It is an exercise in the sociology of knowledge tradition with an emphasis upon the connections between sociocultural situations, science, and world outlooks. The author maintains that traditional positivism, with its focus upon equilibrium and reactivity, has made the human being into a robot for purposes of analysis. He stresses, in turn, the new developments in scientific thought which can be summarized in terms of symbolism and system. The first represents a minor revolution which has reintroduced the problem of the cognitive. The second is the apprehension of organized complexity. Anamorphosis, the evolution of systems toward increasing differentiation and order, is examined, and the ideas are applied to culturology as exemplified by the efforts of Spengler and Sorokin. Spontaneous action, play activity and creative cognition are treated as phenomena demanding a general systems approach.

2. Tom Baumgartner, Tom Burns, and Philippe DeVillé, "Actors, Games, and Systems: The Dialectics of Social Action and System Structuring."

BAUMGARTNER, T., T. R. BURNS, and P. DEVILLÉ
1979   "Work, politics and social structuring under capitalism." In T. R. Burns, L. E. Karlsson, and V. Rus (eds.), Work and Power. London and Berkeley: Sage. Presents a basic model of the capitalist system. It is used to identify and discuss the structure-changing potentialities of various industrial democracy reforms in view of the constraints of multidimensional and multi-level complexities, and power inequalities characteristic for capitalist systems.

BAUMGARTNER, T., T. R. BURNS, and P. DEVILLÉ
1978   "Conflict resolution and conflict development: a theoretical formulation of game restructuring with application to the LIP conflict." Pp. 105–141

in L. Kriesberg (ed.), Research on Social Movements, Conflict and Change. Greenwich, Conn.: JAI Press. Focuses on the dynamic pattern of conflict processes in social life. Shows for a particular management-labor conflict how the material and social context structures the conflict processes, and how human interaction in this context led to the realization of certain transformational potentialities generating a (temporary) conflict resolution.

BAUMGARTNER, T., T. R. BURNS, and L. D. MEEKER

1977 "The description and analysis of system stability and change: multi-level concepts and methodology." Quality and Quantity 11:287–328. Explores the implications of a multi-level theory for social science methodology with its search for functional invariance. Outlines a language and methodological approach appropriate for describing and analysing structural system stability and change.

BAUMGARTNER, T., W. BUCKLEY, T. R. BURNS, and P. SCHUSTER

1976 "Meta-power and the structuring of social hierarchies." Pp. 215–288 in T. R. Burns and W. Buckley (eds.), Power and Control. London and Berkeley: Sage. Develops a conceptual framework for the analysis of social systems with both structure-maintaining and structure-changing processes. Principles of the structuring, i.e., human and environmental production of social relationships and structures, are developed and illustrated with examples from state and empire formation and decay.

BAUMGARTNER, T., W. BUCKLEY, and T. R. BURNS

1976 "Unequal exchange and uneven development: the structuring of exchange patterns." Studies in Comparative International Development 11 (Summer):51–72. Uses a general systems framework to criticize the dominant economic comparative advantage exchange model. Stresses the use of power to structure exchange opportunities, effects and rules. The results are unequal exchange outcomes supporting existing power inequalities. This furthers dependency relationships and generates uneven development patterns.

BUCKLEY, WALTER

1967 Sociology and Modern Systems Theory. Englewood Cliffs, N.J.: Prentice-Hall. The classic application of modern systems theory to the analysis of socio-cultural systems. It emphasizes the complex, adaptive, self-organizing and self-regulating nature of social systems. It stresses system openness, conflict, power and collective behavior as central factors in the explanation of structure-maintaining and structure-changing patterns of social systems.

CANEIRO, R. L.

1970 "A theory of the origin of the state." Science 169:733–738. A concise comparative analysis of early empire formations to stress the importance of the interaction between system boundaries, resource limits and population growth for the emergence of social differentiation and unequal acquisition of structuring power.

DEUTSCH, KARL W.
   1963 The Nerves of Government. New York: The Free Press. A classic development of general systems thinking in political science. Applies the cybernetic model of the error-regulating feedback to politics and governmental action.
GODELIER, M.
   1973 Rationality and Irrationality in Economics. New York: Monthly Review Press. (Translated from French.) A first theoretical attempt to link the study of individual economic behavior within a monoeconomic system and the study of the objective capabilities of change of such a system. Marxist theory is seen as contributing to the development of an economic anthropology.
HIRSCHMAN, ALBERT O.
   1970 Exit, Voice, and Loyalty. Cambridge, Mass.: Harvard University Press. An original and stimulating exposition of two basic mechanisms of system self-regulation. Shows that under modern conditions the exit option—traditionally seen as the economic mechanism—and the voice option—usually identified as the political mechanism—have invaded each other's sphere of application. Discusses the context-dependent use and effectiveness of exit and voice and the role played in this connection by loyalty.

3. Donald Black, "A Strategy of Pure Sociology."

BLACK, DONALD
   1976 The Behavior of Law. New York: Academic Press. A theoretical study of law from the standpoint of pure sociology.
BLAU, PETER M.
   1977 Inequality and Heterogeneity: A Primitive Theory of Social Structure. New York: Free Press. A theoretical work in the spirit of pure sociology. Resembles Black's strategy in several ways.
BRAITHWAITE, RICHARD BEVAN
   1953 Scientific Explanation: A Study of the Function of Theory, Probability
(1960) and Law in Science. New York: Harper & Row. A discussion of the style of explanation used in Black's strategy of pure sociology.
COLLINS, RANDALL
   1975 Conflict Sociology: Toward an Explanatory Science. New York: Academic Press. A theoretical work resembling pure sociology in important respects, but including some psychological components as well.
DURKHEIM, EMILE
   1895 The Rules of Sociological Method. New York: Free Press. An early effort
(1964) to formulate a strategy of pure sociology.
HOMANS, GEORGE C.
   1967 The Nature of Social Science. New York: Harcourt, Brace and World. A discussion of the aims and logic of social science. Although psychologi-

cal in strategy, this is similar to Black's work in its conception of theory and explanation.

KOLAKOWSKI, LESZEK
1966 The Alienation of Reason: A History of Positivist Thought. Garden City, N.Y.: Anchor, 1968. An introduction to the philosophical foundations of modern science. Surveys principles of scientific thought taken for granted in pure sociology.

RADCLIFFE-BROWN A, R.
1948 A Natural Science of Society. Chicago: University of Chicago Press. A discussion of the aims and assumptions of pure sociology, including its relation to other sciences.

SIMMEL, GEORG
1908 The Sociology of Georg Simmel. Edited by Kurt H. Wolff. New York: Free Press, 1960. An early approach to sociology, similar in its level of abstraction to the strategy presented by Black.

WEBER, MAX
1903– The Methodology of the Social Sciences. Edited by Edward A. Shils and
1917 Henry A. Finch. New York: Free Press, 1949. Essays on the role of values, objectivity, and other problems in the scientific study of social life.

4. R. H. Hingers and David Willer, "Prevailing Postulates of Social Exchange Theory."

BLAU, PETER M.
1964 Exchange and Power in Social Life. New York: Wiley. This work in exchange theory is perhaps second only in importance to Homans's works. The scope of concern of this study is broad, and as a consequence, offers an excellent introduction to at least one variant of exchange theory.

EKEH, PETER P.
1974 Social Exchange Theory. London: Heinemann Educational Books. Ekeh's book is a careful review of the varieties of exchange theory and includes a positive critique. The analysis of operant exchange theory is particularly valuable.

EMERSON, RICHARD M.
1969 "Operant psychology and exchange theory." In Robert L. Burgess and Don Bushell, Jr. (eds.), Behavioral Sociology: The Experimental Analysis of Social Process. New York: Columbia University Press.
1972 "Exchange theory, part II: exchange relations and network structures." In Joseph Berger, Morris Zelditch, Jr., and Bo Anderson, (eds.), Sociological Theories in Progress, vol. II. New York: Houghton Mifflin. These two papers offer an introduction to Emerson's position, which is of particular significance for its integration of network and operant theory.

GOULDNER, ALVIN W.
  1960 "The norm of reciprocity: a preliminary statement." American Sociological Review 25:161–178. The basic source on reciprocity is Gouldner's 1960 paper. It remains an excellent analysis today.
HOMANS, GEORGE C.
  1974 Social Behavior: Its Elementary Forms. New York: Wiley. Modern exchange theory in the U.S. is yet largely operant exchange theory and Homans's work is its point of departure.
POLANYI, KARL
  1968 Primitive, Archaic and Modern Economies: Essays of Karl Polanyi. Edited by George Dalton. Boston: Beacon Press. Institutional economists have carried forward important research and analysis on historic systems. One issue is the possible application of microeconomics to precapitalist systems. Polanyi is a leading proponent of the position that the application is unsound.
SAHLINS, MARSHALL
  1972 Stone Age Economics. Chicago: Aldine. An important analysis of exchange relations in primitive systems. It is evident from this work that the application of operant exchange theory to these systems would have great difficulties.
SCHWIMMER, ERIK
  1973 Exchange in the Social Structure of the Orokaiva: Traditional and Emergent Ideologies in the Northern District of Papua. New York: St. Martin's Press. An excellent ethnographic report, noted for its sophisticated conceptualization of incommensurable exchange.
WEBER, MAX
  1947 The Theory of Social and Economic Organization. Glencoe, Ill.: Free Press. The basic work for introduction to Weberian theory. As it relates to exchange theory, it could be pointed out that Weber's treatment of basic concepts has broader potential scope than any exchange formulations yet advanced.

5. James W. Michaels and Dan S. Green, "Behavioral Sociology: Emergent Forms and Issues."

AKERS, RONALD L.
  1973 Deviant Behavior: A Social Learning Approach. Belmont, Calif.: Wadsworth. This is one of the few textbooks written from a behavioral or social learning perspective. Akers introduces his social learning theory of deviant behavior and then applies the perspective to some of the principal types of deviant behavior. The theory integrates Sutherland's explanation of differential association with Skinner's behavioral learning theories.
BURGESS, ROBERT L., and RONALD L. AKERS
  1966 "A differential reinforcement theory of criminal behavior." Social Prob-

lems 14 (Fall):128–147. A paper in which the authors apply the principles of modern behavior theory to Sutherland's differential association theory. The authors show how Sutherland's sociological propositions can be reformulated into a more concise set of statements consistent with the principles of modern behavior. The reformulated propositions, according to the authors, are a better response to the criticisms of Sutherland's original statements.

BURGESS, ROBERT L., and DON BUSHELL (eds.)
 1969 Behavioral Sociology: The Experimental Analysis of Social Process. New York: Columbia University Press. This work, with contributors from sociology and psychology, offers the first collection of theoretical and empirical articles dealing with behavioral sociology. All of the selections are based on an integrated set of behavioral principles. Of special interest is the introduction by George Homans; also of interest are the selections which demonstrate the use of the empirical approach in the analysis of social behavior.

EMERSON, RICHARD M.
 1972 "Exchange theory." In Joseph Berger, Morris Zelditch, Jr., and Bo Anderson (eds.), Sociological Theories in Progress, vol 2. Boston: Houghton Mifflin. In this lengthy, two-part article, Emerson offers a theoretical and rather technical discussion of exchange theory and proposes a theory of social exchange in which social structure is taken as the dependent variable. The author argues that his work, which begins with a given base of psychology, should be thought of as constructionism rather than reductionism.

FRIEDRICHS, ROBERT W.
 1974 "The potential impact of B. F. Skinner upon American sociology." The American Sociologist 9 (February):3–8. A short and provocative paper which briefly discusses and analyzes the behavioral orientation in sociology. Friedrichs notes that behavioral sociology has claimed the allegiance of a rapidly growing group of sociologists and social psychologists, and is very much in harmony with the national research establishment. Of particular interest is the discussion of a conceivable shift from a Parsonian to a Skinnerian orientation.

HAMBLIN, ROBERT, DAVID BUCKHOLDT, DANIEL FERRITOR, MARTIN KOZLOFF, and LOIS BLACKWELL
 1971 The Humanization Processes: A Social, Behavioral Analysis of Children's Problems. New York: Wiley. An interesting blend of both sociology and psychology about the acculturation of children.

HAMBLIN, ROBERT L., and JOHN A. KUNKEL (eds.)
 1977 Behavioral Theory in Sociology. New Brunswick, N.J.: Transaction Books. A collection of writings honoring the contributions of George Homans to behavioral sociology. The contributors follow Homans's approach and develop their ideas within the behavioral framework that

Homans has formulated over the years. This work codifies and expands the behavioral tradition in sociology while also providing some implicit and explicit critical assessments.

HOMANS, GEORGE C.
1961 Social Behavior: Its Elementary Forms. New York: Harcourt, Brace and World. A classic work in the field, about everyday elementary social behavior, which argues that many or most of the empirical generalizations about human behavior may be most easily explained by behavioral psychology and elementary economics. Homans sets up a series of propositions organized around the exchange approach to social behavior; his orientation clearly rejects the Durkheimian position in favor of behavior explanations.

KUNKEL, JOHN H.
1975 Behavior, Social Problems, and Change. Englewood Cliffs, N.J.: Prentice-Hall. In this work Kunkel presents a behavioral perspective of social problems based on a model of humans derived from principles of social learning. Also, the author outlines a set of procedures useful for analyzing particular social problems and their causes. Of particular interest and relevance is the material discussing the behavioral model of human behavior.

SKINNER, B. F.
1953 Science and Human Behavior. New York: Macmillan. An invaluable, early statement by one of the foremost proponents of behaviorism, dealing with the scientific analysis of behavior, considerations of a science of behavior, and the effect of such a science on individuals and groups. The work also contains discussions of the operation of controlling agencies and the control of human behavior.

PART IV. DIALECTICS

1. Richard Appelbaum, "Marxist Method: Structural Constraints and Social *Praxis*."

ALTHUSSER, LOUIS
1969 For Marx. London: Penguin. A good introduction to French structuralist Marxism, although Althusser in more recent writings, has retreated from some of the positions advanced in this early work.

GLUCKSMANN, MIRIAM
1974 Structuralist Analysis in Contemporary Social Thought: A Comparison of the Theories of Claude Lévi-Strauss and Louis Althusser. Boston: Routledge and Kegan Paul. An excellent and informed critique of structuralist Marxism.

HABERMAS, JÜRGEN
1971 Knowledge and Human Interests. Boston: Beacon Press. A significant effort to distinguish the philosophical import of Marx's work and locate it with reference to subsequent development in hermeneutics and psy-

chology, this highly influential work seeks to establish a new anthropology of human nature along the suppositions of critical theory.

LUKACS, GEORG
1971 History and Class Consciousness. Cambridge: MIT Press. This collection of essays, written around 1920 by a leading Hungarian proponent of the *praxis* orientation, reintroduced philosophical Marxism to Marxist intellectuals; its analysis of reification remains of seminal importance in the critical theory tradition.

MARX, KARL
1964 The Economic and Philosophical Manuscripts of 1844. New York: International Publishers. These early writings reveal Marx's initial efforts to reconcile Hegelian philosophy with the science of political economy, developing the humanistic side of his thinking.
1967 Capital, vols. 1-3. New York: International Publishers. The most systematic presentation of Marx's theory of capitalist development and his method. A close reading of Capital is a prerequisite for an understanding of Marx and Marxist thought.
1973 Grundrisse. New York: Vintage. The extensive notes compiled by Marx a decade prior to the publication of Capital, this material constitutes the basis for the later work and contains the most extensive presentation of his methodological thinking.

OLLMAN, BERTELL
1971 Alienation: Marx's Concept of Man in Capitalist Society. New York: Cambridge University Press. A detailed examination of the philosophical and humanistic elements in Marx's work, which seeks to relate dialectics to the philosophy of internal relations.

TUCKER, ROBERT C. (ed.)
1972 The Marx-Engels Reader. New York: Norton. The best short collection of Marx's writings currently available; includes works representative of his economic analysis, philosophical critique, and writings on politics.

WRIGHT, ERIC OLIN
1975 "Alternative perspectives in the Marxist theory of accumulation and crisis." The Insurgent Sociologist 6 (Fall):5-39. An examination of Marx's crisis theory, which focuses on the accumulation and displacement of structural contradictions; contradictions are here treated as internally generated and incapable of satisfactory resolution within the framework of capitalist economic production.

2. David S. Walls, "Dialectical Social Science."

BERGER, PETER L., and THOMAS LUCKMANN
1966 The Social Construction of Reality: A Treatise in the Sociology of Knowledge. Garden City, N.Y.: Doubleday. A model of dialectical social theory from the standpoint of conservative humanism. The authors

synthesize aspects of the thoughts of Marx, Weber, Durkheim, Mead, and Schutz.

BERNSTEIN, RICHARD J.
   1976 The Restructuring of Social and Political Theory. Philadelphia: University of Pennsylvania Press. A consideration of the contributions of empiricism, language analysis, phenomenology, and critical theory to a dialectical social theory.

FAY, BRIAN
   1975 Social Theory and Political Practice. London: George Allen and Unwin. A critique of positivist and interpretive social science, followed by a description of a critical social science that elaborates themes from the Frankfurt School and its successors.

GIDDENS, ANTHONY
   1976 New Rules of Sociological Method: A Positive Critique of Interpretative Sociologies. New York: Basic Books. A sympathetic critique of interpretive social science, moving in the direction of a dialectical methodology. Concludes with a list of "new rules" of sociological method.

GRAHL, BART and PAUL PICCONE (eds.)
   1973 Towards a New Marxism. St. Louis: Telos Press. An anthology consisting primarily of papers presented at a Telos conference in 1970. Contemporary theorizing in the dialectical tradition of Western Marxism, with an emphasis on existential and phenomenological Marxism.

HOWARD, DICK, and KARL E. KARE (eds.)
   1972 The Unknown Dimension: European Marxism Since Lenin. New York: Basic Books. An anthology of contemporary theorizing in the tradition of Western Marxism.

KEAT, RUSSELL, and JOHN URRY
   1975 Social Theory as Science. London: Routledge and Kegan Paul. Positivistic social science is criticized, and a realistic approach to social science is developed. Although sympathetic to structural Marxism, the authors are not hostile to incorporating aspects of interpretive social science into their theory.

O'NEILL, JOHN
   1972 Sociology as a Skin Trade: Essays Toward a Reflexive Sociology. New York: Harper & Row. A collection of essays, several of which explore the relationship of phenomenology and Marxism from a standpoint critical of orthodox Marxism and the Frankfurt School and are sympathetic to a social phenomenology derived in part from Merleau-Ponty.

PACI, ENZO
   1972 The Function of the Sciences and the Meaning of Man. Evanston, Ill.: Northwestern University Press. A major effort to synthesize the later work of Husserl with Marxism, and a primary influence on the development of phenomenological Marxism.

SMART, BARRY
   1976 Sociology, Phenomenology, and Marxian Analysis. London: Routledge and Kegan Paul. An approach to dialectical social science based on a phenomenological Marxism.

3. Mark L. Wardell and J. Kenneth Benson, "A Dialectical View: Foundation for an Alternative Sociological Method."

ADORNO, THEODOR W., et al.
1976 The Positivist Dispute in German Sociology. Translated by Gleyn Adey and David Frisby. New York: Harper Torchbooks. An excellent series of papers, in which some of the more traditional sociologists and philosophers of science debate the central issues in establishing a dialectical method with representatives of the Frankfurt School.

BRAVERMAN, HARRY
1974 Labor and Monopoly Capital. New York: Monthly Review. A recent, highly regarded treatment of the labor process and working conditions in industrial capitalism. Particularly valuable analysis of how the pursuit of profit leads to technological innovations which reduce the skillfulness and meaning of work in capitalist society.

GOLDMANN, LUCIEN
1969 The Human Science and Philosophy. Translated by Hayden V. White. London: Jonathan Cape. Presents criticism of several classical figures in sociology (e.g., Weber) showing how the value-neutrality stance of traditional sociology contains many metatheoretical assumptions.

LEFEBVRE, HENRI
1968 The Sociology of Marx. New York: Pantheon A valuable summary and analysis of Marx's work based on a dialectical reading. Useful for explaining such central concepts of dialectical Marxism as alienation, *praxis*, and totality.

LUKACS, GEORG
1972 History and Class Consciousness. Translated by Rodney Livingston. Cambridge, Mass.: MIT Press. An important and early (1923) statement of the dialectical position, emphasizing its methodological features. Lukacs sees the problem of reification at the core of capitalist domination. He argues that the proletariat's revolutionary role as the identical subject-object of history can end reification. While highly controversial, the book has been an important source within Western Marxism.

MARX, KARL
1963 The Poverty of Philosophy. New York: International Publishers. Attacks Proudhon for maintaining a conventional political and economic point of view. Marx emphasizes the importance of looking at the division of labor and the workshop as products of a particular historical configuration.
1964 The Economic and Philosophic Manuscripts of 1844. Edited by Dirk J. Struik and translated by Martin Milligan. New York: International Publishers. A part of Marx's youthful period, this collection of writings contains the philosophical underpinnings of the dialectical method. Marx develops his *praxis* orientation in this book.

OFFE, CLAUS
1976 Industry and Inequality. Translated by James Wickham. London:

Edward Arnold. Analysis of the achievement principle within capitalism. Offe argues it is an ideology which supports and maintains capitalism. The demands of expanding labor within capitalism are seen as contradicting the achievement principle.

OLLMAN, BENTELL
1971 Alienation: Marx's Conception of Man in Capitalist Society. Cambridge: Cambridge University Press. A recent interpretation, which argues that the philosophy of internal relations is the key to understanding Marx's work, and that alienation is central to Marx's entire work, opposing interpretations which relegate that concept to Marx's early Hegelian period.

PART V. CRITICAL THEORY
1. Michael E. Brown, "Sociology as Critical Theory."

ADORNO, THEODOR, H. ALBERT, R. DAHRENDORF, J. HABERMAS, H. PILOT, and K. POPPER
1976 The Positivist Dispute in German Sociology. New York: Harper & Row. This collection addresses some of the philosophic and methodological issues involved in the attempt to establish the necessity of critical theory and its critique of positivism.

CONNERTON, PAUL (ed.)
1976 Critical Sociology. Middlesex: Penguin. This is the best available collection of articles on the method, substance, and criticisms of the work of the Frankfurt school. It includes a large selection of the classical materials on which critical theory is based. In addition it contains an informative introduction that briefly describes the origins of critical theory and its basic problems. Among the authors are Hegel, Marx, Gadamer, Adorno, and Horkheimer.

HABERMAS, JÜRGEN
1970a "Toward a theory of communicative competence." Pp. 115–148 in H. Dreitzel (ed.), Recent Sociology 2. Patterns of Communicative Behavior. New York: Macmillan. This and other articles in this book introduce some of Habermas's speculations on language. Of special importance is his discussion of the ideal speech situation and his attempt to justify it as a concept essential to the conception of critique.
1970b Towards a Rational Society. Boston: Beacon Press. This collection of writings introduces Habermas's attempt to deal with the political question and to demonstrate the ideological basis of science and technology insofar as they are used to justify the limited rationality of late capitalism and its administration, and to distinguish between his own position regarding the status of science and other critical materialists, particularly Marcuse.
1971 Knowledge and Human Interest. Boston: Beacon Press. This is Habermas's most complete statement of his theory of knowledge and the best

reference for the argument underlying his later work on the evolution of capitalism. The appendix provides an adequate introduction to this difficult but essential work.

1975 Legitimation Crisis. Boston: Beacon Press. This short book presents a fairly recent application of critical theory to the problem of social change in late capitalist society. Habermas criticizes systems theory and attempts to establish a basis for an evolutionary theory of capitalist development culminating in a discussion of the further possibility of critical discourse and critical action. This is one of his more comprehensive efforts to deal with the problems of late capitalism and to integrate sociology, the study of culture, and political economy.

HORKHEIMER, MAX, and THEODOR ADORNO

1972 Dialectic of Enlightenment. Translated by John Cumming. New York: Seabury. This is one of the fundamental texts of critical theory, both because of its broad and profound critique of the sources of ideology in the twentieth century and its illustration, often difficult to penetrate, of dialectical reason at work.

HOWARD, DICK

1977 The Marxian Legacy. New York: Urizen Books. While this book summarizes the work of a number of theorists and does not specifically deal with the scope of critical theory, it has a useful summary of Habermas's work and an excellent discussion of criticisms and possible answers to criticisms. In addition it places Habermas in relation to neo-Marxian thought in general, providing a perspective that complements Jay's book.

JAY, MARTIN

1973 The Dialectical Imagination. Boston: Little, Brown. This is a thorough account of the history of the Frankfurt school, with a good review of its classical literature. It is, in effect, a sociology of critical theory and is the most complete treatment of the topic currently available in English.

POSTER, MARK

1978 Critical Theory of the Family. New York: Seabury. Poster applies the critique of domination to the study of the family and, in so doing, illustrates the power of critical theory in regard to a topic that has been discussed from a number of points of view and in connection with an enormous amount of research. The book also provides a clearly written introduction to the problems of analysis involved in a critical social psychology.

2. Jeffrey A. Halley, "Beyond the Sociology of Art: Recent Interdisciplinary Developments in the Critical Analysis of Culture."

BARTHES, ROLAND

1975 The Pleasure of the Text. Translated by Richard Miller. New York: Hill and Wang. An inventive introduction to some of the themes (e.g., deconstruction) of the French post-structuralists.

BENJAMIN, WALTER
1968 Illuminations. Translated by Harry Zohn and edited by Hannah Arendt. New York: Harcourt, Brace, and World. A valuable collection of Benjamin's essays, including "The Work of Art in the Age of Mechanical Reproduction" and "On Some Motifs in Baudelaire."

GOLDMANN, LUCIEN
1976 Cultural Creation in Modern Society. Translated by Bart Grahl. St. Louis: Telos. This series of posthumous essays is the best introduction to Goldmann's theoretical contributions, in particular, his notions of potential consciousness, the translation consciousness, the transindividual subject, and cultural action.

EAGLETON, TERRY
1976 Marxism and Literary Criticism. Berkeley, Calif.: University of California Press. An excellent and brief survey from the structuralist position.

HORKHEIMER, MAX, and THEODOR W. ADORNO
1972 Dialectic of Englightenment. Translated by John Cumming. New York: Seabury. Contains the seminal essay on rationalization in the "culture industry."

JAMESON, FREDRIC
1971 Marxism and Form: Twentieth-Century Dialectical Theories of Literature. Princeton, N.J.: Princeton University Press. An excellent series of essays interpreting the key figures in Western Marxism (Adorno, Benjamin, Marcuse, Bloch, Lukacs, Sartre).

MARCUSE, HERBERT
1977 The Aesthetic Dimension: Toward a Critique of Marxist Aesthetics. Boston: Beacon Press. Marcuse's latest work characterizes art as a liberating practice that subverts the dominant consciousness.

SANCHEZ VAZQUEZ, ADOLFO
1973 Art and Society: Essays in Marxist Aesthetics. Translated by Maro Riofrancos. New York: Monthly Review. A perceptive critique of dogmatic Marxist conceptions, emphasizing the notion of cultural creation as a material practice.

SOLOMON, MAYNARD
1974 Marxism and Art: Essays Classic and Contemporary. New York: Vintage. The best reader on the subject, containing information on hard-to-find non-orthodox positions (Bloch, Raphael, Bakhtin) and on orthodox (Bolshevik and Zhdanovist) positions.

WILLIAMS, RAYMOND
1977 Marxism and Literature. Oxford: Oxford University Press. Williams presents a profound critique of base and superstructure and reflection theories, and develops a theory of cultural materialism.

3. Sang Jin Han, "Ideology—Critique and Social Science:
The Use of Discursive Method."

ADORNO, T. W., H. ALBERT, R. DAHRENDORF, J. HABERMAS, H. PILOT, and
K. POPPER
1976 The Positivist Dispute in German Sociology. New York: Harper & Row.
This is, mostly, the collection of the papers by Adorno, Popper, Habermas, and Albert, the key participants in the dispute that lasted from 1962
to 1964. In addition a long introduction by Adorno, two short pieces of
critical response by Albert and Popper, a commentary by Dahrendorf,
and a paper by Pilot are included. One should read this text as the initial
announcement of the differences between positivist and critical social
sciences. Enormous self-scrutiny and progress have been attempted since
then by both sides, especially in the works of Albert and Habermas.

ALTHUSSER, LOUIS
1969 For Marx. New York: Vintage Books. As the collection of Althusser's
essays from 1960 to 1965, this text shows the immensity of Althusser's
struggle against Marxist humanism and toward Marxism as a structural
analysis. Althusser's polemic is fundamentally against mechanistic
Marxism and Hegelian or existentialist versions of Marxism. Althusser
uses the concept of "epistemological break" in line with Bachelard and
examines Marx's works and justifies the scientific status of Marxist
analysis. Althusser thus establishes a clean boundary between knowledge
and ideology.

BAUDRILLARD, JEAN
1975 The Mirror of Production. St. Louis: Telos Press. As a critic of orthodox
Marxism, Baudrillard shows the irreducibility of symbolic rationality to
an economic rationality, the pervasive function of signs in modern
capitalism, the mode of subversion of capitalist order in the fields of
language. It is argued that Marxist materialism has unwittingly merged
with capitalism, where a premium is placed upon the economy. This text
can be seen as an exemplar of the semiotic analysis of late capitalism,
which is becoming increasingly popular in France.

FOUCAULT, MICHEL
1972 The Archaeology of Knowledge. New York: Pantheon. This is Foucault's masterpiece, and it establishes the epistemological foundation of
discursive analysis. Though unfinished, this text suggests the archaeological analysis of discourse as an exemplar of the discursive method.
The explicit target of Foucault's criticism is the phenomenological mode
of analysis, but it should be noted that this text is also critical of all forms
of reductionism of language such as Marxist materialism. Against this
reductionism, Foucault shows the reasons that language is important for
science and social formations and the ways in which language may be
understood and analyzed.

HABERMAS, JÜRGEN

1975   Legitimation Crisis. Boston: Beacon Press. Examining the discrete levels of crisis formation in modern capitalism, this text focuses attention on the specificity and the logic of legitimation problems. Basically, Habermas attempts to reconstruct legitimation problems as a "discursive" problem. It is obvious that Habermas raises his polemic against Marxist materialism, systems theory, and Weberian sociology. Habermas argues that none of them is capable of grasping the discursive nature of legitimation problems, which is, in his view, important today. The aim of Habermas's discussion is, therefore, to overcome the limits of Marxism from the point of view of discursive science.

1976a Zur Rekonstruktion des historischen Materialism (Toward a Reconstruction of Historical Materialism). Frankfurt: Suhrkamp. This text is composed of four parts: "Philosophical Perspectives," "Identity," "Evolution," and "Legitimation." Here, as elsewhere, Habermas does not reject Marxist analysis as such, but points out its limits and the way in which these limits can be overcome. Habermas's solution is that the normative structures of society cannot be reduced to the material basis of society, as in Marxism, but must be seen with respect to their own logic of formation and development. This solution is strengthened by many supporting materials to which Habermas draws attention extensively. With this solution Habermas distinguishes two levels of rationalization, instrumental-strategic and communicative, which are characteristic, in his view, of social evolution of human society. Together with *Reading Capital* by Althusser and Balibar, this text provides an important challenge to the orthodox conception of historical materialism.

1976b "Was heisst universalpragmatik?" (What Is Universal Pragmatic?). Pp. 174–272 in Karl-Otto Apel (ed.), Sprachpragmatik und Philosophie. Frankfurt: Suhrkamp. This text represents Habermas's latest and most systematic attempt to develop a theory of communication which serves as the basis of human science and social analysis. In the first part of this work, Habermas examines the methodological problems associated with "rational reconstruction" and in the second part attempts to reconstruct the general structures of communication with specific reference to the validity claims of speech. Habermas's previous discussions on communicative competence, distorted communication, and deep-hermeneutic approach are preserved in a new form and level of generality. Locating the concept of "discursive testing" within the structures of speech, Habermas supports his consensus theory of truth as well as his theory of social evolution. Habermas's project of universal pragmatic now seems to have reached the stage of conceptual maturity, but this does not mean that it is complete.

LORENZER, ALFRED

1974   Die Wahrheit der Psychoanalytischen Erkenntnis (The Truth of Psychoanalytic Knowledge). Frankfurt: Suhrkamp. This is Lorenzer's masterly discursive analysis of the modes of the structuration of personality within the structural contexts of capitalist relationships. Psychoanalysis is reconstructed as a social theory, as a critical-hermeneutic activity which is geared to the emancipation of human society. Lorenzer combines two important elements, structural analysis and the emancipatory interest of science, in a unique manner.

OFFE, CLAUS

1972 Strukturprobleme des kapitalistischen Staates (Structural Problems of the Capitalist State). Frankfurt: Suhrkamp. This text is Offe's powerful polemic against dogmatic Marxism and bourgeois social science. Offe advocates a discursive analysis of state interventionism. For this he examines the methodological problems of discursive analysis and such crucial problems of state activity as structural incompatibility (contradiction), technocracy, legitimation, and the relationship of the state to accumulation. Some of the articles in this book have been translated into English in different places. One who is interested in the theory of the state is encouraged to read Offe's methodological writing, "Structural problem of the capitalist state," in German Political Studies, vol. 1. London: Sage Publications, 1974, pp. 31–57.

RADNITZKY, GERALD

1970 Contemporary Schools of Metascience. Chicago: Regnery. This text is a useful introduction to the Anglo-Saxon philosophy of science and the continential, hermeneutic-critical theory of science. This text is informative, although it does not deal with the metatheoretical thought developed in structuralism and poststructuralism in France. Also, Radnitzky explores and constructs a programatic model of a theory of research based on the hermeneutic-critical theory.

4. John J. Sewart, "Critical Theory and the Critique of Conservative Method."

ADORNO, THEODOR (ed.)

1976 The Positivist Dispute in German Sociology. London: Heinemann Books. Contains a number of landmark papers stating the opposing positions of positivism and critical theory. Included is the classic debate between Adorno and Karl Popper, as well as papers by Dahrendorf, Habermas, and Hans Albert.

ARATO, ANDREW, and EIKE GEBHARDT (eds.)

1978 The Essential Frankfurt School Reader. New York: Urizen Books. A recent anthology containing many important works of the Frankfurt school, which had been untranslated or were difficult to acquire in English. It covers the critique of politics, esthetic theory, cultural criticism, and the critique of methodology. In addition valuable introductory essays by Piconne and Arato and Gebhardt are included.

BERNSTEIN, RICHARD J.

1976 The Restructuring of Social and Political Theory. New York: Harcourt

Brace Jovanovich. A comprehensive scrutiny of the epistemological and normative dimensions of the social sciences. Bernstein carefully dissects the underlying logic of empirical social science, phenomenological analysis, and the critical theory of society proposed by Horkheimer and Habermas. Bernstein's ultimate project is to recover the self-conscious unity of knowledge and human activity.

FAY, BRIAN

1975 Social Theory and Political Practice. London: Allen & Unwin. Critique of positivist social science and its vision of a technological politics. Writing from the perspective of critical theory, Fay explores the possibility of dialectically integrating an interpretative social science into a critical theory of society.

HOWARD, DICK

1977 The Marxian Legacy. New York: Urizen Books. Excellent analysis of the work of Horkheimer, Habermas, Luxemburg, Bloch, Sartre, Merleau-Ponty, Lefort, and Castoriadis. An important critical and original contribution to the status of theoretical and political projects in Western Marxism.

HOWARD, DICK, and KARL KLARE (eds.)

1972 The Unknown Dimensions: European Marxism Since Marxism. New York: Basic Books. Excellent introduction to the tradition of Western Marxism. Theorists dealt with include: Lukas, Korsch, Gramsci, Reich, the Frankfurt School, Benjamin, Sartre, Lefebvre, and Althusser. The introductory essays provide a conscise historical location of Western Marxist thought.

JAY, MARTIN

1973 The Dialectical Imagination. Boston: Little, Brown. An exemplary and invaluable piece of scholarship exploring in detail the intellectual history of the Frankfurt school (1923–1950). An essential beginning point for any serious study of critical theory.

KOSIK, KAREL

1976 Dialectics of the Concrete: A Study on Problems of Man and World. Boston: Reidel. (Volume LII of Boston Studies in the Philosophy of Science.) An excellent critique of reductionistic Marxism and phenomenology from the perspective of a blended Hegelian Marxism and existential phenomenology. Kosik sensitively explores themes such as the part-whole relation, the relation between science and *praxis*, and the importance of labor as a category for recovering a critical perspective on the world as humanly made and therefore possibly different.

LEISS, WILLIAM

1974 The Domination of Nature. Boston: Beacon Press. Useful analysis of the problem of science and technological rationality in relation to critical theory. Provides an in-depth exploration of the religious and philosophical roots underlying the oppressive domination of scientific reason in modern society.

LOBKOWICZ, NICHOLAS
1967 Theory and Practice. Notre Dame, Ind.: University of Notre Dame Press.
Comprehensive analysis of the dual concept of theory and practice,
which are perhaps, the central problem of critical theory. Examines the
development of the concept through the works of Aristotle, Hegel, and
Marx.

O'NEILL, JOHN (ed.)
1976 On Critical Theory. New York: Seabury. A good collection of articles
dealing with various aspects of critical theory. Topics covered range from
the study of politics, music and art, psychoanalysis, the debates between
Habermas and Gadamer, and Hermas and Luhmann, as well as the
linguistic turn in critical theory.

RADNITZKY, GERARD
1973 Contemporary Schools of Metascience. Chicago: Regnery. Excellent
overview of Anglo-Saxon and Continental schools of social and
philosophical thought. Provides an excellent introduction to the basic
issues involved in the traditions of positivism, phenomenology, hermeneutics, and dialectical/critical analyses.

PART VI. THE INDIVIDUAL AND HUMAN CONSCIOUSNESS
1. David R. Dickens, "Phenomenology."

BERNSTEIN, RICHARD
1978 The Restructuring of Social and Political Theory. Philadelphia: The
University of Pennsylvania Press. A good overview for the nonphenome-
nologist of phenomenology's potential import for the social sciences.

CARR, DAVID
1974 Phenomenology and the Problem of History. Evanston, Ill.: Northwestern University Press. An excellent presentation of the overall development of Husserl's philosophy from beginning to end.

GURWITSCH, ARON
1964 The Field of Consciousness. Pittsburgh: Duquesne University Press.
Possibly the clearest technical account of Husserl's analysis of consciousness. An excellent place to begin the study of phenomenology.
1966 "The last work of Edmund Husserl." In Studies in Phenomenology
and Psychology, by Gurwitsch. Evanston, Ill.: Northwestern University
Press. A clear, systematic explication of Husserl's famous Krisis lectures,
which have exerted such an influence on existentialists such as Sartre and
Merleau-Ponty, as well as those who seek to combine phenomenology
with Marxism.

NATANSON, MAURICE
1968 Literature, Philosophy, and the Social Sciences. The Hague: Martinus
Nijhoff. Contains several highly illuminating characterizations of phenomenology in the context of art and literature. Also contains a similar
presentation of existentialism.

PACI, ENZO
1972 The Function of the Sciences and the Meaning of Man. Evanston, Ill.:
Northwestern University Press. The classic statement about the attempt
to combine phenomenology with Marxism.

SCHUTZ, ALFRED
1967 The Phenomenology of the Social World. Evanston, Ill.: Northwestern
University Press. The classic attempt to lay the ground for a phenomenologically based sociology.

STRASSER, STEPHAN
1974 Phenomenology and the Human Sciences. Pittsburgh: Duquesne University Press. An intriguing book which attempts to relate phenomenology to empirical science.

ZANER, RICHARD
1973 The Way of Phenomenology. New York: Pegasus Press. A thorough
analysis of the main features of Husserlian phenomenology. Essential as
a basic text.

2. Joseph A. Kotarba, "Existential Sociology."

ALTHEIDE, DAVID L.
1976 Creating Reality: How TV News Distorts Events. Beverly Hills, Calif.:
Sage. A detailed analysis of television news, based upon extensive
ethnographic research. The author demonstrates how the reality of
events is distorted by the constraints imposed by a commercially and
technologically motivated news perspective that transcends all aspects of
the everyday creation of television news.

ALTHEIDE, DAVID L., and JOHN M. JOHNSON
1979 Bureaucratic Propaganda. Boston: Allyn and Bacon. Grounded in
several ethnographic studies of bureaucratic information management,
this book explains how private and public organizations present positive
and convincing self-images through written reports directed at specific
audiences. Of special interest is the authors' investigative report on the
means used by a large, evangelical religious group to demonstrate
statistical success in attracting "converts."

DOUGLAS, JACK D.
1976 Investigative Social Research. Beverly Hills, Calif.: Sage. The 'classic'
statement on existential/investigative field research methods. Using a
conflict model approach to everyday life reality, the author discusses
techniques (both individual and team-oriented) for using the researcher's
personal experience to break the barrier of evasions, fronts, and misinformation encountered in the field.

DOUGLAS, JACK D., PATRICIA A. ADLER, PETER ADLER, ANDREA FONTANA,
C. ROBERT REEMAN, and JOSEPH A. KOTARBA
1979 Introduction to the Sociologies of Everyday Life. Boston: Allyn and
Bacon. An in-depth discussion and synthesis of the five major varieties of
everyday life sociology (i.e., symbolic interactionism, labeling theory,

existential sociology, the dramaturgical perspective, and phenome-
nology/ethnomethodology).

DOUGLAS, JACK D., and JOHN M. JOHNSON (eds.)
1977 Existential Sociology. New York: Cambridge University Press. The
definitive work in existential sociology. A collection of original essays
portraying the theoretical influences (e.g., Sartre and Merleau-Ponty) on
and the empirical applications (e.g., homosexuality and the chronic pain
experience) of the existential perspective in social science.

FONTANA, ANDREA
1977 The Last Frontier. Beverly Hills, Calif.: Sage. An insightful examination
of the problematic meanings attached to growing old in our society. The
author argues that existing theories of aging, such as disengagement, do
not adequately reflect that process as experienced by the elderly themselves.

JOHNSON, JOHN M.
1975 Doing Field Research. New York: The Free Press. A personal account of
the fusion of feelings and thought in doing field work. This analysis of
the reflexive role of the researcher results in new and innovative views of
objectivity in the social sciences.

KOTARBA, JOSEPH A.
Forth- The Chronic Pain Experience. A thorough inquiry into all aspects of the
com- experience of chronic pain. Topics explored include the effects of chronic
ing pain on self-image and personal relations of the patient, the effects of
intervention by marginal and normal health-care practitioners, and a
comparison of occupational contingencies of chronic pain incurred by
blue-collar workers and professional athletes.

LYMAN, STANFORD M., and MARVIN B. SCOTT
1970 A Sociology of the Absurd. New York: Appleton. An early statement on
the social construction of meaning in a world that is essentially absurd.
Drawing upon the ideas of phenomenologists and existentialists, the
authors explore game frameworks, verbal accounts, "coolness," and time
tracks as members' methods for producing the semblance of social order.

MANNING, PETER K.
1977 Police Work: The Social Organization of Policing. Cambridge: MIT
Press. Based on extensive fieldwork in England and the United States,
this book views policing as "the dramatic management of the appearance
of effectiveness." The popular role of the police as "crime fighters" is
critiqued in light of the limited resources of the police and the unrealistic
expectations placed on them by today's complex society.

3. John O'Neill, "The Mutuality of Accounts: An Essay on Trust."

APEL, KARL-OTTO
1967 Analytic Philosophy of Language and the Geisteswissenschaften. Dor-
drecht: D. Reider. Argues for the compatibility of hermeneutical understanding and causal scientific explanations of human behavior.

CICOUREL, AARON V.
1973 Cognitive Sociology, Language and Meaning in Social Interaction. Harmondsworth: Penguin. Treats the problem of the relation between sociological analysis and the social categories employed by lay members of society.

DALLMAYR, FRED R., and THOMAS A. McCARTHY (eds.)
1977 Understanding and Social Inquiry. Notre Dame, Ind.: University of Notre Dame Press. A useful collection of readings showing idealist, positivist, Wittgensteinian, phenomenological, and ethnomethodological perspectives.

GARFINKEL, HAROLD
1967 Studies in Ethnomethodology. Englewood Cliffs, N.J.: Prentice-Hall. Treats the problem of the relationship between common-sense and social science accounts of institutional rationality and organization.

GIDDENS, ANTHONY
1976 New Rules of Sociological Method: A Positive Critique of Interpretative Sociologies. London: Hutchinson. Critical evaluation of the double hermeneutic of the social sciences.

HABERMAS, JÜRGEN
1971 Knowledge and Human Interests. Boston: Beacon Press. Uses the Frankfurt School critical theory to examine the historical relationship between knowledge and freedom.

O'NEILL, JOHN
1974 Making Sense Together: An Introduction to Wild Sociology. New York: Harper & Row. A defense of the common sense order of everyday life and the values of family and tradition.

SCHUTZ, ALFRED
1967 The Phenomenology of the Social World. Evanston, Ill.: Northwestern University Press. Classical source for the analysis of the structure of common-sense knowledge of persons and society.

TAYLOR, CHARLES
1964 The Explanation of Behavior. London: Routledge and Kegan Paul. A critique of the positivist-reduction of behavior employing ordinary language and phenomenological arguments.

WINCH, PETER
1958 The Idea of a Social Science. London: Routledge and Kegan Paul. A classical source for the argument that common-sense understanding of society is self-sufficient and not merely a poor version of sociological analysis.

4. Don H. Zimmerman, "Ethnomethodology."

BITTNER, EGON
1965 "The Concept of Organization." Social Research, 32:239-55. This article sets forth an ethnomethodological perspective on the study of

organizations. It argues that the notion of organization is a common-sense construct, and as such, is worthy of study in its own right, rather than being employed as a covert resource for sociological studies of organization.

CICOUREL, AARON

1964a Method and Measurement in Sociology. New York: The Free Press. Sometimes construed as a polemic against the use of quantitative methods, this work argues for greater clarity and precision in spelling out the sociologists' models of the social actor underlying the imposition of some metric on social behavior. This book is often cited as a source for the ethnomethodological "critique" of conventional sociology.

1964b The Social Organization of Juvenile Justice. New York: Wiley. An uncompromising, detailed examination of the use of tacit knowledge and background understandings in the construction of accounts of the character and careers of juvenile offenders by juvenile authorities.

GARFINKEL, HAROLD

1967 Studies in Ethnomethodology. Englewood Cliffs, N.J.: Prentice-Hall. Although published more than a decade ago, this collection of seminal studies retains its capacity to deepen the reader's grasp of common-sense reasoning and to inspire insight into its properties. The book is best read from back to front (roughly the order in which the essays were written). Chapter 8 is especially important, for it presents the argument that the domain of common-sense reasoning has its own distinct properties in need of investigation in their own right.

GARFINKEL, HAROLD, and HARVEY SACKS

1970 "On Formal Structures of Practical Actions," in J. C. McKinney and Edward A. Tiryakian (eds.), Theoretical Sociology: Perspectives and Developments. New York: Appleton-Century-Crofts. A difficult article that deals with the notion of "natural language accounts," "indexical expressions," and the distinction between ethnomethodological and conventional sociological interests in social phenomena.

SACKS, HARVEY

1972 "On the analyzability of stories by children." In J. Gumperz and D. Hymes (eds.), Directions in Sociolinguistics. New York: Holt, Rinehart and Winston. An early study concerned with the organization of members' descriptive practices. Sacks points out that it is important to note that the adequacy of a description does not depend in the first instance on its accuracy (the fit between description and thing described), but rather on its situated plausibility (the fit between description and thing described, given what Anyone Knows about such things and the information available.) The study furnishes a clear example of what could be meant by "members methods."

SACKS, HARVEY, EMANUEL SCHEGLOFF, and GAIL JEFFERSON

1974 "A simplest systematics for the organization of turn-taking in conversation." Language 50:696–735. While centrally concerned with the organization of turn-taking in naturally occurring conversation, this lengthy article also provides what might be termed the "members' solution" to the problem of indexicality in the conversational context. The solution hinges on the "context-free, context-sensitive" character of the turn-taking mechanism, which provides for the property of "recipient design," whereby the particular, situated features of conversations and conversationalists are articulated in the turn-by-turn development of a conversation.

SCHUTZ, ALFRED

1962 Collected Papers I: The Problem of Social Reality. The Hague: Martinus Nijhoff.

1964 Collected Papers II: Studies in Social Theory. The Hague: Martinus Nijhoff. In suggesting these two works (there are many more) by Schutz, the intent is to invite the reader to review a body of thought which contributed to the development of ethnomethodology. It is important that such a reading be directed to the ways in which the intellectual heritage in question inspired the development of a new perspective on social phenomena rather than the ways in which the new is nothing more than an extension of the old. A reading of Chapter 8 of Garfinkel's Studies in Ethnomethodology should also suggest that while Schutz had a profound influence on Garfinkel, Garfinkel transformed Schutz's phenomenological analysis into empirical sociological problems.

WEIDER, D. LAWRENCE

1974 Language and Social Reality: The Case of Telling the Convict Code. The Hague: Mouton. Weider's reanalysis of an ethnography of a half-way house for paroled narcotics offenders reveals the structure of members' use of natural language practices to render social conduct accountable.

PART VII. BIOLOGY AND HUMAN BEHAVIOR

1. Saul Feinman, "Biosociological Approaches to Social Behavior."

ALEXANDER, R. D.

1974 "The evolution of social behavior." Annual Review of Ecology and Systematics 5:325–383. An in-depth, sophisticated theoretical consideration of the manner in which social behavior has and can evolve in a wide range of animal species, including social insects, birds, and mammals. The consideration of human sociality is only briefly considered.

BARASH, D. P.

1977 Sociobiology and Behavior. New York: Elsevier. A well-written introduction to the basic ideas and applications of biosociology, mostly as it applies to nonhumans. The final chapter on human applications is especially intriguing but speculative.

DAWKINS, R.
1976 The Selfish Gene. New York: Oxford University Press. A well-written introduction to biosociology, mostly with reference to nonhumans. This book clearly presents the argument that animals behave as if they are controlled and manipulated by genes. The last chapter presents an interesting possibility concerning the evolution of culture.

DURHAM, W. H.
1976 "The adaptive significance of cultural behavior." Human Ecology 2:89–121. This article presents a coevolutionary theory which allows for evolution of genetically and culturally based traits. It is one of the newly generated theories which struggle with the question of where culturally acquired behavior belongs in the scheme of human evolution.

HAMILTON, W. D.
1964 "The genetic evolution of social behavior, I & II." Journal of Theoretical Biology 7:1–52. In this paper Hamilton delineates the recent theory of kin selection and provides a mathematical explication of how this process works.

ORIANS, G. H.
1962 "Natural selection and ecological theory." American Naturalist 96:257–264. This piece lays the foundation for the distinction between ultimate mechanisms and proximate mechanisms. It also provides a useful analysis of how researchers in the same discipline manage to talk past each other in intradisciplinary debate.

TRIVERS, R. L.
1971 "The evolution of reciprocal altruism." Quarterly Review of Biology 47:35–57. Trivers proposes the mechanism by which altruism towards non-kin can be selected. Particularly useful are his delineation of the social conditions under which reciprocal altruism could emerge and his attempt to apply his model to the social psychological literature on altruism.

1974 "Parent-offspring conflict." American Zoologist 14:249–264. An intriguing article which analyzes the interaction of parents and offspring in a new light. It suggests that socialization is not merely the transmission of culture, but is also the parent's attempt to manipulate the offspring.

WEST EBERHARD, M. J.
1975 "The evolution of social behavior by kin selection." Quarterly Review of Biology 50:1–33. The best examination of fitness and selection, this book presents an extremely lucid and concise picture of the components of inclusive fitness and natural selection. The mathematical definitions of fitness and cost/gain ratios are not difficult to follow.

WILSON, E. O.
1975 Sociobiology: The New Synthesis. Cambridge, Mass.: Harvard University Press. An exhaustive and excellent consideration of biosociology. The main examples from animal societies are extensive and fascinating, as are the drawings and photographs. The last chapter deals with humans and is controversially speculative.

2. Penelope J. Greene, Charles J. Morgan, and David P. Barash, "Sociobiology."

DAWKINS, RICHARD
  1967 The Selfish Gene. New York and Oxford: Oxford University Press. Incredibly lucid, this is the best general introduction to sociobiological theory. Dawkins treats human societies as fundamentally different from animal societies, emphasizing the importance of culture and proposing the *meme* as a unit of cultural inheritance analogous to the gene.
GREEN, PENELOPE J.
  1978 "Promiscuity, paternity and culture." American Ethnologist 19:151–159. Kinship terminologies in human cultures are not random and arbitrary but partly explicable on the basis of expected degrees of biological relatedness for given degrees of social kinship.
HARTUNG, JOHN
  1976 "On natural selection and the inheritance of wealth." Current Anthropology 17:607–613. Argues that the greater variance of reproductive success for males and the differential behavior of the X and Y chromosomes may favor patrilineal inheritance. Especially valuable for the comments and reply elaborating the assumptions underlying the analysis.
HRDY, SARAH BLAFFER
  1977 The Langurs of Abu. Female and Male Strategies of Reproduction. Cambridge, Mass.: Harvard University Press.
  1976 "Hierarchical relations among female hanuman langurs (Primates: Colobinae, Presbytis entellus)." Science 193:913–915. Hrdy shows that male-female (or female-male) interactions are profitably viewed as competitive rather than cooperative. The critical observations are that when males take over a troop they systematically execute the infants, and that young females rise in rank over older and sometimes larger female relatives, even though the older females still actively defend the young. Hrdy interprets these results in terms of inclusive fitness and reproductive value.
MAYNARD SMITH, J.
  1976 "Evolution and the theory of games." American Scientist 64:41–45. Reviews the development of the idea of an evolutionary stable strategy. The best behavioral strategy depends on what the other individual will do, and under definable circumstances natural selection will result not in a single "best" strategy, but in a population with a stable mixture of different strategies.
PACKER, C.
  1977 "Reciprocal altruism in *Papio anubis*." Nature 265:441–443. An empirical demonstration of reciprocity in a nonhuman primate, the olive baboon.

TRIVERS, ROBERT L.
1971 "The evolution of reciprocal altruism. Quarterly Review of Biology 46:35–57. Sets forth the preconditions for the evolution of a network of reciprocal altruists and the countermeasures that can be expected to evolve to control "cheating," the nonreciprocation of altruism. Worth reading in the original for its extensive review of the literature on human altruism.

WILSON, EDWARD O.
1975 Sociobiology, The New Synthesis. Cambridge, Mass.: Harvard University Press. Publication of this volume marked the official birth of "sociobiology" as an identifiable theoretical orientation, and it remains central as a source book and review of the field studies of animal behavior available at the time of publication. The treatment of the central theory is not as accessible as Dawkins, and in discussing human social behavior Wilson emphasises the fundamental underlying biology.

3. Theodore D. Kemper, "A Sociology of Emotions: Some Problems and Some Solutions."

ARNOLD, MAGDA B. (ed.)
1970 Feelings and Emotions. New York: Academic Press. Brief, informative articles conveying diverse approaches by psychologists to the study of emotions.

BENSMAN, JOSEPH, and ARTHUR VIDICH
1962 "Business cycles, class, and personality." Psychoanalysis and Psychoanalytic Review 49:30–52. An absorbing theoretical discussion of how location and change of position in the social structure differentially affect the emotional dispositions of rising and falling groups.

FUNKENSTEIN, DANIEL
1955 "The physiology of fear and anger." Scientific American 192:74–80. Exciting, nontechnical report of the early research that led to the norepinephrine-anger and epinephrine-fear hypothesis.

GELLHORN, ERNEST
1967 Principles of Autonomic-Somatic Integrations. Minneapolis: University of Minnesota Press. Probing, technical treatment of the complex interactions between brain, body, and nervous system in the production of emotions.

HAMBLIN, ROBERT L., and CAROL R. SMITH
1966 "Values, status and professors." Sociometry 29:183–196. Seminal discussion and experiment on the nature of status conferral. Provides one important basis for the theory of love relations presented in Kemper (1978).

556   ANNOTATED BIBLIOGRAPHY

HILBRUN, ALFRED B., JR.
1973 Aversive Maternal Control: A Theory of Schizophrenic Development. New York: Wiley. Imaginative theoretical and research application of the power-status (control-nurturance) typology to mother-child relations in the production of schizophrenia.

KEMPER, THEODORE D.
1978 A Social Interactional Theory of Emotions. New York: Wiley. A systematic sociological theory applying the power-status model to emotions, mental illness, love relationships, socialization, aggression, sociophysiology, and research paradigms in experimental social psychology.

LAZARUS, RICHARD S.
1966 Psychological Stress and the Coping Process. New York: McGraw-Hill. An important treatment of the cognitive approach to emotions and coping and of the situational and personality differences that individuate emotional response.

SCHACHTER, STANLEY, and JEROME E. SINGER
1962 "Cognitive, social, and physiological determinants of emotional state." Psychological Review 69:379–399. Classic experiment often cited to refute specificity hypothesis in the psychophysiology of emotions. Extensively analyzed in Kemper (1978).

4. Susan Shott, "The Sociology of Emotion: Some Starting Points."

BERSCHEID, ELLEN, and ELAINE WALSTER
1974 "A little bit about love." In Ted Huston (ed.), Foundations of Interpersonal Attraction. New York: Academic Press. Develops the provocative thesis that situational cues may sometimes induce a person to label intense physiological arousal due to extreme experiences as passionate love.

FOSTER, GEORGE M.
1972 "The anatomy of envy." Current Anthropology 13:165–202. Discusses the difference between envy and jealousy and explores cultural mechanisms developed to control envy.

GOFFMAN, ERVING
1967 Interaction Ritual. Garden City, N.Y.: Anchor Books. A classic exposition of the sources and consequences of embarrassment.

GOODE, WILLIAM J.
1959 "The theoretical importance of love." American Sociological Review, 24:38–47. Analyzes societal means of controlling love in order to prevent disruption of lineages and class strata.

HOCHSCHILD, ARLIE RUSSELL
1975 "The sociology of feeling and emotion." Pp. 280–307. In Marcia Millman and Rosabeth Moss Kanter (eds.), Another Voice. Garden City,

N.Y.: Anchor Books. Focuses on feeling rules and the impact of hierarchies on emotions and their expression.

LEVY, ROBERT I.
  1973 Tahitians. Chicago: University of Chicago Press. Ethnography that includes a discussion of the cultural shaping of feeling and describes the affective "vocabulary of motive" in Tahiti.
MARTINEAU, WILLIAM H.
  1972 "A model of the social functions of humor." Pp. 101–125, in Jeffrey Goldstein and Paul E. McGree (eds.), The Psychology of Humor. New York: Academic Press. Review of the literature on the social function of humor.
SCHACHTER, STANLEY
  1971 Emotion, Obesity, and Crime. New York: Academic Press. Of special interest are Part I, which summarizes four studies concerned with the relationship between cognitive and situational factors and physiological arousal, and Part III, which describes several experiments relevant to the study of emotion and social control.
SIMMEL, GEORG
  1950 The Sociology of Georg Simmel. Glencoe, Ill.: Free Press. Insightfully describes the impact of gratitude on social interaction and social solidarity.
TURNER, RALPH H.
  1970 Family Interaction. New York: Wiley. Presents a theory of love as a means of social control and discusses the impact of culture on certain feelings.

PART VIII. SOCIETY AND THE ENVIRONMENT

1. William R. Catton, Jr. and Riley E. Dunlap, "Environmental Sociology: A New Paradigm."

BUTTEL, FREDERICK H.
  1978 "Environmental sociology: a new paradigm?" The American Sociologist 13 (November):252–256. Buttel argues that traditional theoretical cleavages, e.g., "critical-Marxist vs. functionalist-organicist," among environmental sociologists are more important than their adherence to a new environmental paradigm.
CATTON, WILLIAM R., JR.
  1978 "Carrying capacity, overshoot, and the quality of life." Pp. 231–249, in J. Milton Yinger and Stephen J. Cutler (eds.), Major Social Issues: A Multidisciplinary View. New York: The Free Press. Punctures the defensive assumption common among sociologists that the uniqueness of the human species protects us from ecological principles applicable to other species. Interprets human history in terms of repeated enlargements of the carrying capacity of finite environments, and shows how Homo sapiens has become Homo colossus and now faces the intensifica-

tion of competitive relationships as a result of overshooting sustainable carrying capacity.

CATTON, WILLIAM R., JR., and RILEY E. DUNLAP

1978 "Paradigms, theories and the primacy of the HEP-NEW distinction." The American Sociologist 13 (November):256–259. In response to Buttel's critique (see Buttel reference), the authors argue that the new environmental paradigm represents an ecological world view which differs radically from the world view represented by the human exceptionalism paradigm, and that this paradigmatic cleavage is potentially far more important than traditional theoretical cleavages within sociology.

COTTRELL, FRED

1955 Energy and Society: The Relation Between Energy, Social Change, and Economic Development. New York: McGraw-Hill. Develops an array of sociological implications based on the simple thesis that the things people can do are limited by the energy available for doing them and that the things people will do are influenced by energy-conversion process characteristics. Had this book been more widely read and pondered in its time, sociologists might have been less confounded by the 1970s.

DALY, HERMAN E. (ed.)

1973 Toward a Steady-State Economy. San Francisco: Freeman. A good collection of readings on the concept of a steady-state society which illustrates the need for a new ecologically sound paradigm within economics. In his introduction the author argues that "economists must undergo a revolutionary paradigm shift before they can really come to grips" with the problems posed by a finite earth.

DUNLAP, RILEY E., and WILLIAM R. CATTON, JR.

1979 "Environmental sociology: a framework for analysis." In T. O'Riordan and R. C. d'Arge (eds.), Progress in Resource Management and Environmental Planning, vol. 1. Chichester, England: Wiley. The authors describe the nature of societal-environmental interactions of interest to environmental sociologists. By employing the concept of the ecological complex and by maintaining a distinction between built, modified, and natural environments, they describe a range of interactions which may occur between social phenomena and physical environments.

HARDESTY, DONALD L.

1977 Ecological Anthropology. New York: Wiley. An excellent introduction to anthropological inquiries into human community adaptations to ecological systems. The chapter titled "Carrying Capacity" could be particularly important for reorienting sociologists to real-world constraints long neglected by our discipline.

MICHELSON, WILLIAM

1976 Man and His Urban Environment: A Sociological Approach. Reading, Mass.: Addison-Wesley. Michelson presents a good summary of research by environmental sociologists concerned with human interactions with the built environment, primarily housing and other architecture.

OPHULS, WILLIAM
  1977 Ecology and the Politics of Scarcity. San Francisco: Freeman. An
       excellent and well-documented analysis of how American society's
       dominant values, culture, and institutions developed in an era of
       material abundance, and ". . . are grossly maladapted to the era of
       ecological scarcity that has already begun." Ophuls's grasp of ecological
       and social theories makes this a particularly insightful analysis.
STRETTON, HUGH
  1976 Capitalism, Socialism and the Environment. New York and London:
       Cambridge University Press. Illustrates how policies designed to protect
       environmental quality and cope with scarcity may vary in their distribu-
       tional impacts—i.e., in the distribution of costs and benefits to differing
       social classes. Stretton outlines three general responses to ecological
       constraints (conservative, liberal, and socialist) and presents a detailed
       argument in favor of the latter response.

2. John M. Goering, "The Marxist Perspective and Urban Sociology."

ALCALY, R., and D. MERMALSTEIN
  1976 The Fiscal Crisis of American Cities. New York: Vintage. An excellent
       analysis and critique of the fiscal insolvency of American cities, with a
       special focus on New York. Combines historical, economic, and political
       analyses.
CASTELLS, MANUEL
  1977 The Urban Question: A Marxist Perspective. Cambridge: MIT Press. A
       critique of traditional American urban sociology and Castells's own
       conceptualization of the central Marxist concerns. Includes a useful
       epilogue, plus material on collective consumption and urban social
       movements.
GOERING, J. M. (ed.)
  1978 Comparative Urban Research, vol. 6, no. 2–3 (Fall). This book contains a
       discussion between Marxist and non-Marxist urbanists on the central
       theoretical questions of urban social science and clearly describes the
       theoretical and ideological assets of each view.
HARVEY, DAVID
  1973 Social Justice and the City. Baltimore: Johns Hopkins Press. One of the
       earliest English language critiques of traditional urban sociology and
       geography. The section on socialist alternatives provides a useful addi-
       tion to Castells and suggests further directions for theoretical analysis.
INTERNATIONAL JOURNAL OF URBAN AND REGIONAL RESEARCH
  1977— London: Edward Arnold Publishers. Published since 1977, this is an
       essential source of ongoing theoretical and empirical discussion among
       Marxist urbanists from many countries. It contains invaluable material

on urban policies, planning, and comparative analysis from European, American, and developing nations.

PICKVANCE, C. G. (ed.)

1976 Urban Sociology: Critical Essays. New York: St. Martin's Press. An excellent reader which provides English translations of many important essays, including those of Castells, Lojkine, and Lamarche. Includes a useful introduction and critique by Pickvance.

TABB, WILLIAM K., and LARRY SAWYERS

1978 Marxism and the Metropolis: New Perspectives in Urban Political Economy. New York: Oxford. A well-written reader including an excellent overview by David Gordon. Contains some useful sections on housing and urban development, the fiscal crisis of cities, and on local organizational strategies. The final section includes material on Cuba, China, and the Soviet Union. A bit uneven, but useful for undergraduates as well as graduate students in a variety of disciplines.

3. Bruce London, "Ecology as Macrosociology: A New Look at an Old Perspective."

DUNCAN, OTIS D.

1959 "Human ecology and population studies." Pp. 678–716 in P.M. Hauser and L.F. Schnore (eds.), The Study of Population. Chicago: University of Chicago Press. Introduces the ecological complex (POET) in a discussion of the relationship between human ecology and demography.

1964 "Social organization and ecosystem." Pp. 36–82 in R.E.L. Faris (ed.), Handbook of Modern Sociology. Chicago: Rand McNally. Defines the ecosystem in terms of flows of materials and energy and information, and emphasizes how the presence of humans vastly complicates the operation and evolution of ecosystems.

DUNCAN, OTIS D., and LEO F. SCHNORE

1959 "Cultural, behavioral, and ecological perspectives in the study of social organization." American Journal of Sociology 65:132–146. Advocates the heuristic utility of the ecological approach for the study of certain forms of social organization such as bureaucracy and stratification.

FIREY, WALTER

1945 "Sentiment and symbolism as ecological variables." American Sociological Review 10:140–148. An early statement criticizing classical ecological theory for failure to consider norms, values, and general sociocultural phenomena within its frame of reference.

GIBBS, JACK P., and WALTER T. MARTIN

1959 "Toward a theoretical system of human ecology." Pacific Sociological Review 2:29–36. Introduces an emphasis on sustenance organization into the ecological vocabulary.

HAWLEY, AMOS H.
  1950 Human Ecology: A Theory of Community Structure. New York: Ronald Press. The benchmark reformulation of the ecological theory which overemphasized spatial relationships as a concern of those involved in the development and organization of the community.
  1968 "Human ecology." Pp. 328–337 in D. Sills (ed.), International Encyclopedia of the Social Sciences. New York: Crowell, Collier, and Macmillan. Written by the dean of human ecology, this is the most recent theoretical statement of important ecological concepts and assumptions. It departs somewhat from his earlier focus on the community by now emphasizing the more inclusive social system as the central unit for analysis.
MICKLIN, MICHAEL
  1973 Population, Environment, and Social Organization: Current Issues in Human Ecology. Hinsdale, Ill.: Dryden Press. A collection including the editor's own theoretical statement and many informative articles on population, organization, environment, technology, and their interrelationships.
SCHNORE, LEO F.
  1958 "Social morphology and human ecology." American Journal of Sociology, 63:620–634. Traces the roots of sociological human ecology back to Durkheim's morphological analysis in The Division of Labor and emphasizes that the social psychological drift of American sociology has diverted attention from traditional consideration of social structure as a key dependent variable.
  1961 "The myth of human ecology." Sociological Inquiry, 31:128–139. Argues that ecology is not marginal to sociology, but is a type of macrosociology well-suited to the analysis of social organization.
WILLHELM, SIDNEY M.
  1964 "The concept of the 'ecological complex': A critique." American Journal of Economics and Sociology, 23:241–248. A critique of Duncan's ecological complex as "materialistic," emphasizing its elimination of the concept of social values in particular and "voluntaristic" phenomena in general.

562 ACKNOWLEDGMENTS

Acknowledgments (continued from p. iv)

Penelope Greene, Charles Morgan, and David Barash, "Sociobiology" extracted from a longer manuscript in J. Lockard (ed.), *Evolution and Human Social Behavior*, Elsevier (forthcoming). Reprinted by permission.

Immanuel Wallerstein, "A World-System Perspective on the Social Sciences" *British Journal of Sociology*, Vol. XXVII, September 1976. Reprinted by permission of Routledge & Kegan Paul Ltd. and the author.

The following are reprinted from *The American Sociologist*, Vol. 13, Feb. 1978, by permission of the American Sociological Association and the authors:

Richard P. Appelbaum, "Marxist Method: Structural Constraints and Social *Praxis*," pp. 73–81.

Richard A. Ball, "Sociology and General Systems Theory," pp. 65–72.

Michael Burawoy, "Contemporary Currents in Marxist Theory," pp. 50–64.

William R. Catton Jr. and Riley E. Dunlap, "Environmental Sociology: A New Paradigm," pp. 41–49.

Theodore D. Kemper, "Toward a Sociology of Emotions: Some Problems and Some Solutions," pp. 30–41.

James W. Michaels and Dan S. Green, "Behavioral Sociology: Emergent Forms and Issues," pp. 23–29.

John J. Sewart, "Critical Theory and the Critique of Conservative Method," pp. 15–22.

Don H. Zimmerman, "Ethnomethodology," pp. 5–15.